THE BEST OF

ITALY

3rd Revised Edition

Directed by
André Gayot

Translation and Adaptation
Sheila Mooney

Contributing Editors
Lidia Breda, Milena Ercole, Federico Passi,
Raffaela Rizzo, Gaetano Femiani

Coordination
Sophie Gayot
Assisted by
Stéphanie Masson

Publisher
Alain Gayot

Editorial Staff, Italian Language Guide

Directed by
Giorgio Lindo
Coordination
Federico Umberto d'Amato
Contributing Editors
Bruno Bini, Pino Correnti, Neno Corti, Luigi Cremona, Federico Umberto d'Amato, Gianfranco
Damiani, Walter Del Giudice, Alberto Dell'Acqua, Gigi De Santis,
Rina Durante, Massimo Menta, Giusto Piolatto, Piero Sardo, Paolo Scotto, Enzo Vizzari
Additional Contribution
Annalisa Alberici, Daniela Allemand, Sandro Bellei,
Alessandra Benincasa, Sandro Brandolisio, Bucci Caldarulo, Antonio Chichierchia, Luisa De
Mattia, Luciano Filippi, Luigi Fillipi, Vincenzo Frigo, Guido Gianni, Augusto Jacod, Brunello
Marino, Sandro Masci, Massimo Menta, Pasquale Palma, Stefano Petrecca, Giovanni Ruffa,
Giulio Cesare Saviozzi, Marco Simonetti,
Annibale Toffolo, Costantino Tromellini

Editorial
Claudio Gallo, Antonella Gallo, Loredana Bosio, Roberto Thöni, Lanfranco Fava

Gault Millau

Paris ▪ Los Angeles ▪ New York ▪ San Francisco ▪ London ▪ Munich ▪ Rome

Bring You

Copyright © 1984, 1989, 1995 by Gault Millau, Inc.

All rights reserved including the reproduction
in whole or in part in any form.

Published by Gault Millau, Inc.
5900 Wilshire Blvd.
Los Angeles, CA 90036

Please address all comments regarding
The Best of Italy to:
Gault Millau, Inc.
P.O. Box 361144
Los Angeles, CA 90036

Library of Congress Cataloging-in-Publication Data

Guida d'Italia 1995.   English
    The best of Italy / directed by André Gayot; translation and
adaptation by Sheila Mooney; contributing editors, Lidia Breda...
[et al.]. -- 3rd rev. ed.
        p.   cm.
    Includes index.
    ISBN 1-881066-16-9
    1. Restaurants--Italy--Guidebooks. 2. Hotels--Italy--Guidebooks.
3. Shopping--Italy--Guidebooks. 4. Italy--Guidebooks. I. Gayot,
André. II. Mooney, Sheila. III. Breda, Lidia. IV. Title.
TX907.5.I8G8513   1995
647.9545--dc20   95-17538
                                                            CIP

Printed in the United States of America

CONTENTS

ITALY

A Gift for the Good Life

From the earliest times, Italians have cultivated a taste for the good life. In Tuscany, some 26 centuries ago, the Etruscans decorated their tombs with remarkably lifelike scenes of banquets, games, and revelry—an expression of hope that the next world would be at least as delightful as this one. The prospect of savoring Italy's proverbial *dolce vita* has lured endless waves of invaders, from Barbarians, Normans, and various Bourbons to Napoleonic armies, Baedecker-toting Grand Tourists, and camera-decked sightseers in shorts.

Beauty, more surely than riches, is what makes life sweet. And in Italy, beauty is a birthright, inscribed into the very landscape: in Lombard lakes and Tuscan hills, in majestic Alps and Apennines, in sun-drenched seacoasts that embrace the peninsula from the Gulf of Genoa to the Venetian lagoon. These scenic splendors are matched (some even say surpassed) by the brilliance of Italian art. Beauty endures in the heroic monuments of Rome, it inhabits the faces of a thousand Renaissance madonnas, it echoes in the passionate arias of Verdi, and in the verses of poets from Dante to Montale. Today, as it has for centuries, Italy regales her children and guests with a feast for the senses, and food for the spirit, too.

Do we wax too lyrical? Our enthusiasm may seem excessive in view of Italy's latest traumas—corruption scandals, political disarray, Mafia violence... We don't mean to gloss over the frustrations and, yes, chaos that a traveler may occasionally find daunting or exasperating. But in the end, what lives on in one's memory is always Italy's grace and grandeur, its inimitable style and flavor—the best of Italy. And that is what we have endeavored to present to you in this modest guide.

The Best of Italy focuses on five great cities—Florence, Milan, Naples, Rome, and Venice—including the more noteworthy establishments in such oft-visited outlying areas as Capri (Naples) and Fiesole (Florence). Within each chapter are our keys to the city: honest and (we hope) accurate assessments of places to eat and sleep, hundreds of suggestions on where to shop, where to sit and watch the world go by, sites to discover and explore. You'll also find clues to the culture of each destination in an evocative, in-depth introduction, a wide-ranging choice of museums, and, scattered throughout each chapter, our Citylore vignettes: anecdotes and legends about the city's most remarkable people, customs, artworks, and buildings.

As you read through the restaurant reviews, surely growing as famished as we always seemed to be while editing this guide, you may run across an Italian food term or two that you don't recognize. For just such an occasion, we compiled the "Menu Savvy" section at the back of the book. While this Italian food glossary cannot claim to be exhaustive, we've expanded it to include even more of the items you're likely to see on Italian menus.

André Gayot

SYMBOL SYSTEMS

RESTAURANTS

RATINGS & TOQUES

Gault Millau ranks restaurants in the same manner that French students are graded: on a scale of zero to twenty, twenty being unattainable perfection. The rankings reflect *only* the quality of the cooking; décor, service, reception, and atmosphere do not influence the rating, though they are explicitly commented on within the reviews. Restaurants ranked thirteen and above are distinguished with toques (chef's hats), according to the following table:

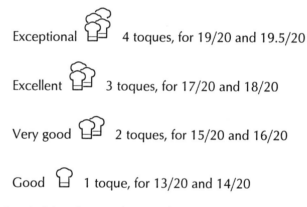

Exceptional   4 toques, for 19/20 and 19.5/20

Excellent   3 toques, for 17/20 and 18/20

Very good   2 toques, for 15/20 and 16/20

Good   1 toque, for 13/20 and 14/20

Keep in mind that these ranks are *relative*. One toque for 13/20 is not a very good rating for a highly reputed (and very expensive) temple of fine dining, but it is quite complimentary for a small trattoria without much pretension.

PRICES

At the end of each restaurant review, prices are given—either **C** *(A la carte)* or **M** *(Menu(s))* (fixed-price meals) or both. A la carte prices are those of an average meal (an appetizer, main course, dessert, and coffee) for one person, including service and a half-bottle of a relatively modest wine. Lovers of Italy's grandest vintages will, of course, face stiffer tabs. The menu prices quoted are for a complete multicourse meal for one person, including service but excluding wine, unless otherwise noted. These fixed-price

5

menus often give diners on a budget a chance to sample the cuisine of an otherwise expensive restaurant.

HOTELS

SYMBOLS & ABBREVIATIONS

Our opinion of the comfort level and appeal of each hotel is expressed in the following ranking system:

Luxurious

First-class

Classic

Practical

Very quiet

Hotel prices given are for the complete range of rooms, from the smallest singles to the largest doubles; suite prices are also given when possible. These prices are per room, not per person. Half-board and full-board prices, however, are per person.

Rms: rooms.   **Stes:** suites.
Pkg: parking.   **Conf:** conference facilities.

RESIDENCES

Some fortunate travelers—business people, actors, models, artists, those on sabbatical—have occasion to require an urban home base for a month or more in Italy. Hotel rooms can become impersonal and a bit cramped for extended stays, and ordinary rentals (apartments and houses) usually require a long-term lease agreement. Enter the *residences*, full-service, hotel-style apartments that are perfect for longer stays. They combine the space and hominess of an apartment with such features as maid service, dry cleaning, and sometimes even concierge services.

PRICES

Sadly, prices continue to creep up, so some places may have become more expensive than our estimates by the time you visit. You're best off expecting to pay a little more—then perhaps you'll be pleasantly surprised!

TOQUE TALLY

Four Toques (19.5/20)

19.5

Antica Osteria del Ponte, *Cassinetta di Lugagnano (see Milan)*
Enoteca Pinchiorri, *Florence*

Four Toques (19/20)

Don Alfonso, *Sant'Agata Sui Due Golfi (see Naples)*
La Scaletta, *Milan*

Three Toques (18/20)

Aimo e Nadia, *Milan*
Alberto Ciarla, *Rome*
Papà Giovanni, *Rome*
Relais La Piscine, *Rome*
La Sacrestia, *Naples*
Sadler-Osteria di Porta Cicca, *Milan*

Ai Tre Scalini, *Rome*

Three Toques (17/20)

Dall'Amelia, *Mestre (see Venise)*
L'Ami Berton, *Milan*
Andrea, *Rome*
Nino Arnaldo, *Milan)*
Bistrot di Gualtiero Marchesi, *Milan*
Calajunco, *Milan*
Casanova Grill, *Milan*
Chez Albert, *Rome*
Cibrèo, *Florence*
Cipriani, *Venise*
Convivio, *Rome*
Galleria, *Milan*
Giannino, *Milan*
Mimì alla Ferrovia, *Naples*
Osteria del Binari, *Milan*
Peck, *Milan*
Relais Le Jardin, *Florence*
Relais Le Jardin, *Rome*
Le Restaurant, *Rome*
Il Sambuco, *Milan*
La Tenda Rossa, *San Casciano Val di Pesa (see Florence)*
La Terrazza, *Rome*
L'Ulmet, *Milan*

FLORENCE

Footloose in the city of flowers

Banners welcome you to Florence, "The European Capital of Culture," the legendary "Cradle of the Renaissance." Glossy tourist brochures invite you to close your eyes and listen to the gentle tapping of Michelangelo's chisel. May we respectfully suggest you open your eyes and read on. What you're hearing is probably the clattering of the taxi that's hauling you up to Piazzale Michelangelo for more money than you'd like to part with. But belly up to the balustrade and take a look at that view. A lump is likely to rise in even the most cynical of throats at the sight of skiffs skimming the surface of the Arno at sunset, with the Ponte Vecchio in the background. So what if the cab ride from Santa Maria Novella station to the top of the hill took an hour? What did you expect? Small-town Florence has been gobbled up by the twentieth century. Toss out a coin and it's liable to land on the head of one of the nearly half-million locals. Each of these proud descendants of Dante now has a car, and they go charging all at once down the narrow, stone-paved streets. Nor can we forget the 400 or 500 tour buses lumbering around town. That's why the noise is so festively appalling. No, this city was not designed for traffic, and the magnificent palazzi are crumbling. During the long, hot summer, *Bella Firenze* chokes on smog alerts, despite the partial closure of the *centro storico*.

So what are we doing here? We're having a grand time, despite the crush— maybe even because of it. For the last millennium, artists and scholars have flocked here to make it happen, or to study how it has happened. Linguists dart in, microphones in hand, to examine the Tuscan tongue, mother of modern Italian. And lovers of food and wine take turns flinging Florentine delights at their palates. Florence flourishes because of its people and its swirling crowds of visitors. Without them it would shrivel. So don't expect small-town treatment: Florence is not a sweet little hamlet you can slip in your pocket. Like Venice and Rome, Florence is coveted by all and owned by none.

Several years ago, the city council created a "pedestrian island" in the heart of the city, where sightseers can promenade undisturbed from the Ponte Vecchio to the Duomo (cathedral), the current limit of the "island." Freedom from the automobile has certainly transformed the Florence experience, liberating the city center from traffic and diesel fumes.

In fact, this tourist compound is now so insidiously pleasant that there is even less incentive to venture out into unknown quarters. But you must. Remember, Florence is also a working city. The centuries-old tradition of merchant banking has spawned thousands of state-of-the-art service-sector and high-tech enterprises. Leather tanning, fashion, and heavy manufacturing fill two-thirds of the community till. The Florentines are master brinksmen balanced between a musty museum town and a metropolis *all'italiana*, full of noise and chaos and— yes—charm. This place is alive and kicking behind its postcard stalls. So fight the pressure of mass tourism as the Florentines do: by seeking out the many smaller, less-publicized sights. An example is the Museo Horne (see *Museums*), a collection of painting and sculpture that would be the pride of any other city. This early Renaissance palazzo is lost in the Florentine superabundance of museums, and besides, the building's several flights of stairs discourage guided tours—so if you go on any day but Sunday (when the museum is closed), you'll likely have this beautiful place to yourself. Or visit another fine, oft-neglected museum, the Bardini-Corsi (see *Museums*) which houses such magnificent trifles as Pollaiolo's *Saint Michael* and Jacopo della Quercia's *Madonna and Child*, as well as 30 drawings by Tiepolo and a couple by Piazzetta.

In the same uncrowded spirit, wander the rest of Florence's "left bank," called Oltrarno—it abounds in less-encumbered but wonderful corners. Another example stands just off the beaten path: the harmonious Renaissance piazza and church of Santo Spirito. In the church (begun in 1444 by Filippo Brunelleschi), near the apse, is a wooden crucifix thought to be an early work by Michelangelo.

Unadorned but not unloved is San Niccolò sopr'Arno, near Piazza Pozzi. This is the real thing, as they say—a working Florentine parish church, a homely cousin of the Duomo. Its one claim to fame is the fact that Michelangelo holed up in the bell tower in 1530, after Florence capitulated to Alessandro de' Medici's imperial troops.

But gloomy interiors do not a city make. Florence is extroverted, its action spills into the streets, squares, and such public gardens as the Boboli. Garden and fountain buffs are delirious here. The scented boxwood labyrinths, fountains, and lily-filled pools have been a source of sunny inspiration for at least four centuries. Eleonore of Toledo, the comely Spanish consort of Duke Cosimo de' Medici, hired Mannerist artists to turn the Pitti Palace and Boboli Gardens into a truly royal abode. A popular favorite is the Bacchus Fountain, which squirts away at the left entrance, nearest the Pitti (it doesn't actually feature Bacchus but Pietro Barbino, Cosimo I's favorite dwarf, riding a huge turtle). Buontalenti's *Grotto* (1583), a self-styled "attempt to reinvent nature," lies a few steps down the garden path. Copies of Michelangelo's marble *Prisoners* hide amid sprays of water and a voluptuous bathing *Venus* by Giambologna (1573). The Kaffehaus—crammed with tourists but still wonderful—is perched on the highest point in the gardens; its spectacular panorama has lured many a thirsty spirit, among them Shelley (he wrote "A View from Pitti Gardens" here). It is an excellent

place to tipple and admire the city from a critical distance. That star-shaped fortress just above is the Belvedere, which the guidebooks say is one of the great achievements in Renaissance military architecture—but young Florentines seem to think it was designed exclusively for *l'amore*. In summer, films are shown in the parade grounds, and spectators flutter around like crazed moths.

Speaking of crazed moths, what's with the Florentines? They are "bizarre and quarrelsome and have been for centuries," as a prominent correspondent recently commented. Florence nurtured the greatest artists of the Renaissance, but the Florentines' love affair with the art of the feud has shackled them to the Middle Ages. Well, the line between the medieval and modern temperament is fine indeed, and not only in Florence. The fiery Tuscan character peppers an otherwise refined sense of self-irony with the pervasive spirit of polemic and politics, even in this age of anti-ideology. And there they go, proving it again. They've kicked up dust and yelled at one another in Piazza della Signoria—over the pavement. For years now the city council has been feuding over the kind of stones to use for the long-overdue repaving of the square, which was finally undertaken in 1985. With characteristic flair, a large sign placed in the square lavished apologies on visitors in four languages while launching accusatory darts at those responsible for the mess. That was fair enough since Piazza della Signoria was born in a bloodbath. Tradition has it that it all started because Buon del Monte de' Buondelmonti jilted his fiancée. So the powerful but humorless Amidei family—in other words, her father—successfully sought revenge on Easter Day 1215, as Buondelmonti dismounted on the Ponte Vecchio. The Guelph and Ghibelline "parties" thus began their merry warring. Until the Guelphs routed the Ghibellines in the mid-thirteenth century, the Piazza della Signoria area was chockablock with Ghibelline house-towers. But following the bloodletting, the victorious Guelphs executed or exiled the Ghibellines, called in the wreckers, and banned all building on the site. Presto: The World's Most Beautiful Square. They paved it in blood-red terra-cotta quadrants bordered by *pietra serena* stone. The current flagstone paving was laid in 1798–a pork-barrel scheme dreamed up by the Grand Duke of Tuscany to quiet the unemployed masses. The Florentines voted overwhelmingly in 1982 to restore the square to its medieval look, but a "typical high-handed maneuver" by a group of "specialists" overrode the citizens—so then it was decided that the flagstones were going back in. Problems arose anew when an extensive Roman *fullonica* (thermal baths used for washing, dyeing, and treating cloth) was discovered under the piazza. The *fullonica* has since been unearthed, mapped, and partly reinterred. To the relief of nearly everyone, the decision to pave over the site with glass tiles was definitively shelved.

Why did the populace groan so desperately at the exciting archaeological find? Because here, alas, there are already too many monuments and relics, too much history. Thirty museums, seventy churches, a dozen monumental cloisters, and just as many *gallerie* (arcades) stun and sometimes even sicken visitors. Strange as it may sound, medical researchers here claim that visitors who see too much beauty, and try to grasp too much history too fast, fall victim to the dreaded "Stendhal Syndrome": a form of visual overload accompanied by temporary loss of memory and depression. Viewed from this standpoint, Florence becomes a fearful place. Even the most innocuous-looking alley may conduct you to a dangerously intriguing site.

"Great art has a price," reply the cynics in the face of shell-shocked tourists. Old Florence hands scoff, seeing in the Stendhal Syndrome simple exhaustion. Whatever the explanation, the best way to avoid this malaise is to prepare yourself before coming to Florence, and once there to sample instead of gorge. Don't let the history break your back with the weight of its riches. Think of the human side of those masters of art and letters who animated *Firenze* during its centuries of glory. People are always calling them "divine," and it's true that they were marvelously talented. But they were also living, breathing people—people who would certainly be amused to know that they and their works have been cowing

millions for centuries. Dante (Dante Alighieri, 1265-1321), Italy's greatest poet, never called his *Comedy* "divine." He pasted the following into the Florentine scrapbook: "Be joyous, Florence, you are great indeed,/ for over sea and land you beat your wings;/ through every part of Hell your name extends!" You can visit Dante's house (Via Santa Margherita at Via Dante) and read the poignant story of his life, and you can see Dante's portrait, from a sketch by Giotto, his contemporary, in the Bargello (Museo Nazionale). It shows a tall, slender man with a bony face, prominent nose, and forceful lips twisted into an expression that has haunted Florentines for centuries. Dante, a dedicated "White" or anti-Papal Guelph, was exiled by the rival Ghibellines and later died in Ravenna; his ornate cenotaph in the church of Santa Croce stands empty. The *Divina* was added to *La Commedia* by a clever publisher in 1555.

According to Dante, Florence was fashion-conscious even 700 years ago. He writes about a miraculously talented painter named Giotto di Bondone (1266–1337) whose work was "all the rage." When you see Giotto's frescoes in Santa Croce, keep in mind that they are widely considered the foundation of Italian and European painting; they served as textbooks for scores of Renaissance painters from Masaccio to Michelangelo. But Giotto's is a real rags-to-riches tale, a shepherd who became the top artist and Architect to the City of Florence. He began the hodgepodge campanile of the cathedral, which people still call "Giotto's tower" when they scramble up it to gawk at the view.

"The rarest and most divine of men" is how Giorgio Vasari, the sixteenth-century painter, architect, and chronicler, described Michelangelo. Michelangelo's work may have been "divine," but he was plagued by grotesquely human troubles. Vasari tells the story of Michelangelo's colossal *David*, a story that's worth keeping in mind as you gaze from afar at its "perfection." Pier Soderini, the gonfalonier—top official—of Florence, took issue with the statue's nose and asked Michelangelo to do something about it. The sculptor, known for his temper, steadied himself and climbed the scaffold.

He made chipping sounds around David's nostrils and tossed down a handful of marble dust he had concealed in his hand. "Is that better?" he barked. "Much better," replied Soderini. "You've given it life!" Vasari himself was no mean artist. Like Botticelli and Michelangelo before him, he studied Masaccio's frescoes in the Brancacci Chapel at Santa Maria del Carmine (they have been restored recently and merit a struggle with the mobs). His own frescoes, paintings on wood, and grand staircase are found at the Palazzo Vecchio. Vasari's greatest achievement, the secret, elevated corridor linking the Uffizi with the Pitti Palace via the Ponte Vecchio, holds a splendid collection of self-portraits by such Italian and foreign greats as Raphael, Andrea del Sarto, Titian, Rubens, Rembrandt, Corot, and Delacroix (unfortunately, it is now closed for restoration).

Certainly, after all that you will want to sit down and stave off the Stendhal Syndrome with a delicious meal. A word to the wise: waiters are often strict. They may refuse to bring you grated cheese for your spaghetti alla buttera ("cowgirl" spaghetti: a palate-bucking blend of spices and oil). They will frown but comply if you order your bistecca alla fiorentina well done. But in a true Florentine trattoria, do not hope to be served a cappuccino after dinner, no matter how you plead. That would be a crime. Ask instead for *un caffè*. And remember: a good Chianti is usually expensive. Cheap Chianti in the familiar straw-wrapped *fiasco* can be just that.

We hope this candid guide will steer you clear of the hyped mediocrity—the overpriced shops, package-tour traps, and lackluster restaurants—and into the heart of excellence *alla fiorentina*.

Lame Horse, Lucky Horseshoe

That cherished, U-shaped metal shoe that hangs over a billion doorways around the world got its start as a lucky charm in Florence. It may be horsefeathers, but the story begins like this: the owner of the Loggia di Orsanmichele, a blacksmith and horse doctor, lost his young son, a saintly boy. One night the dead boy visited his father in a dream and told him to turn his Loggia into a church. The old man—pious but practical—gave it some thought and decided to wait for a sign from on high. A few days later a lame horse was brought in. When the blacksmith lifted up a hoof for a look at its shoe, the hoof came off in his hand. He had no choice but to kill the three-footed mount. As he was raising the club, the horse tapped its leg on the ground and the hoof miraculously snapped back into place. The horseshoe, though, shot off into the blue and went zinging down the street. People have been searching for it ever since. Whenever a horse lost its shoe at Orsanmichele, the chance finder would keep it as a good-luck charm. The habit soon galloped from the humble Loggia to the four corners of the Earth.

Restaurants

Tuscan meals provide the kind of straightforward satisfactions that appeal to untutored palates and epicurean tastes alike. Florentines like to tuck into T-bone steaks grilled juicy and rare, spit-roasted chicken, white beans simmered in olive oil, and thick vegetable soups. Few sauces, few spices, not a single note of exoticism is struck. Yet when the ingredients are first-class, it's hard to imagine anything better than this frugal, wholesome, farmhouse fare. The Tuscans certainly can't, because rich and poor, country folk and city dwellers, they've stuck to virtually the same diet for hundreds of years.

Although their native culinary styles have little in common, like Venice, Florence abounds in "typical" trattorias that specialize in local dishes. The visitor is thus faced with a welter of rustic-looking restaurants, all of whose menus seem to offer exactly the same thing. That's why a guidebook offering reliable recommendations (such as our modest volume) is so invaluable.

Wherever you end up, you are sure to be invited to start your meal with crostini—chopped or puréed chicken liver enlivened with anchovies and/or capers, spread on small slices of toasted bread. Another classic antipasto offering is affettati toscani, a selection of Tuscan cold meats; the assortment will probably include a thick slice or two of finocchiona, a delicious fennel-flavored salami. When it comes time to choose a primo, keep in mind that soups (minestre) are more commonly seen here than minestre asciutte (literally "dry soups": pasta or rice, for instance). Thick with beans and red cabbage or kale, the classic Tuscan ribollita is not for the faint-hearted; the same might be said of another filling soup that combines pasta and chickpeas. Pappa al pomodoro is a simple, oddly comforting "poor man's" soup of breadcrumbs and tomatoes with a healthy dose of garlic.

These fragrant peasant brews are a delicious introduction to the Tuscan kitchen. Yet in autumn, when game and mushrooms from surrounding forests are in plentiful supply, it is hard to pass up pappardelle (golden, eggy pasta ribbons with festive crimped edges) sauced with hare (alla lepre), boar (al cinghiale), or succulent porcini mushrooms.

Main courses in these parts are a carnivore's delight. The renowned bistecca alla fiorentina, cut from flavorful Chianina beef, charcoal-grilled and seasoned with pepper and fruity olive oil, rates star billing on most regional menus, and it can be very good indeed. But it isn't the whole show. Other secondi in the Tuscan tradition are arista (roast pork loin), roast game with sautéed wild mushrooms, grilled chicken alla diavola (flavored with lemon, olive oil, rosemary, and lots of pepper), and such sturdy, countrified dishes as trippa alla fiorentina (stewed in broth with vegetables and herbs), or sausages and beans. (Beans, you will notice, are omnipresent in Florentine cooking—as antipasti, combined with pasta or rice, in soups, and as a side dish—and they have justly been called "the ambassadors of Tuscan cooking.")

It is worth saving room for dessert, since the Tuscan repertory boasts an enticing array of cookies: biscotti di Prato, cavallucci, brigidini, and more. An ancient sweet that is still popular in the region is castagnaccio, a chestnut-flour cake flavored with rosemary. Zuccotto, a Florentine specialty, involves liqueur-soaked cake and a creamy chocolate filling; its shape is inspired, purportedly, by Brunelleschi's dome on the city's cathedral. But should you happen to be in Florence in the fall, the perfect grace note to a typically Tuscan meal of game and wild mushrooms is a wedge of schiacciata, a Florentine flat bread studded with newly harvested grapes.

Speaking of grapes, Tuscany produces some of the finest wines in Italy, particularly elegant, oaky, austere reds that complement the region's red meats, game, and fowl. Chianti Classico is a dependable choice; the riservas are always particularly fine. But do sample Brunello di Montalcino, Carmignano, and some of the unclassified Cabernets, perhaps the most exciting wines now produced in the area: Sassicaia and Tignanello are two excellent examples.

La Baraonda
Via Ghibellina 67 - (055) 2341171
Closed Sun, Mon lunch, at Christmas, Aug. AE, DC.

Elena, who runs the kitchen, used to work in fashion; Duccio, who oversees the dining room, was formerly in textiles. Both are now whole-hearted restaurateurs, and La Baraonda (the name means "cheerful confusion") mirrors the couple's obvious pleasure in their new line of work. The bill of fare offers no antipasti; the dishes proposed are all down-home Tuscan classics: an earthy soup of rice and sausage further enriched with potatoes and cabbage; potato tortelli sauced with lusty boar ragù; meatballs in tomato sauce; and cardoon timbale with chicken-liver salsa. The kitchen's performance is occasionally uneven, reflecting a penchant for improvisation. But Elena's free-wheeling creativity also produces such successful dishes as lasagnette with ricotta and raisins, and tender ham simmered long and gently in fresh milk. Desserts are all homemade, and can be partnered with the house's lush Vin Santo. C 50,000 lire.

Il Barrino
Via Gioberti 71 - (055) 660565
Closed Sun, Aug. All major cards.

Note the new address of this familiar Florentine restaurant. Owner Sandro Franceschetti's team has now hit its stride, presenting a menu (revised every two weeks) based on impeccably fresh ingredients handled with skill and creativity. Among the primi, we like potato ravioli enlivened with pesto, buckwheat pasta with leeks and cheese, and squash blossoms stuffed with anchovy-spiked mozzarella. These good dishes may be followed by crumb-coated red mullet in a garlicky tomato sauce or delicious boned and grilled rabbit with eggplant. The cellar harbors lots of choice bottles posting reasonable prices. C 55,000 lire.

Cammillo
Borgo San Jacopo 57r - (055) 212427
Closed Wed, Thu, 3 wks in Aug, 3 wks Dec-Jan. All major cards.

This is one of the better-known establishments on the Arno's "Left Bank," just a hundred yards or so from the Ponte Vecchio. Young Francesco is the current manager of Cammillo, a restaurant owned for generations by the same family. He supervises a swift-footed staff that serves forth the robust dishes which are Cammillo's signature. For starters, there are tagliolini noodles with tiny peas and truffles or assorted farm-fresh vegetables deep-fried to crackling crispness; main courses include boned squab with wee artichokes, veal cutlet bolognese, and pork with chickpeas and turnip tops. The top-quality olive oil and wine used in the kitchen come straight from the family farm. For dessert, the chestnut-flour fritters with rum-laced ricotta are a real country-style treat. C 65,000 lire.

La Capannina di Sante
Piazza Ravenna (corner of the Ponte da Verrazzano) - (055) 688345
Dinner only. Closed Sun, 1 wk in Aug. All major cards.

Here you'll find the freshest of fresh seafood, simply prepared, and a very attractive selection of Italian white wines. This little trattoria, built entirely of wood, is nestled along the Arno, outside of the usual tourist circuit. The patrons tend to be sleek and fashionable; you can see them on the terrace in fine weather throwing back glass after glass of Ferrari Spumante and dozens of briny Breton oysters. Join them, if you're feeling flush (nothing is cheap here), and order a superb spigola (sea bass) broiled with herbs. In winter, owner Sante Collesanto urges customers to try his spaghetti with seafood and his zuppa di datteri ("sea dates," a kind of mussel from the Tyrrhenian sea) along with a bottle of Ronco delle Acacie, a tasty Friulian white wine. Convivial dinners often last well into the night—in fact, it's better to dine here late than early, to avoid the uncomfortable feeling that someone is waiting to take your table! **C** 100,000 lire (wine incl).

Il Cestello
Hotel Excelsior,
Piazza Ognissanti 3 - (055) 264201
Open daily. All major cards.
The dining room's extravagant, excessive décor contrasts oddly with the virtuous simplicity of Il Cestello's Tuscan menu. There's not an ounce of pomposity in the fabulous salamis and other cured meats, the farmhouse cheeses, the sturdy soups prepared from ancient recipes. Here the bistecca alla fiorentina, served with toothsome white beans, attains a kind of apotheosis...the tripe, the poultry, the gorgeous vegetables display a pristine freshness of the sort one would expect to find in the kitchen of a Tuscan *cascina*. Chef Fausto Monti also prepares a repertory of "international" (read: "hotel") dishes. Need we say that those are not what we come here to enjoy? Excellent wines; supremely elegant, formal service. **C** 100,000 lire. **M** 63,000 lire.

Pretty Poor Place for a Poet to Rest

It's not that there's anything intrinsically wrong with a noisy, chaotic traffic circle like Piazzale Donatello. It just strikes some of us as strange to find Percy Bysshe Shelley buried there, a patch of green in a sea of swirling cars. Not many brave a visit to the poet's resting place, though you can safely take a taxi to the site and ponder the meaning of poetic irony.

Cibrèo
Via dei Macci 118 - (055) 2341100
Closed Sun, Mon, end Jul-1 Sep 1, 1st wk of Jan. All major cards.
The fact that Cibrèo is a fashionable hot spot does not deter true gastronomes from joining the artists, diplomats, and other chic types at this now globally famed restaurant. The name Cibrèo refers to an ancient Tuscan dish of fricasséed cocks' combs and innards in an egg and lemon

sauce, and it signals the owners' commitment to authentic Tuscan cuisine. In the best Florentine tradition, pastas are eschewed here in favor of nourishing soups: the yellow bell pepper purée and the fish soup are exceptional. Owner-chef Fabio Picchi has a penchant for poultry. Birds feature in several of his best dishes: quail breast in chestnut sauce (petti di quaglia con salsa di marroni) and pigeon stuffed with hot-and-sweet fruit. There is also a remarkable larded calf's liver, cooked for a whole day at low heat, and delectable meatballs of veal and ricotta in a zesty tomato sauce. Nor is seafood neglected. We recently sampled a superb mussel terrine, palombo (a variety of shark) alla livornese, and a deeply satisfying inzimino (stew) of calamari and Swiss chard. The vast cellar is impressively stocked with regional wines, and Fabio's wife, Benedetta, crafts all the memorable desserts. **C** 90,000 lire (wine incl).

12/20 Coco Lezzone
Via del Parioncino 26r - (055) 287178
Closed Sun, Tue dinner, last wk of Jul, Aug. No cards.
On a narrow street that runs into the Arno, just a stone's throw from the Ponte Vecchio, is a trattoria with all the "genuine" Florentine atmosphere that you could hope to find. Never mind that the food is just so-so, or that the house wine makes strong men cry; the tourists packed in cheek-by-jowl are convinced that here, at last, they've discovered the real Italy. All the usual dishes are on hand: ribollita (a thick vegetable soup), trippa (tripe) alla fiorentina...bistecca (steak) alla fiorentina must be ordered in advance. The roast pigeon is usually a good bet. Should you decide to order a half-portion of pasta (or anything else), be aware that you will be billed 90 percent of the dish's list price. How's that for hospitality? **C** 90,000 lire (wine incl).

Dino
Via Ghibellina 51r - (055) 241452
Closed Sun dinner, Mon, 3 wks in Aug. All major cards.
A comfortable, animated trattoria where pasta and fine Tuscan beef reign supreme. Sauces for the former contain mysterious herbs and spices, while the latter is served in all its glorious simplicity, embellished

only with a few fragrant drops of olive oil. Owner-manager Dino Casini is one of the city's top sommeliers, and his wine list (or better: wine tome) is astounding. Regional wines are highlighted, from the majestic Brunello di Montalcino to growers' Chiantis (we like the Castello di Ama). A charming place, in sum, with a friendly, smiling staff. C 60,000 lire (wine incl).

Don Chisciotte

Via Ridolfi 4 - (055) 475430
Closed Sun, Aug. All major cards.
Chef Walter's quixotic quest is to create seafood dishes to startle, amaze, and delight his customers. He mischievously sneaks in flavors not specified on the menu—thus, on a recent occasion, our ricotta and salmon dumplings (malfatti) in calamari sauce also tasted of scamorza cheese; and potato gnocchi with squash blossoms and tiny shrimp were liberally spiced with curry. In the first case we found the pairing brilliant, though we normally don't care for seafood and cheese combinations. We were less impressed with the second effort. Main courses include an aromatic gratin of baby squid showered with herbs, delicate monkfish with squash blossoms and zucchini cream sauce, and grouper layered with eggplant and tomatoes to make a kind of fish parmigiano that brims with zesty flavor. We only wish that Walter would use less salmon; and that he would come up with a more original roster of desserts. C 70,000 lire.

Enoteca Pane e Vino

Via San Niccolò 60 - (055) 2476956
Closed Sun (limited menu at lunch), 10 days wk of Aug 15. All major cards.
The setting is most seductive at this noteworthy enoteca and the wine list, as always, is absolutely riveting. You're certain to find a suitable partner for your pumpkin and Pecorino dumplings, lamb and prune tagine, or rosemary-scented baked pasta and beans. C 45,000 lire.

Enoteca Pinchiorri

Via Ghibellina 87 - (055) 242777
Closed Sun, Mon lunch, Aug, 4 days at Christmas. All major cards.
One night in November 1992, someone set fire to the fabulous cellar of legendary wines that Giorgio Pinchiorri and his wife, Annie, had lovingly amassed over the years (37 vintages of Pétrus, 30 of Lafite-Rothschild, the whole gamut of Romanée-Conti, the rarest growths of Tuscany, Piedmont, Lombardy, and the Veneto...). Somehow the couple found the fortitude to start anew, and now the Enoteca Pinchiorri is reborn from its ashes—better even than before. The Enoteca's wine list is as cosmopolitan as the clientele; it boasts prestigious bottles from every fine wine-growing region of the world. The menu, however, is strictly Italian. Led by Annie Feolde, the kitchen team researches long-lost culinary traditions, seeking out ancient regional recipes which are then updated with today's ingredients and cooking methods.
Two young chefs, Italo and Alessandro (whose combined ages don't even add up to 50), lead the preparation of the *Grande Carte*—a staggering sampler of Italy's culinary art—and two eight-course set meals (priced at 150,000 lire). The latter offer excellent value as well as a brilliantly composed progression of tastes. We can still recall the intensely herbal perfume of potato gnocchi stuffed with pesto and paired with tiny squid stewed in white wine; the vigorous savor of tortelli stuffed with cabbage and pancetta and showered with shavings of smoked ricotta; the delicacy of veal sweetbreads enhanced with dried porcini; and the deep, complex flavors of rabbit with walnuts and black olives in a bright carrot purée. Only the fish—in a shellfish sauce touched with anchovy—was a half-tone below the rest. There follows a veritable avalanche of alluring sweets, but (we wager) not even the heartiest trencherman could do justice to them all! C 75-200,000 lire.

Le Fonticine

Via Nazionale 79r - (055) 282106
Closed Sun, Mon, Aug. V, AE.
Emilian and Tuscan influences dominate the menu at Le Fonticine. From Emilia comes the kitchen's knack with pasta—silky, diaphanous, and golden with fresh egg yolks—while the Florentine tradition is evident in the unerring selection of prime meats and perfumed olive oil. So from the all-but-immutable list of offerings, choose a first course of hand-crafted tagliolini, tortelli, or tagliatelle, then follow up with steak alla fiorentina, osso buco, veal kidney, or perhaps a young capon roasted to

savory perfection. Desserts tend to be heavy and caloric; the wine list pays almost exclusive homage to classy Tuscan reds. **C** 65,000 lire.

Il Francescano
Largo Bargellini 16 (Santa Croce)
(055) 241605
Closed Wed, Aug. All major cards.
The patrons, décor, and table settings here are all determinedly trendy, but the Tuscan cooking is as rootsy and genuine as can be. Other assets include a cheerful *zia* ("auntie") who toils away in the kitchen, a smiling and handsome dining-room staff, and jolly Alberto, the owner, who provides his guests with solid sustenance at an honest price—some 55,000 lire with a top-flight bottle of wine. **C** 55,000 lire (wine incl).

Gauguin
Via degli Alfani 24r - (055) 2340616
Closed Sun, Mon lunch, Sep. V, AE.
After your umpteenth blood-rare fiorentina, we bet you'll be ready for a visit to Gauguin, the best vegetarian restaurant in town. It won't feel like penance, either: the atmosphere is elegant and amusing, anything but austere. And the menu is absolutely appetizing, with dishes like cold borscht, semolina gnocchi dressed up with pesto, a peasant-style combination of potatoes and cheese (but the cheese here is real French Camembert), and vegetable croquettes served with a lusty garlic mayonnaise. The wine list is small but perfectly appropriate. **C** 40,000 lire and up.

Leo in Santa Croce
Via Torta 7r - (055) 210829
Closed Mon, Jul 20-Aug 12. All major cards.
Leo is the voluble, ebullient host of this medieval tavern near the church of Santa Croce. House-made pastas and charcoal-grilled meats highlight the long list of Tuscan and Umbrian specialties. From the cellar, why not choose a tasty Umbrian red produced on Leo's family estate? **C** 45-50,000 lire (wine incl).

La Loggia
Piazzale Michelangelo 1
(055) 2342832
Closed Wed, 2 wks in Aug. All major cards.
After admiring the stupendous view from the Piazzale Michelangelo, you can recover from your emotions (and your exertions, if you've made the climb on foot) at La Loggia. Give the "international" offerings a miss, and choose instead from the simpler, seasonal dishes—vegetable soup, charcoal-grilled steak, fish baked in parchment. Lots of tourists fill the huge dining rooms (this is *not* an intimate trattoria), but the food is handled with some care, and there is a mind-boggling cellar of Italian wines. **C** 60-65,000 lire.

A Lume di Candela
Via delle Terme 23 - (055) 294566
Dinner only (exc Sun). Closed 2 wks in Aug. All major cards.
English-style furniture and contemporary paintings decorate this romantic restaurant housed in the remains of a thirteenth-century tower. The cooking is a trifle fussy—the young chefs obviously want to strut their stuff. A recent repast brought ravioli sauced with an elegant lamb ragù; maccheroni topped with a strange but tasty mélange of squid, tomatoes, Pecorino cheese, Sherry, and thyme; delicate scallops poached in Traminer wine; and luscious honey ice cream. **C** 70,000 lire.

The Original Con Artists

The Florentines proudly call Ghiberti's Baptistery door in Piazza Duomo the Portal of Paradise. But they never talk about those two columns of black porphyry backed up against the outside wall. Hundreds of years ago, the people of Pisa gave them as a gift to the rival Florentines, who were getting a lot of bad press for alleged light-fingeredness. The Pisans, offering their expertise, told the gullible Florentines that if they stood behind the magic columns they'd be able to tell a thief from an honest gentleman. The funny thing is, no matter how long the Florentines stood behind those columns, they never quite figured out how to spot an honest man. The Pisans laughed all the way home. And the Florentines never did much to improve their reputation.

La Martinicca

Via del Sole 27r - (055) 218928
Closed Sun, Aug, 1 wk at Christmas. All major cards.

A youthful crew runs this typically Tuscan spot situated in the heart of historic Florence. From cabbage and bean soup (ribollita) to trippa or bistecca alla fiorentina, from cuttlefish stew (inzimino) to baccalà (salt cod) with chickpeas, all the region's classics are on hand, all competently prepared. Yummy desserts; tempting wine list. There are a few fish dishes on offer, but they pump up the bill beyond reason. **C** 50,000 lire (without fish, wine incl).

12/20 Mastrobulletta

Via Cento Stelle 27r - (055) 571275
Closed Sun, Aug. No cards.

Quintessential Florentine "soul food" (ribollita, bread-thickened tomato soup, lampredotto sausage, pot roast, and all manner of offal) is featured here. It's pretty fair cooking at a more-than-fair price. The sweets, however, are no great shakes and the cellar is only middling. **C** 38-40,000 lire.

Alle Murate

Via Ghibellina 52 - (055) 240618
Closed Mon, Aug, Christmas wk. All major cards.

Umberto Montana keeps his menu short, but it's full of bright ideas and is regularly revised. Here's a chef who knows his vegetables; their fresh flavors add a sunny touch to the gramigna pasta with cuttlefish and zucchini, thyme-scented eggplant tortelli and delicate shrimp-stuffed lettuce rolls napped with a silken tomato sauce. Among the main courses, we're partial to sage-scented chicken livers flanked by a tangy onion flan, and tender boned duck sparked with bitter-orange zest. A limited selection of dishes is presented in the adjacent wine bar. There, your bill will be about half of what is charged in the restaurant proper, but some dishes served in the smaller room have struck us as hastily crafted and rashly seasoned. Yet whether you elect to dine in the restaurant or the vineria, you'll be delighted by Umberto's distinctive collection of personally chosen wines. **C** 55,000 lire (30,000 lire in the vineria).

The prices in this guide reflect what establishments were charging at press time.

La Nandina

Piazza Santa Trinità, Borgo SS. Apostoli 64r - (055) 213024
Closed Sun, Aug. All major cards.

Our liking for this snug, centrally sited trattoria owes much to our affection for its owner, Walter Fanucci, a warm and genial host. His menu features typical—not stereotyped—Tuscan dishes executed with rare finesse. Try the memorable pappardelle (wide noodles) paired with duck or hare, delectable salt cod or cuttlefish stew, monumental steak alla fiorentina, and any of the farm-fresh vegetable garnishes. In season, mushrooms and game are given star billing. The clutch of Russian-inspired offerings (borscht, chicken Kiev, chachlik) were taught to Walter long ago by Danilo, a White Russian émigré, and are still piously prepared every day. **C** 45-60,000 lire.

Oliviero

Via delle Terme 51 - (055) 287643
Closed Sun, Aug. All major cards.

Regular visitors to Florence may be familiar with Oliviero; but perhaps they don't know that this long-established restaurant was recently taken over by an energetic and talented chef, Francesco Altomare. By and large, the results are gratifying. Let's get our reservations out of the way first: Altomare keeps his fish on the fire too long; and he gives antipasti and sweets short shrift. But he has few peers when it comes to crafting such lusty Tuscan favorites as tripe with tomato sauce and Parmesan cheese (the best we've sampled this year), pappardelle with a sumptuous duck sauce, potato tortelli topped with a robust rabbit ragù, and chicken-liver ravioli napped with delicate stewed baby onions. Notable, too, is the chicken breast stuffed with spinach and foie gras. Oliviero now proposes an exhaustive list of fine wines, and the service is once again precise and efficient. **C** 60,000 lire.

Il Patio

Hotel Sofitel,
Via de' Cerretani 10 - (055) 2381301
Open daily. All major cards.

Giuseppe Della Rosa puts a personal spin on traditional Italian classics. His scrupulous selection of prime, seasonal ingredients pays big dividends in dishes like penne with bitter greens and tangy Pecorino cheese, pappardelle with a deep-

19

ly flavorful hare sauce, tortellone (a single, sizable pasta dumpling) stuffed with eggplant and mozzarella, or lasagnette brilliantly combined with porcini and shrimp. Seafood lovers should direct their attention to coda di rospo (monkfish) tinged with saffron or turbot roasted with fennel seeds. Still, it's hard to pass over the chicken breast stuffed with fragrant herbs or breast of pigeon served pinkly rare, its juices deglazed with mellow balsamic vinegar. The cellar holds a distinguished collection of wines. C 60-65,000 lire.

Il Profeta
Borgo Ognissanti 83 - (055) 212265
Closed Sun, last 2 wks of Aug. All major cards.
We predict that you will enjoy the good Tuscan dishes served at this comfortable restaurant near the Arno. The sturdy of stomach should order the terrific fritto misto, a regal procession of crispy morsels deep-fried in premium olive oil. Otherwise, first courses run to traditional pastas, and the main event invariably features red meat (except for a few "Continental" offerings, a nod to the many tourists who eat here). The house dessert, zuppa del Profeta, is a visionary interpretation of the that boozy cake-and-custard sweet called zuppa inglese. Try it at your own risk—you may start prophesying in spite of yourself! C 60,000 lire.

Le Quattro Stagioni
Via Maggio 61 - (055) 218906
Closed Sun, Aug, 10 days at Christmas. All major cards.
In another era, Pierino might have been chef at some royal court: he's never happier than when readying a feast or grand occasion (witness his splendiferous fritto misto). The tenor of the times, alas, goes against his natural bent. Everyone is counting calories, or pennies, or both. Still he soldiers on, turning out pluperfect gnocchi, tortelloni, sublime bistecca alla fiorentina, fork-tender stracotto (pot roast), lamb stuffed with artichokes, and an array of appealing desserts. C 50,000 lire (wine incl).

Relais Le Jardin
Hotel Regency,
Piazza Massimo d'Azeglio 3 - (055) 245247
Open daily. All major cards.
Amedeo Ottaviani, who owns and operates this supremely elegant hotel res-

taurant, knows how to bring budding culinary talents to bloom. Young chefs come and go here (and when they leave, it is usually to launch places of their own), but the house style endures: sophisticated, graceful, refined. The current incumbent impressed us mightily with his intelligent technique and pertinent new readings of Italy's gastronomic traditions. A feast here might start with acqua cotta di pesce, a dressed-up version of a humble fish broth; then continue with fine-textured ravioli stuffed with skate, or endive, potatoes, or fennel according to the season. In autumn, tiny pumpkin gnocchetti paired with Tuscan chestnuts could pave the way for a delicate millefoglia composed of layered scallops, scampi, and hake, or for succulent roast pork stuffed with gingered figs and escorted by raviolini in a sweet-sour sauce. Among the lush conclusions we've liked are vanilla soufflé laced with Armagnac and a richly mocha-flavored tortino di caffè e cioccolato. Classy service; catholic cellar. C 100,000 lire.

Checkmate at the Loggia dei Lanzi

When he wasn't penning divine verse, Dante used to play chess with his pal Guido Cavalcanti at the Loggia dei Lanzi. They sat for hours, their legs slung over a wooden bench, oblivious, while local urchins leaped around and needled them unrelentingly. When the poets finally lost patience and jumped up to catch the brats, they often found themselves nailed to the bench by their capes or long coats, which they inevitably ripped to shreds. Sounds like a tailor-made trick...

Sabatini
Via Panzani 9a - (055) 282802
Closed Mon, hols vary. All major cards.
Sober elegance characterizes this handsome old house situated some 200 yards from the Duomo. The classic Tuscan cuisine is in keeping with the traditional, understated surroundings. We suggest you ignore such anomalies as the in-

evitable salmon, pâté de foie gras, and cannelloni oversauced with bechamel, and opt instead for fresh porcini dressed with a tasty variation on tonnato (tuna) sauce, or piquant bow-tie pasta with broccoli, or hearty pasta and beans. Meat courses are superior to the fish, we think, and lamb in particular is cooked to a turn. Though the wine cellar is filled with seductive bottles, their dizzying price tags force us to recommend that you order a good, simple Umbrian red, or the very presentable Orvieto. A retractable roof allows patrons to lunch or dine under an open sky in balmy weather. Charming service. **C** 80-90,000 lire.

12/20 Sostanza-Troia

Via del Porcellana 25r - (055) 212691
Closed Sat, Sun. No cards.
The central location and landmark status of this venerable trattoria makes it look like a good bet. The cheery, chattering waiters and open kitchen seem appealing, too. But the admonition: "Only full meals are served" inscribed on the menu makes one a bit wary; the preponderance of young tourists in the room isn't reassuring, either. The food? Strictly Tuscan, pretty pedestrian. To drink, there's house wine and not much else. Coffee? Forget it... **C** 40,000 lire.

La Taverna del Bronzino

Via delle Ruote 25 - (055) 495220
Closed Sun, Aug. All major cards.
The master portraitist, Bronzino, lived and painted in this house more than four centuries ago. Today, this tavern is the very picture of Tuscan hospitality: in comfortable, timelessly handsome surroundings, veteran waiters juggle platefuls of food that give off all sorts of appetizing aromas. One settles down with a pleasant sense of anticipation. The resolutely regional menu is lengthy and often revised. Fresh pasta—tortelli, tagliolini, ravioli—stuffed or sauced according to the season is reliably satisfying. Among the main courses, osso buco, lamb roasted in wine, veal rolls stuffed with artichokes, chicken curry, and bistecca alla fiorentina are all good choices. Even with a fine bottle from the distinguished wine cellar, the tab remains reasonable. **C** 60,000 lire (wine incl.).

L'Uovo di Colombo

At Vaglia, Via Bolognese 39 (in the courtyard) - (055) 407539
Dinner only (exc Sun & Mon). Closed 2 wks mid Jan, 1st 2 wks of Sep. V, AE.
"Columbus's egg" signifies a simple solution to an apparently unsolvable problem. Problems are few at this eccentric address just outside the city, where patrons are greeted at the entrance by a series of rather naughty photographs, then are seated at marble tables amid vintage cars, antique posters, and other old-time automotive memorabilia. The kitchen's approach is old-fashioned, too: it produces the sort of sturdy, rustic fare that Florentines traditionally favor. After a primo of polenta sauced with wild-boar gravy or spaghetti sautéed with garlic and pancetta, you can move on to one of the excellent main courses that are the highlight here: beef braised in Chianti, stewed local duck, or breast of guinea fowl with mushrooms and field greens. If you can handle dessert, the panna cotta (baked cream) and chocolate cake merit your attention. **C** 50,000 lire.

■ In Bagno a Ripoli   7 km SE

Centanni

Via di Centanni 7 - (055) 630122
Closed Sat lunch, Sun, Aug. V.
The dining room is undeniably charming, and the garden shaded by ancient olive trees is pure delight. But the kitchen has lost its luster of late, forcing us to suspend our rating. Tough tortelli, a botched fiorentina—for 60,000 lire we expect a whole lot better! Centanni's chef used to show imagination as well as skill... What happened? **C** 60,000 lire.

■ In Calenzano   15 km NW

Carmagnini del '500

At Pontenuovo, Via Barberino 238 (exit Prato Calenzano) - (055) 8819930
Closed Mon, 2 wks in Aug, Feb. V, AE, DC.
A huge picture window lets you admire a view of the Apennines while feasting on Renaissance-style Tuscan fare. In addition to the usual crostini (liver canapés), a fine farm-cured prosciutto is offered to start the meal. Irresistible house-made pasta follows, in the form of cannelloni or

tagliatelle, the latter generously garnished with seasonal wild mushrooms. The meats, in particular, have a certain Cinquecento grandeur: tender herbed rabbit, grilled to a turn, or the lordly lamb "del Granduca" are excellent alternatives to the recurrent fiorentina, but that beautifully grilled and seasoned steak is an impressive achievement that beef-lovers will find hard to turn down. The wine cellar is sensational. **C** 50,000 lire.

■ In **Candeli**   7 km E

Il Verrocchio

Villa La Massa, at Candeli, Via La Massa 6 - (055) 666141
Closed Mon, hols vary. All major cards.

We'll spare you the details of our most recent meal on the glorious terrace of this gorgeous villa. We're sure you don't want to hear about a watery dish of pasty ravioli, or about scorched steaks, or unwashed fruit... Suffice it to say that after shelling out some 80,000 lire, we left Il Verrocchio still hungry. Just a fluke? Maybe. But no rating this year. **C** 80,000 lire.

■ In **Carmignano**   22 km W

La Cantina di Toia

At Bacchereto - (055) 8717135
Closed Mon, Tue, Nov. All major cards.

Leonardo da Vinci's grandmother once owned this ancient farmhouse, now the scene of the wildest, woolliest cooking in Tuscany. Chef-proprietor Carlo Persia is a powerhouse of culinary creativity. True, his passion sometimes pushes him overboard into excess, but most of his menu displays a structured complexity that enchants the adventurous palate. We can forgive the incoherence of a dish like young goat spiced with cinnamon, cloves, and juniper, served with herbed gnocchetti, polenta croquettes, and apple strudel (each element, incidentally, is delicious) when in the next moment we are presented with a masterpiece like red and black ravioli stuffed with basil-marinated shrimp in a delectable sauce enriched with morsels of squid and broccoli; or duck lasagnetta with diced fresh vegetables and chestnuts; or a magnificent hare roasted in caul fat and profusely perfumed with fresh thyme. Gustatory thrills

are assured by the Mexican-inspired corn tortilla stuffed with turkey or fried sea bream with coconut rice and fried banana. Desserts are exotic: how about a pineapple filled with sweetened rice and fresh fruit? Or rose and hazelnut mousse laced with Vin Santo? Words don't do justice to these finely wrought culinary conceits. You'll simply have to drive out to this lovely corner of the Tuscan countryside, and see–taste!–for yourself. **C** 50,000 lire.

Da Delfina

At Artimino, Via della Chiesa 1 (055) 8718074
Closed Mon dinner, Tue, Aug. No cards.

Delfina, now 85, has hung up her apron. She tends to her garden these days, while her son, Carlo, and his kitchen team prepare her soul-satisfying repertoire of Tuscan country dishes. Delfina continues to inspire and encourage her successors, and she makes sure that only the freshest seasonal ingredients—most come straight from the family farm—are permitted in the kitchen. Chef Carlo sticks laudably close to his mother's recipes: no "updating" or "free interpretations" here! The fabulous pappardelle alla lepre (wide noodles with hare sauce), the delicate mixed-grain and artichoke soup, the lusty cavatelli with turnip tops are faithful renditions of Delfina's bucolic starters. You could follow them up with a sumptuous dish of baccalà (salt cod), broccoli rabe, and white beans; rabbit with olives and pine nuts flanked by a startling wild-fennel purée; or roast lamb, kid, or spit-roasted farm chicken. The Pecorino and ricotta cheeses come from neighboring farms, and the sweets, though few in number, are all made in Delfina's kitchen. The cellar is small but select; wine buffs won't want to miss the chance to try the tasty Carmignano on its home turf. **C** 50,000 lire.

■ In **Fiesole**   8 km NE

Cave di Maiano
Via delle Cave 16 - (055) 59133
Closed Thu, Sun dinner, 2 wks in mid Aug, 4 days at Christmas. All major cards.

Some fine, sunny Sunday take the road to Fiesole and head for this converted sheepfold, now an adorable country restaurant. The site is sublime: it recalls those serene landscapes one may glimpse through windows painted by Botticelli or Filippo Lippi. On the terrace, shaded by a quincunx of plane trees, Aldo or his nephew, Vanio, recites the day's offerings, usually such typical Tuscan fare as white beans served warm with a drizzle of olive oil or cannelloni with an herbed pork stuffing. The secondi (main courses) comprise the menu's best offerings: pan-roasted farm chicken, an excellent roast pigeon, and in season, all manner of game invariably garnished with porcini mushrooms. Decent cellar, with some good red wines. **C** 50,000 lire.

 Villa San Michele
Via Di Doccia 4 - (055) 59451
Closed end Nov-end Feb. All major cards.

A former convent built in the fifteenth century, the Villa San Michele now attracts a more worldly (and necessarily wealthy) breed of pilgrim. With a light and skillful hand, chef Attilio Di Fabrizio performs minor miracles with the region's meat and produce. In spring, his menu highlights the new crop of tender vegetables; in summer, he accents airy textures and cool flavors; autumn dishes emphasize Tuscany's plentiful game and wild mushrooms. A few classics recur throughout the seasons: risotto enriched with lobster and white beans, for example, or tortelli stuffed with eggplant and goat cheese in a thyme-scented sauce. The restaurant takes pride in the succulent local beef (the bistecca alla fiorentina is exceptional), but steamed sea bass with a tart-sweet orange sauce or turbot swirled with mustard zabaglione offer attractive alternatives. The wine list is enticingly rich, discouragingly pricey. By all means reserve a table on the terrace, where in summer the scent of olive and lemon trees wafts up on every breeze. **C** 120,000 lire. **M** 95,000 lire.

■ In Lastra a Signa   13 km W

 Antica Trattoria Sanesi
Via dell'Arione 33 - (055) 8720234
Closed Sun dinner, Mon, Jul 20-Aug 20. All major cards.

This busy, modest establishment in the center of town serves good local charcuterie, sturdy Tuscan soups and pastas, and a creditable fiorentina (charcoal-grilled steak). In season, game and wild

mushrooms predominate. Ask for the crunchy, mocha-flavored croccantino for dessert. Wines are of the unpretentious, thirst-quenching variety. **C** 50,000 lire (wine incl).

■ In Mercatale Val di Pesa   24 km SW

 Il Salotto del Chianti
Via Sonnino 92 - (055) 8218016
Dinner only (exc hols). Closed Wed, last 3 wks of Jan. All major cards.

This "living room" is intimate, not to say minuscule, but though he may have limited space to seat his patrons, chef Marcello's desire to please knows no bounds. Literally: when he gets wind of an interesting new ingredient, he'll travel miles to get hold of it for his guests. Thus his cheese board is second to none, and his cellar (located a few doors away, and considerably larger than the restaurant) is second only to that of the renowned Enoteca Pinchiorri in Florence (see above). Produce and meats are chosen with admirable discernment. A meal not long ago featured ravioli stuffed with wild asparagus, rustic gnocchetti made with nettle tops, succulent lamb braciolette roasted in caul fat (which bastes and flavors the meat as it melts), and a parfait perfumed with acacia honey. Marcello's spontaneous style occasionally misfires; and we wish he wouldn't put cheese in virtually every dish—several would be far better without. But these cavils are small beer next to the genuine pleasures of dining and drinking—remember that cellar!—at Marcello's Salotto. **C** 50,000 lire.

■ In Montecatini Terme   49 km NW

 Enoteca da Giovanni
Via Garibaldi 25 - (0572) 71695
Closed Mon. V, DC, EC.

Giovanni is an affable, courteous Piedmontese native whose aim in life is to make his patrons happy. His Enoteca has survived being in and out of fashion, several recessions, and all the ups and downs that the restaurant business in Italy has lately been heir to. This enduring popularity can be attributed to Giovanni's terrific risottos, his always prime grilled meats, and such seductive pastas as ravioli in shellfish sauce, tagliolini with shrimp, and maccheroni with duck ragù. We also like the boned pigeon presented in a savory sauce with raisins and pine nuts. In autumn and winter, game is featured along with wild mushrooms and truffles. All the homey desserts are made right on the premises, and the cellar, of course, is top-notch. **C** 90,000 lire (wine incl).

Del Grand Hotel e La Pace
Viale della Torretta 1 - (0572) 75801
Closed Nov-Mar. All major cards.
This hotel restaurant functions like a well-oiled machine. The setting, food, and service meet high standards; the elegant clientele is visibly at ease. Though the menu offers few surprises, it rarely disappoints. Notably good are the trout amandine, linguine sauced with genuine pesto, steamed scallops set atop a silken white-bean purée, turbot simmered in Prosecco wine and strewn with caper blossoms, and saddle of rabbit with field greens. The house recipe for crème brûlée was "stolen" from New York's Le Cirque—by all means, try it! **C** 80,000 lire.

■ In Prato 19 km N

Il Piraña
Via Valentini 110
(0574) 25746
Closed Sat lunch, Sun, Aug. All major cards.
As its name suggests, this restaurant gives top billing to fish. Superlatively fresh seafood stars in imaginative warm and cold antipasto salads, in plump fish ravioli sprinkled with shellfish, in tasty taglierini (long, thin noodles) sauced with squash blossoms and shrimp, and lavish fish soups. Main courses continue the theme with delicate turbot fillets in a light, tomatoey broth dotted with tiny clams, sea bass baked in a crust of coarse salt, or a splendid but daunting mixed grill of fish and shellfish. The chestnut parfait is delicious, but the traditional cantuccini (cookies) di Prato are especially good after a seafood feast. An ample cellar offers many fine Tuscan wines. The service is as classy as the menu, and tab is pretty stiff. **C** 80,000 lire.

■ In Reggello 28 km SE

Le Vieux Pressoir
Villa Rigacci,
at Vaggio, Via Manzoni 76 - (055) 8656718
Closed Tue. All major cards.
Within the walls of this beauteous villa is one of Italy's few French restaurants. Parisian chef David-Pierre Lecomte supervises a menu of Gallic offerings that features a delicious duck breast with citrus fruit, trout in a lightly smoky cream sauce with celery, and a satisfying coq au vin. First courses, on the whole, are less successful; so ignore them and splash out instead on such scrumptious desserts as sautéed apples tucked into a crêpe "beggar's purse" or a crisp pastry "tulip" heaped with white and dark-chocolate mousses. The fairly pricey wine list pays equal homage to French and Italian bottlings. **C** 65,000 lire.

■ In San Casciano Val di Pesa 18 km S

La Tenda Rossa
At Cerbaia, Piazza del Monumento 9
(055) 826132
Closed Wed, Thu lunch, Aug. All major cards.
Creative cooking in a classic setting. The faults to be found here are few: scampi set atop potato mousse lacked verve, we think, and the brodetto served with squid-stuffed cannoli needed a zest of color and heightened taste. But the menu also provides many more exciting moments, witness the lobster ravioli on a heap of tender white beans or sea bream (cooked in its skin for juiciness) paired with onions caramelized in honey and rosemary. Meat dishes are invariably superb. From the plebeian kid stew alla pastorale ("shepherd's style") to the polished squab stuffed with Port-laced giblets and truffles, the flavors are deep, intense, and beautifully balanced. We wonder why the dessert list is so short—luckily, the yummy house chocolates are on hand to satisfy any lingering yen for a sweet. Owner Silvano Santandrea has amassed a sensational cellar, which he will describe to you in loving detail. Adorable service. **C** 100,000 lire and up.

Gault Millau's ratings are based solely on the restaurants' cuisine. We do not take into account the atmosphere, décor, service and so on; these are commented upon within the review.

Quick Bites

CONTENTS

CAFES

Apollo Bar
Via dell'Ariento 41r - (055) 219751
Open 7:30am-1am. Closed Sun.
Come in and admire the splendid wood bar—it resembles the keel of a ship—then join the regulars from the San Lorenzo market who lunch here on good salads and cold dishes. In the evening, students and foreign visitors drop by to listen to music and grab a snack. Owner Sandro Corelli (who also runs the Yab disco, see *Nightlife*) has managed to create an attractive ambience that mixes Florentine flair with a "New York" feel.

Caffè Ricchi
Piazza Santo Spirito 9r - (055) 215864
Open 7am-1am. Closed Sun.
Caffè Ricchi has lots going for it, not least a spectacular view of Brunelleschi's masterpiece, the church of Santo Spirito. But it also boasts a garden where one may enjoy a sandwich or light meal, some ice cream or an aperitivo, to the accompaniment of live music. Inside, the regulars while away an idle hour playing cards or chess.

Giubbe Rosse
Piazza della Repubblica 13/14r - (055) 212280
Open 8am-1:30am. Closed Wed.
A renowned literary café founded in 1890, Giubbe Rosse is best known as the Futurists' favorite watering hole. Since its reopening in 1991, latter-day wits have followed Lenin, Montale, and Gadda who all sipped, supped, and hypothesized here in their day. On offer are tip-top cocktails and aperitivi, good hot and cold dishes, fresh panini (sandwiches), and pastries.

Paszkowsky
Piazza della Repubblica 6 - (055) 210236
Open 7am-1:30am. Closed Mon.
Paszkowsky (the locals say "Pazzoski") is a cultural landmark on a par with Giubbe Rosse (see above), its literary rival on Piazza della Repubblica. Established in 1846, it holds a secure place in the history of Italian art and politics. Come soak up the highbrow atmosphere along with the delicious house hot chocolate, an aperitivo, or a glass of wine from the top-notch cellar. At lunchtime, the bill of fare includes a variety of salads and pastas which generally live up to Paszkowsky's exalted reputation.

QUICK BITES

Bar degli Amici
Via XXVII Aprile - (055) 475087
Open 7am-9pm. Closed Sat.
A dizzying array of hot sandwiches and quick hot or cold snacks is offered in this pleasant spot, located in the northern reaches of Florence. Most of the habitués spurn the tables and eat instead perched on stools at the bar.

25

Birreria Centrale

Piazza de' Cimatori 1r - (055) 211915
Open noon-12:30am. Closed Aug, hols.
  Beer is naturally the beverage of choice at this nineteenth-century brasserie. More than 50 different kinds are on hand to accompany an excellent shrimp and salmon salad, a creditable carpaccio, and unusual (but delicious) venison salami. For dessert, there are regional sweets and a good homemade tiramisù.

Il Boccascena

Viale Europa 49-53 - (055) 685996
Open 5pm-1am. Closed Mon.
  Patterned after a Parisian bistro, where patrons can eat and drink to music, or just order a quick coffee at the bar. The menu spotlights good seafood, with the best oysters in town, mussels, and fish carpaccio. Italian wines dominate a cellar that also includes French, Australian, and American bottles.

Masses in the Open Air

  Ever notice all those decorative little altars dotted around town? There are hundreds of them. They've been there since 1348, when the plague that wiped out tens of thousands of Florentines was at its most virulent. Churchmen of the time decided to build these outdoor altars and decorate them with images of saints to keep up flagging morale. They also wanted to keep the pestilential masses out of churches and in the open air, where there was less chance of spreading contagion.

Boccon Divino

Via Porta Rossa 49r - (No telephone)
Open summer: 10am-10pm; winter: 11am-7pm. Closed Sun.
  Sturdy blond-wood tables and benches create a relaxed atmosphere in this little snack shop, which specializes in crostini alla toscana: canapés topped with artichokes, chicken livers, and various savory spreads. Sandwiches and a rotating roster of pasta and rice dishes are also offered daily.

La Borsa

Via Por Santa Maria 55r - (055) 216109
Open summer: 7:30am-midnight; winter: 7:30am-8:30pm. Closed Sun.
  La Borsa consists of some twenty little tables set out under the portico of the Volta dei Mercati. It's a fine place for a cooling fruit salad on a hot day, or for hearty meal-size salads served in pretty glass bowls. Sandwiches, little pizzas, and a choice selection of beverages round out the menu.

Il Caffè

Piazza Pitti 9 - (055) 2396241
Open 11am-1:30am. Closed Mon, Aug.
  Il Caffè stands opposite the Pitti Palace and Boboli gardens, a convenient stop for a quick lunch—there's a good choice of sandwiches and hot dishes. But the specialty of the house, as the name implies, is coffee: you can sample varieties flavored with mint, cinnamon, or lemon. In the evening, live music is often on tap, but note that dinner is served by advance order only.

Caffè Cibrèo

Via Andrea del Verrocchio 5r - (055) 2341094
Open 8am-1am. Closed Sun.
  Gourmets' eyes brighten and everybody's taste buds snap to attention when they enter this deluxe wine bar, where at any time of day a glass of fine Tuscan red may be accompanied by *recherché* snacks prepared by the same chef who cooks for Cibrèo's excellent restaurant (see *Restaurants*). The cheeses, salamis and other sausages, salmon, caviar, zestful condiments and pickles are all first-rate. Choose a seat in the cozy, wood-paneled café, then make your selection from the reasonably priced menu. The house espresso is not to be missed.

Cantinetta Antinori

Palazzo Antinori,
Piazza Antinori 4 - (055) 292234
Open 12:30pm-2:30pm & 7pm-10:30pm. Closed Sat, Sun.
  Direct from the grower to you: the Antinoris have been winemakers in Tuscany for hundreds of years, and the full range of their production can be sampled here, in the cellar of the family's splendid palazzo. Keep the fine wines company with typical

Florentine fare, good cold meats, or tangy cheeses (many made on the Antinoris' own properties).

Cantinetta dei Verrazzano

Via de' Tavolini 18-20r - (055) 268590
Open 8am-8pm. Closed Sun.

Warm, inviting—and invariably crowded—this wine shop just steps from Piazza della Signoria offers two different settings at a single address. One is wood-paneled, with bottle-lined shelves and a bar displaying ready-to-eat savory snacks; the other, accented with mirrors, presents enticing sweets and stuffed flat breads (schiacciate) which customers order, then take into the adjoining dining room. Don't be put off by the crush: the quality of the food warrants a little effort!

Champagneria

Via Lambrischini 15r - (055) 490804
Open 11am-3pm & 7:30pm-late night. Closed Sun.

Here's a Florentine-style bistro that features excellent wines and appetizing snacks. Good bets include sweet or savory crêpes, fish, focacce, and hearty salads. Don't overlook the list of bubblies—it's the best in town.

I Cinque Tavoli

Via del Sole 26-28r - (055) 294438
Open 8am-3pm & 5pm-1am. Closed Mon.

A convivial mix of students, office workers, and tourists occupy the five tables of this lively brasserie, located between Santa Maria Novella and Piazza della Repubblica. But even if you don't get a seat, you can stand at the bar with a tasty sandwich, cheese-filled foccacia (flat bread), or hamburger hot off the grill, with a glass of excellent English or German beer to wash it down. The low prices attract quite a crowd, so avoid the busiest times if you want a table.

Coffee Shop
di Alessandro Nannini

Via Borgo San Lorenzo - (055) 212680
Open 8am-midnight. Closed Mon.

Nannini, you may know, was once a Formula 1 racer; he is also the scion of Siena's best-known pastry specialists. The bar that bears his name serves a wide selection of premium coffees, which you can accompany with cakes, tarts, doughnuts, or other sweets (all, of course, from the family ovens) for a mid-morning or afternoon break. Lunchtime brings an abundant choice of hot and cold sandwiches. Note the convenient location, near the city's central market.

Dogali

Viale Malta 5 - (055) 679556
Open 9am-7:30pm. Closed Sun.

Fast food, Italian-style, means hot or cold house-made snacks put together virtually as you watch. Dogali is there whenever you're hungry: at lunch, look for meal-sized salads, restorative soups, crostini, or a warming dish of tripe or baccalà; for a bite in between meals, try the hot pizza-dough sandwiches stuffed with ham or vegetables.

Donnini

Piazza della Repubblica 15r - (055) 213694
Open 7am-midnight. Closed Mon.

Centrally located, with pretty tables shaded by broad awnings and a menu of simple, satisfying dishes, Donnini is a haven for the footsore sightseer. The sformati di spinaci (spinach timbales) make an elegant little lunch, and the fruit tarts and tiramisù are a treat. The ice-cream sundaes are fabulous but quite expensive.

Friggitoria N.34

Via Sant'Antonio 50r - (055) 211660
Open 8:30am-2pm & 4pm-8pm. Closed Sun.

An old-fashioned fried-food stand, one of the last in town. Forget about calories just this once, and order up a crisp, satisfying batch of traditional Florentine coccoli (fried bread balls), bomboloni (sweet beignets), and other such fabulous fritters.

Gilli

Piazza della Repubblica 39r - (055) 213896
Open summer: 8am-midnight; winter: 8am-9pm. Closed Tue.

This charming and nostalgic tea room has stood at the same address since 1910, but Gilli's tradition as a purveyor of pastries dates back to the eighteenth century. At the inviting little tables set out on the piazza, you can nibble on the excellent sweets or make a meal of one of the famous house salads and finish with an elaborate and delicious ice cream sundae.

A seductive array of regional Sienese and Florentine cakes appears at teatime. Prices are on the high side: the pastas sell for 13,000 lire, a main dish costs around 22,000 lire.

Harry's Bar

Lungarno Vespucci 22r - (055) 2396700
Open 11am-midnight. Closed Mon.
Not far from Piazza Ognissanti on the Lungarno Vespucci, the Florentine version of Harry's Bar is an elegant spot for a drink or light meal. The paneled interior and soft lights create a cozy, clubby ambience. If a snack or a drink is all the sustenance you seek, head for the bar (on your left as you enter), where sandwiches, fine wines, and Bellinis (of course) are served for prices just slightly higher than in humbler venues.

Italy and Italy

Piazza della Stazione 2r - (055) 282885
Open 10am-1am. Closed Tue.
This well-known chain bridges the gap between American-style fast food and authentic Italian cooking. Luigi Cremoncini, who founded the company, cleverly combined the American atmosphere that Italian adolescents find irresistible with dishes in the homegrown Mediterranean tradition. The result is a menu where burgers meet pasta (spaghetti alla Garibaldi, penne alla Cavour) and fresh meal-size salads. The spacious premises offer ample

A Hole in the Wall for Mr. Moneybags

Unjust tyrant, money-mad banker, and all-around tightwad, Cosimo de' Medici was scolded for his evil habits by Pope Eugene IV and forced to pay for the restoration of the Convent of San Marco, located near the Palazzo Medici. As part of the punishment, he was told to "wall up 10,000 golden florins therein." Even today, passing Florentines train a pious-but-wistful eye on the convent; no one knows if Cosimo complied with the Pope's orders, and, if he did, whether the florins are still holed up in that wall.

seating, even at busy times. Our only reproach is that the wraparound windows make us feel like we're eating in a fishbowl.

Kenny

Via dei Bardi 64r - (055) 212915
Open daily 11am-midnight (Sat & Sun 11am-1am).
The pioneer of fast food in Florence, Kenny serves a bewildering variety of burgers, from the modest to the monumental, along with premium beers and decent patatine (french fries). Service is speedy and delivered with a smile. A quick snack will set you back a mere 10,000 lire.

Marchetti

Via de' Calzaiuoli 102r - (055) 210805
Open summer: 9:30am-12:30am; winter: 10:30am-8pm. Closed Mon.
Places selling pizza by the slice have sprung up all over Florence, but this one gets our vote for its central location and delicious pies, topped with all sorts of imaginative sauces and seasonings. Fresh-tasting salads and several types of crêpes are available as well, along with draft beer, soft drinks, and wine. The premises are roomy and attractive, with lots of seating and (we saved the best for last) a wonderful ice-cream counter.

Nerbone

Mercato Centrale di San Lorenzo, Via di San Casciano - (055) 219949
Open 7am-2pm. Closed Sun.
Tripe and offal are traditional Florentine favorites, and Nerbone is a standard-bearer among the city's purveyors of "variety meats." Situated in the San Lorenzo market hall, this bustling eatery provides shoppers and vendors with lusty snacks of hot sandwiches filled with sausage, or tripe, or terrific boiled beef prepared on the spot. Most people eat on the run, but there are a few tables for the weary. Prices are low for this robust fare, best partnered by a glass of the good house Chianti.

Procacci

Via de' Tornabuoni 64 - (055) 211656
Open 9am-1pm & 4:30pm-7:30pm. Closed Wed.

Amid the fashionable shops of the city's most elegant street you'll find Procacci, the place for panini tartufati. These dainty truffled morsels are to sandwiches what prime rib is to an ordinary burger. So go ahead and order an aperitivo and a panino stuffed with salmon and truffles—a divine! Procacci, which celebrates its 100th birthday in 1995, is also famed as a gourmet grocery, featuring a selection of fine Tuscan foodstuffs.

Queen Victoria

Via Por Santa Maria 34r - (055) 295162
Open summer: 10am-midnight; winter: 10am-11pm. Closed Mon.

Prim little tables are set out on two floors and, in summer, on the terrace. The atmosphere is refined, and the food is good and not too expensive. Choose a full meal or a quick snack from the selection of several pasta dishes, main courses, mixed salads, and ice cream desserts offered daily.

Rose's Bar

Via di Parione 26r - (055) 287090
Open 10:30am-1:30am. Closed Sun.

Rose's is popular with students and working folks, and the crowds here are thickest at lunchtime, when hot and cold starters, stuffed pizzas, variations on carpaccio, and an oft-revised set meal provide speedy, satisfying refreshment.

Lo Spuntino

Via Canto dei Nelli 16r - (055) 210920
Open 8am-midnight. Closed Wed.

The wooden tables, stools, and benches are pretty rudimentary, but they are comfortable enough for a quick snack of pizza (there are more than 30 kinds) sold by the slice, washed down with a soft drink, beer, or glass of wine.

Vineria Torrini

Piazza dell'Olio 2r - (055) 2396616
Open 7am-10:30pm. Closed Sun.

Over 150 years old and still going strong, this venerable wine shop off Piazza del Duomo serves well-loved Florentine dishes—thick soups, herbed roast suckling pig, cheese crostini, Italian salamis. What's more, the competent service is swift enough to rival that of a fast-food chain!

Yellow Bar

Via del Proconsolo 39r - (055) 211766
Open until 1am. Closed Tue.

Not so much a bar as a pub, this spot attracts appreciative crowds for lunch and dinner with its chummy atmosphere, cozy wood furnishings, and cheap eats: steaks, pizzas, burgers, salads, and sweets comprise a bill of fare that has something for every taste and pocketbook.

SWEET SNACKS

■ ICE CREAM

Badiani

Viale de' Mille 20r - (055) 578682
Open 7am-1am. Closed Tue.

All the ice creams at this important gelateria are prepared on the premises by expert artisans. Badiani's specialty is fresh fruit filled with ice cream—the pineapples, lemons, and mandarin oranges are particularly nice—as well as ice-cream cakes, bombes, and frozen mousses. But the shop's crowning glory is its closely guarded recipe for custard-flavored buontalenti ice cream, named for Bernardo Buontalenti, the Florentine architect who invented the creamy dessert for banquets given by the Medicis.

La Bottega del Gelato

Via Por Santa Maria 33r - (055) 296550
Open 8am-8pm (summer 8am-midnight). Closed Tue.

Close to the Ponte Vecchio, this little shop is busy from morning to night with sightseers who, after feasting their eyes on the cultural marvels of Florence, are in the mood for a little oral gratification. The excellent ice creams are made by hand on the premises; if you like caramel, you'll adore the rich, smooth crema caramella flavor. You'll find cannoli, too, filled with ice cream instead of ricotta, and a superb selection of ice-cream cakes.

Cicali

Via de' Banchi 14r - (055) 213776
Open 7am-8pm (summer 7am-midnight). Closed Sun.

In the teeming neighborhood of Santa Maria Novella, you'll find this bar with a separate ice-cream counter and a few gray-and-red marble tables. In addition to the usual range of flavors, Cicali sells delectable pure-fruit water ices and fruit-flavored ice creams. Chocoholics take note: chocolate mousse is a specialty of the house.

Built on the Bleachers

There's a lot more to Florence than meets the eye. The ancient palazzi along Via de' Gondi behind the Palazzo Vecchio are settling into their Roman-ruin foundations. That's what accounts for the pitch of the road, which follows the buried tiers of seats of the Teatro Romano. Nearby Via Torta follows the curve of the 20,000-seat Roman amphitheater lurking below the surface. We'll probably never see either the theater or amphitheater; after all the traumatic digging in Piazza della Signoria, expect the Florentines to let sleeping ruins lie.

Ciolli
Via Ramazzini 35-37r - (055) 677554
Open 9am-1am. Closed Tue.
Ciolli's long-established reputation for fine ice cream is well deserved. Our favorites here are the traditional flavors—chocolate, stracciatella, vanilla, hazelnut, pistachio—and in summer the delectable fruit gelati. The simple, old-fashioned recipes for these yummy treats are prepared right on the premises.

Fiorenza
Via de' Calzaiuoli 9r - (055) 216651
Open 7am-1am. Closed Sun.
Its proximity to Piazza della Signoria brings throngs of sightseers eager for refreshment into this tiny ice-cream parlor. Don't count on sitting down (there are only seven seats) to enjoy Fiorenza's luscious semifreddi (light-textured ice creams) and zuppa inglese (custard, sponge cake, and candied fruit).

Gailli
Piazza del Pesce 3-5r - (055) 296810
Open 2pm-8pm (summer 1pm-1am). Closed Wed.

Smooth fruit-flavored ice creams are the strong suit at this minuscule gelateria situated in the little square just off to the left of the Ponte Vecchio.

Il Granduca
Via de' Calzaiuoli 59r - (055) 298112
Open 8am-midnight. Closed Wed.
The multitudes of shoppers who pass by this ice-cream parlor (strategically set on one of the city's busiest and most fashionable streets) find it difficult not to duck in for a quick cone or a sundae. In addition to the traditional chocolate, vanilla, and strawberry, Granduca also churns out such exotic flavors as mango and kiwi.

L' Oasi
Via Sant'Egidio 5r - (055) 210858
Open 7am-1am. Closed Wed.
Always mobbed until late at night, this pleasant little shop sells its own delicious ice creams. Our favorite flavors are the eggy-rich zabaglione and the tiramisù made with creamy mascarpone cheese.

Perché No!
Via de' Tavolini 19r - (055) 2398969
Open 8am-12:30am. Winter: closed Tue.
Why not sample from the attractive assortment of flavors, which includes several wild-berry varieties prepared lovingly by hand. The tiramisù ice cream, made with triple-creme mascarpone cheese and a lacing of rum, is a popular favorite, as are the yogurt- and rice-based concoctions.

La Sorbetteria
Via Pellicceria 2-4-6r - (055) 284640
Open daily 6am-8pm (summer 6am-midnight).
Tucked away on the left as you leave Piazza della Repubblica, La Sorbetteria is hard to see, but is well worth seeking out. It's one of the few ice-cream shops in Florence where you can sit—indoors or out—and enjoy your treat in peace. More than 35 flavors are available, all produced right in the shop: walnut, Malaga, rum-praline, almond-milk, papaya, and mango are highly recommended. If ice cream seems lonely to you without cake, keep in mind that the next-door annex sells delectable little pastries.

Il Triangolo delle Bermude

Via Nazionale 61r - (055) 287490
Open 10am-midnight. Closed Mon.
Nobody disappears into this Bermuda Triangle—the glass-enclosed setting at a prominent corner location make it a place to be seen. The star attraction is an astonishing blue-hued vanilla-anise-orange ice, but the rose, the rhubarb, and the peanut varieties are also unusual, and tasty to boot. Mousselike semifreddo is the specialty of the house. It comes topped with meringue, filled with glazed-chestnut cream, or spiked with almondy Amaretto. Delish!

Vivoli

Via Isola delle Stinche 7r - (055) 292334
Open 9am-1am. Closed Mon.
Three generations have carried on the tradition of making superb ice creams using the purest and freshest ingredients, with no additives whatsoever. Despite its out-of-the-way location, Vivoli is the city's best-known gelateria, because the quality is unfailingly high and the flavors are so alluring: fig, mulberry, rum-praline, millefeuille, melon, and much more.

Yogen Früz

Via de' Pucci 5a - (055) 282053
Open 9am-1am. Closed Sun.
The name Yogen Früz is your first clue that this establishment is modeled on similar American outfits... "Do-it-yourself" yogurt sundaes are the attraction here. You choose from a vast array of fresh-fruit toppings and frozen yogurts to build yourself a tasty and not-too-caloric treat.

■ PASTRY

Calamai

Via dell'Agnolo 113r - (055) 244826
Open 7am-8:30pm. Closed Wed.
Rich Sicilian sweets, such as cannoli, cassata (pound cake layered with sweetened ricotta and chocolate), and little cream-filled brioches called cremini, are Calamai's particular pride, along with pretty cakes, such as the torta girasole (sunflower cake) and "grandmother's" torte. The candies are toothsome, too: dainty mints, glistening jellies, and exquisite filled chocolates.

Deanna

Piazza della Stazione 55r - (055) 284092
Open 6:30am-midnight. Closed Wed.
This shop's smart gray marble tables and black chairs are invariably occupied, and the oval bar is usually packed as well. But then this is a busy neighborhood, and Deanna's is a particularly inviting place to stop for tea and pastries. Among the treats prepared fresh daily on the premises are luscious, mousselike ice creams, profiteroles, and the famous dome-shaped zuccotto, an ice-cream-and-cake confection inspired by Brunelleschi's cupola for the cathedral of Florence.

Giacosa

Via de' Tornabuoni 83-85r - (055) 296226
Open 7:30am-8:30pm. Closed Sun.
A privileged location amid the city's most luxurious boutiques makes this historic (since 1815) bar/pasticceria an ideal place for a drink—the Negroni cocktail was invented here, in 1920—a dainty snack, or a cup of tea and a pastry. A seductive array of Italian and foreign cakes is charmingly displayed in the front window. A particular favorite is the Sienese specialty, panforte, a dark, spicy, honey-flavored fruitcake. Giacosa's glazed chestnuts are world-renowned.

Migone

Via de' Calzaiuoli 87r - (055) 214004
Open 9am-7:30pm. Closed Sun.
A cheerful array of sugared almonds and other colorful candies lines the shelves, while in the window enticing mounds of cookies tempt passersby. All the specialties of the region are represented: panforte, ricciarelli di Siena (almond cookies), cavallucci (spicy walnut cookies), and cantucci di Prato (orange-flavored almond cookies). This is the place where Florentines buy the stockings stuffed with sweets that are traditional gifts for the Epiphany, on January 6.

Rivoire

Piazza della Signoria 5r - (055) 214412
Open 8am-midnight. Closed Mon.
Obtaining a table here is no mean feat, especially in summer, but your efforts will be amply rewarded. Not only is the view of Piazza della Signoria and the Palazzo Vecchio inspiring, Rivoire's renowned

chocolate is sublime in all its forms: velvety hot chocolate, chocolate-hazelnut cream sold in decorative gift jars, chocolate truffles, rum- or coffee-filled chocolates and, for the purist, tablets of solid chocolate wrapped in distinctive bright yellow paper. Rivoire also produces scrumptious cakes, pastries, and traditional Florentine cookies that are ideal accompaniments for a restorative cup of tea.

Robiglio

Via de' Servi 112r - (055) 214501
Via de' Tosinghi 11r - (055) 215013
Open 8am-7:30pm. Closed Sun.

Robiglio is a traditional cafe and pastry shop with a loyal following in a city notoriously finicky about pastry and sweets. Cornucopian displays of fruit jellies, pralines, caramels, cookies, and tea cakes invite extensive sampling. Everything in the shop is either made on the premises or purchased from top-quality producers. The house specialties, an English-style plumcake and a rustic Italian fruitcake, are handsomely boxed for gift-giving.

San Firenze

Piazza San Firenze 1r - (055) 211426
Open 7am-10pm. Closed Sun.

Two delightful display windows re-create a child's vision of candyland: they overflow with licorice, colorful bonbons, and tiny animals and fruits fashioned from spun sugar or marzipan. Inside, you can sample ice cream, cake, and zuccotto, the famous Florentine dessert that combines both in a high and handsome dome-shaped mold.

Scudieri

Piazza San Giovanni 19r - (055) 210733
Open 7:30am-9pm. Closed Wed.

The dazzling window displays of this elegant pastry shop have a magnetic effect on anyone who beholds them. Since Scudieri is situated in a busy part of town, its terrace and tea room are always filled with eager epicures intent on obtaining some of the shop's famous pastries, chocolates, caramels, chocolate-coated orange peels, fruit jellies, zuccherini con rosolio (liqueur-soaked sweetmeats), and outstanding torrone fiorentino (nougat). Do sample the unusual cornmeal-based amor di polenta, a house specialty.

Sieni

Mercato Centrale di San Lorenzo,
Via dell'Ariento 29r - (055) 213830
Open 8am-7pm. Closed Wed.

All the traditional sweets of Siena can be found here, amid the bustle of the San Lorenzo market. Alongside rich cavallucci cookies and spicy panforte are gleaming fruit tarts, chocolate and maraschino tortes, and in autumn, delicious schiacciate con l'uva—flat cakes garnished with the season's fresh grapes.

The Medieval Skywalkers

Renaissance Florence so fascinates modern-day visitors that few ponder the city's medieval marvels. House-towers—most of them whittled down—still crop up here and there. If you visit the tiny hilltown of San Gimignano you'll get a better idea of what Florence looked like before its Renaissance and miscellaneous other transformations. Once upon a time, there were about 150 house-towers crammed between the Arno and the cathedral. Some of them were real skyscrapers, up to 160 feet tall. Each wealthy family or clan owned one. And friends or political allies generally built their towers near one another. Many such groupings were then linked up with skywalks 150 feet above the pavement. The owners threw parties and waged war from on high, shunting food, weapons, and clansmen to and fro across the walkways. Maybe that's why these uppity families were later scorned for the way they looked down on people. And the house-towers came a-tumbling down.

Hotels

 Albergo Mario's
Via Faenza 89
(055) 216801, fax (055) 212039
Open year-round. 16 rms 80-170,000 lire. V,
AE, DC.
Try to reserve a room on the courtyard, because this street near the central market is a busy one. Mario has taken great pains to make his inn comfortable and attractive, with soundproofing, antiques in the guest rooms, and a convivial bar/TV room.

 **Anglo-American
Hotel Regina**
Via Garibaldi 9
(055) 282114, fax (055) 268513
Open year-round. 108 rms 170-350,000 lire,
bkfst incl. Pkg. V, AE, DC.
Downstairs, mirrored galleries open onto handsome public rooms, decorated in a vaguely English style, and lavish indoor gardens. Upstairs, spacious guest rooms feature authentic period furnishings or handsome replicas, all smelling discreetly of beeswax polish. The Anglo-American offers all the comfort, beauty, and service of a grand hotel that's proud of its long-standing tradition (Tolstoy once slept here).

 Augustus & Dei Congressi
Vicolo dell'Oro 5
(055) 283054, fax (055) 268557
Open year-round. 67 rms & stes. Stes 340-
490,000 lire. Rms 170-350,000 lire, bkfst incl.
All major cards.
Set back on a piazzetta not far from the Ponte Vecchio, this charming hotel stands right in the heart of the historic district. The surroundings are well designed and quiet; the rooms are all attractively decorated, and some have little terraces with views of the city's rooftops. There is also a bright, airy bar downstairs. No restaurant, but some of the best eating houses in Florence are close at hand.

 Azzi
Via Faenza 56
(055) 213806, fax (055) 21806
Open year-round. 12 rms 70,000 lire, bkfst
incl (winter). All major cards.
This tidy, friendly little pensione keeps company with four or five other similarly modest establishments in a turn-of-the-century building on Via Faenza. Most of the guest rooms have double-glazed windows, and all have a little sink (bathrooms are communal). The spacious terrace and common room create a warm, family-like atmosphere. Though not luxurious by any means, Azzi is a quiet, well-run, pleasant place to stay.

 Baglioni
Piazza dell'Unità Italiana 6
(055) 23580, fax (055) 2358895
Open year-round. 190 rms 220-360,000 lire.
Pkg. All major cards.
The Baglioni was renovated a few years back, and some of its broken-down charm was lost in the process, traded in for flashy, show-off luxury (and, let's be fair, much improved comfort). But the hotel still overlooks the Santa Maria Novella cloister, and from the terrace garden and restaurant there is a wonderful view of the Duomo. The meeting rooms draw conventions and business conferences, and the proximity of the train station makes the Baglioni popular with tour groups.

 Berchielli
Lungarno Acciaioli 14
(055) 264061, fax (055) 218636
Open year-round. 70 rms 260-370,000 lire.
Restaurant. All major cards.
The Berchielli, which once hosted jolly crews of bohemians who didn't mind the noisy plumbing, was fully renovated not long ago. Now it is fitted out in splendor to welcome well-heeled tourists who need to be surrounded by marble and wall-to-wall carpeting. Some of the rooms have

retained their terraces, where it's so pleasant to have breakfast in the morning. By all means avoid the rooms overlooking the Arno: the traffic noise is infernal. There is a restaurant on the premises.

An Eye for an Eye

Even back during the glorious Renaissance, people sometimes lost their cool in a heat wave and went on rampages. Florence's populace cast a baleful eye on the behavior of one such crazy, a certain Signor Marrona, who in August 1493 took a pick to every statue of the Virgin Mary in his path. Marrona went so far as to gouge the eye of the *Bambin Gesù* cradled in the arms of the Madonna, in the Tabernacle of the Speziali and Medici on the façade of Orsanmichele. Poor mad Marrona was instantly lynched by a gang of Savonarola's faithful friars. He was stoned, killed, and then his body was dragged all over cheering, heat-sick Florence. The damaged eye of the *Bambin Gesù* was restored soon after but never quite regained its original luster.

Bernini Palace
Piazza San Firenze 29
(055) 288621, fax (055) 268272
Open year-round. 86 rms & stes. Stes 450,000 lire. Rms 270-380,000 lire, bkfst incl. Restaurant. All major cards.

You'll find this slightly faded grand hotel just behind the Palazzo Vecchio, only a few steps away from the Piazza della Signoria. We cannot deny that the place is charming and comfortable, but alas, it is not very quiet. Although the rooms are soundproofed, you can still be awakened by the nasty little Vespa that decides to backfire under your window at 2am. In its favor, it must be said that the Bernini's dining room and bar are both quite attractive.

Calzaiuoli
Via de' Calzaiuoli 6
(055) 212456, fax (055) 268310
Open year-round. 45 rms 100-180,000 lire. All major cards.

For a reasonable amount of money you can enjoy a central location and fashionable address at this pleasant hotel, housed in an ancient edifice with an eighteenth-century façade. The rooms are decorated in contemporary taste, with warm colors. When you book, ask to be lodged on the upper floor to enjoy the fabulous view—and the blessed quiet! Breakfast is served in a pretty room on the first floor.

Claridge
Piazza Piave 3
(055) 2346736, fax (055) 2341199
Open year-round. 32 rms 130-200,000 lire. All major cards.

This small hotel across from Piazzale Michelangelo, well out of the city's center, has a fragrant little garden and the air of a country villa about it. The guest rooms are comfortable and air conditioned, but they are not at all large and the furnishings are undistinguished. The ground-floor lobby and bar, on the other hand, are spacious and tastefully decorated. From the upper floors, guests enjoy fine views of the Arno and the domes and bell-towers of Florence.

Consigli
Lungarno Amerigo Vespucci 50
(055) 214172, fax (055) 219367
Open year-round. 13 rms 110-150,000 lire. V.

Overlooking the Arno but at some distance from the center of Florence, this pensione occupies a fine sixteenth-century building. The public rooms, ceiling frescoes, and handsome parquet floors hint that the house has a glorious past; the present is palpably tinged with nostalgia. Guest rooms are modestly appointed with furnishings that date from the 1930s, but the bathrooms have been modernized.

Croce di Malta
Via della Scala 7
(055) 282600, fax (055) 287121
Open year-round. 15 stes 380,000 lire. 83 rms 150-330,000 lire. Restaurant. Conf. Pool. Garage pkg. All major cards.

Moorish arches, hanging gardens, a lavish patio... tasteful understatement is not the strong suit here. Yet the hotel's old façade, inviting pool, and pervasive tranquility lend it an undeniable charm. Santa Maria Novella is just a few steps away.

Due Fontane
Piazza della Santissima Annunziata 14
(055) 210987, fax (055) 294461
Open year-round. 57 rms 130-200,000 lire, bkfst incl. All major cards.

Not far from the cathedral, across from Brunelleschi's splendid and harmonious Spedale degli Innocenti (Foundling Home), is this very tidy, unpretentious hotel. Relatively inexpensive and close to all the most beautiful Florentine landmarks, it is an ideal choice for people who do not wish to spend a fortune merely for a place to sleep.

 Excelsior
Piazza Ognissanti 3
(055) 264201, fax (055) 210278
Open year-round. 19 stes 892-1,428,000 lire. 186 rms 209-584,000 lire. Restaurant. Conf. Garage pkg. All major cards.

The Excelsior, now part of the Ciga group, is typical of what Italy's grand hotels used to be like, with a vast marble lobby, monumental staircase, and interminable corridors. The somewhat cavernous guest rooms feature huge beds and sturdy furniture, and the bathrooms are luxurious in an austere kind of way. Despite the proliferation of tour groups, the clientele for the most part still seems pretty glossy. The terrace affords an admirable view of Florence, and the bar in the lobby is adorably *vieux jeu*. The Excelsior's restaurant, Il Cestello, is well worth a visit (see *Restaurants*).

Grand Hotel
Piazza Ognissanti 1
(055) 288781, fax (055) 217400
Open year-round. 17 stes 961-1,695,000 lire. 90 rms 373-599,000 lire. Restaurant. Conf. Garage pkg. All major cards.

The Grand Hotel stares across at the Excelsior (see above), which like it belongs to the Ciga group. Should you be tempted to think that the Grand is just a poor relation, check out the room rates. Though on a smaller scale, it is just as luxurious and well equipped as the Excelsior. The bar is quite pretty. Take note that the restaurant serves light meals only.

Grand Hotel Villa Cora
Viale Machiavelli 18
(055) 2298451, fax (055) 229086
Open year-round. 16 stes: prices on request. 32 rms 339-539,000 lire. Restaurant. Conf. Pool. Pkg. All major cards.

This imposing Neoclassical villa once sheltered the exiled Empress Eugénie, and Tchaikovsky and Debussy came here to compose. Though restored, the Villa Cora is still blessed with a certain nineteenth-century extravagance in its design and decoration. The dainty rooms are filled with rugs, crystal fixtures, and furnishings from various periods all piled in together, but the overall effect is cozy and pleasing. Pleasing, too, are the summertime meals served in the garden by the (heated) pool.

The Longest-Running Mass on the Shortest Day of the Year

Some habits die hard. The Florentines' great imperial hero, Hugo of Brandenbourg, passed away tearfully in the "foreign state" of Pistoia some 1,000 years ago. His last wish was to return to his beloved Florence. Well, the Florentines took him seriously. They snatched his body from Pistoia and galloped it home on horseback. Hugo rode in, somewhat stiff, held in the saddle by a trusty servant. And the Florentines' zeal did not end there. They buried Hugo in the Baptistery and held a splendid funeral service, and they've said a funeral mass for him each December 21st ever since. It's brief but of long standing.

 Grand Hotel Villa Medici
Via il Prato 42
(055) 2381331, fax (055) 2381336
Open year-round. 14 stes 565-904,000 lire. 89 rms 260-520,000 lire. Restaurant. Conf. Pool. Garage pkg. All major cards.

To our minds, neither the location (well out of the center of town), nor the pool (not much larger than a bathtub), nor the small garden justify the grand-hotel prices charged at the Villa Medici. But some people may welcome the peace and quiet of the place and enjoy the prospect of dining in the garden.

Hotel Loggiato dei Serviti

Piazza della Santissima Annunziata 3
(055) 289592, fax (055) 289595
Open year-round. 4 stes 270-550,000 lire. 25 rms 110-225,000 lire, bkfst incl. All major cards.

This small, elegant hotel, lodged in a Renaissance edifice opposite Brunelleschi's Spedale degli Innocenti, offers a refined atmosphere, comfortable accommodations, and distinguished service—all for a most reasonable price.

Hotel de la Ville

Piazza Antinori 1
(055) 2381806/5, fax (055) 2381809
Open year-round. 7 stes 600,000 lire. 68 rms 280-398,000 lire, bkfst incl. Pkg. All major cards.

Set on a tiny square smack in the middle of the shopping district, this hotel is well maintained, well run, and endowed with a pool. It is very noisy, however, and the service, though efficient, is just the slightest bit brusque. Most of the rooms overlooking a dark little side street get no sun whatsoever; if you've traveled to Florence to admire the quality of the light, be sure to request a room elsewhere in the hotel.

J and J

Via di Mezzo 20
(055) 2345005, fax (055) 240282
Open year-round. 5 stes 400,000 lire. 14 rms 280,000 lire. Conf. Pkg. All major cards.

The name might sound like a discount store, but this is in fact one of the prettiest hotels in Florence, housed in a converted convent. Bright, comfortable guest rooms overlook a splendid cloister with Doric columns, and sixteenth-century frescoes adorn the hallways. Though they are equipped with modern amenities like air conditioning and color TVs, an indefinable medieval atmosphere pervades the rooms.

Kraft

Via Solferino 2
(055) 284273, fax (055) 2398267
Open year-round. 78 rms 240-340,000 lire. Restaurant. Conf. Pool. Garage pkg. All major cards.

This modern hotel is situated in a neighborhood that has the double advantage of being both quiet and fairly central. In addition to all the usual amenities offered by an establishment of this upscale category, the Kraft boasts a rooftop restaurant and pool, as well as splendid views of the Arno, the Duomo and, in the distance, Fiesole on its hilltop.

Lungarno

Borgo San Jacopo 14
(055) 264211, fax (055) 268437
Open year-round. 12 stes 440,000 lire. 54 rms 220-320,000 lire. Conf. Garage pkg. All major cards.

A modern, comfortable establishment practically on the river, with wonderful views of the old town and the Ponte Vecchio from the guest rooms, the balconies, and the bar. You can expect high-quality service and facilities (but no restaurant), along with an international clientele that includes politicos and entertainers.

Minerva

Piazza Santa Maria Novella 16
(055) 284555, fax (055) 268281
Open year-round. 105 rms & stes. Stes 500-700,000 lire. Rms 265-365,000 lire. Pool. Pkg. All major cards.

Since the Minerva is admirably located just in front of Santa Maria Novella, hotel residents can wander over for a look at the sublime frescoes by Ghirlandaio and Filippino Lippi before they get on with their day. The guest rooms are decently decorated and equipped, without excess. Those at the back of the hotel are the quietest; they overlook the Spanish Chapel and the famous Chiostro Verde (Green Cloister), with its vestiges of frescoes by Uccello. The Minerva boasts a rooftop pool with a panoramic view of Florence.

Morandi alla Crocetta

Via Laura 50
(055) 2344747, fax (055) 2480954
Open year-round. 9 rms 89-149,000 lire. All major cards.

What price charm? The cost is surprisingly low at this tiny, graceful hotel in the center of Florence, owned by Kathleen Doyle-Antuono. The rooms are housed on the first floor of a venerable palazzo, but they offer plenty of modern comfort: telephone, TV, fine bathrooms. Guests can also count on a tranquil atmosphere and simple surroundings enhanced with many elegant touches.

Palazzo Vecchio Petrarca
Via B. Cennini 4
(055) 212182/2281209, fax (055) 216445
Open year-round. 20 rms 65-120,000 lire. Pkg. All major cards.

Despite its proximity to the train station, this little hotel exudes an air of tranquility that is apparent the moment one crosses the front garden to enter the lobby. Many of the simply furnished guest rooms, all with TV, look out onto shady courtyards. Bathrooms are modern, and a few rooms have three beds, an economical solution for families who don't want to devote their entire travel budget to lodging. The hotel has just undergone a full renovation for increased comfort.

Cutting Corners Saves a Fresco

One of the most sensational art discoveries of recent years surfaced during the dig under Florence's cathedral, Santa Maria del Fiore, where archaeologists were searching for the remains of the ancient church of Santa Maria Reparata. They stumbled upon an early fresco featuring the Virgin Mary and Saint John, preserved because the cathedral's builders were in such a hurry—they had cut the fresco down just enough to get on with their job. It goes to show you that haste doesn't always make waste.

Park Palace

Piazzale Galileo 5
(055) 222431, fax (055) 220571
Open year-round. 26 rms & stes. Rms 180-370,000 lire. Restaurant. Pkg. All major cards.

This Neoclassic villa on a square just south of the Boboli Gardens has been fitted out as a modern hotel, yet its charm and harmony remain undiminished. Marble and tapestries lend a touch of luxury, and there are romantic views, a pool, a restaurant, and a lovely garden for strolling. The air-conditioned guest rooms are furnished with restraint, and each bears a name that alludes to art or history.

Caruso, the hotel's bar, is one of the nicest in town.

Plaza Hotel Lucchesi

Lungarno della Zecca Vecchia 38
(055) 26236, fax (055) 2480921
Open year-round. 97 rms & stes. Rms 285-390,000 lire, bkfst incl. Restaurant. Pkg. All major cards.

This century-old Florentine institution with views of the Arno and Santa Croce was given a full-fledged facelift a few years back. The dynamic management laid out lots of money to have the place painted pink and filled with pianos, crystal chandeliers, tall mirrors, thick carpeting... you get the idea. Movie stars feel right at home here. Some of the rooms have terraces where one can have breakfast while admiring a superb view of the Duomo.

Porta Rossa
Via Porta Rossa 19
(055) 287551, fax (055) 282179
Open year-round. 85 rms 86-165,000 lire. All major cards.

Not far from Piazza della Signoria sits this grand old lady of Florentine hotels. As far back as the fifteenth century, weary travelers stopped here for rest and refreshment. With its frescoed ceiling, it is one of the last truly charming hotels in Florence. The plumbing, it's true, is a little wheezy, but we wouldn't change it, or anything else about this fine old place.

Regency
Piazza Massimo d'Azeglio 3
(055) 245247, fax (055) 245247
Open year-round. 5 stes: prices on request. 30 rms 280-520,000 lire. Restaurant. Conf. Garage pkg. All major cards.

Set in a nineteenth-century neighborhood of grand houses and spacious gardens, the Regency is a fine, aristocratic residence that offers peace and quiet along with refined comforts. Some of the rooms are quite large, others are not, but all are furnished with period antiques and decorated in lively, cheerful tones. Service is pleasant and discreet, prices are high; the Regency is affiliated with the prestigious Relais et Châteaux network. For the Regency's restaurant, Relais Le Jardin, see *Restaurants.*

> **The prices** *in this guide reflect what establishments were charging at press time.*

The Original Bonfire of the Vanities

Lorenzo il Magnifico, ruler of Florence, patron of the arts, lover of fine food and comely courtesans, style-setter in the voluble, vain Florence of the roaring Renaissance, died suddenly in 1492. Into the power vacuum stepped Friar Girolamo Savonarola crying, "The party's over." He soon whipped up a crusade to reform the frivolous Florentines, preaching an uncomfortable tightening of the belt and buttoning of the bodice. He even forced the fun-loving citizenry to pile all their paintings, tapestries, books, and beautiful-but-useless miscellanea in Piazza della Signoria.

Savonarola then gleefully torched the priceless pyramid of "vanities" and mounted his pulpit, the self-proclaimed ruler of the city-state. Two years later the tide had turned, and there was another bonfire in the square, this one a kind of gruesome barbecue, with Friar Savonarola and his brethren feeding the flames with their live bodies. A little too late for Savonarola's good, the Florentines repented. They've been doing penance ever since: each May 23rd they lay a wreath of flowers on the spot where the vanities and Savonarola went up in smoke.

Residenza Johanna
Via Bonifacio Lupi 14
(055) 481899, fax (055) 482721
Open year-round. 12 rms 50-95,000 lire. No cards.
Here's a new small hotel with lots of appeal: it's stylish, quiet, impeccably kept, and furnished with taste. A ten-minute walk from the Duomo, the Residenza offers a dozen rooms; five are doubles and one has a private bath (five other bathrooms are at guests' disposal). Charming, though certainly not luxurious, with a pleasant family-style ambience. Special rates can be arranged for longer stays.

Savoy
Piazza della Repubblica 7
(055) 283313, fax (055) 284840
Open year-round. 4 stes 880-1,030,000 lire. 97 rms 240-530,000 lire. Restaurant. Conf. Garage pkg (45,000 lire per day). All major cards.
Conveniently located amid Florence's best-known monuments and landmarks, the Savoy offers comfortable rooms, a decent restaurant, and a classic hotel bar. Yet in spite of the double-glazed windows, noise remains a problem. Although the hotel's facilities are unquestionably practical for business travelers, the Savoy is short on the sort of charm that people traveling for pleasure tend to seek.

Della Signoria
Via delle Terme 1
(055) 214530, fax (055) 216101
Open year-round. 27 rms 195-260,000 lire, bkfst incl. Pay pkg.
Though small, this fully modernized hotel near the Ponte Vecchio offers a superior level of comfort and service. Furnishings are of contemporary Italian design, and the soundproofed guest rooms, while not exactly spacious, are attractive and impeccably equipped.

Tony's Inn Apollo
Via Faenza 77
(055) 284119/214287, fax (055) 210101
Open year-round. 26 rms 120-150,000 lire. All major cards.
This pleasant and picturesque pensione is owned by photographer Antonio Lelli, whose Tuscan portraits and still lifes are prominently displayed on the walls of his tastefully furnished establishment. Ongoing renovation efforts make the guest rooms increasingly attractive and comfortable, and the bathrooms have an inimitable Italian flair. You can count on a warm welcome from the polyglot staff.

Torre di Bellosguardo
Via Roti Michelozzi 2
(055) 2298145, fax (055) 229008
Open year-round. 13 rms & stes. Stes 400-530,000 lire. Rms 230-330,000 lire. Pkg. Pool. All major cards.
Built in the Trecento by poet Guido Cavalcanti—he found the view so seductive he called his tower "Bellosguardo"—this verdant site is just a few minutes' taxi ride from central Florence. The hotel's rooms are all decorated in different styles,

with a host of charming and thoughtful details. The penthouse suite boasts four windows, one for each of the cardinal points.

Villa Belvedere
Via Benedetto Castelli 3
(055) 222501, fax (055) 223163
Closed Dec-Feb. 27 rms 140-280,000 lire, bkfst incl. Pool. Tennis. Pkg. All major cards.
For the price, this family-run villa offers numerous advantages, not the least of which are tennis courts, a pool, and superb views of Florence and Fiesole from the terraces of certain guest rooms. The furnishings are undistinguished, but the rooms are fully equipped with air conditioning and TV, and though there is no restaurant, the bar serves light snacks all day.

Villa Carlotta
Via Michele di Lando 3
(055) 220530, fax (055) 2336147
Open year-round. 27 rms 170-350,000 lire, bkfst incl. Restaurant. Pkg. All major cards.
Well away from Florence's main arteries, yet only a ten-minute walk from the Ponte Vecchio and close to the Boboli Gardens, Villa Carlotta is a paragon of tranquility and blissful comfort. The plant-filled public rooms are conducive to quiet reading or conversation, guest rooms are decorated with graceful simplicity and are fully equipped. What's more, the service is genuinely friendly and there's a restaurant on the premises.

Ville sull'Arno
Lungarno C. Colombo 1-3-5
(055) 670971, fax (055) 678244
Open year-round. 47 rms 180-280,000 lire. Pool. All major cards.
A ten-minute drive east from central Florence brings you to this quiet hotel, which dates back to the fifteenth century. The location makes it particularly convenient for those traveling by car, and by any standard the rates are surprisingly reasonable. Spacious, well-furnished, renovated guest rooms overlook either the Arno or the hotel's garden and pool. There is no restaurant on the premises, but snacks are served at the bar.

> **Prices for rooms and suites** are per room, not per person. Half-board prices, however, are per person.

■ In Candeli   7 km E

Villa La Massa
Via La Massa 6
(055) 6510101, fax (055) 6510109
Open year-round. 5 stes 620-750,000 lire. 35 rms 240-450,000 lire. Restaurant. Conf. Pool. Tennis. Pkg. All major cards.
Built in the eighteenth century on the left bank of the Arno, far from the crush of the city, Villa La Massa was converted into a hotel in 1960. A discreet, aristocratic atmosphere still reigns in the public rooms, where hunting dogs warm themselves before the fire. Sipping tea served by formally dressed waiters, one has the distinct impression of having gone back in time as a visitor to some patrician family's home. The rooms are decorated in a simple, soothing style with furniture that has belonged to the villa for generations. Though the swimming pool is small, the grounds are delightful, shaded by century-old trees. A free shuttle service ferries guests to central Florence. *See Restaurants.*

■ In Fiesole   8 km NE

Villa San Michele
Via Doccia 4 - (055) 59451
Closed mid Nov-mid Mar. 2 stes 1,450-1,800,000 lire. 26 rms 470-990,000 lire. Restaurant. Conf. Pool. Pkg. All major cards.
The origins of this Renaissance convent, fifteen minutes from Florence, date back to the Etruscans. Boccaccio described the site and Michelangelo designed the structure's superb façade. Much more than a hotel, this Relais et Châteaux villa overlooking the Tuscan countryside is a marvel of harmony and serene beauty. Adorned with period furniture, pictures, and tapestries, the public rooms and restaurant (see *Restaurants*) match the landscape for grandeur. The guest rooms go perhaps a little too far in the direction of Hollywood, with round bathtubs and canopied beds fashioned of (over)wrought iron. Leisure pursuits abound: marked trails lead through an oak forest to various historic landmarks; there is a pristine pool in the garden planted with lemon, cypress, and laurel trees; and residents are shuttled on request to a nearby golf course and tennis courts.

■ In **Reggello**   28 km SE

▲▲ Villa Rigacci   ▲♣
Via Manzoni 76 (in Viaggio)
(055) 8656718, fax (055) 8656537
*Closed Jan-Feb. 18 rms 120-260,000 lire,
bkfst incl. Restaurant. Pool. Pkg. All major
cards.*

An aristocratic dwelling erected in the
fifteenth century now houses a supremely
comfortable, quiet, atmospheric hotel.
Surrounded by luxuriant grounds, the Villa
Rigacci boasts coffered ceilings, floors
covered in antique terra-cotta tiles, and a
stupendous fireplace; it is furnished in typical Tuscan style, with country antiques and
wrought-iron pieces. Guest rooms are
cool and spacious. Few in number, they
provide a perfectly tranquil setting for a
relaxing holiday. The Villa's fine French
restaurant is an additional attraction (see
Restaurants).

■ In **Trespiano**   7 km N

▲▲ Villa Le Rondini   ▲♣
Via Bolognese Vecchia 224
(055) 400081, fax (055) 268212
*Open year-round. 44 rms & stes. Stes
300,000 lire. Rms 130-230,000 lire, bkfst incl.
Restaurant. Pool. Tennis. Pkg. All major cards.*

Just a ten-minute drive separates the Villa
Le Rondini from Piazza della Libertà in
Florence, but many of the Villa's guests
prefer to stay right where they are, contemplating the city from the comfort of
their garden chairs (the view is spectacular). Indeed, why should one abandon
the olive trees, the lush private garden, the
pool, the tennis courts, and the restaurant
of this commodious and relaxing villa for
the din and crush of the city, even if the
city in question is the sublime capital of
Tuscany?

APARTMENT HOTELS

Some fortunate travelers—business
people, actors, models, artists,
those on sabbatical—have occasion
to require an urban home base for a month
or more in Italy. Hotel rooms can become
impersonal and a bit cramped for extended stays, and ordinary rentals (apartments and houses) usually require a
long-term lease agreement. Enter the
apartment hotel (or *residence*, as the
Italians say), full-service accommodations
that are perfect for longer stays. They combine the space and hominess of an apartment with such features as maid service,
kitchen facilities, and sometimes even concierge services.

La Fonte
Via San Felice a Ema 29, Poggio Imperiale
(055) 224421, fax (055) 229442
*11 2- & 3- rm apts 3,000-4,000,000 lire per
month. No cards.*

Some of the full-service apartments in
this fifteenth- century Florentine villa feature brick floors and beamed ceilings,
while others are more modern in design.
All boast lovely antique or period furniture,
TVs, and kitchen facilities. The surrounding
park is perfect for a relaxing stroll, and
there is also a pool. A restaurant on the
premises saves the day for people too tired
to cook. La Fonte also functions as a conventional hotel for short-term stays.

Palazzo Ricasoli
Via delle Mantellate 2
(055) 352151, fax (055) 495001
*101 2- & 3- rm apts. 2-rm apts 960,000 lire/wk;
3-rm apts 1,356,000 lire per wk. All major cards.*

This is perhaps the largest *residence* in
the city, and it delivers the kind of atmosphere that most visitors to Florence are
eager to find. That's true, at least, for the
apartments located in the sixteenth-century palazzo. Those in the modern annex
are just as comfortable and well equipped,
but possess less aesthetic appeal. A spacious garden patio divides the two structures, which are blissfully quiet despite
their location near the heavily trafficked
Piazza Martiri della Libertà. The annex
houses tennis courts and a solarium. All
rooms have color TVs and benefit from
daily maid service.

Porte Nuove
Via delle Porte Nuove 57 - (055) 216787
*5 2-rm apts 1,900,000 lire per month. No
cards.*

This tiny *residence* consists of just five
small, moderately priced apartments
rented to long-term visitors (one month,
minimum). All have cooking facilities,
showers, direct telephone lines, TVs, and
simple but pleasing oak furnishings.

Nightlife

CONTENTS

BARS

Apollo Bar
Via dell'Ariento 41r - (055) 219751
Open 8am-1am (Sat 8am-2am). Closed Sun.
    After the bustling central and San Lorenzo markets shut down for the night, the Apollo stays open late. A good-looking flock of young night owls gathers here for fun and chatter.

The Bar
Piazza Libertà 45-46r - (055) 571135
Open 7:30am-1am. Closed Mon.
    This recent arrival bills itself as the city's first "American-style" cocktail bar. Quick lunches (grills, salads, pasta, and such) are also on tap, and in the evening live performances of jazz, Latin, or classical music are featured. The atmosphere is a felicitous mix of old and new that attracts a broad range of customers.

Cabiria Caffè
Piazza Santo Spirito - (055) 215732
Closed Sun.
    At nightfall, this unassuming bar becomes a writhing mass of fun-seeking humanity. A fixture on the Florentine scene, Cabiria exudes a special charm that never palls. In summer, customers jostle for space on the piazza (which, incidentally, offers a sensational view of Brunelleschi's church), where the schmoozing and drinking go on until late at night. In winter, the action moves inside and though the place is always jammed, the mood remains upbeat and jolly.

Dolce Vita
Piazza del Carmine - (055) 284595
Closed Sun.
    Take a bar, add ear-splitting music and a backdrop of non-stop video clips, and you've got (it seems) a recipe for success. La Dolce Vita was an early convert to this formula, and is still one of the top spots in town for seeing and being seen.

Il Piccolo Caffè
Borgo Santa Croce 23r - (055) 241704
Open 3pm-late night. Closed Mon.
    Here's a new address where you can observe the local "underground" in action: sipping cocktails, coffee, or draft beer; flipping through avant-garde magazine (lots of languages available); and listening to the latest indie discs.

Porfirio Rubirosa
Viale Strozzi 38r - (055) 490965
Open until 2am. Closed Mon.
    We're not sure that Porfirio himself would have been happy in a place like this (international playboys like more glitz and glam), but you can't beat the location—right in the center of town—and the drinks aren't bad. The background music runs to dance, soul, and jazz.

Zoe
Via de' Renai 13r - (055) 243111
Open 7am-1am. Closed Sun.
    Brand-new in the San Niccolò neighborhood, with a sleek bar and a hip attitude, Zoe serves up decent quick snacks by day and killer cocktails by night. This venue has already won the approval of a lively crew

41

that stops in for a drink before moving off to one of the dance clubs nearby.

Slaying the Fatted Calf

The world's wildest block party is thrown each June by Florentine soccer players and their fans. For the last 60 years they've followed the fourteenth-century tradition of organizing a soccer tournament, complete with traditional medieval costumes. The four historic neighborhoods—San Giovanni (red), Santa Croce (green), Santa Maria Novella (blue), and Santo Spirito (white)—play three matches. The prize is a calf, which the winner must roast at a street party and share with the losers and everyone else in the winning neighborhood. It's a sporting way to kick off the summer.

DISCOS

Andromeda Club

Via de' Cimatori 13r - (055) 292002
Open until 3am. Closed Sun. Cover charge: 15,000 lire (Mon-Thu), 25,000 lire (Fri-Sat).

Don't expect to hear anything but hardcore dance, house, and new-wave sounds at the Andromeda Club, which boasts twin dance floors, video screens, spectacular lighting effects—there's never a dull moment. The club's central location makes it a favorite with visiting foreigners, so you're bound to hear a familiar language, whatever yours may be. Watch for the special theme-party events that take place during the week.

Full Up

Via della Vigna Vecchia 21r - (055) 293006
Closed Tue. Cover charge: 15,000 lire (drink incl).

This elegant nightclub in the center of Florence was once the rendezvous for the city's classiest revelers. Today the competition has stolen some of Full Up's thunder, but it remains a good choice for a sophisticated evening. Not for the very young.

Manila

Piazza Matteucci, Campi Bisenzio (10 km NW) (055) 894121
Closed Mon-Wed. Cover charge: 20,000 lire (drink incl).

It's well out of the center of Florence, but Manila is such a happening place that it holds its own on the nightlife circuit. Live music, art, fashion, and design shows make Manila much more than just a disco. Every week, "discovery" evenings spotlight new trends in art and music, and frequent theme parties keep excitement high.

Le Nozze di Figaro

C/o Auditorium Flog, Via M. Mercati 24b (055) 490437
Open Fri only. Cover charge: 15,000 lire (drink incl).

This is the club that changed the way Florence looks at nightlife. Le Nozze is a multifaceted disco/cabaret/gallery that draws the culturally curious with art shows and dance, yet keeps hipsters happy with theme parties that exhibitionists simply adore.

Space Electronic

Via Palazzuolo 37r - (055) 293082
Open daily (Mar-Nov) 10pm-2:30am. Closed Mon (Dec-Feb). Cover charge: 20,000 lire (drink incl).

Always the first to launch the hottest trends, this disco introduced video clips from England some twenty years ago, and more recently brought the karaoke craze to town. When it comes to electronic innovations, Space is still tops in Florence, with the best lasers, maxi-videos, and the most spectacular light shows. The DJs obligingly spin whatever sounds the dancers ask for.

Yab

Via de' Sassetti 5r - (055) 282018
Open 10pm-4am. Closed Mon. Cover charge: 15,000 lire (Tue-Thu & Sun, drink incl); 25,000 lire (Fri-Sat; drink incl).

Yab is allegedly a Thai expression meaning "coming together." Many of the regulars are in some way involved with the fashion industry, and the club is at its most crowded and noisy when the fashion-show caravan hits the Pitti Palace. A darling DJ plays old favorites and recent hits

(Thursday is Latin music night) for the energetic throng on the huge, handsomely lighted dance floor. If you'd like to see what the smart set in Florence looks like, drop in here—the party goes on until 4am.

005 Revolution

Via Verdi 57r - (055) 244004
Closed Mon. First drink (oblig): 10,000 lire Tue-Fri & Sun; 25,000 lire Sat.
A mixed bag of rhythms and sounds keeps clubbers on the dance floor of this (literally) underground scene until the wee hours. In addition to occasional live concerts and shows, Revolution hosts cultural events of the sort favored by fashion fauna: film previews, book launches, and the like.

LIVE ENTERTAINMENT

Red Garter

Via de' Benci 33r - (055) 263004
Open daily. Free admission.
Live rock and roll is the rule here. Between sets, taped dance and disco music keep people on the floor, or else a pianist encourages everyone to sing along as he

performs old favorites. The beat goes on until about 1am.

Tenax

Via Pratese 47, Firenze-Peretola (6 km W) (055) 308160
Closed Mon-Wed.
The top rock and pop bands that come through town (except, of course, those which require a stadium-sized venue) play at Tenax, the best live rock club around. Many local new-wave bands got their start here, and on Friday nights Tenax opens its stage to the latest rock trends. Even when the music isn't live, it's lively enough to get everyone dancing around the bright, colorful bar.

Zut

Via Fosso Macinant 3 - (055) 333488
Closed Mon. Free admission Tue-Thu.
Zut (ex-Central Park) is run by the same hip team that operates the trendy Nozze di Figaro club (see above). In summer, Zut is a disco, but when the colder weather sets in, live concerts alternate with the dancing. You'll hear acid jazz, hip-hop, raggamuffin, underground, and tribal sounds; Tuesdays are dedicated to live shows, Saturdays to concerts by foreign bands.

Dynamite Dove
Makes for Explosive Celebration

Easter morning in front of Santa Maria del Fiore is as crazy as New Year's Eve in Times Square. The ear-wracking celebration is known as *lo scoppio del carro*, or the explosion of the cart. It works like this: a cable is strung from the main altar in the cathedral out to the square where the cart is parked; along the cable flies a flaming rocket called the Colombina, which slams into the cart, setting it on fire and exploding its load of firecrackers and Roman candles. The flight of the Colombina ("little dove") is read as an augury for the coming year's crops. Once upon a time the cart was dragged, flaming and booming, by two white oxen, through what is now Piazza della Repubblica and Piazza San Firenze. The tradition is nearly 1,000 years old, inspired by the Florentine Crusader Pazzino de' Pazzi. When he returned in triumph from the Conquest of Jerusalem, he lit the Easter Candle using slivers of stone from the Holy Sepulcher as flint. The event sparked the imagination of the Florentines, who've been putting on a great show ever since.

Shops

CONTENTS

Shops in Florence are open, as a rule, from 9am to 1pm and from 4pm to 7:30 or 8pm. Most are closed on Sunday and on Monday morning. Opening hours are usually extended in the three weeks preceding Christmas. Note, however, that certain shops in the center of town stay open through lunch, from 9 or 10am to 7:30pm. Winter hours are in effect from October through March.

ANTIQUES

Benvenuto Bacarelli
Via de' Fossi 33r - (055) 215457
Open summer: 9am-1pm & 4pm-7:30pm; winter: 9am-1pm & 3:30pm-7:30pm. Closed summer: Sat pm; winter: Mon am.
These large and luxurious premises display paintings, furniture, and objets d'art dating from the sixteenth, seventeenth, and eighteenth centuries.

Bruzzichelli
Borgo Ognissanti 31r - (055) 216196
Open 9am-1pm & 4pm-8pm; winter: 9am-1pm & 3:30pm-7:30pm. Closed summer: Sat pm; winter: Mon am.
Spacious rooms with cross-vaulted ceilings hold fine antique furniture dating from our own century to as far back as the Cinquecento.

Camiciotti
Via Santo Spirito 9r - (055) 294837
Open summer: 10am-1:30pm & 4pm-8pm; winter: 10am-1:30pm & 3:30pm-7:30pm. Closed summer: Sat pm; winter: Mon am.
French antiques from the Second Empire are Camiciotti's stock-in-trade. Every piece is dated and guaranteed authentic, for the buyer's peace of mind.

Fallani Best
Borgo Ognissanti 15r
(055) 214986, (055) 2381419
Open summer: 9am-1pm & 4pm-8pm; winter: 9am-1pm & 3:30pm-7:30pm. Closed summer: Sat pm; winter: Mon am.
Paola Fallana was the first Florentine antique merchant to deal in twentieth-century art objects. One part of her fascinating shop is done in a bold shade of red; there you'll find silver pieces and jewelry by such famous artists as Pomodoro and Afro. The other part, decorated in a more neutral beige, houses larger antiques, sculpture, and fine painting in a wide range of prices.

Gianfranco Luzzetti
Borgo San Jacopo 28a - (055) 211232
Open 9am-1pm & 3:30pm-7:30pm. Closed summer: Sat pm; winter: Mon am.
In pleasant surroundings just steps from the Ponte Vecchio, connoisseurs may inspect a choice stock of antique furnishings, ceramics, paintings, and frames from the Italian Middle Ages and the Renaissance.

Gustavo Melli

Ponte Vecchio 44-48r - (055) 2396568
Open 9:30am-1pm & 3:30pm-7:30pm.
Closed summer: Sat pm; winter: Mon am.
If only to admire the truly splendid view
of the Ponte di Santa Trinita, it would be
worth your while to step into this shop. But
the silver, jewelry, and curiosities from the
eighteenth and nineteenth centuries
deserve the attention of every avid antique
fancier. The cameos are especially fine.
Melli also offers a small collection of late-
Renaissance furniture and art objects.

Giovanni Pratesi

Via Maggio 13 - (055) 296568
Open 9:30am-1pm & 3:30pm-7:30pm.
Closed summer: Sat pm; winter: Mon am.
The entrance to this noted antique
dealer's shop is located on the far side of
the building's imposing street door. Pratesi
specializes in Baroque and Neoclassical
art; his collection, which extends over two
entire floors, includes furniture, statuary,
and pictures.

Zecchi

Via Maggio 54r - (055) 283368
Open 9:30am-1pm & 3:30pm-7:30pm.
Closed summer: Sat pm; winter: Mon am.
Zecchi sells and also restores all manner
of antiques. The shop is full of curious and
exotic merchandise—worth a visit, even if
you don't intend to buy.

BOOKS

Afterdark - English Bookstore

Via de' Ginori 47r - (055) 294203
Open daily 10am-1:30pm & 3pm-7:30pm.
Roomier new premises make this bookshop an even more appealing place to
browse. English-language volumes, both
new and used, line the shelves. American
and British magazines are also available,
and there is a ticket agency for concerts.

*Some establishments change their closing
times without warning. It is always wise to
check in advance.*

The Piglet Is a Boar but Charitable All the Same

Effervescent evenings in flower-filled
restaurants, glittering jewels winking
from the shops on the Ponte Vecchio,
bustling markets, open-air concerts...
these are the marvelous memories
visitors cherish most after a stay in
Florence. All you have to do to ensure
a return trip is toss a coin in the tub at
the feet of the bronze "piglet"—actually a giant boar—in the arcade of the
Mercato Nuovo. If your wish doesn't
come true (but how can you know at
the time?), don't feel that you've
wasted your money. The coins are
collected and given to the Madonna
del Grappa charitable association,
which houses and educates
Florence's waifs.

Alinari

Via della Vigna Nuova 46r - (055) 218975
Open 10am-7:30pm. Closed Wed.
Just across from the admirable Loggia de'
Rucellai is this small but well-known
bookstore, where you may purchase
evocative photographs and photographic
studies of Florence.

B. M.

Borgo Ognissanti 4r - (055) 294575
Open daily 9am-1pm & 3:30pm-7:30pm.
As interesting as it is small, this bookstore
carries a respectable stock of English and
American fiction, Etruscan studies, and
volumes on art, fashion, and travel. The
selection of prints, lithographs, and art
reproductions provides a wealth of
choices for uncommon souvenirs and
gifts.

Edison

Piazza della Repubblica 27r - (055) 213110
*Open daily 9am-8pm (Sun 10am-1:30pm &
3pm-8pm).*
Every book lover in town is overjoyed
with Edison, a new addition to Florence's
cultural scene. A broad selection of

volumes in English and Italian is housed in this spacious, centrally located shop. Panel discussions and book presentations are held regularly on the store's lower level.

Feltrinelli

International, Via Cavour 12-20r - (055) 219524
Via de' Cerretani 30-32r - (055) 2382652
Open daily 9:30am-7:30pm.

Feltrinelli is a publishing giant that operates Italy's biggest and most popular bookstore chain. The International is Feltrinelli's outpost in Florence, with two floors devoted to foreign-language books in English, French, Spanish, and German; the selection ranges from thrillers to erudite art studies. Magazines and video cassettes may be purchased here, too.

"Red Shirts"— Watering Hole of the Wordsmiths

The *Giubbe Rosse* or "Red Shirts" is no elite military corps. It's the name of the fabled artists' and writers' café in Piazza della Repubblica. The Futurist movement was born there, and the late poet laureate Eugenio Montale sipped many an aperitivo at the same tables now spread with hors d'œuvres for you and me. You don't have to be an intellectual to enjoy the olives.

Franco Maria Ricci

Via delle Belle Donne 41r - (055) 283312
Open 10am-1pm & 3:30pm-7:30pm. Closed Mon am; summer: Sat pm.

Elegance and refinement are Franco Maria Ricci's signature. His books are presented as works of art, in stark black-lacquered display cases in a black-and-sand-colored shop. Even if you don't read Italian, the precious, self-consciously aesthetic premises are a marvelous sight to behold.

Idea Books

Via Ricasoli 14r - (055) 284533
Open 9am-1pm & 4pm-7:30pm. Closed Mon; summer: Sat.

In a studious atmosphere of gray stone and white shelving, you may browse to

your heart's content among these handsome volumes on architecture, graphics, photography, fashion, film, and contemporary art. Idea Books is also a reliable source for exhibition catalogs old and new.

Internazionale Seeber

Via de' Tornabuoni 70r - (055) 215697
Open daily 9:30am-7:30pm.

The century-old shelves and furnishings wear their patina proudly. Enormous tables bear piles of new arrivals to leaf through: art, Italian and foreign fiction, and essays. The choice of English-language books is wide and far-ranging.

Paperback Exchange

Via Fiesolana 31r - (055) 2478154
Open 9am-1pm & 3:30pm-7:30pm. Closed Mon in winter.

Plain wooden shelves display an abundance of books in every category (classics, bestsellers, history, philosophy, art...) and in every language—except Italian! The catch is that you have to bring your own used volumes to obtain a voucher for 25 to 50 percent of their original value (depending on type), which you may then exchange for "new" (i.e. different) books. It's a great system if you're not the sentimental type.

DEPARTMENT STORES

Coin

Via de' Calzaiuoli 56r - (055) 280531
Open daily summer: 9am-8pm (Mon 2pm-8pm); winter: 9am-7:30pm (Mon 2pm-7:30pm).

A nationwide chain that sells up-to-date fashions and accessories at reasonable prices.

Standa

Viale de' Mille 140r - (055) 579151
Via Pietrapiana 42-44r - (055) 240809
Via de' Panzani 31r - (055) 283071
Open daily 9am-7:55pm (Mon 2pm-7:55pm).

Like Upim (see below), Standa is a good all-around department store stocked with all the basics, from socks and moderately priced clothing to cosmetics and kitchenware.

Upim

Via Gioberti (corner of Via Cimabue)
(055) 666861
Via Statuto 19 - (055) 475905
Via degli Speziali 3r - (055) 216867
Viale Talenti (corner of Via Liberale da Verona)
(055) 706048
Open daily summer: 9am-8pm (Mon 2pm-8pm); winter: 9am-7:30pm (Mon 2pm-7:30pm).

This national chain of department stores sells a more or less complete range of clothing, personal-care goods, and housewares at mid-range prices.

FASHION

■ CLOTHING

Giorgio Armani

Boutique, Via della Vigna Nuova 51r
(055) 219041
Emporio, Piazza Strozzi 16r
(055) 284315, (055) 215374
Open 10am-7:30pm. Closed summer: Sat pm; winter: Mon am.

The latest designs by the ultimate arbiter of understated chic can be seen, admired, and purchased in his two new shops. High prices for the high-fashion line; slightly smaller tags on the Emporio ready-to-wear.

Conte of Florence

Via Por Santa Maria 35r - (055) 2398611
Open summer: 9am-1pm & 4pm-8pm; winter: 9am-1pm & 3:30pm-7:30pm. Closed summer: Sat pm; winter: Mon am.

Sports fans of both sexes can get decked out here in expensive, top-quality togs: bathing suits, ski (and après-ski) gear, hiking clothes, and outerwear, all with that inimitable Italian flair. Handsome traveling bags to pack your purchases in are sold here as well.

Enrico Coveri

Via della Vigna Nuova 27r - (055) 2381769
Via de' Tornabuoni 81r - (055) 211263
Open summer: 10am-1:30pm & 4pm-8pm; winter: 9am-1pm & 3:30pm-7:30pm. Closed summer: Sat pm; winter: Mon am.

Stylish casual wear for men; imaginative, young-at-heart fashions for women.

Gianfranco Ferré

Via de' Tosinghi 52r - (055) 292003
Open 10am-7:30pm. Closed summer: Sat pm; winter: Mon am.

Ferré's Florentine headquarters flaunt the designer's alluring creations in huge display windows, a magnet for clusters of admiring shoppers. Inside, the store boasts several levels, all filled with gorgeous clothing and accessories in every price range but low.

Backhanded Chiseler

Michelangelo did a little showboating one day in front of the Palazzo Vecchio. He held his chisel behind his back and sculpted the profile of a man into the stone wall just to the right of the door to the palazzo. The face is still there, none the worse for wear.

Gherardini

Via della Vigna Nuova 57r - (055) 215678
Via degli Strozzi 25r - (055) 287950
Open 9am-1pm & 3:30pm-7:30pm. Closed summer: Sat pm; winter: Mon am.

The elegant setting—pastel walls, blond wood, exposed-brick arches—is worthy of Gherardini's fashionable collections of clothing for women and men, and of the shop's vast assortment of status handbags and luggage. At the Via degli Strozzi shop, the merchandise is limited to bags, ties, and scarves.

Gucci

Via de' Tornabuoni 57-59r & 73r - (055) 264011
Open summer: 9:30am-1pm & 3pm-7:30pm; winter: 9:30am-1pm & 2:30pm-7pm. Closed summer: Sat pm; winter: Mon am.

True, you can buy the same finely tailored apparel and G-drenched status accessories for men and women in almost every major city in the Western world—at more or less the same prices—but that doesn't stop a steady stream of international visitors from keeping the salespeople busy here. Gucci's most recent shoe designs (bright patent-leather sandals with ankle straps, for example) combine high fashion with superb craftsmanship.

Happy Jack

Via della Vigna Nuova 7-13r - (055) 284329
Open summer: 9:30am-8pm; winter: 9:30am-7:30pm. Closed summer: Sat pm; winter: Mon am.

A resolutely modern mood pervades the centuries-old edifice that houses Happy Jack, a chic and expensive source for menswear. Here a chap can put together an entire wardrobe, from suits, shoes, and sportswear to outerwear and underwear, all bearing famous labels—Brioni, Zanella, Basile, Valentino, and Les Copains.

Max Mara

Via de' Tornabuoni 89-81r - (055) 214133
Open summer: 10am-2pm & 4pm-8pm; winter: 10am-2pm & 3:30pm-7:30pm. Closed summer: Sat pm; winter: Mon am.

Max Mara's designs for women provide plenty of sleek style for a reasonable amount of money.

A Wagon of War, A Shining Snout, and a Bankrupt Backache

The Loggia del Mercato Nuovo, that Renaissance market arcade streaming with silk, bangles, and touristy trinkets, is famous for its bronze Piglet, whose snout is kept shiny by the strokes of a million passersby. But before its sixteenth-century facelift, the marketplace was originally the garage of the *Carroccio*, a four-wheeled war machine pulled by oxen and equipped with an altar and a giant bell. This clanging contraption was both drummer boy and dispensary for fallen warriors. Another curiosity of the *mercato* is the marble disc on the floor, which marks the uncomfortable spot where bankrupt Florentines were forced to thump their lower backs before the assembled masses. Naturally, one and all were encouraged to hurl insults and jeer at the insolvent souls.

Neuber

Via de' Tornabuoni 17 (in the arcade)
(055) 215763
Open summer: 9am-1pm & 4pm-8pm; winter: 9am-1pm & 3:30pm-7:30pm. Closed summer: Sat pm; winter: Mon am.

Neuber's window displays are soberly traditional; inside, mahogany dominates, accented with gilt molding. This is one of the best-known shops in Florence, patronized by royalty, movie stars, and other celebrities. What draws these august personages is the superbly styled designer clothing for men and women, presented along with a choice selection of English footwear and knits.

Oliver

Via Vaccherreccia 5r - (055) 2396327
Via delle Terme 9r - (055) 287266
Open 9am-1pm & 3pm-7:30pm. Closed summer: Sat pm; winter: Mon am.

Centrally located, with an enviable view of Piazza della Signoria, Oliver (despite its name) turns its back on the English styles that are so popular with conservative Florentines. Instead, it offers youthful, top-quality sportswear and an exceptionally large selection of shirts and blouses.

Principe

Via degli Strozzi 21-29r - (055) 216821
Open summer: 9am-1pm & 4pm-8pm; winter: 9am-1pm & 3:30pm-7:30pm. Closed summer: Sat pm; winter: Mon am.

Located across from the Palazzo Strozzi, with the added advantage of possessing no fewer than fourteen display windows, Principe is one of the city's most influential fashion sources. In keeping with its name, the store has an undeniably aristocratic aura, along with an impressively patrician clientele. Men, women, and children will find every item of clothing they need within Principe's precincts, from outerwear to pajamas and refined accessories. The staff gives sound advice on mixing colors and patterns.

Emilio Pucci

Via de' Pucci 6 - (055) 287622
Open 9am-1pm & 3:30pm-7:30pm. Closed Sat.

Classic elegance is the trademark of this aristocratic Florentine firm, most notably in the supremely feminine evening clothes.

Raspini

Via Roma 25-29r - (055) 213077
Via de' Martelli 5-7r - (055) 2398336
Via Por Santa Maria 72r
(055) 215796
Open summer: 9am-7:30pm; winter: 9am-1pm & 3:30pm-7:30pm. Closed summer: Sat am; winter: Mon am.

The Raspini stores are set in key locations around central Florence, with attractive, contemporary window displays to lure passing shoppers. Avant-garde fashions for dashing young men are featured, and the Via Martelli branch has a special department for children. All the boutiques have an exceptionally wide range of footwear, with a notable selection of English and American styles as well as a value-priced house label.

Mila Schön

Via della Vigna Nuova 32-34r
(055) 294977
Open summer: 9am-1pm & 4pm-8pm; winter: 9:30am-1:30pm & 3:30pm-7:30pm. Closed summer: Sat pm; winter: Mon am.

Distinctive, crisply tailored clothes for day and evening; men's ties are a specialty. The selection is limited but the quality is high.

Ugolini

Via de' Calzaiuoli 68r (women's wear)
(055) 214622
Via de' Calzaiuoli 65r (menswear)
(055) 214439
Open summer: 9am-1pm & 4pm-8pm; winter: 9am-1pm & 3:30pm-5:30pm. Closed summer: Sat pm; winter: Mon am.

In 1921 Ugolini won a British-sponsored, Europe-wide competition for shops that not only sold English goods but cultivated a truly British image as well. To this day the firm offers the very finest quality clothing and accessories from England. Need we say that the look is ultraconservative? But Ugolini also purveys superb hand-sewn Italian evening wear and hand-worked shirts.

Valentino

Via della Vigna Nuova 47r - (055) 293142
Open summer: 9:30am-1pm & 3:30pm-8pm; winter: 9:30am-1pm & 3pm-5:30pm. Closed summer: Sat pm; winter: Mon am.

The selection is fairly small; nonetheless, here you can admire and purchase the cream of the creations of Italy's best-known designer: divine clothing and accessories with eye-popping price tags.

Versace

Via de' Tornabuoni 13r - (055) 2396167
Open 10am-1pm & 3:30pm-7:30pm. Closed summer: Sat pm; winter: Mon am.

In a gorgeously restructured, typically Florentine building you can wander among Versace's sensuous, spirited, resolutely modern Italian fashions for men and women. Subtle they're not, but then "classic elegance" is not everyone's cup of tea. The highly decorative (and instantly recognizable) accessories are especially exciting.

Ermenegildo Zegna

Piazza de' Rucellai 4-7r - (055) 283011
Open 9:30am-7pm. Closed summer: Sat pm; winter: Mon am.

Zegna promotes the "total look" for men, as a cursory inspection of the display windows will convince you. Every item of clothing a man might need—suits, shirts, shoes, ties, underwear, leather jackets, accessories—is available here, and each one bears the stamp of Zegna's personal brand of contemporary elegance. Clothes may be made to measure as well, in a confoundingly wide choice of fabrics.

■ JEWELRY

Befani & Tai

Via Vacchereccia 13r - (055) 287825
Open 9am-1pm & 3:30pm-7:30pm. Closed summer: Sat pm; winter: Mon am.

It is in the studio directly over the little shop (which enjoys a breathtaking view of the Palazzo Vecchio) that Befani & Tai's stunning, one-of-a-kind jewels have been

---

*We're always happy to hear about **your discoveries** and receive **your comments** on ours. We want to give your letters the attention they deserve, so when you write to Gault Millau, please state clearly what you liked or disliked. Be concise but convincing, and take the time to argue your point.*

A Hopping Good Time

Ascension Day in the Parco delle Cascine means picnics, parties, and orgies of sweets. Scores of stands sell candies of all kinds, and others sell an odd piece of merchandise—crickets caged in tiny baskets. The Florentines buy them up like hotcakes, only to release them once they get home. This bizarre custom may be the newest twist on an ancient pagan ritual, or it might be a leftover from the desperate grasshopper hunts of the Middle Ages, when farmers were tormented by the hungry locusts. Still others suggest the festa started when young blades would hang a branch of May-fresh foliage from the jamb of their loved one's door. They would put the tuneful hopper among the leaves to serenade their lady. Apparently, this lazy form of courting was considered cricket in Florence.

crafted for more than 40 years. Its artisans are among the few who still polish their own precious metals and who possess the skills necessary to work with platinum. These craftspeople will happily make pieces to order, even from clients' own designs. In addition to its own production, Befani & Tai sells Art Deco ornaments as well as jewelry from the 1950s.

Blue Point
Via de' Calzaiuoli 39r - (055) 210791
Open summer: 9:30am-7:30pm; winter: 9:30am-1pm & 3:30pm-7:30pm. Closed summer: Sat pm; winter: Mon am.

People who don't like their jewelry classic and prim love what they see at Blue Point. This extraordinary boutique offers necklaces, bracelets, earrings, pins, and watches in every price range. The jewels are enchantingly displayed in a multitude of small vitrines hung from the walls of a midnight-blue, subtly neon-lit gallery.

Mario Buccellati
Via de' Tornabuoni 69-71r - (055) 2396579
Open 9am-1pm & 3:30pm-7:30pm. Closed summer: Sat; winter: Mon.

Famous for its lacy openwork and delicate carving, Buccellati's jewelry is crafted by some of the world's best artisans. A collection of particularly stunning "important" pieces combine flawless gemstones and precious metals in the inimitable Buccellati style.

Burchi
Ponte Vecchio 54r - (055) 287361
Open summer: 9am-7:30pm; winter: 9am-1pm & 3:30pm-7:30pm. Closed Mon.

Opulent watches and lots of massive, heavily worked gold jewelry glitter in Burchi's antique wood-and-wrought-iron display case. The store occupies a strategic site in Florence's shopping district, to the right of Ponte Vecchio as one heads toward Via Guicciardini.

Cartier
Piazza Santa Trinita 1r - (055) 292374
Open summer: 9am-1pm & 4pm-8pm; winter: 9am-1pm & 3:30pm-7:30pm. Closed summer: Sat pm; winter: Mon am.

All of Cartier's "musts" are on hand—watches, baubles, accessories—at their usual high prices.

Faraone Settepassi
Via de' Tornabuoni 25r - (055) 215506
Open 9:30am-1pm & 3:30pm-7:30pm. Closed summer: Sat pm; winter: Mon am.

This superbly elegant shop, which bears the names of two internationally respected jewelers, boasts a string of enticing display cases that wrap around the corner from Via de' Tornabuoni to Via di Parione. Framed in beige and pink marble and illuminated from above with hidden spotlights, the windows resemble nothing so much as a series of little shrines for precious relics. The objects of this elaborate presentation are large, costly ornaments, usually crafted of precious metals combined with enamel or splendid gemstones. At night, the jewels are taken inside and replaced by remarkably true-to-life drawings.

Gherardi
Ponte Vecchio 8r - (055) 287211
Open 9am-1pm & 3:30pm-5:30pm. Closed Mon in winter.

Coral jewelry, figurines, and good-luck pieces (little horns, hearts, tiny animals) are

Gherardi's specialty, but the shop also carries an interesting selection of cultured-pearl jewelry.

Mossa

Via de' Calzaiuoli 52r - (055) 280272
*Open summer: 9am-1pm & 4pm-8pm;
winter: 9am-1pm & 3:30pm-7:30pm. Closed
summer: Sat pm; winter: Mon am.*

This avant-garde jeweler creates drop-dead pieces not only with gems but with semiprecious stones cut in highly original ways. Mossa manufactures a collection of jeweled animal pins—panthers, jaguars, and such—of the type that the late Duchess of Windsor made popular.

Torrini

Piazza Duomo 10r - (055) 284506
*Open 9am-1pm & 3:30pm-7:30pm. Closed
summer: Sat pm; winter: Mon am.*

Torrini is a longstanding tradition in Florence—its trademark, a half cloverleaf with a ram's head, was registered in 1369 by Jacopus Turini. Many of the firm's jewels, from simple pendants to impressive necklaces, are exclusive designs produced by Torrini's own artisans. On view here are the Arcetri watch, the face of which is an antique Florentine coin, and the Zero bracelet (with its patented clasp) in platinum, gold, and diamonds.

■ LEATHER & LUGGAGE

Beltrami

Piazza dell'Olio 1 (showroom) - (055) 213290
Via de' Tornabuoni 44-52r - (055) 287779
Open 10am-7:30pm. Closed Mon am.

Since the early nineteenth century Beltrami has been known for its handsome footwear, and even today the name is synonymous with quality leather accessories, handbags, and luggage. And the firm has extended its line further to include supremely chic leather clothing for women and men, handcrafted by expert tailors.

Bojola

Via Rondinelli 25r - (055) 211155
*Open 9am-1pm & 3:30pm-7:30pm. Closed
summer: Sat am; winter: Mon am.*

The seven superbly dressed display windows at this corner shop near Piazza del Duomo draw a steady stream of oglers and shoppers. Florence is known for quality leather goods, and Bojola is justly proud of the handbags, wallets, and traveling gear that bear the firm's own label. The beautiful umbrellas, walking sticks, and canvas-and-leather bags are also eminently buyable.

Hermès

Piazza Antinori 6r - (055) 2381004
*Open 10am-1:30pm & 2:30pm-7pm
(Mon 3pm-7pm).*

This is the Florentine source for leather goods by the noted French firm; their signature accessories—scarves, scents, watches—and deluxe ready-to-wear are displayed here as well.

Mandarina Duck

Via Por Santa Maria 23r - (055) 210380
*Open summer: 9:30am-7:30pm; winter:
9:30am-1pm & 3:30am-7:30pm. Closed Mon
am.*

Amid all the traditional shops around the Ponte Vecchio, this one stands out, with its bright-yellow pillars guarding the entrance and its high-tech metal shelving inside. Those shelves are lined with the sturdy, contemporary rubber-and-canvas bags and luggage that have made Mandarina Duck so popular, especially with the young.

Ottino

Via de' Cerretani 60-62r - (055) 212139
*Open 9:30am-7:30pm. Closed summer: Sat
pm; winter: Mon am.*

Ottino's spacious showrooms, situated midway between the Duomo and the train station, hold a huge selection of the firm's own make of gorgeous handbags, deluxe luggage, and classy small leather goods, as well as elegant umbrellas, belts, and gloves.

Pollini

Via Por Santa Maria 42r - (055) 214738
*Open summer: 9am-7:30pm; winter: 9am-
1pm & 3:30pm-7:30pm. Closed summer: Sat
pm; winter: Mon am.*

Look for this large, amply stocked leather emporium (luggage, clothing, small leather goods) near the Ponte Vecchio, right in the heart of the city's historic center. Pollini's distinctive yet classic footwear for men and women is featured at another shop, on Via Calimala 12r.

Trussardi

Via de' Tornabuoni 34r - (055) 219902
Open summer: 9am-1pm & 3:30pm-7:30pm; winter: 9am-1pm & 3pm-7pm. Closed summer: Sat pm; winter: Mon am.

Most of these well-made leather goods (bags, briefcases, notebooks) and clothes (skirts, trousers, suits) sport Trussardi's familiar greyhound logo.

Louis Vuitton

Via de' Tornabuoni 47r - (055) 214344
Open 9am-1pm & 3pm-7pm. Closed summer: Sat pm; winter: Mon am.

Louis Vuitton's universally familiar initials are printed on much of the merchandise in this shop: trunks, suitcases, handbags, folders, briefcases, etc. But there are also beautiful bags in green or yellow épi leather, and a wealth of finely crafted accessories.

■ SHOES & ACCESSORIES

Casadei

Via de' Tornabuoni 33r - (055) 287240
Open 9:30am-1pm & 3:30pm-7:30pm. Closed summer: Sat pm; winter: Mon am.

Conveniently situated near the poshest clothes stores on Via de' Tornabuoni, Casadei purveys top-quality boots and shoes that strike a comfortable balance between classic style and up-to-the-minute fashion.

Cresti

Via Roma 14r - (055) 214150
Via Roma 9r - (055) 292377
Via Pietrapiana 73r - (055) 240856
Via de' Martelli 42-44r - (055) 212609
Open summer: 9am-1pm & 4pm-8pm; winter: 9am-1pm & 3:30pm-7:30pm. Closed summer: Sat pm; winter: Mon am.

Four convenient locations sell Cresti's conservative but good-quality footwear. The Via Pietrapiena branch specializes in comfortable shoes for ladies who are no longer young. Women will also find models just for them at all the other branches; men's shoes are stocked at the shops at Via Roma 9r, Via Pietrapiana, and Via de' Martelli; and children's footwear

---

Come on Baby, Light My Lantern

The Rificolone Festival is held each September 7th, on the eve of the Virgin Mary's birthday. The streets of Florence fill with boys and girls carrying long poles topped with paper lanterns. The wildly colored lamps have a candle inside, which often kindles the paper. That's half the fun. The children run amok with the burning lanterns—called *rificolone*—and wind up at Piazza della Santissima Annunziata. The prettiest unburnt lantern wins a prize. The tradition started back in pre-Edison days, when the countryfolk would travel through the night to reach the city before the Feast of the Madonna began, lighting their way with lanterns on long poles.

---

can be found at the other Via Roma and Via de' Martelli branches.

Tanino Crisci

Via de' Tornabuoni 43-45r - (055) 214692
Open 10am-7pm. Closed summer: Sat pm; winter: Mon am.

A deluxe setting for a stunning collection of entirely handmade shoes and boots for women. This footwear is appreciated not only by finicky Florentines but by discerning out-of-town shoppers as well.

Dominici

Via Calimala 23r - (055) 210251
Open summer: 9:30am-8pm; winter: 9:30am-7:30pm. Closed summer: Sat pm; winter: Mon am.

A stark black-and-white sign marks this resolutely modern boutique, cunningly enlarged with mirrors that reflect the name "Dominici" hundreds of times. Fashionable women just adore the firm's bold, even outrageous shoe designs, while their male companions settle for the just slightly more conservative men's styles.

---

*Some establishments change their **closing times** without warning. It is always wise to check in advance.*

Fatina

Via de' Pecori 33r - (055) 214298
*Open summer: 9am-1pm & 4pm-8pm;
winter: 9am-1pm & 3:30pm-7:30pm. Closed
summer: Sat pm; winter: Mon am.*
Buy baby's first shoes or pretty boots for
a young teenager (up to age 15) at this
appealing boutique, where fashion and
orthopedic footwear are both available.
Take note as well of the ecologically sound
shoes for tiny feet: the leathers have undergone no harmful chemical treatments.

Salvatore Ferragamo

Via de' Tornabuoni 16r - (055) 292123
*Open 9:30am-7:30pm. Closed summer: Sat
pm; winter: Mon am.*
Ferragamo is known the world over for
exquisitely crafted, tasteful, and amazingly
comfortable footwear. The broad range of
styles on display may surprise you, if the
only Ferragamos you've ever seen are U.S.
imports.

Fratelli Rossetti

Piazza della Repubblica 43-45r - (055) 216656
*Open summer: 9am-1pm & 4pm-8pm;
winter: 9am-1pm & 3:30pm-7:30pm. Closed
summer: Sat pm; winter: Mon am.*
The posh beige-and-black setting, with
spotlights illuminating the season's newest
styles, is a perfect backdrop for Fratelli
Rossetti's elegant footwear.

Santini

Via de' Calzaiuoli 95r - (055) 2398536
*Open summer: 10am-1:30pm & 4pm-8pm;
winter: 10am-1:30pm & 3:30pm-7:30pm.
Closed summer: Sat pm; winter: Mon am.*
This is Santini's Florentine outpost,
where you'll find sleekly seductive footwear by a designer who is well known to
fashionable Italians.

Ugolini

Via de' Tornabuoni 20-22r - (055) 216664
*Open summer: 9am-1pm & 4pm-8pm;
winter: 9am-1pm & 3:30pm-7:30pm. Closed
summer: Sat pm; winter: Mon am.*
Soft and supple Italian leather gloves, silk
ties, and glowing print scarves are featured
at this long-established shop, and there is
also a superb selection of fine English footwear for men. But what really makes us
swoon are the traditional men's dressing
gowns, in purest silk—divine!

Vitali

Via de' Panzani 20-22r - (055) 284954
*Open summer: 9am-1pm & 4pm-8pm;
winter: 9am-1pm & 3:30pm-7:30pm. Closed
summer: Sat pm; winter: Mon am.*
Along with shoes for both sexes from
famous makers, Vitali presents a noteworthy selection of classic accessories—ties,
belts, small leather goods, and bags.

GIFTS

Riccardo Barthel

Via de' Fossi 11r - (055) 283683
*Open summer: 9am-1pm & 4pm-8pm;
winter: 9am-1pm & 3:30pm-7:30pm. Closed
summer: Sat pm; winter: Mon am.*
The charming model kitchen in the window, complete with brickwork, antiqued
cabinets, and handmade paneling, makes
a convincing advertisement for the
materials inside the shop: salvaged tiles,
such architectural elements as baseboards
and decorative ceiling moldings, and even
the kitchen (or bathroom) sink!

Geographica

Via de' Cimatori 16r - (055) 296637
Open daily 10am-1pm & 4:30pm-8pm.
Unique in Italy, this small shop specializes in highly detailed geographical maps
of every part of the world. Here you'll find
all the publications of the Institute for
Military Geography and the Institute for
Naval Geography, along with the fascinating geological maps edited by Italy's National Geological Service.

I Maschereri

Via de' Tavolini 13r - (055) 213823
*Open 10am-1pm & 3:30pm-7:30pm. Closed
summer: Sat pm; winter: Mon am.*
First admire the pair of window displays
that flank the entrance to this singular
shop. Then prepare to be amazed, when
you step inside, by the huge array of
fabulous masks, some of which are
mysteriously suspended in midair by in-
visible wires: papier-mâché masks of *commedia dell'arte* characters and fantastic
masks for Carnival decorated with
feathers, flowers, and rhinestones.

Officina Profumo-Farmaceutica di Santa Maria Novella

Via della Scala 16r - (055) 216276
Open 9:30am-1pm & 3:30pm-7:30pm (Sat 8:30am-12:25pm & 3pm-6:30pm). Closed Mon am.

The heady fragrance of herbs greets those who enter what is perhaps the most famous pharmacy in the world. Antique glass cases brim over with fascinating potions, balms, and herbal mixtures prepared according to age-old, handwritten recipes that are the Officina's precious (and exclusive) patrimony. Visitors to Florence owe it to themselves to stop by this amazing shop, if only to purchase some pomegranate soap, a flacon of "Elixir di Cina" (reputed to have aphrodisiac properties) or, for those frazzled by traveling in Italy, an herb-based remedy for hysteria. The firm's toiletries enjoy a worldwide reputation.

Oli-Ca

Borgo Santi Apostoli 27r - (055) 2396917
Open summer: 9am-1pm & 4pm-8pm; winter: 9am-1pm & 3:30pm-7:30pm. Closed summer: Sat pm; winter: Mon am.

If you are terrified at the thought of wrapping an important gift, the Oli-Ca staff will do it for you. Bring your parcel to the shop, choose an appropriate paper and ribbon, and you will soon have a most presentable present. For do-it-yourselfers, there are gift boxes in every possible shape and size.

Il Papiro

Via Cavour 55r
Piazza Duomo 24r
Lungarno Acciaioli 45r - (055) 215262 (all shops)
Open summer: 9am-7:30pm; winter: 9am-1pm & 3:30pm-7:30pm. Closed Mon am.

Il Papiro produces lovely handcrafted marbleized and swirl-patterned papers that can be purchased by the sheet; they are also used to cover all manner of useful everyday objects, from picture frames to address books.

Profumeria Inglese

Via de' Tornabuoni 97r - (055) 289748
Piazza dell'Unità d'Italia 13r - (055) 214507
Viale Mazzini 3r - (055) 243802
Open 9:30am-7:30pm. Closed Mon am.

Founded in 1843 by Englishman Henry Roberts, this venerable pharmaceutical firm sells traditional, plant-based, and homeopathic remedies, as well as highly reputed skin creams and natural toiletries for men and women.

Sbigoli

Via Sant'Egidio 4r - (055) 2479713
Open summer: 9am-1pm & 4pm-8pm; winter: 9am-1pm & 3:30pm-7:30pm. Closed summer: Sat pm; winter: Mon am.

Right in the heart of Florence is a terrific source of hand- and machine-made terracotta pots, pitchers, baskets, and planters for your garden. A handsome selection of relatively plain majolica pots is available as well.

LINENS

Loretta Caponi

Borgo Ognissanti 12r & 9-13r - (055) 213668
Lungarno Vespucci 12-16r - (055) 211074
Open summer: 9am-1pm & 4pm-8pm; winter: 9am-1pm & 3:30pm-7:30pm. Closed summer: Sat pm; winter: Mon am.

The beauty of Florentine embroidery has been famous for centuries, but nowadays work of the very finest quality is hard to come by. Loretta Caponi's elegant shop is practically an institution for upper-class Florentine ladies, who come here for their wedding trousseaus and continue to visit, as established matrons, to buy their linens and lingerie. At Borgo Ognissanti 12 you'll find nightgowns and peignoirs as well as bath and table linens, all stunningly embroidered (and personalized, if you order in advance). The second shop (with entrances on Borgo Ognissanti and Lungarno Vespucci) specializes in adorable linens and clothing for infants (and expectant mothers), including christening dresses, tiny shirts, and little embroidered collars that can be sewn onto toddlers' clothes.

Cirri

Via Por Santa Maria 38-40r - (055) 2396593
Open 9am-1pm & 3:30pm-7:30pm. Closed summer: Sat pm; winter: Mon am.

A small shop with a long and respected tradition for quality embroidery, Cirri sells opulent tablecloths for your most important dinners, handkerchiefs simply embroidered with initials or trimmed with yards of lace, delightful clothes for children, and exquisitely feminine blouses and lingerie.

Città di San Gallo

Via Por Santa Maria 60r - (055) 2396249
Open summer: 10am-1:30pm & 4pm-8pm; winter: 10am-1:30pm & 3:30pm-7:30pm. Closed summer: Sat pm; winter: Mon am.
Traditional embroidered designs decorate these handkerchiefs, collars, cradle covers, and adorable bibs for babies. Hand-embroidered silk, linen, and cotton blouses are a specialty.

Ferrini

Via Calimala 5r - (055) 287595
Open summer: 10am-1:30pm & 4pm-8pm; winter: 10am-1:30pm & 3:30pm-7:30pm. Closed summer: Sat pm; winter: Mon am.
Ferrini lures a large audience of potential customers with a ravishing window display of embroidered nightgowns and bed linens. Inside, you can also admire an ample stock of table linens embellished with embroidery. Two distinctly different styles are proposed: a colorful, youthful line of machine-embroidered tablecloths and bath and kitchen towels, and a costly range of silk, organza, or linen tablecloths and napkins enriched with lace and hand-embroidered motifs.

Garbo

Borgo Ognissanti 2r - (055) 295338
Open summer: 10am-1:30pm & 4pm-8pm; winter: 10am-1:30pm & 3:30pm-7:30pm. Closed summer: Sat pm; winter: Mon am.
Dainty lace-encrusted pillows that summon up visions of antique canopy beds; delicate handkerchieves with white-on-white embroidery and lace edging; and silk, linen, or cotton blouses with lacy inserts are just a few of the captivating items you'll covet in Garbo's pretty shop.

Nicol

Via de' Fossi 38r - (055) 214253
Open 10am-1pm & 4pm-8pm. Closed summer: Sat pm; winter: Mon am.
The bright hues of Nicol's displays contrast with those of the far more staid antique dealers that line this street near Piazza Santa Maria Novella. A talented artist-craftswoman creates the splendidly

colored batiks to be found here. Butterflies, tigers, and flamingoes disport themselves on charming cotton panels of every size as well as on pillows, bedspreads, and scarves.

Patrizio

Via della Spada 40r - (055) 280160
Open summer: 10am-1:30pm & 4pm-8pm; winter: 10am-1:30pm & 3:30pm-7:30pm. Closed summer: Sat pm; winter: Mon am.
An antique terra-cotta floor and a coffered walnut ceiling set the tone for this high-class emporium that stands just off fashionable Via de' Tornabuoni. Customers ooh and aah over the rich array of hand- and machine-embroidered linens (machine work is to be found primarily on the terry towels) for table, bed, and bath.

Pratesi

Borgo Ognissanti 3-7r - (055) 292367
Open summer: 10am-1:30pm & 4pm-8pm; winter: 10am-1:30pm & 3:30pm-7:30pm. Closed summer: Sat pm; winter: Mon am.
Like its sister store in Milan, this branch of the Pratesi empire specializes in exclusive machine-embroidered bed and bath linens in superbly coordinated colors. On hand as well are lovely tablecloths (custom-made, if you wish) and adorable smocked dresses for little coquettes.

Spadini

Lungarno Archibusieri 4-6r - (055) 287732
Open summer: 10am-1:30pm & 4pm-8pm; winter: 10am-1:30pm & 3:30pm-7:30pm. Closed summer: Sat pm; winter: Mon am.
This is the place to find divine underthings in pure silk, embellished with hand embroidery and hand-sewn lace inserts. If you can tear yourself away from the lingerie, you'll find some beautiful household linens, also embroidered by hand.

Taf

Via Por Santa Maria 17r - (055) 2396037
Via Por Santa Maria 22r - (055) 213190
Open summer: 10am-1:30pm & 4pm-8pm; winter: 10am-1:30pm & 3:30pm-7:30pm. Closed summer: Sat pm; winter: Mon am.
Via Por Santa Maria 22 is a classic embroidery shop, where small gift items—handkerchieves, place mats, cradle coverlets, and the like—are displayed alongside

more expensive items, such as hand-embroidered nightgowns and ravishing dresses for little girls. Across the street, at number 17, the emphasis is on table linens, of which there is a distinctive selection.

WINE

Enoteca Alessi

Via delle Oche 27-29r - (055) 214966
Open 9am-1pm & 4pm-8pm. Closed Sun (Sat in summer).

This enormous store stocks an imposing selection of Italian wines from all the major wine-growing regions, imported vintages, whiskies, brandies, and any other alcoholic beverage you can think of. And though Alessi majors in wine, it minors in sweets: the entire ground floor is a kind of candyland for discerning gourmets, with all manner of chocolates, cookies, jams, marmalades, and exotic honeys. The enoteca (wine cellar) is appropriately situated underground, and a stunning sight it is. The cavernous room is literally lined with bottles, all maturing quietly in separate cylindrical recesses, with the names of the different regions of origin clearly marked at the top of each shelf. It's a perfect place for a wine buff to browse.

Biagini di Murgia Florio

Via de' Banchi 55-57r - (055) 215686
Open 9am-1pm & 4pm-7:30pm. Closed summer: Sat pm; winter: Mon am.

Set on a busy street that links Piazza Santa Maria Novella to the Duomo, Biagini is a noted purveyor of Tuscan wines. But you can count on finding a good selection of Piedmontese and Venetian vintages here too, along with the odd French or Spanish bottling. Italian and imported liquors are allotted considerable display space, as are Champagnes and Spumantes. Biagini will send gift cases of wine anywhere in Europe. A small sweets section offers an interesting assortment of Florentine and Sienese dolci.

La Bottega del Brunello

Via Ricasoli 81r - (055) 2398602
Open 9am-1pm & 3:30pm-7:30pm. Closed Mon.

All the wines produced in the region around Siena are featured in this wine shop of fairly recent vintage. Star billing, naturally, goes to Brunello di Montalcino. One section of the shop is set up as a tasting area, where you can accompany a glass of good wine with a plate of cheese or cured meats. Also on hand are Siena's famed cakes and cookies, which are perfect for dunking in a glass of sweet Vin Santo.

Bussotti Romano

Via San Gallo 161r - (055) 483091
Open 8:30am-1pm & 4pm-7:30pm. Closed Sat pm.

This tiny wine shop is an annex to the popular brasserie and sandwich shop next door, which is under the same management. The attractive selection of wines comprises Italians and imports, spirits, and bubblies of various origins. White alcohol for preserving cherries, figs, and apricots is in stock, along with a small assortment of gourmet groceries.

Cantina Guidi

Viale de' Mille 69r - (055) 570130
Open 9am-1pm & 4:30pm-8pm (summer: 9am-1pm & 5pm-8pm). Closed summer: Sat pm; winter: Wed pm.

Look for the tile sign decorated with vine motifs that identifies this delightful emporium. Space is at a premium, but every inch is put to good use: shelves extend all the way to the ceiling, and a wooden loft allows customers to reach the uppermost bottles. All of Italy's regional wines are represented, with a special emphasis on Tuscan growths. Forty different whiskies, Italian brandies, and a cheering array of Spumantes round out the selection of wines and spirits. The lower section of the store is devoted to gourmet delicacies: a rich array of teas, extraordinary game "prosciuttos," and exotic tinned foods from many lands.

Plan to travel? Look for Gault Millau's other Best of guides to Chicago, Florida, France, Germany, Hawaii, Hong Kong, London, Los Angeles, New England, New Orleans, New York, Paris, San Francisco, Thailand, Toronto, and Washington, D.C.

La Dolciaria

Via de' Ginori 24r - (055) 214646
Open daily Nov-Mar: 8:30am-1pm & 3:30pm-5:30pm; Mar-Oct: 8:30am-7:30pm.

For well over half a century, La Dolciaria has specialized in the sale of Tuscan wines. Piedmontese growths hold a place of honor as well, in addition to Spumantes, whiskies, and other Italian and imported spirits. The owners also have a weakness for top-quality candies, especially cara-mels, some of which are irresistibly picturesque with their old-fashioned wrappers. If you're fond of them too, take note that wholesale prices are given for quantity purchases.

Enoteca Murgia

Piazza Santa Maria Novella 15r-(055) 293149
Open summer: 9am-1pm & 4pm-8pm; winter: 9am-1am & 3:30pm-7:30pm. Closed summer: Sat pm; winter: Mon am.

Through a tiny doorway under the fifteenth-century Loggia di San Paolo, right across the street from the church of Santa Maria Novella, is this old wine shop, longer than it is wide, with ceilings of exposed ancient brick. Shelves labeled with the names of the premium wine-growing regions of Italy, France, Portugal, and Spain bear a wealth of enticing bottles. A selection of whiskies and Italian brandies is on offer as well, not to mention a full range of festive Spumantes.

Pardi

Via San Gallo 113r - (055) 490361
Open 8:30am-1pm & 3:30pm-7:30pm. Closed Sat pm.

Wines from all over Italy are ·epresented here, led by the most distinguished Tuscan vintages. Fifty whiskies are in stock too, along with Cuban rums, French Champagnes, and the best Italian Spumantes. It takes a lot of space to display all this merchandise, so don't be surprised to see the metal shelves reaching all the way up to the ceiling.

STREET MARKETS

Mercato Centrale

Piazza del Mercato Centrale, Via dell'Ariento
Open 6am-2pm (Sat 6am-8pm). Closed Sun.

In the San Lorenzo district, nearly hidden by the stalls of the clothing market (see below), stands the stately, recently restored iron pavilion—it dates from 1870—that houses the largest food market in Florence. Inside, the scene is a Technicolor marvel that will make any foodie sigh with rapture. Upstairs, stalls are piled high with gorgeous Tuscan vegetables and fruit, while on the ground floor hundreds of merchants hawk meat, fish, premium olive oils, breads, pungent cheeses, wild and cultivated mushrooms, and in season even costly white truffles from Piedmont. To quiet the appetite you're bound to work up while touring the market, stop for a satisfying beef or tripe sandwich at Nerbone's stand on the ground floor.

Mercato Nuovo or Mercato del Porcellino

Piazza del Mercato Nuovo - (055) 283683
Open 9am-6pm. Closed Mon.

Beneath the graceful arcades of the Mercato Nuovo, or straw market, vendors try to interest tourists and passersby in their multifarious merchandise: woven straw hats and baskets, leather goods, carvings, clothing, fabrics, lace, and household items. Tradition has it that the merchants must change places every day. The market is also called the Mercato del Porcellino for the little bronze boar that decorates the fountain on the piazza. Rub the piglet's snout as you pass, to ensure that you'll return to Florence some day.

Mercato di San Lorenzo

Piazza del Mercato Centrale, Via dell'Ariento
Open 7am-7pm. Closed Sun.

What is the appeal, you might ask, of this noisy, crowded, chaotic market? Well, some of us enjoy the sight of a bustling city scene; others are drawn by the prospect of a bargain. At the San Lorenzo market leather gear, knits, and accessories are priced to move, but the labels may or may not be genuine. We suggest you arm yourself with an ounce of healthy skepticism, then go for a look.

> *We're always happy to hear about **your discoveries** and receive **your comments** on ours. We want to give your letters the attention they deserve, so when you write to Gault Millau, please state clearly what you liked or disliked. Be concise but convincing, and take the time to argue your point.*

Museums

Cappella Brancacci

Chiesa S. Maria del Carmine, Piazza del Carmine - (055) 2382193
Open 10am-4:30pm (Sun & hols: 1pm-4:30pm). Closed Tue.

The Brancacci Chapel in the church of Santa Maria del Carmine contains one of the most extraordinary fresco cycles in the history of art, begun in 1425 by Masaccio and Masolino and completed some fifty years later by Filippino Lippi. Now freshly restored, the works can be admired in all their splendor. Masaccio's sublimely expressive *Expulsion of Adam and Eve* and *Tribute Money* exerted an incalculable influence on Renaissance painting.

Cappelle Medicee

Piazza Madonna degli Aldobrandini
(055) 23885
Open 9am-2pm (Sat, Sun & hols: 9am-1pm). Closed Mon.

The museum is part of the grand San Lorenzo complex that includes the Biblioteca Laurenziana, designed by Michelangelo. Visitors may view the grandiose Cappella dei Principi (Princes' Chapel) decorated with rare types of marble and stone; from there, one enters the New Sacristy, Michelangelo's first architectural effort. This funeral chapel holds the Medici Tombs, adorned with Michelangelo's powerfully affecting statues of *Dawn* and *Dusk*, *Day* and *Night*.

Casa Buonarroti

Via Ghibellina 70 - (055) 241752
Open 9:30am-1:30pm (Sun & hols: 9:30am-1pm). Closed Tue.

Michelangelo purchased this house toward the end of his life for his nephew, Leonardo. The Buonarroti heirs donated the house to the city of Florence in 1858. It contains two early marble bas-reliefs by the master: the *Madonna of the Steps* and the *Battle of Lapiths and Centaurs*. On view

as well are a wooden crucifix attributed to Michelangelo and many wax and terracotta models of his sculptural works.

Casa di Dante

Via Santa Margherita 1 - (055) 283343
Open 9:30am-12:30pm & 3:30pm-6:30pm (Sun & hols: 9:30am-12:30pm). Closed Wed.

The house where Dante is said to have been born holds a small collection of documents and pictures dealing with Florence in the great poet's time (1265–1321) as well as several different editions of the *Divina Commedia*.

Cenacolo di Andrea del Sarto a San Salvi

Via San Salvi 16 - (055) 23885
Open daily 10am-2pm.

Andrea del Sarto's masterpiece is a fresco of the *Last Supper* to be found in the refectory of the ancient abbey of San Salvi. The abbey is now a museum that holds a significant collection of sixteenth-century paintings, among which number works by Ghirlandaio and the master colorist, Pontormo.

Cenacolo del Ghirlandaio

Borgo Ognissanti 42 - (055) 2396802
Open Mon, Tue, Sat: 9am-noon.

In the refectory of the convent of Ognissanti is Domenico Ghirlandaio's beautiful fresco representing the *Last Supper* (*Cenacolo*). The adjacent church houses a Botticelli fresco, *Saint Augustine in his Study*, opposite a mural by Ghirlandaio depicting *Saint Jerome*.

Cenacolo di Fuligno

Via Faenza 32 - (055) 23885
Open by appt.

In what was formerly the refectory of the Franciscan convent of Sant'Onofrio, visitors may admire Perugino's fifteenth-century fresco of the *Last Supper*.

Cenacolo di Sant'Apollonia
Via XXVII Aprile 1 - (055) 23885
Open 9am-2pm (Sun: 9am-12:45pm). Closed Mon.
What was once the refectory of the Benedictine convent of Sant'Apollonia is now a museum where frescoes and preparatory sketches by a fifteenth-century Florentine master, Andrea del Castagno, are preserved. On view along with his dramatic *Last Supper* is the series of *Famous Men* frescoes, which were detached from the Villa Pandolfini.

Cenacolo di Santo Spirito
Piazza Santo Spirito 29 - (055) 287043
Open 9am-2pm (Sun & hols: 8am-1pm). Closed Mon.
The refectory of Santo Spirito houses the remaining fragments of Orcagna's great fresco of the *Last Supper* dating from the mid-fourteenth century. The cenacle also contains the Salvatore Romano Foundation, which includes some noteworthy detached frescoes, architectural fragments, and interesting Romanesque and Renaissance sculpture.

Chapterhouse of the Church of Santa Maria Maddalena de' Pazzi
Borgo Pinto 58 - (055) 2478420
Open daily 9am-noon & 5pm-7pm.
In the chapterhouse of the former Benedictine monastery attached to Santa Maria Maddalena de' Pazzi is Perugino's sublime fresco, *Crucifixion and Saints*, painted at the end of the fifteenth century.

Chiostri di Santa Maria Novella
Piazza Santa Maria Novella 18 - (055) 282187
Open 9am-2pm (Sun: 8am-1pm). Closed Fri.
This museum was opened in 1983 as the first phase of a program to salvage works of art and liturgical objects from the city's churches, convents, and monasteries. The monumental cloisters of Santa Maria Novella exhibit frescoes by Paolo Uccello depicting scenes from the Old Testament, Andrea da Firenze's allegorical frescoes inspired by the theological works of Saint Thomas Aquinas, and many precious reliquaries, liturgical vestments, and vessels.

Chiostro dello Scalzo
Via Cavour 69 - (055) 484808
Open Mon & Thu: 9am-1pm.
The small cloister of the Confraternity of Saint John the Baptist is decorated with monochrome frescoes painted by Andrea del Sarto between 1514 and 1526. The cycle depicts episodes from the life of the confraternity's patron, from Zachariah's vision of an angel announcing the birth of a son to John the Baptist's beheading at the hands of Herod.

Collezione Loeser
Palazzo Vecchio - (055) 2768465
Open 9am-7pm (Sun & hols: 8am-1pm). Closed Thu.
The collection of paintings and sculpture donated to the city of Florence in 1928 by historian Charles Loeser includes a wax cast of *Hercules and the Hydra* by Giambologna, a *Madonna and Child* by Lorenzetti, and a fine *Portrait of Laura Battiferri* by Bronzino, as well as interesting Tuscan terra cottas and stuccos.

Donazione Contini Bonacossi
Palazzina della Meridiana, Piazza Pitti
(055) 287096
Open by appt.
The superb collection of paintings, sculpture, furnishings, and objets d'art that belonged to connoisseur Alessandro Contini Bonacossi may be viewed in the Neoclassical Palazzina Meridiana, once the residence of the first king of Italy. Among the splendid works on display are a *Madonna and Child* by Sienese master Duccio di Boninsegna, a portrait by Veronese, Goya's *Torero*, and *Saint Anthony Abbot* by Zurbarán.

Gabinetto Disegni e Stampe degli Uffizi
Via della Ninna 5 - (055) 23885
Open 9am-7pm (Sun & hols 9am-2pm). Closed Mon.
The Drawing and Print Department of the Uffizi Gallery (located on the second floor in the old Medici Theater) is rooted in the collection of Cardinal Leopoldo de' Medici (1617–1655). Additional drawings were acquired over the years, and the inventory now numbers more than 100,000 items. Among the jewels of the collection are preparatory sketches and

drawings by Leonardo, Michelangelo, and Raphael, scores of Old Master drawings from the fourteenth and fifteenth centuries, Venetian drawings from the seventeenth and eighteenth centuries, works by Dutch, Flemish, and Spanish artists, engravings by Dürer and Luca di Leida, and architectural drawings by Brunelleschi.

Galleria dell'Accademia

Via Ricasoli 60 - (055) 2388609
Open 9am-2pm (summer: 9am-7pm, Sun 9am-2pm). Closed Mon.
In 1784 Grand Duke Pietro Leopoldo established the Academy of Fine Arts, endowing it with a collection of paintings for the students to copy. The Academy now houses a staggering number of Florentine pictures from the thirteenth to the nineteenth century (including two works by Botticelli). The museum's glory is the series of seven sculptures by Michelangelo, including the original of his sublime and powerful *David*. This masterpiece was transferred to the Academy from Piazza della Signoria in 1873, and now benefits from new lighting that further enhances the figure's virile beauty.

Galleria d'Arte Moderna

Piazza Pitti 1 - (055) 287096
Open 9am-2pm (Sun & hols: 9am-1pm). Closed Mon.
The Gallery of Modern Art, housed on the upper floor of the Pitti Palace, was inaugurated in 1924. The collections cover 150 years of Italian painting and sculpture, from Romanticism onward. Tuscan holdings are particularly strong, and there is an outstanding group of paintings by the *Macchiaioli* (pointillists), characterized by limpid colors and brilliant luminosity.

Galleria Corsini

Via di Parione 11 - (055) 287629
Open by appt.
The picture gallery in the magnificent seventeenth-century Palazzo Corsini is one of the most important private collections in Italy. In addition to some extremely fine furniture, the gallery conserves remarkable works by artists of the Florentine school of the fifteenth and sixteenth

centuries—Filippo Lippi, Botticelli, Signorelli, Pontormo, and Raphael.

Galleria Palatina

Piazza Pitti 1 - (055) 210323
Open 9am-2pm. Closed Mon.
The Galleria Palatina, also known as the Galleria Pitti, exhibits paintings acquired by generations of the Medici family. The collection, displayed in a series of incredibly opulent rooms, is rich in works from the sixteenth, seventeenth, and eighteenth centuries. Several masterpieces by Raphael (including his lovely *Veiled Woman*) and Titian (*La Bella* and *Portrait of a Gentleman*) are present, as well as works by Tintoretto, Andrea del Sarto, Bronzino, and several foreign artists (Rubens, Velásquez, Van Dyck). The monumental apartments of the Pitti are located just beyond the picture gallery. Of breathtaking splendor, they contain precious tapestries, furnishings, porcelain, and

Mr. America

In 1454 when Florentine nobleman Nastagio Vespucci christened his son Amerigo, he didn't realize that he was also naming a couple of continents. Young Amerigo commenced his career as a merchant in Seville, but soon abandoned commerce for a life of sea-faring and adventure. He met Columbus, and participated in voyages of exploration that reached the coast of what is now Central America in 1501–1502. Five years later, when Vespucci's account of the discoveries was published, geographers suggested that the new territories be called "Amerigo's Land," or America. Vespucci died in Seville in 1512, never having returned to Florence. But he is remembered in his birthplace with a river road, a bridge, and a fresco. The latter, painted by Ghirlandaio, can be seen in the Church of Ognissanti: it depicts the Vespucci family protected by the mantle of the Virgin. The figure on the Madonna's right is none other than Amerigo himself.

artworks amassed by the Medici and the royal houses of Lorraine and Savoy.

Galleria degli Uffizi

Loggiato degli Uffizi 6 - (055) 23885
Open 9am-7pm (Sun & hols: 9am-2pm). Closed Mon.

The Uffizi Gallery glories in the world's richest collection of Italian art, with comprehensive holdings of the Florentine school, from the masters of the Duecento (Cimabue, Duccio, Giotto) to Bronzino, the ultimate court portraitist of the sixteenth century. The Palazzo degli Uffizi, designed by Giorgio Vasari (also known for his Lives of the Painters), was commissioned by Duke Cosimo I de' Medici as an administrative center (Uffizi means "offices"). It was Cosimo's successor, Francesco I, who decided to transform the upper loggia into a museum to house the enormous Medici art collections. Over the centuries, a shrewd policy of acquisitions and exchanges resulted in an unparalleled collection that encompasses antique sculpture (including the Medici Venus), Italian and Flemish tapestries (including Revels at the Court of Catherine de' Medici and Henri II of France), and paintings on wood and canvas that date from the 1200s to the eighteenth century. Subsequent to the 1993 bombing that damaged the Uffizi's third wing and destroyed a number of artworks, many rooms are closed for restoration. At this writing, rooms 26 to 33 and 41 to 45 are inaccessible (they contain works by Raphael, Pontormo, Rubens, Van Dyck, Caravaggio, Rembrandt, Goya, Tiepolo, Canaletto, and Titian's celebrated Venus of Urbino). The justly famed Corridoio Vasariano, lined with artists' self-portraits, is also shuttered, at least until 1996. The museum is not expected to be fully functional until that date.

Museo Archeologico

Via della Colonna 36 - (055) 2478641
Open 9am-2pm (Sun: 9am-1pm). Closed Mon.

Established in 1870 in the handsomely renovated seventeenth-century Palazzo della Crocetta, the Archaeological Museum displays an awe-inspiring collection of Etruscan antiquities. Its Egyptian department is the second most important in Italy, and the Greek and Roman sections are of great interest. Some of the most outstanding holdings are: the François Krater, an archaic Attic vase found in an Etruscan tomb; a red-basalt bust of Pharaoh (seventh-sixth century B.C.); Egyptian polychrome wooden statuettes; a statue of an Etruscan mother goddess seated on a throne; and the bronze Orator, an Etruscan funerary statue discovered in 1566. Don't miss the newly opened Gabinetto delle Gemme, which presents a precious and dazzling collection of Etruscan gold jewelry from the seventh century B.C.

Museo degli Argenti

Piazza Pitti 1 - (055) 212557
Open 9am-2pm (Sun: 9am-1pm). Closed Mon.

More than just silver is featured at this curious museum within the Palazzo Pitti: it also displays magnificent collections of jewels, cameos, carved ivory, and crystal. Many of the objects on view come from the Medici family and date from antiquity and the Renaissance through the eighteenth century.

Museo d'Arte Contemporanea (The Alberto Ragione Collection)

Palazzo Cassa di Risparmio, Piazza della Signoria 5 - (055) 283078
Open 10am-1pm. Closed Tue.

Here is a collection of some 240 modern Italian paintings and sculptures assembled between 1930 and 1945 by Neapolitan engineer Alberto Ragione. It includes works by De Chirico, De Pisis, Marino Marini, Lucio Fontana, Carrà, Renato Guttuso, Emilio Vedova, and Mario Mafai.

Museo Bardini e Galleria Corsi

Piazza de' Mozzi 1 - (055) 2342427
Open 9am-2pm (Sun: 8am-1pm). Closed Wed.

A jewel of a museum, where you can admire works acquired by noted antiquarian Stefano Bardini, who bequeathed his pictures, furniture, tapestries, and extensive sculpture collection to the city of Florence. On the second floor is the Corsi Gallery, which holds some 600 pictures dating from the twelfth century to about 1900. Antonio del Pollaiolo's Saint Michael the Archangel is outstanding.

Museo Botanico

Via Giorgio La Pira 4 - (055) 2757462
Open Mon, Wed, Fri: 9am-noon (1st Sun of the month: 9:30am-12:30pm). Free entry.
With nearly four million specimens in the central herbarium alone, the Botanical Museum of Florence is one of the most important of its kind in the world. The adjacent Botanical Gardens boast a number of trees that are several centuries old.

Museo delle Carrozze

Piazza Pitti 1 - (055) 212557
Open Sat 11am-noon (call for appt).
This interesting little museum, situated in the right wing of the Palazzo Pitti, exhibits important examples of horse-drawn carriages, with a remarkable collection of eighteenth-century vehicles.

Museo della Casa Fiorentina Antica

Palazzo Davanzati, Via Porta Rossa 13 (055) 23885
Open 9am-2pm (Sun: 9am-1pm). Closed Mon.
In the fourteenth-century Palazzo Davanzati, remodeled several times over the years, is housed a fascinating museum that documents how a certain class of Florentines lived and worked from the Renaissance through the eighteenth century. Collections encompass works of art (terra-cotta busts from the della Robbia workshop), furniture (a handsome sixteenth-century painted wardrobe), textiles (antique lace and trapunto embroideries), and household objects.

Museo della Fondazione Herbert P. Horne

Via de' Benci 6 - (055) 244661
Open 9am-1pm. Closed Sun.
Assembled by English connoisseur Herbert Percy Horne (1864-1916), this admirable collection of paintings, sculpture, furniture, and antiquities is housed in the fifteenth-century Palazzo Alberti-Corsi. There are works by Giotto (*Saint Stephen*), Simone Martini, Pietro Lorenzetti, and Filippino Lippi, an *Athlete* sculpted by Giambologna, and drawings by Michelangelo, Raphael, Tiepolo, and Gainsborough. The ensemble is an exquisite reflection of one man's peerless taste and sensibility.

Museo Marino Marini

Piazza San Pancrazio - (055) 219432
Open summer: 10am-1pm & 4pm-7pm; winter: 10am-1pm & 3pm-6pm. Closed Tue.
One of Italy's finest contemporary artists is honored here, in a fine museum opened in 1988. On view are 174 works by sculptor Marino Marini (1901-1980), displayed in ideally spacious, bright surroundings. Most impressive is Marini's *Equestrian Group*, the centerpiece of the exhibition.

Museo Nazionale del Bargello

Via del Proconsolo 4 - (055) 23885
Open 9am-2pm (Sun & hols: 9am-1pm). Closed Mon.
The severe and imposing Palazzo del Podestà, once the residence of the chief of police (*il bargello*), dates from the thirteenth century. It now houses a magnificent collection of fourteenth- to seventeenth-century Tuscan sculpture as well as rich collections of coins, medals, textiles, and objets d'art. Michelangelo's bust of *Brutus*, his *Madonna and Child with Saint John the Baptist* tondo, his *Drunken Bacchus*, and *Young Apollo* (or *David*) can be seen here. Also on view are Cellini's *Ganymede* and several fine works by Giambologna, Verrocchio, and Pollaiolo. An entire room is devoted to Donatello, including his marvelous bronze *David* and his *Saint George*, among others. Notable, too, are the glazed terra-cotta bas-reliefs by Andrea, Luca, and Giovanni della Robbia.

Museo dell'Opera di Santa Croce

Piazza Santa Croce 16 - (055) 244619
Open 10am-12:30pm & 3pm-5pm (Mar-Sep: 2:30pm-6:30pm). Closed Wed.
The museum occupies the refectory and adjacent rooms of the convent attached to the church of Santa Croce. Cimabue's splendid *Crucifix* (restored after having been damaged by the 1966 flood), a gilded bronze *Saint Louis* by Donatello, and detached frescoes by several Florentine masters may be admired here. Through a handsome portal designed by Giuliano da Maiano, one enters Brunelleschi's magnificent Cappella dei Pazzi, which features polychrome decorations by Luca della Robbia.

Museo dell'Opera di Santa Maria del Fiore
Piazza Duomo 9 - (055) 2302885
Open 9am-7:30pm (winter: 9am-5:30pm).
Closed Sun, hols.

A collection of extraordinary richness is exhibited in this small museum, a mandatory stop for anyone who wishes to understand the development of Florentine sculpture. Herein are masterpieces from the Duomo, from Giotto's Campanile, and from the Baptistery. These include fourteenth-century statues from the cathedral's façade, others from the niches on the Campanile, including the prophets Habakkuk and Jeremiah by Donatello, Michelangelo's Pietà, transported here in 1981 from the Duomo, the Baptistery's gilt-and-enameled-silver altar, and Donatello's carved-wood Magdalene. There are also panels from Ghiberti's Paradise Door and a wooden model of Brunelleschi's dome.

Quite a Mouthful

"Put up your duke!" yelled the enraged populace of Florence one grisly July day in 1343. They stormed the Palazzo Vecchio, intent on killing the petty French-born tyrant Gualtieri di Brienne, Duke of Athens and Lord of Florence, who had been taxing them to death. The duke took to his heels and slipped down the staircase to Via della Ninna, leaving behind his notary and Capitano di Giustizia. The mad rabble quickly slaughtered and diced the luckless duo and, still squirming-fresh, ate them in a frenzy of cannibalism. The tale is documented, but difficult to swallow nonetheless.

Museo di San Marco
Piazza San Marco 1 - (055) 23885
Open 9am-2pm (Sun & hols: 9am-1pm).
Closed Mon.

Many of Fra Angelico's finest works may be viewed in this former Dominican monastery (of which the great painter was a friar). Among them are the Crucifixion and a sublimely spiritual Annunciation. The

Pilgrim's House contains the Tabernacle of the Linaioli, with a luminous Virgin Mary and angel musicians in a frame designed by Ghiberti, and an awe-inspiring Last Judgment. The library, an architectural gem designed by Michelozzo, contains a precious collection of illuminated Renaissance manuscripts.

Museo dello Spedale degli Innocenti
Piazza della Santissima Annunziata 12 (055) 2477952
Open 9am-7pm (winter: 8:30am-2pm; Sun & hols: 8:30am-1pm). Closed Wed.

On the first floor of this fifteenth-century foundling hospital is an impressive collection of detached Renaissance frescoes of the Florentine and Umbrian schools. There is an Adoration of the Magi by Ghirlandaio, another by Pontormo, the Madonna of the Innocents by Luca della Robbia, as well as some fine furniture and an exhibit of illuminated manuscripts.

Museo Stibbert
Via Stibbert 26 - (055) 486049
Open 9am-2pm (Sun & hols: 9am-12:30pm). Closed Thu.

The vast and eclectic holdings of the Stibbert Museum were acquired by nineteenth-century connoisseur and Garibaldian hero, Frederick Stibbert. While the furnishings, pictures, and objets d'art are worthy of interest, it is the collection of arms and weapons that merits your close attention. The cortege of fourteen knights and fourteen foot soldiers arrayed in sixteenth-century armor from Italy, Germany, and Spain is a dazzling sight indeed.

Museo di Storia della Fotografia Fratelli Alinari
Palazzo Rucellai, Via della Vigna Nuova 16r (055) 213370
Open 10am-7:30pm. Closed Wed.

Opened to the public in 1985, this photography museum occupies one of the most elegant Renaissance buildings in Florence. The holdings include 350,000 vintage prints, with representative works by virtually all of the master photographers of the nineteenth and twentieth centuries. Antique cameras, lenses, and other equipment complete the picture. The temporary exhibitions hosted by the museum are invariably worthwhile.

Museo di Storia della Scienza

Piazza dei Giudici 1 - (055) 293493
*Open Mon, Wed, Fri: 9:30am-1pm & 2pm-5pm;
Tue, Thu, Sat: 9:30am-1pm. Closed Sun, hols.*

The history of science is documented with scientific instruments from the Medici and Lorraine collections, archives, and a specialized library. Exhibits include Galileo's telescope, the first barometer, an eighteenth-century "electrostatic machine," antique surgical instruments and microscopes. There are also some curious examples of anamorphoses (distorted optical images that appear natural when viewed from a certain angle, or in a curved mirror).

Museo Storico di Firenze Com'era

Via dell'Oriuolo 4 - (055) 2398483
*Open 10am-1pm (Sun & hols: 8am-1pm).
Closed Thu.*

This museum is devoted to "Florence as it used to be," with an evocative collection of prints, drawings, maps, paintings, and photographs that document the city's development and daily life over the centuries.

Palazzo Medici-Riccardi

Via Cavour 1 - (055) 2760340
*Open 9am-1pm & 3pm-6pm (Sun: 9am-1pm).
Closed Wed. (Call for appt).*

Cosimo (il Vecchio) de' Medici commissioned this palazzo from Michelozzo; it is one of the earliest examples of Renaissance architecture in Florence. Completed in 1460, it was subsequently modified according to Michelangelo's design. Within the palazzo, a gallery is decorated with Luca Giordano's Baroque fresco, The Apotheosis of the Medici; the chapel displays another famous (and recently restored) fresco, this one by Benozzo Gozzoli, representing the Journey of the Magi to Bethlehem. The figures in the fresco are portraits of—you guessed it—the Medici family.

Palazzo Vecchio
The Monumental Apartments

Piazza della Signoria - (055) 2768465
Open 9am-7pm (Sun: 8am-1pm). Closed Thu.

Located on the first and second floors of the Palazzo Vecchio (which in medieval times was the seat of government and in the sixteenth century the residence of Cosimo I de' Medici and of his son, Francesco), the Monumental Apartments are sumptuously decorated with splendid frescoes, paintings, sculpture, and other artworks. The Salone dei Cinquecento contains heroic frescoes by Vasari celebrating the Medici and Florence, and Michelangelo's marble *Victory*. Francesco I's Studiolo contains superb Mannerist frescoes and small bronzes by Giambologna. Among the other apartments, the most interesting are the Sala dei Gigli (Lily Room) and Eleanor of Toledo's private quarters, decorated with frescoes by Bronzino and with Giovanni Stradano's fresco cycle, *Deeds of Famous Women*.

Villa Medicea della Petraia and Gardens

Via della Petraia 40 (6 km N) - (055) 451208
*Open Nov-Feb: 9am-4:30pm; Mar-Apr & Sep-Oct: 9am-5:30pm; May-Aug: 9am-6:30pm.
Closed Mon.*

These terraced gardens are graced by a fountain in the center of which stands Giambologna's bronze *Venus*. They afford a splendid view of Florence and the Arno valley. Built in the sixteenth century, the villa is now furnished with Empire and Louis XV pieces, Renaissance tapestries, and seventeenth-century paintings. Particularly worthy of note are the frescoes by Volterrano that decorate the courtyard, representing the opulence of the powerful Medici clan.

An Abundance of History

In the heart of Piazza della Repubblica stands a column that the Florentines call "the column of abundance." Abundance of cars, or cafés, or what? It actually marks the spot occupied in antiquity by the Roman Forum and Capitol. On top of the Roman ruins the medieval ghetto and market were later built. Hundreds of years after that came Piazza della Repubblica, ushering Florence into the twentieth century. If we were you, we wouldn't count on being around for the next renovation.

Useful Telephone Numbers

Florence Area Code: 055

Airports: Peretola, 373498; 30615.
Galileo Galilei (Pisa), (050) 500707;
28088
Ambulance: 212222
City Hall: 284926
City Police Department: 23320
Fire Department: 115
Lost and Found: 367943

Medical Emergency: 118394
Pharmacy: 216761
Police Emergency: 112; 113
Post Office and Telegraph: 160
Radio Taxi: 4390, 4798
State Railway Information: 23521;
288765
Tourist Information: 23320; 2768366
Wake-up Call: 114
Weather Service: 191

Phonebook or Libretto?

The Florentine passion for politics and music can be observed in the city's telephone directory. Nowhere else will you see so many typically Italian cognomens preceded by the names of heroes and heroines. Some are inspired by dramatic moments of history—Marat or Robespierre, Libera, Libero, or Libertà, Italia or Roma, even Lenin, Lenino, Lenina. Other given names echo famous operas or works of literature: we found Ivanhoe, Athos, Aladino, Amleto (Hamlet), Ofelia, Otello, Desdemona, Carmen, Aida, Radamès, Norma, Ernani, Mimì, Musetta, Armida, Tosca, Tristano, Isotta... The bearers of these evocative monikers are usually middle-aged or older. Today's tots tend to be labeled with the local equivalents of Jennifer or Jason. The most common surname in Florence, Innocenti or Degli Innocenti, harks back to the time when foundlings and orphans were sheltered in the Spedale degli Innocenti (Foundling Hospital), designed by Brunelleschi, in Piazza della Santissima Annunziata.

Midnight Sunset

In the cathedral of Florence there ticks a curious clock designed in the fifteenth century by artist Paolo Uccello. Though it runs like, well, clockwork, the hours it marks are those of the Quattrocento—when a rather different notion of time prevailed. The round clockface is set in a square, with four prophets' heads in the corners. It displays not just twelve, but all 24 hours in Roman numerals. Stranger still, the figures are arranged from bottom to top, and the hands travel counterclockwise! Time was reckoned differently back in the Renaissance. The day ended with sunset, which corresponded to the 24th hour; the new day began from that point. In 1750 a well-intentioned soul "repaired" Uccello's clock in accordance with modern methods of measuring time. But a second intervention, in 1973, restored the timepiece to its original—and much more interesting—state.

65

MILAN

Better by Design

Bulging with money muscles and brimming with eyesores, Milan may well greet you with a mote in the eye. Those who were born or emigrated here know that it's polluted, and noisy, and nothing like all the other pretty Italian towns. So why do they stay? *Perché a Milano c'è lavoro*: work and wages. That means action, novelty, dynamism. Beauty takes on other forms. As we write this, the fall designer fashions are swishing down runways all over town. The staccato of stiletto-heeled glamour girls and their crocodile-shod mates is deafening.

Deafening, too, are the image-wise voices of the Milan PR men. Most of the catchy self-styling is inaccurate. "Milan—the city that never sleeps." Well, if it's not sleeping, it's probably working. "Milan—a capital in search of a country." Nope, it's already a city-state, and a very rich one at that (Milan does wish the bureaucracy in Rome would somehow drop dead). A hundred years ago it was called "the most urbane city in Italy," an apt description indeed. The sprawling Province of Milan is Italy's not-so-little engine that could, the locomotive. In industry, finance, fashion, publishing, opera, and art, the Milanese chug along hooting, "We know we can. We know we can." They are style-setters and prodigious toilers, and their exertions account for nearly one-third of the country's national income. Certainly, Milan is one of Italy's most nerve-racked, hard-nosed, chip-on-the-shoulder cities. It is also one of the most endearing and alluring. Hulking Milan attracts talent—the hottest artists and hungry, iron-gloved entrepreneurs—from all over the peninsula.

Most of the city's celebrities past (Da Vinci, Bramante, Stendhal) and present (Armani, De Benedetti, Aulenti, Strehler) hail from somewhere else but made it to the top in Milan. There are probably fewer than 100,000 Milanese who can trace their ancestry back more than a generation or two—not unusual in America but unheard-of in the rest of root-bound Italy.

Milan's Quadrilatero d'Oro, or Golden Rectangle, between Via Montenapoleone and Via della Spiga, is famous the world over for chic shopping and fine restaurants. And everyone has heard of opera at La Scala and drinks at the mosaic-paved Galleria Vittorio Emanuele II. But Milan's international reputation is of recent vintage. Not so very long ago, most people wrote the city off as a dingy place to change trains, a sort of immense Stazione Centrale between Rome or Florence and points north. Milan still has some of the worst traffic jams in Europe. Its buildings have been blackened by foul air. Its humid, Continental climate is one to which only the inhabitants have become impervious. All this is unrelieved by a paucity of parks and open spaces. Still, some improvement seems to be on the way. The historic center is now partially closed to cars without special permits. More than twenty new urban "green spaces" and "pedestrian islands" now bloom among the jumble. Scores of historic buildings have been restored rather than bulldozed. Milan-the-dynamo is slowly, slowly becoming Milan-the-livable. It is tough nowadays to visualize the postwar state of rubble and misery, when 60 percent of the city lay flattened by bombs. Or the industrial boomtown of the 1950s and '60s, when nearly 100,000 industrial workers flooded in each year, most of them long-distance *pendolari*, or commuters, from the South and the depressed agricultural areas of northern Italy. This human tide is what spurred the creation of all those unsightly bedroom communities and satellite cities (Comasina, Gallaratese, Gratosoglio).

Milan likes to bill itself as youthful and bullish on novelty, which it is. But it's also as old as the stones. Hardly anyone seems to know or care that the Quadrilatero d'Oro, for example, is one of the oldest neighborhoods in the *centro storico*, near the site occupied in antiquity by a succession of Etruscans, Ligurians, and an Italic tribe called the Insubres. Today's Romans, steeped in ruins, hate to admit that Milan's history stretches back almost as far as their own. The Cisalpine Gauls moved into this swampy lowland in the sixth century B.C., when they founded Mitta-land ("place in the middle") around a sacred spot under what is now Piazza della Scala or Piazza del Duomo. Foremost among their divinities was, appropriately, a god of business. The hawk-eyed Romans of old foresaw the importance of Mitta-land as a military stronghold and trade center on the northern routes. So they marched in around 61 B.C., and, after waging war for 26 years, subdued the Gauls and built Mediolanum.

Nearly all other ancient Roman cities were built on a checkerboard plan. But Milan—forever an innovator—grew up around radial axes. Its main arteries fan out from a single center like the spokes of a wheel. And since the Middle Ages, the city's hodgepodge has been growing in concentric rings around that magnificent marble mountain, the Duomo. No gridblock of efficiency, this circle-within-a-circle configuration lends itself nevertheless to dynamism. Maybe that's why the wheels within wheels of modern Milan—the circular roadways known as the Cerchia dei Navigli, the Circonvallazione Interna and Esterna—seem in constant, dizzying motion. Or maybe it's just the crazy traffic.

Natives and other boosters love to reminisce damp-eyed about "old Milan." Well, which Milan do you mean? The fortress-city of Federico I Barbarossa? The cruel but creative city-state ruled for centuries by the Viscontis and Sforzas? Or the elegant Napoleonic capital of canals and wide avenues that Stendhal, the great French writer, describes? Only snatches of each—a boggling patchwork—remain.

Each of the dozen or so times Milan has been crunched—by Romans, Huns, Visigoths, Lombards, the French, the Spanish, the Austrians, the Fascists and, most recently, by the Allied Forces in World War II—it has arisen and grown larger. If you netted every good citizen within the city limits, you'd have about 1.4 million busy souls to count. But the greater metropolitan area hosts some 3 million and spills Los Angeles–style into the Lombard Plain. That makes it Italy's second-most-populous city, after Rome.

Zounds—how do you orient yourself in this architectural Babylon? Get onto high ground, maybe, but that's not easy to find. The city is flat and the streets narrow, so there's no perspective—unless, of course, you climb to the top of the cathedral. From the top of the Duomo (open to the public year-round) you can see for miles. On a clear day the Alps poke into view to the north, the Po River and Apennines to the south. The eye naturally stumbles next onto the most imposing pieces of urban furniture. The fourteenth-century Castello Sforzesco, swimming in the greenery of the Parco Sempione, is that ivy-covered mass of bricks to the northwest. Thrice flattened and skillfully rebuilt in the 1890s, it now shelters several excellent museums (Michelangelo's *Pietà Rondanini* and Mantegna's *Virgin and Child in Glory* are there).

The Stazione Centrale over there to the north is probably the most outlandish hulk in town, along with one of the globe's largest covered train stations. The grandiose stone eagles and military motifs are a monument to the Fascist empire's flash-in-the-pan might. It is possibly, along with the Duomo, Milan's most-remembered landmark. Rising next to it is the tallest skyscraper on the horizon, one of the glinting symbols of modern Milan, the sleek Pirelli Tower.

The original skyscraper is the Duomo itself, which was started in 1386 and finished five centuries later. Ever since, in the face of an interminable, colossal, or hopeless project, the Milanese roll their eyes and invoke *la fabbrica dal Dom*, short for *La Divina Fabbrica del Duomo di Milano*, the organization responsible for the construction and day-to-day operation of the cathedral. The job of rebuilding,

69

cleaning, and repairing the Duomo is literally never completed. Big on big, this splendid pastiche of late-Gothic, Renaissance, Baroque, and Neoclassical elements is the third-largest cathedral in the world (after Saint Peter's in Rome and the Cathedral of Seville). The topmost spire scrapes 356 feet, the tacit limit respected by all city builders until the postwar boom. Atop it stands the *Madonnina* winking down at the bustle through her 3,500 layers of gilding, a source, it is said, of inexhaustible inspiration. Inspiration for what?

Well, the Duomo is both the physical and, if you will, the spiritual center of town. Ask how to reach a given destination and a true Milanese will tell you to "Go back up to the Duomo and turn..." It also happens to be one of the quietest corners in this clamorous city, a welcome refuge for the pious and the weary alike. The Duomo doubles as a cathedral and a working parish church, which is one reason why it has never degenerated into a "railroad station" buzzing with tourists. The interior space is enormous (the nave is nearly 150 yards long); light filters through rose windows and some of the finest stained glass anywhere in the world. Anatomy buffs will rejoice at one of the more remarkable specimens of religious art, the statue by Marco d'Agrate (1562) of Saint Bartholomew, martyred by flaying. There's also the chilling reliquary-tomb of Mr. Counter-Reformation, Saint Charles Borromeo (1538–1584). His unsmiling, mummified face stares out from the crystal casket; his lace gloves are still neat and white.

Now it's time to get down into that clutter of red-tile rooftops and cement high-rises you viewed from the roof of the Duomo. Several central neighborhoods have a distinctive flavor: the Brera, known for its high-brow Academy of Fine Arts and the fantastically good Pinacoteca; the Ticinese, where the last of the steaming, uncovered Navigli, or canals, flow; zona Venezia, clicking well-heeled from the lovely Public Gardens to the Quadrilatero d'Oro; Porta Romana, where the Università Statale (state university) and several of the city's best theaters are located; and zona Magenta, which swallows up the Cinque Vie and Sant'Ambrogio.

The immediate surroundings of the Duomo are strewn with architectural nuggets; the Milanese call it *pienissimo centro*. We hope you like to walk, because the only way to explore central Milan is on foot. Taxis are expensive as all get out, and during rush hours at least are prone to *imbottigliamento*, the Milanese equivalent of gridlock. If you're in a hurry, take the Metropolitana Milanese (subway) or, better yet, rattle your bones in one of the old orange electrified trams running around (numbers 29 and 30) or across the center (numbers 1, 4, 8, 13, 15) of town.

Let your nose direct you beyond the Piazza del Duomo in the direction of the Castello Sforzesco. Piazza Mercanti, known for its arcaded Palazzo della Ragione (1230) and the white-and-black marble Loggia degli Osii, will open before you, oddly pungent. At 2 Via Mercanti is the Renaissance Palazzo dei Giureconsulti (1560–1564), whose large clock in the middle of the façade has been there since 1272. But what is that terribly modern odor? Incongruously enough, tranquil Piazza Mercanti, with some of the best-preserved ancient palazzi in town, was the site of the "fast-food gang wars" of the '70s. Several franchise eateries were installed there. Today, the rumbling is over, but the junk food has stayed on and spread: Milan is Italy's fast-food capital.

Even the Galleria Vittorio Emanuele II, one of the western world's most luxurious shopping arcades, has not escaped fast food's influence—some of the best views of the mosaic-floored, glass-domed rotunda are from the second-floor windows of Biffi and Magic cafeterias. Nonetheless, the Galleria, which sparkles with the optimism of the Unification era in which it was built (1865), is still the stuff Milanese café society is made of. We like to sit out at the Camparino café and watch the perennially saber-rattling Carabinieri march by. Savini, one of Milan's best-known restaurants, is right across from Burghy, and several well-stocked bookstores, the telephone office (SIP), and the C.I.T. (a major travel agency) are located there.

"Ridi pagliaccio" they might sing, but the Teatro alla Scala is nothing to laugh at. From the outside it is a surprisingly sober Neoclassical construction, the handiwork of local hero Giuseppe Piermarini (1778). But the fabled interior is indeed a like jewel box, shaped like a horseshoe and upholstered in scarlet. La Scala is a shrine to lyric opera that draws tens of thousands of *devoti* each year, most of them dead serious and dressed to the nines. Unless you reserve years in advance, forget about getting in to see an opera. Your best bet is to collar a scalper or buy standing-room-only tickets on the night of the performance. C.I.T. can sometimes help, and so can certain hotel concierges—it's a matter of timing and good luck.

Well, some things never change: old money dies hard. Beyond La Scala but still in *pieno centro* is the Borgo Nuovo, once called the *Contrada di Sciori*, which in Milanese dialect means "wealthy noblemen's neighborhood." The Borgo is sandwiched between Brera's hip clubs and antique shops on one side, and the Quadrilatero d'Oro on the other. Many of its massive stone dwellings boast unusually fine porticoed courtyards that have remained unscathed by bombs or the wrecker's ball. A favorite pastime is to wander (innocently, of course) into the courtyards to take a peek at the famed columns. No one knows exactly how many columns are hidden behind the heavy street doors in the Borgo Nuovo, the Brera, along Corso Monforte, or on Via Cappuccio; when Stendhal first galloped into Milan, in June 1800, he was told they numbered 20,000.

The fashion avenues of the Quadrilatero d'Oro spill into the corporate heartland of Corso Europa at Piazza San Babila. Here you might share a plastic table with a *paninaro* (a "fast-food freak") or a busy CEO slugging it down at Burghy. The Corso Vittorio Emanuele, which links San Babila and the Duomo, is possibly the liveliest mainstream neighborhood in town, and is now a pedestrian paradise. Adolescents, executives, and Milanese matrons do their *passeggiata* (promenading) cheek by jowl. The maze of surrounding *gallerie* is chockablock with movie theaters, fashionable boutiques, discos, nightclubs, and the largest department store in town, La Rinascente.

It's not surprising that the true survivors of the bombs and building mania are the churches. Piety does not exactly permeate the air, but Milan is profoundly, silently Catholic. So church-hopping—between Sant'Ambrogio, San Lorenzo Maggiore, San Simpliciano, Sant'Eustorgio, Santa Maria delle Grazie, San Satiro and others—is a fine way to leapfrog through the other neighborhoods within the Circonvallazione Interna (inner-ring road). Some of Italy's most remarkable early-Christian and Romanesque structures are in Milan. The city's wealth and the key role it played in the spread of Christianity account for this. Milan hoisted itself into the driver's seat of the Roman Empire in A.D. 286, a "golden era" that lasted until 402. It was from his residence in Milano Romana that Emperor Constantine in 313 proclaimed the Edict of Milan, which allowed Christians the freedom to worship. In 374 the people arose and named Ambrose, the imperial magistrate, Bishop of Milan. The Milanese have been known, in Italian, as *ambrosiani* ever since.

The queen mother of all Lombard churches, the basilica of Sant'Ambrogio, was begun five years later, in 379. Over the centuries it has been enlarged and altered and was partly destroyed in World War II, but it retains its soldier-of-Christ austerity. Inside, don't miss the fourth-century chapel of San Vittore and fifth-century mosaics, or the huge sarcophagus.

As many young Milanese will point out, these days Sant'Ambrogio is known as much for its subway stop (on the green line) and proximity to the Bar Magenta (a fashion-model mecca on Via Carducci) as for its church. Next door is the massive Catholic University, which is graced by two exceptional cloisters, the last work of Bramante in Milan (1498).

One of Bramante's greatest Milan accomplishments is the nearby Santa Maria delle Grazie. While he was cobbling together the cupola, tribunal, and cloister, Bramante befriended Leonardo da Vinci. Leonardo's *Last Supper* (1495–1497) is housed here, sadly faded despite ongoing efforts to restore it.

The bones of the Magi? It is said they are kept at eleventh-century Sant'Eustorgio, a favorite among lovers of relics and lore. Sant'Eustorgio's Portinari Chapel (attributed to Michelozzo) is arguably the finest example of Renaissance church architecture in Milan. The Ticinese neighborhood to which the church belongs swoops from the Navigli at Porta Ticinese to another church, San Lorenzo Maggiore. This church, Milan's oldest, is plopped over a Roman amphitheater (access to the ruins is from behind the altar). In typical haphazard fashion, a tram line runs just in front of the church, cutting it off from its monumental colonnade. These sixteen Corinthian columns, recently restored, once belonged to a third-century Roman bath and are now the haunt of hard-core hipsters who frequent the quirky, "alternative" restaurants and nightclubs, like Le Scimmie and Capolinea.

The Ticinese is up and coming, in direct competition with the better-heeled-but-trendy Brera, perhaps the most aesthetically pleasing neighborhood in town. Brera glitters and jangles within the wedge bounded by the fourth-century church of San Simpliciano, San Marco (much beloved by Mozart), and La Scala. The Pinacoteca di Brera, in the imposing palazzo designed by Richini (1651) and remodeled by Piermarini (1780), has an excellent collection of paintings, including Mantegna's Dead Christ, Raphael's Mar-riage of the Virgin, and Piero della Francesca's Duke of Montefeltro.

No one but a die-hard Beauty and the Beast fan would claim that Milan rivals Rome, Venice, or Florence for charm and looks. That's not why people come here. Milan packs a punch. We hope this modest guide will help you tap into the fountainhead of fashion, art, and fine food, and skirt the blight.

A final postscript: Operation Mani Pulite ("Clean Hands") took root right here in Milan. Italy's industrial capital felt the first tremors of the corruption investigation that has so far engulfed hundreds of the nation's financial, business, and political personalities. The arrogant face that Milan presented to the rest of the world looks less confident now, as scandals and prosecutions enmesh the city's elite. Milan's mood is far from complacent these days. The city seems to be searching for a new spirit, a new identity: the Milan that emerges will surely be more austere and controlled. It may even become less obsessed with appearances and—who knows?—rediscover the meaning of authenticity.

Fishing
for Forgiveness

Enterprising noble maidens of centuries past raised their favorite fry in a fish pond that's now part of the Guastalla Gardens, one of the loveliest parks in central Milan. People often mistake the pool for a fountain. No way—this playful Baroque masterpiece kept trout on the table for the Countess Ludovica Torelli of Guastalla and her cloistered pupils, members of the Regio Collegio convent school for girls. It all started in the mid-sixteenth century when, after years of wild parties and life on the fringe, guilt-stricken Countess Torelli bought the Guastalla grounds. She did the noble thing and cleansed her conscience by building a church, monastery, and girl's school (San Paolo Converso and the Angelic Sisters, who are now in Piazza Sant'-Eufemia). Nowadays, free-floating students from the State University across the street and white collars from nearby offices lounge amid the eighteenth-century statues, the ancient Tempietto, and corner shrines.

Restaurants

Tracking down the treasures of Italian gastronomy is certainly as worthwhile an endeavor as admiring the country's art and architecture, or taking in the incomparable scenery of what we Italophiles are convinced is an enchanted land. The geography, climate, customs, and often the history of a region are revealed in its native cuisine as surely and as distinctively as in the local dialect. The trouble is, locating authentic regional dishes usually requires some effort, though that is more true in some parts of Italy than in others. Take Milan, for example. Nowadays, Lombardy's rib-sticking, long-simmered braises and stews (cassoeula, busecca, stracotto, osso buco), its robust Austrian-accented specialties (by any other name, veal cutlet alla milanese is still Wiener Schnitzel) are thought to be too cumbersome to prepare, too calorie-laden, and too numbing to the digestion of the hard-driving Milanese, who no longer have the leisure to indulge in a three-hour siesta after lunch.

In Lombardy, as elsewhere in Italy, modern eating habits are threatening the province's home-grown cuisine with extinction. For even though the countryside around Milan still abounds in the pigs and cattle that yield meat, lard, butter, and cream for the region's rich traditional cooking, such dishes are now enshrined like relics in a handful of the city's restaurants, some posh, some plain. Given the choice, we prefer the plainer places. "Chefs" tend to citify this country cooking, and their coquettish presentations don't really suit its rough-and-ready character.

Once you've located the ideal trattoria for your Lombard feast (small, not fancy, and family-run—check out our reviews for suggestions), prepare to eat hearty, for a Milanese meal is real trencherman's fare. If you want to be authentic, start out with an antipasto of assorted local salami and cured meats, such as coppa, bresaola, and smoked tongue. For your primo (first course) choose a risotto, polenta, or a thick minestra (soup) instead of pasta, which is not prominent in the traditional Lombardian kitchen. Stubby Arborio rice, the ideal variety for risotto, is still cultivated on the region's well-irrigated plains and appears on Lombard tables braised in broth with saffron, beef marrow, and Parmesan cheese (risotto alla milanese), as risotto al salto (crusty sautéed leftover risotto), or combined with any number of local ingredients, from frogs' legs to asparagus to wild mushrooms. Give a wide berth, however, to such "creative" aberrations as risotto alle fragoline—with wild strawberries.

Typical secondi, or main courses, are the aforementioned slow-cooked specialties as well as such simpler but equally substantial offerings as rostin negàa (a hefty veal chop braised in white wine). Dishes that feature innards, such as busecca (tripe) and cassoeula (all parts of the pig, stewed with vegetables), belong to the category of peasant cooking; but now that they are hard to come by, they have paradoxically acquired the cachet once attached to luxury foods.

And to drink? Good Lombard Pinot Grigio would do well by the more delicate vegetable risottos; sturdier wines from the Oltrepò Pavese (varietals, Barbacarlo, Bonarda) or from the Valtellina (Sassella, Inferno, Grumello, Valgella) will stand up to the rest.

After a meal like this, you may feel too full to tackle anything but a cup of strong coffee. Yet we really can't neglect to mention the fine cheeses produced hereabouts, which you might want to try in lieu of dessert: creamy, veined Gorgonzola, rich and mild mascarpone, pungent Taleggio, or Robiola.

73

Aimo e Nadia

Via Montecuccoli 6 - (02) 416886
Closed Sun, Sat lunch, Aug. All major cards.
The address is far from fashionable, but Aimo and Nadia have succeeded in luring the choicest Milanese society to this godforsaken street. Aimo invariably greets his guests with a little taste of something delicious that Nadia has improvised to whet the appetite: a tiny crostino, say, of baby swordfish sautéed with herbs, or a tidbit of the tenderest Piedmontese beef. These previews provide the first proof that every ingredient in the kitchen is of superlative quality. Aimo scours the land for the very best homegrown foodstuffs (don't look for caviar or Scottish beef here!), on which Nadia then works her own brand of culinary magic. She enhances and highlights the essential goodness of her raw materials, without recourse to complicated techniques. The focus is squarely on intense, immediate flavor. Some examples? How about fresh tuna tartare perfumed with herbs and porcini mushrooms; or broad pappardelle noodles bathed in squab ragù with morsels of pigeon liver; or petals of salt cod strewn over baby field greens—a brilliant dish; or a supremely simple (and simply divine) shoulder of lamb underscored with the vigorous fragrance of rosemary. Desserts are better than ever: we devoured every spoonful of a wild-berry soup embellished with delicate elderberry mousse. All these delights are served by a smoothly skilled staff, while Fabio Scarpitti oversees the fascinating cellar. Prices are steep, but not unreasonable for food of this rare caliber. **C** 100,000 lire.

Alfio

Via Senato 31 - (02) 780731
Closed Sat, Sun lunch, Aug. All major cards.
Tables laden with choice vegetables, seafood antipasti, and whole country hams are the gladsome sight that greets patrons who step into this appealing restaurant. The atmosphere is cheerful and welcoming, and the food is rooted in the grand traditions of Tuscan and Lombard cooking (minestrone, ravioli or bistecca alla fiorentina, risottos, veal scallop alla milanese...). Still, a sizable portion of the menu is devoted to fresh seafood: glossy shellfish, grilled sole, baked scampi, monkfish fragrant with oregano. As you can see, Alfio's is a place for the sort of fresh, direct, and honest fare that never palls—and that's the essence of good Italian cooking. **C** 100,000 lire.

Alfredo al Gran San Bernardo

Via G.A. Borgese 14 - (02) 3319000
Closed Sun, Aug. All major cards.
Milan's renowned breaded veal cutlet will hold no mysteries for you after a dinner at Alfredo Gran San Bernardo. A window in the dining room will give patrons a first-rate view of kitchen proceedings. You may thus observe the cooks at work, coating the thin slices of veal with fine breadcrumbs, frying them quickly at high heat, then enveloping them in a clean cloth to remove every trace of fat. It's an expert rendering of a dish that we have never found particularly inspiring. But costoletta alla milanese is an institution at Alfredo's, which is itself a last bastion of Lombardy's solid, generous farmhouse cooking. The other dishes on the menu are equally familiar to the regulars who order them without even glancing at the menu: minestrone, rigatoni, risotto with artichokes, vitello tonnato (veal with a tuna-mayonnaise sauce). All of it is competently turned out but rather tame—yet that may be why Alfredo is a favorite with so many stressed-out Milanese businessmen, for whom these dishes represent the ultimate in comfort food. **C** 80,000 lire and up.

L'Ami Berton

Via Nullo 14 - (02) 713669
Closed Sat lunch, Sun, Aug, at Christmas. V, AE.
Seafood and vegetables are the mainstays at this exceedingly pleasant, family-run restaurant. From the kitchen come countless imaginative—sometimes inspired—variations on that basic theme: sea bream is paired with tenderly crisp asparagus, delicate sole plays off the bite of bitter greens and crunchy almonds, turbot takes on a woodsy garnish of porcini, sea bass finds a perfect partner in fresh tomatoes, spaghetti sports a sauce of sole fillet and sugar-snap peas...the list is perpetually renewed. To finish, there are excellent sweets and fruit sorbets; the cellar, too, is first-rate. **C** 100,000 lire.

Antica Trattoria della Pesa
Via Pasubio 10 - (02) 6555741
Closed Sun, Aug. No cards.
Walls mellowed by time, lovingly
polished antique furniture, and an atmosphere reminiscent of an earlier age make
this trattoria worth a visit. The resolutely
Milanese cuisine harks back to days when
appetites were more robust. A meal here
might begin with an assortment of salami
or a salad of onions and calf's foot accompanied by puckery sottaceti (pickles).
Risotto alla milanese, tinted with saffron,
would be a natural choice to precede a
hearty portion of osso buco with its traditional garnish of lemon peel, parsley, and
garlic. Thoroughly Milanese, too, are such
dishes as braised beef with polenta, a
flavorful, sage-scented veal chop called
rustin negàa, and cassoeula, a hearty pork
and vegetable stew. If you can con-
template dessert, we suggest you try the
high and handsome vanilla soufflé.
C 50,000 lire.

 Nino Arnaldo
Via Carlo Poerio 3 - (02) 76005981
*Closed Sat lunch, Sun, Aug, at Christmas. All
major cards.*
Nino Arnaldo's fresh and inventive cooking draws an appreciative clientele of well-
heeled diners to his freshly refurbished
restaurant in a residential section of Milan.
Nino scours the market daily for the
makings of his very personal cuisine, and
his efforts indeed pay off. Irreproachable
freshness was the keynote of our delicious
tagliatelle with scampi and wild chiodini
mushrooms. Excellent, too, (though a bit
messy) was fried rabbit flavored with
honey and Port. Nino shows equal skill
when handling rich ingredients (we loved
sea bass paired with asparagus) or
humbler ones (mackerel fillets sparked
with capers and fresh tomatoes). But like
many a creative cook, he sometimes sends
out a flop: salmon with grapefruit, for example. But never mind. Like us, you'll forgive such slight missteps when you taste
his sensational homemade ice creams and
sorbets; the frozen zabaglione is a poem!
We've been given to believe that the wine
cellar is due for an overhaul—good news,
for the present selection isn't worthy of the
food it accompanies. **C** 90,000 lire.

 **Arrow
La Trattoria del Pesce**
Via Mussi 13 - (02) 341533
Closed Sun, Aug. All major cards.
Here's a reliable address for a seafood
feast, at about half the price charged at
Milan's tonier restaurants. Journalists,
politicos, and business execs love Piero
and Eligia's warm welcome and their tasty
(though hardly innovative) cooking. Try
the tagliolini with fresh anchovies, then
order the "catch of the day" along with a
bottle from the nicely stocked cellar. The
homemade pastries are a treat.
C 60,000 lire.

 Aurora
Via Savona 23 - (02) 89404978
Closed Mon, hols vary. AE, DC.
Shimmering crystal, glowing woodwork... the surroundings irresistibly recall
the stately old cafés of Turin. That's no
coincidence, for Aurora specializes in the
traditional cuisine of the Piedmont region.
For starters, treat yourself to bagna cauda,
a creamy hot sauce flavored with
anchovies and white truffles, served with
a bouquet of raw vegetables for dipping.
Pasta offerings include thin tagliolini with
porcini mushrooms and plump agnolotti
bathed in meat juices. Tiny cheese fritters
are an appetizing alternative to pasta and
an ideal preamble to that glorious Piedmontese specialty, fritto misto (a procession of more than half a dozen different
crisply fried foods), which must be ordered
in advance. Equally opulent, though a bit
less caloric, bollito misto consists of a
savory array of boiled meats, poultry, and
vegetables. Should you still have room for
dessert, be advised that Aurora employs a
master pastry chef. Excellent regional
wines are available, as well as a superb
Piedmontese grappa (brandy). In fine
weather, be sure to book a garden table.
M 38,000 lire (set lunch), 50,000 lire and
up (dinner).

 Bagutta
Via Bagutta 14 - (02) 76002767
*Closed Sun, 2 wks at Christmas. All major
cards.*
Milan's stony façades conceal an abundance of greenery, but to find it, you have
to know where to look. Bagutta's regular
patrons know that just a few steps away
from a dark, narrow street they can enter

a delightful garden full of bird song, trees, and pretty tables. A huge showcase of antipasti puts diners in the mood for a relaxed, cheerful meal of rigatoni alla Bagutta (with cream and chicken giblets), followed by a classic osso buco or—our favorite—a delicious veal scallop paired with mozzarella and anchovies. The fish, we find, is most often overcooked. If the weather does not permit a garden idyll (Milan is famous for its fog), the indoor rooms are cozy and comfortable, amusingly decorated with caricatures of famous Italians. **C** 60,000 lire and up.

Il Baretto
Via Sant'Andrea 3 - (02) 781255
Closed Sun (& Sat dinner in Jul), Aug. All major cards.

Just off Via Montenapoleone, in one of the city's most elegant enclaves, stands this English-style establishment, long a favorite with sleek business people and chic trendsetters. Behind the bar, a passage leads to a tiny dining room with red banquettes and yellow-clothed tables. The food is good—light and refined, with a faintly Venetian tint in such dishes as tiny squid with artichokes, smoked swordfish served with a zingy horseradish sauce, risotto flavored with radicchio, or baccalà (salt cod) alla vicentina. Reservations are indispensable, since the aforementioned fashionable fauna regard certain tables as their personal turf. Impeccably trained waiters, familiar with the preferences of their regular customers, provide smooth service. **C** 75,000 lire.

Battivacco
Osteria della Barona
Via Bardolino 3 - (02) 8138825
Closed Mon, 1st 3 wks of Jan, last 3 wks of Aug. No cards.

This restored farmhouse at the city's rustic southern limit has cozy dining rooms perfect for romantic tête-à-têtes, and an ancient wisteria to shade its pretty garden: even if the food were indifferent, Battivacco would surely have a loyal following. But in fact, the restaurant boasts a talented chef who interprets a traditional Lombard repertory with a pleasingly personal touch. Salt cod with beans is an original way to start off a meal, but the pastas, like tortelli stuffed with duck meat or with lean pork, are distractingly good; so is the risotto alla

milanese (a model of its kind). Main courses include a classic osso buco, polenta with melted cheese, and in season, a profusion of specialties featuring mushrooms, truffles, and game. Desserts are proudly proclaimed to be homemade. The cellar holds more than 150 different Italian and French wines. **C** 60,000 lire.

Bice
Via Borgospesso 12 - (02) 76002572
Closed Mon, Tue lunch, end Jul-beg Sep, 2 wks at Christmas, 4 days at Easter. All major cards.

The Milanese elite meet and eat at Bice, a celebrated, always jam-packed restaurant set smack in the center of the city's deluxe shopping district. The sleek décor runs to mellow woodwork and fine pictures, and can be admired in either of the small rooms to the left and right of the entrance. But no regular would dream of accepting a table anywhere but in the central dining room, with its comfortable divans lined up against the walls. Tuscan specialties are the kitchen's strong suit: to start, there are hot crostini (canapés), tasty fennel sausages and salami, and robust pasta and beans alla toscana. Owing to the crush, no doubt, the cooking is sometimes a bit slapdash; so it pays to stick to the simpler main courses—like the grilled steak served with a side of artichokes and potatoes. Not all of the desserts are made in Bice's kitchen; among those that are, we like the hot apple tart. The cellar rates four stars for its incredible selection. **C** 80,000 lire.

Biffi Scala
Piazza della Scala - (02) 866651
Closed Sat lunch, Sun (Sat & Sun in summer), Aug, 2 wks at Christmas. All major cards.

Just a couple of steps away from the famous Teatro alla Scala, this café/restaurant glitters with a glamorous post-opera crowd. As for the food, well... it is by turns pretentious (tournedos Rossini, need we say more?) and cheerfully simple. Maltagliati pasta topped with chunks of eggplant and mozzarella or pennette fired up with Tuscan peperoncino are guaranteed to revive the most tearful witness to Butterfly's travails; and a nice bowl of onion soup will set you right up after hours of suffering along with Boris Godunov. Risotto and osso buco, both alla milanese, are popular options. Peach Melba is the opera buff's natural choice for dessert, but the house tart isn't bad either. Decent wines. **C** 75,000 lire. **M** 50,000 lire (lunch), 60,000 lire (dinner).

 ### Bistrot di Gualtiero Marchesi
Via San Raffaele 2 (7th floor) (02) 877120
Closed Sun, Mon lunch, Aug. All major cards.
Gualtiero Marchesi, a culinary cult figure in Italy, operates his main restaurant, a lavish Relais et Châteaux establishment, in the Lombard country town of Erbusco. His Milanese outpost is perched high up on the seventh floor of the Rinascente department store. In addition to the gastronomic enticements it offers, the Bistrot also provides a startling view of the Duomo's uppermost spires: the gilded Madonnina seems close enough to touch. Marchesi's menu ranges wide, listing fish, hearty regional fare, vegetarian dishes, and a few innovations typical of this chef's vibrant style. Recent repasts have yielded a famously tasty salad of cuttlefish, baby octopus, and mixed shellfish dressed with mellow balsamic vinegar, tender eggplant ravioli redolent of fresh marjoram, a pluperfect veal cutlet alla milanese—crisply crumbed outside, succulent within—and a lusty combination of chicken and sweet peppers. Cheeses and desserts meet a similarly high standard, and the cellar holds plenty of exciting possibilities. **C** 60-70,000 lire.

 ### Boccondivino
Via Carducci 17 - (02) 866040
Closed Sun, Aug, 1 wk at Christmas. V, AE.
The tiny dining room and minuscule cellar that compose this agreeable establishment could never hold the numerous patrons who manage to squeeze in, were they all planning to order a proper meal. But as the name of this restaurant/wine bar indicates (Boccondivino: mouthful of wine or mouthful of divine—you pick), the point here is to imbibe a selection from the vast array of discerningly chosen Italian (and imported) wines. Yet the food, simple as it is, proves to be very good indeed. Start with a sampling of the superlative sausages or pâtés, follow up with a plate of fresh pasta, then turn your attention to the fabulous cheese board, laden with more than 50 prime specimens

accompanied by excellent bread or polenta. Owner Luigi Concordati will be happy to guide you through the labyrinthine wine list. **C** 50,000 lire (and up, depending on wine).

 ### Boeucc
Piazzetta Belgioioso 2 - (02) 72020224
Closed Sat, Sun lunch, Aug. All major cards.
This restaurant is a monument to the glory of classicism, an eighteenth-century edifice set on a charming square whose noble palazzi are home to members of the Milanese aristocracy. The décor is classical, too, with just a hint of rococo, all dusky-rose walls and rich draperies. The long, conservative menu holds few surprises, but the dishes are competently turned out. Among the antipasti, fried olives all'ascolana are noteworthy, and an unusual rice minestrone served at room temperature makes a perfect primo for a warm day. If you can't imagine skipping pasta, try the delectable tortelloni stuffed with greens. Afterward, the typically Milanese procession of cutlets, chops, steaks, stews, and tripe may seem like heavy going, but baby lamb chops alla milanese with porcini can revive even a flagging appetite. Then not one, but two dessert trolleys roll up to the table, laden with sweets that may just tempt you to stretch your tummy to the limit! The interesting wine list provides lots of options for every budget. Obliging, stylish service. **C** 60-90,000 lire.

La Brisa
Via della Brisa 15 - (02) 86450521
Closed Sat, Sun lunch, Aug. All major cards.
The kitchen works in two very different veins: one gives priority to vegetables and fish, for a cuisine as light as *una brisa*; the other highlights robust Milanese classics (pot roast, veal cutlet, tripe, stewed pork and vegetables...). We lean toward the lighter line, where the complex flavors of herbs successfully stand in for rich sauces, and low-calorie steaming replaces sautéing in fat. The chef's homemade pastas are positively ethereal (try the herbed, pumpkin-stuffed tortelli), and if you follow up with lemon-baked sea bass or couscous with fish and vegetables, you won't feel the least twinge of guilt for finishing with a bright fruit tart. The selection of wines is small but attractive. **C** 50,000 lire and up.

Buriassi

Via Lecco 15 (corner of Via Casati) (02) 29523227
Closed Sat lunch, Sun, Aug. V, AE.

Classic elegance is the Buriassi style: food and surroundings alike are calculated to pamper and please Milan's well-heeled bourgeoisie. The dining rooms are softly lit, the better to dramatize owner Guido's showmanship as he flambés his famous beef fillet, sliced at tableside and finished in a sauce of porcini mushrooms and truffles. Other dishes are more subdued, in the Ligurian-Lombard tradition: we like the pasta with pesto (the basil's bite is smoothed with the addition of lettuce leaves), rigatoni in a rich yet pungent sauce of bottarga and Taleggio cheese, and a light, sapid sea bass with a pristine vegetable garnish. When it's time for dessert, Guido whips out the chafing dish again, to flame raspberries or chestnuts in whisky. The cellar is handsomely stocked, but the house wine is not to be neglected. C 60,000 lire. M 55,000 lire (tasting menu).

Liberty's Ancestor

Take a close look at the upper portion of the Duomo's central portal, and you'll notice a sculptural group called *The Two Ladies of the Law*. A sharp-eyed observer will be struck by the resemblance between the figure on the left and the Statue of Liberty in New York harbor. The only differences are that the Duomo's Lady raises a cup instead of a torch, and a cross where her American lookalike holds the tables of the law. Intererestingly, the Milanese sculpture by Camillo Pacetti was completed a full 76 years before *Liberty Enlightening the World!*

Calajunco

Via Stoppani 5 - (02) 2046003
Closed Sat lunch, Sun, hols vary. All major cards.

"Come back in the evening," the waiter told us, "and you'll see that the atmosphere is much more chic." As it was, we thought the lunchtime crowd looked pretty smart in this cool, summery blue-and-white décor. Owner Renato Carnevali came over to our table to recite the day's offerings. Have no hesitation about sampling the full range of the wonderful hot and cold antipasti: sautéed zucchini, shellfish salads, tuna balls in tomato sauce with sweet peppers, octopus and artichoke salad, marinated fresh sardines... Seafood, indeed, gets top billing here, and the menu changes so often that we're at a loss to recommend specific dishes. But if they're available, do try the pumpkin-stuffed ravioli tinged with cuttlefish ink, or sea bream sparked with just a touch of lemon. Nearly everything we tried at Calajunco was fresh and flavorful, with a certain unpretentious elegance about it. If meat is your dish, we can recommend the veal scaloppine alle Sette Isole (baked with mozzarella, tomatoes, and basil). Desserts deserve your notice too, particularly the almond semifreddo swirled with hot chocolate, the chocolate and ricotta cassatella, and the fig tart. Impressive cellar. And yes, the waiter was right: the ambience is even more alluring in the evening. Reservations are indispensable. C 80,000 lire and up. M 85,000 lire (tasting menu).

Canova

Via Hoepli 6 - (02) 8051231
Closed Sun, Aug. All major cards.

Wildly creative when it comes to furniture and fashion, the Milanese are inexplicably conventional in the culinary realm. It's as if they were afraid of betraying their dear mammas if they ate something new. At Canova, however, the kitchen brigade lives by Brillat-Savarin's maxim, namely that the discovery of a new dish is as important as the discovery of a star. And so it is that with the exception of a few standards, the menu casts aside the traditional litany of Milanese classics in favor of such unhackneyed fare as risotto with eel and bay leaves, sturgeon braised in red wine, or delicate calf's brains escorted by crisp artichokes. The ingredients used here are prime, and the cooking style is confident and precise, with no needless flourishes. We found that the desserts looked better than they tasted, however, and the new owners should give the wine list a thorough overhaul. C 110,000 lire.

Al Capriccio
Via Washington 106 - (02) 48950655
Closed Mon, Aug. V, DC.
"I don't love getting up before the crack of dawn, but when my customers' rave about the freshness of my fish, I feel it's worth the effort." Oreste knows that the early bird gets his pick of the morning's catch at the San Martino market. He brings this briny bounty home to his wife, Lucia, who turns it into a rousing roster of fish soups, shellfish salads, and all manner of seafood pastas and risottos. Her main courses—baked sea bass, roasted monkfish, grilled sea bream—are handled simply and with skill. If you're in a mood to splurge, order the fritto misto, a golden mixed fry of light, crisp, ever-so-tasty morsels. Pull the cork on a bottle of cool Orvieto or Torre di Greco, and settle down to a fine fish feast! **C** 50,000 lire.

 Casanova Grill
Hotel Palace,
Piazza della Repubblica 20 - (02) 29000803
Open daily. All major cards.
Casanova, that elegant Venetian libertine, would doubtless have approved the graceful setting in the restaurant that bears his name. The mirrors, marble fireplace, handsome sconces, fragile (uncomfortable!) chairs, and warm color scheme all attest to the decorator's taste and skill in dealing with an awkwardly proportioned room. The chef interprets the Italian repertory with a vivid spark of imagination, evident in bow-tie pasta sautéed in chicken ragù with tender fava beans or risotto intriguingly flavored with smoked trout and faintly bitter turnip greens. Main courses are polished and beautifully presented: turbot in a potato crust, lamb noisettes coated with crushed almonds, or calf's liver with shallot vinegar. Desserts show similar sophistication (nougat semifreddo, puff pastry layered with fresh berries...). The wine list is most attractive, as are the patrons, who don't seem in the least put off by the vertiginous prices. **C** 110-130,000 lire.

 Don Carlos
Grand Hotel et de Milan,
Via Manzoni 29 - (02) 723141
Dinner only (exc Sun). Closed 2 wks in Aug. All major cards.
The curtain just rang up on this opulently rehabbed hotel dining room, named for Verdi's starcrossed hero. But guests needn't worry: nothing tragic occurs in the kitchen, which performs an exclusively Italian repertoire highlighted by sublime olive oil, pristine vegetables, and pungent regional herbs. A recent recital featured squash blossoms stuffed with greens in a sprightly basil sauce, and lively herbed tortelli drizzled with browned butter. Not one for virtuoso turns, the chef prefers the uncomplicated harmonies of baked or roasted fish and simply grilled meats. Let's hope that as he gains confidence, the menu will acquire a more distinctive timbre. The cellar is still quite young, but the prices, you'll notice, are already full-grown. **C** 100,000 lire.

 Don Lisander
Via Manzoni 12 - (02) 76020130
Closed Sun, 10 days in Aug, 2 wks at Christmas. All major cards.
After a smooth transition from the former owners to the new, Don Lisander remains a favorite with international celebrities, fashion designers, and the big guns of the business world. An unusually handsome restaurant (it occupies what was once the Trivulzio family chapel), Don Lisander provides solid Lombard sustenance for those die-hard fans of risotto and osso buco, as well as lighter fare for less voracious appetites: elegant carrot ravioli in lettuce sauce, for example, or fish ravioli in a chervil-scented shrimp sauce. Grilled fish and meat make the most successful main courses of meals that can be enjoyed—weather permitting—on an inviting terrace with a splendid view of the Trivulzio gardens. The cellar harbors a rare selection of Barolos, Brunellos, and Barbarescos, as well as a full complement of French wines. Reservations are recommended (they're imperative in summer). **C** 80-90,000 lire.

 Duomo
Grand Hotel Duomo,
Via San Raffaele 1 - (02) 8833
Closed 3 wks in Aug. V, AE, EC.
Ablaze with silver and crystal, the vista of immaculately clothed tables stretches out over spacious, luminous dining rooms. These posh premises, and the glossy patrons who haunt them, are attended by a cadre of suavely efficient waiters. It's the

glamorous hotel restaurant of one's dreams... What about the food, you say? It's far better than one has a right to expect. Both the "international" offerings and the regional Italian dishes are prepared with style and skill. We make no secret of our preference for the latter. Indeed, why pick smoked salmon when delicious native bresaola and premium prosciutto are on offer? Similarly, our choices in the first-course category run to risotto or silken handmade pasta rather than omelets and the like. The kitchen sends forth a fabulous Neapolitan rib steak alla pizzaiola, full of lusty flavor; the lasagna, too, is truly exceptional. Remember to save room for the fragile pastries, all made in-house, and note that the cellar overflows with distinguished vintages from Italy and abroad. **C** 45,000 lire and up.

Franca, Paola, Lele
Viale Certosa 235 - (02) 38006238
Closed Sat, Sun, Aug, at Christmas. V.

Well out of the downtown area, near the Turin highway, this family-run trattoria is worth seeking out. The rustic dining room holds only a few tables, at which lucky diners can look forward to first-rate country cooking. Lele himself, a jovial host, oversees the service and wine cellar. He has firm ideas about what people should eat, and his advice is sound. He is sure to press upon you a generous sampling of farmhouse salami (from the family farm) and homemade duck or goose pâté. If a warming bowl of soup is what you hanker for, Lele will proudly produce his wife's superb leek-and-bean combination or, in season, her extraordinary pasta and bean brew. Among the pasta dishes, the hard-wheat tagliatelle sauced with butter and sage is sublimely simple—the quality of the ingredients shines through. Daily specials may include stewed rabbit on a bed of incredibly flavorful polenta (the corn is ground specially for the restaurant) or fragrant roast kid with herbs. If it's available (and you've got the appetite), by all means try the stuffed pancetta: it fairly bursts with deep, complex flavors. Like the rest, desserts are crafted by hand and are worthy of your interest. Follow Lele's advice, and order a bottle (or two) of his delicious Cabernet Sauvignon Farra d'Isonzo. But be forewarned: the prices are less

countrified than the setting and the food! **C** 70,000 lire.

Francesco
Via Festa del Perdono 4
(02) 58307404
Closed Sun, 2 wks in Aug & at Christmas. All major cards.

Strategically sited between the university and the courthouse, Francesco is an obvious favorite with Milan's magistrates and professors. Here they can give their busy brains a break, while treating their taste buds to squash-blossom risotto, expertly cooked fresh fish (the fried calamari are toothsome morsels indeed), or seasonal game and mushrooms prepared according to traditional recipes. A few Sardinian offerings appear on the menu: malloreddus (shell pasta), sheep cheeses, and austere island wines. Desserts are baked in-house and are perfectly delicious. **C** 40-50,000 lire. **M** 35,000 lire.

Galleria
Hotel Principe di Savoia,
Piazza della Repubblica 17 - (02) 6230
Closed Sat. All major cards.

The remodeled hotel is extravagantly (indeed, ostentatiously) decked out in lavish fittings: marble, velvet, gilding appear at every turn. Happily, the Galleria's quieter elegance offers a respite from all this in-your-face luxury. The menu is something of a hybrid: innovative, highly refined dishes alternate with down-to-earth Lombard specialties. Adventurous palates will want to try duck sausage in a delicate shrimp ragù or ginger-spiced sea bream sparked with rice vinegar, while culinary conservatives may take refuge in minestrone di riso alla milanese or soothing osso buco served with the traditional gremolada topping of lemon zest and garlic. Appetites perk up afresh when the dessert list arrives. Only the wine list comes in for a small criticism—it just doesn't match the level of the food. **C** 100,000 lire.

Al Genovese
Via Troilo 14 (corner of Via Conchetta) - (02) 8373180
Closed 2 wks in Aug, 10 days at New-Year's day. All major cards.

Liguria's fresh, vibrant cooking is showcased here, in a menu that fairly beams with Riviera sunshine. Starters are so tempting that we could make a meal of them alone. Just consider: chickpea-flour pancakes (panisses) topped with zesty marinated cuttlefish, thin slices of smoked gurnard with cardoons, zucchini brightened with pesto and a sprinkling of toasted pine nuts, a savory terrine of anchovies and Swiss chard... Yet it would be a shame to miss out on the other courses, which display plenty of Mediterranean verve. To be honest, the red mullet we tried recently was overcooked, and potato ravioli came with some tired-looking artichokes. Still, the tiny calamari in fresh tomato sauce and the stuffed lettuce leaves set afloat in a sapid chicken bouillon are the best we've ever tasted. Desserts, on the whole, lack spark. **C** 90,000 lire. **M** 50,000 lire & 85,000 lire (tasting menu).

Gianni e Dorina Il Pontremolese

Via G. Pepe 38 - (02) 606340
Closed Sat lunch, Sun, Jul 25-Sep 15, at Christmas. All major cards.

Tuscan, Emilian, and Ligurian influences combine in the full-bodied fare of Pontremoli, a regional cuisine that is not often encountered in Milan. Spurred by curiosity and a hearty appetite, we recently feasted here on testaroli mushrooms dressed with pesto, lasagnette noodles made with chestnut flour sauced with smooth ricotta cheese, a heap of unspeakably crisp, light codfish fritters, an earthy sauté of country sausage, beans, and radicchio, and rabbit stewed with fat, glossy black olives. Dorina, the owner, looks after her guests with maternal benevolence (she'll even season your dish of tripe and beans with a fillip of her own superb olive oil); she also presides with pride over a fabulous, award-winning wine cellar. **C** 65,000 lire.

Giannino

Via Amatore Sciesa 8 - (02) 55195582
Closed Sun, Aug. All major cards.

In surroundings that, for Milan, are astoundingly spacious (there's even a delightful garden for summer dining), owner Antonio Mirate and his team serve forth a mix of Milanese, Tuscan, and Neapolitan specialties. In other words, the lengthy but handily executed menu stretches from North to South, from risot-

to, veal cutlet, and osso buco, via pasta e fagioli and bistecca alla fiorentina, to beef in pizzaiola sauce and sartù di riso (a complicated rice timbale, one of the glories of the Neapolitan table). Each day also brings its complement of specials *del giorno*—unpredictable, and usually worthy of interest. Exceptional cellar; unexceptionable service. **C** 90-110,000 lire. **M** 70,000 lire (lunch).

Joia

Via P. Castaldi 18 - (02) 2049244
Closed Sat lunch, Sun, Aug. All major cards.

Pietro Leeman's *alta cucina naturale* delivers bold, pure flavors in dishes that are rigorously conceived and executed with uncommon skill; the man is indubitably one of Italy's most fascinating chefs. Vegetables, cheese, and fish—no meat—combine to create a menu that is utterly unique. Typical of Leeman's cerebral style is a starter called "six cubes": tomato aspic; spinach and raisins; stuffed tofu; ricotta-walnut mousse; chickpea pâté enveloped in gold leaf; and raw cucumber. Cooked and uncooked ingredients, suave and acidic flavors, muted and brilliant colors play off each other in this artful composition, which pleases eye and palate alike. Or consider Leeman's dessert "tower" built of vanilla ice cream, hazelnut mousse, strips of chocolate, and zabaglione glazed under the grill: it's a sweet symphony of contrasting temperatures and textures. We have fond memories too of his smoked eggplant pâté and of scallops baked in parchment with chickpeas. If you're game for a gastronomic adventure, we suggest you book a table right now! **C** 50-60,000 lire.

A Precious Tear

During a gala reception in honor of Napoleon held in the sumptuous Palazzo Litta, Barbara Litta was so overwhelmed by the imperial presence that she shed a tear of emotion. To recall this moving episode, a pearl was set into the mosaic floor of the palazzo's Red Room, on the very spot where the noble lady's teardrop fell.

Mastro Ghirlandaio

Hotel Michelangelo,
Via Scarlatti 33 (corner of Piazza Luigi di Savoia)
(02) 6755
Closed 2 wks in Aug. All major cards.

Endless remodeling makes the premises seem oddly precarious; the abbreviated menu contributes to a general air of uncertainty. But veteran chef Bruno Fovanna acquits himself admirably in these difficult conditions, enticing his clients with an array of house-made pastas and pastries, fresh fish, and an appetizing list of daily specials. The menu *del giorno* is not only your best bet gastronomically speaking; it also makes economic sense! C 100,000 lire. M 75,000 lire (wine incl.).

Al Matarel

Via Solera Mantegazza (corner of Corso Garibaldi) - (02) 654204
Closed Tue, Wed lunch, Jul. No cards.

Tradition is a byword at this venerable temple of Lombard cuisine. You may want to fast for a few days before you attack a meal that begins with fabulous salami and prosciutto, or the cartilaginous nibbles known as nervetti, long a favorite among northern Italians. Go on from there to sample such rustic fare as busecchina (a thick soup of chestnuts boiled in milk), polenta and cream, or an authentic, saffron-tinged risotto alla milanese. Main courses are equally hearty: there's bussecca (a local classic based on calf's tripe), cassoeula (stewed pork and vegetables), or the grandiose braised veal chop known as rustin negàa. Desserts—hot zabaglione, torta di pane, zuppa inglese—are regionally rooted as well, and not particularly light! The cellar highlights premium wines from Piedmont, Lombardy, and the Veneto. C 40,000 lire and up.

Montenapo

Via Montenapoleone 12 - (02) 784650
Closed Sun, Aug, Jan 1-10. All major cards.

The culinary customs of the Piedmont region hold no secrets for Ivo, who learned all about them in his mother's and grandmother's kitchens. He offers guests a bouquet of refreshing salads to start off a meal; they segue into a delicate risotto garnished with squash blossoms, golden tagliatelle with porcini mushrooms, or quill-shaped pennette pasta with zucchini. The menu lists some appealing seafood options (the rosemary-scented shrimp are

delicious), but it's in the meat dishes that Piedmont's superb truffles and mushrooms feature most prominently. The cheese board is laden with all sorts of treats—aged Parmesan with pears, Gorgonzola with walnuts—that complement the cellar's fabulous cache of Barolos, Dolcettos, and Barbarescos. C 60-80,000 lire (dinner). M 30,000 lire (lunch).

Moon Fish

Via Bagutta 2 - (02) 76005780
Closed Sun, hols vary. V.

The Milanese sister of a similarly named New York spot, Moon Fish serves nothing but sparkling fresh seafood. Start out your feast with shellfish—shipments arrive every day—then try the excellent sea bass, prepared alla genovese, alla pugliese, alla fortemarmina... any way you say it, the fish is delish, enhanced with the kitchen's superlative extra-virgin olive oil. You can also look forward to tasty desserts, and a cellar awash in refreshing white wines. C 55-65,000 lire.

Gli Orti di Leonardo

Palazzo delle Stelline,
Via A. De Togni 6-8 - (02) 4983476
Closed Sun, 3 wks in Aug. All major cards.

One of Milan's smartest restaurants stands in an elegant old residential neighborhood, down in the cellars of the Palazzo Atellani. Behind the palazzo, a delicious garden holds what remains of a vine given to Leonardo da Vinci by his patron, the powerful Ludovico Sforza, hence the restaurant's name ("Leonardo's gardens"). You could start out on a bright, fresh note with a chive-showered tartare of sea bass and marinated salmon, or prefer the elegant richness of duck breast stuffed with foie gras and game mousse. If the risottos and soups don't inspire you, move right on to turbot baked alla mediterranea with zucchini, asparagus, and flavorful little tomatoes, or veal piccata under a mantle of Chiavenna cheese. An interesting vegetarian menu is also available, and the cellar is nicely composed. C 50,000 lire and up.

Osteria del Binari

Via Tortona 1 - (02) 89406753
Dinner only. Closed Sun, 3 wks in Aug. AE.

Just behind the Porta Genova train station (*binari* are railroad tracks), set in the shade of tall plane trees, is this polished little restaurant whose eclectic menu borrows from the Piedmontese and Lombard traditions. Seasonal antipasti precede plump, homemade agnolotti bathed in rich meat juices or potato gnocchi perfumed with speck (smoky, salted pork) and porcini mushrooms. Fish fresh from the morning market features in the lighter main courses, but many diners prefer the more substantial specialty of the house: beef tenderloin prepared in a variety of ways, often enriched with truffles and fragrant wild mushrooms. In winter, a lordly array of boiled meats is wheeled up to the tables, accompanied by all manner of zesty condiments. Piedmont is renowned for its pastries, and the assortment presented here does credit to that tradition. The prestigious cellar holds a wealth of Piedmontese wines, along with bottles from the rest of Italy and France. **C** 50-60,000 lire.

Osteria Corte Regina
Via Rottole 60 - (02) 2593377
Closed Sat lunch, Sun, Aug. V, AE.

A rustic little oasis amid the encroaching concrete, this pretty hostelry offers a warming fireplace in winter and a garden for summer dining. Though the menu is traditional, as one would expect in this setting, the young chefs have managed to lighten and modernize Lombardy's robust specialties. To begin, try their delicious herbed gnocchi, or ravioli with a delicate stuffing of lake char, or a dainty cake of sautéed risotto surrounded with crayfish. Notable among the main courses is a version of cassoeula made with goose instead of pork, but the kitchen's way with fish is hard to resist. Owner Giancarla Virtuani is justifiably proud of the cheese trolley, loaded with specimens produced on her family's estates. Excellent sorbets round out the picture, along with a wide-ranging cellar of fine Italian wines. **C** 65,000 lire.

Osteria da Francesca
Viale Argonne 32 - (02) 730608
Closed Sun, hols vary. V.

The intimate, homey atmosphere that reigns in this little restaurant draws a faithful crowd of actors and actresses from the TV studios nearby. They clamor for the comforting handmade pâté and fresh pastas that Francesca and her son, Maurizio, prepare in the little kitchen. The rest of the menu varies with the seasons and the market's bounty, but the fresh fish and roasted meats are dependably good. By all means save room for the homemade desserts. Nuccio, Francesca's husband, does double duty as host and sommelier—the Franco-Italian wine list deserves your close attention. **C** 50,000 lire.

Paper Moon
Via Bagutta 1 - (02) 76022297
Closed Sun, hols vary.

Here's a delightful address. Smartly dressed Milanese patrons pause to inspect the colossal array of antipasti before taking their seats in the lively ground-floor dining room or in the quieter space upstairs. The pappardelle (broad egg noodles) Paper Moon are deservedly popular, but the polenta with mushrooms makes a pleasing change of pace from pasta. From there, we like to go on to the tasty grilled swordfish or a wafer-thin slice of pounded beef (battuta di manzo). Desserts are prettily presented, and there's a goodish range of wines. **C** 50,000 lire.

Peck
Via Victor Hugo 4 - (02) 876774
Closed Sun, hols, 1st 3 wks of Jul, Jan 1-10. All major cards.

An appetizing selection of prepared foods can be purchased to take out or to be enjoyed on the spot at Peck's large counter, where a choice range of French and Italian wines may be ordered to accompany them. Downstairs, a handsome and very comfortable dining room sports a slightly chilly modern décor: marble floors, white walls, and blond wood chairs. Based on excellent ingredients, the Franco-Italian dishes are generally well done, but small slipups sometimes mar the effect—overcooking is the most frequent flaw. But we enjoyed an elegant saffron-tinged aspic of salmon and mushrooms, and a supremely fresh sea bass alla mugnaia with golden sautéed potatoes. Typically Milanese dishes come off best: we savored a pluperfect minestrone and the risottos—all prepared to order—rated unreserved raves. To wind things up, there's a sumptuous cheese board and a mouthwatering array of Peck's own pastries. **C** 90,000 lire. **M** 55,000 lire, 80,000 lire.

Al Porto

Piazza Cantore - (02) 8321481
Closed Sun, Mon lunch, Aug. All major cards.
Some perseverance may be needed to locate this creditable little seafood spot, but it's worth the effort. Just look for the place with the anchor on the door. The décor is nautical, though without excess, and the food is simple, carefully prepared, and very, very fresh. For an extensive sampling of what's available, order the fritto misto—fried smelts, shrimp, prawns, and squid—as an antipasto; move on, if you're so inclined, to a dish of pasta or risotto with seafood (mussels, clams, cuttlefish); and then enjoy a generous mixed grill of the day's freshest fish. With a dry white Orvieto, it amounts to an uncomplicated but memorable meal. **C** 80,000 lire.

I Quattro Mori

Via San Giovanni sul Muro 2
(02) 878483
Closed Sat lunch, Sun, 3 wks in Aug. All major cards.
Stendhal declared that Italians possess a special knack for happiness. And indeed, when you see all those contented Milanese taking their ease on the spacious, shaded terrace of Quattro Mori, you have to admit he had a point. The establishment's harmonious architecture recalls the villas built in grander days by the local gentry. Harmonious, too, in its simplicity, is the fine food that comes from chef Sisto's kitchens. The brief menu highlights prime ingredients, like the superb fish displayed near the restaurant's entrance—obviously the catch of the day. Seafood is always a good choice: we have fond memories of a bracing octopus salad, perfect fish ravioli with baby artichokes, and toothsome monkfish perfumed with oregano. If fish is not your meat, then sample the pan-roasted kid redolent of rosemary and garlic, or the sturdy Tuscan sausage with beans. With a tingly, slightly *frizzante* white wine and some fruit to finish, you will discover that one needn't be Italian to be happy (though being in Italy helps, *non è vero?*). **C** 65,000 lire (wine incl).

A Riccione

Via Taramelli 70 - (02) 6686807
Closed Mon, Aug. All major cards.
The two adjacent dining rooms, windowless and with tiled floors, would be doomed to gloominess were it not for the series of portraits on the walls. The ladies in question, painted by master colorist Gentilini, do a creditable job of brightening this rather posh seafood restaurant. Milan is not a fishing port, of course, but it is ideally situated to profit from both Mediterranean and Adriatic catches. Irreproachably fresh fish is the basis of Riccione's straightforward menu: sole, monkfish, turbot, and bream are offered either grilled, sautéed in butter, or napped in a fresh-tasting sauce of tomatoes and white wine. Nothing fancy, nothing fussy, just good seafood simply prepared. A recent meal provides a typical example: seafood salad dressed with divinely fragrant oil, then tagliolini topped with firm scampi, followed by a hefty portion of sweet, firm John Dory. With the eminently drinkable house white wine, it was a satisfying—though not inexpensive—meal. **C** 100,000 lire (wine incl).

Rigolo

Largo Treves (corner of Via Solferino)
(02) 86463220
Closed Mon, Jul 15-Aug 15. All major cards.
The Simoncini brothers are Tuscan natives, but their restaurant now shows less of a regional slant than in years past. Their updated menu features lighter and (let's face it) more digestible fare than the old model did. Tuna pâté spiked with green peppercorns is a refreshing antipasto. Autumn appetites will warm up to a soothing wild-mushroom soup, but spaghetti with clams can be had year-round, and a different risotto is offered every day. Main-course choices include sea bream baked in parchment and swordfish Robespierre (read: raw); mixed grill is a house specialty, as is a delicious dish of beef tenderloin with porcini mushrooms. French and Italian wines figure on the wine list, along with an extensive selection of grappas (brandies). **C** 40,000 lire.

Sadler
Osteria di Porta Cicca

Ripa di Porta Ticinese 51
(02) 58104451
Dinner only. Closed Sun, 1 wk in Jan, 3 wks in Aug. All major cards.
Owner-chef Claude Sadler serves his cerebral, surprising creations in unpretentious surroundings near the Ticino harbor.

Sadler's devotion to prime ingredients is nothing short of obsessive. He chooses the sweetest, firmest shrimp to combine with crunchy little artichokes in a basil-scented antipasto that truly revs up the appetite. Supremely fresh braised sea bream is encased in potato slices and served with grilled radicchio. When they're in season, white truffles from Alba inspire Sadler to create unforgettable dishes. But even without truffles, his breast of guinea fowl all'ossolana, curried turbot with lentils, or monkfish in a velvety bean-based sauce leave behind luscious, lingering memories. Desserts are as innovative as the rest: we marveled at the lightness of chestnut-flour crêpes with pine nuts and raisins; and we didn't leave a crumb of the flaky strudel served with velvety fig ice cream. The wine list rises to the same high standards, with plenty of tantalizing bottles on hand. Tables here are few, so remember to book in advance. **C** 100,000 lire.

Il Sambuco

Hotel Hermitage,
Via Messina 10 - (02) 33610333
Closed Sun, Sat lunch, at New Year's, 1st 3 wks of Aug. All major cards.

Here's a rare find: a cheerful, welcoming family-run restaurant housed in a luxury hotel! And a mighty good restaurant it is. Achille Maccanti and his daughter, Alessandra, attend to their guests' comfort in a handsomely decorated dining room, while Francesca Maccanti performs *con brio* in the kitchen. Francesca's in-depth knowledge of seafood (she ran a noted seaside restaurant near Ferrara for many years) stands her—and us—in good stead when it comes to sniffing out the most succulent scampi and shrimp, pearly scallops, and fish full of authentic, briny flavors. Her spaghetti heaped with clams, zucchini, and tomatoes, her black tagliolini (they're tinted with squid ink) combined with cuttlefish and fresh peas, or an incomparably fragrant sea bream baked in parchment all provide stunning proof of her skill. Meat and even game appear on the menu, and they are anything but afterthoughts, witness a savory ragoût of locally raised rabbit with olives and pine nuts. Keen-flavored fruit sherbets close the meal on a bright, refreshing note, and the cellar is stocked with many accessibly priced bottles. **C** 100,000 lire.

San Fermo

Via San Fermo della Battaglia 1
(02) 29000901
Closed Sun, Mon dinner, Aug, 1 wk in Jan. All major cards.

At noontime, the bar does duty as a lunch counter for quick, one-course meals. In the evening, more leisurely repasts are served in the charming little dining rooms. A Milanese accent is perceptible in the eggy pastas sauced with braised pumpkin or with puréed artichokes and fresh ricotta cheese. The veal cutlet milanese is a crisp, succulent rendition of that often botched local specialty. Confirmed fish lovers can opt for grilled swordfish, turbot baked with tomatoes and olives, or octopus steamed in aromatic broth. Equally fresh and unfussy, though a trifle heartier, are the rib of beef with grilled vegetables or roasted beef tenderloin with mozzarella. When autumn rolls around, porcini mushrooms and truffles lend their bosky savor to a wide array of dishes. Desserts don't get short shrift here: a whole menu is devoted just to sweet finales. The wine list is limited, but composed with discernment. **C** 65,000 lire (dinner, wine incl).

San Vito da Nino

Via San Vito 5 - (02) 8377029
Closed Fri, Aug. V.

Elegant napery, sparkling crystal, fine china... nothing is too good for Maria Grazia Musella's patrons, who are always warmly welcomed and extravagantly pampered. The menu spotlights Milanese dishes, but also gives nods in the directions of Naples, Piedmont, and France (chicken in Champagne sauce). Among the attractive starters are a full-flavored house pâté and premium local charcuterie. Meats hold the place of honor among the main courses, with superlative grills, beef braised in Barolo wine, and game in season. Amaretto cake and orange-scented crêpes Suzette are rich but irresistible endings. The wine list boasts excellent Italian and French bottlings. **C** 80,000 lire.

> *Remember to call ahead to* **reserve your table,** *and please, if you cannot honor your reservation, be courteous and let the restaurant know.*

A Loge at La Scala

When the curtain was first raised on the Teatro alla Scala in 1776, the splendid theater was not exclusively reserved for operatic performances. Masked balls and all sorts of festivities took place there as well. Revelers would drink, feast, and gamble the night away in charmingly decorated boxes, or loges. After La Scala was hit by bombs, these loges were largely destroyed. The sole survivor is number 15, called the *palco degli specchi*, delightfully adorned in its period furnishings of mirrors, gilding, and tapestries.

Savini

Galleria Vittorio Emanuele
(02) 72003433
Closed Sun, Aug. All major cards.

Not far from the Gothic fantasia of Milan's Duomo, Savini occupies a prominent place in the imposing iron-and-glass Galleria Vittorio Emanuele, often called "the drawing room of Milan." These vast premises hold well-dressed, well-spaced tables adorned with glowing silver and served by squadrons of waiters and maître d's. The Milanese gentry, who frequent the place with some assiduity, are apparently more attuned to such niceties than they are to imaginative cooking. The menu is eclectic and more than a bit fusty; appetizers and first courses clearly outclass the rest (the risotto alla milanese, in particular, scores high). Stick to simple dishes, like the excellent carpaccio prepared tableside, or plain grilled fish, and you are likely to have a rewarding meal. The dessert cart is a stunner, but we advise you to admire it with your eyes only. Superb wine list; shocking prices, except for the two prix-fixe menus. **C** 120,000 lire. **M** 60,000 lire, 85,000 lire (dinner).

The prices in this guide reflect what establishments were charging at press time.

La Scaletta

Piazza Stazione Genova 3
(02) 58100290
Closed Sun, Mon, Aug. AE.

The nearby train station is so dreary that you might be tempted to hop a freight and leave the scene. But resist that temptation and head over instead to this alluring little restaurant for some of Italy's most exciting and creative cooking. Shy, retiring Pina Bellini opened her restaurant in 1980 at the urging of her son, Aldo. To everyone's astonishment, she began to turn out wildly unconventional, utterly distinctive fare that keeps Milan's most adventurous (and knowledgeable) palates begging for more. Assisted nowadays in the kitchen by a young southern Italian chef, Pina continues to amaze us with an inexhaustible imagination and sure-handed skill. Her ingredients, style, and (allow us the term) soul are purely Italian. But over years of eating our way through the Boot, we've never tasted anything like Pina's zuppetta di nervetti alla crema di cipolla (chewy nuggets of calf's foot in a velvety onion cream), or risotto Tagliapietra (the vegetables and herbs mimic the colors of Murano glass). She sauces spaghetti with tangy black olives and caramelized tomatoes (the long cooking intensifies their sunny sweetness); she brings veal and plump snails together in an unprecedented rendition of cutlet alla milanese. Saffron ice cream or a snowy yogurt tortino strewn with wild berries are just two of the splendid desserts she's recently dreamed up. By now, you're probably dreaming too! If you want to see if the reality measures up, just remember to reserve your table well in advance (as much as a month ahead in high season), line your wallet with wads of lire, and prepare yourself for an unforgettable gastronomic experience. **C** 100-130,000 lire.

La Segosta

Via Gozzi 6 - (02) 70123465
Closed Wed, Aug. All major cards.

Seafood is what the jolly waiters serve to most of La Segosta's elegantly arrayed tables. There's a superb house prosciutto to start things off, and unreconstructed carnivores can always order the tenderloin of beef, but fish is what the kitchen does best. After a briny, bracing platter of oysters or mixed shellfish, you can tuck into a first-rate risotto al nero (blackened with cuttlefish ink) or pappardelle noodles with porcini mushrooms and firm, pink scampi. For your main course, you won't go far wrong if you pick the fish of the day, whatever it might be. The homemade pastries have their charm, but the wine list tempts us even more. **C** 45,000 lire and up.

Stendhal
Via San Marco (corner of Via Ancona) (02) 6572059
Closed Mon lunch, 3 wks in Aug. All major cards.
Pier Luigi Pizzi, a celebrated set designer who studied with the incomparable Visconti, is responsible for the elegant décor of Stendhal, a restaurant at which Milan's considerable fashion community gathers, along with theater folk and journalists from the *Corriere della Sera*. The kitchen plys this colorful crowd with such delightful starters as miniature pizzas (pizzette), artichoke timbales, and clever little rolls of smoked trout, followed by an array of satisfying risottos, pastas (the tagliatelle are especially good), or soups. Main courses run to fresh fish (swordfish Robespierre, for example) or tasty grilled meats. Homemade ice creams and sherbets are appealing, but the crisp meringue napped with chocolate sauce is a knockout. Interesting cellar, too. **C** 50-60,000 lire.

Suntory
Via Giuseppe Verdi 9 - (02) 862210
Closed Sun, 10 days in Aug, Christmas hols. All major cards.
Although it is "made in Italy," the Japanese food served at Suntory is as authentic as any you'll find this side of Tokyo, a fact that the high proportion of Asian clients would appear to confirm. Start off with deep-fried seaweed tidbits, a variety of raw fish, or a green salad dressed with soy, then follow with a classic sukiyaki, tempura, sushi, or sashimi. Patrons sip beer, hot sake, or cool Italian white wine while watching the chef perform his culinary legerdemain at the central grill. All the ingredients are of pristine freshness, the premises are suitably exotic, and the light, delicate fare is a great antidote to an overdose of fettuccine and tiramisù. **C** 80-100,000 lire.

A Devil of a Column

There aren't many old-time oddments as bedeviling as the Roman column kept in the courtyard of the basilica of Sant'Ambrogio. It has fascinated and frightened the Milanese for nearly 1,600 years, ever since Lucifer himself drove his horns into it and lashed it with his saber-sharp tail. He was enraged, they say, by Saint Ambrose's devil-may-care contempt for Satan. Back in the gory days of the Viscontis and Sforzas, each governor-elect gave Satan's column a bear hug while swearing to abide by the law. Even ruthless Gian Galeazzo Visconti, the first Duke-tyrant of Milan, gave the marble a trembling embrace and told the Devil to go to hell.

Taverna della Trisa
Via F. Ferruccio 1 - (02) 341304
Closed every other Sun, Mon, Aug. V, AE.
The sideboard covered with climbing gear and the menu written in Trentine dialect (with an Italian translation) might lead you to believe that you've fallen into the worst kind of tourist trap. Not at all. The mountain hospitality you'll find here is as genuine as the Trentine specialties: wild-duck pâté or an assortment of cold game rouse the appetite as thoroughly as a hike in the Alps. Traditional pastas include strangolapreti ("priest stranglers": small pasta nuggets) and pumpkin-filled tortelli in a sauce with bits of smoky ham. Veal rolls stuffed with chicken giblets is a main course worth a try, but how can one resist smoked lake trout in horseradish sauce or crayfish culled from a mountain stream? There's (slightly heavy) homemade strudel for dessert, and regional wines to wash it all down. **C** 50,000 lire.

Il Teatro
Hotel Four Seasons, Via Gesù 8 - (02) 77088
Dinner only (exc Sun). Closed Aug, 2 wks at Christmas. All major cards.
Il Teatro is the ambitious new restaurant of the luxuriously restored Four Seasons

Hotel. Veteran chef Giacomo Gallina puts his well-trained kitchen brigade through its paces, sending forth complex, creative fare: oysters swaddled in phyllo pastry and accented with red-onion aspic, risotto spiked with citron and caviar, or chickpea-flour crêpes wrapped around a filling of radicchio and scallops. And that's just for starters! More sophisticated still are turbot baked with wild-rose hips, or a version of saltimbocca in which an escalope of rabbit replaces the veal and smoked goose breast stands in for the usual prosciutto. Still, a hotel restaurant cannot serve "challenging" food alone. The menu also embraces a classic risotto "Vecchia Milano" enhanced with bone marrow, ravioli wrapped around a stuffing of pumpkin, crushed amaretti, and minced mustard-preserved fruit (an old Lombard specialty), and lipsmacking glazed pork shanks with lentils and baby onions. Desserts are uniformly excellent; the cellar, understandably, still betrays its youth. **C** 100,000 lire.

La Topaia
Via Argelati 46 - (02) 8373469
Closed Sun, Aug. V, AE, DC.
Not far from the canal, near the Porta Ticinese, is this friendly little spot where light-hearted groups of diners enjoy generous, unpretentious cooking in a verdant bower. There is no menu; instead, the chef suggests a selection of antipasti (perhaps a salad of tuna or octopus, a mushroom tart or vegetable terrine), assorted pastas (with pesto or seafood sauces), followed by hefty portions of perfectly grilled fish or meat. All this, plus a pleasant little wine, won't cost an arm and a leg. Our only complaint is that even at night it can get pretty hot under that arbor. **C** 50,000 lire.

Il Torchietto
Via Ascanio Sforza 47 - (02) 8372000
Closed Mon, hols vary. V, EC.
The stars come out to dine at this well-known Milanese venue (Gianni Versace, Nastassia Kinski, lots of soccer personalities, journalists...), though things have been quieter since the "Clean Hands" scandals came home to roost. But whatever else may change, the menu remains faithful to the specialties of the Mantua region, famous for its charcuterie (excellent coppa) and pumpkin-stuffed tortelli. Among the main courses, look for the beef tenderloin with basil and capers. A classic torta sbricciolona (crumbly cake of cornmeal and almonds) makes a tasty finale, but chocolate addicts will want to try the mousse with a zabaglione sauce. **C** 60,000 lire.

Trattoria Masuelli San Marco
Viale Umbria 80 - (02) 55184138
Closed Sun, Mon lunch, 3 wks in Sep. No cards.
A family-run trattoria nearly 70 years old, this is one of the city's last outposts for real homestyle Lombard and Piedmontese cooking. The surroundings are appropriately rustic (ignore the roar of urban traffic just outside the door) for a meal of acciughe (anchovies) in salsa or a robust soup of chickpeas and spareribs, followed by one of the main-course specials, which change daily: bollito misto (mixed boiled meats) with mostarda (a fruit-mustard relish), cabbage leaves stuffed with savory meatballs, merluzzo (cod) with polenta... On Wednesdays, Fridays, and some Saturdays you can indulge in the pleasures of a Piedmontese bagna cauda: an opulent assortment of vegetables with a hot, truffled dipping sauce. Carafes of house wine are available as well as a selection of bottles from Piedmont wineries. **C** 50-60,000 lire (wine incl).

L'Ulmet
Via Disciplini (corner of Via Olmetto) (02) 86452718
Closed Sun, Mon lunch, Aug, 2 wks at Christmas. V, AE.
Whenever the chef goes on holiday, he brings back an exotic touch or two to rev up his traditional Lombard repertoire. He recently treated us to a a terrific recipe for lake char in a sweet-sour marinade, velvety pumpkin soup spiked with Amaretto, and an inspired combination of crayfish and endive in a bisque-like sauce. But we like his latest dessert discovery best of all: it involves a cinnamon-scented filling of figs and ricotta in fresh, hand-rolled potato pasta—yum! Still, we think he should rework his tortelli stuffed with zucchini and shellfish (the flavors are pale), and refrain from keeping delicate scallops too long on the fire. **C** 80,000 lire.

■ In **Brugherio**   14 km NE

La Guzzina
Via Brugherio 3 (Edilnord)
(039) 879632
Closed Tue, Aug. All major cards.
This eighteenth-century farmhouse, miraculously spared by voracious developers, is an enchanting spot for a romantic dinner. The chef has a deft touch with seafood, which appears all over the menu. Good gratinéed oysters or tiny stuffed squid will start off your meal very nicely, and things will continue in the same pleasant vein if you sample the spaghetti sauced with grouper or fish soup alla tarantina. Expertly grilled sea bass and sea bream are fine, light main courses, but the chef has a secret passion for traditional Lombard cuisine that shows up in such dishes as cassoeula (stewed pork and vegetables) and rustin negàa (a veal chop braised in white wine and sage). The cellar holds some tasty wines from Apulia. **C** 60,000 lire and up.

■ In **Cassinetta di Lugagnano** 25 km SW

Antica Osteria del Ponte
Piazza G. Negri 9 - (02) 9420034
Closed Sun, Mon, Aug, Dec 25-Jan 9. All major cards.
The setting is utterly bucolic: a disused canal, a towpath overgrown with wildflowers, an arched stone bridge with an ivy-covered hunting lodge at one end, and at the other an antique inn. Ezio Santin has transformed this osteria into an idyllic, elegant restaurant, where gastronomic pilgrims from the world over dine side by side with members of the Milanese gentry. What draws them here is the sublimely delicate and nuanced cooking produced by the self-taught Santin, a passionate chef with the soul of an artist. He fashions his dishes with seamless technique, pointing up the essential flavor of his rigorously selected ingredients. Other chefs may be bolder or more imaginative, but few can match the pristine harmony of Santin's very personal cuisine, inspired by the flavors of Liguria and the Mediterranean. Like us, you'll be dazzled by pasta rings stuffed with sole, shellfish, and baby beets; or by the haunting savor of lasagnette sauced with onions, leeks, and black truf-

fles; or by a flawless risottino that incorporates jewel-bright seasonal vegetables. To follow, there might be a brilliantly simple roast red mullet, fragrant with fresh thyme, flanked by a vivid tomato flan; or baby kid baked in a web of caul fat for richness and abetted by the delicate crunch of almonds. Young Maurizio Santin, a star pupil of pastry king Gaston Lenôtre, crafts the ineffable desserts, and Renata Santin oversees a genial, professional staff. **C** 130-150,000 lire.

■ In **Certosa di Pavia**   27 km S

Vecchio Mulino
Via del Monumento 5 - (0382) 925894
Closed Sun dinner, Mon, Aug. All major cards.
In a little courtyard adjacent to the stupendous Charterhouse of Pavia are two heavenly dining rooms and an Edenic garden where you can succumb to the temptations of sinfully good traditional cuisine. The locally made charcuterie is a seductive antipasto, but only a saint could resist the appetizing fresh vegetable terrines. Risotto with frogs' legs, tagliolini sauced with Taleggio cheese, and ravioli stuffed with a mix of duck, leeks, and eggplant are all devilishly delicious first courses. And what follows is no less tantalizing: venison cutlets with thyme and juniper, braised rabbit, farm-bred duck or guinea hen, and an array of the region's celestial cheeses (don't miss the Gorgonzola). The homemade desserts (cinnamon mousse, strawberry savarin) are divine, and the wine list offers an impressive litany of the best Italian bottlings, along with an infernally good assortment of local brandies. **C** 60-70,000 lire.

So What's Your Sign?

Just as you enter the Duomo, look down and admire the amazing Zodiac sundial designed by astronomer Antonio de Cesaris in 1786, which lies parallel to the cathedral's central door. When sunbeams manage to cut through Milan's usual blanket of fog, they fall precisely on the current month's sun sign.

Quick Bites

CONTENTS

CAFES

Caffè Rico

Corso Garibaldi 65 - (02) 862092
Open 6am-8pm. Closed Sun.
Not much bigger than a hole in the wall, but this is the place for the best espresso in town. Feeling jumpy? Then order the decaf; and if you're homesick, there's even an American-roast coffee to chase away the blues.

Caffè Moda Durini

Via Durini 14 - (02) 76021188
Open 10am-7pm. Closed Mon am.
Set in a fashion gallery crammed with enticing boutiques—Missoni, Ferré, Ferretti, Nicoletta Ruggiero, Sportmax—Caffè Moda is an ideal place to map out your shopping strategy over a cup of espresso or a snack.

Caffè Del Domm

Via Dogana 1 - (02) 875598
Open 7am-8pm. Closed Sun.
Mecca for cappuccino fans! You can savor a cup of the creamy brew in the decorative indoor room, or seated at one of the little outdoor tables. A full range of spirited drinks and other beverages is on hand, as well as a menu of meal-sized salads at lunch.

Camparino

Piazza Duomo 21 - (02) 86464435
Open 7:30am-9pm. Closed Sun.
Campari, Italy's famous bittersweet aperitivo, was born here in 1867. This is a fine place to sample the stuff, cut with soda water or served straight up (*liscio*), or in a delicious Negroni cocktail (gin, Campari, Cinzano). What's more, the tables out front provide a prime vantage point for eyeing the sleek natives as they hustle through the Galleria Vittorio Emanuele.

Tagiura Caffè Mokito

Via Tagiura 5 - (02) 48950613
Open 7:30am-8:30pm. Closed Sun.
This spot is many things to many people: a café, bar, tobacco shop, restaurant, trattoria, wine bar... Cold snacks are available all day long, and the sandwiches are terrific, especially the eggplant panino, the vegetarian variety filled with simmered greens, or the Greek-style chicken sandwich. In the early evening, habitués cluster around the bar, chatting and sipping an aperitivo.

QUICK BITES

L'Acerba

Via Orti 4 - (02) 5455475
Open noon-3pm & 6pm-midnight. Closed Mon.
The handsome stone floor and fine antique furnishings call to mind an old-fashioned café, but L'Acerba's famed vegetarian menu is utterly modern. The food quickly puts to rest any prejudices one might harbor about meatless cuisine. And what variety! More than 100 kinds of fruit and vegetables are used to make quiches, crêpes, and desserts—all delicious. Regular and herb teas are, with fresh

fruit juices, the only drinks available, but they are very good indeed. The incredibly lavish brunch must be experienced to be believed.

Amico Motta

Piazza Duomo, at Via Orefici - (02) 72002211
Piazza San Babila, at Corso Vittorio Emanuele (02) 76002248/47
Piazza Cinque Giornate 10 - (02) 5450513
Corso Buenos Aires, at Piazza Lima (02) 29401109
Open 7:30am-midnight. Closed Fri (Piazza Duomo), Tue (Piazza Cinque Giornate), Mon (Piazza San Babila), Wed (Corso Buenos Aires). Open daily Oct-Christmas.
Come on, now! Did you really travel to Italy to eat burgers and hot dogs? This chain of large and lively fast-food restaurants also serves warm, chewy foccacine and piadine—authentic Italian flat breads—with a host of toppings, along with a wide choice of desserts.

Brek

Via Cino del Duca 5 - (02) 76023379
Corso Italia 3 - (02) 72021679
Via Lepetit 20 - (02) 6705149
Open 11:30am-3pm & 6:30pm-10:30pm. Closed Sun.
Select from a variety of cold dishes—salads, top-quality cold cuts and cheeses—or choose a full hot meal served cafeteria-style in two spacious, comfortable, and attractive dining rooms. Among the desserts, the creamy mousses deserve special mention.

Brunch di Gualtiero Marchesi

Piazza Duomo, La Rinascente department store, 7th floor - (02) 877159
Open 11:45am-11:45pm. Closed Sun.
A taste of Marchesi (Italy's top celebrity chef) for people in a hurry. Nab a table and enjoy the view of the Duomo's spires as you munch on a hearty salad or robust regional dish (the offerings are regularly renewed). Appetizing cheeses, salamis, pastas, and r isottos round out the list, and there's always a tempting array of desserts. The house wine is tasty, too (good thing: it's the only kind available).

Burghy

Piazza Duomo 17 - (02) 86460435
Open 11am-11pm. Closed Mon.
Burghy was the first hamburger chain to get a foothold in Italy, and it is now the nation's largest. There are a dozen franchises scattered throughout Milan, but this one near the Duomo is the mother of all Burghys.

Il Cantinone

Via Agnello 19 - (02) 86461338
Open 7am-8:30pm. Closed Sun, Aug.
A dizzying range of panini stuffed with tasty Tuscan treats: try the sandwich filled with grilled sausage, or with pancetta, or with Florence's famous finocchiona salami. On Tuesdays, homesick Florentines can feast on cecina (chickpea porridge), another dish typical of the region.

Ciao

Corso Europa 12 - (02) 76021142
Via Meravigli 2 - (02) 8900375
Corso Buenos Aires 7 - (02) 29401109
Via Fabio Filzi 8 - (02) 66986020
Open 11:30am-3pm & 6pm-11pm. Closed Mon (Corso Europa), Fri (Corso Buenos Aires), Sat (Via Meravigli & Via Fabio Filzi).
The quality is high and the choices extensive in these attractive cafeteria-style restaurants. An impressive variety of hot and cold dishes lets you put together just the kind of meal you're in the mood for.

La Crêperie

Via Correnti 21 - (02) 8375708
Open daily noon-1am.
If a sandwich isn't the ticket, why not try a crêpe? Or two: one filled with savory Gorgonzola and walnuts followed by a chocolate-banana crêpe for dessert. To accompany them, try one of the brightly colored fruit or vegetable shakes (frullati) that are a specialty of the house.

De Santis

Corso Magenta 9 - (02) 875968
Open 11:30am-3pm & 7pm-1am. Closed Sun.
This is the granddaddy of Milan's *paninerie*, or sandwich shops, if you prefer. De Santis uses interesting types of bread and original fillings to make its 150 regular and open-faced sandwiches; we especially like the salmon, the shrimp, and the French cheese varieties. To wash them down, try one of the several Italian wines on hand.

Find the address *you are looking for, quickly and easily, in the index.*

El Tumbun de San Marc

Via San Marco 20 - (02) 6599507
Open 8am-1am. Closed Sun.
Milan's first pub, founded in 1963, is an enjoyable spot in the very center of town, with a big, polished wood bar. A lively crowd comes here in the evening to hoist a Guinness or two, and dine on such sturdy fare as bean soup, grilled ham, or crêpes del Tumbun. At lunchtime, panini (sandwiches) and cold snacks are on tap.

Goblin

Via Orti (corner of Via Commenda)
(02) 5469355
Open daily 11am-3pm & 6:30pm-3am.
Spaghetti lovers share this address near Porta Romana only with their nearest and dearest, for the premises are mighty small. But the list of spaghetti sauces goes on and on; they're all prepared by Roberto, a passionate student of the subject. Among his creative toppings you'll find one that involves air-dried boar and pineapple, another that pairs shrimp with avocado, and a third that sports the colors of Milan's soccer club (red and black). To drink, there's Canadian lager and a white (wheat-based) beer. Quick meals of salads and sandwiches are served at lunchtime.

Grand'Italia

Via Palermo 5 - (02) 877759
Open noon-2:45pm & 7pm-1:30am. Closed Tue.
There's always a crowd in this large, likable eatery, ordering up slices of pizza, chewy stuffed foccace (flat bread), and Grand'Italia's delicious and filling meal-size salads. This the place to come for fast food Italian-style. Of course you'll find the usual array of hamburgers and salads; the novelty is that you can order a plate of risotto or handmade pasta sauced with tomatoes, pesto, or with zucchini and peppers—*evviva!*

Margherita

Via Moscova 25, at Via San Fermo
(02) 6590833
Open 12:30pm-3pm & 7pm-2am. Closed Sun.
You can drop in at this warm, attractive eatery at just about any hour for a sandwich (there are 30 options) or a full meal selected from the short but varied menu. Offerings include hot starters and entrées, several variations on the carpaccio theme (thin-sliced raw meat or fish, diversely garnished), meal-size salads, and for dessert, oven-fresh cakes.

Monistrol Pub Guinness

Piazza Leonardo da Vinci 10 - (No telephone)
Open 7:30am-8:30pm. Closed Sun.
Students and profs from the nearby School of Architecture and Polytechnic Institute are in the habit of settling down comfortably on the leather sofas of this pleasant English-style bar for breakfast, lunch, or a convivial aperitivo.

Pane e Farina

Via Pantano 6 - (02) 8693274
Open noon-3pm & 7pm-1am (Sun 7pm-1am). Closed Sat.
What sets this cafeteria/pizzeria apart from the rest is the fact that all the hot dishes are cooked to order. Grilled meats are a specialty.

I Panini della Bagi

Corso Vercelli 23 - (02) 4814032
Open 7:30am-8pm. Closed Sun.
This tiny bar is renowned for its 60 kinds of panini. The fillings for these fresh, tasty sandwiches vary according to the season. Signora Bagi also serves a short list of hot and cold daily specials as well as delectable desserts that she makes herself.

Panino Giusto

Corso Garibaldi 125 - (02) 6554728
Piazza Beccaria 4 - (02) 76005015
Open noon-3:30pm & 6:30pm-1am. Closed Sun (Corso Garibaldi), Mon (Piazza Beccaria).
There's nary a smoker in sight around the clean-lined wooden tables—that's because smoking is prohibited at Panino Giusto. Instead, clean-lunged folks enjoy the excellent regular and open-faced sandwiches made with care and a good deal of imagination (the bresaola and goat cheese combo is great). To drink, there's draft beer or modest Italian wines.

Quadronno

Via Quadronno 34 - (02) 58306612
Open 7am-2am. Closed Mon.
At midpoint of the bustling Corso di Porta Romana you'll find this famous sandwich shop—a *paninoteca* with a long

list of appetizing options. The "Francesino" is stuffed with salmon, the "Primavera" with Prague ham, French cheese, and tomato, and the "Quadranno" overflows with a zippy filling of tongue, tomato, Tobasco, and mayo. But our special favorite is the "Palma d'oro," an award-winning mix of bresaola, bottarga (dried mullet roe), game pâté, and a secret sauce!

Taverna Morigi

Via Morigi 8 - (02) 86450880
Open noon-3pm & 7:30pm-1am. Closed Sun.
The sleek, shiny surface of modern Milan will seem far away when you settle into this vintage tavern: the dark-wood bar, faded red tablecloths, low lights, and smoke-stained walls hark back to another age. Drink in the atmosphere along with a glass of Moscato, Barbaresco, or brawny Barolo. On the solid side, there are excellent charcuteries and cheeses for a light lunch or snack.

Tecoteca

Via Magolfa 14 - (02) 58104119
Open 6:30pm-1am. Closed Mon.
Given over almost entirely to the pleasures of tea, this relaxing tea room offers more than 40 varieties, all directly imported from their countries of origin (not, in other words, from England!). Herb teas, fruit juices, and even a few wines and beers are served, but don't even ask for anything fizzy and sweet: soda pop is anathema here. Occasional art exhibits and book presentations make the modern, unaffected décor even more attractive.

SWEET SNACKS

■ ICE CREAM

Big del Gelato

Corso di Porta Romana 92 - (02) 58314364
Open 11am-8pm. Closed Mon.
Big was among the first ice-cream shops to experiment with new taste sensations. It still stocks a strange selection of flavors, which vary according to the mixmaster's whimsy. One day he'll offer saffron-risotto ice cream, and another he'll be inspired by

an apéritif (how about Campari sherbet?) or a flower. The creative frenzy extends to elaborate sculptural compositions (rendered in ice cream, of course) which are guaranteed to floor your guests at dessert time.

Bottega del Gelato

Via Pergolesi 3 - (02) 29400076
Open 9am-10pm (Mar-Oct 9am-midnight). Closed Wed.
Jewel-toned ices are the house specialty. Such exotic flavors as lychee, medlar, and avocado were found here before they became the rage in fashionable restaurants. Dainty and delicious, the fresh fruits filled with sherbet are a treat.

Cremeria Buonarroti

Via Buonarroti 9 - (02) 48007930
Open 7:30am-midnight. Closed Mon.
Classic flavors are favored in this traditional ice-cream shop, but dependable quality makes up for any lack of fantasy. The praline bowl filled with fruit-flavored ices is pretty spectacular by any standard, and the zuccotto (ice-cream cake) and meringata (meringue shell filled with ice cream) merit special mention as well.

Cremeria Dante

Via Dante 6 - (02) 876033
Open 9am-midnight. Closed Mon.
The modern setting offers no clue that this familiar and much-loved Milanese institution is more than 60 years old. No strange or exotic flavors here, just the classic favorites churned with care and made with the best ingredients.

Cristal

Via Ascanio Sforza 11 - (02) 58103929
Open 5:30pm-2am. Closed Mon, Sun am.
Picture this: a stately barge gently rocking on the waters of the Naviglio, live Baroque or Renaissance music, and a whole menu of ice cream concoctions to choose from. Isn't it romantic?

Ecologica

Corso di Porta Ticinese 40 - (02) 58101872
Open 1pm-midnight. Closed Nov-Feb.
At this friendly holdover from the hippie era, the ice creams have an appealing homemade look and incorporate such healthful ingredients as yogurt, wheat

93

germ, honey, sesame seeds, and... chocolate (a great source of magnesium, you know!).

Il Gelartista

Piazza Sempione 2 - (02) 3496967
Open 1pm-midnight. Closed Mon.

Opened by a group of natural-foods enthusiasts, this ice-cream shop guarantees the purity and authenticity of every ingredient used in its kitchens: organically grown fruit, cane sugar (replaced by honey where possible), and eggs from free-range chickens. The fresh-fruit sherbets are especially attractive.

Gelateria Sartori

Piazza Luigi di Savoia (corner of Via Pergolesi) (No telephone)
Open daily Mar 1-Oct 1: 10am-1am.

Not an ice-cream shop in the usual sense, this is a charming little stand established on the right side of the Stazione Centrale. Sartori owes its renown to a couple of delectable specialties: icy and refreshing lemon granita, and nocciolato, a luscious ice cream that tastes richly of hazelnuts. And there are 24 more yummy flavors to try.

Grasso

Via Andrea Doria 17 - (02) 6694456
Open 8:30am-midnight (Sat & summer 8:30am-1:30am). Closed Mon.
Via Cellini 1 - (02) 5454224
Open 9am-12:30pm & 3:30pm-8pm (summer 3:30pm-midnight). Closed Tue.

Grasso is a traditional gelateria that prepares a classic line of ice cream or sherbet sundaes as well as more recent inventions, such as the tropical fruit extravaganza (which bears a marked resemblance to Carmen Miranda's headgear) and the refreshing combination of wild-berry ice creams. The Via Doria location boasts an inviting outdoor terrace.

Jack Frost

Via Lazzaretto at Via Casati - (02) 6691134
Open 10am-11pm (Mar-Oct 10am-1am). Closed Wed.

Unusual and perfectly yummy ice-cream cakes are sold here in individual portions, in such wonderful flavors as glazed chestnut, chocolate, and mocha. For reasons we cannot fathom, these varieties

are available only in the colder months, but year-round Jack Frost makes some 70 other flavors of ice cream (at least 50 are available on a given day), including hazelnut (good and crunchy, with lots of nuts), tiramisù made with rich mascarpone cheese, and an American-style coconut-chocolate ribbon. Less rich but just as luscious are the fresh-fruit sherbets.

Leonarduzzi Gelato

Via Saffi 7 - (02) 4390302
Open 7am-10pm. Closed Mon.

The owner takes justifiable pride in the quality of his all-natural ingredients, which he churns into more than a dozen scrumptious flavors. We're particularly fond of his yogurt, banana, and walnut varieties. If you like cake with your ice cream, try the homemade panettone or brioche. Hand-dipped chocolates are sold here too, along with a very good cup of espresso.

Marghera

Via Marghera 33 - (02) 468641
Open 9am-midnight. Closed Wed.

Despite the shop's confined quarters, Marghera sells delicious ice cream in a wealth of flavors (we tallied more than 70 at our last visit).

Passerini

Via Victor Hugo 4 - (02) 86464995
Open 7:30am-8pm. Closed Wed.

Famous since the '20s for the finesse and intense flavors of its ice creams—the blackberry variety is legendary for its richness and depth—Passerini continues to come up with sublime new creations, such as frozen filled persimmons and grated-coconut ice cream. Passerini's cakes and ice-cream sculptures are known for their imaginative appeal.

Pozzi

Piazzale Cantore 4 - (02) 89409830
Open 8am-1am. Closed Mon.

Pozzi is the dean of Milan's ice-cream shops. In warm weather its spacious terrace is packed with folks enjoying fanciful sundaes or dishes of Pozzi's miraculously unctuous butterscotch ice cream.

The prices *in this guide reflect what establishments were charging at press time.*

Rachelli

Piazza Gramsci 3 - (02) 3315151
Open 8am-11pm (summer 8am-1am). Closed Mon.
Piazza Baracca 10 (corner of Corso Vercelli) (02) 48003821
Open 8am-8:30pm. Closed Wed.
The two house specialties are tartufi (frozen chocolate truffles topped with whipped cream) and zuppa inglese (cake soaked in rum custard), but we're partial to the colossal Coppa Rachelli, a sundae that brings together chocolate ice cream, Marsala-spiked custard, whipped cream, and crumbled glazed chestnuts. The Piazza Baracca address is small but very elegant, and is not far from the center of Milan.

Rossi

Viale Romagna 23 - (02) 730492
Open 9:30am-12:30pm & 3:30pm-11pm. Closed Mon am.
All the dreamy flavors are made in-house, but special mention goes to the rich chocolate ice cream and the snowy fior di latte (cream) variety. Though Rossi is not in the center of town, the quality of the ice cream is definitely worth a detour.

Solferino

Via Solferino 18 - (02) 6592098
Open 8am-8pm (summer 8am-midnight). Closed Sun.
Here the temptations bear such names as "milk and honey," "mascarpone" (imagine: an ice cream made of rich triple-creme cheese!), and "sweet kiss," all invented and prepared with a pleasing touch of whimsy.

Toldo

Via Sacchi 6 - (02) 86460863
Open 7am-8pm. Closed Sun.
The owners get their kicks turning all their favorite flavors into ice creams. Cinnamon and Mont Blanc (chestnut and cream) are two recent creations of which we heartily approve. And on a hot day, there's nothing like Toldo's Tropicana sundae, a cocktail of exotic fruit-flavored ice creams.

Umberto

Piazza Cinque Giornate 4 - (02) 5458113
Open 9:30am-2pm & 4pm-7:30pm (Mar-Sep 9:30am-7:30pm). Closed Sun.

Every day brings a new crop of flavors at this tiny but well-known and proudly traditional gelateria.

Viel

Foro Bonaparte 71 - (02) 878004
Corso Buenos Aires 15 - (02) 29516123
Open 9am-1am (Sat 9am-2am). Closed Wed (Foro Bonaparte), Tue (Corso Buenos Aires).
Viel proposes an alluring array of homemade ice creams, but the house specialty is fresh fruit whipped into refreshing shakes (frullati). The bright fruit salads also make a cool, low-calorie treat.

■ PASTRY

Ambrosiana

Via Rugabella 1 - (02) 86454811
Open 7am-8pm (Sun 8am-8pm). Closed Sat.
With half a century of experience to its credit, Ambrosiana is famed throughout Milan for its exquisite sweets. By all means try the buttery Sormonte puff pastry or the irresistible caramelized beignets. Light meals are served at lunch, and the barman's expertly mixed cocktails are popular at aperitivo time.

Biffi

Corso Magenta 87 - (02) 48006702
Open 8am-8pm. Closed Mon.
Though it was refurbished not long ago, Biffi has retained the original 1920s furnishings that date back to the founding of this posh tea room. All the pastries, including that famous Milanese specialty, panettone (a sweet yeast bread), are baked in an old-fashioned wood-fired oven. Prices are high.

Caffè Rue de Rivoli

Via Rivoli 2 - (02) 875454
Open 7:30am-8pm. Closed Sun.
A delightful French-style café, with tiny tables and delicate pink-silk seats, a polished wood bar and curtains at the windows. Classic and flavored teas from France, England, and China may be accompanied by dainty cakes and desserts for an afternoon break. At lunchtime, salads and cold dishes are offered.

> **Find the address** *you are looking for, quickly and easily, in the index.*

Clivati

Viale Coni Zugna 57 - (02) 89403338
Open 8am-1:30pm & 3pm-8pm. Closed Mon.
In addition to a selection of traditional Italian pastries, Clivati takes particular pride in its Torta Primavera (a delicate filling of fruit-studded whipped cream), Torta Greca (an almond crust with a filling of filberts and crushed amaretti cookies), and dark, chocolatey Gran Gianduja dessert.

Conca

Corso Magenta (corner of Via Carducci)
(02) 8057463
Open 8am-7:30pm. Closed Sun.
An enticing array of fresh, fragrant brioches is always on display at this tiny pastry shop. The fruit tarts are irresistible too, and may be devoured on the spot, at a little bar tucked away in a corner of the shop.

Cova

Via Montenapoleone 8 - (02) 76000578
Open 8am-8pm. Closed Sun.
For more than 150 years, Cova has dispensed divinely delicious pastries and chocolates to well-heeled Milanese gourmands. It remains to this day an elegant gathering place for a cosmopolitan crowd that dotes on the handmade sweets, the splendid Victorian silverware, and the attentive service. Deluxe sandwiches and classy cocktails are served here, too.

Cucchi

Corso Genova 1 - (02) 89409793
Open 7am-10pm. Closed Mon.
The pastries on display at this bustling tea room are mostly of the traditional sort, though the pineapple torte rings a more modern note. Cucchi offers freshly made candy as well: we'd like to draw your attention in particular to the pralines and the delightful old-fashioned jellies.

Excelsa

Piazza De Angeli 7 - (02) 463251
Open 7:30am-midnight. Closed Mon.
If your craving for tea and cakes comes on after most people have finished their dinner, you can depend on this capacious and comfortable *sala da tè* for fresh, delicious sweets and ice creams served until late at night.

Freni

Corso Vittorio Emanuele 4 - (02) 804871
Via Torino 1 - (02) 877072
Via Chiossetto 5 - (02) 76000970
Open 8:30am-11pm. Closed Wed.
When you enter, it seems that by a stroke of some magic wand the world has been transformed into sweet, fragrant, pastel marzipan. If almond-paste objects and animals are too cloying for your taste, Freni also purveys rich pastries in the extravagant southern Italian tradition.

Gattullo

Piazzale di Porta Lodovica 2 - (02) 58310497
Open 7am-10pm. Closed Mon.
The Torta Primavera, filled with pastry cream and tropical fruit, is the most popular offering here, but the pride of the house is the sculptural Torta Carlina, a cascade of miniature cream puffs and strawberries. On balmy days, you can gorge on these treats at an outdoor table.

Marchesi

Via Santa Maria alla Porta 13 - (02) 862770
Open 8am-8pm. Closed Sun pm, Mon.
From the nineteenth-century sign to the elegant antique furnishings, nothing has changed at Marchesi for generations. The elaborate confections produced here for a loyal clientele are as deliciously old-fashioned as the setting.

Panarello

Piazza San Nazaro in Brolo 15 - (02) 58307049
Via Speronari 3 - (02) 86462264
Open 8am-1pm & 3pm-8pm. Closed Tue (Piazza San Nazaro in Brolo), Mon (Via Speronari).
The Genoese owners are masters of biscotti di Lagaccio, a Ligurian cookie flavored with aniseed. The Ligurian version of panettone is worth trying too, as are the pretty wreaths fashioned from sweet pastry.

Paradiso

Corso di Porta Vigentina 10 - (02) 58314668
Open 8am-1:30pm & 3pm-9pm (Sun 8am-9pm). Closed Mon.
A heavenly address for adventurous gourmands who like to taste anything new and different. One day the kitchen produces a deliciously gooey chocolate-chestnut tart; another day you may come

across a torte of pears and cocoa cream or a feuilleté filled with pears, pine nuts, and chocolate. A luscious carrot cake and even lusher Sachertorte are always on hand. Like the name says, this place is Paradise!

Piave

Viale Premuda 42 - (02) 799435
Open 7am-9pm. Closed Mon.
Piave's drawing card is a line of dietetic sweets from which (depending on the type) either proteins, glutens, or sugars have been banished. The desserts are a boon for diabetics and dieters who crave an occasional treat.

Ranieri

Corso Garibaldi 33 - (02) 86462211
Via San Giovanni sul Muro 4 - (02) 8900920
Via Moscova 7 - (02) 6595308
Corso Italia 22 - (02) 86453057
Open 8am-7:30pm. Closed Sun pm, Mon.
Ranieri's display is an embarrassment of riches, but if we had to elect a few favorites, our first candidate would be the sublime zuppa di frutta (pastry cream, whipped cream, and fresh fruit, available by advance order only), followed by the zesty lemon torte, the glistening fruit tarts, the almond-rich Caprese cake, and an unusual savory version of Milan's famous sweet bread, panettone.

San Carlo

Via Bandello 1 - (02) 4812227

Open 6:30am-8:30pm. Closed Mon.
The premises may seem lilliputian, but there's a huge cache of sweet treats to discover inside. The orange and lemon pastries are pure delight, and chocolate lovers are sure to home in on the rich, wickedly delicious Trulles Torta. If you can't wait to devour your purchases at home, you may enjoy them at the little bar along with a cup of good espresso.

Sant'Ambroeus

Corso Matteotti 7 - (02) 76005447
Open 8am-8pm. Closed Mon.
Much more than mere desserts, the cakes, pastries, and ice creams conceived by the Sant'Ambroeus staff are stunning, one-of-a-kind works of dessert art. They may be sampled in the shop's refined little tea room.

Taveggia

Via Visconti di Modrone 2 - (02) 798687
Open 7:30am-9pm. Closed Mon.
Many Milanese lawyers have adopted the habit of strolling to Taveggia for an aperitivo, for it's conveniently sited near the city's courthouse. The atmosphere in the tea room (check out the authentic 1930s furniture) is cozy and pleasant, just right for nibbling on golden panettone, lemon cake, or a soothing dish of rice pudding.

What a Lovely Echo

Once upon a time, in the charming countryside ringing the industrious Renaissance city of Milan, there was a delightful little old villa where a pretty noblewoman named Clelia Simonetta strangled her pink-cheeked lovers in lustful delight. Lots and lots of them. Happily, another legend has it that the park behind her villa was endowed with the most extraordinary echo, able to repeat the word *amore* as many as 40 times. It is not clear whether the echo sounded before or during the strangling. During the last war a bomb fell right on this magnificent house of ill repute. Villa Simonetta, now part of the Sempione neighborhood (in drab Via Stilicone), has been restored and houses a music school. The pupils appreciate its fine acoustics and lovely echo.

Hotels

Antica Locanda Solferino
Via Castelfidardo 2
(02) 6592706, fax (02) 6571361
Closed 2 wks in Aug. 11 rms 150,000 lire. All major cards.
This traditional hostelry in old Milan combines a restaurant specializing in Lombard cooking and just under a dozen guest rooms (advance reservations are indispensable). The latter are on the second floor, up a steep, creaky staircase. The rooms offer such amenities as private baths and TVs, and the tastefully chosen nineteenth-century furniture and antique linens lend them a wonderfully cozy and intimate atmosphere. Breakfast in bed here is a real treat.

Ariosto
Via Ariosto 22
(02) 4817844, fax (02) 4980516
Closed Aug. 74 rms 123-179,000 lire. All major cards.
In its category, the Ariosto is undoubtedly one of the best hotels in town, housed in a lovely "Liberty" (Art Nouveau) palazzo close to the exhibition grounds. The guest list is a mix of British travelers and people in show business. Rooms are decorated in a fresh blue-and-white scheme; those at the back overlook a small garden dotted with birch trees. The reading room invites guests to linger in the comfy armchairs, and there is an attractive meeting room downstairs with exposed-brick walls.

Ariston
Largo Carrobbio 2
(02) 72000556, fax (02) 7200914
Closed Aug. 42 rms 167-234,000 lire. Garage pkg. All major cards.
The Ariston can make the singular boast that it is Milan's first "ecological" hotel. The building was fully restructured, and in the process all harmful substances and pollutants were reduced to a minimum.

Bedding, wall coverings, upholstery, adhesives, and furniture are all manufactured from natural materials. The air inside the hotel is treated with a special purifying and ionizing system that eliminates pollutants. In the bar area, a special fountain dispenses water at the temperature of one's choice, with just the amount of acidity and bubbles one prefers. The bicycles parked by the door are for hotel residents to use for sightseeing or pedaling to a business appointment! The hotel is located in the heart of Milan's historic district. No restaurant.

Capitol
Via Cimarosa 6
(02) 48003050, fax (02) 4694724
Open year-round. 96 rms 162-290,000 lire. Restaurant. Conf. Garage pkg. All major cards.
Located in an upscale residential zone, the Capitol is close to the elegant shops of the Corso Vercelli and the Milan Trade Fair site. The hotel comprises two buildings joined by a passageway; more than half of the well-equipped rooms overlook a tranquil inner courtyard. Furnishings are understated, modern, and comfortable. The hotel's grill is open nightly.

Carlton Senato
Via Senato 5
(02) 76015535, fax (02) 783300
Closed 3 wks in Aug. 79 rms 238-316,000 lire, bkfst incl. Pay pkg. All major cards.
Set back from Via Senato, the Carlton Senato is housed in a beautiful old palazzo. The location is enviable: right in the heart of the Golden Rectangle shopping district, close to the Villa Reale gardens and the Contemporary Art Pavilion. The staff is friendly, and the bar, furnished with antiques, is a pleasant place for a quiet drink. Though not large, the rooms are comfortable, and those overlooking Via Spiga are perfectly quiet.

Hotel Carlyle Brera
Corso Garibaldi 84
(02) 29003888, fax (02) 29003993
*Open year-round. 106 rms 330-395,000 lire,
bkfst incl. Pay pkg. V, AE.*
This modern hotel in the arty Brera district opened its doors in 1991. It provides a soothing ambience, with a restful salmon-pink color scheme. Half the rooms overlook Corso Garibaldi; all offer first-rate amenities, including satellite TV. Certain accommodations are reserved for non-smokers and for the disabled. The hotel bar welcomes guests until 1am. The subway (Linea 2) is conveniently close by. The hotel is scheduled to close for the month of August, 1995 for renovations.

 Century Tower Hotel
Via Fabio Filzi 25b
(02) 67504, fax (02) 66980602
*Open year-round. 148 rms 250-320,000 lire,
bkfst incl. Restaurant. Pay pkg. All major cards.*
The Century stands near the Stazione Centrale and draws a clientele made up chiefly of business travelers, who appreciate the up-to-date conference facilities. This member of the Concorde hotel group offers modern, functional accommodations decorated in understated tones of green and brown. The breakfast included in the room rate is an American-style buffet; there is a restaurant on the first floor.

 Dei Cavalieri
Piazza Missori 1
(02) 8857, fax (02) 72021683
*Open year-round. 7 stes 500,000 lire.
170 rms 265-313,000 lire. Restaurant. Pay
pkg. All major cards.*
The Dei Cavalieri leans against ancient Roman walls in the very heart of Milan's historic center, just minutes away from the Duomo and the Teatro alla Scala. The hotel itself was recently remodeled in contemporary style and offers all modern facilities. Tones of green and bordeaux dominate the guest rooms which are decorated with comfortable blond-wood furnishings.

 Diana Majestic
Viale Piave 42 - (02) 29513404
*Closed Aug. 94 rms 225-320,000 lire. Garden
dining. Pkg. Garage nearby. All major cards.
U.S. information number: 1-800-221-2340.*

Built early in this century in the distinctive Liberty style, the Diana Majestic is a favorite with fashion folk (many designers show their collections here). The hotel revels in a leafy garden with fountains and an unbeatable location in one of the city's liveliest sections, near Porta Venezia. All the usual services and amenities are available, including a cocktail bar with a garden view. Do take time to admire the beautiful lobby and the lounge. When you book, ask if rooms 322 or 325 are available: they provide the loveliest accommodations.

 Duca di Milano
Piazza della Repubblica 13
(02) 6284, fax (02) 6555966
*Open year-round. 18 stes 655,400 lire.
81 junior stes 474,600 lire. Restaurant. Conf.
Garage pkg. All major cards.*
The Duca di Milano was formerly an annex of the Principe di Savoia, but is now a hotel in its own right and a total restructuring in 1990 enhanced its nostalgic Victorian look. A member of the Ciga hotel group, the Duca benefits from a U.S. reservation service that can be reached at 1-800-221-2340. Traveling executives particularly appreciate the extensive office services available here. The impeccably equipped bedroom/sitting room suites are ideal for small meetings and working lunches. Located in Milan's business district, the hotel is close to the major shopping streets as well.

 Excelsior Gallia
Piazza Duca d'Aosta 9
(02) 6785, fax (02) 66713239
*Open year-round. 10 stes 1,000,000 lire and
up. 240 rms 360-415,000 lire. Restaurant.
Conf. Garage pkg. All major cards.*
This imposing edifice across from the midtown train station, built in the '30s, is one of Milan's best-known institutions. The oversized public rooms are tastefully done in a modern style; guest rooms are diversely decorated and offer every comfort. Seven superbly equipped conference rooms are available for meetings. The Baboon bar (you read that right) hosts a piano player nightly, and the fitness center boasts a sauna, work-out room, and beauty salon. Despite ongoing renovations, the ambience here is surprisingly serene.

99

Four Seasons
Via Gesù 8
(02) 77088, fax (02) 77085000
Open year-round. 16 stes: Executive ste 750,000 lire; Cloister ste 1,500,000 lire; Visconti ste 2,400,000 lire. 12 junior stes 680,000 lire. 70 rms: Deluxe dbl rm 550-610,000 lire. Restaurant. Conf. Pkg. Prices exclusive of 13% VAT.

The Four Seasons occupies a prestigious address in Milan's most fashionable district. The superbly restored building dates back to the fifteenth century, and was once home to a monastery. Each room and suite in this impossibly swank hotel is individually decorated with Italian flair: gleaming blond woodwork, Fortuny fabrics, and exclusive designer furnishings create a sumptuous setting for work or relaxation. Guests are pampered with every imaginable amenity, from 24-hour room service to a library of film cassettes in all sorts of languages (televisions in the rooms are naturally equipped with VCRs). A professional secretarial service, chauffered limousine, and private faxes in the rooms are just a few of the facilities provided by the Four Seasons' Business Center. Two restaurants, including the lavish Teatro (see *Restaurants*).

Galles
Via Ozanam 1
(02) 29404250, fax (02) 29404872
Open year-round. 5 stes 380,000 lire. 100 rms 195-260,000 lire. Pkg. All major cards.

The Galles is a charming small hotel that sits pretty just steps away from Corso Buenos Aires, one of Milan's best-known shopping streets. Housed in a handsomely restored turn-of-the-century palazzo, this link in the Best Western hotel chain plays host to people traveling for business or pleasure, and even counts a few rock stars among its patrons (David Bowie and Neil Young have both stayed here). A terrace garden affords a splendid view over the rooftops of Milan; the mansard on the upper floor boasts a small terrace with a Jacuzzi. Among the first-rate business facilities are computers, video-conference equipment, and a meeting room that holds 120 people.

Gran Duca di York
Via Moneta 1a
(02) 874863, fax (02) 8690344
Closed Aug. 30 rms & stes. Stes 290,000 lire. Rms 165-190,000 lire. V, AE.

The Gran Duca di York occupies picturesque premises that once lodged foreign visitors to the Biblioteca Ambrosiana. Guests from abroad still favor this hotel, whose lobby is decorated with armor, helmets, and swords from the age of chivalry. Two rooms, numbers 8 and 20, give onto an enclosed balcony that is utterly charming. Business travelers appreciate the duly equipped conference room and the hotel's proximity to the Stock Exchange.

Grand Hotel Brun
Via Caldera 21
(02) 45271, fax (02) 48204746
Annual closings vary. 24 stes 600,000 lire and up. 306 rms 250-300,000 lire. Restaurant. Conf. Garage pkg. All major cards.

The hundreds of rooms in this attractive, modern establishment have done much to relieve Milan's chronic hotel-room shortage. It is some distance from the city's center, but the rooms are flawlessly equipped and prettily decorated (more so than the public areas), each in a different way. Complete business facilities are available, and there is a pleasant piano bar for relaxing in the evening. Note that the hotel sometimes closes its doors in August.

Grand Hotel Fieramilano
Viale Boezio 20
(02) 336221, fax (02) 314119
Open year-round. 238 rms 280-350,000 lire, bkfst incl. Restaurant. Pay garage pkg. All major cards.

This vast hotel complex across from Milan's important Fiera (exhibition grounds) was designed to house the innumerable visitors who attend the center's many trade fairs. Downtown Milan is easily accessible via public transportation. For all its size, the hotel is amazingly peaceful. The public areas are spacious and functionally furnished, while the guest rooms have all the expected amenities, including hair dryers and telephones in the bathrooms. A restaurant serves regional specialties, and there is an agreeable cocktail bar.

> Remember to call ahead to **reserve your room**, and please, if you cannot honor your reservation, be courteous and let the hotel know.

Grand Hotel et de Milan
Via Manzoni 29
(02) 7231411, fax (02) 86460861
Open year-round. 8 stes 678-1,120,000 lire. 96 rms 497-599,000 lire. Restaurants. Conf. Garage pkg. All major cards.
The Grand Hotel, founded in 1865, stands just a hundred yards from La Scala. It was Verdi's residence for more than 30 years. Nostalgia buffs will love the period antiques that furnish the public areas of the hotel; indeed, the entire hotel was recently refurbished from stem to stern in nineteenth-century style. Avid shoppers should note that the Grand Hotel stands right at the heart of Milan's fashion district. For an account of the Don Carlos restaurant, see *Restaurants.*

 Hermitage
Via Messina 10
(02) 33107700, fax (02) 33107399
Annual closings vary. 12 stes 480,000 lire; Junior ste 400,000 lire. 120 rms 265-330,000 lire, bkfst incl. 3 rms for disabled & non-smokers. Restaurant. Pay garage pkg. All major cards.
Here's a sparkling new hotel that offers refined luxury to discriminating patrons. Marble, polished walnut woodwork, elegant fabrics meet the eye at every turn. Each comfortable guest room is equipped with a Jacuzzi. In addition to an excellent restaurant (see *Restaurants*), there are commodious conference rooms for working and a pleasant garden for relaxing.

Hilton
Via Galvani 12
(02) 69831, fax (02) 66710810
Open year-round. 2 stes 900-2,000,000 lire. 321 rms 300-480,000 lire. Restaurant. Conf. Garage pkg. All major cards.
Conrad Hilton declared that the three essential factors to consider when building a Hilton were location, location, and location. Consequently, the Milan link in the Hilton chain is just a couple of minutes from the train station in the center of the business district, and a quarter of an hour from the Duomo. The décor of the guest rooms is rather sober, but they are comfortable and flawlessly equipped. Three floors of rooms (fourth, fifth, and sixth) just emerged, bright and new, from a thorough renovation. The plush bar is a fine place to relax or do business.

Skulduggery at San Bernardino's Chapel

We make no bones about it—this is the creepiest collection of human crania in the city. Candles flicker as the faithful kneel before assorted skeletal remains artfully fashioned into crucifixes and dangling knicknacks. They're all crammed into the Baroque chapel of San Bernardino alle Ossa on Piazza Santo Stefano. The church's main attraction, the skulls are billed as having been lopped off Christian shoulders by marauding Arian heretics or godless Goths. More likely, they were tossed out by the ancient Brolo hospital next door. Pirated or not, these skulls and crossbones are sure to tingle your spine.

Liberty
Viale Bligny 56
(02) 58318562, fax (02) 589061
Closed 2 wks in Aug. 3 stes 260,000 lire. 49 rms 160-230,000 lire. Garage pkg. All major cards.
The Liberty provides elegant lodgings in the Porta Romana neighborhood. The décor is accented with stained glass and fine marquetry furniture; concern for guests' comfort is obvious in the breakfast and reading rooms, furnished with deep armchairs, antique chests, Persian carpets, and bouquets of fresh flowers. Bay windows frame a view of a garden, and beyond a vintage Milanese edifice which now serves as a garage for guests' convenience.

Manzoni
Via Santo Spirito 20
(02) 76005700, fax (02) 784212
Closed Aug, at Christmas. 3 stes 280,000 lire. 50 rms 152-198,000 lire. Bkfst 19,000 lire. Pay garage pkg. All major cards.
A trendy clientele appreciates this hotel's convenient proximity to Via Montenapoleone, Milan's designer wonderland. The entire hotel was just remodeled in contemporary style. Guest rooms are

101

amazingly quiet, given the location, and provide all the usual amenities.

Michelangelo

Via Scarlatti 33
(02) 6755, fax (02) 6694232
Open year-round. 7 stes 720-860,000 lire. 305 rms 320-500,000 lire. Restaurant. Conf. Garage pkg. All major cards.

Like so many modern, impersonal hotels, this one has no distinguishing characteristics (it could just as easily be located in Peru), but it does possess a large garage, which is quite an advantage in car-choked Milan. After a full overhaul completed in 1992, the comfortable, impeccably appointed rooms feature pastel walls and walnut furniture; the granite bathtubs boast hydromassage equipment. As for the business facilities, they are second to none, and the hotel also provides free shuttle service to Linate and Malpensa airports. For a review of the hotel's restaurant, Mastro Ghirlandaio, see *Restaurants*.

Palace

Piazza della Repubblica 20
(02) 6336, fax (02) 654485
Open year-round. 10 stes 700-1,500,000 lire. 204 rms 280-500,000 lire. Restaurant. Conf. Business center. Garage pkg. All major cards. U.S. reservation number: 1-800-221-2340.

Another of the Ciga group's fine hotels, the Palace is a handsome, high-class establishment set squarely in the heart of Milan's business district. An ambitious renovation program is now complete: the hotel boasts a new marble façade, freshly refurbished Empire-style rooms fitted with delightful amenities, and the public spaces include terraces, gardens, and a solarium. An impressive Business Center was inaugurated in 1994. Even the bar, which we used to find a bit fusty, sports a spiffing new look. A noted restaurant, the Casanova Grill, completes the picture (see *Restaurants*).

Palazzo delle Stelline

Corso Magenta 61
(02) 4818431, fax (02) 58207540
Closed Aug. 103 rms & stes. Stes 300,000 lire. Rms 150-220,000 lire. Restaurant. Pay pkg. All major cards.

This hotel is the near neighbor of Santa Maria delle Grazie, the church where Leonardo painted his famous *Last Supper*. Fitted out in the wings of an age-old cloister, the rooms are quiet and very bright, with modern beechwood furniture and watercolors of old Milan on the walls. Bathrooms are equipped either with showers or Jacuzzi bathtubs. The serene mood of the place is augmented by the presence of a garden, where da Vinci himself pottered about, cultivating his grapevines. The Palazzo also houses a conference center and several public and private institutes. Gli Orti di Leonardo, a well-known restaurant, is located on the premises (see *Restaurants*).

Pierre

Via De Amicis 32
(02) 72000581, fax (02) 8052157
Closed Aug. 4 junior stes 690,000 lire. 45 rms 230-500,000 lire, bkfst incl. Restaurant. Pay garage pkg. V, AE, DC.

The Pierre is a highly polished little jewel of a hotel, housed in an eighteenth-century palazzo near the basilica of Sant'-Ambrogio. Guests revel in the intimate luxury of antique furnishings, classical and contemporary artworks, marble-clad bathrooms, embroidered bed linens—all this plus a blessedly tranquil ambience. The service is impeccable, and includes 24-hour flower delivery, a restaurant, and a piano bar. A private limousine service is provided for an extra charge, and room service operates around the clock.

Principe di Savoia

Piazza della Repubblica 17
(02) 6230, fax (02) 6595838
Open year-round. 47 stes 900-1,900,000 lire. 250 rms 340-580,000 lire. Restaurant. Conf. Pool. Garage pkg. All major cards. U.S. reservation number: 1-800-221-2340.

The refreshing greenery of Piazza della Repubblica is surrounded by several hotels that belong, like this one, to the Ciga group. Well out of the city's center, the Principe di Savoia offers peace, understated luxury, and an efficient staff. Newly emerged from a thoroughgoing renovation, the accommodations are exquisitely comfortable and stylish. The public rooms, too, received a needed facelift: accented with handsome regional antiques, they are now plush and inviting. For guests' entertainment, the hotel houses a piano bar, a brand-new pool located on the top floor, Caffè Doney for light meals and afternoon tea, and a fine restaurant, the Galleria (see *Restaurants*).

Ramada Grand Hotel
Via Washington 66
(02) 48521, fax (02) 4818925
*Open year-round. 11 stes 600,000 lire.
312 rms 190-250,000 lire. Restaurant. Pay
garage pkg. All major cards.*
Visitors to the Milan Trade Fair (Fiera)
should note the address of this spanking-
new hotel. Beyond the imposing marble-
clad entrance guests discover a lobby
dotted with palm trees, an obliging and
efficient staff, and first-class accommodations. The restaurant serves meals nonstop from 11am to midnight.

 Spadari
Via Spadari 11 - (02) 72002371
*Closed Aug, Christmas hols. 2 junior stes
450,000 lire. 40 rms 300-380,000 lire. Pay
pkg. All major cards.*
Here's a lovely place to stay in the very
center of Milan: the little balconies offer a
splendid view of the Duomo and its forest
of spires. Relatively new (it opened in
1991), the Spadari is Italy's first "Art
Hotel," modeled after similar establishments in Paris and Germany. The hotel
is furnished as if it were the private home
of an art collector: works by contemporary
painters and sculptors grace each of the
guest rooms, which are tastefully
decorated with pastel fabrics and modern
blond-wood furniture. Even the singles are
spacious, for a change! Television chan-
nels in three languages are available via
satellite.

RESIDENCES

Some fortunate travelers—business
people, actors, models, artists,
those on sabbatical—have occasion
to require an urban home base for a month
or more in Italy. Hotel rooms can become
impersonal and a bit cramped for extended stays, and ordinary home rentals
usually require a long-term lease agreement. Enter the apartment hotel (or
residence, as the Italians say), full-service
accommodations that are perfect for
longer stays. They combine the space and
domestic comfort of an apartment with
such features as maid service, kitchen
facilities, and sometimes even concierge
services.

Borgonuovo
Via Borgonuovo 1
(02) 6438541, fax (02) 66104091
*15 apts. Studios 3,500,000 lire per month;
2-rm apts 4,800,000 lire per month. V, AE,
DC.*
For an extended stay in the city, a full-service apartment is often a more economical
solution than a hotel. The Borgonuovo
occupies an entire nineteenth-century
palazzo on one of Milan's most
fashionable streets. Its clientele runs to
top-level managers, actors, and designers
who appreciate the establishment's discreet elegance. Apartments are cleaned
daily (except holidays), and a dry-cleaning
service is available.

Garibaldi
Corso Garibaldi 72/1 - (02) 6599127
*15 studios 1,800,000 lire. 15 2-rm apts
2,300,000 lire. Garage pkg. V, AE.*
Make yourself at home in the central,
arty Brera district close to the Moscova
subway stop. The Garibaldi is done up in
a modern, functional style with carpeted
floors and simple furniture. Electricity,
telephone bills, and 9% VAT are not included in the room rates.

Maria Theresia
Via Bocchetto 15 - (02) 8057673
*36 studios & 2-rm apts. Studios 2,500,000 lire
plus 9% VAT; 2-rm apts 3,000,000 lire plus
9% VAT. All major cards.*
This elegant and exclusive establishment,
located in the heart of the business district,
equidistant from La Scala and Il Piccolo
Teatro, is as much a favorite with actors
and opera singers as with bankers and
CEOs. The housekeeping service operates
daily, and there is an efficient dry cleaner
in the building. Renovations are currently
underway.

Missori
Via Albricci 4 - (02) 809741
*150 studio, 2- & 3-rm apts. Studio 2,950,000 lire;
2-rm 3,750,000 lire. No cards.*
Ideal for business people, the Missori
boasts a central location. Fittings are basic,
but functional. A deposit of 1 million lire is
required.

> **Find the address** *you are looking for, quickly
> and easily, in the index.*

Residence
de La Gare

Via M. Macchi 49 (corner of Via Pergolesi)
(02) 6690524, fax (02) 66741284
22 apts 3,000-3,200,000 lire per month. Pay garage pkg. V, AE, EC.

Many residents appreciate the warm, welcoming atmosphere that reigns in this residence near the Stazione Centrale. The accommodations are brand-new, accented with marble and parquet floors. Luxurious amenities include air conditioning, bathtubs with hydromassage, armored doors, safes, and 24-hour doormen. Faxes and cellular phones are available, too.

Ripamonti

Via dei Pini 3 Pieve Emanuele (Mi)
(02) 90761, fax (02) 90720229
839 2- to 4-rm apts 1,450-3,500,000 lire. Pay garage pkg. All major cards.

The Ripamonti stands at the outer edge of Milan proper. The facilities are legion: business center, shopping center, a sports complex with a pool and tennis courts are all close at hand. Residents all enjoy private terraces, and there is self-service restaurant conveniently located on the premises. A shuttle ferries guests to the subway stop.

Romana

Corso di Porta Romana 64 - (02) 58309793
100 studios, 2- & 3-rm apts. Rms 2,750-4,500,000 lire per month. V, AE, DC.

Here you can rent what is doubtless the largest suite in town: four sumptuous rooms with a garden view (6,000,000 lire per month). The more modest apartments are quite attractive, too, and they're certainly more affordable; all are fully equipped and decorated with care. Centrally located, the Romana is preferred by many singers, actors, bankers, and business executives who make extended stays in Milan. Chambermaids come in five days a week; parking and a dry-cleaning service are offered.

Ostello Piero Rotta

Viale Salmoiraghi 1 - (02) 39267095
Closed at Christmas-New Year's. 350 beds. Family rms 66,000 lire. Rms 20,000 lire. Student ID required. No cards.

This hostel is open to members of the International Youth Hostel Federation (membership costs 15,000 lire per year, and may be paid at the hostel). One of the largest establishments of its type in Italy, it provides low-cost, short-term (three days maximum) lodging for young people and students. Families are welcome here, too— a floor is reserved just for them. Accommodations are spartan and functional, with six beds to a room; separate quarters are provided for men and women. Bathrooms are communal, and individual lockers line the halls. True, it isn't the Ritz, but for travelers on a shoestring budget (and with valid student ID), this is a dandy place to stay.

Holy Moses,
a Snake!

Talk about an object worming its way into the heart of the Milanese... In the basilica of Sant'Ambrogio there's a most beloved bronze serpent that is said to have been sculpted on the express order of Moses. That's right, he is supposed to have used it to keep the cobras at bay while he wandered in the deserts of Egypt. Archbishop Arnolfo brought it to Milan from Istanbul in the year 1002 and had it mounted on a lovely Roman marble column, the third on the left in the basilica's nave. Until the advent of pharmaceuticals, Milanese matrons lined up by the dozen with their tapeworm-infested kiddies in front of Moses' snake in hopes that it would put a stop to their *bambini*'s bellyaching.

Nightlife

CONTENTS

BARS

American Bar Coquetel
Via Vetere 14 - (02) 8360688
Open 8am-2am. Closed Sun, Aug 1-Sep 6.
This trendy venue in the Navigli district had hardly hatched before it became a rallying point for hip young Milanesi. The crowd starts to gather in the garden across the street around 6:30pm, then moves en masse into the bar to sip cocktails, premium whiskies and rums, "killer" punches, or alcohol-free fruit drinks. Things are quieter around lunchtime, when sandwiches, snacks, and light meals are served.

Bar Basso
Via Plinio 39 - (02) 29400580
Open 8am-1:15am. Closed Tue.
Since the 1950s, cocktail fanciers have flocked to this classic bar. In addition to perfectly mixed drinks, the resident "chemist" will also prepare, at your request, the celebrated ice cream–based specialty of the house, called *mangia e beve* ("eat and drink"). It's a knockout! You may partake of these refreshments either amid velvet-covered armchairs and crystal lamps, or in an equally comfortable but less formal room with rustic furnishings.

Il Baretto
Via Sant'Andrea 3 - (02) 781255
Open 10am-1am. Closed Sun.
Look around at the sleek patrons for an accurate picture of the hottest trends in Italian fashion. Il Baretto is a convenient place to pause during a shopping spree for a drink or a bite. The (expensive) menu proposes salads, shrimp curry, risotto alla milanese, and baccalà (salt cod) alla vicentina.

Bar Giamaica
Via Brera 32 - (02) 876723
Open 9am-2am. Closed Sun.
All that's changed at this club since the days of its celebrity are the windows of the little veranda that looks out over the street. As for the rest, owner Elio Mainini is his same gruff and mischievous self, and the place remains a favorite with artists and intellectuals. There are a lot more young people and tourists than in the old days, however. At lunchtime, patrons have to wait their turn to be seated, and at drinks time they stand in clusters around the crowded tables. But that jostling camaraderie is just what pulls in the crowds, year after year.

Bar Magenta
Via Carducci 13 - (02) 8053808
Open 7:30am-3am. Closed Mon.
Inspect the fashionable natives in their natural habitat, here at one of the city's hippest bars. Aperitivo time is best for people-watching, but you can also drop in for lunch or a light, late-night snack. Admire the Art Nouveau interior as you hoist a beer—a dozen different varieties are available on tap.

> *Some establishments change their* **closing times** *without warning. It is always wise to check in advance.*

Be-Bop

Via Col di Lana 24 - (02) 8376972
Open 8pm-2am. Closed Mon.

The TV screens on the wall are now the only reminder of the club's short-lived attempt to lure an adolescent crowd. Be-Bop is much quieter now, and the management prefers to define it as a "café-restaurant." People stop in for a drink and for tasty meal-size salads, pasta, and grills. The excellent pizzas are prepared with soy flour, which makes them especially light and digestible. Orders may be placed, we are amazed and pleased to report, right up until closing time.

La Belle Aurore

Via Castelmorrone (corner of Via Abamonti) (02) 29406212
Open 8am-1am. Closed Sun.

The decorator aimed to create a "Paris bistro" look, and we must admit that the attempt was pretty successful. The black and white tiles on the floor, the marble tables and Thonet chairs, the mirrors, and the *pâte de verre* bottles make a suggestively Gallic setting. Step up to the antique wooden bar for a classic cocktail or one of the bartender's original concoctions. Good salads and innovative dishes are served at any time of the day, but we are particularly attached to the breakfast ritual here, which consists of excellent croissants, coffee, and the morning paper.

Blues Bikers

Via Brioschi 7 - (02) 8372816
Open 7pm-2am. Closed Sun.

This is no ordinary beer house. It's a kind of club for motorcycle enthusiasts, complete with videos and photos all devoted to the manly art of biking.

Bodeguita del Medio

Via Col di Lana 2 - (02) 89400560
Open 7pm-2am. Closed Sun.

Named for a mythical bar in Hemingway's Havana, this Milanese copy is manned by an extremely adroit mixmaster, Gualtiero Menoni. He knows Cuba like the back of his hand: that's where he learned to concoct the killer cocktails that have made this place famous. Be careful not to get carried away on a tasting spree—your head will not thank you come morning.

Caffè Milano

Piazza Mirabello 1 - (02) 29003300
Open 12:30pm-2:30pm & 6:30pm-1am. Closed Sun.

Caffè Milano rose from the ashes of the late, lamented Oreste, long a Milanese landmark. Come in for a typically Lombard lunch (a set menu is offered at noon) or later on for cocktails or drinks, all served in a musical ambience. The late-night menu is limited to pastas, salads, and light snacks.

Caffè Vecchia Brera

Via dell'Orso 20 - (02) 86461695
Open 7am-2am. Closed Sun.

Tables for two, candlelight, music in the background: here's a romantic spot for a drink (the barman knows his cocktails) after the movies or a show. Light snacks are on tap, too: the sandwiches, pastries, and crêpes rise well above the ordinary.

Cap Saint Martin

Via De Amicis 9 - (02) 8394145
Open 1pm-2am. Closed Sun.

Cap Saint Martin has carved out its niche as a favorite haunt of Milan's young trendies. Oil lamps and wooden tables create an attractive setting with a nautical flavor; the soft lighting allows you to observe your neighbors discreetly as you nurse a cocktail or aperitivo. When the weather turns fine, the scene moves outdoors: drinks and snacks are served at little tables overlooking the Columns of San Lorenzo.

Entropia

Via De Amicis 34 - (02) 867639
Open 8pm-2am. Closed Tue.

Close to the Porta Ticinese, this restaurant-brasserie is a magnet for card players. You may not be familiar with their rules (*risiko* is the game here), but you might learn a trick or two just watching. On tournament nights the atmosphere gets pretty intense.

Happy Rock Café

Viale Tibaldi 1 - (02) 58105888
Open 8:30pm-2:30am. Closed Mon.

A rolling roster of rockers play here live every Wednesday night. The musical menu ranges from blues to Latino rhythms. The music is played just the way the customers like it: loud. Mirrored tabletops and low lights lend the place some atmosphere, and the food—snacks, salads, sweets, and crêpes—is better than you'd expect.

Julien Bar (ex-La Nave)

Via Maggi 6 - (02) 3490459
Open 11am-3pm & 7pm-3am. Closed Sun.
Jazz fills the air, tropical cocktails flow from the bar, the multicultural menu features foods from every land but Italy... The newly rehabbed Julien Bar draws an eclectic crew of fun-lovers who know how to party!

Louisiana

Via Fiori Chiari 17 - (02) 86465315
Open noon-3pm & 6pm-2am. Closed Mon.
Jazz plays in the background, photos of vintage jazz greats decorate the walls, and the bartender dispenses Hurricanes, Daiquiris, and other explosive rum-based drinks. A menu of spicy Cajun specialties is featured downstairs; upstairs, by reservation, you can dine on the chef's Creole creations.

Manhattan

Via Verri 3 - (02) 76023566
Open noon-3pm & 8pm-3am. Closed Sun.
Manhattan faces a pretty indoor garden, where a rare Japanese fighting fish swims quite peaceably in his pond. At noon, quick single-course lunches are served. Come evening, the menu expands (plan on spending about 30,000 lire, without wine) at the only late-night restaurant in midtown Milan. The surroundings are elegant but not ostentatious, and the cocktails are mixed with care. Live piano music in the evening.

Matricola Irish Pub

Viale Romagna 43 - (02) 2363498
Open 7am-10pm. Closed Sun.
This authentic Irish pub in Milan's student quarter sports a polished wood bar, outsized mirrors, and gleaming brass trim. Hibernian fare is featured at lunchtime, but the menu shrinks thereafter to just sandwiches. Evenings, after all, are meant for downing pints of Guinness in a noisy, cheerful atmosphere.

> The prices *in this guide reflect what establishments were charging at press time.*

The Old Fox Pub

Via C. da Sesto 23 - (02) 89402622
Open 11:30am-2:30pm & 6pm-12:30am. Closed Sun.
A genuine English pub, or at least a faithful reproduction of that beloved British institution, with the requisite brass and leather fittings, light and dark beers, and excellent whiskies. The habitués dote on the menu of sandwiches and other pub grub offered daily.

Osteria del Pallone

Via Gorizia 30 (corner of Via Alzaia Naviglio Grande) - (02) 58105641
Open noon-2am. Closed Mon.
A spruce little place, lovingly furnished with turn-of-the-century antiques, this tavern is especially cozy and inviting in winter. Sweet and savory delicacies, including fabulous Italian charcuterie and cheeses, are served along with expertly mixed drinks and premium beers (Guinness is a big favorite). A colorful crowd shows up on the last Sunday of each month, when the Naviglio antique market spreads out its wares nearby.

Portnoy Café Letterario

Via De Amicis 1 (corner of Corso di Porta Ticinese) - (02) 8378656
Open 7am-2am. Closed Sun.
This is the first and, apparently, only café willing to undertake the heavy responsibility of acting as Milan's official intellectual headquarters. It's a bright, pleasant place, furnished in an urbane postmodern style. The establishment covers two floors, linked by a spiral staircase: one is devoted to serious drinking (try the Caipirina cocktail), the other to equally serious literary debate and discussion. A special event—meetings with authors, poetry readings, lectures—is scheduled nearly every day. Light meals are served at midday only.

Radetzky

Corso Garibaldi 105 - (02) 6572645
Open 7:30am-1:30am. Closed Sun.
From morning coffee to nightcaps, from croissants to an after-theater oyster feast, Radetzky caters to every appetite at almost any hour. Given the quality of the sustenance and the elegance of the setting (marble, antiques...), the prices are most reasonable. And the barman is an ace: his

cocktails must be among the most beautifully presented in town.

Resentin Café

Via Mercato 24 - (02) 875923
Open 4pm-2am. Closed Sun.

On the site of the former Gabriele bar, once a famous artists' rendezvous, stands the Resentin Café, a watering hole with roots in the Trentino region. The owner is Trentine, as are the 35 different grappas (Italian grape brandies) on tap, the wines, the Spumante, and the rugged, robust mountain fare. Even the atmosphere has a distinctive northern coziness, as if there were always snow on the ground outside.

Ronchi

Via San Maurilio 7 - (02) 867295
Open 12:30pm-2:30pm & 9:30pm-1:30am. Closed Sun.

What was once an ancient wine cellar is now a restaurant and bar that brims with picturesque charm. Homestyle Italian dishes make up the lunch menu, while in the evening charcuterie, foccace (stuffed flat breads), and cheeses accompany a list of wonderful wines. Live guitar and piano music add to the pleasure.

Al Teatro

Corso Garibaldi 16 - (02) 864222
Open 4pm-1am. Closed Mon.

Across the street from the Teatro Studio, this popular club goes full tilt from cocktail hour until closing time. Surrounded by antiques in a slightly bohemian setting, patrons down drinks, pastries, and appetizing little snacks. In fine weather, some tables are set outdoors on the lively Corso Garibaldi.

Who's Who

Via Arena 5 - (02) 58106121
Open 8pm-2am. Closed Mon.

The monks who lived here in the seventeenth century would be startled to see their austere quarters transformed into this polished place of refreshment. Patrons sit beneath coffered wood ceilings and sip colorful fruit-based cocktails, French teas, and soothing herbal infusions.

> *Some establishments change their* **closing times** *without warning. It is always wise to check in advance.*

DISCOS

Carrobbio

Via San Vito 26 - (02) 86451087
Open 10pm-2:30am. Closed Mon. Cover charge: 15,000 lire (drink incl); 20,000 lire (Sat).

A new scene for Milan's fun seekers, situated just steps from the Duomo. A small entrance leads into a basement club, where cleverly placed mirrors seem to enlarge the space. Next to the dance floor, notice the ancient relics of Milan's Roman and medieval past, illuminated by throbbing colored lights. The DJs spin oldies as well as house, techno, and disco sounds.

City Square

Via Castelbarco 11 - (02) 58310682
Open Fri & Sat 11pm-3am; Sun 3pm-6:30pm. Cover charge: 20,000 lire (Fri); 25,000 lire (Sat).

A huge vintage movie house and theater was transformed to create City Square, arguably the biggest disco in town. An eclectic program of house, rock, '70s pop, and heavy metal appeals to a broad range of tastes. But late on Friday nights, the DJs pull out their collection of oldies and the dancing goes on until the wee hours. Live concerts by name bands and singers are scheduled periodically.

Gimmi's

Via Cellini 2 - (02) 55188069
Open 10pm-2am. Closed Mon, Wed. Cover charge: 30,000 lire (drink incl).

Disco music and live concerts alternate in this American-style club, decorated with sketches of jazz greats. The acts range from young up-and-comers to established performers. Reservations are a must.

Hollywood

Corso Como 15 - (02) 6598996
Open 10:30pm-3am. Closed Mon. Cover charge: 20,000 lire (Tue-Thu & Sun); 25,000 lire (Fri-Sat).

At this currently hot disco, sedate couples and professorial types can be seen on the dance floor early in the evening. But the temperature rises considerably after midnight, with the arrival of a flashier crowd of models and ad mavens.

Ipotesi

Piazza XXIV Maggio 8 - (02) 8322160
Open 10pm-3am. Closed Mon, Wed. Cover charge: 12,000 lire (Tue, Thu, Fri, Sun); 15,000 lire (Sat).

Spread out over two levels, with lots of room to dance, Ipotesi works on the hypothesis that people (even the university types who gather here) just love to shake their booty. The music evolves over the evening, with techno, house, and acid jazz all represented. Frequent theme evenings spice up the action.

Madame Claude

Piazza Giordano 1 - (02) 76022062
Open 10:30pm-3:30am. Closed Sun. Cover charge: 20,000 lire (Mon-Thu); 25,000 lire (Fri-Sat).

A plush little nightspot, with private tables that can be booked in advance. A frisky mix of underground sounds and oldies gets clubbers up and dancing.

Nepentha

Piazza Diaz 1 - (02) 86464808
Open 9pm-3am. Closed Sun. Cover charge: 20,000 lire (drink incl).

Nothing but the pounding beat of pure, hard-line disco is ever played on these premises. Most of the dancers belong—in one way or another—to Milan's sizable fashion community. Note that the restaurant (a most elegant and quite pricey affair) is open and operative right up until closing time.

Rolling Stones

Corso XXII Marzo 32 - (02) 733172
Open daily 11pm-3am. Cover charge: 20-25,000 lire (drink incl).

Milan's young hipsters have given Rolling Stones their stamp of approval. They throng here to dance to jazz, disco, house, and revival sounds—the beat changes nightly. The club also hosts live performances by name singers and bands.

Sabor Tropical

Via Molino delle Armi 18 - (02) 58313584
Open 10pm-2am. Closed Mon, Wed. Cover charge: 12,000 lire (Tue, Thu, Sun); 20,000 lire (Fri-Sat).

The Latino beat will move you up and out to the floor, to mambo, merengue, and cha cha the night away. The newly renovated Sabor Tropical also stages live concerts, dance performances, and risqué revues.

Shocking Club

Bastioni di Porta Volta 12 - (02) 6595407
Open from 10:30pm. Closed Mon. Cover charge: 20,000 lire (Tue-Thu & Sun); 25,000 lire (Fri-Sat).

Currently Milan's premier nightspot, the Shocking stays open until the last revelers decide to call it a day. Models, intellectuals, musicians, and actors mix on the huge dance floor, moving to a beat that modulates from house, to pop, to current hits. Air conditioning keeps the temperature cool, even when the ambience heats up around midnight.

UB

Via Gatto (corner of Viale Forlanini) (02) 70107329
Open Tue, Thu, Fri, Sat. Cover charge: 20,000 lire (Tue, Thu); 25,000 lire (Fri-Sat).

This former perfume factory is now a trendy club. A big trendy club: 1,000 square meters hold a dance floor, a "food zone" for snacks and midnight crêpe feasts, and a private VIP area curtained off from the curious gaze of the hoi polloi. The merrymakers range from young aristocrats to veteran nighthawks, with a sprinkling of ravers and other "alternative" types. The resident DJs program a mix of house, rock, fusion, and blues.

LIVE ENTERTAINMENT

Bukowsky Pub

Via Santa Sofia 21 - (02) 58305955
Open daily 8:30pm-2am.

A relative newcomer to the city's nocturnal circuit is this English-style pub, already popular for its excellent selection of draft beers. Jazz, blues, or rock performers entertain nightly.

Ca' Bianca Club

Via Lodovico il Moro 117 - (02) 89125777
Open daily 8:30pm-2am. Annual membership: 100,000 lire; 1st drink: 25,000 lire.

The entertainment is always first-rate, whether its a cabaret act, a jazz or blues concert, or a song recital. Lots of local celebrities can be spotted at this posh nightclub, where you can dine in comfort before the show (the restaurant is open to the general public, but reservations are indispensable). For dinner and a show, expect to pay about 90,000 lire.

Capolinea

Via Lodovico il Moro 119 - (02) 89122024
Open 8pm-1:45am. Closed Mon.
This is a mandatory stop for all the best European and international jazz musicians. Even if the program doesn't include a world-famous group, you can be sure that the music will be excellent, often superb. The restaurant stops serving around midnight, but little snacks are on tap until closing time.

Espace Zimba

Via Besenzanica 3 - (02) 40091900
Open 8pm-2am. Closed Mon. Cover charge: 10,000 lire.
Often referred to as the "tropics of Milan," Zimba showcases African-rooted rhythms, along with a little samba and a little reggae. Live music and dance concerts are featured frequently and draw enthusiastic audiences of Africans and West Indians. The food and drinks match the musical themes: tropical cocktails and Caribbean fare are the mainstays.

Grand Hotel Pub

Via Ascanio Sforza 75 - (02) 89516153
Open 8pm-2am. Closed Mon.
New talent (often promising young female singers) is presented regularly at this well-known cabaret, though established names also make regular appearances on the Pub's stage. In summer, the garden nearly doubles the club's capacity.

Grilloparlante

Alzaia Naviglio Grande 36 - (02) 89409321
Open 8pm-2am. Closed Tue.
Night owls in the know come to roost beneath the sloping roof of this inviting club. Soft lights and intimate tables set the scene for talented musicians who perform rock, R & B, jazz, or Brazilian rhythms. The club's restaurant serves first-rate northern Italian fare.

Mirò

Vicolo Fiori 2 - (02) 876016
Open until 2am. Closed Mon. Cover charge: 15,000 lire.

No reference to painter Joan Mirò is intended. The club takes its name from the initials of owners Mimmo and Roberto, who have succeeded in drawing a celebrity-studded crowd (TV personalities, singers, and the like) to their joint venture. Live music is performed nightly, but the really big shows are on Tuesdays and Thursdays, when Mimmo's band takes over the stage.

Le Scimmie

Via Ascanio Sforza 49 - (02) 89402874
Open 8pm-2am. Closed Tue.
Among the clubs of the new generation, Le Scimmie ("Monkeys") is one of the hippest. It has captured a loyal audience with an excellent program of diverse live and recorded jazz, scheduling the best of the new groups alongside established names. Dinner is served far into the night.

Tangram

Via Pezzotti 52 - (02) 89501007
Open 9pm-2am. Closed Sun.
A terrific spot for open-minded music fans who are happiest when they hear it live. Tangram's stage hosts blues and jazz bands as well as funk and rock groups. Most of the musicians are young, but the standards are high, and it's fun to be among the first to discover a bright new performer. While you listen, you can nurse a beer or a drink, and order a sandwich or sweet snack.

Zelig

Viale Monza 140 - (02) 2551774
Open 9pm-2am. Closed Mon. Cover charge: 20,000 lire (for cabaret; drink incl.).
Discover the newest talent on Milan's lively cabaret scene at a club that has launched several nationally known performers. Even if your Italian is too rusty to understand the jokes and the lyrics, stop in anyway for a quick drink at the bar, or to chat and listen to good recorded music in another little room off to the side.

NIGHTCLUBS

Astoria

Piazza S. M. Beltrade 2 - (02) 86460960
Open 10pm-4am. Closed Sun.

Astoria's golden days were back in the '50s and '60s, but it remains a fixture on the city's club circuit. Nostalgia buffs will love the grand staircase swathed in bordeaux velvet and the "classical" statues. Not many Milanesi in sight here, but plenty of tourists (and B-girls).

La Porta d'Oro

Piazza Diaz 3 - (02) 863680
Open daily 10pm-4am.
Behind this "Golden Door," one of the most famous nightspots in town, you'll find clusters of tourists (as well as a few Milanese business execs) applauding the striptease *artistes* and variety acts.

William's

Foro Bonaparte 71 - (02) 877218
Open daily 10:30am-4am.
William's packs them in nightly with sequin-spangled revues imported from Las Vegas and Paris. From jugglers to ventriloquists, acrobats to strippers, the performers are all class acts. The room is irresistibly decked out in a florid '60s style, with yards of red velvet, cushy armchairs, and silk-shaded lamps. Patrons include a large proportion of foreign visitors; the club's 40 hostesses make sure they don't feel lonely for long.

PIANO BARS

Club Due

Via Formentini 2 - (02) 86464807
Open daily 8pm-3am.
Milanese night owls have nursed their insomnia for years at this solidly established club in the Brera district. Downstairs, the karaoke craze has caught on; but upstairs the piano bar offers a mellow, intimate setting, with low tables and low lighting.

El Brellin

Vicolo Lavandai (corner of Alzaia Naviglio Grande 14) - (02) 58101351
Open 8pm-2am. Closed Sun.
The pianist has mastered an impressive repertory of international standards, which you may enjoy over a late supper (served until midnight) in this seductive setting. Reservations are advised.

Gambrinus

Viale Beatrice d'Este 7 - (02) 58301791
Open 6pm-2:30am. Closed Sun.
At this warm, elegant nightspot with comfortable, low sofas and discreet lighting, you can nibble on savory little snacks, sip a cocktail, and listen to good music.

Magia Music Meeting's

Via Salutati 2 - (02) 4813553
Open 10am-3pm & 7pm-3am (Sat 7pm-3am). Closed Sun.
Musicians, record producers on the prowl for fresh talent, and artists of all descriptions forgather at Magia Music Meeting. Emerging young bands try out their acts on an encouraging public. Upstairs, recorded music and rock videos round out the entertainment.

Momus

Via Fiori Chiari 8 - (02) 8056227
Open 8pm-2am. Closed Sun.
Here's a posh, intimate spot for a late supper. A singer and pianist contribute to the romantic mood.

Patuscino

Via Madonnina 21 - (02) 807264
Open daily 9:30pm-3am.
This tiny club is usually jammed with a happy, youthful crowd. The singer and trio boast a repertory that includes compositions from the '30s to the '60s, with a special affection for Milanese songs. Terrific cocktails and midnight pasta feasts.

Ponte di Brera

Via Brera 32 - (02) 876723
Open 10pm-2am. Closed Sun.
Situated a floor above the Bar Giamaica (see *Bars*, above), this was Milan's pioneer piano bar, and it is still a favorite with the city's night people. Maestro Renato Sellani makes the music, and it is not unusual, at evening's end, for the mood to switch from magical and poetic to hot and swinging.

Sayonara

Via I. Nievo 1 - (02) 436635
Open 4pm-2am. Closed Mon.
A quiet, elegant bar in the American mode, where piano music is performed from 10pm on. A perfect place for cocktails close to the Fiera exhibition grounds.

Shops

CONTENTS

Milan's shopkeepers rest on Sundays, except for the three weeks preceding Christmas. Many shops also remain closed on Monday mornings, opening for their usual afternoon hours—generally around 3:30pm. Note, however, that some stores in the center of Milan have adopted an uninterrupted schedule, opening from about 10am to 7:30pm.

ANTIQUES

Tino Bellini

Via Madonnina 12 - (02) 86462086
Open 9:30am-1pm & 3:30-7:30pm. Closed Mon am.

The fine sixteenth- and seventeenth-century pieces presented here come from central Italy, principally Tuscany. Some of the furniture is crafted in solid walnut, while other pieces sport strange and amusing tempera motifs. Handsome sculptures, some dating from the eighteenth century, are often to be found in the shop, as are precious French and Italian tapestries.

Antonella Bensi

Via Santo Spirito 15 - (02) 76023007
Open 9:30am-12:30pm & 3pm-7pm. Closed Mon am.

Here's an elegant shop specialized in European silver and parlor games from the eighteenth and nineteenth centuries. A select group of antique Italian furniture is offered for sale as well.

Mauro Brucoli

Via della Spiga 46 - (02) 76020361
Open 9:30am-7:30pm. Closed Mon am.

Mauro Brucoli deals in two areas of specialization. The first is blond-wood furniture in Neoclassic, Empire, and Directoire styles, and the second is pieces of all types from the period between 1790-1850, including silver, porcelain, furniture, and pictures, from Italy and elsewhere.

Il Cirmolo

Via Lanzone 16 - (02) 867173
Open 9:30am-12:30pm & 3pm-7:30pm. Closed Mon.

In Via Lanzone antique dealers are packed cheek by jowl; Il Cirmolo, specialized in country pieces, is one of the best. You're sure to admire the collection of cupboards, tables, chests, and small household items crafted by artisans of long ago.

L'Oro dei Farlocchi

Via Madonnina 5 - (02) 860589
Open 9:30am-1pm & 3pm-7pm. Closed Mon am.

This stunning shop is the animal (figurine) kingdom, realm of the porcelain bear and the bronze rooster. No matter what their age or origin, the effigies collected here are droll and witty, with interesting histories. Dedicated collectors will be thrilled, of course, but mere browsers may be inspired to start collecting, too, so charming are these artful creatures. In addition to animals, the stock extends to all manner of strange and wonderful antique curios.

La Piazzetta degli Antiquari

Via Turati 6

Gathered in a tiny square on Via Turati (near Piazza della Repubblica) are eight antique shops that offer a trove of silver, religious icons, and precious antique furniture, as well as less unwieldy treasures: majolica pieces, small carpets, and fine old pictures.

The Washerwoman's Last Stand

Shaky but still standing is the last public scrub-your-own laundry in Milan. It's the only example of what the buildings used to look like around here two or three centuries ago—a sort of rough-and-ready tile-roofed barn architecture. It's called *il Brellin della lavandaia* and stands just off the Alzaia Naviglio Grande (the canal towpath) at the heart of the studiously down-at-heel, nightclub-dotted Ticinese neighborhood. We don't recommend *il Brellin* for delicate fabrics, as the canal water that fuels it is pretty rough.

Roberta e Basta

Via Fiori Chiari 2 - (02) 861593
Open 9:30am-12:30pm & 3pm-7:30pm. Closed Mon am.

Furniture and objects from the 1920s and 1930s, all selected with unerring taste, are the core of this shop's holdings. The collection of lamps is particularly rich, including many rare and signed pieces.

Sabatelli

Via Fiori Chiari 5 - (02) 8052688
Open 9:30am-1pm & 3:30pm-7:30pm. Closed Mon.

Situated in the arty Brera district, this gallery majors in antique picture frames dating from the Cinquecento to the Liberty (Art Nouveau) period.

Subert

Via della Spiga 22 - (02) 799594

Opan 10am-1pm & 3pm-7:30pm. Closed Mon.

One of Milan's best-known antique dealers specializes in splendid furniture from the early eighteenth century to the Neoclassical era. The impressive inventory embraces period objets d'art and rare scientific instruments.

Il Tempo Ritrovato

Corso Garibaldi 3 - (02) 876194
Open 10am-1pm & 3:30pm-7:30pm. Closed Mon.

Don't be fooled by first impressions. Yes, the shop's entrance is as sleek and modern as can be, but the real heart of the place beats in the back rooms overlooking the courtyard. There, in a setting of antique floors and vaulted ceilings, you'll find mostly Italian furniture and objets d'art from the eighteenth and nineteenth centuries. The pieces are carefully chosen and meant for daily use rather than mere display, and all blend beautifully with contemporary décors.

La Tenda Gialla

Via Castelfidardo 2 - (02) 29000981
Open 10am-1pm & 3pm-7:30pm. Closed Mon am.

Pieces from early in this century are featured in this delightful store. The interesting, often amusing collection includes jewelry, lamps, American costume jewelry from the '30s and '40s, glass, boxes, posters, and a variety of objects that are useful or just plain decorative. A limited selection of furniture is available as well, primarily small tables, armchairs, and settees.

BOOKS

American Bookstore

Via Camperio 16 - (02) 878920
Open 10am-7:30pm (Sat 10am-1pm & 2:30-7:30pm). Closed Mon am.

For a selection of English and American books that ranges far and wide.

L'Archivolto

Via Marsala 2 - (02) 6590842, (02) 29010444
Open 10am-1pm & 3:30pm-7:30pm. Closed Mon.

113

Books on architecture, urbanism, design, and local history are showcased here. Along with the foremost Italian and foreign writings on those subjects, L'Archivolto stocks a choice selection of antiquarian books, drawings, and prints (including many handsome prints of Milan) and hosts frequent exhibitions.

Dell'Automobile

Corso Venezia 43 - (02) 76006624
Open 9am-12:30pm & 3pm-7pm. Closed Sat pm.
Speed demons may take home volumes devoted to their beloved Ferraris, Maseratis, and—yes—Fiats from this exemplary bookstore, which also stocks shelves of road maps and tourist guides in a variety of languages, foreign and familiar.

Al Castello

Via San Giovanni sul Muro 9 - (02) 875347
Open 9:30am-1:30pm & 3:30pm-7:30pm. Closed Mon am.
A small, elegant bookshop that specializes in volumes on collecting. What's more, the owners practice what they preach, staging worthwhile exhibits of collectibles and handcrafts. Those interested in the applied arts will appreciate the selection of lavishly illustrated books on fashion, fabrics, graphics, illustration, advertising, and design, all fields in which Italian artists excel.

Cavour Internazionale

Via Fatebenefratelli 23 - (02) 6595644
Open 9:30am-7:30pm. Closed Mon am.
English- (and other) language novels and poetry collections are stocked in cheerful profusion here. Art books and exhibition catalogs are a specialty, and there's an enticing section full of old and rare volumes.

Centro Botanico

Via dell'Orso 16 - (02) 86464474
Open 10am-1pm & 2pm-7pm. Closed Sat.
Books are not the sole attraction at this airy, be-frescoed botanical center—its exhibitions of rare flowers and plants draw avid gardeners who can't read a single word of Italian. As for the opulently illustrated volumes on gardens and gardening, the pictures are worth a thousand words.

Cooperativa Librai Lombardi

Pinacoteca di Brera, Via Brera 28 - (02) 877809
Open 9am-6pm (Fri-Sat 9am-2pm; Sun 9am-1pm). Closed Mon.
The Cooperativa does business at a counter inside the Pinacoteca di Brera Museum, selling Italian and foreign art books, monographs and exhibition catalogs as well as an impressive selection of slides of works on view in the museum.

Del Corso

Corso Buenos Aires 49 - (02) 29516798
Open 9am-7:30pm. Closed Mon am.
This huge book emporium stocks a vast assortment of volumes, but we think its art and photography section merits particular mention. Travelers take note: Del Corso also stocks a wealth of guidebooks.

Einaudi

Via Manzoni 40 - (02) 76005164
Open 9am-1pm & 3:30pm-7pm. Closed Mon am.
Appropriately situated on a street named for one of Italy's finest writers, Einaudi occupies Milan's cultural high ground. Little schlock is on sale at this intellectuals' bookshop, where you'll find a gratifying selection of English-language volumes, art books, and exhibition catalogs.

English Bookshop

Via Ariosto (corner of Via Mascheroni) (02) 4694468
Open 9am-7pm. Closed Mon am.
Literate Brits abroad (and Americans who believe that "English" is their native language) will find a complete selection of reading matter here.

FMR (Franco Maria Ricci)

Via Durini 19 - (02) 798444
Open 9:30am-1pm & 3pm-7:30pm. Closed Mon am.
Is this a temple or a bookstore? A bit of both, really. Franco Maria Ricci is a contemporary high priest of high culture, who produces books that many consider to be works of art. Limited editions are printed in Bodoni type on handmade paper, and bound in black and gold silk. Among the collectors' volumes here, sold amid marble and ivory columns, are books on such noted artist/personalities as Erté and Tamara de Lempicka.

Feltrinelli

Corso Buenos Aires 20 - (02) 29400731
Via Manzoni 12 - (02) 795826
Open daily 9am-7:30pm.
On the ground floor a fully stocked newsstand greets all comers with the daily of their choice, while upstairs an abundance of fiction, history, philosophy, and biography titles (in English and other languages) awaits those lucky enough to possess a longer attention span.

Gallini

Via Gorani 8 - (02) 72000398
Open 10:30am-12:30pm & 3pm-7pm. Closed Mon am, Sat.
Whether your taste runs to classic or contemporary, the sheet music you're seeking is surely in stock at this commendable little establishment. Of course, you'll find books, too: antique volumes as well as modern histories and biographies of musicians and composers.

Del Giallo

Piazza San Nazaro 3 - (02) 58307802
Open 9:30am-12:30pm & 3:30pm-7:30pm. Closed Mon am.
For chills, thrills, and mystery in your native language (or in Italian) this is the place. Out-of-print and hard-to-find editions make this bookshop a browsing paradise for mystery addicts. Don't miss the original cover drawings done for publisher Mondadori's thriller series—they'll slay you!

Hoepli

Via Hoepli 5 - (02) 864871
Open daily 9am-7pm.
This is Milan's biggest and best-stocked bookstore, with everything from avant-garde literature and do-it-yourself manuals to high-priced, limited-edition art books. The foreign-language selection is large and wide ranging.

Marco

Galleria Passarella 2 - (02) 795866
Open 9:30am-7:30pm. Closed Mon am.
The handy newsstand section of this large, centrally located bookstore stays open late and stocks a variety of international dailies and magazines.

Di Milano

Via Meravigli 18 - (02) 86453154
Open daily 9:30am-7:30pm (Sat 9:30am-1pm & 3pm-7:30pm; Mon 3pm-7:30pm).
An obligatory stop for Milan's many fans. The city's history, culinary traditions, proverbs, and legends will be an open book to you after a visit to this shop. Also on hand are picture books illustrating the beauties of Milan, guidebooks, and calendars.

Alla Porta Romana

Corso di Porta Romana 51 - (02) 5510948
Open 9:30am-1pm & 3pm-8pm. Closed Mon am.
For an interesting assortment of books in English as well as in French and Italian, this shop is a good bet. Specialized sections are devoted to archaeology, art, sports, and graphics.

San Babila

Corso Monforte 2 - (02) 799219
Open 9am-1:30pm & 3pm-7:30pm. Closed Mon am.
The owner and the manager of this notable bookshop are exceptionally cultivated individuals who will guide you knowledgeably through their stock of Italian and foreign literature, essays, and volumes on art, antiques, and collecting.

Dello Spettacolo

Via Terraggio 11 - (02) 86451730
Open 9:30am-1pm & 3pm-7pm. Closed Mon am.
This bookstore subscribes to the belief that there's no business like show business. Witness the Italian and foreign tomes on theater, dance, the circus, puppets, and even television that overflow the shelves of this *simpatico* shop.

Il Trovatore

Via Poerio 3 - (02) 76001656
Open 9:30am-12:30pm & 3pm-7pm. Closed Mon am.
All to the glory of the lyric art, this bookstore sells rare and antique volumes on opera and singers as well as sheet music and librettos. Owner Tiziana Vercesi prides herself on her ability to track down elusive editions for her clients.

DEPARTMENT STORES

Coin

Piazza Cinque Giornate 1a - (02) 55192083
Corso Vercelli 30 - (02) 48005160
Piazzale Cantore 12 - (02) 58104385
Piazzale Loreto - (02) 2826179
Open 9:30am-12:45pm & 3pm-7:30pm. Closed Mon am.
This large department store, part of a nationwide chain, specializes in not-too-pricey clothing for the whole family.

Fiorucci

Galleria Passarella 1 (corner of Corso Vittorio Emanuele) - (02) 76003276
Open 10am-7:30pm. Closed Sun, Mon am.
Four floors of fun, frivolous, fashionable merchandise. Look on the upper level for jeans and colorful knitwear; the lower floors house in-shop boutiques that feature an eclectic array of housewares and decorative accents, fashions for men and women, stationery, and toiletries.

La Rinascente

Piazza Duomo - (02) 88521
Open 9:30am-7:30pm. Closed Mon am.
Akin to America's Bullocks and Macy's, La Rinascente is a large, mid- to upper-range department store known for good service. Clothing, shoes, hosiery, lingerie, housewares, cosmetics, jewelry—it's all here. The store's own label, Ellerre, signs a good-looking and fairly priced line of fashions for men, women, and kids.

Standa

Via Torino (corner of Via Palla) - (02) 864489
Piazza Cairoli - (02) 878437
Corso Buenos Aires 35 - (02) 279297
Via Sarpi 33 - (02) 317252
Piazza IV Novembre 5 - (02) 67071872
Corso Vercelli 8 - (02) 4690329
Open 9am-7:30pm (Corso Vercelli 9am-12:55pm & 3pm-7:30pm). Closed Mon am.
A reliable, middle-of-the-road department store that can be counted on to supply the basics in clothing, accessories, and other necessities of life.

Upim

Via Torino (corner of Via Spadari)
(02) 86460945
Via Cuneo (corner of Via Marghera)
(02) 4814800
Corso XXII Marzo 15 - (02) 5456176
Piazzale Loreto 5 - (02) 26143389
Corso San Gottardo 29 - (02) 8357392
San Babila (corner of Corso Venezia)
(02) 76020736
Open daily 9:30am (9am at Via Cuneo & Corso San Gottardo)-7:30pm; Mon 2:30pm (1pm at Via Torino, Corso Buenos Aires & San Babila)-7:30pm.
Like Standa (above), Upim is a moderately priced, mid-level department store that's recommended for everyday essentials.

Thieves at the Court of Miracles

Oh Bej, Oh Bej shout the hawkers at Milan's patron saint's fair, held each December 6-8 in Piazza Sant'-Ambrogio. Once upon a time it was packed with one-of-a-kind stands selling precious antiques, vintage toys, unusual clothing, and down-home snacks like roasted chestnuts and saffron risotto. Today, it would take a miracle by Saint Ambrose to bring the good buys back, but the *Fiera degli Oh Bej, Oh Bej* is jumping all the same. It just goes to prove that wonders will never cease.

FASHION

■ CLOTHING

Adriana Mode

Corso Buenos Aires 65 - (02) 29405258
Open 9:30am-12:30pm & 3:30pm-7:30pm. Closed Mon am.
Glamorous fashions for women. From impressive suits to extravagant evening clothes, everything here is culled from the best international designers' collections. Adriana also carries its own exclusive line of blouses and knits in both classic and utterly up-to-the-minute designs.

Giorgio Armani Boutique
Via Sant'Andrea 9 - (02) 76003234
Open daily 10am-1:30pm & 3pm-7:30pm (Sat 10am-7:30pm; Mon 3pm-7:30pm).
Armani's top range of supremely sophisticated, streamlined clothing and accessories for men and women are displayed in a tony, tasteful setting of blond wood.

Giorgio Armani Emporio Bambino
Via Durini 27 - (02) 794248
Open 10am-1:30pm & 3pm-7:30pm (Sat 10am-7:30pm). Closed Mon am.
Now you can dress your little ones in the same divine Armani duds in which you outfit yourself—assuming, of course, that money is no object.

Giorgio Armani Emporio Uomo e Donna
Via Durini 24 - (02) 76003030
Open daily 10am-7:30pm (Mon 3pm-7:30pm).
Armani's "Emporio" carries somewhat sportier clothes than the parent boutique, at prices that are a trifle easier to swallow.

Bardelli
Corso Magenta 13 - (02) 86450734
Open 9:30am-1pm & 3pm-7pm. Closed Mon am.
Tweedy British elegance for men and women. Stylish suits and shirts (including some custom-tailored items), sportswear, and knits are featured in the menswear section, while women are pampered with the best Italian and imported ready-to-wear.

Luisa Beccaria
Via Formentini 1 - (02) 876840
Open 10am-1:30pm & 2:30pm-7:30pm. Closed Mon am.
This shop is an exclusive showcase for smart, subtle clothing executed in stunning fabrics by young Milanese designer Luisa Beccaria. In addition to her utterly feminine—but never saccharine—women's wear, a delightful line of clothes for children is sold in the boutique next door.

Laura Biagiotti
Via Borgospesso 19 - (02) 799659
Open 10am-1:30pm & 3pm-7:30pm. Closed Mon am.
Superbly cut clothing in luxurious fabrics (cashmere, linen) for men and women. Though by no means cheap, Biagiotti's designs are less expensive here than in the U.S.

Bianca e Blu
Via De Amicis 53 - (02) 8361139
Open 10am-12:30pm & 3:30pm-7pm. Closed Mon am.
There's the feel of a designer's atelier about this shop, which is exclusively devoted to clothing created by Monica Bolzoni. Her extraordinary suits and dresses, displayed in a little gallery, are cleverly balanced between classics with a French haute-couture flavor and more contemporary, "Milanese" pieces. Beautiful accessories.

Biffi
Corso Genova 6 - (02) 89402426
Via Filzi 45 - (02) 67072175
Open 9am-1pm & 3pm-7:30pm. Closed Mon am.
Biffi is the city's best source of fearlessly fashionable clothes, with a selection that tilts toward the avant-garde without sacrificing wearability. Neither sex is neglected: women will find designs by Azzedine Alaïa, Norma Kamali, Irié, Sybilla, Pour Toi, Yamamoto, and Fusco, while the menswear comes from CP Company, New York New York, and Guido Pellegrini.

Boggi
Via Dante 17 - (02) 86463562
Open 9:30am-12:30pm & 3pm-7:30pm. Closed Mon am.
Men who favor a classic, Anglo-Italian look can be assured of finding just the togs to suit them here. Especially attractive are the Shetland and cashmere sweaters in a rainbow of tints, and the soft, wide-wale corduroy trousers. In addition to shirts and ties for the office, Boggi sells good-looking weekend wear, too.

Brigatti
Corso Venezia 15 - (02) 76000273
Open 10am-7pm. Closed Mon am.
In business for more than 100 years, Brigatti has a solid family tradition as purveyors of sportswear and sporting equipment. At the turn of the century, it was the

first in Milan to sell golf clubs, and it still boasts a top-notch workshop, should your putter need repair. In addition to sports gear, you'll find fine Harris tweed caps, luxurious cashmere sweaters, and superb footwear.

Brusadelli

Via Manzoni 15 - (02) 86464018
Open 10am-1:30pm & 2:30pm-7pm. Closed Mon am.
At Brusadelli's elegant women's wear boutique, you'll find famous-label clothing and an appealing line of exclusive designs, some classic and some contemporary. Don't leave without a look at the wonderful accessories.

Enrico Coveri

Via San Pietro all'Orto (corner of Corso Matteotti) - (02) 76005977
Open daily 9:30am-1:30pm & 2:30pm-7:30pm (Mon 3pm-7:30pm).
Stylish casual wear for men; youthful, imaginative fashions for women.

Dolce & Gabbana

Via della Spiga 2 - (02) 76001155
Open 9:30am-12:30pm & 3:30pm-7:30pm. Closed Mon am.
These provocative Sicilian stylists don't follow fashion, they make it. Their no-holds-barred designs have seduced Madonna, among others; even better, the clothes are not only hip, they're beautifully made.

Effebieffe

Via Marsala 7 - (02) 6598069
Open 9:30am-1pm & 3pm-7:30pm. Closed Mon am.
A mouthwatering collection of English knits, from cashmeres in every weight to handmade Shetland sweaters (in no way comparable to the ubiquitous machine-made article) is displayed here, along with classically styled suits for men and women, cut from first-rate English fabrics, and accessories (silk ties and cravats, socks and so on) crafted with distinctive British flair.

Eliogabalo

Corso di Porta Ticinese (corner of Piazza Sant'Eustorgio) - (02) 8357290
Open 9:30am-1pm & 3pm-7:30pm. Closed Mon am.

The store's trademark is youthful, slightly adventurous fashion for hip young men and women. The clothes are original (though not wild), affordable, and accessorized with wit and humor. Stylish shoes complete the look.

Erreuno

Via della Spiga 15 - (02) 795575
Open daily 10am-7pm (Mon 3pm-7pm).
Fresh, attractive, sometimes whimsical women's wear. Erreuno's clothes are quite the rage in fashion-conscious Milan.

Etro

Via Montenapoleone 5 - (02) 76005049
Open 9:30am-1pm & 3:30pm-7:30pm. Closed Mon am.
Etro's sumptuous, sophisticated cashmere creations get star billing in this chic boutique. Snuggly cardigans for women and luxurious dressing gowns for men are arrayed alongside luscious accessories: shawls in jewel-tone wool challis, silk ties, leather bags and belts.

Fendi

Via Sant'Andrea 16 - (02) 76021617
Open daily 10am-1:30pm & 2pm-7:30pm (Mon 3pm-7:30pm).
Extravagantly priced, gorgeously detailed clothing and fabulous furs are the Fendi sisters' signature.

Gianfranco Ferré

Via della Spiga 11 - (02) 794864
Open daily 10am-1:30pm & 2:30pm-7pm (Mon 3pm-7pm).
Stunning, high-priced, quintessentially Italian clothing and accessories (including shoes) for women and men are enticingly displayed in Ferré's flagship store.

Alberta Ferretti

Via Montenapoleone 21 - (02) 76003095
Open daily 10am-1:30pm & 2:30pm-7pm (Mon 3pm-7pm).
More and more a name to be reckoned with, Ferretti's line of meticulously finished clothing for women ranges from casual jeans to flirty party frocks.

Gemelli

Corso Vercelli 16 - (02) 48000057, (02) 433404
Open 9am-12:30pm & 3pm-7:30pm. Closed Mon am.

Contemporary classics and sportswear for men and women are Gemelli's specialty. You'll find lots of clothes sporting major designer labels, including cashmeres by Fissore and Malo Tricot and styles by Blumarine and Thierry Mugler. Men can purchase ready-to-wear by Cerruti, Hitman, Filippo Alpi, and Henry Cotton or patronize the shop's custom tailor, who makes beautifully personalized shirts, jackets, and overcoats.

Isa Genolini

Via Boccaccio 45 - (02) 4812739
Open 9:30am-12:30pm & 3pm-7pm. Closed Sat.
Milan's smart set comes to Isa Genolini's lovely shop (it's housed in a handsome old palazzo) for drop-dead evening clothes and impeccably tailored, ladylike suits.

Guardaroba

Via Solferino 9 - (02) 86452847
Open 9:30am-7:30pm. Closed Mon am.
We admire the exclusive designs produced by Guardaroba's own manufacturers, in a young, spirited style that pleases chic Milanese matrons as much as it does their daughters. Decidedly youthful sportswear for men is offered as well, along with trendy accessories. Porselli's pretty and comfortable ballerina flats are available here in a wide range of colors.

Gucci

Via Montenapoleone 5 - (02) 76013050
Open daily 10am-7:30pm (Mon 3:30pm-7:30pm).
Gucci's complete line of finely tailored apparel for men and women—but not its famous shoes and bags—is sold at this spacious, two-level shop. The neighboring store (Via Montenapoleone, 2) can supply you with all the shoes and G-stamped leather goods you'll ever need. Thankfully, Gucci's latest bags, wallets and accessories make more discreet use of the logo.

Krizia

Via della Spiga 23 - (02) 76008429
Open daily 10am-1:30pm & 2:30pm-7pm (Mon 3pm-7pm).
Famous for bold knitwear, Krizia produces playful outfits and loads of stylish accessories for the whole family—and this large shop stocks the complete collection. Prices are high but not daunting.

Marisa

Via Cino del Duca 2 - (02) 76021054
Via Sant'Andrea 10 & 1 - (02) 76001363, (02) 76001416
Via della Spiga 52 - (02) 76002082
Open 10am-1pm & 2:30pm-7pm. Closed Mon am.
These three boutiques fairly burst with fashionable women's wear. The first has a young, avant-garde slant with designs by Moschino, Rifat Ozbek, and Physic du Rôle. The second is just as stylish, in a more refined and classic mode: cashmeres by Fissore and collections by Aspesi Fusco e Jil Sanders. The Via della Spiga store sells elegantly understated fashions.

Enrica Massei

Via Brera 11 - (02) 862540
Open daily 10am-7pm (Mon 3pm-7pm).
The place for cashmere: softest sweaters, clingy dresses, and cozy shawls.

Missoni

Via Sant'Andrea - (02) 76003555
Open 10am-1pm & 2:30pm-7pm. Closed Mon am.
These renowned knits in jewel-like colors, with their touchable textures and decorative patterns, are covetable but ever so costly.

Neglia Le Diable

Corso Venezia 2 - (02) 795231
Open 10am-1:30pm & 3pm-7:30pm. Closed Mon am.
This shop is a must for men who like to dress in a classic style sparked with a touch of contemporary flair—the sort of look that gives Milanese men their inimitable chic. The sportswear and accessories are exceptionally attractive.

Oldani

Via Serbelloni 7 - (02) 76001087
Open 10am-7:30pm. Closed Mon am.
Oldani offers decidedly classic styles, with a pronounced preference for the understated look of fine British tailoring. The handsome suits for men and women are Oldani exclusives, made from superb Italian and English fabrics, and the woolens and knits are lovely.

119

Renna Sport

Piazza Diaz 1 - (02) 8053728
Open 9:30am-7:30pm. Closed Mon am.
Known for fabulous leatherwear (its own label as well as such famous names as La Matta), Renna Sport offers classic fashions for men and women and some very classy sportswear from such top designers as Armani, Allegri, and Moschino.

Mila Schön

Via Montenapoleone 2 - (02) 781190
Open daily 10am-7:30pm (Mon 3pm-7:30pm).
Schön creates handsome, distinctive clothes for day and evening; cashmere shawls, handsomely tailored suits, and men's silk ties are a specialty.

Ken Scott

Via Montenapoleone 10 - (02) 76023211
Open 10am-7pm. Closed Mon am.
Since he burst on the scene in the late '60s, Ken Scott has drawn lots of attention in Milan with his signature floral prints. Discover his fabrics, ready-to-wear, leather goods, umbrellas, and household linens in this charming shop on fashion's high street.

Pupi Solari

Piazza Tommaseo (corner of Via Mascheroni) (02) 463325
Open 10am-1:30pm & 2:30pm-7pm. Closed Mon am.
One can sense the very personal taste behind the clothes presented in this elegant yet comfortable boutique. Though classic, the designs have a pleasing freshness about them. The cordial staff will prepare a cup of tea for you to sip while making your selection. The children's section is equally charming.

Luciano Soprani

Via della Spiga 19 - (02) 781469
Open daily 10am-1:30pm & 3pm-7:30pm (Mon 3:30pm-7:30pm).
An established star on Italy's fashion scene, Soprani designs well-crafted, up-to-the-minute women's wear at prices that won't impoverish you. Don't miss the shoe collection.

Nanni Strada

Via Gesù 4 - (02) 76014321
Open daily 9:30am-7pm.

Designer Nanni Strada's personal style is a savvy mix of elegance and common sense. Her latest line is a collection of traveling clothes, the summer models executed in splendid Solbiati linen (with pleating reminiscent of Fortuny's turn-of-the-century styles), the rest in silk and pleated wool. This is simple, supremely wearable clothing designed to need little ironing. Handsome quilted or embroidered jackets complete the attractive collection.

La Tenda

Via Solferino (corner of Galleria San Marco) (02) 6575804
Open 9:30am-1pm & 3pm-7:30pm. Closed Mon am.
Women's wear with wit and polish. La Tenda's clothes for day, night, and sport include Grazia Fava's extraordinary (and hard-to-find) creations, as well as designs by Moschino, Virginia, and Bogey's.

Tincati

Piazza Oberdan 2 - (02) 29518358
Via Verri 1 - (02) 76002498
Open 9:30am-7pm (10am-7:30pm Via Verri). Closed Mon am.
Impeccable taste is everywhere in evidence at Tincati, where classic British tailoring prevails. The men's department features shirts by Truzzi and Burini; cashmere sweaters; suits and outerwear by Brioni, St. Andrew's, Aquascutum, and Burberry; handmade shoes; exclusive sport jackets cut from English cloth; and Ralph Lauren's Polo sportswear line. The women's wear is equally select, with such famous labels as Byblos, Aspesi, and Basile.

Trussardi

Via Sant'Andrea 5 - (02) 76020380
Open daily 10am-1pm & 2:30pm-7:30pm (Mon 3:30pm-7:30pm).
Once known strictly for its greyhound-logo leather goods (which are still as commendable as ever), Trussardi has expanded its line to include a full range of smart non-leather clothing and accessories.

Valentino

Via Santo Spirito 3 (women's wear) (02) 76006478
Via Montenapoleone 20 (menswear) (02) 76020285

Open daily 10am-7pm (Mon 3pm-7pm).
If you're jetting off for dinner with Monaco's royal family or tea with Princess Di, you'd best stop first at Italy's most famous designer's for a suitably impressive ensemble. The prices reflect Valentino's peerless craftsmanship and his tremendous stature in the fashion world.

Versace

Via della Spiga 4 (women's wear) - (02) 705451
Via Verri (corner of Via Montenapoleone) (menswear) - (02) 76008528
Open daily 10am-7pm (Mon 3pm-7pm).
Sensuous, spirited Italian fashion for men and women. We're particularly fond of the menswear (notably the hip sports jackets and dashing suits) and the look-at-me accessories for both sexes.

■ DISCOUNT DESIGN

Salvagente

Via Fratelli Bronzetti - (02) 76110328
Open 10am-12:30pm & 3pm-7pm (Wed & Sat 10am-7pm). Closed Mon am.
The trek out here is worth your while, for this is Milan's oldest established discount warehouse. Sure, not every item is a winner but a little rummaging among the orderly racks of clothing and accessories will surely yield a few designer goodies at unbeatable prices. Lots of big names are represented.

Emmi Curradi

Via Alberto Mario 32 - (02) 48193605
Open daily 10am-7pm (Mon 4pm-7pm).
End lots and samples with high-fashion labels (all the best Italian designers are on hand) are marked way, way down.

■ JEWELRY

Anaconda

Via Bergamini 7 - (02) 58303668
Open 10:30am-2pm & 3pm-7:30pm. Closed Mon.
Anaconda's clean-lined, contemporary creations in silver, a combination of silver and gold or, like a recent group of necklaces, in raw silk and gold, are striking and unusual. Like the best minimalist art, these ornaments are modern and spare, yet somehow poetic.

Maria Grazia Baldan

Via Fiori Chiari 14 - (02) 86463559
Open 10am-1pm & 3pm-7:30pm. Closed Mon.
Every jewel that leaves Maria Grazia Baldan's luxurious workshop is unique. Her highly individual style has an indefinably Asian flavor; some particularly lovely pieces combine antique Chinese jade with ivory and semiprecious gemstones from India. Custom orders are accepted.

Gianmaria Buccellati

Corte di Via Montenapoleone 12 - (02) 799944
Open 9:30am-1pm & 3pm-7:30pm. Closed Mon am.
Every jewel in the shop is personally designed by Gianmaria and his son, Andrea, then produced according to age-old methods by master craftsmen. Precious stones, gold, and silver combine in a wondrous variety of classic and modern ornaments.

Mario Buccellati

Via Montenapoleone 4 - (02) 76002153
Open 9:30am-12:30pm & 3pm-7:30pm. Closed Mon am.
It is said that the renowned writer, Gabriele D'Annunzio, always purchased gifts for his many mistresses at Buccellati. We can't imagine any lady refusing a finely wrought bracelet or gemstone ring from this prestigious firm, whose origins date back to the Renaissance. Buccellati is also noted for its silver flatware and serving pieces, and for delightful animal figures carved in sterling.

Calderoni

Via Montenapoleone 8 - (02) 76001293
Open 10am-1pm & 3pm-7:30pm. Closed Mon am.
Calderoni has crafted supremely refined jewels for over a century, specializing in opulent creations that partner the rarest gems with precious metals.

Desart

Via Albricci 2 - (02) 8053829
Corso Buenos Aires 61 - (02) 29405004
Open 10am-1pm & 3:30pm-7pm. Closed Mon am.
James Riviere is one of the most respected names in contemporary jewelry

design. He was one of the first to combine precious metals with such "lesser" materials as leather and unusual minerals like titanium. His creations for men have been epoch-making as well. Geometrical forms and a certain sculptural quality distinguish Riviere's designs.

Il Discanto

Via Turati 7 - (02) 29003557
Open 9:30am-1pm & 3pm-7:30pm. Closed Mon am.

Il Discanto is an exclusive showcase for antique ethnic jewelry. The pieces are chosen with rare taste and connoisseurship from all over the world, with the majority hailing from Africa and the Orient. Look for gorgeous coral, antique amber, and Indian gold pieces.

Falliva Panizzi

Corso Magenta 5 - (02) 804829
Open 9am-12:30pm & 3pm-7:30pm. Closed Mon.

Falliva Panizzi's eye-catching window displays have already won several awards, with their dramatic arrangements of jewels and mysterious protagonists in theatrical settings. The ornaments themselves are anything but commonplace: luxurious but unostentatious, classic yet unmistakably modern.

Faraone

Via Montenapoleone 7a - (02) 76013656
Open 10am-7pm. Closed Mon.

Faraone is one of Milan's foremost jewelry firms. In addition to classic and contemporary designs in precious metals and stones (the necklaces are stupendous), this firm crafts remarkable ornaments that combine gold and silver with other metals, such as steel. The antique department displays an interesting selection of English plate from the seventeenth to the early twentieth century.

Marangoni

Viale Papiniano 38 - (02) 4812275
Open daily 9am-12:30pm & 2:30pm-7:30pm.

For nearly 50 years, the Marangoni family's atelier has produced ornaments and accessories for the Teatro alla Scala as well as fancy buttons, buckles, and belts for famous French and Italian clothing designers. But Marangoni also sells beauti-

fully crafted costume jewelry to the general public; some of the pieces have a pronounced antique flavor, while others sport a contemporary look.

Merù

Via Solferino 3 - (02) 86460700
Open 9:30am-12:30pm & 2:30pm-7:30pm. Closed Mon am.

The Merù brothers' tiny boutique is a gold mine of youthful fashion jewelry. We loved the romantic enameled pieces, the assorted earrings ranging from microscopic studs to huge hoops, and the clever necklaces and bracelets that boyfriends can wear, too. An atelier next door will produce custom pieces on request.

Misani

Piazza Liberty 8 - (02) 793903
Open 10am-1pm & 3pm-7:30pm. Closed Mon.

Ivo Misani's creations are jeweled sculptures that combine gold (often hammered gold) with materials that provide a strong contrast, such as Plexiglas or leather. The men's line is striking, particularly the watches, which combine gold with steel or semiprecious stones.

L'Orafo nel Tempo

Via Gonzaga 5 - (02) 72010654
Open 9:30am-1pm & 3:30pm-7:30pm. Closed Mon.

The jewels presented in these shops are all faithful reproductions of archaeological finds from ancient civilizations—Aztec, Egyptian, Greek, Etruscan, and Roman. It is startling to see how extraordinarily modern these designs seem, even though they're thousands of years old.

Pomellato

Via San Pietro all'Orto (corner of Corso Matteotti) - (02) 76006086
Open 9:30am-12:30pm & 3:30pm-7:30pm. Closed Mon am.

The Pomellato name and style are internationally known. Alongside the jewels and its famous gold chains, Pomellato displays such luxuries as superb silver tea services, silver flatware, boxes, and gift items for men (buckles, pens, studs, and the like) fashioned from silver and gold, all in exquisite taste.

Scavia

Via della Spiga 9 - (02) 76021610
Open 10am-1pm & 3pm-7:30pm. Closed Mon am.

Sara Scavia and her son, Fulvio, are the designing minds behind this contemporary collection of jewelry and clocks, all handcrafted in unusual materials.

■ LEATHER & LUGGAGE

Il Bisonte

Via Madonnina 10 - (02) 86460145
Open 10am-1pm & 2:30pm-7:30pm. Closed Mon am.

This Florentine firm is famous for youthful designs executed in rugged leathers. Everyone has seen and admired Il Bisonte's luggage, shoulder bags, and briefcases in untreated leather, but not everyone knows that for winter the firm stocks a small collection of nicely cut, warm and cuddly sheepskin coats for men and women.

Bocci

Via San Pietro all'Orto (corner of Corso Vittorio Emanuele) - (02) 76020839
Open 10am-1:30pm & 2:30pm-7pm. Closed Mon am.

From chic leather slippers to impressive leather trunks, from shaving and makeup bags to tasteful luggage pieces in every imaginable size (in modern aluminum or soft, squashy leather), here you will find a wealth of handsome accessories for traveling with class. The men's department also carries a select assortment of briefcases.

Bonera

Via Pirelli 17 - (02) 66986488
Open 10am-2pm & 3pm-7pm (Sat 10am-12:30pm & 3pm-7pm). Closed Mon am.

Traditional styles for sport and formal occasions predominate at Bonera, but fashion trends are not ignored. Suitcases and traveling bags are a specialty, and we like the wide assortment of belts and small leather goods. There's a fully stocked men's department, too.

Coppola e Toppo

Via Manzoni 20 - (02) 76021459
Open 9am-1pm & 3:30pm-7:30pm. Closed Mon am.

Exceptionally lovely evening bags are the attraction here, many of them hand-embroidered or all aglitter with handsewn sequins. For day, there's a good selection of classic and sport bags, including some handsome designs by Redwall.

Circus Minimalist

Staggering, isn't it, that an Imperial seat the likes of Milan has no Roman ruins? Actually, there are a few half-submerged antiquities in town. One of the largest Roman circuses ever built is hiding under the following *Vie*: Brisa, Morigi, Medici, Torchio, Circo, Cappuccio, and Luini. It peers out with a marble eye at the intersection of Via Circo and Via Torchio, a stone's throw from another relic, an Imperial Palace (in Via Brisa) that is now little more than a royal mess.

Eve

Via Mascheroni 12 - (02) 468732
Open 9:30am-1pm & 3:30pm-7:30pm. Closed Mon am.
Via Solferino 11 - (02) 8052931
Open 9:30am-1pm & 3pm-7pm. Closed Mon am.

Soft, roomy leather bags; clean-lined, sophisticated city bags in glamorous colors; elegant briefcases and luggage in all sorts of sizes and shapes—this stylish shop is a gold mine for chic leather accessories that are always in step with the latest fashions.

Furla

Via Orefici 11 - (02) 8053944
Corso Venezia 21 - (02) 780714
Open 9:30am-1pm & 3pm-7:30pm. Closed Mon am.

Furla's exceptionally broad selection of day and evening bags comes in appealing colors and high-fashion shapes. We also like the attractive collection of belts and the (small) group of luggage pieces in leather or a sporty combination of leather and fabric.

Monday, like Sunday, is a day of rest for many shopkeepers.

123

Prada

Galleria Vittorio Emanuele 63 - (02) 876979
Via della Spiga 1 - (02) 76008636
Via Sant'Andrea 21 - (02) 76001426
Open daily 10am-1:30pm & 2:30pm-7pm (Mon 3pm-7pm).

A stylish emporium for leather accessories, established in Milan since 1913, Prada occupies the oldest shop in Milan's Galleria. The merchandise is diverse and eminently tasteful: crocodile bags, glove-soft leather bags, and youthful leather-and-fabric designs. An eye-catching display of travel bags stands in one corner, and in another is a choice collection of shoes for men and women. Prada's elegant ready-to-wear has captured the interest of a growing number of high-fashion customers.

Serapian

Via Jommelli 35 - (02) 2826041
Open 8am-noon & 2pm-7pm. Closed Sat am.

Serapian's is not to be found in the Golden Rectangle of chic Milanese shops—it is a factory outlet that sells fine leather goods at terrific prices. The huge selection comprises casual and dressy bags (we particularly admire the woven-leather styles and the sporty canvas designs with leather fittings), attractive wallets, change purses, and other small leather goods. Don't miss the covetable leather luggage, leather jackets, and sheepskin coats for men and women—the workmanship is first-rate.

Simone

Viale Coni Zugna 58 - (02) 58101325
Corso Genova 6 - (02) 89403990
Open 9am-12:30pm & 3pm-7:30pm. Closed Mon am.

This is the place for leather bags and accessories geared to young, fashion-conscious shoppers. Styles range from the whimsical to the sophisticated, with a nifty choice of suitcases and slouchy leather "grips" that harken back to another age. In the men's department, take a look at the painstakingly crafted briefcases and portfolios.

■ SHOES

Bagnara

Via San Vittore 2 - (02) 86452526
Open 9:30am-7:30pm. Closed Mon am.

Once upon a time, only custom footwear was available at Bagnara. Today, while the tradition of handcraftsmanship continues, ready-made shoes for women are also available: exclusive creations in a youthful yet classic vein.

Tanino Crisci

Via Montenapoleone 3 - (02) 76021264
Open 9:30am-1pm & 3pm-7:30pm. Closed Mon am.

Timeless style and quality workmanship are the firm's signature. The shoes are fashioned of superb skins and are favored by the discriminating Milanese: you'll see the "Bettina" model on many sleek, feminine feet; the classic "Argo" lace-up is prized by well-dressed men.

Diego Della Valle

Via della Spiga 2 - (02) 76002423
Open 10am-1:30pm & 2:30pm-7:30pm. Closed Mon am.

Yes, this is the man who invented the "J. P. Tod" shoe, a distant cousin of the familiar Wallabee. But take a look at Della Valle's other sophisticated and original creations, and at the designs by Romeo Gigli and Azzedine Alaïa. For men, there is an elegant line of footwear by Gatto.

Salvatore Ferragamo

Via Montenapoleone 3 - (02) 76000054
Via Montenapoleone 20 - (02) 76006660
Open daily 10am-7pm (Mon 3pm-7pm).

Exquisitely crafted, with beautiful hand-detailing, these shoes are quietly elegant and comfortable, too. Back in the '60s Audrey Hepburn and Sophia Loren went wild for Ferragamo's designs. The first address is for women, the second for men. Along with shoes, you'll find such lovely leather goods as briefcases and bags; the end-of-season sales are not to be missed.

Figini

Piazza San Babila 3 - (02) 76022937
Via Spadari 3 - (02) 86462048
Open 9:30am-1pm & 3pm-7:30pm. Closed Mon am.

Many of Figini's models are designed in-house and produced by local craftspeople. The men's shoes are resolutely classic, albeit with a sporty touch, just the way Italian gentlemen like them. The women's line includes some prestigious labels and tends to be closely pegged to current fashion trends.

Fratelli Rossetti

Via Montenapoleone (corner of Corso Matteotti) - (02) 76021650
Corso Magenta (corner of Via Nirone)
(02) 86454284
Open 10am-7:30pm. Closed Mon am.
This prestigious footwear "Made in Italy" is famous throughout the world. Top-quality leathers, superb workmanship, and a unique style that combines fashion with wearability distinguish the classic and sporty designs as well as the firm's more elegant (and expensive) creations.

Alfonso Garlando

Via Madonnina 1 - (02) 874679
Via Piero della Francesca 13 - (02) 33101198
Open daily 10am-7:30pm (Mon 3pm-7:30pm).
A huge collection of shoes and boots for both sexes in an equally vast range of sizes. One of the first to jump on the color bandwagon, Garlando chose to bet on outrageous shades rather than on extreme styles. And its rainbow-hued shoes were an instant success. Evening slippers and delicate footwear and bags for brides are a specialty. The Via Madonnina store always carries a selection of shoes at sale prices.

Lario 1898

Via Montenapoleone 21 - (02) 76002641
Open 10am-7pm. Closed Mon am.
Lario fashions choice, glove-soft leathers into restrained, polished styles. The selections for men are soberly sporty, and nary a high heel, bangle, or bow can be spotted in the entire women's collection.

Santini

Via Montenapoleone 1 - (02) 76001958
Open 10am-7pm. Closed Mon am.
This highly original footwear is made for women for whom fashion's dictates are law. Always attuned to the latest trends, Santini's designers aren't afraid to experiment with different leathers, fabrics, colors, and forms.

Sebastian

Via Borgospesso 18 - (02) 780532
Open 10am-7pm. Closed Mon am.

Sebastian's specialty is custom-made shoes for women; there are 150 models and myriad materials (fabric, calf, kid...) to choose from. An order generally takes about two months to complete. Surprisingly, the price is not much higher than what you'll pay for high-quality ready-made shoes. Men's shoes are available as well, but most of the (mainly classic) designs are ready-made.

Spelta

Via Solferino (corner of Via Pontaccio)
(02) 8052592
Open 9am-1pm & 3pm-7:30pm. Closed Mon am.
Spelta launched the craze for ballerina slippers, both plain and with a strap across the instep. The firm still produces them in prodigious quantities, and they're sold here in an extraordinary assortment of colors. The other designs on view are quite attractive in the same youthful, comfortable, casual vein.

Mario Valentino

Via Montenapoleone 10 - (02) 798113
Open daily 9:30am-7pm (Mon 3pm-7pm).
Flamboyant footwear and stylish leather gear.

La Vetrina di Beryl

Via Statuto 4 - (02) 654278
Open 9:30am-1pm & 3pm-7:30pm. Closed Mon am.
A strange but somehow successful mix of avant-garde shoes and traditional British and American footwear. On the one hand (or should we say foot?), you'all find designs by Stéphane Kélian, Robert Clergerie, Romeo Gigli, Martine Sitbon, Sibylla, Tokio Kumagai, and Emma Hope, while on the other, you'll see such mainstream labels as Clark, Saxon, Grenson, and Sebago.

Vierre

Via Montenapoleone 27b - (02) 76001131
Corso Vittorio Emanuele 7 - (02) 781804
Open 10am-1pm & 3:30pm-7:30pm. Closed Mon am.
The customers are young, but they know what they want and they follow trends attentively. Designs by Casadei and Soprani share space with fashion-forward footwear by Stéphane Kélian, Claude

Montana, Accessoire, Tokio Kumagai, and such emerging Italian stylists as Pellinacci, Paciotti, Lorenzo Banfi, along with some of the top English and American shoe designers.

FOOD

■ GOURMET SHOPS

Bellini

Via San Pietro all'Orto 17 - (02) 76002057
Open 8am-1pm & 4pm-7pm. Closed Mon pm.
Amazingly, this wonderful grocery filled with appetizing smells and intriguing packages has managed to resist the incursion of luxury boutiques, which have supplanted most of the other shops in the neighborhood. Here you can still find loose spices, jars of chocolates and caramels sold by the *etto* (100 grams, or a little over three ounces), and a noteworthy assortment of Italian and German honeys. All the top-quality merchandise is selected with care.

C'era Una Volta

Corso Genova 1 - (02) 8390308
Open 9:30am-1pm & 4pm-8:30pm. Closed Mon.
Once upon a time (*"c'era una volta"*), there was a gourmet grocery that held more treasures than Ali Baba's cave... Among the riches on display are French jams made with Provençal honey, Italian honey from the Castello di Volpaia, dried or oil-packed porcini mushrooms, truffles and truffle paste, and all sorts of cookies packaged in handsome tin boxes. Impressive gift baskets, containing the epicurean treats of your choice, are prepared to order.

Cignarelli

Corso Buenos Aires 65 - (02) 2043564
Open 8am-1pm & 3:30pm-7:30pm. Closed Mon am.
All Milan knows that Cignarelli stocks an extraordinary variety of caramels, hard candies, licorice, and sugar decorations. But fewer people are aware that this is one of the last remaining sources of such old-fashioned grocery items as real mint extract and powdered vegetable dyes for coloring food safely and naturally. A delightful place to browse.

Gaboardi

Piazza Tricolore 2 - (02) 794603
Open 8am-1pm & 3:15pm-7:15pm. Closed Mon am.
Gaboardi carries everything from essential groceries and household and grooming products to fine wines, liquors, and such gourmet goodies as candied fruit, nougat, Italian and imported cookies, and tip-top English marmalades.

Galli

Via Hugo 2 - (02) 86464833
Corso di Porta Romana 2 - (02) 86453112
Open 8:30am-1pm & 2:30pm-8pm. Closed Mon am.
If you get your buzz from sweets, make a beeline for Galli, source of the honeyed treats that all Milan adores: marrons glacés (glazed chestnuts), crunchy pralines, juicy fruit jellies, jewel-like candied fruit, and—to give homemade desserts a romantic touch—delicate sugared violets.

Monforte

Corso Monforte 18 - (02) 799234
Open 8:15am-1pm & 3:30pm-7:15pm. Closed Mon pm.
This sizable establishment stocks just about everything you can think of, from dried fruit (the selection is truly amazing) to grooming products, and every item is of top quality.

Parini

Via Borgospesso 1 - (02) 76002303
Open 8:30am-1pm & 3pm-7pm. Closed Mon am.
A landmark grocery store, nearly 100 years old, Parini is noted for its appetizing delicacies and foodstuffs. The entrance level is exclusively devoted to caramels, the very best that Italy and France have to offer. Downstairs is a golden array of some 30 different cold-pressed extra-virgin olive oils, jars of oil- or vinegar-packed vegetables (with no other preservatives), colorful sauces, condiments, and jams. Parini also carries a line of diet foods and all-natural cookies, fine French and Italian wines, and an exceptional range of grappas (Italian grape brandies).

Peck

Via Spadari 9 - (02) 86461158
*Open 9:30am-1pm & 3pm-7:30pm. Closed
Mon am.*
Peck is the pick of Milan's delicatessens,
where gourmets gather to purchase prime
charcuterie, tasty carry-out dishes, and all
manner of treats for the taste buds. The
eye-popping displays alone are worth a
visit. Peck is not to be neglected if you
want to put together a picnic or hotel-
room feast.

Salumaio di Montenapoleone

Via Montenapoleone 12 - (02) 76001123
*Open 8:30am-1pm & 3:30pm-7:30pm.
Closed Mon am.*
Windows crammed with epicurean
edibles are unusual along this stretch of
tony fashion boutiques. But the celebrated
Salumaio is a high-class outfit too: a taste
of the wares will convince you. Choose
from an alluring array of sausages and
salamis, cheese quiches, fresh pasta, and
colossal cooked or air-dried prosciutto.

Soana

Corso Magenta 1 - (02) 86452725
*Open 8am-1pm & 3:30pm-7:30pm. Closed
Mon pm.*
The owner of this singularly attractive
shop is passionate about the products he
sells. He personally seeks out the extra-virgin olive oils and natural honeys that fill his
shelves, purchasing them only from small-
scale producers who do all their work by
hand. Just as much care is taken in the
selection of the 82 varieties of teas, all sold
loose. Other delights to be found at Soana
include caramels, pâtés, and savory
sauces.

■ WINE

La Botte

Via Giacosa 11 - (02) 2610316
Piazzale Susa (corner of Via dell'Ongaro)
(02) 744695
*Open 9am-12:30pm & 3pm-7:30pm. Closed
Mon.*
Bulk wines may not sound very appealing, but those offered at this wine shop just
might change your mind. Nine different
wines are available, from vineyards in Tuscany, Friuli, Emilia, and the Veneto. All

represent excellent value and may be purchased in five-liter (or more) containers. La
Botte's selection of spirits is small but
choice, with especially fine grappas, Cog-
nacs, and whiskies.

Casati

Via Carducci 9 - (02) 86452009
*Open 8am-12:30pm & 3pm-7:30pm. Closed
Mon am.*
Housed on Via Carducci for the past
decade, Casati's origins stretch back even
further: it has been a Milanese fixture since
the nineteenth century. With some 2,000
wines in stock—primarily Italian, with a
worthwhile choice of French and Spanish
bottlings—the shop is a fascinating place
for wine buffs to browse. Champagnes
and spirits are available, too.

Cotti

Via Solferino 42
(02) 29001096, fax (02) 29001222
Open 8am-1pm & 3pm-8pm. Closed Sun.
Another wine merchant's that dates from
the last century, this place has been
managed by the Cotti family since the
1950s. Part of the shop is reserved for
tastings, the rest for retail wine sales. A
thousand labels are usually in stock, along
with 200 types of grappa (Italian grape
brandy), a staggering collection of 300-
odd whiskies, and all the top brands of
Cognac, Armagnac, Calvados, and Champagne.

Moscatelli

Corso Garibaldi 93 - (02) 6554602
*Open 10:30am-7:30pm & 9:30pm-2am.
Closed Sun.*
Run by the Moscatelli family for more
than 135 years, this unusual enoteca specializes in—what else?—Moscati (Italian
Muscat wines), both sparkling and still,
from every part of the Boot, including the
isle of Elba. An interesting selection of
other Italian wines and spirits is available
as well.

N'Ombra de Vin

Via San Marco 2 - (02) 6552746
Open daily 8:30am-1pm & 4pm-7:30pm.
Situated just next to the splendid church
of San Marco, this wine shop occupies
what was formerly the refectory for a community of Augustinian monks. N'Ombra

de Vin has earned the title of "Milan's University of Wine" thanks to the high level of the wine-tasting and gastronomy courses it sponsors. The shop itself stocks about 700 wines, classified in an orderly fashion according to region and type. Champagnes and spirits are offered as well.

So What's Your Sign?

Just as you enter the Duomo, look down and admire the amazing Zodiac sundial designed by astronomer Antonio de Cesaris in 1786, which lies parallel to the cathedral's central door. When sunbeams manage to cut through Milan's usual blanket of fog, they fall precisely on the current month's sun sign.

Ricerca Vini

Via Monti 33 - (02) 460471
Open 8am-1pm & 4pm-7:30pm. Closed Mon am.

The 75 Italian wines that bear the "Ricerca Vini" label are discoveries that merchant Angelo Betti has unearthed in their region of origin and bottled himself in Milan. The advantages of this operation are obvious: relatively low prices, strict quality control, and a stock limited to wines from regions where the harvest was most successful in a given year. Ricerca Vini also carries wines from well-known bottlers, along with a fine assortment of Italian and foreign spirits.

Ronchi

Via San Vincenzo 12 - (02) 89402627
Open 9:30am-noon & 3:30pm-7:30pm. Closed Mon am.

Maria Luisa Ronchi, Italy's top female sommelier, represents the fifth generation of a wine-merchant dynasty that stretches back to 1865. Her inventory embraces hundreds of premium Italian and French growths, as well as some rare rums, Ports, and whiskies. Don't overlook the mouthwatering range of Italian gastronomic specialties and natural foods.

Solci

Via Morosini 19
(02) 55195725, fax (02) 5458122
Open 9am-1pm & 3:30pm-7:30pm. Closed Mon am.

While the proprietor gives pride of place to Italian wines, he is no chauvinist. Many of the 1,300 wines in stock come from France, Germany, Spain, Hungary, Portugal, and as far away as the United States and South Africa. Tastings are held from time to time in the little tavern downstairs.

Verdi & Pancani

Corso Italia 6 - (02) 876191
Open 8:10am-1pm & 3pm-7:30pm. Closed Mon am.

In addition to the Chiantis produced at its Cerreto Guidi property, this wine merchant displays something like 2,000 bottlings, among them the very best Italian, French, German, Greek, and Portuguese wines. Good selection of spirits, too.

Vino Vino

Corso San Gottardo 13 - (02) 58101239
Via Pasubio 6/8 - (02) 6554246
Open 9:30am-1pm & 4pm-7:30pm. Closed Mon am.

Both shops are furnished with spartan austerity, to focus your entire attention on the stock of rigorously selected Italian and French wines. These rare vintages share shelf space with a superb collection of premium whiskies and Armagnacs. Comparative tastings of wines and spirits are organized frequently to introduce new arrivals to the shop's loyal clientele.

GIFTS

L'Affiche

Via Unione 6 - (02) 804978
Open 10am-1pm & 3pm-7:30pm. Closed Mon am.

Milan's first poster gallery remains the largest and best stocked. A rich selection of Italian and imported art posters is on display, but this shop also produces interesting graphics and silkscreen prints. All may be purchased framed or unframed, as you like.

L'Albero delle Mele

Via Sacco (corner of Via Marghera)
(02) 4695789
Open 10am-1pm & 3:30pm-7:30pm. Closed Mon am.
The owner will give you a guided tour through her stock of traditional and novel board games from all over the world, and she'll offer expert advice on which game is particularly suited to your temperament.

Albrizzi

Via Bagutta 8 - (02) 76001218
Open 10am-12:30pm & 3pm-7:30pm. Closed Mon am.
At this elegant bookbinder's shop you can obtain handsome datebooks, notebooks, and albums bound in costly colored papers and luxurious leathers. Among the most precious objects here are Ettore Sobrero's extraordinary miniature bookshelves.

Avant de Dormir

Via Turati 3 - (02) 6599990
Open 10:30am-7pm. Closed Mon am.
Teapots and teacups rock back and forth, a folding table mimics a grand piano, and glass headgear turns out to be a collection of lamps. Zany designers Marina and Kobi Weisendanger transform functional household items into surrealistic, wonderfully droll objets d'art.

Bianchi

Via Montebello 7 - (02) 6555108
Open 8:30am-12:30pm & 3:30pm-7:30pm. Closed Mon am.
Milan's most romantic flower arrangements come from master florist Raimondo Bianchi. He composes bridal bouquets that are sheer poetry.

Carpe Diem

Viale Tunisia 1 (corner of Corso Buenos Aires) - (02) 29517833
Open 9:30am-1pm & 3pm-7:30pm. Closed Mon am.
A one-stop gift-shopping center, where whimsy rules, quality is high, and prices attractive. Alongside pretty handcrafted items are picture frames and photo albums, exotic stationery, unusual knits, and masses of clever baubles sure to please and amuse the most discerning individuals on your gift list.

Città del Sole

Via San Clemente (Piazza Fontana)
(02) 72022667
Open 9:15am-7:15pm (Sat 9:15am-1pm & 3pm-7:15pm). Closed Mon am.
Via Dante 13 - (02) 86461683
Open 9am-1pm & 3:15pm-7:15pm. Closed Mon am.
You'll find more than just Monopoly at this House of Games. The inventory includes hundreds of diversions for adults: board games, games to play alone, electronic and video games, war games, scale models to assemble, card games, dominoes, puzzles, and a curious selection of what might be called "artistic pastimes"—materials for making woodcuts and colored sand to drizzle decoratively into glass bowls.

Controbuffet

Via Solferino 14 - (02) 6554934
Open 10am-1:30pm & 3pm-7:30pm. Closed Mon am.
This sort of shop is a relatively recent phenomenon, but it caught on quickly with the design-conscious Milanese. Tableware, bibelots, lamps, jewelry, and such functional objects as telephones and clocks are carefully selected for their beauty and originality. It's a good place to choose a clever gift.

Coronel Tapiocca

Via Torino 68 - (02) 8052746
Open 10am-2pm & 3pm-7:30pm. Closed Mon am.
You, too, can make like Indiana Jones. Just stop in at "Colonel Tapioca's" and kit yourself out with matches that light in the rain, miniature packets of freeze-dried food, a waterproof wallet that can be strapped to your ankle, assorted knives of varying sizes...and you're ready for adventure!

10 Corso Como

Corso Como 10 (in the courtyard)
(02) 29002674
Open 10am-7:30pm. Closed Mon am.
This offbeat shop is tucked away in one of old Milan's picturesque courtyards. A sort of new-age bazaar, it's filled with curious clothing for women and men, ethnic jewelry, exotic yet useful household items, fabrics, plant-based remedies,

129

toiletries, and cosmetics. Art exhibitions are staged on the upper floor; and in warm weather, drinks are served at little tables set out in front of the shop—it's a fun, funky place to note on your shopping itinerary.

I Giorni di Carta

Corso Garibaldi 81 - (02) 6552514
Open 9:30am-1pm & 3:30pm-7:30pm. Closed Mon am.
The only stationery shop in Milan truly worthy of this city's impeccable shopping reputation. An exhilarating variety of letter and notepapers, impressive fountain pens, and a palette of inks are aligned on the shelves, where one may also find beautifully bound address books and notebooks. And there are some unusual decorative objects made from paper that are not necessarily useful, but appealing just the same.

Legatoria Artistica

Via Palermo 5 - (02) 861113
Open 9:30am-7pm (Sat 9:30am-1pm & 3pm-7pm). Closed Mon am.
Who would not love to receive one of these gorgeous—handmade!—photo albums, crafted from Varese or flower-print paper? Smaller, but just as giftable, are the boxes (lots of sizes), picture frames, diaries, and pencils sold here, all covered with beautiful decorative papers.

Lorenzi

Via Montenapoleone 9 - (02) 76020593
Open 9am-12:30pm & 3:30pm-7:30pm. Closed Mon am.
What began as a cutlery shop has evolved into an elegant and multifaceted emporium for exquisite shaving equipment, travel kits filled with luxurious grooming accessories, pipes and smoking paraphernalia, tableware, and various accoutrements for wine buffs. Executed in metal, horn, and other choice materials, many of these creations are designed by Aldo Lorenzi and are available here exclusively.

Makeupstudio

Via Madonnina 15 - (02) 862747
Open 10am-7:30pm. Closed Mon am.
Diego Dalla Palma's upscale makeup mart is a busy place, with photographers and models constantly running in to purchase the novel cosmetics and accessories that have made this place famous. You can try out all the products right on the spot and count on knowledgeable advice from the friendly sales staff.

Nava

Via Santa Cecilia - (02) 76004832
Open 9am-1pm & 3pm-7pm. Closed Mon.
This great little shop stocks high-class supplies for the rising young executive. The exclusive line of Nava office paraphernalia includes sophisticated appointment books designed by Bob Noorda, "power" pens, calendars, sleek Porsche Design leather goods, smokers' accessories, and snazzy eyeglasses.

Nimius Museum Shop

Via Durini 23 - (02) 76023687
Open 10am-7:45pm. Closed Mon am.
Nimius started out as a shop for trendy designer gifts, but the range of merchandise has expanded to include classy clothing for men and women, fragrances by Fragonard, and leather accessories signed Bottega Veneta or Prada.

Penelopi 3

Piazza San Marco 1 (corner of Via Solferino) (02) 6599640
Open 10am-2pm & 3pm-7pm. Closed Mon am.
Here you'll find a profusion of quirky, offbeat, and ethnic accents for the home: the colorful doormats, whimsical kitchen utensils, wooden toys, and amusing bags all make highly acceptable gifts.

Profumo

Via Brera 2 - (02) 72023334
Open 9:30am-12:30pm & 3:30pm-7:30pm. Closed Mon am.
Finally, a perfume shop where even men feel perfectly welcome and comfortable. What's more, they'll find top-quality scents, skincare products just for them, alongside an abundance of scented coquetries and cosmetics for women. Hard-to-find labels are featured, such as England's Czech & Speake, France's Comptoir du Sud Pacifique and, from New York, skin and hair treatments from Kiehl's. And don't miss the covetable shaving and bath accessories and fragrances for the home.

Roncoroni
Via Broletto 39 - (02) 86464454
Open 10am-7pm. Closed Mon am.
A shop for all the essential (but disposable) equipment that the hostess with the mostest desires: confetti (of course), paper plates, cups and napkins, and much more. What sets these supplies apart is their sophisticated design, especially the items themed for the Christmas and Carnival holidays.

Savinelli
Via Orefici 2 - (02) 876660
Open 9am-1pm & 3pm-7pm. Closed Mon am.
A pipe-smoker's paradise. Savinelli is a must for meerschaum and briar lovers, or for anyone who wants to see the world's smallest pipe, or the largest (carved from an enormous South African squash). Dunhill pipes are well represented, as are Tyrolean models and others that would have suited Sherlock Holmes. A full range of accessories is on display, including many types of tobacco and a lighter with a flame inclined to the correct 45-degree angle.

Timbrificio Piave
Viale Piave 28 - (02) 29522306
Open 8:30am-12:30pm & 2:30pm-7pm. Closed Sat.
You'll leave a lasting mark with the stamps produced in this unusual shop. No matter how bizarre and no matter how baroque, any stamp you desire will be made to your specifications. Metal plaques are a specialty too, and there is an attractive selection of writing accessories and office supplies. This shop gets our stamp of approval!

Torriani
Via Mercato 1 - (02) 866519
Open 9am-12:30pm & 2:30pm-7:30pm. Closed Mon am.
One of the oldest toy stores in Milan, Torriani is also one of the very few that will minister to old or damaged dolls. The store stocks an amazing array of tricks, jokes, and novelties, and you'll find a large selection of Carnival masks and fireworks as well.

Turi
Via Cerva 10 - (02) 76002947
Open 9am-7:30pm. Closed Mon am.

Shoes that are coddled with Turi's polishes (in an astounding range of colors), creams, and brushes have an excellent shot at immortality. Spot removers for every type of leather are on hand, in addition to such necessities as beautifully carved wooden shoe trees and traveling pouches that can accommodate some twenty pairs of shoes.

HOMEWARES

Caracalla
Via Cerva 19 - (02) 76002195
Open 10am-1pm & 3pm-7pm. Closed Mon am.
Caracalla, appropriately enough, is exclusively devoted to the bath. You'll admire the lovely and unusual ceramic tiles for bathroom walls and the dizzying selection of accessories, including glass by Barovier & Toso, and divine little antique accoutrements to make the bath the most inviting room in the house.

Cassina
Via Durini 18 - (02) 76020745
Open 10am-7pm. Closed Mon am.
The "Great Masters" collection brings together reissues of timeless designs by Le Corbusier, Mackintosh, Asplund, and Frank Lloyd Wright. More recent creations are also on view, including frankly futuristic seating and tables by such innnovative designers as Vico Magistretti and Mario Bellini.

De Padova
Corso Venezia 14
(02) 76008413, fax (02) 783201
Open 10am-1:30pm & 2:30pm-7:30pm. Closed Mon am.
Designs by top international furniture manufacturers are showcased at this sleekly modern emporium. The Edizioni line reproduces handsome functional objects from the nineteenth century (including clean-lined Shaker items) as well as handsome pieces by noted contemporary designers.

*Some establishments change their **closing times** without warning. It is always wise to check in advance.*

131

Dilmos

Piazza San Marco 1 - (02) 29002350
Open 9:30am-1pm & 3:30pm-7pm. Closed Mon am.

Here's an exciting collection of the best in contemporary furniture and a choice array of reproductions of designs by modern masters. Thus, alongside pieces by Breuer, Giò Ponti, and Gaudí, you may view the most recent creations of Mendini, Sottsass, Castiglioni, Santachiara, and one-off works by Ceroli and Luigi Ontani.

Frigerio

Corso Europa 11 - (02) 794462
Open 9:30am-12:30pm & 3pm-7:30pm. Closed Mon am.

Frigerio is the exclusive retail outlet for six famous northern European design firms: Thonet, Avarte of Finland, Interlübke (modular units and office furniture); Cor (armchairs, sofas, and handmade pieces); Artifort of the Netherlands (known for the Lagos chair); Tecta (quirky Bauhaus-style furnishings characterized by asymmetric lines), and Form (Viennese modernism, with pieces designed by such masters as Loos and Hoffmann).

High-Tech

Piazza XXV Aprile 12 - (02) 6590515
Open 10am-7pm. Closed Mon.

Known throughout the world for trendsetting contemporary furniture and accessories, High-Tech is the firm that brought industrial design into the home. Lofty creative standards continue to distinguish this innovative company. An entire section of the shop is devoted to kitchenware and table décor.

Lyda Levi

Via Durini 7 - (02) 780414
Open 9am-1pm & 3pm-7pm. Closed Mon am.

Famous for handcrafted rattan and wicker furniture in an appealing range of colors, Lyda Levi sells tables and chairs for indoor or outdoor use. All are exquisitely designed.

Liliana Longo

Corso Italia 47 (in the courtyard)
(02) 58313098
Open 9am-1pm & 3pm-7pm. Closed Mon am.

Liliana Longo's showroom occupies a stunning space in an 1876 building that features a neo-Renaissance arcade. You're sure to admire the enormous range of wall coverings, upholstery fabrics, flowered chintzes, and imaginatively printed linens and silks that would give any room a refined, romantic look.

Mirabello

Largo Treves 2 - (02) 6555629
Open 9:30am-1pm & 3pm-7:30pm. Closed Mon am.

This seductive shop presents an assortment of bed linens sufficiently vast to indulge any whim. Many of the comforters and sheets are made with sublime fabrics to Mirabello's own specifications. Blankets by Agnona, Marzotto, and Sannwald (in pure cashmere!) are obtainable here, as are unusual handmade Scandinavian lap rugs and shawls.

Officine Alessi

Corso Matteotti 9 - (02) 795726
Open 9:30am-1pm & 3pm-7pm. Closed Mon.

Rev up your kitchen with architect-designed accoutrements by Aldo Rossi, Ettore Sottsass, Richard Sapper, and more. The kettles, colanders, and coffeepots are sleek, chic, and furiously fashionable. Expensive, too, of course.

Pedano

Viale Umbria 120 - (02) 7383735
Viale Umbria 126 - (02) 7425411
Open 9:30am-12:30pm & 3:30pm-7pm. Closed Mon am.

For several years now, internationally known craftsman and sculptor Pino Pedano has designed and produced handsomely simple modular furniture for the home and office. The pieces have a strong, contemporary look: Pedano invented the *millefogli* table, with a stratified top displaying several natural wood tones, and lacquered legs. Prices are reasonable.

Spazio Erreti

Via Fatebenefratelli 34 - (02) 29002730
Open 9:30am-1:30pm & 3pm-7:30pm. Closed Mon am.

Erreti's specialty is rustic furniture from the Trentino and Alto Adige regions. In plain natural wood or decorated with painted motifs, the pieces have a strong, simple beauty; the tastefully chosen selection is both appealing and functional.

Sofas stuffed with goose down, Murano lamps, and the Kartell furniture line are on display as well as tropical-wood furniture from Brazil and Indonesia.

Tanzi

Via Fatebenefratelli 9 - (02) 29003692
Corso Monforte 19 - (02) 783697
Open 10am-1:30pm & 2:30pm-7pm. Closed Mon am.
Some 40 well-reputed design firms are represented here, along with Tanzi's own line of sofas, armchairs, and occasional and kitchen furniture.

Vetrerie di Empoli

Via Borgospesso 5 - (02) 76008791
Open 10am-1pm & 2:30pm-7:30pm. Closed Mon am.
Via Pietro Verri 4 - (02) 76021656
Open 10am-7pm. Closed Mon am.
The Via Borgospesso premises—a palazzo adorned with eighteenth-century frescoes—are quite nearly as interesting as the merchandise. Here, and in the newly restructured Via Verri shop, a display of Tuscan glass vases, lamps, decorative accents, and tableware glitters enticingly.

STREET MARKETS

To get the most out of Milan's open-air markets, remember to go early, before the crowds become unmanageable; keep your wallet and papers in a safe place; and give the merchandise a close look before you buy. Some stands do indeed offer remarkable bargains, notably in designer clothing and famous-label footwear at incredibly low prices. Here is a list of Milan's biggest and best-known street markets:

Papiniano Market

Viale Papiniano
Open Tue & Sat 9am-1:30pm.

Via Osoppo Market

Via Osoppo
Open Thu & Sat 9am-1:30pm.

Piazza Mirabello Market

Piazza Mirabello
Open Mon 9am-1:30pm.

Via Pagano Market

Via Pagano, Largo V° Alpini
Open Fri 9am-1:30pm.

Bastioni di Porta Nuova Market

Bastioni di Porta Nuova
Open Sat 9am-1:30pm.

Piazzale Martini Market

Piazzale Martini
Open Wed 9am-1:30pm.

■ AND ALSO...

The Brera Antique Market (Mercatino dell'Antiquariato di Brera) is held in Via Fiori Chiari and in Via Brera on the third Saturday of every month except July and August. Collectors come to find old silver and Art Deco jewelry.

The Senigallia Flea Market (Mercato delle Pulci di Senigallia) takes place every Saturday along the Darsena on Viale G. D'Annunzio. The merchandise is a very mixed bag: you'll find second-hand clothing, attic treasures, old books, and the like.

The Navigli Antique Market (Mercatone dell'Antiquariato dei Navigli) is as attractive for its canal-side setting as for the merchandise on display. The latter is far from negligeable, however: some 100 stands offer a varied array of bric-a-brac and antiques on the last Sunday of each month.

The Oh bej, Oh bej Fair is an old Milanese tradition, held in honor of Saint Ambrose, the city's patron. It takes place every year on December 6–8 in the streets around the basilica of Sant'Ambrogio. For real antiques, look around on Via Gnecchi; other stands propose a jumble of handcrafts, exotic knickknacks, and street food.

*We're always happy to hear about **your** discoveries and receive **your** comments on ours. We want to give your letters the attention they deserve, so when you write to Gault Millau, please state clearly what you liked or disliked. Be concise but convincing, and take the time to argue your point.*

Museums

The *Carta Museo* available from Milan's Tourist Office is an electronic card valid for six months that provides easy, convenient access to the following museums: **Museo Nazionale della Scienza e della Tecnica, Museo del Duomo, Museo del Cinema, Museo Teatrale alla Scala, Museo Poldi-Pezzoli, Società Belle Arti ed Esposizione Permanente** as well as to the twelve public (*civico*) museums listed below. The card costs 28,000 lire, and may be obtained from the Tourist Office (Azienda di Promozione Turistica, or APT) at 1 Via Marconi, just off Piazza del Duomo.

Acquario Civico
Viale Gadio 2 - (02) 86462051
Open 9:30am-5:30pm (Sun 10am-noon & 2pm-6pm). Closed Mon.
This is the largest aquarium in Italy, with numerous exhibits of fresh and saltwater fish, tropical fish, and invertebrates. The collection of mollusks includes more than 35,000 specimens.

Civica Galleria d'Arte Moderna
Via Palestro 16 - (02) 76002819
Currently closed for restoration.

Civiche Raccolte d'Arte Antica
Castello Sforzesco - (02) 62083284
Open 9:30am-5:30pm. Closed Mon.
This museum presents sculpture from the early Christian era to the late Renaissance, paintings from the fifteenth to the eighteenth century (with significant works by Mantegna, Giovanni Bellini, Tintoretto, and Lorenzo Lotto), as well as a fine furniture collection. Perhaps the most moving piece is Michelangelo's last work, his unfinished *Pietà Rondanini*.

Civiche Raccolte d'Arte Applicata e Incisioni
Castello Sforzesco - (02) 62083284

Open 9:30am-5:30pm. Closed Mon.
Known for its collection of rare musical instruments and the Bertarelli bequest (fine engravings), the museum also exhibits Chinese ceramics, gold altar vessels, antique textiles, sacred vestments, and costumes from the eighteenth and nineteenth centuries. Among the museum's most remarkable holdings are the sixteenth-century *Tapestries of the Months*; unfortunately, the room in which they are displayed is frequently closed.

Civico Gabinetto Numismatico
Castello Sforzesco, Torre del Filarete
(02) 62083284, fax (02) 62083944
Open by appt.
An impressive collection of more than 150,000 Greek, Roman, and Italian coins. The latter collection boasts coins minted in Milan under Charlemagne and specimens struck under the Viscontis and the Sforzas.

Civico Museo Archeologico
Corso Magenta 15 - (02) 86450665
Open 9:30am-5:30pm. Closed Mon.
Milan's Archaeological Museum is housed in a former Benedictine monastery. It contains prehistoric, Greek, Etruscan, and Roman art and artifacts, including a superb torso of *Hercules*, a head of the *Empress Agrippina*, and a Bronze Age vase from Cyprus in the form of a bull.

Civico Museo Archeologico
Prehistoric & Egyptian Departments
Castello Sforzesco, Cortile della Rocchetta
(02) 62083284
Open 9:30am-5:30pm. Closed Mon.
Also in the museum complex of the Castello Sforzesco are the important prehistoric and Egyptian collections of the Archaeological Museum. Pre- and protohistoric relics include bronze tools dating from 1400 B.C., while the Egyptian

section presents sarcophagi, statuary, and papyruses from the New Kingdom to the Ptolemaic Era.

Civico Museo d'Arte Contemporanea

Palazzo Reale, Piazzetta Reale 12
(02) 62083914
Open 9:30am-5:30pm. Closed Mon.
This museum occupies the first-floor rooms of the eighteenth-century Palazzo Reale, the former residence of the Spanish and Austrian governors of Milan. The collections focus on post–World War II Italian art, with works by Giorgio De Chirico, Lucio Fontana, and Umberto Boccioni, among others.

Civico Museo di Milano & Museo Civico di Storia Contemporanea

Via Sant'Andrea 6 - (02) 783797
Open 9:30am-5:30pm. Closed Mon.
The Museum of Milan reconstitutes three centuries of Milanese history with its collection of maps and artists' renderings of the city, portraits and busts of notable citizens, and an exhibit of typical Milanese costumes. The Museum of Contemporary History documents the period between World Wars I and II with photographs, posters, letters, newspapers, and personal memorabilia of politicians and Resistance fighters.

Collezioni del Museo del Cinema della Cineteca Italiana

Palazzo Dugnani, Via Manin 2 - (02) 6554977
Open 3pm-6pm. Closed Sat-Mon.
The cinema museum commemorates the birth and development of motion pictures, with a fabulous collection of photographs, documents, and personal mementoes. A specialized library is also available for research.

Museo Bagatti Valsecchi

Via Santo Spirito 10 - (02) 76006132
Open 1pm-5pm. Closed Mon.
Stepping into this Renaissance palazzo is a little like stepping back in time. Recently opened to the public, this museum is housed in a former patrician residence; the twenty rooms present many superb pictures, including Giovanni Bellini's celebrated *Saint Justine.*

Mysterious Baths

That's the evocative name of the Giorgio De Chirico fountain tucked in the Parco Sempione in front of the Palazzo della Triennale. The fountain looks like a wacky swimming pool floating in a sea of grass. An inscrutable stone swan cruises by several metaphysical mystery figures splashing for eternity, whatever that means.

Museo del Giocattolo

Ripa di Porta Ticinese 27 - (02) 8322103
Open 9:30am-12:30pm & 3pm-7:30pm. Closed Mon, Aug, Easter, Dec 24-31.
Delightful displays of dollies, tin soldiers, and cunning wooden playthings from the nineteenth and twentieth centuries form the backbone of the Toy Museum's collection.

Museo della Basilica di Sant'Ambrogio

Piazza Sant'Ambrogio 15 - (02) 86450895
Open 10am-noon & 3pm-5pm (Sat & hols 3pm-5pm). Closed Tue, Easter Mon, Aug, Dec 24-26.
This museum holds items of historic and artistic importance from the early Christian basilica of Sant'Ambrogio, the origins of which go back to the fourth century. Notable are relics from the sarcophagus of Saint Ambrose, fragments of an early Christian mosaic, and two paintings by Bernardino Luini.

Museo della Basilica di Santa Maria della Passione

Via Bellini 2 - (02) 76021370 (Church sacristy)
Open 10am-noon & 3pm-5pm (hols 3pm-5pm). Closed Sat, Easter, Easter Mon, Dec 24-26, Aug.
On display are paintings, sculpture, and liturgical objects from the Renaissance basilica of Santa Maria della Passione, the second-largest church in Milan, after the Duomo. The sacristy itself is decorated with admirable frescoes by Bergognone and Petarzano.

Museo Cenacolo Vinciano

Piazza Santa Maria delle Grazie 2
(02) 4987588
Open 8am-1:45pm. Closed Mon.

It was here, on a wall of the refectory in this former Dominican monastery, that Leonardo da Vinci painted The Last Supper. Despite restoration efforts, the painting is a pale reflection of what one can now only imagine was its original splendor.

Spouting Off About the Local Brew

"Here's mud in your eye," say the habitués of this mineral "health" spring as they slug back bucketfuls of water. The stuff smells like rotten eggs and pours out of a fountain in the middle of the Parco Sempione behind the Castello Sforzesco. So here's to your health! Even the water department says it's okay to drink.

Museo delle Cere

Stazione Centrale - (02) 6690495
Open daily 8am-11pm.

Milan's wax museum is about as amusing as such places generally are. It is peopled with famous figures from antiquity to our own day, who are placed in detailed period settings. If you have some time to kill while waiting for a train, you probably won't mind idling away an hour here.

Museo Civico Navale Didattico

Via San Vittore 21 - (02) 48010040
Open 9:30am-5pm. Closed Mon.

The Italian Association of Naval Veterans has put together a remarkable source of historical and technical documentation on ships and sailing. Among the exhibits are reproductions of famous ships, war vessels and ships used for polar and other exploratory expeditions.

Museo Civico di Storia Naturale

Corso Venezia 55 - (02) 62085405
Open 9:30am-5:30pm (Sat & hols 9:30am-6:30pm). Closed Mon.

Rare fossils, giant quartzes, a 90-pound topaz, an incredible collection of stuffed birds, and Italy's sole dinosaur skeleton (*Kritosaurus notabilis*) are on view at Milan's Museum of Natural History.

Museo del Duomo

Piazza Duomo 14 - (02) 860358
Open 9:30am-12:30pm & 3pm-6pm. Closed Mon.

A fascinating collection of historical documents, objects, and artifacts relating the long history of the Duomo is presented here. Exhibits encompass architectural plans and models (including a stupendous sixteenth-century carved wooden replica), liturgical objects, stained glass, vestments, tapestries, and paintings. But the most outstanding holdings are in sculpture, with Lombard Gothic, French, and Rhenish examples.

Museo Manzoniano— Manzoni House

Via Morone 1 - (02) 86460403
Open 9am-noon & 2pm-4pm. Closed Sat, Mon, hols.

In the house where the great novelist and poet Alessandro Manzoni lived from 1814 to his death in 1873 are displayed documents, manuscripts, books, and portraits, along with some personal belongings. The bedroom and study are furnished with pieces actually owned by the author of *I Promessi Sposi*.

Museo Nazionale della Scienza e della Tecnica Leonardo da Vinci

Via San Vittore 21 - (02) 48010040
Open 9:30am-4:50pm. Closed Mon.

Milan's huge Science Museum, spread out over three different buildings, aims to promote knowledge of the origins and history of scientific thought and to illustrate the progress of technology. Many crucial advances in industrial development from the last three centuries are on display, along with fascinating documents relating to Leonardo's own scientific activity.

Museo Poldi-Pezzoli

Via Manzoni 12 - (02) 794889
Open 9:30am-12:30pm & 2:30pm-6pm. Closed Mon.

Gian Giacomo Poldi-Pezzoli, a nineteenth-century connoisseur of art and antiques, bequeathed his home, his collections of books, furnishings, rare objects, weapons, and armor, and an incomparable gallery of paintings to the city of Milan. Among the masterpieces on view are works by Botticelli, Pollaiolo, Man-tegna, Piero della Francesca, and Francesco Guardi. This is a true gem among Milanese museums.

Bullish on Turin

Want to get a rise out of a real Milanese? Tell him you know about the mosaic bull in the pavement of the Galleria Vittorio Emanuele. It's good luck to stroke your shoe—somewhat disrespectfully—on the tender underparts of this potent symbol of rival Turin. But tread lightly! The Milanese have been scuffing here madly for so many decades that the bull these days is looking more like an ox.

Museo-Studio Francesco Messina
Via San Sisto 10 - (02) 86453005
Open 9:30am-5:30pm. Closed Mon. Tram 19.
Collected here in the former Church of Saint Sixtus are paintings and sculptures by noted contemporary artist Francesco Messina.

Museo del Risorgimento
Via Borgonuovo 23 - (02) 8693549
Open 9:30am-5:30pm. Closed Mon.
Assembled in the fine Neoclassical Palazzo Moriggia are documents, paintings, portraits, engravings, arms, and other artifacts relating chiefly to the history of Italy from the eighteenth century to 1870, and the national movement for political unity (*il Risorgimento*). Interesting personal memorabilia of Napoleon are on view as well as some splendid portraits of the great Italian hero, Garibaldi.

Museo Teatrale alla Scala
Piazza della Scala 2 - (02) 8053418
Open 9am-noon & 2pm-6pm (May 1-Oct 31: Sun 9:30am-noon). Closed Sun (Nov 1-Apr 30).
No opera buff will want to miss these fascinating exhibits of memorabilia devoted to the lyric arts, the theater, and La Scala itself. Its history is related through grand portraits and drawings of famous singers as well as musical instruments and personal relics of such composers as Lizst and Verdi.

Museo del Tesoro del Duomo
Piazza Duomo - (02) 808229
Open daily 9am-noon & 2pm-6pm.
The cathedral's treasury holds stupendous sacred vessels wrought in gold, silver, and ivory, dating from the fourth to the seventeenth centuries. On display are an ivory diptych from the Carolingian era, a fourteenth-century French Gothic chalice, and two superb seventeenth-century silver statues of Saint Charles Borromeo and Saint Ambrose.

Pinacoteca Ambrosiana
Piazza Pio XI 2 - (02) 86451436
Closed for restoration until early 1996.
This rich collection of paintings and drawings is based on a bequest by Cardinal Federico Borromeo, who in 1609 built the palazzo that houses the Pinacoteca. Augmented over the years, the collection emphasizes Lombard and Venetian paintings and includes masterpieces by Leonardo, Botticelli, Raphael, and Caravaggio.

Pinacoteca di Brera
Via Brera 28 - (02) 722631
Open 9am-5:30pm (hols 9am-12:30pm). Closed Mon.
The Brera, one of the finest art museums in Italy, was declared a national picture gallery by none other than Napoleon (whose statue greets gallery goers in the courtyard) and was opened to the public in 1809. It presents an exceptional collection of Italian painting from the fourteenth to the twentieth century. Particularly rich are holdings of Venetian art of the sixteenth to eighteenth centuries (Crivelli, the Bellinis, Carpaccio, Mantegna, Tintoretto, the Tiepolos, Guardi), and of Lombard and Emilian painting of roughly the same era. The important Jesi and Jucker collections, located in a new wing of the museum, offer a splendid overview of twentieth-century Italian painting and sculpture. After years of restoration work, the three famous Napoleonic rooms have reopened, bringing pictures by Tintoretto, Tiepolo, Moretto, Veronese, and Savoldo back into the public's admiring eye.

Useful
Telephone Numbers

Milan Area Code: 02

Airport Information: Linate and Malpensa, 74852200
Ambulance: 7733
City Hall: 6236
City Police Department: 77271
Dental Emergency : 865460
Fire Department: 115
Lost and Found: 878710

Pharmacy, 24-Hour: (02) 6690735 in Stazione Centrale
Police Emergency: 112; 113
Post Office and Telegraph: 160; 186
Public Transportation Information: 875491
Radio Taxi: 8585; 8388; 6767; 5251
State Railway Information: 67500
Tourist Information: 861287
Wake-up Call: 114
Weather Service: 167

The Petrified Florist

Scattered around central Milan are dozens of turn-of-the-century palazzi dripping with wild floral motifs, an architectural style known as "Liberty." The zaniest of all is at 11 Via Bellini, opposite the Conservatory of Music. The bogglingly meticulous architect Alfredo Campanini designed and built it for himself in 1904. The heavy street door is flanked by two Amazonian caryatids with their hair dangling Rapunzel-style. The entry and stairwell are bursting with colorful details: murals, stained glass, wrought-iron grates, and gates, and handrails. Real creepers twine over their stone counterparts in a mad profusion. Topping it all are the wackiest chimneys in town. They pop through the roof and twirl skyward, like the gnarled trunks of some exotic, long-extinct tree.

Year
of the Dragon

Milan's Chinatown, the largest and longest established in Italy, is a low-key clutch of restaurants and shops strung along Via Paolo Sarpi and offshoots. But on the last wintry Sunday of February a conspicuously long dragon—more than 150 feet—raises its folkloristic head of papier-mâché and does its snaky thing. Take a peek and duck! You've got to move fast or you're likely to be trampled by frozen spectators scattering to warmer quarters.

NAPLES

Siren-Song City

Naples is a mad, marvelous metropolis washed up on the shores of the Mediterranean in what is surely one of the most beautiful spots on earth. A crescent bay, a warm blue sea dotted with verdant isles, majestic mountains rising as a backdrop... So where's the catch?

As you dive into town, whether you drive by the dragons on the beltway, wing in over the sultry Campania plain, or steam in off the swelling sea into the Neapolitan labyrinth, prepare yourself for a site etched by the passing of plagues, wars, bombings, and earthquakes. It's a good idea to breathe deeply and drink in all of nature's delights surrounding this sprawling city before you enter it. Because Naples will *not* leave you indifferent. It is at once soulful, elegant, gorgeous, brutally ugly, painfully noisy, cloister-quiet, crammed with art treasures, and crippled by timeless poverty. The most densely populated metropolis in Italy, Naples teems with life like an overstocked trout pond.

People, cars, the city itself, go up and down, up and down across the hills and into the sea. There are elevators and funiculars and snaking staircases everywhere. Higgledy-piggledy palazzi teeter over swarming streets, traffic swirls in a chaos of color and light. Everything seems to happen outdoors—courting, eating, arguing, buying, selling, and sipping coffee, lots of coffee. The bazaar-like market stalls in Piazza Garibaldi or Via Toledo overflow with scarlet tomatoes, the bright shells of *frutti di mare*, silk scarves, and twinkling amulets. The amulets—horn of antelope, a crescent moon with a face on it, a hand with the index and little finger extended and the other fingers doubled down—swing with equal frequency over swarthy chests and well-turned wrists, attracting and diffusing the pervasive evil eye (*la jettatura*).

In the midst of this ferment, squadrons of motor scooters loaded with whole families zip by, through bumper-to-bumper traffic jams. And everywhere, everyone seems to be strolling endlessly, methodically, arms linked and fingers wagging. The fabled Neapolitan promenade means one pace forward, a half-pace back. This showy shuffle is part of the collective effort to appear constantly at ease, never rushed, no matter how hurried, worried, or miserable they might be. With a fatalistic shrug of the shoulder and a good dose of irony, the Neapolitans will say, "There's always the sun, the sun and the sea."

In the tumbledown, pungent port, fleets of rusty fishing boats bob. In a further cove, flotillas of aircraft carriers and destroyers glint in the merciless sun. Nearly naked youths trot along the sea-walk, and crowds of *scugnizz'* (street urchins) clamber over the rocks along the waterfront. Ignoring the "No Swimming" signs, they dive like dolphins through the murky waters. Troops of perma-tanned speedboaters lay siege to the classy watering holes in the Borgo-by-the-sea. And the hydrofoils skate from Mergellina to the fashionable islands of Capri and Ischia across the gulf. Above it all, to the east, twin-peaked Vesuvius looms large, belching out smoke in the mind's eye, sometimes capped in snow, a constant reminder of the frailty of all this human life and its precarious institutions. It does make the head spin.

You can call it Babylon-by-the-Bay or compare it to Calcutta, but Naples remains Naples, the original melting pot. The peculiar Neapolitan alloy is part Marsii, Samnite, Lucanian, Arabian, and Greek. Muses, sirens, nymphs, dryads, naiads, and countless other ancients, real or imaginary, set up shop here around 700 B.C. In the Middle Ages, their fecund offspring welcomed the Normans, Swabians,

Provençals, and Spaniards, plus an occasional northern Italian—all of them conquerors of the kingdom of Naples. The result is this semi-Oriental hodgepodge, which just happens to be governed for the time being by a nation-state known as Italy. The Neapolitans are the epitome of southern Italians. That is to say, they belong first to a family, then a clan, then a city, the only *real* city: Naples. They have successfully thwarted authority for several thousand years, so don't be surprised when you see them driving the wrong way on one-way streets or doing the exact opposite of what signs state, signals flash, or bans forbid.

The blight of poverty and corruption is extremely hard to ignore in Naples and probably shouldn't be ignored, since it is fundamental to the Neapolitan experience. Certainly, beauty and strength flank the Neapolitan "condition" of misery. But it's also dangerously tempting to overromanticize the wit-sharpening, hungry life of fascinating neighborhoods like the *bassi*. These first-floor one-room homes often double as tiny windowless shops. Until recently, the men would drag their mattresses into the street and sleep there, while the women and children all slept together on one huge bed at the back of the *basso*. The front door is always open, and as you walk by you cannot help looking in. A lamp often burns before an image of the Madonna, and old women sit together knitting and gossiping. There's little reason not to look in; the people who live here are used to it. They seem to enjoy the attention. While they often snap at fellow Neapolitans, they love foreigners. Hospitality—as in the Orient—is a way of life. You will probably find strangers doting on you, guiding you, reassuring you. It can be unnerving, all this warmth and good cheer, unless you warm up a tad yourself.

Most people here are passionate and outspoken. Don't confuse all the shouting and gesticulating with a show of anger. The Neapolitans' infamous reputation as perpetrators of violent crime is usually exaggerated. And local Mafia gangs pick each other off, leaving the tourists alone. All you have to worry about is fending off pickpockets and *scippatori*—the purse and package snatchers who often operate on Vespa motorbikes. You'd be surprised just how comfortable a money belt can feel in Naples. And ladies, leave your bag in the hotel, especially if you plan to tour the Porta Capuana area near Spaccanapoli, "the split of Naples" at the city's heart, running like a part down the ancient Roman Decumanus Maximus. The same street changes name six times in less than a mile. On it, sumptuous palazzi (the Sant'-Angelo, the Monte di Pietà, the Marigliano) share roofs with squalid tenements. It is grand, decaying, and dirty—one of the most fascinating districts in Italy.

Huge and serpentine, Naples is unlike any of the other marvelous human hives on the Peninsula. It spreads practically unbroken from the Bay of Pozzuoli to the Punta di Campanella, swallowing up Castellammare and Vico, all the way to Sorrento. Here and there a grove of cascading oranges or a vineyard has survived. Just off what used to "the foulest beach in the world" is the splendid Villa Pignatelli, a lovely park on the Riviera di Chiaia. Sections of the old city walls and gates are still intact, although not always obvious to the casual stroller. The pairs of round, crenellated towers along the bastions from Aragonese days are with few exceptions, in dire need of a savior—someone to clean them and repair them and protect them from the wild traffic and smog.

A sudden calm descends on chaotic Naples in the afternoon, from 1pm to 4pm, when siesta time rolls around. If you can stand the heat, this is the best time to sneak a peek at hidden courtyards off Corso Umberto, or find a seat in a fine caffè, like the ornate Caffè Gambrinus (in Piazza San Ferdinando), one of the oldest in town. The Galleria Umberto, an elaborate nineteenth-century shopping arcade, is a favorite place to rest tired feet and sample the local brew. Coffee-drinking in Naples is a fine art, another import from the Orient. The machine used in Neapolitan homes and many restaurants and caffès is nothing like the Moka Espresso so common in the rest of Italy. The Neapolitan coffee pot is actually two pots united, with a basket for the grounds in between. The coffee is steamed, then the machine is flipped and the coffee drips down into the bottom pot. This requires a good deal of time. But what's the rush? In Naples, coffee is always served with a glass

141

of water to slake the thirst. And if you like it unsweetened, you must ask for a *caffè amaro*. Otherwise, the bartender will automatically add the sugar.

Even the coffee houses are semiabandoned on Sunday afternoons. Is Vesuvius erupting or what? Everyone is yelling *calcio!* Soccer matches are followed with religious fervor in Naples. The stadium is always packed. Those who can't get in physically tune in on the radio or TV. Groups of fans clog streets, shouting and commenting, invoking San Gennaro and the Madonna. Piazza San Giovanni a Carbonara (also known as Santa Sofia) regularly becomes an impromptu soccer field, with multiple matches that turn into a sort of cheerful free-for-all, especially on Sundays. Sometimes the buses—which are notoriously unreliable—stop in the middle of a run as the driver rushes to find out who's winning.

Siestas and soccer matches slow all means of transport save one—your legs. Many of the streets and alleys of old Naples are too narrow for vehicles anyway. A good way to get around Naples is by taxi; just make sure the meter is in gear, and be prepared for Grand-Prix-style maneuvers. An ancient electrified tram runs from the central train station to the port at Mergellina, offering a colorful, crowded, and noisy ride that's a slice of untouristy Neapolitan life. The subway's older line runs from the station to points west, stopping at Piazza Cavour (for the Museo Nazionale), Piazza Amedeo (for one of the funicular railways to the hills), and Mergellina; another, newer, line mounts from Piazza Vanvitelli on the Vomero to the hospital zone in the city's northern reaches. The Funicolare Centrale climbs from the Piazzetta Duca d'Aosta, by the Galleria Umberto, to the Vomero, a leafy residential area high on the hills, with magnificent views of the city. The excellent Circumvesuviana train runs from the central station south, stopping in Pompeii, Herculaneum, and Sorrento. A cable car and bus link Herculaneum to the lip of Vesuvius.

As you can imagine, the most stupendous panorama of the Naples area is from the volcano. But is it safe? The last time Vesuvius blew its top was in 1944, and since then the smoke has stopped gushing out. Don't let the apparent calm fool you. Any Neapolitan will tell you that the only thing between you and the molten lava is San Gennaro. His statue towers like a benign traffic cop on the slopes of Vesuvius—to keep the lava at bay. His bones have been trotted out on various occasions and waved at the volcano to make it behave. It seems to have worked. But throw a little salt over your shoulder and clasp your antelope horn just to be safe.

You will quickly discover that among the superstitious Neapolitans, San Gennaro is a saint for all seasons. He's right up there with the Madonna and the greats of soccer in the Neapolitan pantheon. The martyred bishop's freshly spilled blood was bottled by a devout spectator and has been a major attraction for the last 1,700 years or so. It is stored in an unusual silver reliquary in the Chapel of San Gennaro (in the cathedral). Twice a year, in May and September, the divine substance liquefies and starts to froth in its crystal ampule. Skeptical? Well, the Neapolitans do not question its authenticity. And so far, modern science has failed to come up with a rational explanation for the miracle. Woe unto us if the blood fails to liquefy! It happened in 1527, and 60,000 Neapolitans died in the plague. A dry-blood year is a very bad omen for the city. Admittedly, in other years, when Naples was under siege or when hundreds of thousands died of starvation, or cholera, the blood bubbled and flowed as expected. But that means nothing to San Gennaro's faithful.

What about earthquakes, tidal waves, and all those buried cities of old? Victims of pre-San Gennaro Vesuvius fill the National Archaeological Museum—a must-see, and alone worth the trip to Naples. It houses more of Pompeii and Herculaneum than the actual archeological sites. The volcano vomited lava and ash on the grand old Roman bathing resorts in A.D. 79. Amazingly enough, not everything went up in smoke. The nuts, olives, and other tidbits from the Herculaneans' last supper are artfully displayed, along with buttons, and pins, and manicure sets from the boudoirs of Pompeian beauties. The Grand Masters Gallery is home of the *Farnese Hercules* and the *Farnese Bull*, the largest sculpture group from antiquity. Sprouting just to the north of the National Museum is Capodimonte, with its marvelous picture galleries (masterworks by Masaccio, Bellini, and Botticelli are on the second floor), surrounded by a wooded park with fine views.

Beyond the museums and monuments, life pulsates in the piazzas and caffès, the restaurants and dance halls, and that is where the Neapolitans are seen at their best. Their favorite hour is dusk. In the twilight, in the age-old central city, they fling their shutters open and appear at windows. They slip out into the cooling streets, men and women and extended families, and promenade conspicuously through the boggling scenery. In the dance halls, where the accordions drone and leap from key to key, the *tarantella* survives despite the disco. It is the most Neapolitan of dances, a love story enacted on the floor. The partners war and woo, pet and bill, warble and coo. And you can see the ancient madness induced by the tarantula bite—the origin of the dance—in the their eyes. Only a melancholy melody in a minor key, accelerating imperceptibly into a heart-plucking *pizzicato*, can cure them.

There's no point in being a wallflower in Naples. You've got to get out and polish the paving stones, if not the dance floor. Those who take the time to get to know Naples almost always get bitten by the bug, and wind up loving the city. Indeed, Napoli has a bite all its own—a nibble that stirs the heart. The goal of this candid guide is to be your back-pocket San Gennaro, to whisk you into the best of Naples—the warmth, the wonder—and keep you out of the web of what is best left unsavored.

The Head

What would Naples be if it had a Body and not a Head? There it is in white marble, larger than life, staring out from the grand staircase at Palazzo San Giacomo (city hall). The head has a name—Donna Marianna—and a full head of hair neatly parted down the middle. Some say Donna Marianna is really the siren Parthenope (legendary founder of the city), and others insists she's Venus, goddess of pulchritude and the pleasures of the flesh. The head popped up during the 1500s (no one remembers where), but was sculpted in the Greco-Roman era, some time just before or after Christ. It has become a symbol of Naples and source of popular myths. For about 400 years the head surveyed one of the city's most bustling working-class neighborhoods. Then, one fateful day in 1954 a lightning-fast team from the public-works department struck with pick and shovel. They pried the head from its pediment and rushed it to a warehouse. It disappeared for years (restoration) and surfaced in 1960 in the Rotonda of Via Caracciolo (to celebrate the Olympics). Then it was housed in the municipal museum until 1962, when it turned up on the staircase at city hall. The rest of the head's history is of interest primarily to stamp collectors. In 1975 the Republic of San Marino reproduced Donna Marianna on a 50-lira stamp to celebrate the International Philatelic Exposition at Palazzo Reale in Naples. About one million Heads of Naples then took to the sky, winging their way into the stamp books of the world.

Restaurants

Vibrant, exuberant, a riot of vivid colors, keen scents, and fresh flavors: the best Neapolitan cooking is as gratifying to the spirit as it is to the palate. Brilliant sun produces luscious fruit; rich volcanic soil yields taut-skinned vegetables bursting with flavor; and the teeming Bay of Naples ensures a bounty of seafood. Happily, the local character tends to make the most of nature's generosity, inventing pretexts for enjoying the pleasures of food at nearly every hour of the day, in addition to regular meal times. What may be the best coffee in Europe is brewed here, a perfect foil for lush, cream-filled pastries. And Naples, you'll recall, is the birthplace of pizza—the original snack food—and the cradle of some of humanity's most gifted *gelatai* (ice-cream makers).

In Naples, good places to eat are legion. They tend to be small, crowded with habitués, and unrecorded by guidebooks (our own list is representative but not exhaustive). So don't be afraid to follow your nose into any eatery that strikes you as *simpatico*. You can usually count on being welcomed with the Neapolitans' legendary warmth. What's more, their inbred theatrical bent (which naturally comes to the fore in a restaurant), makes eating out in this town a joyful, many-layered social and linguistic experience.

Displayed near the entrance of many *ristoranti* is a colorful, abundant assortment of antipasti: raw anchovies (alici crudi) in a lemon marinade, octopus salad, shrimp, tuna, glistening eggplant or mushrooms sott'olio (in olive oil), fried zucchini blossoms, roasted red and yellow peppers, and more. If you crave something warm, there are pizzette (little pizzas) or bruschetta (chewy bread toasted, rubbed with garlic, sprinkled with olive oil, and topped with fresh tomatoes). These tasty little nibbles rouse the appetite and prepare the palate for the two major themes on which a Neapolitan meal provides so many seductive variations: the garden and the sea.

Myriad forms of hard-wheat macaroni dominate the pasta course: spaghetti, linguine, rigatoni, fusilli... One good way to enjoy them is alla napoletana, sauced with tomatoes and a bright spark of basil; another is alla pescatora, garnished with a heap of mixed mussels, cockles, and shrimp; still another is with a sauce of the local clams, known as vongole (remember that *real* vongole—the ones that cost the most—have little "horns," like snails). Lavish fish soups are an alternative to pasta, and are often a chef's special source of pride.

The Neapolitan way with seafood is simplicity itself. Shellfish are sautéed in oil with herbs, fish are usually roasted, grilled, poached (in acqua pazza—"crazy water"—sea water with tomatoes, herbs, and garlic) or baked in parchment. If the fish is of top quality, and if the cook knows when to take it off the fire (overcooking is the worst thing that happens to seafood in Naples), the result can be sublime. Swordfish, fresh tuna, and tiny red mullet are the varieties to sample, but sea bream, sea bass, octopus, and squid are also excellent hereabouts.

Fish may hold the center stage, but meat has its place in the Neapolitan kitchen. Veal scallops, especially, appear with any number of fresh-tasting sauces: alla pizzaiola (with tomatoes and oregano), al limone, piccanti (with anchovies and capers).

Mozzarella di bufala, made with the milk of water buffalo, is a prized local specialty. Neapolitans enjoy it alone or with tomatoes as an antipasto, in deep-fried sandwiches (mozzarella in carrozza) as a snack or a starter, as a topping for pizza, or melted over veal scallops or eggplant.

144

Extravagant sweets like sfogliatelle (flaky feuilletés filled with sweetened ricotta), which beckon to passersby from pastry-shop windows, are best appreciated on their own at midmorning or teatime. To close a meal, the best (and most typically Neapolitan) choice is a selection of the splendid local fruit: fat green and purple grapes, perfumed peaches, downy apricots presented in a bowl of cool water.

Seafood and vegetables call for white wines, and Campania provides some fine examples. Forget the Lachryma Christi (the name is more poetic than what's in the bottle), and call instead for a flavorsome Fiano di Avellino or a Greco di Tufo, white wines with plenty of character. Most restaurants propose a house wine, usually a light-bodied Ischian white, which goes down easy but is hardly memorable. If red wine is what you want, a local variety worth tasting is Ravello, dry and full-bodied. *Buon appetito!*

Amici Miei

Via Monte di Dio 77 - (081) 7646063
Closed Sun dinner, Mon, Aug. All major cards.

When the final curtain falls at the nearby Teatro Politeama, many of the theater goers head straight for a table in one of the two little dining rooms of Amici Miei ("My Friends"). A plate of assorted charcuterie gets things under way, followed by very good risottos or homemade pasta in myriad forms: orecchiette ("little ears") with chickpeas, fusilli dressed with seasonal vegetables, pappardelle sauced with lamb ragù. Steaks and chops come sizzling from the coals with a lively accompaniment of grilled radicchio. The fruit tarts look fresh and attractive, but the chocolate cream is the chef's pride, made from an ancient Neapolitan recipe. The cellar stocks good regional wines. C 50,000 lire.

La Bersagliera

Borgo Marinaro 10 - (081) 7646016
Closed Tue. All major cards.

Everybody knows La Bersagliera, with its vast terrace stretched out over the quays of Porto Santa Lucia. The moment dusk falls, the huge neon sign blazes out into the Neapolitan night. Tall turn-of-the-century mirrors reflect the diners who stream in from all corners of the city. The new owner, Signor Agostino, has revamped La Bersagliera's menu with recipes from

another age: try the intriguing salad of fifteen herbs and plants tossed with premium olive oil, then move on to the Renaissance extravaganza known as "the abbess's timbale," or lightly fried spinach and ricotta croquettes, or turkey cutlet showered with almonds. Offerings from the restaurant's glory days (it used to be the haunt of artists and international film stars) include very good spaghetti with mussels, octopus salad, and deep-fried mozzarella. For dessert, don't miss the tart topped with wild berries and rose petals. C 50-55,000 lire (wine incl).

La Cantina di Triunfo

Riviera di Chiaia 64 - (081) 668101
Closed Sun, Aug. No cards.

Tina and Carmine Triunfo have made a triumphant success of their Cantina: it's one of the city's jolliest dinner spots—and one of the best. Tina gives a creative spin to popular Neapolitan dishes, and she also dusts off some of the elaborate, time-consuming recipes that once graced the tables of the local bourgeoisie. The concise menu changes often, for she hews closely to the seasons and the tides. If it's on offer, you must try Tina's pasticcio di pesce, a lush oven-baked amalgam of fish, potatoes, artichokes, and zucchini; still more baroque and typically Neapolitan is the timpano di scàmmaro: molded macaroni and mussels bound with a sauce of shrimp, mushrooms, and tiny peas. She also turns out a warming soup of beans and crumbled chestnuts; linguine topped with squid, raisins, and pine nuts; and a magnificent pastry-wrapped eggplant flan set on a bed of creamy Provola cheese. Desserts display irresistible Southern flair: there's orange and almond tart, blancmange made from a medieval recipe, and a curious—delicious!—torta of eggplant and chocolate. Carmine, who oversees the dining room, will tell you just what bottle to choose from his glorious collection of little-known growers' wines. C 40,000 lire (wine incl).

La Cantinella

Via Cuma 42 - (081) 7648684
Closed Sun, Aug. All major cards.

Portable telephones are obviously regarded as "power accessories" by the young executives eager to impress the clients they bring to lunch at La Cantinella.

This restaurant has long been reputed as the city's finest; with its air-conditioned veranda and spectacular view of Mount Vesuvius and the Bay of Naples, it is surely one of the most attractive. Unfortunately, the cooking no longer warrants the high ratings of yore. The tables, however, are elegant indeed, laid with lovely china and silver; the wine list, too, is a handsome piece of work, with a very nice selection of French and Italian bottlings. By all means, come in to savor the atmosphere—just don't expect the food to rise above the ordinary. **C** 80-90,000 lire.

 ### Casanova Grill
Hotel Excelsior,
Via Partenope 48 - (081) 7640111
Open daily. All major cards.

The Casanova Grill may indeed be the restaurant of the most luxurious hotel in Naples, but it doesn't exactly pack them in. It's a shame, really, because the chef has a deft way with the region's fine produce: he turns these fresh ingredients into such authentic Neapolitan classics as eggplant parmigiana, maccheroni al ragù (a savory meat sauce), anchovy terrine, incomparably crisp deep-fried delicacies, and gloriously flavorful fish. The "Continental" dishes don't compare to the rest, though they are as good here as in any other hotel dining room. Desserts, mostly of the lavish, Southern variety, are worth saving room for. **C** 100,000 lire.

 ### Al '53
Piazza Dante 53 - (081) 341124
Closed Thu, Aug 10-25. No cards.

The mood here is casual and laid-back, but the food possesses a certain majesty. The sheer abundance of antipasti is impressive: fried tidbits, seafood salads, little pizzas, and marinated vegetables pave the way for linguine with fish sauce, sartù di riso (an elaborate affair involving rice molded around a filling of meatballs and vegetables), and zuppa forte (a restorative winter soup that incorporates every edible part of a pig). Afterward comes a procession of stupendous sausages, colorful meat-stuffed sweet peppers, and grilled chops, steaks, or cutlets in the zesty tomato sauce known as pizzaiola. Regal desserts; modest but irresistibly tasty local wines.
If the room is full, try for a table at Dante e Beatrice, also on Piazza Dante. The am-

bience, menu, and prices are virtually indistinguishable. **C** 50,000 lire.

Footloose Fountain

The *Fontana dell'Immacolatella* has been running for centuries—in various locations all over the center of Naples. Three elegant arches leaping over pairs of Tritons and caryatids, the fountain was cobbled together by various illustrious artists, among them Pietro Bernini and Michelangelo Naccherino. Back in the seventeenth century it flanked the Palazzo Reale, a lively meeting place in the very heart of the city. But in 1815 the water was shut off and the fountain carted to the port. It was reassembled near the harmonious palazzo—crowned with a statue of the *Immacolatella*, or Immaculate Virgin—designed by Domenico Antonio Vaccaro. Here it plashed away for over half a century and earned its felicitous nickname. But alas, progress came chugging along, spewing smoke and cinders. The fountain was removed to make way for the railroad. It wound up in the nearby Villa del Popolo. Nowadays you can listen to its waters play along the curve of Via Partenope and Via Nazario Sauro.

 ### Ciro a Mergellina
Via Mergellina 18-21 - (081) 681780
Closed Mon. All major cards.

We'll stick our necks out and say that for our money, the pizza served here is the best in Naples (which pretty much amounts to saying it's the best in the world). Also worth sampling are the traditional "Sunday dinner" dishes and the "poor man's" fare that are the complementary components of the Neapolitan table. Splendid vegetables filled with complex stuffings of meat and herbs, a profusion of deep-fried morsels (don't overlook the unforgettable fried sea bass), elaborate baked pastas and timbales share the limelight with crunchy potato croquettes, mozzarella in carrozza, and the aforementioned pizzas (we won't even attempt to describe them: they must be tasted to be believed). The wheeling, whirling waiters who serve these good things provide plenty of free entertainment. The average bill hovers around 50,000 lire, but you'll pay less if you choose pizza, more if you opt for sea bass and other expensive fish. **C** 50,000 lire.

Ciro a Santa Brigida

Via Santa Brigida 71 - (081) 5524072
Closed Sun (& Sat in Jul), Aug. All major cards.
Ciro is an old-time Neapolitan establishment which has moved gracefully into the modern age: the menu is printed out daily by computer! But the food is as traditional as can be. Generous seafood antipasti lead into heartwarming pastas and soups. If you find it on the menu, by all means sample the zuppa maritata, a rustic blend of assorted greens and pork in a finely flavored broth. Authentic Neapolitan pizza topped with mozzarella di bufala is a treat. Mozzarella is prepared in carrozza (deep-fried) as well, accompanied by zesty marinated zucchini. If you're in Naples around Christmas, New Year's, or Easter, come here to sample the city's festive and distinctive holiday fare. The limited wine list highlights tasty, unpretentious regional bottles. **C** 60,000 lire.

Il Delicato
Largo Sermoneta 34 - (081) 667047
Closed Sun, 10 days mid Aug. All major cards.
It's not the display of glistening fresh fish and madly expensive shellfish that draws crowds to Il Delicato; nor is it for a table on the airy terrace that people wait in line. No, what the noisy groups and quieter couples are after is a table in the (often stifling) dining room, and a few traditional dishes that they order without even a glance at the ornate menu. What they crave is pizza, or manfredi (broad eggless noodles) with ricotta, or peppery penne all'arrabbiata, or the famous deep-fried squash blossoms. Now, we find the latter—and the rest of the fried items—a trifle greasy, but we seem to be in the minority. If the pastries have run out (or even if they haven't), we recommend that you finish up with some sun-gorged seasonal fruit. The decent house wine won't add too much freight to the bill. **C** 60,000 lire.

Don Salvatore

Via Mergellina 5 - (081) 681817
Closed Wed. All major cards.
This picturesque tavern boasts a terrace on Mergellina just steps from the pleasure port as well as two cool white dining rooms and straightforward regional fare. The dishes are written on the menu in Neapolitan dialect: presutte e muzarelle (prosciutto and mozzarella), inzalata e purpe (octopus salad), and tubetti con le cozze (stubby macaroni with mussels). The fish comes right out of the Bay of Naples; do sample the luscious fravaglie (tiny fried red mullet), much moister than the larger grilled specimens. Memorable, too, are mazzancolle (shrimp) in chickpea purée, braised squid, and sculpin in an orange-scented sauce. The wine list is encyclopedic, the work of owner Tonino Aversano. Because this passionate pro wants others to know and love Italian wines as much as he does, Aversano offers his treasures at very attractive prices—and the variety of grappas (Italian brandies) in stock is boggling. **C** 60,000 lire.

Ettore
Via Santa Lucia 56 - (081) 7640498
Closed Sun, Aug. No cards.
Don't be daunted by the line of would-be customers that clusters outside of Ettore's eatery. Your patience will be amply rewarded by one of the best pizzas you'll ever put a tooth to: piping hot, generously topped, with a chewy, yeasty crust. The calzone (a folded-over pizza here called "pagnotello") has its fans, and the spaghetti sauced with seafood also comes highly recommended. If a fabulous fritto misto is your idea of a treat, don't miss the Neapolitan version offered here: it features fried mozzarella, eggplant, potato croquettes, rice balls, and more. You can finish up with homemade bigné (beignets) filled with sweet pastry cream, or gorgeous fresh fruit. **C** 40-55,000 lire (with fish, less with pizza).

Gallo Nero
Via Tasso 466 - (081) 643012
Open Tue-Sat dinner, Sun lunch. Closed Aug. All major cards.
This magnificent nineteenth-century villa set in the hills overlooking Mergellina possesses several dining rooms, all charmingly arranged like little salons. Since there is no written menu and the offerings change

San Gennaro's Bomb Shelter

Everyone knows about the wondrous powers of this most Neapolitan of saints. San Gennaro is friend to the man in the street and the lady on the sidewalk, a wise counselor to the rich and poor alike, and first-rate when it comes to doing battle with the Bourbon bureaucracy. But hardly anyone knows where his house is—that is, the place he was born (in A.D. 272). You can visit it at 41 Via San Gregorio Armeno, site of the delightful Baroque Palazzo dell'Accademia Ercolanese (early 1600s), which was piled on top of San Gennaro's home. During the last world war, terrified neighbors used the ancient ruin—a sort of crypt—as a bomb shelter (the stairway in the back of the courtyard leads down to it). Many a neck was saved, thanks again to San Gennaro.

almost daily, the maître d' plays an essential role in orchestrating a meal at Il Gallo Nero. Pino Musto is equal to the task, modulating the succession of courses with a keen sense of textures, colors, and flavors. On a recent evening, we started out on a crisp, ethereal note with an assortment of fried tidbits and arancini (little rice balls), followed by a delicately refreshing salad of marinated octopus and artichokes, and an explosively tasty cassuoletta of braised cuttlefish, squid, potatoes, and baby tomatoes. After an interlude of linguine with mussels and capers came swordfish rolls with a chili-fired seafood stuffing—a resounding success. The food is remarkably light, since the chef uses oil sparingly; we only wish that he would take his seafood off the stove half a tick sooner. Desserts leave no lingering memory, save for the coffee and gianduia (chocolate-hazelnut) tartlets. There's an attractive cellar, and the piano bar on the veranda is an ideal place to bring the evening to a close. **C** 70,000 lire.

Da Giovanni
Via Domenico Morelli 14
(081) 7643565
Closed Sun, Aug. V, AE.

Tonino Falco puts his guests immediately at ease, with good-humored Neapolitan hospitality and elegant variations on traditional Neapolitan food. If they're on offer, try the imperial prawns paired with peppery arugula; pasta with spollichini (tender country beans) is another good way to start off. Main courses focus on the freshest imaginable fish, presented in acqua pazza (sea water, tomatoes, herbs), in fragrant marinara sauce, or simply grilled to moist perfection. Bollito misto (mixed boiled meats) is a dish rarely seen in these parts, and Da Giovanni's version makes a delicious change of pace from seafood. Top dessert honors go to the oven-fresh tarts topped with cherries on a layer of pastry cream or fragrant wild strawberries. Decent cellar. **C** 65,000 lire (wine incl).

Gorizia
Via Bernini 29 - (081) 5782248
Closed Wed, Aug. No cards.

Perched high on the Vomero hill, for decades Gorizia has been a mecca for pizza lovers. The pizza napoletana, baked in a wood-fired oven, is in a class by itself. For variety, you could also sample the zesty mushroom and anchovy version, or try something entirely different: octopus alla Luciana, for example. Tasty local wines; lavish traditional sweets. Expect to pay 10-15,000 lire for pizza and a beverage, 50,000 lire for a full meal. **C** 50,000 lire.

Hotel Cavour
Piazza Garibaldi 34 - (081) 283122
Closed Sun, 2 wks in Aug. All major cards.

A good hotel restaurant is a rare commodity in Naples. All the more reason, then, to encourage the efforts of the Hotel Cavour. In addition to a place to sleep, guests are offered well prepared, satisfying, not exclusively Neapolitan cooking. You'll find a wide range of pastas and superbly fresh fish handled with a pleasing touch of personality. Be sure to taste the mozzarella di bufala, a particular source of pride. The cellar, however, is mighty mundane. **C** 60,000 lire.

Mimì alla Ferrovia
Via Alfonso d'Aragona 21
(081) 5538525
Closed Sun. All major cards.
You can't miss Mimì's: it's lit up with lots of neon on an unprepossessing street not far from the railway station. Show up with an appetite, and throw away your watch— a meal here shouldn't be picked at or rushed! You can order a steaming bowl of pasta e fagioli (pasta and beans) for a song, or spend a princely sum on a splendid grilled lobster. The Giugliano brothers spare no effort for their customers; in addition to such classics as linguine garnished with a startling array of local shellfish, they propose some personal creations inspired by the market and the catch of the day. Don't ruin your meal with the house wine, a gassy white from Ischia; ask for the wine list instead. The generous food, friendly service, and reasonable prices attract a mixed clientele of families, young couples and (usually boisterous) groups of friends. **C** 50-70,000 lire.

 Mimì-Gi
Centro Direzionale, Isolato G, Galleria Le Gemme - (081) 5625182
Closed Sun, Aug 10-20. All major cards.
Business travelers whose work takes them to the city's new Centro Direzionale, should note this address, an offshoot of the Mimì described above. It is both a *tavola calda* serving ready-made, swiftly served specialties, and a restaurant offering dishes prepared to order. There's an appealing daily menu that often highlights fresh fish, and a tempting array of antipasti and sweets that display the same high quality for which the mother house is famous. **C** 40,000 lire.

 Osteria Enoteca da Tonino
Santa Teresa a Chiaia 47 - (081) 421533
Lunch only (dinner also on Fri & Sat Oct-May). Closed Sun, Aug. No cards.
Tonino and Nina Acanfora run one of the oldest taverns in Naples, a tiny two-room affair with just eight tables. The handwritten menu proposes the sort of old-fashioned Neapolitan home cooking one hardly ever encounters these days—in or out of the home! There are heartwarming pastas, combined with cauliflower, or pumpkin, or chickpeas. On a given day, you might find ziti sauced with meaty ragù napoletano (and followed, logically, by

braciole: thin-sliced beef rolled up around a garlicky filling); rich gattò di patate (a potato cake enriched with cheeses and bits of salami); or molded anchovies perfumed with fresh oregano. Tonino seats patrons according to what he instinctively feels are their "affinities," so a lunch here promises to be more than just a gastronomic adventure! Rock-bottom prices. **C** 15,000 lire.

 Il Pozzo
Via Fratelli Magnoni 18 - (081) 668333
Closed Sun. No cards.
Nostalgic, "popular" dishes are executed here with polished technique. Each day brings a profusion of flavorsome antipasti (we're particularly fond of the boned pig's trotters, cubed and fried to golden crispness) and zesty pastas, like linguine allo scammaro, topped with green and black olives, anchovies, capers, and Pecorino cheese. Riso brusciato—rice cooked in a mediocre red sauce—elicits no enthusiasm, but the tortino of orange-fleshed zucca squash in a faintly sweet pastry crust is a rare and wonderful dish. Tasty, too, are strips of tender braised beef in a nice, tight sauce. Chef Antonio takes special care with desserts: try the tangy fruit sherbets or the dark bitter-chocolate cake. Choose your wine from the good list of local bottlings. **C** 50,000 lire.

I Quattro Caini
Via Cinzia 41 - (081) 7674949
Closed Mon, 3 wks in Aug, 3 days at Christmas. All major cards.
In Naples, where word of mouth can make or break a reputation, the presence of large crowds in a restaurant is usually a sign of high quality. There's almost always a cheerful crush in I Quattro Caini, a typically Neapolitan spot where you can munch on genuine garlic bread (with just a whisper of garlic and lots of fruity olive oil) or tiny pizzas garnished with baby sardines, before digging into a heaping plateful of spaghetti with seafood or rigatoni alla mammà, rich with ricotta and mozzarella cheeses. Main courses are mostly seafood; we enjoyed the sunny flavor of mazzancolle con aglio e peperoni (large shrimp with garlic and sweet peppers). Peppe, the cook, turns out yummy pastries, and the cellar holds many varieties of tasty Campanian whites. **C** 60,000 lire.

15 Rosiello

At Posillipo, Via Santo Strato 10
(081) 7691288
Closed Wed, 2 wks in Aug. All major cards.
From Rosiello's wisteria-shaded terrace you can drink in a picture-postcard vista of bella Napoli: Sorrento, the islands, lordly Mount Vesuvius... The kitchen, commendably, does its best to complement the seductive surroundings. Taste the fresh, milky mozzarella paired with the tiniest of tomatoes, or silken prosciutto partnered with fragrant figs and vintage Parmesan. Baby squid fried to golden crispness make a lovely first course, but then so do sea snails (lumachine di mare) simmered in an herbal broth. If you can't do without pasta, go for the linguine with octopus or prawn sauce. In addition to locally caught fish, which are poached, baked, or braised, there is a savory pan-roasted rabbit, or braciola (a thin beefsteak) folded around a stuffing of pine nuts and raisins. Whatever you choose, do save room for the almond or marmalade tarts, or the classic Neapolitan ricotta cake called pastiera. **C** 75,000 lire (wine incl).

14 Rosolino

Via Nazario Sauro 5 - (081) 7649873
Dinner only. Closed Sun, Aug. All major cards.
The large panels of colored glass that decorate the bar and dining room, the overhanging balcony and the stage where a comely chanteuse croons at her piano all call to mind one of those big movie houses of yore. But Rosolino is indeed a restaurant, a great favorite with the upper reaches of Neapolitan society. The food is traditional, from the antipasti laid out in splendor on a large buffet to the scaloppine al limone and the sumptuous fried sea bass (spigola fritta). The prices are well beyond those charged by neighborhood trattorias, which this place is emphatically not. After dinner, you can take to the dance floor (polished to a blinding shine) and quaff Spumante or Champagne, which the management thoughtfully keeps on ice for you, just in case. Next door, the Posto Accanto restaurant (same kitchen, same management) serves lunch as well as dinner, for less money (about 50,000 lire). **C** 80,000 lire.

The prices *in this guide reflect what establishments were charging at press time.*

18 La Sacrestia

Via Orazio 116 - (081) 664186
Closed Mon (Sun in Jul), 3 wks in Aug. All major cards.
For what seems like ages now, this garden terrace in a posh residential district on the heights of Posillipo has been a favorite with fashionable Neapolitans and pretty Americans accompanied by their local *cavalieri serventi*. Among the attractions are a stupendous view of the bay, utterly polished service, and a bright, comfortable dining room for days when the weather turns inclement. This year, we spent less money and enjoyed our meal more than ever before. The kitchen, it seems, has charted a new course, eschewing costly ingredients and putting an inventive spin on the menu. There's no *déjà vu* about the lusty likes of pasta and potatoes enriched with smoked Scamorza cheese, famously tasty bucatini (hollow spaghetti) sauced with puréed, wine-braised onions, lightly pickled shrimp dusted with flour and fried to a golden turn, sea-sweet sole paired with barely cooked baby artichokes, or bluefish poached in a zesty broth flavored with pancetta and garlic. At dessert time, the offerings revert to tried-and-true Neapolitan favorites—pastiera, babà, sweet fritters—to which chef Mariano occasionally adds an imaginative touch of his own. **C** 80,000 lire.

12/20 Vini e Cucina

Corso Vittorio Emanuele 762
(081) 660302
Closed Sun, Aug 20-30. No cards.
If the 60 seats of this trattoria across from Mergellina station fill up so quickly, it's because everybody loves authentic Neapolitan home cooking. People come from all over the city to this modest eatery—the décor was just spruced up a year or two ago—for a bowl of zuppa primavera (peas, fava beans, artichokes...), or pasta e fagioli (pasta and beans), linguine alla puttanesca (the zingy sauce features capers, olives, garlic, hot pepper), and a simple grill of beef or pork. Tripe is the specialty of the house, but it is only available in the cooler months when the essential ingredients of the dish are in prime condition. Start off your meal with a whole mozzarella poised on a bed of fresh greens, and end it with the famous torta caprese, drink the frisky white Cam-

panian wine, and you will begin to understand the importance of life's humbler pleasures. **C** 20,000 lire (wine incl).

Zi' Teresa
Borgo Marinaro 1 - (081) 7642565
Closed Mon, 2 wks in Aug. All major cards.
At the turn of the century, the beautiful Teresa Fusco hawked cakes and mineral water on Borgo Marinaro; later, she sold cooked food to the fishermen who took Teresa's specialties out with them on their boats. Before long, Zi' ("Auntie") Teresa was running the most famous restaurant in Naples, with patrons that included Toscanini, D'Annunzio, and international celebrities. After a long decline, this address is on the upswing owing to the efforts of the Della Notte brothers. Freshly revamped, it's now a luxurious spot. The food is still uneven, but you won't go far wrong if you order the tubetti del Borgo (stubby macaroni garnished with mussels, crabmeat, and tiny tomatoes), baby octopus braised in its juices with tomatoes, and any of the zingy, fresh lemon desserts. The region's wines are well represented. **C** 60,000 lire.

■ In **Amalfi**   62 km S

La Caravella
Via Matteo Camera 12 - (089) 871029
Closed Tue, 3 wks in Nov. V, AE.
Tiny red mullet (fragaglie) grilled in lemon leaves makes an auspicious beginning to a lunch at La Caravella. To follow, why not sample linguine dressed with pesto amalfitano (a savory mélange of capers, olives, oil, and a hint of anchovy), then move on to fresh fish sparked by a light, lemony (too lemony?) little sauce and surrounded by a bouquet of seasonal vegetables. Citrus also features prominently in the mousse, soufflé, and biscottini offered for dessert. The cellar's better than it used to be, but the décor could stand further improvement. **C** 60,000 lire.

Da Gemma
Via Frà Gerardo Sasso 9
(089) 871345
Closed Wed, mid Jan-mid Feb. All major cards.
Gemma is gone, but her sons Marco and Franco carry on in this restaurant just across the street from Amalfi's splendid cathedral. The dreamy summer terrace boasts a panoramic view of the region's

breathtaking scenery. It's a perfect spot to enjoy uncomplicated seafood: shellfish salads and sautés, linguine with scampi, cold poached sea bass, and a mixed grill of the day's catch. Do try the tangy Provola cheese grilled over hot coals and served on a dark-green bed of lemon leaves. Desserts are delicious and homemade, and the appealing wines come from Campania and Sicily. **C** 60,000 lire.

Sirens on a Drag Strip

Once upon a time... the gates to the city opened under monumental archways, like Porta Capuana and Porta Nolana (both near the train station these days). Giant metal dragons have taken their place. They stand on the feverishly fast expressway and let drivers know they are crossing the city limits. The designers claim that the dragons are both an aesthetic enhancement and a lucky charm, a means of protecting the city from evil (like the snake carved on the Parthenon). We don't know about that, but at least the dragons are better than billboards. The brace behind them, by the by, is a metal silhouette shaped like the siren Parthenope, the mythical founder of Naples.

Santa Caterina
Hotel Santa Caterina,
At Pastena, S.S. Amalfitana - (089) 871012
Open daily. All major cards.
The menu pays homage to the sort of food apparently preferred by the denizens of luxury hotels: oysters, salmon, shrimp are all present and accounted for. But we recommend that you choose instead from the daily specials (*proposte del giorno*); not only are they in tune with the setting (the view of Amalfi will take your breath away!), they also showcase the gorgeous local produce. The day's list might feature tagliolini swathed in a keen-flavored lemon sauce or laganelle topped with asparagus tips, followed by a soul-satisfying brodetto di pesce: just-caught fish briefly braised in a tight tomato sauce with

a garnish of sea-sweet clams. The desserts number among the region's best. **C** 75-100,000 lire.

■ In Bacoli   24 km W

L'Altro Cucchiaro
Porticciolo di Baia - (081) 8687196
Closed Mon, Aug 10-30. V, AE.
The elegant surroundings, warm wood paneling, rich draperies and gleaming silver are a delight to the eye. The patrons of this upscale fish house are numerous and loyal, making reservations indispensable. Local waters furnish the ingredients for every course save dessert: fresh anchovies for a lively antipasto, then linguine with crab or risotto al mare, and for the main event, lobster or the day's catch, either baked in parchment or seared on the grill. The chef's popular chocolate-almond cake provides a fine, rich finish. The wine list offers a winning selection of regional whites that make superb companions for seafood. **C** 60,000 lire.

Love at First Sight

Right in the tender heart of Naples, where the ancient Greco-Roman fabric of streets was never rent, stands the thirteenth-century church of San Lorenzo Maggiore, in Piazza San Gaetano. Beyond the artistic merits of the place, it's worth a visit for sentimental reasons. Giovanni Boccaccio, Italy's greatest storyteller, fell head over heels in love with Fiammetta there. The course of Italian and English literary history—Chaucer learned his trade by reading Boccaccio's Decameron—was altered by his palpitations.

La Misenetta
Via Lungolago 2 - (081) 5234169
Open daily May-Jul. Closed Wed from Sep-Apr, Aug, Christmas-Jan 3. V, AE.
Come to this lovely spot near the coastal lagoon of Lake Misena (a site celebrated by the immortal poet, Virgil) for a memorable seafood feast. Another great poet, Giuseppe Ungaretti, gave the restaurant its name. You'll doubtless be inspired too by the fine food served by owner Salvatore Di Meo. Prime local ingredients from sea and farm are put to exemplary use in dishes that have an indefinable French flair, owing to the influence of Salvatore's wife, Nicole. To start, taste the spectacular fish pie embellished with sweet-pepper sauce, or risotto enriched with zucchini and shrimp, or bucatini (hollow spaghetti) sauced with eggplant and fresh mozzarella, then proceed to monkfish in a saffron-stained sauce, scampi enhanced with a salsa of pale-green lettuce and melon, or a superlative steamed sea bass. The sherbets and other sweet finales are all crafted in-house, and Salvatore has few peers when it comes to matching wines with this wonderful food. **C** 80-90,000 lire.

■ In Capri   90 min by ferry, 40 min by hydrofoil

Aurora
Via Fuorlovado 18 - (081) 8370181
Closed Nov-Apr. V, AE.
Crusty, crackling, fragrant pizzas—the best on the island—are the specialty of the house. The décor is simple: Just a few celebrity photos (Roger Moore, Anita Ekberg, Luchino Visconti) smile down from the walls. But nobody seems to mind. What folks come here for is that famous pizza as well as for spaghetti with big, meaty mussels, marinated zucchini with lobster, grilled scampi, and delicious stuffed squid. The ideal companion for this rustic fare is a cool bottle of Greco di Tufo, a Campanian white wine with lots of fruit and character. Reservations are a must. **C** 40-50,000 lire.

12/20 La Canzone del Mare
Via Marina Piccola 93 - (081) 8370104
Lunch only. Closed Nov-Mar. V, AE.
The toniest spot for lunch on the isle of Capri, frequented by jet-setters and celebrities. At the lovely outdoor tables, fleet-footed waiters greet patrons with a pitcher of white-wine sangria loaded with peaches, pineapple, and melon, accompanied by an appetizer of crunchy little fragaglie (deep-fried red mullet). From there, you'll progress to linguine dressed with crabmeat or zucchini, or penne with eggplant and tomatoes, followed by braised squid or baked fresh fish. For dessert, we like the bright raspberry tart or the torta caprese. **C** 70,000 lire.

La Capannina
Via delle Botteghe 14
(081) 8370732
Closed Wed (exc in Aug), beg Nov-Mar 20-25. V, AE, EC, MC.
Always seasonal, dependably fresh, the menu at La Capannina varies from day to day. Among the bounty of appetizing dishes we've savored lately are a lively assortment of sautéed shellfish, linguine tossed with a tasty sauce of scorfano (Mediterranean rockfish), a light minestrone featuring a gardenful of baby vegetables, famously good stuffed squid, and rabbit alla caprese. Polish off your bottle of local wine with a bit of cheese, then ask for some of the delicious house-made almond cake. **C** 60,000 lire.

 I Faraglioni
Via Camerelle 75 - (081) 837020
Closed Mon, mid Oct-Apr 1. All major cards.
In the beginning, I Faraglioni was probably nothing more than a fishermen's bar. Its lowly appearance hasn't changed much, so passersby may not realize that it is one of the island's better restaurants. And there is no lack of passersby: tourists trek along Via Camerelle on their way to the panoramic view at Tragara point, and when we've dined here, every one of them, it seems, inspected the contents of our plates. Of course, that does not diminish the quality of what's on them. I Faraglioni's fish is beautifully fresh and firm, and the pastas are prepared in any number of enticing ways. The best meat on Capri is to be had here; the beef fillet prepared with potatoes and sweet peppers is a real treat. Don't neglect to book ahead. **C** 60-70,000 lire.

 Luigi ai Faraglioni
Strada dei Faraglioni - (081) 8370591
Closed Oct-Easter. V, AE.
The most enchanting place to swim and lunch on sautéed clams, grilled or poached fish, and a salad of tomatoes and mozzarella is at Luigi's. To drink, don't overlook the house wine, a likable local white. The strangely shaped Faraglioni rocks and the islet that closes the little bay form a uniquely beautiful setting. Before or after lunch, you can (for an extra charge) sunbathe and swim at Luigi's adjoining private beach. If you don't feel inclined to attempt the steep climb back to Tragara, a boat will ferry you to Marina Piccola. **C** 60,000 lire and up.

 Paolino
Via Palazzo a Mare 11 - (081) 8376102
Closed Wed (exc in seas), Oct-Jun. No cards.
The prettiest restaurant on the island is situated halfway between Marina Grande and Capri. Sheltered beneath a bower of lemon trees, diners enjoy a light-hearted ambience along with their refreshing vegetable antipasti (beans, eggplant, zucchini...), seafood salad, and grilled fish moistened with fragrant olive oil. Don't miss the little fried mozzarella balls ("bombe") with prosciutto and fresh tomato sauce. The house wine, a vigorous Tiberio, only adds to the charm of this delightful spot. Reservations are indispensable. **C** 60,000 lire and up.

■ **In Ischia**   *80 min by ferry, 40 min by hydrofoil*

 Damiano
At Ischia Porto, Superstrada S.S. 270
(081) 983032
Dinner only. Hols vary in winter. No cards.
A fresh scent drifts in from the pine wood nearby, while diners watch evening settle over Ischia's busy port. Forthright regional food with no unnecessary furbelows is Damiano's trademark. Seafood dominates the antipasti (sautéed clams and mussels, fresh octopus or prawn salads), as well as the main courses (there's an excellent sea bass soup), with spaghetti in scampi sauce or gnocchi al pesto as an intermezzo. Nicely turned-out desserts. The cellar holds some interesting southern Italian wines. Take care to book your table in advance. **C** 70,000 lire.

 Gennaro
At Ischia Porto, Via Porto 66
(081) 992917
Closed Tue (off-seas), Oct-Easter. All major cards.
Fine, fresh seafood handled with a minimum of fuss may be enjoyed in this pretty little portside trattoria. Zesty arugula topped with shrimp or aromatic marinated anchovies introduce Gennaro's particular specialty: a myriad of pasta dishes starring seafood in clever combinations (terrific linguine with clams and radicchio). The proceedings continue with the catch of the day—the poached sea bass with olives and capers tops our list of favorites.

Homemade sweets run to babà au rhum and profiteroles. The island's white wines are attractive accompaniments. **C** 50-60,000 lire.

Giardini Eden

At Ischia Ponte, Via Nuova Cartaromana - (081) 993909
Closed Oct-Apr. No cards.
This admirably well-equipped establishment boasts a garden terrace, a pool fed by hot springs, a solarium, and a jewel of a restaurant. The chef regales the guests with personalized versions of traditional Campanian dishes. Ischian beans add a countrified touch to the elegant antipasto salad of lobster and prawns; simpler but so satisfying are the airy squash-blossom fritters. Pastas are dressed with lobster, rare vongole rosse (red clams), or with humbler—but just as tasty—toppings of vegetables or mozzarella and basil. We don't know if seafood featured in the original Garden of Eden, but they play a starring role in this one. The house specialty is spigola all'acqua pazza: sea bass gently poached in a flavorful herbed fumet. Crustaceans and shellfish abound, and can be prepared just about any way you like. With a cool bottle of white wine and a slice of perfumed melon to finish, you may just think you've discovered paradise. **C** 70,000 lire.

■ In Pompei   26 km

Il Principe
Piazza Longo 8 - (081) 8505566
Closed Mon, Aug, 1 wk at Christmas. All major cards.
After exploring the fabulous ruins of Pompei, you may well want to treat yourself to a first-rate meal. Chef Franco Aliberti favors vigorous flavors that rouse and revive: his spaghetti seasoned with anchovies and capers, and his linguine boiled in fish fumet then tossed with tiny scampi and squid are two convincing cases in point. Fresh fish features on the menu year round (however, we found our sole al limone a tad overcooked), and the colder months bring a notable bounty of game (owner Marco Carli is a keen hunter). Biscotti and tiny tartlets top the dessert list; the sorbets are skippable. Unexpectedly classy service; impressive cellar. **C** 75,000 lire and up.

■ In Positano   57 km S

La Cambusa

Piazza A. Vespucci - (089) 875432
Open daily. All major cards.
Positano's singular charms attain critical mass at La Cambusa: enchanting scenery, social cachet, and sparkling seafood come together to create an exciting ambience. So admire the view and check out the sleek patrons as you tuck into the array of delectable antipasti: seafood salad, lemon-marinated anchovies, irresistible little balls of pearly ricotta or fresh cacio cheese... They'll set up your appetite for a sauté of tiny shrimp or wonderful spaghetti garnished with just-picked zucchini. Splendidly fresh fish—ricciola, orata, sargo and other Mediterranean denizens—are presented roasted or poached; but the chef takes special pride in his vibrant rockfish soup (zuppa di scorfano). Lush fruit tarts provide a sweet coda to a very good meal. The wine list is short but perfectly apropos. Reservations are indispensable. **C** 70,000 lire.

Chez Black
Via Brigantino 19 - (089) 875036
Closed Nov-Jan. All major cards.
Salvatore Russo, alias Black, runs this shipshape establishment decorated like a luxury yacht. You'll want to dive right into the briny seafood antipasti (note the cuoricini, "little hearts— filled with fish or vegetables), then come up for air and a plate of farfalle (bow-tie pasta) sauced with sun-gorged tomatoes and sweet crabmeat, or stubby macaroni embellished with lobster. The day's haul of fine, fresh fish is prepared grilled, fried, or oven-roasted—sea bass or turbot baked with potatoes are particularly tasty. Black serves up wonderful pizzas, too, and the house wine (Bianco di Black) holds its own among the pricier bottles on the list. Outstanding ice creams cap the meal. **C** 60,000 lire (wine incl).

La Sponda

Hotel Le Sirenuse,
Via Cristoforo Colombo 30 - (089) 875066
Closed mid Nov-Mar. All major cards.
The spectacle of Positano by moonlight, viewed from La Sponda's magnificent terrace, is an unforgettable scene. One could almost forgive the kitchen were it to treat food as a mere afterthought... Fortunately,

no such leniency is required. La Sponda presents traditional Neapolitan dishes based on superlative local ingredients culled from garden, farm, and sea. Exhilarating flavors mark such antipasti as grilled baby tomatoes, braided fresh mozzarella, lemon-marinated cheese balls, and delicate seafood salad, all served with focaccine (little rolls) hot from the oven. After linguine heaped with shellfish or tagliatelle al limone, diners can move on to herbed sea bass or a light, crispy dish of fried red mullet and squid. Jewel-toned fruit sherbets make a bright finish to a graceful, elegantly served dinner. Interesting cellar. Reservations are indispensable. **C** 100,000 lire.

■ In Sant'Agata Sui Due Golfi 57 km S

Don Alfonso

Piazza Sant'Agata - (081) 8780026 *Closed Mon & Tue (Mon only in summer), Jan 10-Feb 25.* AE, DC, EC.

Livia and Alfonso Iaccarino, owners of southern Italy's finest restaurant, are perfectionists. They have a private pipeline of superlative ingredients, each used to advantage at its seasonal peak. Tomatoes, eggplant, zucchini, peppers, green and white beans, marjoram, basil, oregano...all arrive in the kitchen fresh from the Iaccarinos' Punta Campanella farm. The oil that perfumes their dishes is an extra-virgin "essence" made from individually harvested olives; the egg pasta is rolled by hand; artisans produce the hard-wheat macaroni; seafood is supplied by fisherman friends. Inspired by this incomparable bounty, Alfredo creates dishes bursting with vivid color and unexpected nuances of flavor. What could be more light and delicious than puffy lobster fritters with a sweet-sour sauce? Or an ethereal ricotta soufflé with a sauce of nettle tops? Or more deeply satisfying than al dente fusilli topped with a rosemary-scented rockfish ragù? And there's more: sweet-pepper cannelloni, swordfish gratinéed with mustard and a whiff of lavender, an opulent combination of rockfish, crustaceans, and shellfish (*lo scrigno di Boccadoro*)... The desserts share the same bright tastes and airy textures that are Don Alfonso's trademarks. The cellar? It's stupendous, with a stock ranging from robust Barolos

to flowery Sauternes. **M** 75,000 lire (traditional menu), 90,000 lire (tasting menu).

■ In Sorrento 48 km S

Caruso

Via Sant'Antonino 12 (Piazza Tasso) (081) 8073156 *Closed Mon (exc in summer). All major cards.*

Veteran chef Antonio Cosentino seasons his version of *cucina napoletana* with a touch of fantasy. True, some dishes lack polish but his menu brims over with character and flavor. Lobster ravioli swathed in broccoli sauce is typical of the kitchen's bright ideas (though the pasta should have been a shade thinner); the single raviolo stuffed with smoky Provola cheese was flawless. Cosentino gets high marks for his lightly pan-fried John Dory in a zippy anchovy sauce, triglie (red mullet) al Gragnano, and a splendid timballetto that brings together rockfish, porcini mushrooms, and tiny shrimp. You'll surely want to have a go at the lavishly laden dessert cart; don't miss the torta Caruso, a lush duo of oranges and walnuts. The exemplary service is does credit to the posh surroundings. **C** 70,000 lire.

'O Parrucchiano

Corso Italia 71 - (081) 8781321 *Closed Wed.* V, MC.

It is a real shame that such a handsome establishment (a multilevel greenhouse) with a long tradition of good food and warm hospitality should decline into a canteen for harried sightseers and tour groups. That, alas, seems to be the direction in which this place is heading. The gnocchi and spaghetti we had so often heard praised were marred by heavy sauces. An assortment of fritti arrived lukewarm, their crispness just a memory. Ravioli di gamberetti e salsa di vongole tasted neither of shrimp nor of clams, but of mint and Provola cheese (not bad, but not what we expected). Only the local version of dolmas—rice cooked in fig-leaf wrapper—recalled the time when 'O Parrucchiano was famous for top-notch Campanian cooking. Here's hoping that those memorable meals have not disappeared forever. **C** 60,000 lire.

Find the address *you are looking for, quickly and easily, in the index.*

Quick Bites

CONTENTS

QUICK BITES

Brandi

Salita Sant'Anna di Palazzo 1 - (081) 416928
Open noon-4pm & 7pm-1am. Closed Mon.
  This pizzeria is the birthplace of pizza margherita, the most popular pizza on earth. On a fine June day in 1889, Raffaele Esposito was summoned by his sovereign to the Capodimonte Palace and commanded to prepare his specialty. Don Raffaele made three different pizzas, but Queen Margherita showed a particular preference for the one garnished with tomato, mozzarella, and basil—the pizza to which she gave her name. It's still a royal treat today: fragrant, crispy, and fresh from the oven.

La Crêperie

Via G. Donadio 1-3 - (081) 5781430
Open daily 8:30pm-2:30am.
  The menu is fairly catholic, extending to sandwiches, canapés, salads, and desserts (note the Eiffel Tower ice-cream sundae...). But owner Gigi Rosolia specializes in crêpes, crafted according to an authentic Breton recipe. If French fare is not what you've come to Italy to eat, try the pizza-crêpe, a culinary compromise that bows to local tradition.

Ettore

Via S. Lucia 56 - (081) 7640498
Open noon-midnight. Closed Sun.

Arguably the busiest pizzeria in town, but the swift, efficient service means you won't have to wait too long for a table. You'll swoon over pizza topped with genuine mozzarella di bufala and fresh, tiny tomatoes; or the unforgettable pagnottiello, a baked sandwich stuffed with mozzarella and prosciutto; or an opulent vegetarian fritto all'italiana, composed of croquettes, breaded mozzarella, eggplant, and zucchini, all deep-fried to ineffable crispness.

Friggitoria del Vomero

Via D. Cimarosa 44 - (081) 5783130
Open 9:30am-2:40pm & 5pm-10pm (Sat until midnight). Closed Sun.
  Traditional Neapolitan specialties combined with today's "fast-food philosophy." The Friggitoria is a favorite with students and working people on their break. If you, too, feel a yen for a crispy fried treat, step up to the counter for some rice balls (arancini di riso), puffy fritters, stuffed vegetables, or irresistible little deep-fried pies filled with greens, cheese, or meat. Also on offer are delectable pizzas topped with squash blossoms (in season) or spinach. Caloric? Well, yes; but so satisfying!

Happy Rock

Via Bausan 51 - (081) 411712
Open 7:30pm-1am. Closed Tue.
  The formula is simple and very successful: appealing and original sandwich combinations paired with a good glass of wine. Pink walls, lots of mirrors, music, and a sociable crowd create a lively ambience.

Hard Rock

Via Ascensione 26 - (081) 416064
Open 8pm-1am. Closed Mon.
  Yet another haven for hamburger lovers. The Hard Rock has extra cachet, however, for it's also known as the springboard that has launched local musicians to national

fame. In addition to grills and such, the menu features some interesting and original rice dishes.

Intra Moenia

Piazza V. Bellini 70 - (081) 290720
Open daily 10:30am-2am.

Intra Moenia is a intellectuals' caffè close to the ancient walls that mark the site of the Greco-Roman settlement of Neapolis. A studious atmosphere reigns: patrons sip and nibble as they pore over their books or newspapers. In summer, open-air concerts are hosted here, and the menu expands to include heartier dishes.

Lombardi

Via Benedetto Croce 59 - (081) 206496
Open noon-3:30pm & 7pm-midnight. Closed Sun.

The genuine article is what you'll find here: guaranteed authentic Neapolitan pizza, baked in the traditional manner. The throngs of students and tourists drawn to this stretch of Spaccanapoli by its high concentration of schools, cultural institutions, historic landmarks and sites fill Lombardi to the bursting point. Believe us, the pizzas are worth the struggle to get a spot at the counter.

Luise

Piazza dei Martiri 68 - (081) 417735
Via Toledo 266 - (081) 497852
Open 8:30am-3:30pm & 5pm-8:30pm (Piazza dei Martiri); 9am-9pm (Via Toledo). Closed Sun.

Though the fare at both addresses is speedily served for quick consumption, "fast food" it isn't. More in the tradition of the old-fashioned rosticceria (takeout shop) or tavola calda, Luise offers pasta and pastries as well as more refined snacks, like open-faced salmon sandwiches.

McDonald's

Via G. Sanfelice 16 - (081) 5529185
Open 10am-11pm. Closed Mon.

McDonald's staked out its Naples outpost in a strategic site between the historic port district and the university neighborhood. The familiar formula gets a fresh twist here: alongside the Big Macs you'll find a display case of "McMediterranean" antipasti and Italian fare. Even though there are tables on three levels, the place is a mob scene on Saturdays and Sunday evenings.

L'Oca Verde

Via Bausan 28 - (081) 414865
Open 8pm-1am. Closed Tue.

Situated on a little street that opens onto the busy Riviera di Chiaia near the Pignatelli Museum, this salad bar is a magnet for groups of young people who like the intimate, welcoming atmosphere as much as the refreshing and original menu.

La Salsa

Piazza Amedeo 15 - (081) 419440
Open 8pm-2am. Closed Mon.

A central location, a lively ambience, a list of spicy Mexican dishes and snacks: that's the recipe for La Salsa's merry mix. Of course, there's another "secret" ingredient—the pitchers of sangria and beer that wash all the zesty food down!

Steak House

Piazzetta A. Falcone 23 - (081) 5782306
Open 7pm-2am. Closed Mon.

A German-style eatery where robust grilled meats top the bill of fare. The mixed assortment (piatto misto) brings a gargantuan platter of quail, turkey, pheasant, guinea hen, and chunks of pork, served with a plethora of garnishes. Only parties of two or more are served here—probably because the portions are so huge!

Trianon

Via Pietro Colletta 46 - (081) 5539426
Open 9am-4pm & 6pm-10:30pm. Closed Sun am.

This pizzeria is an institution in the busy Castelcapuano district, seat of the city's judicial offices. We plead guilty of overindulgence on the Trianon's stellar specimens: all manner of tasty garnishes top crusts that strike an ideal balance between crispness and chewiness.

Vinarium

Via Cappella Vecchia 7 - (081) 7644114
Open daily noon-4:30pm & 7pm-2am (Sat & Sun 7pm-2am; Mon noon-4:30pm).

The cellar boasts a broad range of 250 different wines, which may be uncorked beside a quick, light meal of salads or open-faced sandwiches. Special mention

157

goes to the Caprese cake, our favorite dessert.

Vineria del Centro

Via Paladino 8a - (No telephone)
Open 8pm-3am. Closed Mon.

A two-level wine bar, where singles gather at the bar downstairs, while groups of friends eat and chat comfortably at tables upstairs. The enticing wine list includes some notable reds produced in the region, as well as bottles from Tuscany and the Veneto. But there are some delightful little Spumantes on offer, too, perfect partners for a light snack or slice of fruit tart.

SWEET SNACKS

Attanasio

Vico Ferrovia 2 - (081) 285675
Open 6:30am-8pm. Closed Mon.

The fragrance that tickles visitors' noses, as they step down from the train at the Naples station, emanates from Attanasio. For 80 years, this firm has purveyed fresh-baked sfogliatelle (flaky pastry stuffed with sweetened ricotta and candied fruit), pine-nut cookies, almond cakes, and torta caprese to an appreciative public.

Bilancioni

Via Posillipo 238b - (081) 7691923
Open 8am-10pm (Sat 8am-1pm). Closed Wed.

Owner Pietro Bilancioni started out as a child actor, playing with the likes of Vittorio De Sica. But he abandoned the screen to learn the ice-cream trade, and wisely apprenticed with the best teachers in Naples. Bilancioni graduated to his own shop, now the city's most fashionable *gelateria*, where his hazelnut-cream, custard, and nutella (chocolate-hazelnut) flavors attract hosts of enthusiastic fans.

Caflisch

Via dei Mille - (081) 416477
Via Chiaia 143 - (081) 404588
Open 8am-8:30pm. Closed Wed.

Founded long ago by an enterprising Swiss, Caflisch manages to keep up with the times—having added a catering service and a fast-food section—while maintaining the traditions that have made its reputation. The overall excellence of the pastries

and ice creams make it hard to single out just a few for praise. But we will admit to a fondness for the intensely flavorful mocha cake, the fragrant pastiera (a traditional Neapolitan cake based on ricotta and wheat simmered in milk, once made only for Easter but available here year-round), and the Scazzette di Cardinale, a delectable concoction topped with cardinal-red wild strawberries. If you hanker for something cold and sweet, be advised that Caflisch is famous for its spumone (molded ice cream) and coviglie (frozen parfaits).

Carraturo

Via Arangio Ruiz 75 - (081) 681795
Open daily 8am-2pm & 3pm-8pm.

You'll stop dead in your tracks before the profusion of sweet indulgences displayed in Carraturo's window. The firm is famous for its darling little Mignons (assorted petits-fours) and luscious Torta Carraturo, an extravagant confection filled with cream and profiteroles.

Cimmino

Via Filangieri 12 - (081) 418303
Open 8am-9pm. Closed Tue.

A time-honored rendezvous for shoppers who have exhausted the better part of their resources on Via Chiaia and Via dei Mille, the city's premier shopping district. There's nothing like a baba imbibed with good rum or—depending on the season—a cup of hot chocolate or a chocolate sundae to recharge batteries worn down by a session of conspicuous consumption.

Daniele

Via Scarlatti 104 - (081) 5564804
Open 8am-9pm. Closed Tue.

This spacious eatery on the heights of the Vomero hill offers multiple options for sweet or savory snacking: at the bar, the tavola calda (snack bar), the restaurant, or the pastry counter. Those in the know say that Daniele's babas are among the best in Naples—garnished with whipped cream and strawberries, they are alluring indeed. And without exception the cakes are, as they say hereabouts, squisiti: absolutely delicious.

Fontana

Riviera di Chiaia 12 - (081) 664311
Open 7:30am-9:30pm. Closed Tue.

Shall we call this excellent address a pasticceria or an ice-cream shop? True, Fontana's fame originated with its fabulous frozen desserts, particularly the Testo di Moro (Moor's Head), which is a veritable hymn to chocolate. But it has not escaped our notice that the pastries elicit a good deal of enthusiasm; special mention goes to the airy cream puffs chock-full of thick cream.

Moccia

Via San Pasquale a Chiaia 21 - (081) 411348
Open 8am-9pm. Closed Tue.
Breads share equal billing with pastries here, and the entire roster of specialties is highly recommended. The breads are a joy to behold, in a profusion of shapes and sizes: round pagnotte, little panini, long, slim bastoncini and fruste, and rustic cafoni ("bumpkins"), so called because they were formerly brought in from the countryside. Crusty or tender, French-style or Tuscan-style, alla siciliana or alla fiorentina... there are breads for every taste and mood. Moccia's pastries are just as irresistible, especially the zeppole di San Giuseppe, Continental cousins to the homely doughnut. Excellent ice creams, too.

Pintauro

Via Toledo 275 - (081) 417339
Open 8am-8pm. Closed Tue (Sun & Wed in summer).
Step across the threshold of this doll-size bakery and you're immediately in front of the counter; and right behind the counter is the oven door. It's only a few square meters all told, but Pintauro is acclaimed for its delicate sfogliatelle (a confection born in Sicily but perfected in Naples), filled with sweetened ricotta and citron, which connoisseurs claim are unforgettable. And so they must be, since the shop has been a Neapolitan success story since the eighteenth century.

Principe

Via dei Mille 91 - (081) 416477
Corso Vittorio Emanuele 595 - (081) 416633

Open 8am-9pm. Closed Mon.
Principe purveys traditional Neapolitan sweets (excellent pastiera, or ricotta cake) and such savory treats as frittatine di maccheroni: firm, golden-brown omelets made with spaghetti or vermicelli, Parmesan, and herbs. The Via dei Mille site caters to a slightly more sedate crowd than the other location, closer to Mergellina, where a decidedly youthful ambience prevails.

Riviera

Riviera di Chiaia 183 - (081) 665026
Via dei Mille 60 - (081) 405622
Open 8am-10pm. Closed Mon.
Most of the customers make a beeline for the seasonal fruit tarts and almond pastries, but visitors to Naples should not overlook the typically Neapolitan pastiera (ricotta cake), fragrant with orangeflower water. Riviera's pastiera is always served moist and golden, as tradition dictates. But if you swear solely by chocolate, by all means order the Tartufo, a dense, dark ice cream-and-cake concoction dusted with cocoa—it's a revelation.

Scaturchio

Piazza San Domenico Maggiore 19
(081) 5516944, fax (081) 5517031
Open 8am-8pm. Closed Tue.
This shop has been a landmark in the heart of old Naples since the turn of the century, and it figures on the must-see lists of savvy tourists from all over the world. After admiring the neighborhood's magnificent old churches and palaces, they—like numberless Neapolitan natives—follow their noses to Piazza San Domenico Maggiore and Scaturchio's fragrant displays of babas, cassata (pound cake layered with sweetened ricotta), sfogliatelle (ricotta-filled pastries), liqueur-soaked brioches, Moors' Heads, and more. If, from this embarrassment of riches, you must choose only one treat, opt for the Ministeriale, a specialty of the house: a chocolate log filled with rum-laced cream.

---

*We're always happy to hear about **your** discoveries and receive **your comments** on ours. We want to give your letters the attention they deserve, so when you write to Gault Millau, please state clearly what you liked or disliked. Be concise but convincing, and take the time to argue your point.*

159

Hotels

Britannique

Corso Vittorio Emanuele 133
(081) 7614145, fax (081) 669760
Open year-round. 6 stes 260,000 lire. 86 rms 180-240,000 lire. Restaurant. Conf. Garage pkg. All major cards.

The Britannique is a Neapolitan institution, its noble façade rising from the slope of the hill topped by the Villa Floridiana and its enchanting gardens. The hotel also boasts a little garden of lush Mediterranean flora, which protects the guests' unobstructed views of the bay and Mergellina. Nicely equipped and quite comfortable, the rooms are decorated in a turn-of-the century style. Service is impeccable.

Excelsior

Via Partenope 48
(081) 7640111, fax (081) 7649743
Open year-round. 12 stes 500-900,000 lire. 90 rms 192-360,000 lire. Restaurant. Conf. Garage pkg. All major cards.

Behind a handsome turn-of-the-century façade, the Excelsior is a perfect example of a luxury hotel in the grand tradition. Guest rooms on the upper floors enjoy fabulous views of the Castel dell'Ovo and Capri; rooms overlooking the port have Mount Vesuvius as a backdrop. All are spacious and display the charm habitually associated with hotels of the Ciga group. In addition to the usual amenities, the Excelsior provides business facilities and a babysitting service. For an account of the hotel's Casanova Grill, see *Restaurants*.

Grande Albergo Vesuvio

Via Partenope 45
(081) 7640044, fax (081) 7640044
Open year-round. 16 stes 500-1,300,000 lire. 151 rms 250-380,000 lire. Restaurant. Conf. Garage pkg. All major cards.

Rebuilt just after the war, the old Vesuvio was beginning to show its age. A full-scale renovation, we are glad to say, has put everything right. Request a room on one of the upper floors—they are less noisy—and don't miss the eye-popping view of Capri. All the rooms are decorated in subdued style and punctuated with antique pieces; they are also equipped with double-glazed windows. Service is courteous and attentive, in the best Italian tradition. The ninth-floor restaurant is named for the legendary tenor Enrico Caruso, a frequent guest at the Grande Albergo Vesuvio.

Grand Hotel Oriente

Via Armando Diaz 44
(081) 5512133, fax (081) 5514915
Open year-round. 2 stes 300,000 lire. 130 rms 175-230,000 lire. Restaurant. Conf. Garage pkg. All major cards.

The Oriente occupies an enviable location close to the old city and the best shopping streets. Thoroughly revamped just a few years ago (the rooms are now fully soundproofed), the hotel's charm remains intact; it's a delightful place to stay in the center of Naples. Director Salvatore Maturi makes certain that his guests feel right at home, thanks to the attentions of an obliging staff.

Holiday Inn

Centro Direzionale, Isola E6
(081) 2250111, fax (081) 5628074
Open year-round. 32 stes 320,000 lire. 298 rms 185-240,000 lire. Restaurant. Conf. Garage pkg. All major cards.

The futuristic Centro Direzionale, the new business center of Naples, is home to this recent addition to the Holiday Inn hotel chain, designed by Japanese architect Kenzo Tange. Business travelers are sure to appreciate the many services provided, including a shuttle to the airport (which is only five minutes away), a fitness center, and a welcoming Italian restaurant. Maximum comfort and convenience, close to all of the city's major arteries.

Hotel delle Terme

Via Agnano Astroni
(081) 5701733, fax (081) 7626441
Open year-round. 62 dbl rms 175-220,000 lire. Restaurant. Conf. Pkg. All major cards.

This is a 1960s–style hotel swaddled in the greenery of the ancient Agnano springs (*terme*) on the southwestern edge of Naples. Palm trees and Mediterranean flora create a soothing scene for a relaxing sojourn that can, if you wish, include spa treatments at the hot springs. In summer, theatrical and musical events are held in the hotel's lovely grounds, and the racetrack is close by.

Mercure Angioino

Via De Pretis 123
(081) 5529500, fax (081) 5529509
Open year-round. 85 rms 165-225,000 lire. Restaurant. Conf. All major cards.

A few steps away from the Teatro San Carlo and Castel Nuovo, the Angioino occupies a strategic position in the historic center of Naples. Avid shoppers and sightseers alike appreciate the location, near the city's top boutiques and the ferries that serve the islands of the bay. The hotel is of recent vintage, with all the usual amenities. Certain rooms are reserved for non-smokers. The restaurant is housed in the magnificent Villa Virgiliana.

Paradiso

Via Catullo 11
(081) 7614161, fax (081) 7613449
Open year-round. 3 stes 295-400,000 lire. 71 rms 160-260,000 lire. Restaurant. Conf. Garage pkg. All major cards.

Among his clients Vincenzo Di Donato counts both business people and couples on holiday. A romantic at heart (what Neapolitan isn't?), he assigns to the latter the rooms that open onto ravishing little terraces full of flowers and sunshine, with views of Mount Vesuvius, ideal for long, lazy, tête-à-tête breakfasts. Situated in a modern neighborhood of upscale apartment buildings, just fifteen minutes from the airport, the hotel was recently remodeled and redecorated; the rooms are now tastefully furnished in a contemporary style that is both fresh and cozy. The Paradiso gives you loads of charm for your money, along with smiling, friendly service.

Santa Lucia

Via Partenope 46
(081) 7640244, fax (081) 7648580
Open year-round. 12 stes 380,000 lire. 95 rms 210-300,000 lire. Restaurant. Conf. Garage pkg. All major cards.

The Santa Lucia had begun to seem a little faded, a little worn; its name was no longer mentioned when discussing the finer hotels in Naples. Fortunately, the Santa Lucia has a new lease on life, thanks to a thorough, intelligent renovation. The elegant lounges feature fine pictures and carpets, and there is a romantic piano bar in which to relax. Guest rooms have been redecorated and their amenities improved; the bathrooms are fresh and new. We prefer the accommodations with bay views to those overlooking Via Santa Lucia, which sometimes vibrate to the rhythm of the heavy traffic outside. The service is friendly and efficient.

Terminus

Piazza Garibaldi 91
(081) 286011, fax (081) 206689
Open year-round. 6 stes 320,000 lire. 172 rms 180-250,000 lire. Restaurant. Conf. Garage pkg.

Knowledgeable travelers have long been fond of the Terminus, a hotel built in 1919 and completely renovated in 1992. The rooms now provide all the amenities one could desire and the location—close to the Stazione Centrale and just minutes by taxi from the airport—is ideal for visitors who prefer to do without a car. From the panoramic restaurant on the top floor, diners can admire the rooftops of Naples. Among the services on offer are a beauty spa and an airport shuttle.

■ In Amalfi

63 km S

Grand Hotel Excelsior

Via Papa Leone X
(089) 830015, fax (089) 830255
Closed Nov-Mar. 4 stes 230-290,000 lire. 93 rms 115-230,000 lire. Restaurant. Conf. Pool. Pkg. All major cards.

The Excelsior occupies an enchanting site on a sheer cliff above the sea, with a private beach accessible via a long (long) stairway or a private elevator. On days when one feels too lazy to face the trip, the beautiful swimming pool is tempting indeed. There is dancing on the terrace in

161

the evening. The rooms are spacious and attractive, with private balconies and sublime panoramic views.

 Luna
Via P. Comite 19
(089) 871002, fax (089) 871333
Open year-round. 5 stes 180-230,000 lire. 50 rms 100-180,000 lire. Restaurant. Conf. Pool. Garage pkg. All major cards.

This thirteenth-century monastery was once the home of Saint Francis of Assisi; its inner courtyard, of Byzantine cast, is surrounded by circular corridors and Romanesque arches. Breakfast is served there in fine weather; guests may enjoy dinner on the lovely terrace. All the rooms have private baths, and there is a pool on the premises as well as a discothèque.

 Santa Caterina
Via Nazionale 9
(089) 871012, fax (089) 871351
Open year-round. 7 stes 500-1,000,000 lire. 63 rms 180-450,000 lire. Restaurant. Conf. Pool. Garage pkg. All major cards.

Some old-timers here remember the nights in 1944 when Glenn Miller and Artie Shaw played for the American soldiers who had requisitioned the hotel. Santa Caterina has been considerably modernized since then, but somehow the charming old atmosphere lingers on. The stylish, comfortable rooms feature marquetry furniture, hydromassage in the bathtubs, and spacious terraces with wonderful views of the Amalfi coast. Luxuriant terraced gardens lead down to the sea, but indolent guests can be ferried up and down by elevator if they wish. The restaurant serves fresh fruits and vegetables gathered in the hotel's citrus grove and kitchen garden. In addition to a seawater pool, there are facilities for all sorts of water sports—windsurfing, waterskiing, sailing. For an account of the Santa Caterina's eponymous restaurant, see *Restaurants.*

■ **In Capri**   90 min by ferry & 40 min by hydrofoil

 Europa Palace
Via Capodimonte 2b, Anacapri
(081) 8370955, fax (081) 8373191
Closed Nov 30-Apr 1. 5 stes 270-470,000 lire. 88 rms 160-340,000 lire. Restaurant. Conf. Pool. Pkg. All major cards.

A modern hotel built in typical Caprese style, the Europa Palace basks in a glorious setting of luxuriant palms and tropical plants. The accommodations are exquisitely comfortable; most of the guest rooms boast balconies overlooking the Bay of Naples, and the suites are sumptuous. A truly impressive array of facilities is provided: beauty spa, fitness center, Turkish baths, covered pool, and more. In summer, barbecue lunches are served by the pool; dinner may be enjoyed on the delightful terrace.

 Grand Hotel Quisisana
Via Camerelle 2
(081) 8370788, fax (081) 8376080
Closed Nov 1-Apr 1. 14 stes 800-950,000 lire. 136 rms 300-600,000 lire. Restaurant. Conf. Pool. Tennis. All major cards.

Certainly the largest and most prestigious of Capri's hotels, the Quisisana pampers guests with recently renovated rooms and duplex suites featuring antique furnishings, terraces, and such amenities as individual safes, along with the usual color TVs and air conditioning. The clientele is of the pearls (for her) and yachting cap (for him) variety that haunts the world's luxury resort hotels. They are an oddly anachronistic sight when, at cocktail hour, dressed to the nines, they settle out on the terrace en masse. Amply equipped for meetings and conventions, the Quisisana provides impeccable service by a large, well-trained staff, along with pools (covered and un-), tennis courts, a fitness center, beauty salon, and a restaurant.

La Palma
Via Vittorio Emanuele 39
(081) 8370133, fax (081) 8376966
Open year-round. 80 rms 120-370,000 lire. Restaurant. Conf. All major cards.

With its flower-bedecked terraces lit up late into the night, the Palma is a lovely place to stop for a drink when the chic caffès on the Piazzetta are full. Then you can move on to the hotel's disco and later, perhaps, to a soothing session in the sauna to bring the evening to a close. The elegance of the guest rooms, lounges, and restaurant, along with its facilities and fine service, would make the Palma an ideal place to stay if it weren't for one thing: the noise. The rooms, which give directly onto a street just 500 yards from the Piazzetta, are air conditioned, but not all are soundproof. Light sleepers, take note!

Palatium

Via prov. Marina Grande 225
(081) 8376144, fax (081) 8376150
Closed Nov 30-Apr 1. 46 rms 180-390,000 lire. Restaurant. Conf. Pool. All major cards.

From the harbor, you can already make out the palm trees surrounding the Palatium, as well as the hotel's distinctive façade (it's painted a fiery Pompeian red!). Compact and run with an admirable eye to detail, this hotel offers spacious, discreetly attractive accommodations. Guest rooms open out on a pretty swimming pool from tiny, flower-decked patios where leisurely breakfasts are served. When it's time for an aperitivo, residents repair to the splendid terraces that afford an incomparable view of the Bay of Naples. Sun-worshippers may indulge their passion on the private beach below or in the hotel's solarium. Boating excursions can be arranged on request.

La Pazziella

Via P.R. Giuliani 4
(081) 8370044, fax (081) 8370085
Open year-round. 3 stes 250-500,000 lire. 17 rms 180-300,000 lire. V, AE.

This old Caprese home converted into a small hotel stands right in the center of the island amid lush greenery. The spacious rooms are nicely arranged and blissfully quiet. The public rooms, furnished with antiques and fine paintings, include a well-stocked library. Guests have free use of a nearby hotel pool.

Punta Tragara

Via Tragara 57
(081) 8370844, fax (081) 8377790
Closed Nov-Mar. 31 stes 330-450,000 lire. 4 rms 240-320,000 lire. Restaurant. Conf. Pool. V, DC, MC.

With its seawater pool, inviting cocktail bar, fine restaurant, and spa—and with its stunning cliff-face location offering wide-angle views of Capri's coastline and the Faraglioni rocks—the Punta Tragara is the kind of place where guests feel so comfortable that they are disinclined to wander. The principal flaw in this paradise is the interior decoration: dull beige and brown tones in the lobby, gaudy red and blue (with gold lanterns) in the bar, an odd juxtaposition of marble floors and carpet-

ing. The overall effect is jarring. Similar lapses mar the otherwise comfy, fully equipped suites.

La Scalinatella

Via Tragara 8
(081) 8370633, fax (081) 8378291
Closed Oct 21-Mar 19. 26 stes 440-580,000 lire. 4 rms 370-460,000 lire. Restaurant. Pool. Tennis. No cards.

The most refined (if not the most luxurious) of Capri's hotels is so discreet that unless you know it's there, it could easily escape your notice. For its loyal clientele, this is just another of La Scalinatella's numerous charms. The guest rooms are terraced along the steep hillside, among oleanders and masses of fragrant flowers. All are exquisitely decorated in white and shades of blue, and each features a terrace with a view of the sea and the strange Faraglioni rocks. All the amenities one expects of a luxury hotel are on hand, along with the personal, caring service that only the cream of such establishments can provide.

■ In Ischia   80 min by ferry & 40 min by hydrofoil

Grand Hotel Punta Molino

Lungomare C. Colombo 23
(081) 991544, fax (081) 991562
Closed Nov-Mar. 5 stes. 77 rms. Full board 220-340,000 lire. Half-board 190-310,000 lire. Restaurant. Conf. Pool. Pkg. All major cards.

Converted into a hotel some 25 years ago, this former mill overlooks the ocean, with a fragrant pine wood as a backdrop. Colorful furniture, tiles, and hangings decorate the public rooms downstairs. Residents are unlikely to spend much time in their fully equipped rooms, for there are two pools (one fed by hot springs), restaurants, a private beach, and a spa to occupy their vacation time. Facilities for waterskiing and other sports are also provided.

Il Moresco

Ischia Porto, Via E. Gianturco 16
(081) 981355, fax (081) 992338
Closed Oct-Apr. 3 stes 330,000 lire. 69 rms 180-270,000 lire. Restaurant. Conf. Pool. Pkg. All major cards.

The Moresco is a strategically located hotel that coddles guests with every comfort and caring service. Surrounded by a

t pine wood, the interior is
ied in warm, Mediterranean hues;
... imer, a cascade of bougainvillea
adds to the romantic charm of the pure
white façade. After a day of exploring or
sunning, guests settle on the poolside terrace for cocktails, under the benevolent
eye of manager Franco Conte.

🏠 Mezzatorre 🌲🏖
Forio D'Ischia, Via Mezzatorre
(081) 986111, fax (081) 986025
*Closed Oct-May. 6 stes 380,000 lire. 52 rms
200-290,000 lire. Restaurant. Conf. Pool. Pkg.
All major cards.*
The Mezzatorre resembles an ancient
watchtower as it clings to a promontory
nearly hidden beneath exuberant
southern flora. Situated in a tranquil setting
a few kilometers from Ischia's main port,
the hotel is an ideal spot for a restful or
sporting holiday. Guests can ride horseback, waterski, enjoy the heated pool, or
clamber among the rocks on the coast
below. Each of the attractive rooms and
suites affords a splendid panoramic view.

🏠 Regina Isabella
Lacco Ameno, Piazza Santa Restituta
(081) 994322, fax (081) 900190
*Closed Oct 30-Apr 23. 17 stes. 117 rms. Full
board 250-530,000 lire. Ste supp 95-
200,000 lire. Restaurant. Conf. Pool. Tennis.
Golf. Garage pkg. All major cards.*
Nestled in an enchanting landscape, this
hotel is an elegant example of classic
Italian hotel-keeping. It offers every resort
facility, from tennis courts and swimming
pools to private beaches and hot springs.
The handsomely furnished guest rooms
are fully equipped with air conditioning
and all the usual luxury-hotel amenities.
Equipment for all manner of water sports
is provided. Suites are available in the
Royal Sporting annex.

🏠 San Montano
Lacco Ameno, Via Montevico
(081) 994033, fax (081) 980242
*Closed Nov-Feb. 2 stes 361,000 lire. 65 rms
214-268,000 lire. Restaurant. Conf. Pool. Tennis. Golf. Pkg. All major cards.*
Set between the island's green hills and
the azure sea, this hotel commands a
breathtaking view of Ischia's striking volcanic landscape. Guests may take the cure
at the thermal spa, swim in a pool fed by
hot springs, play tennis, or merely stroll
around the lovely, peaceful grounds. The

Italian taste for elegance and comfort is
evident in both the well-equipped guest
rooms and the public rooms downstairs.
Sightseeing excursions are arranged on
request.

■ In Positano 57 km S

🏠 San Pietro
Via Laurito 2
(089) 875455, fax (089) 811449
*Closed Nov-Mar. 7 stes 680-1,500,000 lire.
53 rms 400-630,000 lire. Restaurant. Conf.
Tennis. Pkg. All major cards.*
Some 30 years ago, it was decided to drill
through Positano's cliffs to create "a window on the sea." Today, the San Pietro's
rooms, salons, restaurant and pool are all
dug out of volcanic rock. It took eight
years to finish the first 30 rooms, which all
feature huge picture windows, and
another year to complete the elevator that
ferries guests to the private beach. The
décor is an extravagant mix of antique,
Baroque, and eighteenth-century elements, with oversize tubs in the
bathrooms and giant beds in the
bedrooms. The service is on a scale with
the sumptuous surroundings.

🏠 Le Sirenuse
Via C. Colombo 30
(089) 875066, fax (089) 811798
*Open year-round. 4 stes 580-1,300,000 lire.
58 rms 360-560,000 lire. Restaurant. Conf.
Pool. Pkg. All major cards.*
A superb seventeenth-century chest in
the lobby and a carved wooden pharmacy
counter in the bar are just two of the many
striking antique pieces displayed around
this luxurious establishment. The guest
rooms all overlook the ocean; the beds are
enveloped in sheer curtains, eighteenth-
century paintings have been affixed to the
ceilings, and the bathrooms are the last
word in refinement. It's no wonder Liz
Taylor makes a point of staying here when
she's in Positano! For a detailed account
of La Sponda, the hotel's restaurant, see
Restaurants. Le Sirenuse recently launched
a cooking school, where you can learn all
the secrets of *la cucina napolitana*. Courses
are taught in Italian, with English translation. Contact the hotel for dates and rates.

> **The prices** *in this guide reflect what estab-
lishments were charging at press time.*

■ In Ravello
66 km SE

Caruso Belvedere
Via San Giovanni del Toro 52
(089) 857111, fax (089) 857372
*Open year-round. 2 stes 248,000 lire and up.
22 rms 140-270,000 lire. Restaurant. Pkg. All
major cards.*

To seduce the divine Greta Garbo, the great conductor Leopold Stokowski carried her off to room 21 of the Caruso hotel. We wonder how much time they spent admiring the sea view from their terrace... Just over 100 years old, the Caruso is a listed landmark and though the rooms provide considerable comfort they are far from high-tech. But the atmosphere is delightfully romantic, especially in the garden planted with cypresses and oleanders, and on the terrace, where guests sip preprandial drinks while admiring the winding coastline.

Palumbo
Via San Giovanni del Toro 28
(089) 857244, fax (089) 858133
*Open year-round. 3 stes 540-720,000 lire.
18 rms 340-520,000 lire. Restaurant. Conf.
Tennis. Garage pkg. All major cards.*

This beautiful, historic hotel proudly displays its impressive guest list which includes Wagner, Ingrid Bergman, and William Randolph Hearst. The lovely rooms feature handmade faïence tiles in the bathrooms and ravishing antique furnishings. The service is smooth and professional, overseen by Swiss-born owner Marco Vuilleurmier. Prices are astonishingly reasonable, given the stunning beauty, tradition, and high level of comfort.

■ In Sorrento
48 km S

Excelsior Vittoria
Piazza Tasso 34
(081) 8071044, fax (081) 8771206
*Open year-round. 10 stes 519-945,000 lire.
100 rms 251-424,000 lire. Restaurant. Conf.
Pool. Garage pkg. All major cards.*

This ravishing nineteenth-century villa was heavily damaged by the 1980 earthquake. The owners have made herculean efforts to restore the rooms to their original beauty. One has only to examine the hand-painted ceilings, beautiful woodwork, and marble stairways to understand the amount of will, patience, and hard work that the operation has required. Ask to visit Enrico Caruso's suite (number 448), where you may view the maestro's piano and the music he was working on at the moment of his death. Be sure to take a stroll in the gorgeous grounds. Sophia Loren and Ronald Reagan both have stayed at the Excelsior Vittoria (no, silly, not together!).

Imperial Tramontano
Via Vittorio Veneto 1
(081) 8782588, fax (081) 8072344
Closed mid Jan-mid Mar. 14 stes 350-450,000 lire. 105 rms 180-290,000 lire. Restaurant. Conf. Pool. Pkg. V, AE.

Built around the Villa Stongoli, birthplace of Renaissance poet Torquato Tasso, this hotel is situated in the center of Sorrento. Many poets, in fact, have sojourned in this lovely spot: Keats, Byron, Shelley, Lamartine, Longfellow, Leopardi... The list goes on! One side of the hotel overlooks the sea, and the other opens onto a shady garden and a pool. The recent renovation efforts respected the original style of this charming establishment—the glass-roofed indoor courtyard is strikingly lovely—while providing it with modern conveniences.

Parco dei Principi
Via Rota 1
(081) 8784644, fax (081) 8783786
*Closed Nov-Mar. 4 stes: prices on request.
173 rms 200-315,000 lire. Restaurant. Conf.
Pool. Pkg. All major cards.*

The guest rooms enjoy views of the ocean or of the extensive grounds dotted with century-old trees. An elevator whisks residents down to the private beach, where one can have a leisurely lunch in summer, and there is a seawater pool as well. During the summer season, the piano bar is a convivial place to while away the evening. A thorough-going renovation has improved the décor and comfort of the accommodations.

> *We're always happy to hear about* **your discoveries** *and receive* **your comments** *on ours. We want to give your letters the attention they deserve, so when you write to Gault Millau, please state clearly what you liked or disliked. Be concise but convincing, and take the time to argue your point.*

Nightlife

CONTENTS

BARS

City Hall Café
Corso Vittorio Emanuele 137 - (081) 669400
Open 8pm-2am. Closed Mon.
    One of the first places in Naples to jump on the giant video-screen bandwagon, City Hall Café serves dinner and snacks until late at night.

Dizzy Club
Corso Vittorio Emanuele 19-20
Open 8pm-2am. Closed Wed.
    Just contemplating the list of 150 different cocktails is enough to make our head spin! The offerings change weekly, so one need never sip the same drink twice. As you sample these works of the bartender's art, you can play cards or chess, or watch as the habitués match wits.

Gambrinus
Via Chiaia 1-2 - (081) 417582
Open 8am-1:30pm & 4:30pm-11pm. Closed Tue.
    Enjoy the view of the Teatro San Carlo and Piazza Plebiscito (now closed to traffic, what a brilliant idea!) as you soak up the ambience of this historic caffè, a favorite rendezvous for coffee and conversation. You can commune with the spirits of D'Annunzio and Verdi and sample an excellent granita di caffè (coffee ice) or a cup of espresso and a delectable pastry. Light meals are also served.

DISCOS

Acquarius
Via dei Mille 40 - (081) 413881
Open 10pm-3am. Closed Sun-Wed.
    Formerly labeled La Mela (which is what many folks still call it), this club now sports a New Age name. Admission is for couples only; the music is mainly dance, with a few nods to hits from the '70s. Reservations are a must.

Blanche
Gradini Amedeo 12 - (No telephone)
Open 11pm-3am. Closed Sun, Mon, Wed.
    Eccentric, extravagant looks abound at this high-energy venue, favored by teenagers and a mixed gay (male and female) crowd. Drag shows are staged on Tuesdays and Thursdays; on Saturdays the DJ plays kitsch and camp hits from the last twenty years—it's a mob scene!

Chez Moi
Via del Parco Margherita 13 - (081) 407526
Open 11pm-4am. Closed Mon.
    Happy groups of dancing fools meet in nearby Piazza Amedeo before they head to Chez Moi, a popular disco near the funicular station at the bottom of the Vomero hill.

Damiani
Statale Domiziana (55 km W) - (081) 8661202
Open 8pm-2am. Closed Mon.
    Sometimes it's fun to get out of the city and wind up the evening in a natural setting. Damiani is a trendy disco in the historic Campi Flegrei ("Burning Fields")

some 50 kilometers west of Naples, where in summer you can dance outdoors next to the pool.

Kiss Kiss

Via Sgambati 47 - (081) 5466566
Open Fri-Sun.
In this huge, wild disco, those who can stand the decibel levels let loose on the dance floor from Friday to Sunday. Dance and rock-music videos, projected onto gigantic screens, set the electric mood.

Piazza di Spagna

Via Petrarca 101 - (081) 7694882
Open 10pm-3am. Closed Mon-Wed.
Do you wanna dance? Then this freshly renovated club is the place to be. A spectacular staircase punctuates the spacious dance floor. Live bands perform on Thursday nights.

Il Tongue

Via Manzoni 207 - (081) 7690800
Open Sat & Sun: 10pm-3am.
A fairly young crowd has taken over what is obviously one of the most popular discos in town, open for dancing from Friday to Sunday.

NIGHTCLUBS

Accademia

Via Porta a Posillipo 43 - (081) 7692500
Open Fri-Sun: 10pm-4am.
Like many other Neapolitan nightclubs, this one is open only on weekend nights as a rule, though special midweek events are occasionally scheduled. Accademia is one of the city's top discos, but it is also a bar, restaurant, and crêperie.

Lido Club 21

Via Nazario Sauro 21b - (081) 404079
Open Fri-Sat: 10pm-4am.
The age-old art of striptease is practiced by seasoned pros at this well-known Neapolitan nightspot.

My Way

Via Cappella Vecchia 30 - (081) 7644735
Open Fri-Sun: 11pm-4am.

The revelry goes on from Friday to Sunday in this atmospheric disco and piano bar, set below street level. Centrally located but a bit off the city's traditional nightlife circuit.

The Body

They stumbled upon it in the 1600s while demolishing the foundations of an ancient monastery: a headless body wrapped in a tunic and lying on its back, its left arm leaning on a sphinx, the right holding a cornucopia, a couple of babies at its breast. No one could figure out if it was a man or a woman. It looked like a fertility goddess. But the experts decided it was a man, a marble statue from the Greco-Roman era symbolizing the Nile. They deduced that the Egyptian merchants once established in Naples (in the Vico Alessandrini neighborhood) wanted it there to remind them of home. No one knows how it wound up under the monastery. In 1657 it was cleaned, fitted with a head, flowing hair, and beard, and reinstalled in the niche in which it was found. It has been known for centuries as the Body of Naples, centerpiece of the animated Piazzetta Nilo, about a hundred yards from Piazza San Domenico Maggiore.

New Zeppelin

Via Manzoni 176 - (081) 640923
Open Fri-Sun: 11pm-4am.
This disco and nightclub caters to a very young crowd, as the rows of motorbikes parked in front of the club every weekend attest.

Notting Hill

Piazza Dante 88a - (081) 5492694
Open 11pm-3am. Closed Mon, Tue.
Every night owl in town knows this address. Established in 1992, Notting Hill occupies a former movie house and now plays host to every advanced rock band that comes through Naples.

167

Al Pruneto

Via Boccaccio 1 - (081) 7695748
Open Sat-Sun: 9pm-2am.
Gilded youth from the Posillipo quarter gather at this crowded disco on weekend nights to drink, dance, and show off their new clothes. You have to look very hard to spot a face that looks much older than 25.

PIANO BARS

Airone

Via Petrarca 123 - (081) 5750175
Closed Wed.
This classic piano bar is a popular spot in the panoramic hills of Naples. Even in winter, a lively crowd keeps the atmosphere warm and exuberant.

Bar dell'Ovo

Via Partenope 6 - (081) 7644280
Closed Tue.

Talking Heads

There's a slice of Neapolitan history for everyone at Palazzo Reale in monumental Piazza del Plebiscito. Along the façade of the palazzo are eight niches under arches that, until the nineteenth century, buttressed the building. Since then they have contained statues of the founders or most illustrious members of the various dynasties that ruled Naples. From left to right we see, in chronological order, Roger the Norman, Frederick II of Swabia, Charles I of Anjou, Alphonse I of Aragon, Charles V, Charles of Bourbon, Joachim Murat, and, last but not least, Victor Emmanuel II. Their posture has often been the target of ridicule. Supposedly, the statues talk to each other at night, exchanging of all sorts of insults. No one claims they're great works of art, but the Neapolitans seem to like them all the same, perhaps better dead than alive.

From Friday to Sunday, this agreeable watering hole turns into a piano bar. You can relax with the music and a drink until the wee hours, within sight of the glorious Bay of Naples.

La Cachaca

Via Petrarca 29 - (081) 7690490
Open 9pm-4am. Closed Tue.
Live acts appear frequently in the attractive surroundings of this well-known piano bar. It's a favorite nightspot with avid sports fans and athletes, particularly members of the Naples soccer team.

Caffè Megaride

Via Eldorado 1, Borgo Marinaro
(081) 7645300
Closed Tue.
Of all the nightspots on Borgo Marinaro, this is the one that the locals love best. The scent of the sea, expertly mixed drinks, and soft music make for a heady cocktail that you can sip until the wee hours.

Caffè Nobile

Largo Principessa Pignatelli 217 - (081) 400390
Closed Mon.
Aviator Umberto Nobile is glorified here (his photograph is plastered all over the place). Barman Mauro Paradisi concocts sophisticated cocktails, which you may savor in the piano bar—the music goes on until 2am. Light snacks are also served.

De X Cafè

Piazzetta Ascensione 26-27 - (081) 404476
Closed Tue.
Fresh pasta and other Mediterranean-style snacks are just one more reason to give this place a try. The main attraction is pianist Luciano Cipriani, who sings Italian and American songs. He will, if prodded, break out into an operatic aria.

'A Fenestella

Via Marechiaro 23 - (081) 7690020
Closed Wed.
On Saturday nights, this usually sedate seafood restaurant is transformed into an animated *ristopiano*, featuring live piano music and Neapolitan songs. Beautiful seaside surroundings.

Il Gabbiano

Via Partenope 26 - (081) 411666
Closed Sun.

Set amid the luxury hotels on Via Partenope, Il Gabbiano is a favorite with the tourist population. The low lights and cozy sofas in the piano bar create a pleasant atmosphere for an enjoyable, relaxing evening.

Il Gallo Nero

Via Tasso 466 - (081) 643012
Closed Sun eve, Mon.

Handsome nineteenth-century furnishings adorn this admirable villa, which houses an elegant restaurant (open for dinner and late suppers) as well as a plush, quiet piano bar.

Le Grotte Risto-Club

Vico Vasto a Chiaia 28 - (081) 400501
Closed Mon.

The furnishings are rustic but the service is urbane at this restaurant and piano bar, located just a short distance from Via dei Mille and its many enticing shops.

Guinness Club

Via Chiarini 17 - (081) 5936712
Closed Mon.

This restaurant-cum-piano bar is located in the Fuorigrotta quarter, not far from the stadium. Not limited to a single age group, the crowd is ebullient and welcoming, even to unfamiliar faces.

Villa Scipione

Via Scipione Capece 4-6 - (081) 640206
Closed Mon.

Splendid salons and terraces with panoramic views of the surrounding hills enchant the patrons of Villa Scipione. Formerly a private residence, the villa is now an elegant restaurant and piano bar.

Zabadak Club

Via G. Martucci 44 - (081) 7612147
Closed Wed.

A classy cohort of VIPs and executives gather here to sip tropical cocktails and nibble on appetizing little snacks. Don't be surprised if they suddenly join the pianist and burst out in song!

Tough Egg to Crack

The Castel dell'Ovo (Egg Castle) is the most visible and most visited fortress in Naples. It towers over the panoramic Via Partenope and Borgo Marinaro, between grand hotels and renowned restaurants.

The first occupant of the site was lucky Lucius Licinius Lucullus, Roman consul. His wild feasts made his name a byword for extravagance ("Lucullan") in several languages. He built a party house there, on the nob that used to be an island. But the Romans' party ended with a bang and then a whimper, and the spot fell into the hands of a less-than-fun-loving monastic community. In 1128 the monks were hustled out by a Norman junta, which proceeded to build the awesome citadel (enlarged over the centuries). The castle was recently remodeled and is now a convention center and showroom/gallery.

The name itself is a puzzler no one has figured out. Why call it the Egg? The easy answer is its presumed former oval shape, but there's no proof of that. So the Neapolitans prefer a lively legend in which the unlikely name of Virgil comes up. Virgil, they say, was not just a poet, he was a sorcerer as well. He hung a glass amphora containing a magic egg from the rafters of a room in the castle to protect it from bad luck. Unfortunately, during the reign of Queen Joan I, the egg went bust and the castle fell to rubble in a matter of seconds. When it was rebuilt, it was decided that Virgil's egg would be replaced with a golden one, not so easy to crack. And the castle's been solid ever since. The story is slightly scrambled, but it goes over easy with the locals, who never swallow their facts hard-boiled.

Shops

CONTENTS

Neapolitan shopkeepers rest on Sundays, except for the three weeks preceding Christmas. From January 17 until March 13, and from June 14 until October 9, shops in Naples also close their doors on Saturday afternoons. Otherwise, hours are as listed.

ANTIQUES

Adiar
Via Cavallerizza a Chiaia 57 - (081) 421674
Open daily 9am-1:30pm & 4:30pm-8pm.
Mirella Iacono and Clara Topa oversee a startlingly vast stock of antique furniture, picture frames (highly desirable!), statues, and rugs. Adiar is an excellent source for hard-to-find Staffordshire statuettes. Twice a year, the city's "First Ladies of Antiques" mount eagerly awaited exhibitions of Southern ceramics and hand-knotted rugs.

Arte Antica
Via Ferrigni 9 - (081) 7646897
Open daily 9am-1:30pm & 4:30pm-8pm.
Members of the Falanga family have collected and sold paintings, porcelain, and antique furniture since the beginning of this century. Their shop features a pleasing mix of Neapolitan and other Italian pieces and some French antiques, primarily from the eighteenth century.

Gennaro Brandi
Via Domenico Morelli 11 - (081) 7643906
Open daily 9am-1:30pm & 4:30pm-8pm.
In business for more than a century, Brandi specializes in important pieces, such as the magnificent eighteenth-century red-olivewood writing desk from Lombardy that we recently spied in the shop, alongside a Neapolitan reproduction of a Louis XVI commode, executed in rosewood and ebony with mother-of-pearl inlays.

D'Amodio
Via D. Morelli 6 bis - (081) 7643872
Open daily 9am-1:30pm & 4:30pm-8pm.
Antimo D'Amodio inherited his taste for antiques from his father; his integrity and expertise are legendary. He presents Neapolitan pieces and a superb collection of majolica, which is his particular specialty. He showed us an outstanding set of travel accessories produced by the Real Fabbrica Ferdinandea. Speaking of royal, when Queen Elizabeth visited D'Amodio she was presented with a handsome cup decorated with naval vessels flying English flags.

Mario D'Angelo
Via Bisignano 23 - (081) 7648385
Open daily 9am-1:30pm & 4:30pm-8pm.
Formerly a set designer for television, Mario D'Angelo is also a sought-after interior decorator who collects and sells precious seventeenth-century paintings and objects. If you crave a picture by Luca Giordano, Giuseppe Recco, or a Flemish master, by all means come to this shop to inspect the fine religious subjects, landscapes, and still lifes on view.

Fabbrini
Vico Satriano 2 - (081) 7643753
Open daily 9am-1:30pm & 4:30pm-8pm.
  Guido Fabbrini started out as a private collector, later became a consultant, and then made the big move: he is now one of the city's best-known dealers in twentieth-century antiques. His special passions are glass, Art Nouveau, and Art Deco, as you'll see from the superb collection he has amassed of furniture, mirrors, lamps, statuettes, and bibelots. A section of the shop is reserved for French and American costume jewelry of the '40s and '50s.

Florida
Via Domenico Morelli 13 - (081) 7643440
Open daily 9am-1:30pm & 4:30pm-8pm.
  Standing amid splendid desks, inlaid tables, and a captivating collection of silver, majolica, and porcelain, it is a pleasure to while away an hour talking about art and antiques with Riccardo Fanelli. A native of Milan who has lived in Naples for almost 50 years, he specializes in furniture from Campania and Sicily dating from the seventeenth and eighteenth centuries and the early years of the First Empire.

Salvatore Iermano
Via Gaetani 27
Via Domenico Morelli 30 - (081) 7643913
Open daily 9am-1:30pm & 4:30pm-8pm.
  After admiring the eighteenth-century *presepi* (Nativity scenes) at the San Martino museum, you may be struck with a yen to collect crèche figures yourself. Generally about a foot high, with remarkably expressive terra-cotta faces, the shepherds and other figures fashioned in the eighteenth and early nineteenth centuries are superb examples of Neapolitan craftsmanship. Salvatore Iermano's shop holds an especially fine collection of these crèche figures, along with a selection of antique furniture and decorative objects.

Madama Luna
Via San Carlo 20 - (081) 407091
Open daily 9am-1:30pm & 4:30pm-8pm.
  In their refined little shop across from the Teatro San Carlo, the Barbaros present solid country antiques as well as an eclectic group of pieces from Asia and others from Central America.

Maison Suisse
Via Filangieri 29
(081) 421765, fax (081) 426924
Open daily 9am-1:30pm & 4:30pm-8pm.
  The antique and the modern mix it up at Maison Suisse. Right next to a handsome eighteenth-century chair stands a contemporary sofa; a Ching vase is placed side-by-side with a crystal bibelot only a few weeks old. Whatever their age, what the objects and furniture have in common is an uncommon elegance of design.

Tullerie
Via Bisignano 57 - (081) 402851
Open daily 9:30am-1:30pm & 5pm-8pm.
  Tullia Gargiulo was one of the first to ride the modern wave that has since swept the world of antiques. She displays many exclusive pieces—furniture, picture frames,

Philosophers on Memory Lane

  The long, narrow street called Spaccanapoli splits the city down the middle (*spaccare* means to split). The central section, site of the old Greco-Roman city, goes by the name of Via San Biagio dei Librai. History floods out of its doorways. At number 31 is the house of the great Neapolitan philosopher, Giambattista Vico, whose *Scienza Nuova* was the genesis of modern historical study. (Until Vico came along, "history" dealt only with the lives of great men and/or accounts of the unfolding of God's will.) Vico's father, a *libraio*, or bookseller, had his shop there. Giambattista was born among the dusty pages on June 23, 1668.
  Down the way is the splendid Palazzo Filomarino, with a Baroque doorway and a Renaissance courtyard. Another famous philosopher—Benedetto Croce—spent his greatest years there. The Italian Institute for Historical Studies, a Croce creation, now has its headquarters in the palazzo. As the saying goes, a visit to Spaccanapoli is literally a stroll down memory lane.

vases, silver, fabrics—designed by Klimt, Hoffmann, and Fortuny. The late Rudolf Nureyev purchased furnishings for his Positano residence here at Tullerie.

■ AND ALSO...

Two open-air antique markets worth visiting are the *Mercatino Antiquario*, held on the third weekend of each month in the *Villa Communale*, between the Riviera di Chiaia and Via Caracciolo; and the *Mercatino Antiquario* held on the second weekend of each month on *Via Costantinopoli*, near the Museo Nazionale.

BOOKS & PRINTS

Casella
Via Carlo Poerio 92 - (081) 7642627
Open daily 9am-1:30pm & 4:30pm-8pm.
Casella is an old and respected name in the Neapolitan book world. From modest beginnings, the firm has risen to occupy elegant quarters that resemble a drawing room more than a shop. Collectors, or anyone who loves rare books and fine prints, are certain to admire the antiquarian books, autographs, and engravings offered for sale.

Colonnese
Via San Pietro a Maiella 33 - (081) 459858
Open daily 9am-1:30pm & 4pm-7pm.
Old and rare books are accorded the place of honor in this curious shop, but they are flanked by many other venerable items that will set collectors' eyes alight: prints (including many views of old Naples), antique photographs, playing cards with ethnic motifs, crèche figures, postcards, and assorted bric-a-brac. It's a charming place to while away an hour between sightseeing sessions.

Deperro
Via dei Mille 17 - (081) 418687
Open daily 9am-1:30pm & 4:30pm-8pm.
Old guidebooks of Naples used to call Deperro the city's most fashionable bookstore. It continues in that fine tradition today, selling the latest art books and

a sumptuous selection of volumes on Naples and its environs, culture, art, and traditions.

Fiorentino
Calata Trinità Maggiore 36 - (081) 5526628
Open daily 9am-1:30pm & 4pm-7:30pm.
Philosopher and statesman Benedetto Croce used to patronize this wonderful bookstore, as did his compatriot Malaparte, and publishing genius Luigi Einaudi. Fiorentino takes particular pride in its selection of antiquarian volumes and its exhaustive collection of tomes on architecture.

Grimaldi
Via Bausan 61 - (081) 406021
Open 9:30pm-1pm & 4:30pm-7:30pm. Closed Mon am.
Rare editions dealing with the history of Naples are Grimaldi's specialty, but the shop also sells French and English antiquarian books. Precious old engravings, prints, and maps are sold here, too; we particularly admired the early nineteenth-century lithographs that illustrate scenes from Neapolitan life. A catalog is available upon request.

Guida
Via Port'Alba 20-23 - (081) 446377
Via G. Merliani 118-120 - (081) 5560170
Open daily 8am-7pm.
This is without a doubt one of the best-stocked bookstores in a city abounding in bookstores. If you don't find what you want, they'll special-order the volume in question for you. Take note that the colorful Via Port'Alba is home not only to many *librerie* but also to some excellent *pizzerie*—after an extended browse along the booksellers' windows, you can fortify yourself with a fragrant pizza marinara or margherita, fresh from the oven.

La Libreria dei Ragazzi
Largo Ferrantina a Chiaia 1 - (081) 404826
Open 9am-1:30pm & 4:30pm-8pm. Closed Sat pm.
Even the tiniest tots can browse through the charming, colorful children's books arranged on low, easy-to-reach shelves. The store also stocks a good assortment of games that will amuse little ones (and please adults, too).

Libri & Libri
Via G. Carducci 32 - (081) 417152
Open daily 9am-1:30pm & 4:30pm-8pm.
A modern book emporium established in 1989, where cultural events are often held, including the Libri & Libri book and publishing awards.

Marotta
Via dei Mille 78 - (081) 418881
Via G. Porzio, Centro Direzionale
(081) 5625262
Open daily 9am-1:30pm & 4pm-7:30pm.
Marotta's huge shop window contains hundreds of books, all displayed to advantage. Most of the recent publications on view are Italian, but a fair sampling of foreign-language books is available as well.

Treves
Via Toledo 250 - (081) 415211
Open daily 8am-1:30pm & 4:30pm-8pm.
Set on the city's principal thoroughfare, where the action is nonstop from morning to night, Treves is known not only for its well-stocked bookshelves but for its excellent music section. A record or cassette of Neapolitan folk songs is a wonderful way to bring back memories of a trip to *bella Napoli.*

DEPARTMENT STORES

Coin
Via Alessandro Scarlatti 100 - (081) 5780111
Open daily 9am-1:15pm & 4:15pm-7:45pm.
Coin is notable for its selection of inexpensive clothing and accessories in tune with the latest fashion trends. In addition, you'll find a full range of department store merchandise—if you need to stock up on essential supplies, this is just the place.

La Rinascente
Via Toledo 343 - (081) 411511
Via Diaz 38 - (081) 5523983
Open daily 9am-1:15pm & 4:15pm-7:45pm.
Italy's largest and best-stocked department store features good-quality merchandise—including its own line of clothing—at reasonable prices. A reliable source for both basics and fashion.

Standa
Via Diaz 24 - (081) 5525393
Via Solimene 143 - (081) 5780480
Open daily 9am-1:15pm & 4:15pm-7:45pm.
The Standa chain stocks lower- to middle-range department-store standards. Come here for cosmetics, toiletries, stationery, and such.

Upim
Via Diaz (corner of Piazza Matteotti)
(081) 5523354
Via dei Mille 59 - (081) 417520
Via Scarlatti - (081) 5562817
Via A. Doria 40 - (081) 5934477
Open daily 9am-1:15pm & 4:15pm-7:45pm.
Need a pair of socks, an undershirt, a carry-all, or a bathrobe? You'll find it at Upim, and it won't cost you too much.

Square Drawing Room

They call it the *Salotto*, or Drawing Room because Piazza dei Martiri is the most elegant square in Naples. In the center is a circular flower bed planted around a column with four lions at its base. Around the square stand the palazzi of the patrician families, the Partanna and Calabritto. Neapolitans like to rendezvous at the foot of the column for a friendly chat. The *passeggiata* (ritual stroll) often starts there, as do the sorties of the serious shoppers who swoop down to Via Chiaia, Via Filangeri, and Via dei Mille, the designer showcase.

FASHION

■ CLOTHING

Barone Pio
Via Pessina 36 - (081) 5498841
Via Merliani 51 - (081) 5788371
Open daily 9am-1:30pm & 4pm-7:30pm.
Full-figured women come here in search of quality fashion that fits. Barone's styles combine excellent tailoring and fetching

colors in sizes significantly larger than those worn by emaciated cover girls.

Benetton

Via dei Mille 41 - (081) 5499664
Open daily 9am-1:30pm & 4:30pm-8pm.
Although Benetton's bright, cheerful, young-in-spirit knits and sportswear are now as ubiquitous in the U.S. as in Italy, it's still fun to buy them at the source. The prices are just a bit lower than in the States.

Blasi

Via dei Mille 27 - (081) 415283
Open daily 9am-1:30pm & 4:30pm-8pm.
This spacious, elegant shop is well known in Naples and beyond for its first-rate clothing and accessories. Discriminating men and women count on owner Nicola Blasi (whose forebears handed down to him his indisputable sartorial flair) to provide personalized service, including expert advice on choosing fabrics and colors.

Cacharel

Via Calabritto 5 - (081) 7643821
Open daily 9am-1:30pm & 4:30pm-8pm.
Cacharel's bright, sporty French women's wear is well suited to sunny Naples.

Livio De Simone

Via D. Morelli 15 - (081) 7643827
Open daily 9am-1:30pm & 4:30pm-8pm.
Women love Livio De Simone's vibrantly hued sportswear, made of print fabrics in sophisticated colors that are perfect for casual occasions. The beachwear and swimsuits are particularly pretty, but the shirts and trousers are attractive too (beautiful, luminous yellows and blues), and every piece is nicely finished.

Emporio Armani

Piazza dei Martiri - (081) 425816
Open daily 9am-1:30pm & 4:30pm-8pm.
Armani's Naples branch keeps southern Italians dressed with the same terribly sophisticated flair as their fashionable countrymen to the north. This boutique focuses on Armani's more relaxed lines for men and women.

Fendi

Santa Caterina a Chiaia 22 - (081) 421387
Open daily 9am-1:30pm & 4:30pm-8pm.

Known throughout the fashion world for their sumptuous furs, the Fendi sisters also design a full range of chic, fearsomely expensive ready-to-wear. Gorgeous leather accessories and clothing are also a specialty.

Gianfranco Ferré

Via dei Mille 1 - (081) 406367
Open daily 9am-1:30pm & 4:30pm-8pm.
Stunning, high-priced, quintessentially Italian fashion for women and men from the "architect of fashion," Gianfranco Ferré. Shoes are included in the ultracontemporary line.

Giorgio

Via Calabritto 29 - (081) 7644122
Open daily 9am-1:30pm & 4:30pm-8pm.
Giorgio Ricciardi is quite a character. After a stint with Nicola Trussardi, he's back in Naples, heading a smart boutique in the heart of the shopping district. Giorgio plies his customers with music, advice, and irrepressible good humor. He clothes both men and women with a classic, elegant look. Nothing loud or aggressive, and no men's suits: Giorgio deems that only a custom tailor can do that job right.

Gucci

Via dei Mille 56 - (081) 414084
Open daily 9am-1:30pm & 4:30pm-8pm.
Exquisitely tailored apparel and status accessories for men and women. The sportswear for women is noticeably less fusty than in years past (you'll drool over the silk floral-print blouses).

London House

Via Filangieri 26 - (081) 403908
Open daily 9am-1:30pm & 4pm-7:30pm.
When this haberdashery was founded in the 1920s, every well-dressed Italian man considered English tailoring to be the height of sartorial elegance. Hence the name of this shop, now run by Mariano Rubinacci, son of its founder, who continues to follow the British creed of fine fabrics cut to create an impression of ease and nonchalance, and finished with a meticulous eye to detail.

Angelo Marino

Via Santa Caterina 74 - (081) 416234

Via dei Mille 6 - (081) 414225
Open daily 9am-1:30pm & 4:30pm-8pm.
For stylish menswear, young (and not-so-young) Neapolitan dandies have traditionally relied on Angelo Marino. You can see them standing in front of the shop's windows, discussing the relative merits of a suit, shirt, or topcoat. Inside, an obliging staff offers sound advice and personalized service.

Maxi Ho

Via Nisco 23-27 - (081) 427530
Open daily 9am-1:30pm & 4:30pm-8pm.
The big names in high-fashion menswear are gathered together in this stunning space. Exclusive casual clothes, classic and sporty sweaters, trendy or businesslike shirts—every item is tasteful and beautifully made, by Yamamoto, Dolce & Gabbana, Gaultier, Gigli and the rest of the *Vogue Uomo* crowd. Another shop, just for women, is located across the street.

Down with Rome, Long Live Toledo!

The street in Naples is and always has been Via Toledo. Many a traveler has waxed lyrical about its lively market and swirling crowds. Nowadays traffic is controlled and the number of street hawkers has been cut, but Via Toledo is still a favorite meeting place. Don Pedro de Toledo christened the street, so to speak, in the first half of the sixteenth century. After Italian Unification, when Rome became the capital in 1870, Via Toledo's name was changed to Via Roma. But the Neapolitans went on calling it Via Toledo, with all due respect to the city of the Caesars. A few years ago, the city council decided to clean off the ancient street signs and reinstate the beloved name. Via Toledo forever!

Mediterraneo

Vico Satriano 10 - (081) 7647360
Open daily 9:30am-1:30pm & 4:30pm-8pm.

Designer Cristina Di Stasio reigns over a sober, clean-lined shop where her women's wear is attractively displayed. Inspired by the Mediterranean, she creates evocative clothing—blouses, suits, silks, pareos—that is always just a step ahead of the fashion pack. Reasonable prices.

Eddy Monetti

Via dei Mille 45 (menswear) - (081) 407064
Piazza Santa Caterina 7 (women's wear)
(081) 403229
Open daily 9am-1:30pm & 4:30pm-8pm.
The house logo—a carriage drawn by a prancing horse—symbolizes the easy elegance of yesteryear, an elegance that Eddy Monetti keeps alive in his classic clothing for men and women. Refined fabrics, impeccable tailoring, and close attention to detail are Monetti's trademarks. The Santa Caterina shop features women's wear, while the Via dei Mille location is a bastion of masculinity.

Old England

Via Toledo 229 - (081) 417055
Via G. Filangieri 15d - (081) 414382
Open daily 9am-1:30pm & 4:30pm-8pm.
In matters of personal style, Neapolitan men have traditionally favored the classic English look that combines comfort with elegance. This store is a veritable corner of London set down in southern Italy, complete with all the marvelous tweeds, woolens, and cashmeres that distinguish the classiest British clothing.

Pour les Amis

Piazza dei Martiri 28 (menswear)
(081) 7643103
Via Alabardieri 23 (women's wear)
(081) 413357
Open daily 9am-1:30pm & 4:30pm-8pm.
Friends, indeed. True to its name, this store pampers customers and makes certain that they have sound advice on colors, styles, and coordinates. The women's store, on Via Alabardieri, presents a range of home accents, fabrics, embroidery, and curtains as well as clothing.

Raffaele Ricciardi

Via Carducci 57 - (081) 400309
Open daily 9:30am-1:30pm & 4:30pm-8pm.
This boutique quickly earned a reputation as one of the most stylish shops in

Naples. Designer clothes for women and men are alluringly displayed downstairs, while the upper floor is home to a magnificent collection of luxurious furs.

Amina Rubinacci

Via dei Mille 16 - (081) 415672
Open daily 9:30am-1:30pm & 4:30pm-8pm.
In Paris, Amina is known as the "Queen of the Knit." As a sweater artist, she's in a class by herself. For the young set, there are delicate pastel tints and chromatic brights, while their elders can snuggle up in more sober shades of black, beige, blue... Amina's "oyster" sweater has become a status symbol among fashion insiders (Inès de la Fressange, that icon of chic, is an assiduous customer).

Gabriella Spatarella

Via Filangieri 23 - (081) 401703
Open daily 9am-1:30pm & 4:30pm-8pm.
Knits—especially her stunning sweaters—and leatherwear are Gabriella Spatarella's specialties. This feminine boutique is done up in ivory and white, and the staff provides personalized service as well as stylish clothing and accessories for fashion-conscious women of all ages.

Staffelli

Via C. Poerio 12 - (081) 7646922
Open daily 9:30am-1:30pm & 4:30pm-8pm.
Designer Ernesto Esposito is also an art collector (Andy Warhol used to be a chum). His notions about women's clothing are daring, perhaps a bit provocative. Even the accessories, from belts to shoes, are avant-garde—the better to lure young fashion plates who want to put together a distinctive look that can't be copied.

Stefanel

Corso Umberto I 27-29 - (081) 5526972
Open daily 9am-1:30pm & 4:30pm-8pm.
A competitor to the incredibly popular Benetton, Stefanel carries a similarly colorful line of casual unisex sweaters, T-shirts, jackets, and other youth-oriented sportswear. Moderate prices.

Valentino

Via Calabritto 1 - (081) 417236
Via Filangieri 68 - (081) 417711
Open daily 9am-1:30pm & 4:30pm-8pm.

At this showcase for the creations of Italy's best-known designer, you can peruse his eye-catching clothes and accessories (and gasp at the eye-popping prices).

Versace

Via Calabritto 7 - (081) 7644210
Open daily 9am-1:30pm & 4:30pm-8pm.
Gianni Versace's designs for men and women need no introduction. Though flamboyant, the clothes are impeccably cut from the finest fabrics—whether it's silk twill for the wild print shirts or pink lamé for a micromini. Even the accessories require a significant investment, but they pay out high-fashion dividends.

■ JEWELRY

Theo Brinkmann

Piazza Municipio 21 - (081) 5520555
Via dei Mille 72 - (081) 414475
Open daily 9am-1:30pm & 4:30pm-8pm.
In the historic Piazza Municipio, where you may admire the Palazzo San Giacomo and the majestic Castel Nuovo, Theo Brinkmann's display windows glitter enticingly. His exclusive creations and tradition of fine workmanship have won him a loyal following in Naples and beyond. Be sure to check out the superb selection of timepieces.

Ileana Della Corte

Via Santa Lucia 65 - (081) 7648765
Open daily 9:30am-1:30pm & 4:30pm-8pm.
Ileana Della Corte combines white gold and diamonds to make jewels that even a czar would covet. Coral inspires her too, to create lovely rings, necklaces, and cunning little charms and pendants. Each piece, however classic, bears a special detail that is Ileana's alone. Princess Anne recently received a silver and lapis box from this shop; and Mickey Rourke wears a ring that Ileana designed.

Fiaba

Via Toledo 241 - (081) 412101
Open daily 9am-1:30pm & 4:30pm-8pm.
Fiaba shops are sprinkled around the downtown shopping district, displaying truly amazing quantities of fun jewelry. The necklaces, bracelets, earrings, and

pins don't cost the earth and will make even last season's outfit look up to date.

Knight

Piazza dei Martiri 52 - (081) 7643837
Open daily 9am-1:30pm & 4:30pm-8pm.
In what is perhaps the most elegant square in all of Naples, the Knight family (of English origin but long established in the city) offers a choice collection of fine jewelry and silver to shoppers of discriminating tastes (and considerable means).

The Catacombs

The labyrinths of Naples are not just above ground. Many neighborhoods are built over caverns, tunnels, and abandoned rock quarries, some of which have not been explored since antiquity. The most interesting hole in the ground is, of course, named after San Gennaro (Saint Januarius), where the bones of Naples's patron saint were once kept. San Gennaro's catacombs began in the second century as a small cemetery and became the official Christian burial ground. They occupy two floors divided into vast halls and ambulatories, some with delicate frescoes. Access is from the avenue next to the church of the Madre del Buon Consiglio (a recent imitation of a Roman basilica). Guided tours are held on weekends.

Monetti

Via dei Mille 12 - (081) 411468
Via Santa Brigida 60 - (081) 5523867
Open daily 9:30am-1:30pm & 4:30pm-8pm.
Monetti presents Pomellato's prestigious jewels and trinkets, as well as an opulent line of timepieces by Rolex, Vacheron Constantin, Piaget, and Cartier.

Nappa

Via Filangieri 65 - (081) 413143
Open daily 9am-1:30pm & 4:30pm-8pm.
Run for three generations by the same family, which not only sells but also designs fine jewelry, Nappa is considered one of the city's most reliable jewelers. A knowledgeable staff can discuss jewelry and silver with authority and will patiently answer questions about gem quality or workmanship. Whether classic or contemporary, the objects and ornaments on view at Nappa are uncommon—and of uncommonly high quality.

Vendome

Piazza dei Martiri 31 - (081) 7643240
Open daily 9:30am-1:30pm & 4:30pm-8pm.
Vendome is the newest jeweler in Naples, and has already made its mark with fascinating exhibitions on Van Cleef and Fabergé. Gabriella Naso presides over the glittering array of tasteful, distinctive jewelry, in which pearls occupy a place of honor.

■ SHOES & ACCESSORIES

D'Aria

Via dei Mille 71 - (081) 415309
Open daily 9am-1:30pm & 4:30pm-8pm.
Neapolitans know their shoes; at one time, footwear fashioned in the shadow of Mount Vesuvius was the most prestigious that money could buy. Times have changed, of course, and now even in Naples one finds shoes made in South Korea. This shop, however, sells only classic, top-quality Italian footwear for men and women.

Salvatore Ferragamo

Piazza dei Martiri 56 - (081) 415454
Open daily 9am-1:30pm & 4:30pm-8pm.
Exquisitely crafted, comfortable footwear in restrained yet fashionable styles.

Galiano

Via Cavallerizza 59 - (081) 426286
Open daily 9am-1:30pm & 4:30pm-8pm.
Button, button, who's got the button? This store sells what seems like thousands of them every day, since thrifty Neapolitans are fond of sprucing up last season's coat with a new set of buttons. The crowds are so thick here that it's hard to get near the counter, but persevere—you may come across some old, rare specimens that would be just the thing to jazz up a vintage jacket.

177

Giannotti

Via Toledo 321 - (081) 406078
Open daily 9am-1:30pm & 4:30pm-8pm.

Here are lovely handbags in reptile, calf, crocodile, and a wide range of fabrics, for evening, daytime, and casual wear. The array of luggage and accessories—belts and such—is especially tempting at sale time.

Iorio

Via Chiaia 86 - (081) 416115
Open daily 9am-1:30pm & 4:30pm-8pm.

Specialty shops are a vanishing breed, so we are particularly pleased to have found this little gem. Its sole purpose is to sell slippers to those who appreciate the small yet not insignificant pleasure of trading their shoes for something more comfy the moment they walk in the door. The selection of colors and styles could not be more complete. After a period of eclipse, slippers have made a comeback as people rediscover the joys of cocooning.

Lerre

Via Calabritto 21 - (081) 7643884
Open daily 9:30am-1:30pm & 4:30pm-8pm.

You've surely admired Lerre's shoes on the covers of Vogue. The footwear manufactured by this century-old firm is designed for fashionable, active women who like to stand out from the crowd. A New York art dealer, known for her chic, once purchased eighteen pairs of Lerre's elegant pumps in one fell swoop!

Eugenio Marinella

Piazza Vittoria 287 - (081) 7644214
Open daily 9am-1:30pm & 4:30pm-8pm.

Fine neckties are, of course, available in most good men's stores. But if you want a tie that is truly exceptional, follow automotive tycoon Gianni Agnelli's example and let Eugenio Marinella advise you on your choice of color and pattern. The neckwear sold in this highly reputed but discreet little shop is made of top-quality silk; ties can also be custom-made to your specifications.

Must de Cartier

Via Calabritto 8 - (081) 7644250
Open daily 9am-1:30pm & 4:30pm-8pm.

Cartier's timeless "Must" collection of watches, jewelry, and chic leather accessories are displayed here with all the taste that the pieces demand.

Nazareno Gabrielli

Via Chiaia 142 - (081) 417863
Open daily 9am-1:30pm & 4:30pm-8pm.

One of Italy's foremost leather-crafters, Nazareno Gabrielli produces a covetable line of beautifully finished handbags, travel gear, wallets, and more. Look for the firm's famous luggage in a signature mix of leather and tweed.

Fratelli Piccini

Via Chiaia 145 - (081) 417654
Open daily 9am-1:30pm & 4:30pm-8pm.

The window displays handsome leather bags, but Piccini Brothers is noted above all for its beautifully crafted umbrellas. If you regard that particular accessory as something more than just protection from a downpour, make a point of visiting this charming shop.

Piscopo

Via San Pasquale a Chiaia 17
Open daily 9am-1pm & 4:30pm-8pm.

Blue hatboxes bearing the prestigious Lock & Co. label are neatly arranged on Maria Piscopo's shelves. Around the shop you'll see wooden "blockheads," used to shape these fine hats to customers' measurements. Among Piscopo's many well-known clients is Prince Francesco Caravita di Sirignano, considered the last of the Neapolitan dandies.

Pistola

Via Santa Caterina 12 - (081) 422058
Open daily 9am-1:30pm & 4:30pm-8pm.

Naples is famous in Italy and abroad as a center for quality leather gloves. But paradoxically, the city's mild climate means that Neapolitans rarely wear gloves, and therefore most of the shoppers who come to Pistola are foreign tourists or Italian out-of-towners. They love the shop's superb selection of lined and unlined styles for men and women, available in a glorious range of colors and skins.

Salvatore Spatarella

Via Calabritto 1 - (081) 7643794
Open daily 9am-1:30pm & 4:30pm-8pm.

The owner comes from a family that has a solid tradition of leather merchandising, with shops all over town. This one is perhaps the most prestigious of all: the shoes, handbags, and luggage are classic in design, flawlessly finished, and priced in accordance with their excellent quality.

San Carlo–Worth Crowing About

Just over 250 years ago the famed Teatro San Carlo opera house opened for business—November 4, 1737, the name day of Charles of Bourbon, who commissioned the theater (designed by Medrano and built by Angelo Carasale). And it became a sensation overnight (the first opera performed there was Metastasio's *Achille in Sciro*). But in 1816 a raging fire left the San Carlo in ruins. It was rebuilt in record time by Antonio Niccolini, and many preferred the new theater to the old. That indefatigable traveler, Stendhal, was so enthralled that he came again and again after the reopening. He wrote pages describing the fascination he felt, the awe inspired in him by the silver and gold of the auditorium, the sky-blue boxes, and the ornamented parapet, which together produced "the impression of magnificence... superb illumination, sparkling with lights, which make every bit of gold and silver shine..." And so on. We suggest you take a look yourself; the San Carlo is pretty good at singing its own praises.

La Tienda
Via dei Mille 63 - (081) 415249
Open daily 9am-1:30pm & 4:30pm-8pm.
The very same fabrics designed by Saint Laurent, Dior, Ungaro, Valentino, and Mila Schön for their costly creations can be purchased by the meter at La Tienda. The vast assortment of fabulous silks, wools, satins, cottons, linens, and brocades is guaranteed to set a seamstress's creative juices flowing. The shop is also home to a small collection of costume jewelry and accessories.

Mario Valentino
Via Calabritto 10 - (081) 7644262
Piazza Trieste e Trento 56 - (081) 418638
Open daily 9am-1:30pm & 4:30pm-8pm.
The "other" Valentino, renowned for flamboyant footwear and stylish leather gear.

FOOD

■ GOURMET SHOPS

Codrington & Co.
Via Chiaia 94 - (081) 418257
Open daily 9am-1pm & 4:30pm-8pm.
This historic emporium was founded by an English family who settled in Naples a century ago. Centrally located under the Ponte di Chiaia, Codrington's is a gourmet bazaar, a delightful shop for rummaging, and it is unlikely that you will leave the premises empty-handed. Spices, teas, condiments, sauces, and vinegars from all over the world are on display, many bearing curious, exotic labels. There is an especially fine selection of English marmalades, many of which can be found nowhere else. The range of merchandise extends from English saddle soap and shoe creams to a fascinating array of kitchen utensils and gadgets.

Coloniali
Via Consalvo 74 - (No telephone)
Open daily 9am-1:30pm & 4pm-7:30pm.
Like the colonies its name evokes, this shop seemed on the verge of extinction. We are pleased to report that it has reemerged in new quarters under new management, with an even more impressive line of all the ingredients an ambitious home baker might need. Candied violets, orangeflower water, and all manner of decorations and flavorings—including the most esoteric—are sold here, and precious advice on how to use them all is dispensed free of charge.

Drugs
Via Aniello Falcone 388-390 - (081) 643382
Open daily 8am-1:30pm & 4:30pm-8pm.
There's nothing old-fashioned about Drugs, a grocery store that bears a marked

179

resemblance to its New World counter-parts. In addition to the usual cookies, caramels, coffees, syrups, jams, and ice creams that are the mainstays of traditional *drogherie*, you'll also find the detergents and household cleansers to which Italian women are as loyal as American housewives are to their Tide or Joy.

Gay Odin

Via Toledo 291 - (081) 421867
Via Chiaia 237 - (081) 422824
Via Vittoria Colonna 15 - (081) 418282
Via Giordano 21 - (081) 5783380
Open daily 9am-1:30pm & 4pm-7:30pm.

If, like us, you are intemperately fond of chocolate, take careful note of these ad-dresses: they are the retail outlets of a first-rate local chocolate manufacturer. The great debate currently raging in Naples has the Nudi and the Tronchetti (two of the many varieties of chocolates here) vying neck and neck for the title of popular favorite. For our part, we think the Cozze are tops. And in addition to these terrific chocolates, Gay Odin carries excel-lent powdered cocoa, licorice, and hard candies of every shape and hue.

Tortora

Via Piedigrotta 53 - (081) 667003
Open daily 9am-1:30pm & 4pm-7:30pm.

Confetti—sugar-coated almonds—ac-company every significant event in a tradi-tional Italian lifetime. Births, baptisms, first communions, and weddings are all marked by a wide and generous distribu-tion of the pastel confections to friends and relatives. Tortora is one of Naples's premier suppliers; the tiny premises are stocked with improbable quantities of confetti as well as precariously balanced jars and boxes of top-quality hard candy and other sugarplums.

Dal Vecchio

Via Cavallerizza 32 - (081) 414568
Open Mon-Sat: 8am-8pm.

Time seems to have stood still in this charming, old-fashioned shop. Crossing the threshold of Dal Vecchio is almost like plunging into the past: the display cases and shelves are all antiques, and the groceries are piled up, as was once the custom, in a picturesque jumble of boxes, sacks, and crates. But the favorite tea or coffee, the rare spice or special candy you request will be produced from the ap-parent chaos in record time, by the friend-ly owner or one of his family members.

■ HERBALISTS

La Bottega dell'Erborista

Via Bellini 68 - (081) 5499677
Open daily 9am-1:30pm & 3pm-8pm.

After admiring all those pictures and statues of gorgeous gods and goddesses at the National Archaeological Museum or the Academy of Fine Arts, turn your atten-tion to your own looks and stop in here (it's quite close to the museums) to indulge in some of this herbalist's all-natural soaps, oils, and essences. The staff will also prof-fer reliable advice on herbal remedies for insomnia, coughs, and sore throats. If you are already perfectly divine and never have a problem falling asleep, stop in anyway for a jar of delicious honey or a bag of barley-sugar caramels.

L'Erba Voglio

Via Orazio 141a - (081) 7142323
Open Mon-Sat: 9:30am-1:30pm & 4:30pm-8pm.

Erba voglio is the wonder herb that grows on the Posillipo hill; it is reputed to cure all sorts of little ills. You'll find it here, in this spruce little shop, along with macrobiotic foods, plant-based cosmetics, and herbal teas. The courteous, professional staff is on duty to advise you.

Aux Herbes Sauvages-Mességué

Piazza San Pasquale 29 - (081) 7642428
Open daily 8:30am-1:30pm & 4:30pm-8pm.

For the ever-more-numerous disciples of herbal guru Maurice Mességué, this shop provides the entire line of cosmetics and food products dreamed up in the great man's laboratories. New items bring in the faithful from the far corners of the city, who purchase them unquestioningly. Mességué's natural products—brewer's yeast, jams, cereals—are expensively pack-aged and command luxury prices.

> *Some establishments change their **closing times** without warning. It is always wise to check in advance.*

Idea Verde

Riviera di Chiaia 9 - (081) 682444
Open daily 8:30am-1:30pm & 4:30pm-8pm.

At this cheerful, unusual shop you can purchase an herbal-tea mixture, a house plant, or a bouquet of flowers to delight a friend. This herbalist-florist had the notion that macrobiotic foods, plant-based cosmetics, tulips, chrysanthemums, and rhododendrons should all live together in perfect harmony. And a beautifully *idea verde* ("green idea") it is!

La Mandragola

Via Fiorelli 9b - (081) 413906
Open daily 8:30am-1:30pm & 4:30pm-8pm.

Named for the mysterious mandrake, an herb whose forked root bears a strange resemblance to the human form, this serious herbalist offers culinary and medicinal herbs, plant extracts, essences, tinctures, and distillations as well as a range of natural food products: honey, seaweed, whole-grain bread, and the like. Outside, window displays provide much useful information on the properties of herbal medicines and treatments. The shop occupies quarters in a fashionable part of town, next to a garden whose century-old trees set an appropriately natural tone.

La Strega

Vicoletto Belledonne 5 - (081) 413140
Open daily 9am-1:30pm & 4:30pm-8pm.

The "witch" to which the shop's name alludes is in fact a personable lady who seems at home among the salutary herbs and creams that fill her fresh, white boutique. Her particular brand of magic deals with keeping skin soft and smooth; she will concoct a special cream just for you, taking into account your age and lifestyle. Is it by chance that her shop is located on a street named for "beautiful ladies"? It's just a few steps away from the city's premier shopping district.

Il Vaso di Pandora

Via Kerbaker 56 - (081) 5561327
Open 8:30am-1:30pm & 4:30pm-8pm. Closed Sat pm.

As you may recall, hope was all that remained in Pandora's box after the ills of the world had escaped from it. And hope is just what the proprietors of Il Vaso di Pandora hold out to their many customers: hope of improving their health or their looks with natural plant-based remedies and cosmetics. Situated in a busy shopping center in the residential Vomero district, this elegant herbalist's shop is staffed by friendly salespeople on whom you can count for excellent advice.

Poets' Hole in the Wall

Whether they rest in peace or in pieces is immaterial—it's the thought that counts. Virgil and Leopardi, the great Latin and Italian poets, were separated by millennia but lie shoulder to shoulder in Naples, or so it is said. Their tombs are in a stone wall in a park near the Mergellina station (next to the tunnel to Fuorigrotta), though no one is really sure whether Virgil's or some other Roman's ashes repose in the Augustan-age columbarium. And it's unlikely that the second tomb contains the remains of Leopardi, who died in 1837 during a cholera epidemic in Naples and more likely wound up in a mass grave. But ceremonies in honor of the poets are always held at this spot at the foot of the green Posillipo hill.

■ WINE

Arfè

Via Santa Maria in Portico 37 - (081) 669153
Open 9am-2pm & 4:30pm-7:30pm. Closed Thu pm.

Located in the neighborhood of a lively market where hucksters hawk a little of everything, this wine shop is a busy place at any time of day. The window displays feature a host of domestic and imported gourmet indulgences, excellent charcuterie and cheeses, and wine bottles bearing elaborate labels. Inside, however, you can find an attractive selection of more affordable, perfectly estimable little wines from good producers.

Bacco

Vico San Domenico Maggiore 1
(No telephone)
Open eve only, from 8pm.

The opening hours are irregular, for Bacco opens only when owner Gennaro Di Maio feels like greeting customers and uncorking a bottle or two. And what a scene! Antiques, classical statues—and tables attached by chains to the wall and ceiling! In this eccentric setting, patrons hoist glass after glass of delicious wines sold by the carafe. Jolly ambience.

Cavin

Calata Villa del Popolo - (081) 260464
Open daily 9am-6pm.

The Di Meglio brothers distill lipsmacking lemon-based liqueurs, notably several varieties of limoncello, a dessert cordial that is deservedly much in demand. They'll also introduce you to their choice range of spritzy Spumantes, lush Marsalas, and fine Italian wines.

Corcione

Via Filangieri 75 - (081) 417772
Open 9am-2pm & 5pm-8pm. Closed Thu pm.

Like many another *salumeria* (delicatessen) in downtown Naples, this one carries an ample stock of wines and spirits. The bottles in the window boast celebrated labels and seem to lord it over the hams, jars of marmalade, and tins of tomatoes with which they are displayed. But the best bottles, of course, are kept inside, in cool spots well out of the sun.

Enoteca Belledonne

Vico Belledonne a Chiaia 18 - (081) 403162
Open Mon-Sat: 9:30am-1:30pm & 4:30pm-8pm.

In the heart of Naples's artist quarter, this tiny wine shop stocks an impressive inventory. We come here for local wines, some produced on the island of Ischia, others in the shadow of Mount Vesuvius. By all means sample the tasty Falanghina, a variety that is currently all the rage.

Enoteca del Buon Bere

Via Turchi 13 - (081) 7647843
Open 8:30am-1:30pm & 4:30pm-7:30pm. Closed Thu pm.

The sight of so many shelves fil'ed with perfectly aligned bottles bearing diverse and fascinating labels is sure to provoke a shiver of delight in any oenophile. What's more, this shop near the oceanfront in the hotel district also sells caviar, foie gras en terrine, good Norwegian smoked salmon and vintage (naturally!) Champagne... all the provisions for an unforgettable picnic.

Da Luigi

Via Arangio Ruiz 54 - (081) 682529
Open 8am-2pm & 4pm-8pm. Closed Thu.

The sign says that this is a fruit store, but like many other such establishments, Luigi's stock in trade has diversified over the years. So in addition to the baskets of apples, pears, and flawless tropical fruit on which the shop's reputation is based, you'll find an ample assortment of judiciously selected (primarily Italian) wines.

La Maison du Vin

Vico Figurella a Montecalvario 47
(081) 413111
Open 9am-1:30pm & 4pm-7:30pm. Closed Thu.

Despite its French name, La Maison du Vin does not exclude wines from Italy—or, for that matter, from Spain and Portugal. The tiny street on which it stands runs off Via Toledo, just across from the headquarters of the Banco di Napoli.

Fratelli Montagna

Via Santa Lucia 20a - (081) 204647
Open 8am-1:30pm & 4:30pm-8pm. Closed Thu.

The flashy sign out front announces that this is the place for *vini e liquori*. But inside, the atmosphere is hushed, to suit the precious bottles accustomed to the cool silence of a cellar. You'll find an ample assortment of Italian wines as well as a small foreign delegation of imports. The owners have a marked preference for red wines, of which they stock some truly exceptional examples.

Pisaniello

Largo Vasto a Chiaia 88 - (081) 418390
Open 9am-2pm & 4pm-8pm. Closed Thu pm.

Like many of its customers, we wish that Pisaniello would find more spacious quarters. Yet in a very few square yards of floor space, this well-known emporium manages to stock an amazing quantity of wines, spirits, mineral waters, beers and olive oils. And not only is the inventory large, it is first-class: local wine buffs know that this is *the* place to find a very special bottle.

Rigoni

Via Guglielmo Sanfelice 39 - (081) 5520888
Open daily 8am-7pm.
This shop is hard to define, but then that's the source of its charm. Part delicatessen, part snack bar, part wine shop, it is always full of customers and has a delightful, old-fashioned air. The unfailingly cordial staff will advise you on your selection from the wide array of carefully chosen wines, spirits, and beers. You'll find Rigoni right in the center of town, just a few yards away from the police station.

A Herculean Task

They look like a bunch of half-burnt easy-to-light fireplace logs. Actually, they're the famed Papyruses of Herculaneum, now housed in Palazzo Reale's Officina dei Papiri Ercolanesi. They were discovered during the eighteenth century, about 1,700 years after they were written, in an excavation at Herculaneum. Like Pompeii, Herculaneum was covered by ash, stones, and molten lava in A.D. 79 following the eruption of Vesuvius. The machine used to unroll the papyruses, invented by Antonio Piaggio in the late 1700s, is also on display. It allowed researchers to read the works of Greek and Latin Epicurean philosophers written on the rolls. At the time, it took about one month of solid work to unroll one inch of papyrus without destroying the rest. The unique collection is open to the public weekday mornings.

Vinarium

Via Cappella Vecchia 7 - (081) 7644114
Open 9am-1:30pm & 4:30pm-8pm. Closed Sat am.
On a quiet little street that leads off Piazza dei Martiri (an open-air "drawing room" of the type that Italian architects

have always designed so well) stands a wine shop that is a real treasure trove for connoisseurs. Expect to pay top lira for these premium wines and spirits.

Vinicola

Via Consalvo 108 - (081) 610301
Open 9am-1:30pm & 4:30pm-7:30pm. Closed Thu pm.
Whatever you're thirsty for, you can find it here: mineral waters, fruit juices, beers, wines, and spirits are all in plentiful supply, at prices noticeably lower than in the midtown stores.

GIFTS

Arethusa

Riviera di Chiaia 202b -(081) 411551
Open daily 9:30am-1pm & 4:30pm-7:30pm.
Posters for every taste occupy one part of this shop, including Michel Bedard's colorful works peopled with crocodiles and geese, or Van Utens's renditions of Renaissance landscapes. The bestseller is *Napolicromia*, a poster designed and printed in-house.

L'Arte della Cera

Via Bellini 13 - (081) 349582
Open daily 9am-1:30pm & 4:30pm-8pm.
The art of candlemaking has been practiced on these premises for nearly 100 years. The candles come in a beguiling variety of shapes—fruits, animals, flowers. Some even serve purposes other than merely providing a romantic glow, from warding off the evil eye to absorbing cigarette smoke. Depilatory wax may be purchased here as well.

Bottega della Carta

Via Cavallerizza 22 - (081) 421903
Open daily 9am-1:30pm & 4:30pm-8pm.
Among the eye-catching party supplies—Japanese and Venetian lanterns, masks, colorful wrapping paper, and Carnival disguises—you'll also find some lovely crèche figures that make an appropriate souvenir or gift to bring back from a trip to Naples.

Bowinkel

Piazza dei Martiri 24 - (081) 7644344
Open daily 9:30am-1:30pm & 5pm-8pm.
Since 1879 Bowinkel has purveyed antique and modern prints, in addition to artistic bibelots and objets d'art (figurines, watercolors, fans, handcrafted picture frames...). Paintings and antique prints are also expertly restored here.

Caruso

Via L. Giordano 182 - (081) 5782480
Open daily 9am-1:30pm & 4pm-7:30pm.
A shop on the cutting edge: Caruso sells knives for collectors (with handles of horn, precious wood, or steel), as well as more proletarian types for kitchen and pocket. If your blade needs sharpening, bring it on in.

Clinica dell'Accendino

Piazza Carità 5 - (081) 5520595
Open daily 9am-1:30pm & 4:30pm-8pm.
This clinic guarantees a new life for your lighter, no matter how old (it'll even fix Granddad's old Zippo). Clever and unusual supplies for pipe smokers are available, too.

Ferrigno

Via San Gregorio Armeno 8 - (081) 5523148
Open daily 9am-1pm & 4pm-7pm (at Christmas 9am-7pm).
Via San Gregorio is "Nativity street," and Giuseppe Ferrigno's shop is one of the best. All of his crèche figures—shepherds, magi, and more contemporary characters—are crafted lovingly by hand, according to time-honored tradition. Maestro Riccardo Muti is among the many admirers of Ferrigno's fine workmanship.

Liberti

Via Cesareo Console 23 - (081) 416269
Open daily 9am-1:30pm & 4:30pm-8pm.
A dizzying array of jewelry and decorative objects in coral, tortoise shell, and mother-of-pearl is featured at Liberti. Even a limited budget can buy pretty, inexpensive coral good-luck charms guaranteed to ward off the evil eye.

Liutofficina

Vico San Pietro a Maiella 6 - (081) 290852
Open daily 9am-1pm & 4pm-7pm.
Guitars, violins, cellos: this minuscule shop is chockablock with stringed instruments, which the owner restores and repairs. This is one of the city's few sources for handcrafted Neapolitan mandolins, once so common, now quite rare.

Lustrascarpe

Via San Carlo 9 - (No telephone)
Open daily 9am-1:30pm & 4:30pm-8pm.
"When there's a shine on your shoes, there's a melody in your heart," or so the song says. See for yourself! Settle into a comfortable chair under the arcades of the Umberto I gallery (across from the Teatro San Carlo) and find out what a top-notch shine by a real pro can do for both your shoes and your morale.

Nel Regno di Pulcinella

Salita Arenella 56 - (081) 5786450
Open daily 9am-7pm.
Lello Esposito's workshop is a wonderland of colorful masks and delightful objects celebrating the Neapolitan theater, and the character of Pulcinella in particular. The mischievous miss appears in many guises: mask, statue, pendant, and more. All make charming gifts or souvenirs.

Ospedale delle Bambole

Via San Biagio dei Librai 81 - (081) 203067
Open daily 9am-1:30pm & 4:30pm-8pm.
The "chief surgeon" at this Doll Hospital is Luigi Grassi, who operates with plaster, wax, papier-mâché, wood, and wire to make antique dolls (who may be missing an eye or an arm) as good as new. No mechanism is too complex for Grassi, who has helped many patients regain their power of speech or locomotion. We salute this expert artisan who belongs to a vanishing breed.

Del Porto

Via Santa Lucia 165 - (081) 415093
Open daily 9am-1:30pm & 4:30pm-8pm.
Visitors to Naples have long sought out the beautifully crafted coral jewelry and objects made just south of the city in Torre del Greco. The coral trade is based in the traditional tourist areas around Santa Lucia, near the big oceanfront hotels. Del Porto's shop is more than a century old, and its coral carvings (along with its watches and graceful ceramic vases) are of reliable quality.

Tattoo

Calata San Marco 24 - (081) 5511018

Open daily 9:30am-1pm & 4:30pm-7pm.
Here's a gift that will leave a lasting mark!
Giuseppe Serra forsook his criminal law
practice to practice the more satisfying (he
avers) art of the tattoo. The Cure provide
the background music in this tiny
workshop, where Serra decorates various
body parts with eagles, butterflies, dolphins, hearts—or whatever tattoo your
heart desires.

LINENS & LINGERIE

Salvatore Balbi
Via Chiaia 258 - (081) 418551
Open daily 9am-1:30pm & 4:30pm-8pm.
Colorful shirts, sweaters, socks,
nightwear, and underwear for men are the
centerpiece of Salvatore Balbi's artistic
window displays. Classy robes and
pajamas are a specialty, and some of the
hosiery sports motifs that would impress
an art critic!

La Cage
Largo Ferrandina 10 - (081) 403811
Open daily 9am-1:30pm & 4:30pm-8pm.
From potholders to sheets, tablecloths to
bedspreads, every type of household linen

is can be found here in an impressive
range of fabrics: raw silk, batiste, linen,
cotton, and more. An entire section of the
shop is dedicated to babies; we found the
embroidered cradle sheets and tiny quilts
absolutely irresistible. A friendly sales staff
is eager to help and advise.

Carmagnola
Via Chiaia 261 - (081) 417710
Open daily 9am-1:30pm & 4:30pm-8pm.
This little shop continues to sell the sort
of old-fashioned underthings that are
designed with comfort—not seduction—in
mind. No silk teddies here, girls, just cotton
and wool undershirts that have a certain
cozy charm and are delightfully warm in
winter.

D'Andrea
Via Santa Brigida 34 - (081) 5510621
Open daily 9am-1:30pm & 4:30pm-7:30pm.
Tasteful, top-quality household linens
and underthings for men, women, and
children have been the D'Andrea family's
specialty since 1836. It would be hard to
find a larger range of styles and sizes than
in this store near Piazza Municipio.

Horsing Around
with Piazza del Plebiscito

One of the most splendid squares in Naples is Piazza del Plebiscito, home
of Palazzo Reale and the Neoclassical church of San Francesco di Paola.
There are two giant equestrian statues in the square, one dedicated to
Charles of Bourbon and the other to his son Ferdinand. Charles's statue is
the result of changing horses in the middle of a reign. It was sculpted by
Canova, but not for Charles; the man on top was supposed to have been
Napoleon. Canova took so long to make it that, in the meantime,
Napoleon's kingdom fell, and the Bourbons returned to power. Ferdinand
of Bourbon appropriated the horse—the only finished part of the work—and
ordered Canova to make a statue of Charles, his father, to sit in Napoleon's
place. As of June, 1994 the piazza was closed to traffic; it is now particularly
beautiful at night.

Museums

Acquario Stazione Zoologica di Napoli

Villa Comunale, Via Caracciolo - (081) 406222
Open 9am-5pm. Closed Mon.
Set in the gardens of the Villa Comunale, the magnificent municipal Aquarium presents some 200 species of fish and marine plants from the Bay of Naples. The strangely moving frescoes of fishing scenes that decorate the library, the work of nineteenth-century German artist Hans Von Marees, are worth a visit, too.

Galleria dell'Accademia di Belle Arti

Via Bellini 36 - (081) 341032
Open daily 9am-2pm.
The picture gallery of the Fine Arts Academy houses works by nineteenth-century Neapolitan and other southern Italian artists. Particularly charming are the landscapes and marine views by members of the Posillipo school; works by Camille Corot and Louis Cabat are exhibited as well.

Museo dell'Appartamento Storico del Palazzo Reale

Piazza Plebiscito 1 - (081) 413888
Open 9am-2pm. Closed Mon.
The Palazzo Reale dates from 1600, though it was extensively renovated and rebuilt in the following century. The rooms of the royal apartments are filled with exquisite furniture (note the eighteenth-century porcelain-covered work table, a gift from Marie-Antoinette to her sister Marie-Caroline), art objects, and precious Beauvais tapestries. The palace's picture gallery features paintings from the Neapolitan and French schools.

Museo Archeologico

Piazza Museo 19 - (081) 440166
Open 9am-2pm. Closed Mon.
The Archaeological Museum of Naples is one of the most important in existence.

The collections afford a broad and fascinating view of how people lived in antiquity, with holdings that range from Roman copies of Greek sculpture to domestic implements and mechanical devices. Housed here, in more than 100 rooms, are antique statues amassed by the Farnese family, mosaics, and the choicest paintings and artifacts from Pompei and Herculaneum. A visitor would need to return several times to admire all the riches displayed here, but those short of time should make sure to see the collection of antique marbles. It includes a superb replica of Polyclitus's celebrated bronze *Lance Bearer*, an Augustan copy of a relief by Phidias representing *Orpheus, Eurydice and Hermes*, a Roman copy of the *Venus Callipyge* that once stood in Nero's house, and the *Farnese Bull*, the largest sculptural group to have come down to us from antiquity. And the mosaics are unforgettable: note the *Cat Catching a Quail* and the fine *Battle of Alexander and Darius*. On the upper floor are more superb sculptures, the splendid picture gallery, and a riveting collection of bronzes, vases, and a 115-piece table service unearthed at Pompeii.

Museo Artistico Industriale

Piazza Salazar 6 - (081) 405969
Open Thu during school terms: 9:30am-1pm.
This tranquil little museum displays an eclectic collection of Oriental and Western ceramics and porcelain, as well as archaeological material, Egyptian artifacts, and interesting examples of Neapolitan tile floors from the fifteenth century to the present.

Museo delle Carrozze

Villa Pignatelli, Riviera di Chiaia 200
(081) 669675
*Open 9am-2pm (Sun & hols 9am-1pm).
Closed Mon.*
Entirely given over to exhibits of late-nineteenth-century Italian, French, and

English carriages, with all their marvelous accessories, this delightful museum occupies five vast rooms in a charming garden pavilion on the Villa Pignatelli grounds.

Museo Civico Principe Gaetano Filangieri
Via del Duomo 288 - (081) 203175
Open 9am-2pm (Sun & hols 9am-1pm). Closed Mon.
Housed in the Renaissance Palazzo Cuomo are the fine Filangieri collections of mostly Italian paintings, of European and Oriental weapons, of majolica and porcelain, of exquisite furniture and rare coins. Remarkable exhibits include the Spanish, Italian, and Burgundian swords and daggers in the Sala Agata di Paternò as well as paintings by Luca Giordano, Bernardino Luini, and the *Head of John the Baptist* by José Ribera.

Museo della Canzone Napoletana
Via Amato di Montecassino 7 - (081) 5444426
Private museum, open Sun by appt.
Salvatore and Regina Tolino, fervent boosters of the city's rich theatrical and musical traditions, oversee this unusual museum, composed of three drawing rooms filled with memorabilia, manuscripts, photographs, and sheet music. As visitors wander through the exhibits, they hear famous selections of Neapolitan songs play in the background.

Museo Etnopreistorico
Castel dell'Ovo - (081) 7645688
Open Tue & Fri 7pm-9pm.
The items on display document the cultures of peoples who even today live in conditions that qualify as "prehistoric." Other interesting exhibits tell of peasant life and culture, with special reference to the island civilizations of southern Italy.

Museo e Gallerie Nazionali di Capodimonte
Parco di Capodimonte
(081) 7410801/81, fax (081) 7413102
Open 9am-2pm (Sun & hols 9am-1pm). Closed Mon.
The highly important collection of masterpieces housed in the eighteenth-century royal palace of Capodimonte is based on works amassed by the Farnese

dukes of Parma. Among the dazzling paintings on view are Simone Martini's *Saint Louis of Toulouse Crowning Robert of Anjou King of Naples*, Masaccio's dramatic *Crucifixion*, the *Transfiguration* by Giovanni Bellini, *Portrait of Pope Paul III with his Nephews Ottavio and Alessandro Farnese* by Titian, Cranach's somber *Christ and the Adulteress*, and works by Botticelli, Correggio, Parmigianino (*Girl with a Sable (Antea)*), Holbein, El Greco, Caravaggio. The museum also includes a gallery of nineteenth-century Neapolitan pictures, the vast De Ciccio collection of majolica, glass, enamel, and bronzes (Pollaiolo's *David*), and an impressive display of eighteenth-century porcelain from the Capodimonte factory.

Museo di Mineralogia dell'Università
Facoltà di Scienze, Via Mezzocannone 8
(081) 202061, fax (081) 206801
Open daily 9am-2pm.
Of significant interest here is the collection of "Vesuviana," which runs to 1,000 specimens found on and around the celebrated volcano that dominates the Bay of Naples. Noteworthy, too, are the quartz crystals, which are among the largest in the world.

Museo Nazionale della Ceramica Duca di Martina
Villa Floridiana, Via Cimarosa - (081) 377315
Open 9am-2pm (Sun & hols 9am-1pm). Closed Mon.
The museum occupies a splendid Neoclassical palazzo on the Vomero, with a panoramic view of Naples. Inside is an unparalleled collection of European and Oriental porcelain and majolica amassed by Placido di Sangro, Duke of Martina. Outstanding pieces include a Medicean porcelain pitcher, a group of walking sticks with porcelain, ivory, crystal, and malachite pommels, and some fine enamels.

Museo Nazionale di San Martino
Certosa di San Martino, Largo San Martino 5
(081) 377005
Open 9am-2pm (Sun & hols 9am-1pm). Closed Mon.
The splendid Charterhouse of Saint Martin, which has stood atop the Vomero hill

since the days of the Anjou dynasty, was so extensively renovated in the seventeenth century that it has become one of the foremost examples of Baroque architecture in Naples. The museum that occupies the former monastery is dedicated to Neapolitan history, geography, art, and culture. One of the most spectacular exhibits is the Cuciniello crèche, with its hundreds of shepherds, angels, and animals.

Museo Principe Diego Aragona Pignatelli Cortes

Riviera di Chiaia 200 - (081) 669675
Open 9am-2pm (Sun & hols 9am-1pm). Closed Mon.
This superb Neoclassical house is decorated in the manner of a patrician residence, with exquisite period furniture, porcelain, Chinese vases, sumptuous table services, and eighteenth-century Neapolitan paintings and drawings. The garden boasts a collection of rare and exotic plants.

Museo di Santa Chiara

Convento di Santa Chiara, Via Benedetto Croce - (081) 205561
Open 8:30am-12:30pm & 4pm-6:30pm (Sun & hols 8:30am-12:30pm).
A modest collection of archaeological finds, epigraphs, early medieval fragments, and fifteenth-century frescoes is presented here, along with some pieces of fourteenth- to eighteenth-century sculpture. But the best reason to visit the Santa Chiara cloister is its delicious eighteenth-century garden, replete with arbors and splendid majolica-covered walls, benches, and pillars.

Museo di Storia del Costume

Piazzetta Mondragone 18,
C/o Istituto Mondragone
Open 9am-2pm. Closed Sun, hols.
The Istituto Mondragone dates back to 1655, when it was established as a school for poor young noblewomen. Since then, the institute has assembled a collection of silk and gold embroidery, fine textiles, and sacred vestments that reflects the history of clothing in Naples. This singular museum is a must-see for fabric fanciers.

Museo Storico Musicale

Conservatorio di Musica,
Via San Pietro a Maiella 35 - (081) 459255

Open 9am-1pm. Closed Sun, hols.
This conservatory of music is situated in the fourteenth-century monastery of San Pietro a Maiella. The small collection features portraits (*Cimarosa* by Elisabeth Vigée-Lebrun) and personal memorabilia of the composers Bellini, Scarlatti, and Rossini.

Museo di Zoologia

Facoltà di Scienze,
Via Mezzocannone 8 - (081) 206318
Open by appt.
The university's Museum of Zoology is worth a visit for the glimpse it affords of how museums were arranged in the last century. The specimens of various birds and beasts are kept in wonderful glass-fronted marquetry cases.

Orto Botanico

Botanical Gardens, Via Foria 223 - (081) 449759
Open by appt.
Established by Joseph Bonaparte in 1807, the Botanical Gardens of Naples contain examples of local flora, tropical plants, ferns, and specimens of particular scientific interest.

Pinacoteca dei Girolamini

Convento Padri Girolamini,
Via del Duomo 142 - (081) 449139
Open 9am-7pm. Closed Sun, hols.
The small picture gallery housed in the sixteenth-century monastery of the Girolamini fathers exhibits a collection of seventeenth-century religious paintings by Andrea di Salerno, Zuccaro, Guido Reni (*The Flight into Egypt*), Solimena, and followers of Caravaggio.

Pinacoteca del Pio Monte della Misericordia

Via Tribunali 253 - (081) 445517
Open by appt.
This collection of fine religious paintings occupies several rooms in the Palazzo del Monte. Ribera's *Saint Anthony Abbot* is one of the most distinguished works on view here.

Raccolta d'Arte della Fondazione Pagliara

Istituto Universitario Suor Orsola Benincasa,
Via Suor Orsola - (081) 412908

Open by appt.
It is worthwhile to request permission to view this exceptional private collection, which includes works by El Greco and by Neapolitan artists of the sixteenth, seventeenth, and eighteenth centuries.

■ In Amalfi   62 km S

Museo Civico
Piazza Municipio - (089) 871066
Open 8:30am-1:30pm & 2:30pm-7:30pm. Closed Sun.
The prize of this little museum, housed in Amalfi's city hall, is the *Tavole Amalfitane*, the world's oldest code of maritime law. A collection of ancient navigational instruments is also displayed (Flavio Gioia, considered a native of Amalfi, invented the marine compass in the eleventh century).

■ In Anacapri   90 min by ferry

Villa San Michele
Viale Axel Munthe - (081) 8371401
Open summer 10am-6pm; winter 10am-3pm.
This villa was built about 100 years ago by a Swedish doctor and writer, Axel Munthe, who wrote a captivating description of his beloved San Michele. Today its rooms hold a collection of seventeenth-century furniture, antiquities (mosaics, bas-reliefs, terra cottas), and sundry art objects, arranged just as Munthe left them. From the garden, there is a breathtaking view of the island.

■ In Capri   90 min by ferry

Museo del Centro Caprese Ignazio Cerio
Piazzetta Cerio 5 - (081) 8370858
Open Mon, Wed, Fri: 10am-noon.
The castle where the notorious Queen Joan I resided in the fourteenth century now houses a collection of archaeological material and fossils assembled by Ignazio Cerio, a doctor and naturalist. Something to occupy a rainy morning!

Museo Diefenbach
Certosa di San Giacomo - (081) 8376218
Open 9am-2pm (Sun & hols 9am-1pm). Closed Mon.

Capri's most significant architectural work is this fourteenth-century charterhouse. Among its many fascinating features, the monastery contains a small, curious museum of visionary seascapes by K. W. Diefenbach, a Symbolist painter who lived on Capri at the turn of the century.

■ In Ischia   80 min by ferry

Scavi e Museo di Santa Restituta
Piazza Santa Restituta, Lacco Ameno
(081) 995045
Open daily 8:30am-1pm & 4pm-6pm.
Adjacent to and beneath the sanctuary of Santa Restituta, site of a fourth-century basilica, this museum presents Greco-Roman and early Christian material: funerary urns, clay temple vessels and other religious objects, coins, and a Greek loom. Visitors may also examine an archaeological excavation and view the remains of a Greek ceramic workshop, complete with kilns (fifth to second century B.C.) as well as Roman tombs and a Christian burial ground. Some 70 display cases hold finds that date from the prehistoric era to the Middle Ages.

■ In Pietrarsa   10 km

Museo Ferroviario Nazionale
Corso S. Giovanni a Teduccio - (081) 472003
Open 9am-noon. Closed Sun, hols.
Why not while away a morning inspecting a nineteenth-century locomotive, antique trains and signals, and a rich collection of documents that attest to the evolution of railroad technology?

■ In Pompei   24 km SE

Antiquarium
Pompei Excavations - (081) 8610744
Open daily 9am-1 hour before sunset.
The most striking displays in Pompei's Antiquarium are the plaster casts of victims—both people and animals—of the explosion of Vesuvius in A.D. 79. But there are also fascinating relics of Dionysian cults, along with incredibly evocative household items, fascinating artworks, and architectural fragments.

189

Museo Vesuviano

Piazza Longo 1 - (081) 8631000
Open daily 9am-12:30pm.

This unique little museum contains material from in and around Mount Vesuvius, in addition to paintings and drawings that depict the eruptions of the volcano, and Christian relics from Pompei.

Tesoro del Santuario della Madonna del Rosario

Piazza Longo 1 - (081) 8631000
Open daily 8am-2pm & 5pm-6:30pm.

The treasury of this modern (1891) sanctuary, a pilgrimage church, consists of priestly vestments, gold and silverwork, ceramics, porcelain, ivory, cameos, and sundry curious coins, medals, and books.

■ In Portici   9 km S

Orto Botanico

Botanical Gardens,
Via Università 100 - (081) 7390624
Open daily 9am-6pm.

An interesting variety of medicinal herbs is cultivated on the grounds of the city's palazzo. In neighboring gardens, visitors may admire examples of eighteenth-century garden design and fountains.

■ In Ravello   66 km SE

Antiquarium

Villa Rufolo - (089) 224322
Open daily 9:30am-1pm & 3pm-7pm (winter 2pm-5pm).

The antiquarium displays funerary urns, inscriptions, architectural fragments, and gargoyles, in several rooms of the Arabo-Sicilian-style Villa Rufolo. The panoramic gardens also boast handsome exotic plants, pines, and cypresses.

Museo del Duomo

Piazza del Duomo - (089) 857212
Open daily 9:30am-1pm & 3pm-6:30pm.

Ravello's eleventh-century cathedral contains a beautiful pulpit designed by Niccolò di Bartolomeo da Foggia in 1272, and a smaller pulpit, or ambo, decorated with mosaics and dating from about 1130. The museum itself, located in the crypt of the Duomo, holds a number of artworks,

including two paintings by Giovanni Filippo Criscuolo: *Saint Sebastian* and *Mary Magdalene.*

■ In Sorrento   47 km S

Museo Correale di Terranova

Via Correale 48 - (081) 8781846
Open summer 9:30am-12:30pm & 5pm-7pm; winter 3pm-5pm. Closed Nov, hols.

An outstanding collection of fifteenth- to eighteenth-century Neapolitan and Sicilian furniture may be admired here. Some of the later pieces, ornamented with majolica or marble, are particularly lovely. Among the paintings on view are many land and seascapes by nineteenth-century Neapolitan artists, but the museum also possesses pictures by Breughel and Rubens.

Burn the Belfry!

In mid-July Neapolitans get all fired up and pretend to burn the campanile of the church of Santa Maria del Carmine in Piazza Mercato. The phony fire is a tradition from the nineteenth century when the Bourbon king's court would arrive under a hail of fireworks to celebrate the feast of the *Madonna Bruna* (a fourteenth-century cult object). The kings and the fireworks are no longer, and the Neapolitans hated them anyway, so why not torch the bell tower?
But the piazza is worth a visit any time of the year. The church is a thirteenth-century gem that has been embellished over time and stuffed with the tombs of the greats. The square itself has a rich, if bloody, history; for centuries it was the royal choppery where many a visitor lost his head. It started in 1268, when Charles I of Anjou had Corradino of Swabia and Frederick of Baden, Duke of Austria, beheaded (they're buried in the church). In 1647 the popular revolt led by Masaniello against the Spanish oppressors began in Piazza Mercato (he's in the church, too).

Useful Telephone Numbers

Naples Area Code: 081

Airport: Napoli Capodichino, 7091111; flight information: 7092815; lost luggage: 7092813
Ambulance: 7520696; 7520850
City Hall: 7951111
City Police Department: 7513177
Ferry and Hydrofoil Service, (Beverello Quay): 5513882; 5513352; 5527209;
(Mergellina): 7611004; 7612348
Fire Department: 115
Medical Emergency: 7513177
Pharmacy: 192
Police Emergency: 112; 113
Post Office and Telegraph: 5511456
Radio Taxi: 5707070; 5564444
State Railway Information: 5543188
Tourist Information: 5523328
Wake-up Call: 114
Weather Service: 191

Garibaldi Slept Here

Everyone calls the Palazzo dei Principi Doria d'Angri, just off Via Toledo, "Garibaldi's place." The heroic liberator slept soundly here on September 7, 1860, after a hard day's work ridding Naples of the Bourbons and uniting Italy. That night a huge crowd gathered below the windows and celebrated—in total silence. No one wanted to disturb Garibaldi's sleep. The palazzo was built in the eighteenth century by Luigi Vanvitelli and his son, Charles. It stands on Largo VII Settembre, named for the day of the hero's snooze.

Villa of Ill Repute

One of Naples's best known and most misunderstood villas is Palazzo donn'Anna, built in 1642 by architect Cosimo Fanzago for the wife of the Spanish viceroy. Its seaboard location at Posillipo is enchanting, with the waves lapping at majestic walls that rise over a warren of caverns. The palazzo's balconies and terraces boast sweeping views of Vesuvius, Capri, and the Sorrento coast. But that's not why it's so famous. Neapolitans stubbornly refuse to admit that the Palazzo donn'Anna is not the den of depravity of Queen Joan II of Anjou (who died more than 200 years before the palazzo was built). This last queen of the Anjou dynasty thrilled all of Naples with her hot blood and fabled insatiability, and has kept tongues clacking for the last 500 years. In the fifteenth century, her pleasure house, the Villa delle Sirene, probably sat where donn'Anna Carafa's palazzo now dips its innocent feet in the gentle surf.

ROME

City of a Thousand Fountains

" Rome is a mother who asks for nothing, and expects nothing from you in return." That is how Federico Fellini, who knew a thing or two about the city in which he filmed *La Dolce Vita* and *Amarcord*, described the Rome that dazzled and dazed him with its splendid indifference when, as a young provincial fresh from Emilia-Romagna, he first encountered *La Città Eterna*. In its 2,700-year existence, Rome has seen it all: "The Tiber has watched popes and emperors come and go," as old Roman sages say.

When trains from points north pull into the Stazione Termini, they pass along the tall red-brick wall built by the Emperor Aurelian late in the third century. It protected Rome throughout the Middle Ages and up until 1870, when Victor Emmanuel's troops broke through to capture Rome for the Kingdom of Italy. The same Aurelian Wall marked the limits of Rome when, as capital of the Roman Empire, it boasted three million inhabitants (today's population hovers around 2.7 million). In 1309, however, ten centuries after the wall's construction, with the papacy exiled in Avignon, only 20,000 Romans dwelled within its limits. Since that low point, the capital of a unified Italy has made up for lost time. True, growth has been anarchic, and post–World War II expansion has come under control only recently. But part of Rome's appeal is the fact that its monuments lead us straight to the heart of a long, complex, tormented history, indelibly etched on this ancient body of brick and stone.

There are some cities—in Italy and elsewhere—that seem more like museums or mausoleums than living urban centers. Strolling through them is like leafing through a picture book; they seem meant to be admired, like objects in a showcase.

Florence, for example, presents its every relic duly polished and labeled, served up to satisfy visitors' voracious appetite for "culture"; people solemnly pay their respects at each monument as if they were visiting an elderly aunt. Rome's magnificence is more muted, and its landmarks less spic-and-span; but here at least, a visitor never has the stifling impression of wandering through an eerily lifeless "museum-city." With its realistic view of what urban life entails, Rome's city government resists creating too many pedestrian zones off-limits to normal traffic. Nowhere in Rome has the natural flow of the city's lifeblood been blocked. Nor are the churches of Rome mere shrines for sacred art: they are vital cells of religious life where a visitor can discover how Romans really worship and pray. Rome is first and foremost a city of people, not of monuments.

Roman history covers an immense span. Some of its oldest landmarks have a curiously timeless quality, as if they existed in their own perpetual present. Nero's Domus Aurea (Golden House), for example, was buried by the construction of the Emperor Trajan's Baths just twenty years after it was built; yet we can see the Domus Aurea today, virtually intact, and share the amazement of the early-Renaissance archaeologists who first uncovered it. Yet most Roman monuments have lived an uninterrupted existence throughout the centuries.

Rome began to overflow its ancient boundaries only 100 years ago. Before then, builders simply stacked new layers of construction over old ones within the Aurelian Wall, which outlined the city in blood-red brick. Endless rebuilding made the layout of roads and streets a random, maddening crazy quilt—and produced a unique metropolis where visitors see the centuries collide before their eyes, in kaleidoscopic confusion.

As travelers emerge from the train station, they are confronted by the immense Baths of Diocletian (A.D. 298-306), that rise up just opposite, across the Piazza dei Cinquecento. Michelangelo transformed the central hall of the baths into a church, Santa Maria degli Angeli (Our Lady of the Angels); part of the remaining structure became a Carthusian monastery and the rest became an astronomical observatory, and then a movie theater. Today, the site is home to the bronzes and marble statues of the National Roman Museum. People too serious about organizing their sightseeing around the theme of Rome's historical development are bound to retrace their steps again and again, with only a glut of confused recollections for their pains.

In Rome, what Stendhal, that indefatigable tourist, called the visitor's "duty to see" is best abandoned in favor of another duty: the duty to *look*. It is an art every traveler should cultivate.

Who wouldn't be tempted, at the first ray of dawn on their first day in Rome, to head straight for Piazza Navona, perhaps the most famous square in the world? Despite what many guidebooks say, the name Navona has nothing to do with ships ("nave" in Italian). Rather, it refers to the circus or arena erected by the Emperor Domitian in A.D. 86 for games and athletic contests (the Latin phrase *campus agonis*, meaning field of competition, is the origin of the piazza's name).

At seven o'clock on a summer morning, Piazza Navona fills up with blue and ocher light, and with a fresh coolness that sends shivers running over the skin. The news dealer opens his stand. The woman who runs the Tre Scalini bar waits in the doorway for her staff to arrive. In the middle of the square, a slow-moving street sweeper pushes his broom at a pile of papers, burst balloons, and the debris of mechanical birds that little boys were flying in the square the day before. Suddenly, as if at a silent signal, some unseen hand turns on the water: the fountains gurgle and begin to flow.

Unlike Piazza del Campidoglio on the Capitoline Hill, designed by Michelangelo

to glorify power, and unlike Saint Peter's Square, constructed as a stage for Christianity's grand and solemn ceremonies, Piazza Navona was built with no particular purpose in mind—purely for esthetic pleasure. The square sprang up, you might almost say, spontaneously, in the image of Rome itself.

Some ten yards below ground, the arcades of Domitian's stadium support Piazza Navona; the arcades rest on a substratum of volcanic rock buried beneath twenty yards of silt deposited by the Tiber, which flooded the square every winter until it was channeled in 1910. This site was littered chiefly with ruins in the fourth century, when the Christian emperor Constantine plundered the stadium, sending a booty of marble and bronze masks to his new capital, Constantinople. Then, for nine centuries it served as a battleground for the feudal lords who built fortified castles all around the site to proclaim their wealth and power. In shrunken medieval Rome, it was the city's center of gravity, bustling with markets and commercial activity. Successive demolition and construction have always respected the original elongated ellipse of Domitian's stadium.

Last reconstructed in the 1650s, Piazza Navona provided endless inspiration for such seventeenth- and eighteenth-century painters and engravers as Israël Silvestre and Bernardo Bellotto, whose works depict the piazza's changeless décor and immutable colors: the intense blue of the cloudless sky, the grayed-out white of travertine marble, and every imaginable shade of ocher and ivory. Over the centuries, travelers who have come to Piazza Navona to admire Bernini's Baroque fountains and the church of Sant'Agnese in Agone (designed by Bernini's archrival, Francesco Borromini) have heard and repeated the same amusing, slightly malicious legends. It is said that the statue personifying the River Plate on Bernini's Fountain of the Four Rivers raises his hand to protect himself from the imminent collapse of Borromini's church. And the figure of the Nile allegedly hides his head to avoid contemplating Borromini's "dreadful style." But the statue of Saint Agnes, in defense of the church dedicated in her name, is said to place her hand on her heart to pledge that Borromini's structure will always stand fast.

True to its origins, the site of Piazza Navona has kept its recreational status and is even now a center for Roman festivities. Until 1867 the piazza was flooded every August. The lower classes swam and cavorted, while society folk watched the picturesque scene from their carriages. At other times, fashionable ladies and gentlemen promenaded on the piazza, elbow-to-elbow with strolling musicians, itinerant performers, and pulpit-less preachers. Ambassadors and princes of the Church held elaborate revels in the piazza; fireworks and tournaments thrilled the crowds. Not so long ago, mothers still brought their brood to Piazza Navona on the feast of the Epiphany for the traditional chase of la befana, the wicked witch who at Christmas puts coal in naughty children's stockings. Before Christmas, merchants used to sell crèches, figurines, and puppets on the piazza.

Currently, the most moving reminder of those celebrations is the arrival at Christmastime of shepherds from the Abruzzi, who gather each evening in Piazza Navona after crisscrossing the city all day playing their traditional fifes and bagpipes. With their pointed, beribboned hats and their sheepskin coats, they resemble the nineteenth-century brigands who used to terrorize travelers on the road from Rome to Naples. These piferari (pipers) at first seem out of their element in the frenetic modern capital that Rome has become. And yet their presence hints at an essential aspect of Roman life: the importance—and the very real proximity—of the countryside and of nature.

The food, the farm produce, and the rustic cuisine of Latium provide the first clue that fields and farms are not far off. In ancient and medieval times, country folk came to Rome to sell their wares at the Forum Boarium (cattle market); fishermen hawked their catch behind the Roman Forum; herbs and vegetables were even grown within the city limits. Until quite recently, vineyard owners from the Castelli would sell their own Frascati from horse-drawn carts at Campidoglio market. Though they are now gone, waiters still plunk down wide-mouthed carafes of that fresh, white wine at every trattoria in Rome.

Since time immemorial, wheat has been the cornerstone of the Roman diet. Bread in particular had a sacred character: it was "the gift of Ceres," the goddess of grain (meat, on the other hand, had no divine patron). Ceres, who made the wheat grow, was worshipped by all Romans because everyone, in every social class, eats bread. Over the centuries, methods for preparing wheat have evolved (Rome's legionaries carried their ration of grain on their backs; they ground it, combined it with water and salt, and cooked it on a hot stone, a method still used in rural Romagna), but it continues to reign supreme on Roman tables. Legend has it that Marco Polo learned to make noodles from the Chinese. However true that may be, it is clear that at some point the Romans threw over their traditional polenta (made of wheat flour, not corn) for pasta, and things haven't been the same since. To see how powerful Ceres still is in Roman life, just look into a panificio (bakery), where pasta is made and sold by the kilo, wrapped up in coarse yellow paper; or into more elegant shops, where straw baskets are piled high with mountains of tortellini, ravioli, fettuccine (Rome's favorite form of pasta), lasagne, and bundles of spaghetti.

Not so long ago, it would have been difficult to find a butcher in all of Rome who sold mutton. The few who did catered to the very poor—no self-respecting Roman of means would dishonor himself by putting mutton on his table, for his guests would be sure to turn up their noses at what they considered the meat's strong, unpleasant smell. In his Gallic Wars, Caesar wrote that while his men were laying siege to the town of Avaricum in Gaul, a shortage of wheat forced them to eat sheep rounded up from neighboring farms. The disgusted soldiers seem to have passed on their repugnance to generations of descendents. Yet Romans are inordinately fond of abbacchio, the mild-tasting milk-fed lamb that is served in all the better trattorias, especially at Eastertime.

Game from the surrounding countryside is a popular Roman favorite. In fall and winter it abounds in the city's markets and restaurants—less, perhaps, than in the nineteenth century when travelers marveled at the plentiful quails, larks, woodcocks, partridges, hares, and boar that Roman cooks prepared with singular brio. However, excessive hunting has killed off much of the region's game birds, so that the quails on most menus are domestic, not wild. But even the farming of game birds has an ancient precedent: in imperial Rome, quail and other species were raised in aviaries to supply the huge local market.

Rites from a pre-Christian past explain the ceremonial preparation of certain dishes at specific times of the year. Though they may not know why, today's Romans—like their ancestors—faithfully eat snails on Midsummer's Eve, ravioli on Mardi Gras, semolina gnocchi and macaroni after the harvest in October, and broccoli, nougat, and eggy brioche at Christmastime. These country customs are still very much a part of life in Rome, the *Urbs*, the archetypal city.

The sight and sound of water running in Rome's thousand fountains are another tangible sign of nature's presence in the city. From grandiose fountains on grand public squares to more modest fountains in the courtyards of ancient palazzi, fountains have flowed in Rome since antiquity. The city's oldest fountain, which dates back to ancient Rome, stands across from the church of Santa Maria in Trastevere. Restored by Bramante in the early sixteenth century, the fountain has moved little in 2,000 years, going only from the edge of the square to the center. But that is the exception rather than the rule, since Romans take a perverse pleasure in moving their fountains around as if they were pieces of furniture! The fountain that now flows in Piazza Nicosia was once at home on Piazza del Popolo; the one near the Pantheon was built for Piazza Navona. Two immense granite basins in Piazza Farnese, which hail from the Baths of Caracalla, were originally intended to stand before Palazzo Venezia, but they finally fetched up in Palazzo Farnese. We could go on, but you get the idea.

Perhaps the most typically Roman of the city's myriad fountains are Bernini's Fountain of the Rivers, on Piazza Navona, and Niccolò Salvi's recently restored Trevi Fountain. Both combine water and stone, nature and artifice, in a way that perfectly illustrates the lavish Baroque architecture

that the building campaigns of sixteenth- and early-eighteenth-century popes made Rome's predominant style.

Indeed, the sovereign pontiffs did their utmost to put a specifically Christian stamp on Rome. Christianity is omnipresent here, not only in the catacombs, the early Christian basilicas, and the multitude of churches. No, what sets Rome apart is the determination and the munificence with which the popes (after their return from Avignon in 1420) pursued their goal of imposing a religious significance on every aspect of the Holy City. Martin V, the first pope elected after the Avignon exile, planned a system of roads that would radiate from the Vatican (where plans were already afoot to replace the old basilica constructed under Constantine) and encircle all of Rome's districts. The project finally triumphed late in the sixteenth century, when Sixtus V accomplished the papal dream of Christianizing ancient Rome. The Vatican's basilica, too far removed from the city's center, was no longer the system's linchpin; that role was assumed by another ancient patriarchal basilica, Santa Maria Maggiore on the Esquiline Hill. From there an immense "Way of the Cross" radiated, a network of new roads linking all the basilicas and churches visited by pilgrims who thronged to Rome from every corner of Christendom.

The crossroads of this huge network were marked with obelisks salvaged from piles of ancient ruins; triumphal columns dating from antiquity were topped with statues of saints: Saint Peter was placed on the summit of Trajan's Column, while Saint Paul crowned the Column of Marcus Aurelius on Piazza Colonna. By the seventeenth century, Rome was completely renovated, rebuilt, and transformed into the capital of Christendom, taking unto itself, in Christian terms, the age-old pagan belief in the sacredness of the very soil upon which the city stood.

The impression Rome gives is not of a place where people settled, made their homes, and eventually built temples and churches to their gods, but of a city where men and women appeared on a scene already occupied by sanctuaries and places of worship. To get to the heart of Rome, one must try to grasp the meaning of its innumerable holy sites, both Christian and pagan—of the crosses, the tiny chapels housed in niches of old palazzi, so like the shrines set up to honor pagan deities in the homes of ancient Rome. In Rome, a visitor shouldn't try to separate the relics of antiquity from the still-unblemished splendor of the city's Renaissance and Baroque heritage. For they are linked by a web of secret connections that over millennia has ensured the survival of this extraordinary entity, the Eternal City.

The Incomparable Compared

It's impossible to resist the temptation to compare and judge two masterpieces of Baroque church architecture that stand practically side by side: Gian Lorenzo Bernini's Sant'Andrea al Quirinale and Francesco Borromini's San Carlo alle Quattro Fontane. Bernini, the acclaimed master of his day, spent twelve years on his labor of love and produced this sublime, harmonious, and yet magnificent church, which features the first-ever elliptical interior. And then there's Borromini, who lived his life in Bernini's shadow, and ultimately committed suicide. Only after years of lonely struggle did he manage to prove his worth. The plan of San Carlo alle Quattro Fontane is revolutionary: a four-sided parallelogram packaged in curves. The Romans call the church by an affectionate diminutive, San Carlino, because it was designed to be compact enough to fit inside a single column under the dome of Saint Peter's. Borromini's brilliant architectural devices speak volumes for his tormented genius—from the elliptical dome, which seems to hover in thin air, to the one-of-a-kind windows. From the standpoint of modern architecture, it is Borromini who casts the longest shadow. But, you're right, why compare?

Rules for a Triumph

Since Rome's power rested on military might, the state's highest honors were understandably reserved for its generals. The ultimate distinction was a "Triumph": a ritual procession to the Capitoline Hill that glorified the warrior's valor and skill. But winning a major battle was not enough to earn a Triumph; several more exacting conditions had to be met. Only a victory which increased Rome's territory and in which at least 5,000 foreign adversaries had perished could be considered grounds for a Triumph. (Note that no civil war battle, however bloody or glorious, could count). If these conditions were met, the victorious general could make a formal request for a Triumph. He then swore a solemn oath before the Senate, who authorized the ceremony with a special law. The Arch of Constantine near the Colosseum, the Arch of Septimius Severus and the superb Arch of Titus in the Roman Forum, and the masterpiece of sculpture that is Trajan's Column in the Forum of Trajan are all triumphal monuments that date from Rome's imperial era.

Restaurants

Real Roman cooking is not to be found in hotel dining rooms; nor in the city's glittering "international" restaurants (the sort that specialize in such culinary kitsch as "penne alla vodka"); nor in establishments where *cucina creativa* (nouvelle cuisine, Italian-style) is the order of the day (though many of these have won deservedly high marks in this very book). There's nothing fancy or refined about the kind of food favored by scores of generations of Romans. In fact, it's pretty primitive: many dishes are based on innards, on such "found" vegetables as wild greens and mushrooms, on game, and simply roasted pork or lamb. This gutsy, substantial fare is best sampled in modest inns and trattorias that offer the classic roster of specialties prepared alla romana, the closest this region comes to possessing a codified cuisine.

It has been observed that antipasti are a relatively recent addition to Roman menus, and it's true that they are more like hors d'œuvres to be idly nibbled at than an essential part of the meal. They run to fresh vegetable or seafood salads, assortments of mixed salami and prosciutto, or pinzimonio: raw vegetables dipped in olive oil, salt, and pepper.

As in all of Italy, the proceedings really get under way with the primo. If soup is your preference, there's stracciatella alla romana (a kind of egg-drop soup, with the added interest of Parmesan cheese). For a more robust starter, you can try gnocchi alla romana, tiny oven-browned semolina dumplings drizzled with butter and cheese.

Yet in Rome, the primo is almost always synonymous with pasta. Fettuccine, a traditional favorite, comes alla romana (sauced with tomatoes, ham, mushrooms, and chicken giblets), or with thick cream, or ricotta and pepper. Tonnarelli (square spaghetti), another egg-based pasta, is often garnished with basic yet famously tasty sauces of broccoli rabe or arugula sautéed in olive oil with plenty of garlic. Manufactured hard-wheat pastas are as popular in Rome as they are in all of southern Italy. Bucatini (hollow spaghetti) all'amatriciana is a standby in most trattorias; the sauce is a blend of tomatoes, pancetta, hot peppers, and tangy Pecorino cheese. But spaghetti alla carbonara (with eggs, bacon, and Parmesan cheese) or ajo e ojo (with garlic-infused olive oil) are also typically Roman.

One dish you are unlikely to encounter outside of Rome is rigatoni alla pajata, ridged tubular pasta served with a sauce of chopped veal innards, tomatoes, onions, garlic, and a hint of clove. We've already alluded to Romans' fondness for offal, traceable, it is said, to the days when the imperial and papal courts, ambassadors, prelates, and princelings consumed huge quantities of meat, but only the choicest cuts; innards and offal were sold off cheaply. Even today, such dishes as coda alla vaccinara (oxtail stew), trippa alla romana, cervella fritta (fried brains), and lamb's head are distinctively Roman.

Of course, if "variety meats" (as offal is euphemistically called) are not your cup of tea, other options are available. Abbacchio—milk-fed lamb—and porchetta—suckling pig—are two quintessentially Roman secondi. Their delicate flavor, underlined but not overwhelmed by garlic, herbs, oil, and (sometimes) a drop of white wine, is a revelation. And there is saltimbocca alla romana, which is about as "sophisticated" as Roman cooking gets: a veal scallop paired with a thin slice of prosciutto and a sage leaf, dredged in flour, sautéed in oil, served with the pan juices deglazed with white wine.

Of all the prime, flavorful vegetables—onions, beans, peas, broccoli, peppers, spinach, chicory—cultivated in the fertile countryside of Latium (the province of which Rome is the capital), artichokes are undoubtedly the best-loved. Prepared alla romana they are braised with parsley, garlic, and mint; but they are perhaps even more typically Roman when prepared alla giudia (Jewish-style): flattened out and deep-fried, so that the result resembles a beautiful bronze-tinged flower. Deep-frying is a cooking method traditionally practiced in Rome's Jewish community. Today, in certain trattorias around the old Ghetto, you can make a meal of superbly crisp fritti, starting with deep-fried zucchini blossoms and ending up with light, puffy ricotta fritters.

Cheeses are another treasure of Roman gastronomy. Like foods made from wheat, dairy products do not require a blood sacrifice. Virgil's shepherds learned to make ricotta, that pearly white, fresh ewe's-milk cheese, from Roman shepherds. We don't know if the ancients were familiar with mozzarella, but they certainly were adept at making Pecorino, a hard, tangy sheep's-milk cheese. And they also knew how to preserve cheese by smoke-curing it; the result was the ancestor of modern-day caciocavallo, a favorite in Rome and southern Italy.

That much-loved ricotta is the base of some of the region's best desserts: ricotta pie, studded with candied fruit, or fresh ricotta slathered with honey, an age-old (dating from Virgil) treat that would make a suitable prelude to a tour of Rome's ancient monuments. Latium's vineyards produce light, white table wines like those from the Castelli Romani: Frascati, Marino, and Colli Albani. Red wines are few, but definitely worth tasting: if you run across it, make a point of trying Fiorano Rosso, a wine produced near Rome from Cabernet Sauvignon and Merlot grapes.

Agata e Romeo

Via Carlo Alberto 45 - (06) 4465842
Closed Sun, Mon lunch, at Christmas. All major cards.

Now here's a find. Agata, an exceptionally gifted cook, serves personalized, updated versions of dishes rooted in the culinary traditions of Rome and Campania. She takes the trouble to seek out superior ingredients: bacon from Colonnata for her divine pasta all'amatriciana,

Pachino tomatoes, premium Pecorino, fragrant olive oil... The results of these efforts are gratifying indeed. We can warmly recommend her pasta with broccoli and skate, superb game-stuffed ravioli (in season, of course), and colossal fritto misto of fresh fish and vegetables. Romeo oversees the elegant little dining room with inimitable flair, and helps guests choose from the extensive wine list. M 50,000 lire (lunch), 75,000 lire (dinner).

Alberto Ciarla

Piazza San Cosimato 40 - (06) 5818668
Closed Sun lunch. All major cards.

Alberto Ciarla runs the best—and most beautiful—seafood restaurant in Rome. A few years back, he launched a palate revolution among the city's gourmets, insisting that there were more ways to serve fish than just fried or in soups. He then declared war on overcooked seafood, and even proved to his patrons that raw fish, properly presented and seasoned, is a peerless delicacy. What is Albert up to now? His latest idea is to replace meat with fish in a series of familiar Roman dishes: thus he pairs beans with—seafood—sausage, and uses sea bass or salmon instead of veal in his unorthodox (but very tasty) versions of saltimbocca and piccatina. Ciarla's cellar is awash in premium white wines, the best possible partners for this lively, original fare. C 90-100,000 lire (wine incl). M 70-90,000 lire (tasting menu).

Alfredo

Piazza Augusto Imperatore 30
(06) 6878734
Closed Sun. No cards.

Yes, folks, this is the birthplace of fettuccine Alfredo. The dish was invented by the present Alfredo's grandfather, in response to his pregnant wife's craving for something buttery and rich. The version served today by Alfredo III is indisputably the best in town, uncontaminated by peas, prosciutto, or (heaven help us) chicken giblets! It is also the best dish on Alfredo's menu, though the artichoke starter is very fine, and there is an appetizing mixed fry, too. Good cellar; honest prices. The service is delightfully vieux jeu. C 55-65,000 lire.

Some establishments change their closing times without warning. It is always wise to check in advance.

Andrea
Via Sardegna 26 - (06) 4821891
Closed Sun, Aug 10-30. All major cards.

Handsome embossed wallpaper and bottle-green woodwork lend a sober elegance to the décor of this restaurant near Via Veneto. But it's the display of enticing antipasti set out near the door that draws customers in, their taste buds jumping with anticipatory joy. Don't even bother with the long, confusing menu and wine list. Let host Aldo di Cesare be your guide. Should he propose his fabulous lobster salad or, in season, the equally sensational salad of raw porcini mushrooms, white truffles, and Gruyère, stop him right there and put in your order. Both dishes are extraordinary in their simplicity—their sole drawback is that they are hard acts to follow. Yet ricotta-stuffed ravioli, flawless in a suave, tomato-tinctured sauce, and straccetti di manzo (thin slices of beef quick-sautéed with tangy arugula, slivers of truffle, and tiny cubes of melting mozzarella) are both superb. Best-of-class in the dessert category goes to a medley of wild berries served with pistachio ice cream. The cellar is stocked with many rare and enticing wines. C 80-110,000 lire.

 Antico Bottaro
Passeggiata di Ripetta 15
(06) 3240200
Hols vary. All major cards.

We prefer this vegetarian restaurant to its twin on Via Margutta, for its more attractive surroundings. The bill of fare (to our taste) is a trifle too repetitive, but the antipasti fulfill their appetite-whetting purpose, and the zucchini parmigiana, asparagus timbale, and vegetable mixed fry display bright, fresh flavors. Wine, thank goodness, is held in high regard here, witness the interesting, varied cellar. There is also a selection of beers and excellent cider. For best value, consider the copious tasting menu. C 75,000 lire.

Antico Falcone
Via Trionfale 60-62 - (06) 3723400
Closed Tue, Aug. No cards.

For an eyeful of local color. Neither the premises nor the patrons of Antico Falcone change much over the years; needless to say, the menu is immutable. You start out with a sampling of supplì al telefono (deep-fried rice croquettes stuffed with melted mozzarella), before moving on to such Roman classics as involtini al sugo (veal birds in a rich gravy) or stewed oxtail with celery, washed down with the sturdy house wine. Note that on March 19, the feast of Saint Joseph, the restaurant (indeed, the entire *quartiere*) celebrates with a fantastic "fritter fest." Don't miss it! C 50,000 lire (wine incl.).

 Il Bacaro
Via degli Spagnoli 27 - (06) 6864110
Dinner only. Closed Sun, 3 wks in Aug, 3 days at Christmas. V, AE, MC.

Just a handful of marble tables are set for guests in this discreetly luxurious tavern. Among the good pastas on offer are penne con bottarga (mullet roe) and orecchiette lavished with an exceptionally fragrant pesto. Main courses are rather less orthodox, witness the smoked goose with a sauce based on kiwi fruit, veal scallop with apples, or the assortment of smoked fish. For the rest, you can count on excellent cheeses, uncomplicated desserts, and astutely chosen wines from the Veneto. C 40,000 lire.

Bonne Nouvelle
Via del Boschetto 73 - (06) 486781
Closed Sun, 2 wks in Aug. All major cards.

This thoroughly Italian restaurant is "good news" indeed for seafood lovers. Giuliano De Dominicis chooses prime, rigorously fresh specimens at the market, then entrusts them to the skillful hands of Liliana, a jewel of a cook. She, in turn, transforms this bounty into simple dishes that display clear, expertly balanced flavors, as in her divinely light tagliolini topped with squash blossoms and firm, fragrant shrimp; or tiny, tender squid sautéed with just a little wine and a whiff of garlic. A few meat dishes are also available (first-rate trippa alla romana, veal stewed with fresh peas). Chestnut ice cream and crème brûlée deserve their reputation as the sweet specialties of this quietly elegant spot. The cellar is small but select; and the service attentive yet discreet. C 60,000 lire.

Camiscioni
Via Sardegna 135 - (06) 4742218
Closed Sun (& Sat in summer), 10 days in Aug. All major cards.

Here in the heart of Rome, just steps from Via Veneto, Pierluigi Camiscioni makes it possible to enjoy a full—delicious!—meal with wine for the eminently reasonable sum of 40,000 lire. This elegant little address is perfect for business lunches or romantic dinners. And the food? Well, you'll begin with "tastes" of several different vegetable antipasti, then segue into one of the four or five excellent pastas on offer (the list changes daily) before tucking into a tasty chicken with peppers, baccalà (salt cod) with raisins and pine nuts, wine-braised rabbit, splendid veal birds (a house specialty), or meat loaf with julienne carrots and celery. To finish, there are homemade biscottini and ciambellone to dunk in the last drops of your wine—a Vernaccia from the Marches, perhaps. **C** 40,000 lire (wine incl).

Peter, Paul, and the Doors

The Basilica of San Giovanni in Laterano, shaded by Rome's oldest and tallest obelisk, is chockablock with marvels, some of them musical. The bronze doors of the central portal don't squeak, they sing, and rather tunefully at that. Another auditory oddity is the tomb of Pope Sylvester II, who is reputed to have been something of a sorcerer. An ancient tradition has it that Sylvester's gravestone sweats and screeches on the eve of each pontiff's death. The basilica (which, incidentally, is the cathedral of Rome) also contains the venerated relics of Saints Peter and Paul.

 Cannavota

Piazza San Giovanni in Laterano
(06) 77205007
Closed Wed, Aug 1-20. AE, DC.

This lively trattoria set in the teeming cathedral neighborhood offers lots of Roman atmosphere and good, fresh seafood. Bits of tender marinated octopus and other little salads start things off, followed by outstanding house pastas: penne all'arrabbiata con i gamberetti, for example (pasta and shrimp fired up with a dose of hot pepper). A few meat dishes

find their way into the main course selections, but we recommend the sautéed prawns and the assortment of grilled fish. Desserts are mundane (stick to the gelati), but there is an interesting line-up of wines, with choices from Friuli, Latium, and Sicily. Excellent value. **C** 45-55,000 lire.

 **Il Cardinale**

Via delle Carceri 6 - (06) 6869336
Closed Sun, Jul 15-Sep 12. All major cards.

Giovanni Sentuti obviously inherited his family's knack for running first-rate restaurants (his father presides at the well-known Papà Giovanni, see below). Here in his intimate, nostalgic little establishment, he turns traditional Roman ingredients into dishes with a pleasing, innovative touch. Giovanni recently fed us cuffiette pasta sauced with a lusty tripe ragù; on another occasion, he treated us to vermicelli alla contadina, topped with a gardenful of fava beans, zucchini, and fresh peas. Other appealing offerings include a pan-roast of anchovies and Belgian endive, osso buco with potatoes, and an array of unconventional salads that Giovanni dreams up every day. If only he would dream up a few more desserts (we never want to see another crème brûlée)! The wine list is most alluring, however, and prices are reasonable. **C** 50,000 lire.

Checchino dal 1887

Via di Monte Testaccio 30
(06) 5746318
Closed Sun, Mon, Aug, Christmas wk. All major cards.

Monte Testaccio isn't the eighth hill of Rome, it is an imposing (98-foot-high) mound of pottery shards (formed by broken fragments of wine and oil amphoras), piled up over 500 years by Roman slaves. Checchino, a century-old trattoria, adjoins this unusual eminence, and its wine cellar, dug out of the terracotta fragments, enjoys a constant temperature, winter and summer, of 48 degrees Fahrenheit. Located near the slaughterhouse, Checchino preserves the culinary traditions of Rome's poorer classes, offering some dozen dishes based on cheap cuts of meat and a variety of innards. This is nourishing, robust food, impeccably prepared: tripe alla romana, stewed oxtail with celery and raisins, rigatoni con la pajata (with calf's innards), fagioli e cotiche (beans and caul fat). The recipes came down to owner Elio Mariani from his great-grandmother, and though they are prepared with less fat now than in granny's time, they still hardly qualify as *cuisine minceur*. And strangely—considering that the demand for offal is not exactly intense—the food isn't particularly cheap. Never mind—Checchino is one of a kind. A special menu of cheeses and desserts, all partnered with an ideal wine, supplies the grace note for an unforgettable meal. **C** 80-90,000 lire.

 ### Chez Albert
Vicolo della Vaccarella 11 (06) 6865549
Closed Sun (exc lunch by reserv), Aug. All major cards.
Chez Albert reproduces the cheerful, convivial atmosphere of an intimate French bistro. From bouillabaisse à la provençale to choucroute à l'alsacienne, cassoulet à la toulousaine, and fondue à la bourguignonne, no region of France has been slighted (though Albert displays a special fondness for Provence). All these dishes are creditably handled and based on superlatively fresh ingredients. To finish, try that quintessential bistro dessert, tarte aux pommes. The wine list is thoroughly Gallic, too. **C** 80,000 lire.

 ### Convivio
Via dell'Orso 44 - (06) 6869432
Closed Sun, Aug. All major cards.
In their small, serene dining room, the Troiani brothers invite you to sample from an ambitious menu that is surely one of the most creative in Rome. True, some of the dishes are a trifle fussy, but you'll have no complaints if, from among the wide choice of antipasti, you choose marinated sea pike (aguglia) presented on a bed of fennel with a sprinkling of mustard seeds and a suave hint of fig essence, or broccoli layered with pungent Pecorino cheese in a sauce of mild garlic flecked with prosciutto. The innovations don't stop there: consider the extraordinary fillet of John Dory in an herbal crust, further embellished with a sophisticated sauce of shellfish and spinach, or a lusty tortino of pig's trotters, duck liver, and leeks brightened with a touch of raspberry vinegar. Less convincing is the cloying sauce of clams, shallots, and scallions that comes with the

taglierini; and a creamy bean soup is marred by Pecorino ravioli that are several shades too sharp. The chef's inspiration doesn't flag at dessert. A crunchy basket filled with banana mousse or a roasted peach with vanilla ice cream and minted strawberry sauce make splendid finales. A final word of praise is in order for the cellar, which features white wines chosen with as much discernment as the reds. **M** 80,000 lire (tasting menu).

 ### Coriolano
Via Ancona 14 - (06) 44249863
Closed Sun (& Sat in Jul), Aug. All major cards.
The cutting edge of Rome's political and business communities likes the stylish service and surroundings of Coriolano, a plush establishment just beyond Porta Pia in the city's eastern section. In addition to such typically Roman specialties as tripe, stewed oxtail, and baby lamb, the menu lists several pasta dishes featuring such premium ingredients as fresh porcini mushrooms and truffles. Fresh sole, sea bass, and shellfish arrive daily from Formia, a port in southern Latium. The food is good, traditional fare carefully prepared with high-caliber ingredients. Superb wine list. Prices are high, but we think they're justified. **C** 100,000 lire.

 ### La Cornucopia
Piazza in Piscinula 18 - (06) 5800380
Closed Sun, Aug 6-Sep 4. V, AE, EC.
This charming haven for seafood fanciers is located in the Trastevere district across from the Isola Tiberina. Tables on the vine-covered terrace offer views of the enchanting Piazza in Piscinula; the setting is preferable, we think, to the pink-and-green décor indoors. But while the dining room's candy-box colors left us cold, we warmed up immediately to the lavish display of antipasti and homemade breads and cakes on the bar. After you pick and choose, your selection will be brought to your table immediately. There's marinated sea bass, stuffed squid in a delicate sauce, and tiny shrimp with black olives and potatoes. The pasta course brings pennette with sardines and fennel, spaghetti with grouper and eggplant, or shrimp-stuffed black ravioli (tinted with cuttlefish ink). The centerpiece of any meal here is the fish of the day. On a recent visit, we struck lucky with a superb steamed turbot bathed in a briny sauce of fresh clams with

a swirl of artichoke purée on the side. Ricotta pie (pastiera) and apple-walnut cake are homey, comforting desserts. C 65,000 lire (wine incl).

La Cupola
Hotel Excelsior,
Via Veneto 125 - (06) 4708
Open daily. All major cards.
It's unusual to find regional cooking in the restaurant of a high-class hotel like the Excelsior, particularly since the region in question is Rome, whose gastronomy is not what one would call refined. But the Cupola's kitchen hews closely to the local repertoire, proposing orthodox versions of bucatini all'amatriciana, spaghetti alla carbonara, chicken with peppers, and abbacchio brodettato (lamb in egg and lemon sauce), served with nicely handled seasonal vegetables. A few "Continental" offerings are available for unadventurous palates. Desserts are appealing on the whole, but the cellar is just average. C 100-110,000 lire.

12/20 Dino e Toni
Via Leone IV 60 - (06) 39733284
Closed Sun. V, AE.
This spotless little trattoria, just steps away from Saint Peter's, is run by two energetic young Italians. The menu's slant is resolutely Roman (and therefore robust), but fresh fish is featured every Tuesday and Friday, and the antipasti based on prime seasonal vegetables are always refreshing and light. Don't even glance at the limited wine list—just order a carafe of the house red or white. In summer, tables spill out onto the sidewalk to create a delightful dining-room-with-a-view. C 35-38,000 lire (wine incl).

Il Drappo
Vicolo del Malpasso 9 - (06) 6877365
Closed Sun, Aug. AE.
With Valentina back in the kitchen, this likable Sardinian spot near Via Giulia seems to be on the upswing. Starters and most of the fried offerings are still too greasy for our taste, but Valentina's skill is evident in the delicious and unusual main dishes: squid with an exotic fruit-and-vegetable stuffing, sweet-and-sour pigeon, crispy-skinned roast suckling pig and tangy rabbit with olives and capers. Though we find them heavy, the ricotta-filled fritters (sebadas) soaked in bitter honey have

many fans. Charming décor; interesting island wines. C 60,000 lire.

12/20 Elettra
Via Principe Amedeo 74
(06) 4745397
Closed Sat, Aug. V, AE.
The vicinity of the Termini train station is, one might say, lacking in charm. But this restaurant is almost worth a special trip to that neck of the woods. Inside, you'll find a bright, tidy dining room and a corps of regulars, neighborhood folks and reporters who work nearby, all of whom relish Elettra's lusty cooking. Homemade fettuccine (that most Roman of pastas) comes with cubes of country-cured ham, a splash of cream, and a sprinkling of citron juice; osso buco boasts a winy sauce and a garnish of creamy risotto. And this is surely the only place in Rome where you can drink a wine made from the owner's grapes, grown just a stone's throw away (not every vintage, we should add, is

Now It's Time to Tell the Truth!

In the portico of the church of Santa Maria in Cosmedin is a famous mask that wears the truculent features of a river god. It is known as *la Bocca della Verità*, or Mouth of Truth. Legend has it that those suspected of perfidious deeds were made to thrust their hand into the mouth. If they lied, it would snap shut, shearing off their hand. But a clever ruse saved at least one lecherous lady accused of cuckolding her husband. As she was being led to the test, her lover, disguised as a slovenly madman, embraced her wildly in front of the crowd. She thrust her hand into the snapping mouth and calmly swore that she'd never in her life known the embrace of anyone but her husband... anyone, that is, but the poor madman who had just hugged her! Nowadays the mouth seems to have lost its power, much to the relief of Rome's libertine ladies and gentlemen.

equally successful!). The house pastries are a pleasant surprise, and so is the moderate tab. **C** 40-45,000 lire.

Les Étoiles

Hotel Atlante Star,
Via Vitelleschi 32 - (06) 6879558
Open daily. All major cards.

A terrace with a stupendous view of Saint Peter's and the Vatican is not the least of this restaurant's charms. But food is what we're paid to appraise, so *a tavola, if you please!* Chef Paolo Preo, a native of Treviso, officiated for two decades at the noted Toulà restaurant (see below). He has brought to Les Étoiles a classic repertoire of Italian *cucina borghese*, with a few rousing touches from the popular traditions of Venice and Rome. The combination makes for exciting meals. They might begin with sardines in a zesty "saor" marinade, succulent quail on a bed of radicchio with a piquant mustard sauce, or a fat artichoke stuffed with ricotta, Pecorino, and herbs. You could then proceed to a fabulous ink-hued cuttlefish risotto (perhaps the best of many we've sampled in a long career), followed by minted baby lamb with its liver in a grappa-spiked sauce or an impeccably fresh fish prepared with simplicity and skill. Among the many ways to conclude, our favorite is the tiramisù–a dessert we generally despise, but which is beautifully wrought in Preo's kitchen. To make your pleasure complete, there is an exceptional wine list. **C** 70-90,000 lire.

12/20 Felice

Via Mastro Giorgio 29 - (06) 5746800
Closed Sun, 2 wks in Aug. No cards.

Forget about calories and cholesterol when you visit Felice, a typical trattoria in the newly trendy Testaccio district. Visibly, the regulars here have long abandoned any notion of trimming their waistlines! The portions of these traditional Roman dishes (fettuccine, anchovies, oxtail, braised lamb) are large enough to feed a family, the sauces are a trifle fatty, but the deep, old-fashioned flavors are absolutely authentic—and so is the atmosphere. Proletarian prices. **C** 35,000 lire.

> **Find the address** you are looking for, quickly and easily, in the index.

La Fontanella

Largo Fontanella Borghese 86
(06) 6871092
Closed Mon, Aug. No cards.

A fine place to stop for lunch, conveniently set in Rome's elite shopping district. Peppe, the charming owner, will revive your flagging spirits with handily executed dishes made from top-flight ingredients. Do try his generous tagliolini with shellfish and bottarga or, in a more rustic vein, the comforting pasta e fagioli. Political and business scandals have taken their toll on Rome's fashionable restaurants; consequently, tables at La Fontanella are now easier to come by than once upon a time. **C** 60-70,000 lire.

Gemma alla Lupa

Via Marghera 39 - (06) 491230
Closed Sat, Jul 20-Aug 20. No cards.

Gemma (alone since the death of her husband, Maurizio) is a jewel of a cook who has the Roman repertory down pat. For the most flavorful bucatini all'amatriciana (hollow spaghetti with tomatoes and unsmoked bacon), the most fragrant tripe alla romana, the lightest rigatoni con la pajata (with calf's innards), and the lustiest coda alla vaccinara (stewed oxtail), rush over to this homey little spot the minute you get to Rome (it's right near the train station). Along with a few dishes native to regions other than Rome (Venetian seafood risotto, Emilian pumpkin tortelli), Gemma serves a few specialties of her own, like sumptuous pan-roasted veal, preceded by spaghetti bathed in the meat's fragrant cooking juices. Memorable food, good wine, and friendly service at unbeatable prices. **C** 25-35,000 lire.

Dei Gigli d'Oro

Via de' Gigli d'Oro 2-3-4
(06) 68308104
Closed Sun, Mon lunch, Aug 11-31, 3 days at Christmas. All major cards.

Congratulations to Claudio and Vincenzo, who recently celebrated their restaurant's first birthday. We'd have to add our encouragements, too, for this dynamic young duo's unstinting efforts. Not long ago they served us a splendid meal that featured sea bass encased in a golden crust of potatoes and zucchini, sautéed rabbit in a creamy sauce heightened with shallots and leeks, tender guinea fowl steamed over a shallot- and sage-scented broth, and a savory stuffed sole. Pasta? Of course! Here it's prepared with light, thoroughly degreased sauces. The current roster includes penne with a zesty garnish of anchovies and Pecorino, farfalle (bow-ties) with smoked ricotta and pancetta, and plump bombolotti stuffed with pungent radicchio. And there's more to like: the cellar is choice, the surroundings gracious, and the bill comes in under 60,000 lire. **C** 60,000 lire.

Giovanni
Via Marche 19 - (06) 4821834
Closed Fri, Aug. All major cards.
Run by the same family for half a century, Giovanni boasts a low-key elegance and generous homestyle cooking that continues to please large numbers of well-groomed Roman and foreign patrons. The food is soothing and familiar rather than imaginative, but the family recipes are skillfully executed with the best possible ingredients. Stracciatelle alla romana (chicken broth to which an egg-and-cheese batter is added) is a warming and authentically Roman way to start things off, but when they are in season, how can one resist the broiled porcini mushroom caps drizzled with olive oil? Friday brings fresh Adriatic seafood, and any day is right for the house specialty, abbacchio: baby lamb roasted with no added seasoning to veil its delicate natural flavor. Seasonal fruit or a crisp millefeuille are your best bets among the desserts. An appealing Verdicchio and a heady Rosso Piceno are served by the carafe. **C** 90-100,000 lire.

Giuseppe al 59
Via Angelo Brunetti 59 - (06) 3219019
Closed Sun, Aug. AE.
This Bolognese enclave near Piazza del Popolo attracts a select clientele of socialites, Socialists, journalists, and other strategists with the rich cuisine of Emilia-Romagna. No specialty of that food-loving province is omitted: mortadella sausage, golden tagliatelle, gramigna con salsiccia (macaroni and sausage), and plump tortellini are all on hand. The main-course winner, in our estimation, is the stupendous trolley of mixed boiled meats, which a cheerful waiter will roll right up to your table. Creamy zabaglione and assorted mousses wrap up a gratifying meal. Wines

from Romagna are, naturally, the house favorites. **C** 55,000 lire.

Gualtiero
Via Lucrino 2 - (06) 86206811
Closed Mon, last 2 wks of Aug. No cards.
Gualtiero's uncompromising eye never fails to spot the market's best seafood and vegetables. He prepares this bounty with restrained simplicity, but when it's time to serve, Gualtiero's exuberant personality comes to the fore. He plies his patrons with course after irresistible course—even the heartiest trencherman ends up throwing in the *tovagliolo* (his napkin, that is). Our latest spree kicked off with the freshest possible boiled crab, simply dressed with oil and lemon; a sauté of tiny clams and tellins (another, rarer, mollusk); and spaghetti topped with seafood (but alas! the undercooked pasta refused to absorb the delectable sauce). There followed an eggplant frittatina, gorgeously fresh red mullet, and grilled beef with equally meaty porcini mushrooms. A little dessert? Why not? Vanilla ice cream lavished with berries was the grace note to this feast. The cellar holds a fine cache of white wines, but there are some tasty reds, too, which complement the polenta with pork or sausage that Gualtiero prepares in winter. Note that excellent pizzas, with unusual toppings of Gualtiero's devising, draw appreciative crowds here in the evening. **C** 65,000 lire.

Lounge del Roman Garden
Hotel D'Inghilterra,
Via Bocca di Leone 14 - (06) 672161
Closed Sun. All major cards.
The venerable Hotel D'Inghilterra houses this charming restaurant, where we recently enjoyed a fine prix-fixe lunch that is quite a remarkable value. For the moderate sum of 45,000 lire, you can choose two courses from a list that includes a refreshing salad of Belgian endive, bean sprouts, green apple, and shrimp; eggplant rolls stuffed with creamy ricotta; or a crisp "tempura" of shellfish and artichokes followed by a delicate dessert. The cooking is impeccable, as is the refined service. And the elegant atmosphere is included at no extra cost. **C** 45,000 lire.

Da Lucia
Vicolo del Mattonato 2 - (06) 5803601
Closed Mon, Aug. No cards.
Silvana and Sandra do the cooking, and Ennio runs the dining room of this typical

Trastevere inn—so who, we wonder, is Lucia? No matter. The attraction here is earthy, full-flavored *cucina romana*, served with a minimum of fuss. After sampling the appetite-rousing antipasti, you might plump for the fantastic pasta with beans (or chickpeas, depending on the cook's whim), cuttlefish with tiny green peas, authentic baccalà, or satisfying chicken and peppers. Friday brings a wonderful country vegetable soup of the sort that Horace or Juvenal might have savored in their day. Desserts are skippable, but the cellar has improved and the prices are disarmingly modest. **C** 30-35,000 lire.

Mariano
Via Piemonte 79 - (06) 4745256
Closed Sun, hols vary. All major cards.
Mariano is a convivial, quintessentially Roman trattoria that comes into its glory in the hunting season. Although the fine fish and succulent meats served here year-round are above reproach, the rich bounty of game, wild mushrooms, and truffles that arrives in the fall and winter seems to inspire the kitchen to reach new heights. Pappardelle (wide noodles) with hare may be followed by pheasant in a Cognac-laced sauce or Umbrian wood pigeon in a rich broth dotted with tortellini. Main courses come with outstanding crisp-cooked vegetables, like the memorable puntarelle (bitter greens) with anchovy sauce. The cellar is well stocked with sturdy red wines that are ideal accompaniments for game. **C** 50,000 lire.

Mimì
Via Gioacchino Belli 59 - (06) 3210992
Closed Sun, Jul 15-end Sep. All major cards.
Gianni Dies knows a thing or two about seafood. First of all, how to choose the very freshest fish and crustaceans, and second, how to bring all their bracing, briny flavors to the fore. He eschews complicated cooking in favor of such straightforward methods as steaming, poaching, and grilling. We particularly like his colorful insalata di mare (seafood salad), rigatoni baked in parchment with fresh shellfish, an exemplary risotto al nero (stained black with cuttlefish ink), tasty stuffed squid alla napoletana, and superb poached sea bass. The wine list won't impress you, but it was obviously designed with seafood in mind. Prices are pegged to the fish market's current rates; on average, you'll spend about 60,000 lire. **C** 60,000 lire.

Montevecchio

Piazza di Montevecchio 22
(06) 6861319
Dinner only (exc Mon). Closed 2 wks at Christmas, 3 wks in Aug. V, AE, EC.
On those evenings when atmosphere counts as much as food in your choice of a restaurant, consider booking a table at Montevecchio. While the cooking is more than respectable—bombolotti verdi (green pasta stuffed with ham and spinach), strudel ai porcini, and roasted kid are reliably good—what lures us back here time and again is the prospect of whiling away a warm Roman night on this singularly charming piazzetta. **C** 70,000 lire.

Nino
Via Borgognona 11 - (06) 6795676
Closed Sun, Aug. All major cards.
The wood-paneled premises are a warm setting for simple, soul-satisfying Tuscan food. A dinner of regional ham and fennel-flavored salami followed by ribollita (bean and cabbage soup) and a bistecca alla fiorentina (the steak is actually "imported" from Florence) will set you up for anything life may throw at you. In season, you can conclude with Tuscany's favorite chestnut cake; otherwise, try the tiramisù (a rum-laced concoction of cream cheese and ladyfingers). Wines are predominantly Tuscan, and the Chiantis are uniformly fine. **C** 50,000 lire.

L'Ortica
Via Flaminia Vecchia 573
(06) 3338709
Closed Sun dinner, Mon, hols vary in Aug. All major cards.
Too often, what passes for Neapolitan cooking is a mere caricature that borders on culinary kitsch. The genuine article is hard to find, especially outside of Naples. That's why we're so pleased to have discovered Vittorio Virno's L'Ortica. Here you can savor the authentic, soul-satisfying pleasures of real mozzarella di bufala, pizza di scarola (more pie than pizza, filled with escarole), a splendid mold of cheese-enriched mashed potatoes called gattò di patate, and zesty marinated eggplant or peppers. And they're just the starters! Afterward come such baroque Neapolitan specialties as sartù (a rice timbale filled

with tiny meatballs) and a vast array of pastas, including penne sauced with real southern pomodorini and piquant Provolone or spaghetti alla tropea (with onions and salted ricotta). These, in turn, are followed by superlative lamb or sparkling fresh fish (with the accent on "blue" varieties: anchovies, sardines, mackerel...), all escorted' by splendid vegetables. A feast at L'Ortica is necessarily concluded with a sensual Southern sweet, and accompanied by a bottle of excellent Campanian wine from the extensive cellar. C 70,000 lire.

Papà Baccus
Via Toscana 36 - (06) 4742808
Closed Sat lunch, Sun, hols vary. All major cards.

There are plenty of Tuscan restaurants in Rome, but for our money this one is the best. Italo Cipriani procures prime ingredients from his native Casentino: golden tagliatelle, farm-cured hams, sausages, cheeses, and of course, ineffably fragrant olive oil. The rest of his raw materials come straight from the market, giving his menu a fresh, seasonal slant. We recently sampled some magnificent ravioli stuffed with fish, eggplant, and shrimp, and a memorable combination of bosky porcini mushrooms set atop thin slices of beef tenderloin. First-rate cheeses, lovely desserts, and a wide-ranging cellar are additional reasons to visit Papà Baccus. In summer, you can request a table on the pretty outdoor terrace. C 60-80,000 lire.

Papà Giovanni
Via dei Sediari 4 - (06) 6865308
Closed Sun, part of Aug. All major cards.

Renato Sentuti's poetic temperament shines through every facet of the minuscule restaurant he inherited from his father, papà Giovanni. Sip an aperitivo of Fragolino—a delicate wine with a strawberry finish—while examining the cheerful clutter of photos, postcards, and old wine bottles that make up the whimsical décor. Then turn your full attention to your plate, folks, because the food here is simply sublime. Starter salads (the ingredients fresh that morning from the Campo de' Fiori market) perfectly perform their role of rousing the taste buds. One superb example combines thin slices of pear, slivers of Pecorino cheese, mint, basil, and

arugula seasoned with a splash of chilled Spumante. The pastas are astonishing. Coffee-flavored fettuccine is swathed in a sauce of creamy mascarpone cheese scented with sage; tiny ravioli stuffed with thirteen herbs are sprinkled with garlic-infused olive oil. Roast baby lamb, its reduced juices heightened with Marsala and a pinch of cocoa, is a sensational version of the traditional Roman abbacchio. Desserts—particularly the pure fruit-juice sorbets—are on a par with the rest: fresh, light, and handsomely presented. Renato is a passionate oenophile with a fondness for the light-hearted wines of his native Latium: Frascati, Cerveteri, Formia, and the marvelous Marino Rosso Vigna del Vassallo. Two words of warning: tables must be booked well in advance; and some readers have complained that the service meted out to "non-habitués" is not always warm. C 80,000 lire and up.

Paris
Piazza San Callisto 7a - (06) 5815378
Closed Sun dinner, Mon, hols vary. All major cards.

Here in the heart of Trastevere, Dario Cappellanti practices the art of "friggitoria giudia", a method of deep-frying long identified with Rome's Jewish community. Dario learned the tricks of his trade at Piperno, once the capital's foremost Jewish restaurant, and he has mastered all the fine points of producing incredibly light and crisp fried artichokes, codfish fillets, squash blossoms, and potato croquettes. Other enticing options include skate with broccoli, tagliarini sauced with squash flowers and shrimp, and terrific little gnocchetti with fish ragù. For dessert, we recommend one of the vivid fruit sorbets. Good wine list; appealing prices. C 55-60,000 lire.

Quirino
Via delle Murate - (06) 6794108
Closed Sun, 3 wks in Aug. V, AE.

In existence for more than 100 years, Quirino combines contemporary comfort with antique charm. The cooking has a dual personality too, owing to the Roman and Sicilian roots of the proprietors, Assia and Giovanni. Truth to tell, we prefer the Sicilian side of the menu, for its zesty stuffed sardines, swordfish in a sprightly salmoriglio sauce redolent of oregano, bistecca (steak) alla palermitana, and such scrumptious island sweets as homemade cassata and cannoli. Interesting cellar; friendly service. **C** 50,000 lire.

Relais Le Jardin

Hotel Lord Byron,
Via Giuseppe de Notaris 5 - (06) 3220404
Closed Sun, hols vary. V, AE, DC.
Veteran chef Antonio Sciullo has presided over this luxurious Relais for fifteen years. With only the occasional lapse, he's managed to keep standards high while evolving a diverse, appetizing repertoire that keeps Rome's notoriously demanding diners happy and intrigued. The amazingly long menu (100 dishes, no less) currently highlights traditional fare rooted in Latium and Abruzzi. Among the starters, we like the silken boar "prosciutto" served with morsels of liver, olives, and a brandy-spiked fruit compote; and the bright zucchini blossoms stuffed with greens, Pecorino cheese, and a lively touch of mint. We followed those up with grouper in a delicate tomato broth with meaty, sweet peppers; and honey-glazed pork spiced with a whiff of ginger and presented with sweet-and-sour baby peas. We can also vouch for the richly flavored mocha tortino swirled with a beguiling sage-and-anise sauce. Fabulous cellar; stylish service in keeping with the posh atmosphere. **C** 120,000 lire.

Relais La Piscine

Hotel Aldrovandi Palace,
Via Aldrovandi 15 - (06) 321626
Closed Sun (exc for residents), Aug. All major cards.
Chef Jean-Luc Fruneau combines echoes of his Breton heritage and influences gleaned from his Sicilian spouse, to produce one of the most surprising and exciting menus in town. We were bowled over, not long ago, by the subtle layers of flavor in an escalope of foie gras set off by a teasingly tart sauce of berries and balsamic vinegar; a companion, meanwhile, raved about a vividly hued pumpkin risotto enriched with pearly morsels of sea scallops. For adventurous lovers of pasta, Fruneau proposes squid ink–stained tagliarini enhanced by tiny calamaretti, clams, and the slightly bitter tang of chicory. Our fish course brought baked sea bream redolent of wild fennel and drizzled with chili-infused extra-virgin olive oil; that dish was nearly surpassed by succulent beef tenderloin gratinéed with bone marrow and a bouquet of herbs, in a sauce of woodsy morels and aged Marsala. For dessert, Fruneau has devised an irresistible series of hot and cold chocolate confections—heavenly! And so, incidentally, are the surroundings: in summer, the magnificent dining room of the Hotel Aldrovandi is extended by a poolside patio. As you will surely have surmised, the Relais's cellar and service are flawless. **C** 85-115,000 lire.

Le Restaurant

Le Grand Hotel,
Via V.E. Orlando 3 - (06) 4709
Open daily. All major cards.
Grand indeed and quite costly, too, is the bill of fare presented to the patrons of this luxurious hotel dining room. Chef Ivan Catenacci, worthy successor of Escoffier (who inaugurated the Grand Hotel's kitchens), sends forth impeccably crafted dishes based on ingredients of exceptional quality. You may prefer, however, to pass over the impressive *carta* and opt instead for the oft-renewed *menu del giorno*. After a satisfying pasta (orecchiette sautéed with prosciutto and Pecorino, spaghetti tossed with strips of beef and rosemary, or pasta e fagioli al pesto toscano, for example), you can choose from an equally attractive list of main courses; a recent day brought mazzancolle (shrimp) al curry, saffron-spiced sole, salmon showered with pistachios, chicken with citrus fruit, and glazed veal with baby onions. A sweet from the imposing dessert trolley rounds out a meal served with style in surroundings of absolute comfort. **C** 120,000 lire.

La Rosetta

Via della Rosetta 9 - (06) 6861002
Dinner only. Closed Sun, Aug. All major cards.
This is one of Rome's best-known and best-liked restaurants, situated in the lively Pantheon district; don't dream of visiting without a reservation. Seafood has made La Rosetta's reputation; when diners walk in, even before the headwaiter can say *buona sera*, they are greeted by an artistic and very appetizing display of fresh fish and crustaceans. Antipasti are generally cold (lots of seafood salads) and often raw (marinated fish). Among the primi, we

especially like the delicate spaghetti with scampi, zucchini blossoms, and Pecorino cheese or the more gutsy pasta with fresh sardines. Fish prevails in the main courses, too. Try a classic grilled turbot with oysters, red mullet perfumed with sage, or striped bass baked in a salt crust. Here, as so often happens in Italy, people wind up a seafood meal with a refreshing fruit salad—and a stiff hit of grappa (the assortment on hand is quite impressive). The wine list, incidentally, presents a selection of crisp whites from Latium, Friuli, Tuscany, and the Trentino–Alto Adige; the bottle of your choice will be poured by one of the well-bred, well-trained waiters who make eating here such a pleasure. **C** 100,000 lire.

Sans Souci
Via Sicilia 20 - (06) 4821814
Closed Mon, Aug. All major cards.
A blinding blaze of crystal, silver, and gold stuns the eye. Is it a set for a Hollywood musical? No, it's the Sans Souci, one of Rome's flashiest restaurants. The confusion is understandable, though, because nary a Roman is to be spotted on the premises. The natives have long since abandoned the site to rich foreigners who dote on the fussy, "French" cuisine. In all justice, it must be said that the food is skillfully prepared (pâté de foie gras with a sweet wine sauce; Champagne sorbet; fish cooked with split-second accuracy). The kitchen isn't stingy with the truffles, either, and the wine cellar is a veritable treasure trove. But these pleasures are dearly bought: you can expect to leave behind a fistful of 10,000 lire notes. **C** 90-140,000 lire.

La Tana del Grillo
Via Alfieri 4 (corner of Via Merulana) (06) 70453517
Closed Sun, Mon lunch. AE, DC.
La Tana's new setting doesn't hold a candle to its previous splendid quarters, but the menu, thank goodness, hasn't changed. It still features the rich and savory cuisine of Ferrara, a city famous for its excellent pork specialties, such as meltingly tender salama da sugo (sausage), the pumpkin-filled ravioli called cappellacci di zucca, and eel prepared in a host of clever ways. When eel is in season, La Tana del Grillo serves it marinated as an antipasto, as well as roasted or stewed in wine. Justly famed as well is the gran bollito, or mixed

boiled vegetables and meats, accompanied by mostarda, a tangy fruit preserve. Ricotta pie is notable among the array of homemade desserts. The cellar offers wines from Emilia-Romagna, Ferrara's home province. Make a point of sampling the nocino, a homemade walnut liqueur. **C** 55,000 lire.

Taverna Giulia
Vicolo dell'Oro - (06) 6869768
Closed Sun, Aug. All major cards.
Four hundred years of Roman history have done little to dim the appeal of this pleasant tavern, which continues to stand serenely near a bend in the Tiber. The same savory and nourishing fare has appeared on the menu for decades: trenette, lasagne, or ravioli in sauces of onion, basil, walnuts, or tomato, followed by fragrant tripe alla genovese, stracotto (braised beef), or osso buco, with a silky, orange-scented crème brûlée for dessert. While we might like a new dish to appear now and then, we can't argue with the quality or the generous portions for which the Taverna is renowned. The lively wines of Liguria are very attractive and easy to drink. **C** 50-70,000 lire.

La Terrazza
Hotel Eden,
Via Ludovisi 49 - (06) 4743551
Open daily. All major cards.
The Eden, a landmark among Roman hotels, reopened its doors in 1994, much to the joy of the posh crowd who regularly patronized the hotel's high-perched dining room. From the extraordinary terrace spreads a view of the city's monuments, patrician villas, and gardens—an enchanting sight to be sure. The kitchen is now in the young but capable hands of Enrico Derflinger, who formerly cooked for the Prince and Princess of Wales (back when they were "happily" wed) as well as for President Bush. We, too, can now vouch for his skill, after sampling from a menu that includes hand-rolled pasta topped by a savory sauce of fish and leeks; lasagnette baked with fragrant pesto; fresh porcini swaddled in vine leaves; and jumbo shrimp intriguingly combined with plums and a touch of tarragon. The special "menu romano" features delicious fettuccine al vino rosso con salsa amatrice (the latter consisting of tomatoes, bacon, and

Pecorino cheese), as well as a famously tasty braise of spiced lamb with potatoes. Among the tempting desserts, minted mango mousse and a warm torta di riso (rice cake) stand out in our memory. The cellar still wants stocking, but there are plenty of fine bottles on hand. **M** 80-100,000 lire (lunch, wine incl), 120-140,000 lire (dinner, wine incl).

Toulà
Via della Lupa 29b - (06) 6873750
Closed Sun, Aug. All major cards.
Near the Caffè Greco and Rome's fashionable boutiques, Toulà celebrates Italy's *alta cucina* in a refined setting of handsome furniture and paintings, sumptuous flower arrangements, and discreet lighting. The restaurant is very popular with sleek, prosperous Romans who feel quite at home here, so reservations are a must, particularly in the evening. The menu displays a few discreet Venetian touches: the tiny sole and sardines in a sweet-and-sour marinade, velvety cream of shellfish soup, excellent risottos (served nice and wet, as in Venice), and perfect calf's liver with onions all merit special mention. The classic desserts are as beautiful as they are good. The wine list is extensive and varied, but it offers no bargains. **C** 90,000 lire.

Ai Tre Scalini
Rossana e Matteo,
Via SS. Quattro 30 - (06) 7096309
Closed Mon. All major cards.
Set in a deserted street not far from the Colosseum, Rossana and Matteo's Tre Scalini is home to some of the city's finest food: creative, subtle, and full of seductive surprises. Rossana, a sturdy Bologna native (and former civil engineer), draws her inspiration from the fine raw materials she culls from the market each morning. She laughs when asked to share the secret of her fresh, spontaneous cooking: "I do it for the sheer joy of dreaming up new dishes!" And indeed, every day brings a procession of such ingenious offerings as Greek jambalaya (lobster, oysters, peppers, rice, and fiery-hot sausage), crab served warm in a piquantly spicy sauce, or ravioli stuffed with smoked ham, radicchio, and Taleggio cheese. A recent dinner in hunt season brought forth a splendid pasticcio of boar with celery-root purée, and a succulent rack of venison encrusted with herbs, flanked by a zucchini-blossom soufflé. Not the least of the many pleasures to be savored here are the wines that Matteo chooses from his extensive cellar to complement Rossana's cooking. Politicians, financiers, and even a few prelates may be counted among the ever-growing number of the couple's fans. Competition for tables is fierce, so be sure to reserve yours well in advance. Less expensive, lighter fare is now served in the new basement dining room. **C** 70-80,000 lire.

Vecchia Roma
Severino il Pugliese,
Viale Manzoni 52-54 (corner of Via Principe Umberto) - (06) 4958493
Closed Sun, part of Aug. No cards.
It would be tough to find better value for your dining dollar than here at Severino's popular trattoria. After a light salad of tomatoes and basil or a heartier starter of orrechiette con broccoli, you may choose to follow one of two culinary traditions: that of the owner's native Apulia (all manner of seafood; fava beans with chicory), or that of the Roman countryside (tripe, roast baby lamb, beef braised with olives and pine nuts). Whichever route you choose, the food is certain to be nicely prepared and fresh tasting, thanks largely to Severino's home-grown vegetables. And every dish is so generously apportioned that you may not have room for dessert. As it happens, that is no great loss. Even when things get hectic here, you can count on service with a smile. **C** 25,000 lire.

The Toast of the Town

Roman café society isn't what it used to be, but Rome's most celebrated coffeehouse, Caffè Greco, is still the toast of the town. It's been brewing espresso and cappuccino for the greats since the eighteenth century. Goethe, Byron, Liszt, Wagner, and Gogol were a few of the regulars at 86 Via Condotti. Romans claim it's one of the true monuments of the eternally caffeine-craving city. It's certainly worth visiting to see what all the (ahem) brew-haha is about.

Quick Bites

CONTENTS

CAFES

Alemagna
Via del Corso 181 - (06) 6792887
Open 7am-9:45pm. Closed Sun.
Noisy, crowded, and utterly Roman, this large café and pastry shop is a fine place to pause for a coffee break or a quick meal. The Italian-style cafeteria also provides takeout service.

Bar del Tennis
Viale dei Gladiatori 31, Foro Italico
(06) 3219022
Open summer: 8am-2am; winter: 8am-11pm. Closed Mon.
A splendid place to sit in the sun and a great favorite with kids cutting class on days when they'd rather work on their tans than read Kant. When the tennis championships are in full swing, it's hard to get near the bar, which becomes the focus for the social goings-on. The Italian-style cafeteria service is nonstop in summer, but it operates only at traditional mealtimes in winter.

Caffè Greco
Via Condotti 86 - (06) 6782554
Open 8am-midnight. Closed Sun.
Founded in 1760, Caffè Greco is a historic Roman rendezvous. The coffee served here may not be the best in the city, but the warmly inviting little rooms and

unique ambience warrant a visit. The very "literary" crowd that frequents the place, the imperturbable and stylish waiters, the walls covered with memorabilia combine to create a fascinating scene.

La Caffettiera
Piazza di Pietra 65 - (06) 6798147
Open 7am-9:30pm. Closed Mon.
A corner of sunny Napoli in the center of Rome. Sit down to a cup of authentic Neapolitan coffee and a rum-soaked baba, served by distinguished waiters in this handsome, wood-paneled caffè. Lunch and snacks are also proposed, including arancini and crocchette di patate (rice or potato croquettes), Italian omelets, and pizza.

Doney
Via Veneto 145 - (06) 4821790
Open 8am-midnight. Closed Mon.
The mythical Via Veneto immortalized by Fellini in *La Dolce Vita* is just a memory now. Yet it looks like a renaissance is in the making for this "street of dreams," symbolized by the recent reopening of Doney and Harry's Bar (see below), after a long eclipse. Romans can once more duck into Doney's for their morning coffee, sip an aperitivo in the beautiful interior, or join friends at an outdoor table to indulge in a snack or treat (the good pastries and ice creams are all made on the premises). Brunch, served from noon to 3pm (45,000 lire including beverages), is a new addition to Doney's repertoire.

Ombre Rosse
Piazza Sant'Egidio - (No telephone)
Open 7pm-2am. Closed Sun.
One of Trastevere's most engaging spots, especially in warm weather when the outdoor terrace beckons irresistibly. An aperitivo is served here with all the appropriate flair. And theater goers favor Ombre Rosse for a bite before or after the show.

Parnaso

Piazza delle Muse - (06) 8079741
*Open 7:30am-9pm (summer 7:30am-1am).
Closed Wed.*

On warm summer nights, this stylish venue is a haven for denizens of the fashionable Parioli district. These distinguished Romans flock to Parnaso in summer to enjoy the cool breezes that drift through the garden. Sometimes groups of as many as twenty crowd around a single table, laughing, talking, and drinking the evening a-way. In the shank of the night, when the noise and happy confusion hit their peak, you can escape from it all just by casting an eye at the distant lights of Via Olimpica, off where the Tiber flows in a quiet, unspoiled setting.

Rosati

Piazza del Popolo 5 - (06) 3225859
Open 7:30am-midnight. Closed Tue.

In fine weather, the little tables of this sizable and elegant caffè/pasticceria overflow onto the celebrated Piazza del Popolo. For generations, Rosati has been *the* place where people meet for a last drink and gossip before turning in. Saturday nights are especially animated, when Rosati becomes a stage for Rome's flamboyant nocturnal fauna.

Sant'Eustachio

Piazza Sant'Eustachio 82 - (06) 6861309
Open 8:30am-1am. Closed Mon.

Enviably situated in the triangle formed by the Pantheon, Piazza Navona, and Piazza di Torre Argentina, this noteworthy address attracts innumerable coffee lovers with some of the best espresso in town. The price of a cup is a little higher here than elsewhere, but elsewhere you can't get this marvelous brew. The cappuccino and granita di caffè (coffee ice) are worthy of your interest as well.

Tazza D'Oro

Via degli Orfani 84 - (06) 6792768
Open 7am-8:15pm. Closed Sun.

This "Golden Cup" holds coffee only—don't even dream of asking for tea! The rich brew dispensed at the bar is aromatic and clean-tasting: surely one of the city's best espressos. Beans scooped from jute sacks that line the walls are roasted and ground on the premises, so that you can purchase some of the fragrant Brazilian blend to savor at home. For a coffee-flavored sweet (with quite a kick) try the frozen granita di caffè topped with whipped cream.

Vanni

Via Frattina 94 - (06) 6791835
Via Col di Lana 10a-b-c - (06) 3223642
Open 7am-midnight. Closed Mon.

Any one of the tables aligned on busy Via Frattina provides an ideal observation post for studying the passing scene while indulging in a cappuccino, cakes and tea, or an aperitivo. Native Romans, wide-eyed and weary tourists, veteran reporters, and cultural VIPs maintain the time-honored habit of meeting for drinks or a quick snack at Vanni, where they find the same high caliber of food and service as in decades past. The Via Frattina location is more modern but just as lively as the original Vanni, on Via Col di Lana. The latter's proximity to the Teatro delle Vittorie and the RAI television network makes it a favorite with actors and other celebrities.

QUICK BITES

Antonini

Via Sabotino 21-29 - (06) 37517845
Open 7am-9pm. Closed Mon.
Piazza Mazzini 9-10 - (06) 3217502
Open 7am-10:30pm (summer 7am-midnight). Closed Mon.

Sweet or savory, the choice is yours. This bakery is equally reputed for its open-face sandwiches and dainty tea cakes. The former are topped with shellfish, meat, and all sorts of appetizing sauces. Many customers willingly forgo a formal lunch in

Keyhole With a View

Saints alive! This is paradise for Pope-watchers. The most extraordinary view in Rome is at the keyhole of the Villa dei Cavalieri di Malta's door, on the Aventine Hill. Place your pupil to the hole and there it is—splendid in the sunlight, twinkling in the night—the gigantic dome of Saint Peter's!

favor of an assortment of these delicious tartine, as they are called. And the fame of Antonini's pastries (especially the lush Saint Honoré) has spread far beyond the Prati district. A second Antonini, recently opened on Piazza Mazzini, is a popular meeting place for lunch or cocktails in summer.

Babington's English Tearoom

Piazza di Spagna 23 - (06) 6786027
Open 9am-8:30pm. Closed Tue.

A Piazza di Spagna fixture for nearly a century, this establishment was founded by Misses Cargill and Babington, whose endeavor it was to provide their traveling compatriots with a traditional tea room, faithful in every detail to the ones they had left behind in England. And so it remains to this day, with its small wooden tables, straw placemats, and slightly uncomfortable chairs. Ladies sip tea and converse in hushed tones while middle-aged waitresses smile reassuringly and offer cakes and muffins (and Christmas pudding in season), all made according to immutable, top-secret recipes. So when in Rome, do as Lauren Bacall, Claudette Colbert, and Dustin Hoffman have done before you: pause in your busy day of shopping and sightseeing for tea and scones or brunch (served all day, 40,000 lire) at Babington's—frightfully expensive—English Tearoom.

Birreria L'Orso Elettrico

Via Calderini 64 - (06) 3966202
Open 8pm-2:30am. Closed Mon.

At this likable Italian-style beer house furnished with rustic wooden tables, judiciously chosen brews (on tap or in bottles) wash down pasta, crêpes, bruschetta, hearty mixed salads, and excellent french fries served with a secret homemade sauce.

Birreria Tiroler Keller

Via Vitelleschi 23 - (06) 6869994
Open 7pm-1am. Closed Mon.

Nostalgia for Mitteleuropa is as thick as the fragrant sausages and dried hams served in this warm, friendly Slavic tavern not far from Saint Peter's. The featured specialties are rich and tasty fondues, available in cheese, Chinese, and bourguignon versions.

Birreria Viennese

Via della Croce 21-22 - (06) 6795569
Open noon-midnight. Closed Wed.

Since 1937, the Birreria Viennese has stood on this splendid street, which links Via del Corso to Piazza di Spagna, Rome's traditional social center. Hunting trophies line the walls, their glassy eyes gazing longingly, one imagines, on the happy crowds of beer drinkers clustered around the bar. The food has a pronounced Tyrolean accent: smoked pork knuckle, all sorts of sausages, sauerkraut, and such.

Bottega del Vino da Bleve

Via S. Maria del Pianto 9a-11 - (06) 6865970
Open 9am-1pm & 4:30pm-8pm. Closed Sun.

A quiet and attractive spot, this wine shop in the former ghetto becomes a wine bar at lunchtime, serving great farmhouse cheeses and salamis, as well as salads and a hot dish or two, partnered with wines served by the glass.

Burghy

Piazza della Rotonda 14-15 - (06) 6875643
Open 10am-midnight (Sat 10am-1am). Closed Wed.
Via Barberini 2-16a - (06) 4871257
Open 11am-1am (Sat 11am-2am). Closed Tue.
Via Cola di Rienzo 156 - (06) 6874225
Open noon-midnight. Closed Mon.

For quite a while, the Burghy on Piazza della Rotonda was the most talked-about fast-food place in town—not because the "cuisine" was controversial, but because many Romans questioned the propriety of permitting a hamburger house to operate right across from the Pantheon, one of the city's most revered monuments. Despite the polemics, Burghy's gaudy parasols remain in place, beneath a large marble plaque that explains (in Latin) how the piazza had been cleared of the peddlers' stands and other eyesores that, while the popes ruled Rome, had been allowed to disfigure this sacred site. *Plus ça change...*

Calisè

Via Col di Lana 14 - (06) 37515395
Open noon-1am. Closed Sat-Sun at lunchtime.

In summer, this attractive little establishment is particularly appealing, when a bouquet of pretty, parasol-shaded tables is arranged outdoors. Calisè specializes in panini: some 40 different sandwiches are offered, many of them named for cartoon characters.

Ciampini

Piazza San Lorenzo in Lucina 29 - (06) 6876606
Open 7:30am-9pm. Closed Sun.
A perfect spot for a quick bite at lunchtime: excellent sandwiches are served at the bar or at little tables set up inside and (come summer) outdoors. Ciampini also offers a quality breakfast-on-the-run, with first-rate coffee and cornetti (croissants).

La Crêperie

Via Galvani 11 - (06) 5743814
Open 8pm-1:30am. Closed Mon.
This wee crêperie offers no fewer than 200 kinds of sweet and savory crêpes: one of them is sure to satisfy your craving for a mid-night snack! In warm weather, tables spill out of this tiny establishment onto the sidewalk.

Cul de Sac 1

Piazza Pasquino 73 - (06) 68801094
Open 12:30pm-3pm & 7:30pm-12:30am. Closed Mon at lunchtime.
An encyclopedic wine list and an appetizing choice of quality cheeses and cured meats (a sight better, we think, than the pâtés and soups) draw a smart, youngish crowd to this minuscule wine bar behind Piazza Navona. From your table, you can admire the staggering collection of more than 1,000 bottles lined up against the walls.

Euclide

Via Flaminia 8.200 km marker - (06) 3330695
Largo di Vigna Stelluti 1-4 - (06) 36307865
Via F. Civinini 119-127 - (06) 8078017
Open 7am-10pm (7am-11pm Via Flaminia). Closed Mon (Via Flaminia), Tue (Largo di Vigna Stelluti), Wed (Via Civinini).
Despite its size and the diversity of its operations—catering, snack bars, baked goods—all the Euclide shops produce fare that is unfailingly fresh and inviting. The Via Flaminia branch is the largest, with a pleasant little terrace where you can munch pizzas as well as exquisite sweets. On Largo di Vigna Stelluti, Euclide specializes in house-made cakes, pastries, and ice cream, while the Via Civinini shop, in the smart Parioli district, is reputed for its tempting snacks and sandwiches.

Dar Filettaro a Santa Barbara

Largo dei Librari 88 - (06) 6864018
Open 5pm-10pm (summer 5pm-10:30pm). Closed Sun.
This tiny fried-food stand is tucked away at the edge of the Campo de' Fiori. Until you've eaten some of the crispy strips of deep-fried baccalà (salt cod) that make this eatery's reputation, you cannot claim to be a genuine Roman, or to have seen the "real" Rome. In summer, these crispy treats may be enjoyed at little tables set out front on the piazzetta.

Lazzareschi-Caffè Vigna Clara

Piazza Stefano Jacini 20-21 - (06) 36303074
Open 7:30am-11pm (summer 7:30am-mid-night). Closed Wed.
Vigna Clara is one of Rome's more elegant residential districts, well out of the city's center, and this spacious pastry shop/caffè/caterer is a neighborhood institution. An appetizing array of cold dishes and delicious sweets is on offer throughout the day. Everything is irreproachably fresh, prepared right on the premises.

McDonald's

Piazza di Spagna 46-47 - (06) 69922400
Open 10am-midnight. Closed Mon.
The American fast-food colossus was not exactly welcomed with open arms when it set down stakes in the heart of old Rome. (A famous designer complained vociferously that the proximity of the restaurant's ventilation shafts to her atelier would have her expensive creations reeking of grease.) In point of fact, the Piazza di Spagna link in McDonald's chain is not an eyesore (the little marble tables set out on either side of the central atrium are quite attractive). A marble plaque, requisitioned, we suppose, from some old Roman street, warns the population (in antique Italian) not to litter the site under penalty of a fine. It's quite witty, and certainly appropriate.

Mister George

Via del Moro 17 - (06) 588288
Open 9:30am-2am. Closed Wed.
Another American outpost, this one in the quaint Trastevere district. The bill of fare features such Yankee staples as bagels, waffles, and Philadelphia cheese steaks. A traditional Sunday brunch may be enjoyed at little outdoor tables, and there is a range of take-out dishes, too.

Il Nuovo Zio d'America

Via Ugo Ojetti 2 - (06) 8272741

Open 7am-midnight. Closed Mon.

You can get anything you want at the "American Uncle" restaurant. The ultra-modern Talenti district is home to this eclectic eatery that attempts to be all things to all people: a bar, a restaurant, a pizzeria, a pastry shop, a coffee house, a wine bar, and a tea room. You can expect to find friendly service and a lively young crowd of regulars.

Paladini

Via del Governo Vecchio 29 - (06) 6861237
Open 7:30am-8pm. Closed Sun.

Paladini started out in 1914 as a bakery, later became a full-service grocery store, and now—in a brilliant stroke—purveys hot-from-the-oven pizza crust, which customers can top as they like. The choices encompass various salamis, all sorts of cheeses, arugula and other greens, and even chocolate-hazelnut spread, so you can have pizza for dessert! A bright idea for a tasty snack on the run.

Panatela

Piazza della Cancelleria 87 - (No telephone)
Open noon-3pm & 8pm-1am (Sat-Sun 8pm-1am).

Sandwiches, Italian-style: a panoply of fresh, tasty panini, filled just about any way you like. If it's a sweet treat you seek, try a tempting just-baked torta (cake). To wash your snack down, there's draft beer, wine, or fresh fruit juice.

Pannocchi

Via Bergamo 56-58-60 - (06) 8552109
Open 7am-8:30pm. Closed Mon.

Pannocchi is a venerable pasticceria in the gracious Porta Pia neighborhood. We recommend a stop here for breakfast, when the sweet rolls and glazed doughnuts called "bombe" are at their best, or for a quick stand-up lunch of focaccine (stuffed flat bread) or sandwiches at the bar.

St. Andrew's Pub

Vicolo della Cancelleria 36 - (06) 6832638
Open 9:30am-1:30am. Closed Wed, Sun at lunchtime.

Here's a cozy Scottish pub (note the tartan-covered walls), improbably situated in the Campo de' Fiori district. Sturdy Scots' specialties can be washed down with good draft beer, or you can stick to the Italian menu offered at lunch (13,000 lire). In the afternoon, St. Andrew's proposes typical teatime fare.

Il Simposio

Piazza Cavour 16 - (06) 3211502
Open 11:30am-3pm & 6:30pm-12:30am. Closed Sat at lunchtime, Sun.

Piero Costanti is a familiar figure to the city's oenophiles. His wine shop stocks a rich and discerning selection of bottles, and the adjoining wine bar—separated from the shop by a wrought-iron screen—provides the opportunity for immediate sampling. To accompany these premium vintages, there are 80 cheeses from around the world, soups, and savory tarts. Cheesecake is a standout among the desserts. For a full meal, expect to pay about 30,000 lire, more if your taste runs to rare and costly wines.

Teichner

Piazza San Lorenzo in Lucina 17 - (06) 6871449
Open 8:30am-8pm. Closed Sun.

Teichner is a deluxe little gourmet grocery, a wine bar, and coffee house all in one. Noted especially for its intense, top-quality espresso, Teichner also draws crowds at noontime with tasty dishes served in a flash. If you aren't in a huge hurry and the weather is fine, nab a table on the lovely Piazza San Lorenzo.

Boning Up on Franciscan History

The Capuchin Fathers' church, Santa Maria della Concezione, in Via Veneto, is home to an unusual cemetery. Skulls, tibiae, fibulae, femurs, and whole skeletons of about 4,000 friars overflow the chapels under the church. It's an unsettling yet elegant allegory of death, and an invitation to ponder the present: "That which you are, dear visitor, we were. That which we are, you shall be." Don't miss the masterpieces tucked away in the sacristy: *Saint Michael and the Dragon* by Guido Reni and *Saint Francis* by Caravaggio.

Trimani Wine Bar
Via Cernaia 37b - (06) 4469630
Open 11:30am-3:30pm & 5:30pm-midnight.
Closed Sun.

A superb wooden bar topped with Carrara marble, small tables, and halogen lighting form the modern, understated backdrop for enticing snacks (smoked fish, salads, first-rate cheeses, crostini, cured meats...) or full meals, all irrigated by wines from Trimani's legendary collection.

SWEET SNACKS

■ ICE CREAM

La Douce Vie
Via Boncompagni 49-51 - (06) 4744994
Open 6am-9:30pm. Closed Sun.

Just around the corner from the famed Via Veneto, La Douce Vie is an up-and-coming ice-cream emporium that offers a score of irresistible, all-natural, house-made treats. The cremas, or custard-based specialties, are smooth and sublime.

Il Gelato di San Crispino
Via Acaia 56-56a - (06) 70450412
Open 3pm-2am. Closed Tue.

This relative newcomer (opened in 1992) is currently one of Rome's hottest places for ice cream. San Crispino presents a festival of delectable flavors and original toppings to satisfy the greediest gelato fanatics.

Giolitti
Viale Uffici del Vicario 40 - (06) 6991243
Viale Oceania 90 - (06) 5924507
Open 7am-midnight. Closed Mon.

Colossal, colorful, copious: Giolitti's ice-cream sundaes are a challenge to the heartiest appetites (we dare you to swallow the last spoonful of an "Eiffel Tower"!). Even in the wee hours the place is jammed with a festive crowd of nocturnal merrymakers looking to put a sweet finish to their evening.

Palazzo del Freddo di Giovanni Fassi
Via Principe Eugenio 65-67 - (06) 4464740
Open noon-midnight (Sun 10am-midnight).
Closed Mon.

For Romans, the name Fassi is synonymous with ice cream. This modernist gelateria opened in 1924, and since then has faithfully indulged the city's appetite for cold, sweet treats. Fassi's confections are uniformly scrumptious, and are still crafted according to time-tested methods; the internationally renowned cassata, tartufo, and Caterinetta (semifreddo rich with custard-based ice cream, chocolate, and zabaglione) are musts.

Herbal Panaceas and Antiplague Remedies

The sure way to fight heartburn and headache is to take a swig of Friar Basilio's acqua antisterica or *antipestilenziale*, from the ancient Pharmacy of Santa Maria della Scala (in Piazza della Scala). This is Rome's last convent pharmacy, and it has been in the same, second-floor location for centuries. (Underneath is the modern pharmacy of the same name, run by monks. Ask them if you can visit the upstairs.) There are huge marble vases that once contained the marvelous, mystery brew known as teriaca or triaca, a kind of cure-all. The walls of the pharmacy are covered by cabinets containing some 230 types of dried herbs, all expertly arranged in labeled drawers. Portraits of medicine's greats hang here and there: Hippocrates, Galen, and the celebrated herbalist, Fra Basilio.

Pellacchia
Via Cola di Rienzo 103-105-107 - (06) 3210807
Open 6am-1pm. Closed Mon.

Since 1923, Pellacchia has catered to the local passion for gelato. The tables set out on the boutique-lined Via Cola di Rienzo lure weary shoppers to take an ice-cream break. Our favorite offering here is the cool coffee granita topped with a dollop of whipped cream.

---

*Some establishments change their **closing times** without warning. It is always wise to check in advance.*

Pica

Via della Seggiola 12 - (06) 68803275
Open 8:45am-1pm. Closed Sun.
Ice cream, in its infinite variety, is Pica's raison d'être. Every fresh flavor is made the old-fashioned way, with no concession to "industrial" methods. In summer, swarms of sweltering Romans vie for tables at this little gelateria (one of the oldest in town), to get their fair share of the delicious house specialties. The zuppa inglese and creamy cinnamon ice cream are tops.

Tre Scalini

Piazza Navona 28 - (06) 68801996
Open 8am-1am. Closed Wed.
Those in the know don't come here to sit out front and admire the spectacular view of one of the world's most imposing squares. No, the real cognoscenti are the ones who rush inside, and before they even look for a place to sit, order a tartufo al cioccolato. The chocolate truffle, a rich, dark, and addictive confection topped with a drift of whipped cream, is the true reason that God created Tre Scalini.

Lo Zodiaco

Piazzale del Parco Mellini 90, Monte Mario (No telephone)
Open daily 9am-2am (Tue 3pm-2am).
An enchanting panorama—a full 360-degree view of the Eternal City—is just one of Lo Zodiaco's attractions. The other is ice cream. We can't think of a better way to spend a sunny Sunday than to sit here, admiring the scenery, while spooning into a Coppa Cosmica (ice cream and fruit lavished with whipped cream) or Coppa Universo (four kinds of custard gelato topped with whipped cream). More abstemious sorts can order just a coffee or a beer.

■ PASTRY

Bella Napoli

Corso Vittorio Emanuele II 246-250 (06) 6877048
Open 7:30am-9:30pm. Closed Sat.
Genuine Neapolitan pastries and sweets are the attraction at this fragrant little bakery: sfogliatelle (filled flaky pastries), pastiera (ricotta cake), and smooth ice creams in a rainbow of flavors. Terrific coffee, too: strong and aromatic.

Bernasconi all'Argentina

Largo di Torre Argentina 1 - (06) 68308141
Open 6:30am-11pm. Closed Mon.
At this long-established, traditional Roman pastry shop, the renowned sweets and ice creams are all concocted right on the spot, and they are gloriously fresh and delicious. A pause at Bernasconi has become for many an obligatory prologue to a quintessentially Roman evening of art, conversation, emotion, and a little epicurean indulgence.

Boccione

Via del Portico d'Ottavia 2 - (06) 6878637
Open 8am-8pm. Closed Sat.
This street was once a boundary of the Roman Ghetto, where thousands of Jews lived segregated in the close confines of a walled enclave, from 1555 until late in the nineteenth century. Boccione sells such fragrant, traditional delicacies as ricotta cakes, crunchy amaretti cookies, and Jewish pastries filled with candied fruit.

Cavalletti

Via Nemorense 181 - (06) 86324814
Open 7:30am-1:30pm & 2:30pm-8:30pm. Closed Tue.
Cavalletti is famed for its millefoglie, a masterpiece of ethereal puff pastry layered with luscious pastry cream (the strawberry variety is our particular favorite). Christmas cakes and pastries are also specialties of the house.

Il Cigno

Viale Parioli 16a - (06) 8082348
Open 7am-11pm. Closed Mon.
This is an attractive place to pause for a pastry, some ice cream, or a quick hot meal in one of the smartest districts of Rome. In summer, little tables are set up outside, offering an ideal vantage point for scrutinizing the chic passersby.

Cottini

Via Merulana 286 - (06) 4880391
Open 7am-11pm. Closed Mon.
An excellent pastry shop situated in a busy neighborhood, Cottini offers not only delicious sweets but a wide selection of savory snacks as well.

> **The prices** *in this guide reflect what establishments were charging at press time.*

Europeo

Piazza San Lorenzo in Lucina 33
(06) 6876304
Open 7am-midnight. Closed Wed.
Scrumptious Sicilian sweets are the specialty of this pleasant bar and pastry shop. Everyone raves about Europeo's warm chocolate-filled croissants, which are famed throughout the city.

Giuliani

Via Paolo Emilio 67a - (06) 3243548
Open 8:30am-8pm. Closed Sun pm.
Something for every sweet tooth: tantalizing chocolates, glazed chestnuts, Easter eggs, and old-fashioned fruit jellies.

Gran Caffè
Esperia Ruschena

Lungotevere dei Mellini 1 - (06) 3204449
Open 7:30am-9pm. Closed Tue.
Close to Piazza Cavour and the hulking Palazzo di Giustizia (courthouse), this venerable pastry shop and tea room recently marked its 50th birthday, proud of the accomplishments that have endeared it to Rome's sweets-loving citizenry. The Gran Caffè Esperia Ruschena is the birthplace of panettone romano (a golden sweet bread), and to this day the ovens regularly turn out inventive—even fantastic—pastry creations. To accompany them, order a cup of creamy, delicious cappuccino.

Marinari

Piazza Santa Emerenziana 20
(06) 86219332
Open 6:30am-9pm. Closed Mon.
After a hard day of shopping, this traditional pasticceria, with its extensive assortment of pastries and cakes, is a perfect place to rest and enjoy a richly deserved treat. You'll find Marinari in the so-called Africano neighborhood, between Viale Libia and Viale Eritrea.

Mondi

Via Flaminia 468a - (06) 3336466
Open 6:30am-10pm. Closed Mon.
This is the most popular spot for pastry or ice cream in the picturesque Ponte Milvio area. Or should we say pastry *and* ice cream? Mondi specializes in delectable hybrids of gelato and cake. These confections are so distractingly good that Constantine and Maxentius, who fought a bloody battle on this site in the fourth century, might have resolved their differences with a helping of zuccotto (a dome-shaped mold of ice cream and pound cake: a surefire way to sweeten testy tempers) had Mondi been in existence back then.

Romoli

Viale Eritrea 140-142-144 - (06) 86325077
Open 6am-2am. Closed Mon.
If you see cars triple-parked at one in the morning, you'll know you're at the right place: this is another venue where Rome's midnight ramblers stop for a last indulgence before they head home. Warm croissants satisfy the sober-minded, and ice cream or pastry extravaganzas are popular with the young and carefree, who emerge from their late-night revels with cheeks charmingly smudged with chocolate or cream.

San Filippo

Via di Villa San Filippo 8 - (06) 8079314
Open 7am-midnight. Closed Mon.
Old-timers remember when King Farouk would fly into a rage here, because he couldn't find a chair to fit his royal posterior—but he stayed anyway, for San Filippo's legendary ice cream. Federico Fellini, when feeling indolent, would send over a taxi to fetch his gelato. Sounds like a chic, sleek Roman venue for the *dolce vita* crowd? You're only half right. The San Filippo is no showplace, but the glitterati (and the rest of us) have thronged in since 1947 for delectable fruit-flavored ice creams that are second to none.

Svizzera Siciliana

Piazza Pio XI 10-11 - (06) 6374974
Open 7:30am-9pm. Closed Mon.
Native Sicilians give Siciliana their highest accolade when they proclaim its cassata (pound cake layered with sweetened ricotta and iced with chocolate buttercream) "as good as mamma's!" But cassata is not the only reason to visit this far-famed pasticceria: there's the Montblanc (chestnut purée and meringue), the cream-filled Saint-Honoré, and a splendid Sachertorte made with real Swiss chocolate. Yum!

219

Hotels

Accademia
Piazza Accademia di San Luca 75
(06) 6792266, fax (06) 6785897
Open year-round. 55 rms 190-235,000 lire, bkfst incl. All major cards.
A comfortable, pleasantly modern hotel situated just steps away from the Trevi Fountain. In addition to the usual amenities, the rooms are also equipped with safes and satellite television. An efficient, professional staff provides first-rate service. The American-style breakfast buffet is spread in a bright, cheerful room.

Adriatic
Via Vitelleschi 25
(06) 6869668, fax (06) 6893552.
Open year-round. 32 rms 50-130,000 lire. V, AE, MC.
This unpretentious pensione is located near the Piazza del Risorgimento in the vicinity of Saint Peter's. The rooms are tidy and fairly modern; 26 have private baths, the rest share bathrooms. Television and air conditioning are available on request, for a supplemental fee. Breakfast is not served in the hotel.

Albergo Sole
Via del Biscione 76
(06) 6879446, fax (06) 6893787
Open year-round. 62 rms 70-140,000 lire. No cards.
With its pretty indoor garden and terraces, the Albergo Sole offers charm as well as affordable lodgings in the desirable Campo de' Fiori district. Anglophones with only rudimentary Italian will be pleased to note that the staff speaks English. The rooms are quite comfortable, but only half have private bathrooms. Breakfast is not served in the hotel.

Aldrovandi Palace

Via U. Aldrovandi 15
(06) 3223993, fax (06) 3221435

Open year-round. 18 stes 700,000 lire and up. 125 rms 300-500,000 lire. Restaurant. Conf. Pkg. All major cards.
In the very heart of the posh Parioli district, across from the Villa Borghese gardens, this hotel has all the elegance and luxury of a traditional patrician palazzo. It offers extensive grounds for strolling among venerable pines, an indoor solarium, a sauna, and stunning antique furnishings. The warm, comfortable guest rooms boast every amenity, from air conditioning to Jacuzzis to phones in the bathrooms. Charming service, and a first-rate restaurant, the Relais La Piscine (see *Restaurants*).

Alpi

Via Castelfidardo 84a
(06) 4441235, fax (06) 4441257
Open year-round. 34 rms 110-190,000 lire, bkfst incl. All major cards.
Equidistant from Via Veneto and the Termini station, the Alpi offers a respectable level of comfort and quiet. The service occasionally seems disorganized, but the staff is friendly.

Ambasciatori Palace
Via Vittorio Veneto 62
(06) 47493, fax (06) 4743601
Open year-round. 8 stes 450-600,000 lire. 103 rms 230-420,000 lire. Restaurant. Conf. Garage pkg. All major cards.
This beautiful establishment, one of the oldest on Via Veneto, is constantly being renovated and refined. In addition to the usual amenities (air conditioning, color TV...), safes were recently installed in the guest rooms, along with thick satin bedspreads, marble tiles in all the bathrooms, and Jacuzzis in the pricier rooms and suites. The grand entrance and lobby were just handsomely restored. The service is first-class, and the rates are pretty reasonable, considering the elegant address.

Atlante Star
Via Vitelleschi 34
(06) 6873233, fax (06) 6872300
Open year-round. 10 stes 520-2,250,000 lire.
70 rms 255-405,000 lire. Restaurant. Conf.
Garage pkg. All major cards.
From the moment one crosses the ornate
but somewhat narrow entrance of this
well-situated hotel (the roof garden offers
a fine view of Saint Peter's), it is clear that
lack of space is a problem. The rooms are
colorful, nicely equipped, and decorated
with an eye to detail, but they are not large.
Business travelers will appreciate the
hotel's office facilities and the convenient
free shuttle to and from Leonardo da Vinci
airport. Excellent restaurant, Les Étoiles
(see *Restaurants*).

 Barocco
Piazza Barberini 9
(06) 4872001, fax (06) 485994
Open year-round. 1 ste 550,000 lire. 27 rms
280-380,000 lire, bkfst incl. All major cards.
The extensively (and tastefully)
renovated Barocco boasts a convenient
and charming location on Piazza Barberini. The guest rooms are decorated
with cherrywood furniture and understated fabrics; the bathrooms are clad in
luxurious Trani marble. If you feel the urge
to splurge, book the fourth-floor suite,
which offers a breathtaking panoramic
view. Discreet, attentive service.

 Bernini Bristol
Piazza Barberini 23
(06) 4883051, fax (06) 4824266
Open year-round. 16 stes 600-800,000 lire.
110 rms 260-450,000 lire. Restaurant. Conf.
Garage pkg. All major cards.
This exceedingly plush establishment
was constructed to host newly wealthy families
on the Roman leg of their Grand Tour. The
slightly antiquated air of the lobby contrasts with the modernity of the fully
renovated guest rooms, which are bright,
spacious, and functional; the bathrooms
are lined with marble. Accommodations
on the top floor possess garden terraces
overlooking Piazza Barberini and its
famous fountain. Avoid, if you can, the
rooms on Via Barberini, which are not
perfectly quiet despite double glazing.
And make a point of visiting the Bristol's
cocktail bar to admire its superb antique
tapestries. Throughout the hotel, you can
count on deluxe Italian service.

Borromeo
Via Cavour 117
(06) 485856, fax (06) 4882541
Open year-round. 1 ste 300,000 lire and up. 28
rms 130-235,000 lire, bkfst incl. All major cards.
Strategically situated near the
Metropolitana and the Termini rail station,
the Borromeo is also close to the basilica
of Santa Maria Maggiore. This little three-
storey palazzo dates from 1850, and was
converted into a hotel in 1993. Rooms are
comfortable and pleasantly furnished; windows are double glazed for extra quiet.
Guests can relax in the elegant lounges after
partaking of the attractive breakfast buffet.

Campo de' Fiori
Via del Biscione 6
(06) 68806865, fax (06) 6876003
Open year-round. 27 rms 77-160,000 lire,
bkfst incl. All major cards (exc AE).
A rooftop terrace with a splendid view of
the old city is thoughtfully furnished with
deck chairs and little tables. True, you'll
have to climb six flights of stairs to enjoy it
(there is no elevator), but the panorama is
well worth the effort. At press time, only
nine of the pleasant rooms had private
baths, but plans are afoot to provide
modern plumbing in all of the accommodations. The picturesque Campo de'
Fiori market, open every morning, is just
around the corner.

Carriage
Via delle Carrozze 36
(06) 6793312, fax (06) 6788279
Open year-round. 24 rms 205-260,000 lire,
bkfst incl. All major cards.
Not far from Piazza di Spagna, this
charming hotel offers small, well kept, and
tastefully decorated guest rooms. The
lounges, too, are elegant and inviting.

Celio
Via Santi Quattro 35c
(06) 70495333, fax (06) 7096377
Open year-round. 10 rms 120-170,000 lire,
bkfst incl. All major cards.
Here is a tiny but most appealing hotel
close to the Colosseum. Guests benefit
from a tranquil atmosphere and rooms
equipped with air conditioning, satellite
television, minibar, and safe. Generous
breakfasts are served in the rooms at no
extra charge, and for your entertainment,
there are VCRs and a film rental library of
some 500 cassettes (150 in English).

Columbus

Via della Conciliazione 33
(06) 6865435, fax (06) 6864874
*Open year-round. 105 rms 185-245,000 lire,
bkfst incl. Restaurant. Pkg. All major cards.*
On the broad Via della Conciliazione
that stretches between the Tiber and Saint
Peter's, the Columbus occupies an imposing Quattrocento palace. The splendor of
that age is evident in the hotel's public
rooms, which boast ceiling frescoes,
marble columns, and walls hung with rich
velvet. The guest rooms are less grand but
pleasing just the same; every amenity is
provided. A garden and resident parking
are located in an enclosed courtyard.

Crowne Plaza Minerva

Piazza della Minerva 69
(06) 69941888, fax (06) 6794165
*Open year-round. 16 stes 800-1,400,000 lire.
118 rms 350-535,000 lire. Restaurant. Conf.
Pkg. All major cards.*
The colorful awning that greets guests at
the Crowne Plaza is the work of noted
architect Paolo Portoghesi. One of the
most prestigious links in the Holiday Inn
chain, the Crowne Plaza is lodged in a
historic palazzo dating from 1626, with a

Money Meltdown in the Forum

Talk about money burning a hole in
your pocket... Back in the days of the
Caesars, in the Basilica Emilia inside
the Roman Forum, the money
changers sorted their shiny lucre in the
shade of a long arcade. The bottom
fell out of the market when the Goths
swept in to sack Rome, in A.D. 410.
Like crazed floor traders, the defense-
less but fearless servants of Mammon
held out to the last moment. They
dashed away just as the invaders
began their pillaging, and in the
process dropped coins all over the
marble floor. When the flames of the
burning city spread to the basilica, the
tremendous heat melted the bronze
coins, which left gray-green marks on
the paving stones that are still visible
today.

spectacular terrace. As for the rooms, they
provide all the comfort and little extras of
a luxury hotel in addition to a wide array
of services.

Diana

Via Principe Amedeo 4
(06) 4827541, fax (06) 486998
*Open year-round. 2 stes 260,000 lire.
185 rms 155-210,000 lire, bkfst incl. Restaurant. Conf. All major cards.*
This spacious hotel near the Teatro dell'-
Opera and the Termini station was
remodeled in 1993. The lobby and public
rooms are attractively furnished, as are the
guest rooms, which still look spanking
new. The suites are equipped with Jacuzzis. In addition to a restaurant offering
special "diet" menus, there is a bar where
light snacks are served at any time of the
day.

Eden

Via Ludovisi 49
(06) 4743551, fax (06) 4821584
*Open year-round. 11 stes 1,100-
2,000,000 lire. 102 rms 390-590,000 lire.
Restaurant. Conf. All major cards.*
The Eden occupies a privileged site near
the Villa Borghese and Via Veneto.
Reopened in September 1994 after extensive renovations that had lasted well over
two years, the hotel now pampers guests
with every luxurious amenity. Precious antiques grace the public rooms, which have
been decorated with an admirable eye to
detail. And with a sure sense of refined
hospitality, the management has seen to it
that rooms are absolutely quiet (a rare trait
in Rome) and beautifully equipped.
What's more, bathrooms are sumptuous
and the service truly distinguished. Venture up to the terrace for an exceptional
view of the city and a fine meal at La
Terrazza (see *Restaurants*).

Excelsior

Via Vittorio Veneto 125
(06) 4708, fax (06) 4826205
*Open year-round. 45 stes 900-1,500,000 lire.
282 rms 350-540,000 lire. Restaurant. Conf.
Garage pkg. All major cards.*
Via Veneto was not much more than a
country road when this hotel opened in
1906; people used to come here to taste
the fresh farmhouse cheese made nearby.
Since then, the street has gone Hollywood, as the Excelsior's décor amply
demonstrates. The immense lobby is car-

peted in oceans of blue, with Venetian chandeliers, velvet chairs, and enormous bouquets placed on imposing, bronze-legged tables. Each guest room is decorated in a different style and, in the suites, every stick of furniture is of museum quality. Perfect comfort, stylish service. For an account of La Cupola, the hotel's fine dining room, see *Restaurants*.

 ### Forum
Via Tor de' Conti 25-30
(06) 6792446, fax (06) 6786479
Open year-round. 6 stes: prices on request. 75 rms 260-385,000 lire, bkfst incl. Restaurant. Pkg. All major cards.
Its exceptional location—in a medieval tower amid the Fori Imperiali—terrace garden, plush furnishings, numerous amenities, and affable service all justify the high prices charged at this commendable establishment.

 ### Genova
Via Cavour 33
(06) 476951, fax (06) 4827580
Open year-round. 91 rms 243-346,000 lire, bkfst incl. All major cards.
Recently remodeled in an understated, pleasing style, the Genova is a reliable address in this busy neighborhood near the Termini station. The air-conditioned rooms are generally comfortable, but those overlooking Via Cavour are somewhat noisy—and in Rome, street noise winds down late and starts up early.

Giulio Cesare
Via degli Scipioni 287
(06) 3210751, fax (06) 3211736
Open year-round. 90 rms 280-380,000 lire. Conf. Pkg. All major cards.
Formerly an aristocratic residence and now a first-class hotel, the Giulio Cesare stands across from Piazza del Popolo on the far side of the Tiber. Manager Eugenio Pandolfi has taken enormous pains with the decoration of this establishment, placing superb Persian carpets and antique furniture (handsome Louis XVI consoles and writing desks, for example) in all the public rooms, halls, and lobby. The guest rooms are exceptionally comfortable and done up in different styles, with attractive marble bathrooms and all the small details and personal touches that only caring, professional management can provide.

The garden/bar is a delightful spot in fine weather.

 ### Le Grand Hotel
Via Vittorio Emanuele Orlando 3
(06) 4709, fax (06) 4747307
Open year-round. 36 stes 800-1,500,000 lire. 134 rms 320-520,000 lire. Restaurant. Conf. Garage pkg. All major cards.
As imposing as an embassy, this hundred-year-old edifice, now a Ciga hotel, is a great favorite with members of the diplomatic corps and with Italian and foreign government officials. The Grand Hotel is also the preferred residence of heads of state, princes, and potentates sojourning in Rome. The austerely monumental lobby, with its marble columns, Venetian chandeliers, high, frescoed ceilings, and rich carpets, livens up at teatime when waiters pass around trays of sandwiches to the genteel strains of harp music. The guest rooms are exceedingly luxurious. The place is positively thick with marble, bronze, expensive bibelots, paintings, and antiques. A seriously posh clientele frequents the hotel's three cocktail bars and gourmet dining room, Le Restaurant del Grand Hotel (see *Restaurants*).

Gregoriana
Via Gregoriana 18
(06) 6797988, fax (06) 6784258
Open year-round. 19 rms 180-280,000 lire, bkfst incl. All major cards.
The Gregoriana occupies a seventeenth-century building that was once a convent, in a quaint street behind Trinità del Monte. Inveterate shoppers favor this location for its convenient access to the alluring boutiques of Via Frattina, Via Condotti, and Via Borgognona; the rest of us are drawn by its proximity to the verdant grounds of Villa Medici and Villa Borghese. Some of the guest rooms boast small terraces; all the accommodations are intimate and attractive. Breakfast is served in the rooms at no extra charge.

 ### Hassler
Piazza Trinità dei Monti 6
(06) 6782651, fax (06) 6789991
Open year-round. 15 stes: prices on request. 85 rms 400-620,000 lire. Restaurant. Conf. Garage pkg. V, AE, MC.
Poised atop the Spanish Steps, the Hassler enjoys a breathtaking view of

Rome—its rooftops, its flowery terraces, the Pincio gardens, the Villa Borghese and, far below, Piazza di Spagna. This century-old hotel is an oasis of hushed, aristocratic luxury at the heart of Rome's sightseeing district. The lobby, guest rooms, and princely penthouse suite are decorated with Old Master paintings, Persian rugs, Venetian mirrors, and embroidered linens. The hotel's Rooftop restaurant serves Sunday brunch as well as lunch and dinner, and the Hassler bar is a prime spot for cocktail-hour people-watching.

D'Inghilterra
Via Bocca di Leone 14
(06) 69981, fax (06) 69922243
Open year-round. 21 stes 573-916,000 lire. 84 rms 300-480,000 lire. Restaurant. Conf. V, AE, DC, MC.

The ghosts of Franz Liszt, Mark Twain, Hans Christian Andersen, and Ernest Hemingway still linger in this old palazzo, a hotel since 1850. The antique furnishings and bibelots lend a unique charm and intimacy to this elegant establishment. All the rooms are decorated in different styles, and the suites afford enchanting views of the Piazza di Spagna neighborhood. Among the public rooms, the yellow salon is particularly splendid, with its collection of Neapolitan gouaches; the Lounge del Roman Garden restaurant (see *Restaurants*) features engaging trompe l'oeil murals. The romantic atmosphere that reigns here is not broken by the chattering of large parties of sightseers, for groups are not accepted.

Locarno
Via della Penna 22
(06) 3610841, fax (06) 3215249
Open year-round. 1 ste 280,000 lire and up. 37 rms 150-230,000 lire, bkfst incl. Conf. All major cards.

Housed in a handsome Art Deco building just behind Piazza del Popolo, the Locarno has long been a favorite with actors, artists, and intellectuals. The comfortable lounges (and some of the rooms) are decorated with furniture from the Twenties and Thirties. In winter, guests may gather around a cozy fireplace; in fine weather, the splendid terrace affords a romantic view of Rome's rooftops. This warm, welcoming establishment also boasts a quiet little garden where breakfast may be served. The hotel bar is open from 6:30am to midnight; bicycles are available to guests for freewheeling tours of the city.

Lord Byron
Via Giuseppe De Notaris 5
(06) 3220404, fax (06) 3220405
Open year-round. 9 stes: prices on request. 29 rms 300-540,000 lire. Restaurant. Conf. Garage pkg. All major cards.

On an almost bucolic little street in the elegant Parioli district, amid patrician dwellings, private villas, and gardens, stands one of Rome's most tranquil hotels. Downstairs in the lobby and public rooms, the décor is pure 1930s. The guest rooms and suites are spacious and quite comfortable, but the furnishings do not always display flawless taste. Neither the reception nor the service is notable for its warmth. Our verdict: the Lord Byron is good, even very good, but it could be better. It is a member of the Relais et Châteaux and The Leading Hotels of the World associations. For a review of the hotel's excellent Relais Le Jardin restaurant, see *Restaurants*.

Majestic
Via Veneto 50
(06) 486841, fax (06) 4880984
Open year-round. 6 stes: prices on request. 94 rms 380-580,000 lire, bkfst incl. Restaurant. Conf. All major cards.

Frank Sinatra, Luciano Pavarotti, Placido Domingo have all signed the Majestic's guest register. This palatial hotel on Via Veneto reopened in the early 1990s after a radical remodeling. Today, it sports an eccentric décor that mixes rare antiques with emphatically patterned fabrics that some would call "colorful"—and others might qualify as "loud." The commodious guest rooms are furnished in various styles, but all the bathrooms are clad in white Carrara marble and offer Jacuzzis in the tubs. The Majestic's distinctive personality and exclusive ambience account for the high prices.

Margutta
Via Laurina 34
(06) 3223674, fax (06) 3200395
Open year-round. 21 rms 134,000 lire, bkfst incl. All major cards.

The Margutta is a small hotel that offers very good value, given its convenient location, just off the busy Via del Corso between Piazza del Popolo and Piazza di Spagna. The guest rooms are decorated with dark wood furniture and wrought-iron beds; though small, the bathrooms are well equipped (there's a hairdryer in each). A cordial staff provides attentive service.

🏠 Mozart
Via dei Greci 23
(06) 69940041, fax (06) 6784271
Open year-round. 31 rms 175-215,000 lire, bkfst incl. All major cards.
The Mozart's accommodations are a trifle small, but they are cozy and individually decorated. The hotel's ideal location—in a pedestrian zone between Piazza del Popolo and Piazza di Spagna—makes this an address worth noting. The antique dealers of Via del Babuino and many fashionable boutiques are close at hand. You can count on courteous service and a friendly atmosphere.

🏠 Piazza di Spagna
Via Mario de' Fiori 61
(06) 6793061, fax (06) 6790654
Open year-round. 16 rms 120-220,000 lire. All major cards.
Signora Cinzia has been looking after her guests for well over 30 years now. She now presides over newly refurbished (and thus slightly more pricey) premises, well situated in a picturesque neighborhood just a few steps from Piazza di Spagna and Rome's best shopping.

🏠 Pincio
Via Capo le Case 50
(06) 6790758, fax (06) 6791233
Open year-round. 16 rms 120-220,000 lire, bkfst incl. All major cards (exc DC).
This modest hotel is a fairly inexpensive place to stay near Piazza di Spagna. The rooms, spread out over four floors, are simple and strictly functional, with tired-looking furnishings. Yet the rooftop terrace, where breakfast is served in fine weather, is a definite asset.

🏠 Regno
Via del Corso 330
(06) 6792119, fax (06) 6789239
Open year-round. 25 rms 170-250,000 lire, bkfst incl. All major cards.
With its inviting lounges and spacious rooms decorated with walnut furniture and muted blue-gray fabrics, the Regno is a pleasant, comfortable headquarters for visitors to the Eternal City. Guests wake up to an American-style buffet breakfast, and may relax in the sun-drenched roof garden–solarium.

🏠 La Residenza
Via Emilia 22-24
(06) 4880789, fax (06) 485721
Open year-round. 7 junior stes 280,000 lire. 21 rms 120-248,000 lire, bkfst incl. V, MC.
This tasteful little dwelling with aristocratic airs provides comfortable accommodations that are reasonably priced, considering the posh address. While the reading rooms and lounges are furnished in a warm, welcoming fashion, a little redecorating wouldn't hurt the guest rooms. Buffet breakfast; hospitable staff.

🏠 Rome Cavalieri Hilton
Via A. Cadlolo 101
(06) 35091, fax (06) 35092241
Open year-round. 16 stes 1,000-2,400,000 lire. 360 rms 330-620,000 lire. Restaurant. Conf. Pool. Tennis. Garage pkg. All major cards.
This mammoth hotel complex stretches out over fifteen acres atop Monte Mario, with a stupendous view of Rome. Among other amenities, the Hilton offers two tennis courts, a jogging track, a marvelous pool and solarium, Turkish baths, a sauna, and a massage service. The recently renovated guest rooms all have balconies and marble bathrooms. Room service is available around the clock, and there is an attractive cocktail lounge and piano bar near the hotel's main entrance. The Giardino dell'Uliveto restaurant is a pleasant spot for an aperitivo or lunch.

Pilferage in the Pantheon

A real wolf in Good Shepherd's clothing was Pope Urban VIII (Maffeo Barberini). He heisted the bronze from the Pantheon's ceiling, melted itdown, recast part as cannons for the papal fortress at Castel Sant'-Angelo, and used the rest for the famed *baldacchino*, or canopy, at Saint Peter's. Even today, in the face of vandalism from on high, Italians quote the Latin saying, *"Quod non fecerunt barbari, fecerunt Barberini"* ("What the barbarians didn't swipe, the Barberini clan did").

Sant'Anselmo ♨♠

Piazza Sant'Anselmo 2
(06) 5783214, fax (06) 5783604
*Open year-round. 46 rms 100-186,000 lire,
bkfst incl. All major cards.*

Here in a lovely (and quiet!) residential neighborhood on the Aventino, the Sant'-Anselmo occupies a tranquil piazzetta. The hotel offers nicely furnished rooms, two of which have private terraces. On fine days, breakfast is served in the garden planted with orange trees.

Scalinata di Spagna

Piazza Trinità dei Monti 17
(06) 6793006, fax (06) 69940598
*Open year-round. 16 rms 200-350,000 lire.
All major cards.*

This minuscule hotel perched atop the Spanish Steps offers the same splendid view as the palatial Hassler but at a considerably lower cost. A warm, romantic atmosphere prevails, and though it is no longer a pensione in the classic sense, the Scalinata remains so popular that its comfortable, old-fashioned rooms (equipped with doll-sized bathrooms, minibars, and air conditioning) must be reserved far in advance for the high season. While breakfasting on the garden terrace, residents can drink in a view of Roman rooftops and Piazza di Spagna.

Senato

Piazza della Rotonda 73
(06) 6793231, fax (06) 69940297
*Open year-round. 51 rms 166-220,000 lire,
bkfst incl. All major cards.*

The Senato is a venerable establishment enviably located directly across from the Pantheon. It was the favorite of Sartre and Simone de Beauvoir, who appreciated the charm of the place and its comfortable and spacious rooms. The lobby and public rooms are now freshly refurbished.

Del Sole al Pantheon

Piazza della Rotonda 63
(06) 6780441, fax (06) 69940689
*Open year-round. 3 stes: prices on request.
26 rms 300-420,000 lire, bkfst incl. All major
cards.*

The Renaissance poet Lodovico Ariosto and Italian operatic composer Pietro Mascagni once lived—at different times—in this handsome Renaissance edifice, which was recently remodeled in a most intelligent manner. The hand-decorated coffered ceilings have been preserved, while welcome amenities have been added: there are Jacuzzis in all the rooms and double glazing in the windows. A superb view of the Pantheon and a truly hospitable staff make this a fine place to stay in the very heart of Rome.

Teatro di Pompeo

Largo del Pallaro 8
(06) 68300170, fax (06) 68805531
*Open year-round. 12 rms 190-240,000 lire,
bkfst incl. Conf. All major cards.*

The name on the sign alludes to the ruins of a Roman theater dating from 55 B.C., upon which the hotel stands. Archaeological vestiges excavated from the site are on view in the breakfast room. Guest rooms are cozy, with wooden beams and simple décor; the double-glazed windows ensure peaceful nights. A courteous staff delivers cheerful service. And note the hotel's desirable location, between Campo de' Fiori and Piazza Navona.

Della Torre Argentina

Corso Vittorio Emanuele 102
(06) 68333886, fax (06) 68801641
*Open year-round. 52 rms 144-250,000 lire,
bkfst incl. Conf. All major cards.*

Housed in a late-eighteenth-century palazzo, this hotel was fully renovated a few years back and boasts a first-rate location near Largo Argentina. The guest rooms and lounges are nicely kept, and the personnel provides service with a smile.

Turner

Via Nomentana 29
(06) 8541716, fax (06) 8543107
*Open year-round. 37 rms 195-250,000 lire,
bkfst incl. All major cards.*

The English painter, William Turner, would surely be pleased by the hotel that bears his name, set in the Nomentano district just beyond Porta Pia. Reproductions of the artist's works are everywhere present of course, but there are also (genuine) antique furnishings, marble and stucco adornments in the lounges and lobby, and fine linens in the individually decorated guest rooms. All these details contribute to a charming atmosphere. Residents are treated to delicious fresh pastries at breakfast.

♨♠
This symbol indicates hotels that offer an exceptional degree of peace and quiet.

♠♠ Venezia
Via Varese 18
(06) 4457101, fax (06) 4957687
Open year-round. 61 rms 130-205,000 lire, bkfst incl. All major cards.
Family-style hospitality prevails in this tidy, tastefully decorated hotel. Charming antiques, Murano lamps, eighteenth-century candelabra, and precious bibelots delight the eye at every turn. Though not large, the guest rooms are comfortable and prettily furnished, with double-glazed windows. Breakfast consists of a generous American-style buffet.

♠♠ Villa Florence   ♣♥
Via Nomentana 28
(06) 4402966/4402992, fax (06) 4402709

Three Naked Nymphettes

On the nob of the Aventine Hill stands the church of San Saba. The spot is known largely as a lover's lane, because of its splendid views. But the church is graced by several nuggets of art worth a look-see, among them the thirteenth-century *cosmati* pavement of inlaid marble. Yet what really catches our eye is the cycle of frescoes on the left side of the church that tells the story of the life of Saint Nicolas of Bari. One panel shows—oh my—three nude girls. And—gads—they're in bed together! But hold on, there's an explanation. No moral turpitude after all. The girls' stone-broke father can't afford to give his daughters a dowry, so no one will marry them; they're faced with lives of sure perdition. Saint Nicolas to the rescue! There he is, leaning in the window. No, he's not a Peeping Tom—he's leaving a sack of gold coins for the father. For the dowry, of course.

Open year-round. 32 rms 190-240,000 lire, bkfst incl. Pkg. All major cards.
Guests may relax in the quiet garden or attractive public rooms of this turn-of-the-century palazzetto in the Nomentano district. The best rooms are those in the central building, decorated in an appealing nostalgic style. (One is graced with a Liberty-style stained-glass window and heavy walnut doors.) Other accommodations are housed in little cottages and have considerably less cachet. All the rooms, however, offer many amenities including television, minibar, and air conditioning.

♠♠ Villa Glori
Viale del Vignola 28
(06) 3227658, fax (06) 3219495
Open year-round. 38 rms 190-259,000 lire, bkfst incl. All major cards.
Quiet surroundings and tasteful, modern furnishings distinguish this hotel. The Villa Glori occupies an imposingly aristocratic dwelling in the Flaminio district, a short walk from Piazza del Popolo and Rome's historic center.

♠ Villa delle Rose
Via Vicenza 5
(06) 4451788, fax (06) 4451639
Open year-round. 37 rms 130-185,000 lire, bkfst incl. All major cards.
A period villa hard by the Termini station, with a pocket-sized garden and lounges that wear their age gracefully. Though individually decorated, the guest rooms are less charming—impersonal, really. Four of them are air conditioned.

♠ Villa San Pio   ♣♥
Via Sant'Anselmo 19
(06) 5783214, fax (06) 5783604
Open year-round. 59 rms 100-186,000 lire, bkfst incl. All major cards.
Villa San Pio, an annex of the nearby hotel Sant'Anselmo (see above), provides quiet, comfortable accommodations in the capital. Guest rooms are uniformly pleasant, and the garden is a lovely spot for a sunny breakfast.

---

*We're always happy to hear about **your discoveries** and receive **your comments** on ours. We want to give your letters the attention they deserve, so when you write to Gault Millau, please state clearly what you liked or disliked. Be concise but convincing, and take the time to argue your point.*

227

APARTMENT HOTELS

Some fortunate travelers—business people, actors, models, artists, those on sabbatical—have occasion to require an urban home base for a month or more in Italy. Hotel rooms can become impersonal and a bit cramped for extended stays, and ordinary home rentals usually require a long-term lease agreement. Enter the apartment hotel (or residence, as the Italians say), full-service accommodations that are perfect for longer stays. They combine the space and domestic comfort of an apartment with such features as maid service, kitchen facilities, and sometimes even concierge services.

Aldrovandi
Via Aldrovandi 11
(06) 3221430,
fax (06) 3222181
Studios & 2-rm apts 2,500-5,000,000 lire per month.

Minutes from Via Veneto, in an elegant district of patrician villas and luxuriant gardens, this vast residence occupies a fine nineteenth-century palazzo. The apartments are furnished with an eye to the functional, but charming details have not been neglected; the overall impression is one of warmth and comfort. A pool and a restaurant number among the Aldrovandi's luxurious facilities. Alas, there is no parking garage.

Di Ripetta
Via di Ripetta 231
(06) 69921088, fax (06) 3203959
Studios, 2- & 3-rm apts 3,200-6,500,000 lire per month (plus tax).

Set smack in the middle of the perpetual gaiety and near-chaos of Piazza del Popolo, these full-service apartments are housed in a seventeenth-century palazzo. A delicious atmosphere of quietude emanates from the garden courtyard at the center of the structure and from the luminous arcades that surround it. As for the apartments, they are commodious and tastefully decorated, with color TVs and air conditioning. Residents may relax in the roof garden or the pleasant cocktail bar downstairs. A garage and a message service are available as well.

Palazzo al Velabro
Via del Velabro 16
(06) 6792758, fax (06) 6793790
34 2- to 5-bed apts 5,268-10,506,000 lire per month.

At the foot of the Palatine Hill stands this ancient palazzo, which was completely remodeled and modernized to house 34 full-service apartments. It is a *residence* of rare elegance, surrounded by fascinating landmarks and huge gardens in one of Rome's most peaceful and historic areas. Inside, an air of discreet efficiency reigns. The bright, spacious apartments afford splendid views, and pains have been taken to create a pleasant décor and well-designed kitchens and baths.

Brotherhood of the Last Wish

The church of San Giovanni Decollato—Saint John the Beheaded—used to be the headquarters of the Confraternity of Mercy, a brotherhood charged with the preparation and postmortem service of condemned criminals on death row. You can visit their small museum in the church. It contains the tools of their trade: baskets for severed heads, lamps for the night watch of the condemned, knives used to cut the hangman's rope, paper and pens for copying down last wishes, wills, and testaments. Fortunately, in Italy today there is no longer a need for the brotherhood to perform this thankless task.

Nightlife

CONTENTS

BARS

Bar della Pace
Via della Pace 3 - (06) 6861216
Open noon-3am. Closed Mon.

Just around the corner from Piazza Navona's effervescent nightlife, the Bar della Pace stands in a superb Renaissance enclave that features a small jewel of a church, Santa Maria della Pace (home to Raphael's *Sybils* and a cloister designed by Bramante). This turn-of-the-century bar, with its marble, wood, and mirror décor, is chic and utterly sedate by day, but at night, along with Bramante and the Bar del Fico, it forms part of Rome's Golden Triangle, where the party goes on until the wee hours. Business types come in for an early-evening aperitivo, artists and intellectuals drop by after 10pm, and midnight brings the local versions of very young rockers.

Bar del Fico
Piazza del Fico 27 - (06) 6865205
Open 8pm-2am. Closed Sun.

Restored and reopened a few months back, after a long eclipse this tiny bar is aiming to reclaim its position on Rome's nightlife circuit. Young hipsters pile in to listen or dance to the background music; tables set out on the piazza accommodate the weekend spillover.

La Bevitoria
Piazza Navona 72 - (06) 68801022
Open 1pm-2am. Closed Sun.

After touring the high-voltage venues on Via della Pace, head for La Bevitoria, a perfect place to wind down with a quiet nightcap. A wood-paneled wine bar with a beamed ceiling and a fascinating display of bottles, it provides a sophisticated setting conducive to conversation. It's not a bad choice either for a sunlit aperitivo: as you sip, you can soak up the atmosphere of one of the world's most beautiful squares.

Bramante
Via della Pace 25 - (06) 68803916
Open 5pm-2am. Closed Wed.

Neighbor and rival of the Bar della Pace, just across the street. Bramante boasts bright, spacious premises with a clever *trompe-l'œil* mural that dominates the seating area. The crowd is definitely eclectic: while La Pace caters to habitués, this spot draws young fun seekers out to party on a Saturday night. It's a lively scene that warrants a look-in.

Harry's Bar
Via Veneto 150 - (06) 4883117
Open 11am-1am. Closed Sun.

Harry's Bar is back, after a two-year absence from the Via Veneto scene. The interior is sprucer than ever, decked out in gleaming wood paneling and antique mirrors, with a convivial bar manned by Marco Graziosi, the young and charming mixmeister. Cocktails for two (accompanied, on occasion, by live piano music), a prandial aperitivo, mid-morning coffee, or tea on the outdoor terrace are just a few of the delightful options. Lunch and dinner are served as well (noon to 3pm and 7:30 to 11pm), backed up by a worthwhile wine list.

Hemingway

Piazza delle Coppelle 46 - (06) 6864490
Open 10pm-3am. Closed Tue.

Hemingway's is a classic in the annals of Roman high-life, a reputation it richly deserves. Small and swank, it sports luxurious carpets, inviting sofas, low lights, and a saloon-style bar where patrons nurse drinks and chat with friends. Both selective and democratic in its admissions policy, Hemingway's is the sort of bar where established show-biz celebrities can rub shoulders with young up-and-comers and elegant unknowns.

Jonathan's Angels

Via della Fossa 16 - (06) 6893426
Open 1pm-2am. Closed Mon.

Colorful, that's how we'd describe this place—and the crowd that hangs out here! Kitsch? You bet: angels and saints' statues fill the two rooms, and an oddball assortment of souvenirs festoons the frescoed walls. Join the (very) young hipsters for a drink in room number one, then head back to room two for dancing. The scene is upbeat, fun, and flamboyant. Another surprise awaits you in the restrooms, which are—shall we say?—unique! Be sure to duck in for a pee...k.

Radio Londra

Via Monte Testaccio 65b - (06) 5750044
Open 9pm-3am. Closed Mon. Cover charge: 5,000 lire.

The old Testaccio district, once solidly working class, is Rome's current entertainment mecca: live-music venues, trendy restaurants, cinemas, and theaters are sprouting like *funghi* after the rain. A recent arrival is Radio Londra, a—literally—cavernous disco/bar carved out of the hillside. When we say this place is a showcase for hard rock, we don't just mean the music! The short menu offers salads, hamburgers, and a few vegetarian dishes to nibble while you listen.

Selarum

Via dei Fienaroli 12 - (06) 5806587
Open 9pm-1am. Closed mid Oct-Apr.

This delightful garden in the heart of Trastevere is just the right place to while away a summer evening, to the strains of (often live) Brazilian music. To go with the cool sounds, even cooler refreshments:

ice cream, colorful cocktails, spritzy Spumante.

Tartarughino

Via della Scrofa 2 - (06) 6864131
Open 9:30pm-3:30am. Closed Sun.

Rome's high-society and high-finance sets like to hobnob at this classy piano bar. Jackets and ties are obligatory for any male who wishes to while away a long, relaxing evening at the club's restaurant (the food is classic Italian; count on a tab of 90,000 lire with wine) or in the bar, where a pianist offers renditions of tunes from the 1950s to today.

Victoria House

Via Gesù e Maria 18 - (06) 3201698
Open 6pm-1am (Sun 5pm-midnight). Closed Mon.

Soft lighting and velvet-lined walls set the cozy mood at Victoria House, the bar best known for having introduced Romans to the ritual of "Happy Hour" (6pm to 9pm, Saturdays and Sundays until 8pm). English is spoken here by the friendly young staff, and by many of the patrons as well, who stop in after work or a shopping spree. Beer is the beverage of choice, with a wide selection of premium brands to choose

A Theatrical Piazza and an Imaginary Dome

The graceful Rococo Piazza Sant'-Ignazio, designed in 1727 by Raguzzini, opens like the wings of a theater. In the middle of this feat of joyous architecture stands Maderno's solemn church (1650) of Sant'Ignazio di Loyola. Inside is a masterwork of *trompe l'œil*. The grand dome far above the main altar isn't a dome at all but a brilliant optical trick, a play of perspective painted on a flat surface. Even the vault's fine fresco, also the work of artist Andrea Pozzo, is a study in false perspective—it portrays Saint Ignatius, the founder of the Jesuits, stepping into Paradise.

from, either on tap or in bottles; the food is decidedly English. Victoria House stands on a street that links Via del Corso to Via Babuino, a district chockablock with antique shops and artisans' ateliers, where Anglo-Saxons seem to feel particularly at home. Not far from here are the Keats and Shelley House and Byron's former residence.

CABARETS

Il Puff

Via Zanazzo 4 - (06) 5810721
Open 8:30pm-12:30am. Closed Mon. Cover charge: 34,000 lire (drink incl).
Popular singer Lando Fiorini often sings a traditional repertory of Roman songs in the club's piano bar. Dinner is served in the attractive dining room from 8:30pm (about 50,000 lire buys you dinner and wine), and the show starts at 10:30pm.

Salone Margherita

Via Due Macelli 73 - (06) 6798269
Open 9:30pm-midnight. Closed Sun. Cover charge: 48,000 lire (drink & spaghetti at intermission incl).
This classic Roman cabaret is the realm of Oreste Lionello, a noted comic performer. If your Italian is good, this place is worth a try. Even if your vocabulary is limited to *ciao* and *arrivederci*, you can still have a drink and indulge in some amateur sociology while you check out the audience.

DISCOS

Alien

Via Velletri 13 - (06) 8412212
Open 11:30pm-4am. Closed Mon. Cover charge: 30,000 lire (Tue-Thu & Sun, drink incl); 35,000 lire (Fri-Sat, drink incl).
The décor is classic disco: ambient dimness punctuated by psychedelic lighting. Inspired by Ridley Scott's sci-fi thriller, Alien attracts a youngish crew (22 to 40, we'd say) sprinkled with show-biz personalities. The elite have a private room at their disposal; the rank and file congregate at three bars and on two dance floors, the smaller of which is reserved for rock, with

a preference for sounds from the '70s and '80s.

Big Bang & Tatum

Entrance to Big Bang disco:
Via Schiaparelli 31 - (06) 3221251
Open 11pm-3am. Closed Sun-Mon. Cover charge: 30,000 lire (Tue-Thu, drink incl); 35,000 lire (Fri-Sun, drink incl).
Entrance to Tatum restaurant and disco/bar:
Via Luciani 52 - (06) 3221251
Open noon-4pm & 8pm-4am. Closed Mon. Cover charge: 25,000 lire (Tue-Thu, drink incl); 30,000 lire (Fri-Sun, drink incl).
Like most of the city's top clubs, this one offers several entertainment options: a disco for night owls with happy feet, and a new disco/bar called Tatum, where a lower decibel-level makes it possible to chat over cocktails. Tatum also houses a restaurant that serves an inexpensive menu (12,000 lire) for lunch and dinner, as well as late-night pizzas to re-stoke weary dancers.

Divina

Via Romagnosi 11a - (06) 3611348
Open 11pm-4am. Closed Sun. Cover charge: 30,000 lire (drink incl).
Relax on the comfortable red sofas of Divina's intimate bar while Enrico Giarretta accompanies singer Franco Califano on the piano—it's a surefire recipe for a romantic evening in Rome. Divina also doubles as a disco, favored by an ebullient crowd in their mid-20s to mid-30s. Theme evenings and special events keep things interesting.

Follia

Via Ovidio 17 - (06) 68308435
Open 10:30pm-4am. Closed Mon. Cover charge: 20,000 lire (Tue-Thu, drink incl); 35,000 lire (Sat-Sun, drink incl).
Directed by the dynamic duo of Flamini and Lofaro (recognized by aficionados as "the guiding lights of Roman nightlife"), Follia draws the 20 to 30 set. A saxophone riff invites clubbers to step up to a platform covered with transparent tiles, which glitter underfoot while dancers move to the music. In the piano bar, people listen (and dance) to popular Italian tunes. The atmosphere is bright, light, and laid-back.

Some establishments change their **closing times** *without warning. It is always wise to check in advance.*

Gilda

Via Mario de' Fiori 97 - (06) 6784838
Open 11pm-4am. Closed Mon. Cover charge: 30,000 lire (Sun, Tue-Wed, drink incl); 35,000 lire (Thu, drink incl); 40,000 lire (Fri-Sat, drink incl).
Dedicated to Rita Hayworth, whose huge portrait gazes down glamorously at the club's denizens, Gilda is home to Rome's current "Dolce Vita" set. Actors, singers, and other show-biz types, athletes, and artists from Italy and abroad make up the mix; lots of politicians turn up here too—they're not afraid to strut their stuff on the dance floor, to underground and disco sounds. *Trompe-l'œil* palm trees and waterlilies highlight the "tropical garden" décor, which also features comfy sofas and a couple of bars. In the Gilda Swing piano bar, Italian and international hits are performed live; one night a week is devoted to salsa and merengue—Gilda would surely have approved!

Jackie O'

Via Boncompagni 11 - (06) 4885457
Open daily 9pm-4am. Cover charge: 20-40,000 lire (drink incl).
Jackie O' is a successful disco that carved out its niche in the '70s, when Via Veneto was an international nightlife mecca. Princess Margaret recently hosted a party here, a sure sign that Jackie O' remains a stalwart on Rome's nocturnal circuit—it may not be the hippest spot in town, but Jackie O' is a class act. The club's restaurant opens at 9pm, and there is live music in the piano bar.

New Open Gate

Via San Nicola da Tolentino 4 - (06) 4824464
Open 11pm-4am. Closed Mon, Tue, Wed. Cover charge: 30,000 lire (drink incl).
Note that this is indeed an "all-New" Open Gate: the old one, a familiar Roman nightspot, has undergone a total metamorphosis under the artistic direction of Spaniard Paola Cuervo. She is the driving force behind the *movida* which has lately revitalized Rome's club scene. A rudimentary décor of weathered iron and glass houses two distinct environments: the larger dance floor is dedicated to garage and tribal rhythms, the smaller to acid jazz, funk, and soul. An "alternative" club, the New Open Gate is a showcase for Rome's more extravagant nocturnal fauna.

Notorius

Via San Nicola da Tolentino 22 - (06) 4746888
Open midnight-4am. Closed Tue. Cover charge: 40,000 lire (Fri & Sat, drink incl); 20,000 lire (Sun, Mon, Wed, Thu) per drink at bar, 35,000 lire for table service.
One of the hottest clubs of the '80s, Notorius has survived in the far more difficult circumstances of the '90s, maintaining its rep as a favorite with Rome's fashionable set.

Le Stelle

Via Beccaria 22 - (06) 3611240
Open 10:30pm-3am. Closed Mon. Cover charge: 30,000 lire (drink incl); 35,000 lire (Sat, drink incl).
Still swinging after all these years... Le Stelle draws a well-bred, well-dressed, well-heeled crew of youthful dandies and stunning young women, who dance, joke, and drink till dawn in this noisy, densely crowded club.

LIVE ENTERTAINMENT

Akab

Via di Monte Testaccio 69 - (06) 57300309
Open 10pm-4am. Closed Mon. Cover charge: 15,000 lire (Tue-Thu, drink incl); 20,000 lire (Fri-Sun, drink not incl).
A live-music venue that is also a disco-bar, Akab owes its growing success to an eclectic programming mix. On a given night, the bill might feature excellent acid jazz, funk, soul, or reggae rhythms. This trendy Monte Testaccio spot is where Rome's young hipsters come to hear what's cool and what's hot.

Alexanderplatz

Via Ostia 9 - (06) 3729398
Open 9pm-2am. Closed Sun. Cover charge: 12,000 lire.
Rome's one and only club devoted exclusively to live jazz performed by top musicians. It's an intimate (just 130 seats), inviting room that has hosted the likes of saxophonist Harold Ashby and the Swing-

ing Ladies. If you like, as you listen you can also dine by candlelight (35-40,000 lire).

Alpheus
Via del Commercio 36-38 - (06) 5747826
Open 10pm-3am. Closed Mon. Cover charge: 10-30,000 lire.
Never a dull moment at Alpheus, a multifaceted venue that offers a wide range of live entertainment. Four different shows are presented each night in the club's three rooms. The evening kicks off with cabaret or live bands playing soul, Latino, ethnic, jazz, or New Age sounds. Later on, the two larger rooms turn into a disco, while the smaller space hosts another live music performance. Clubbers wander at will from one section to another, sampling from all the options. Each space has a separate bar, and out in the garden, the Pizzeria Alpheus serves snacks until 3am.

Big Mama
Vicolo San Francesco a Ripa 18-(06) 5812551
Open daily 10pm-2am. Cover charge: 10-35,000 lire.
Big Mama's specialty is concerts by established bands, but the club is also known as a place to discover the best young up-and-coming jazz and blues acts.

Caffè Latino
Via del Monte Testaccio 96 - (06) 5744020
Open 10pm-4am. Closed Mon, Aug-mid Oct. Cover charge: 20,000 lire.
In the late '80s Caffè Latino was one of the first live-music venues to put down stakes in the Testaccio district. Ever since, it has attracted a growing number of fans who crowd in to hear blues, jazz, or hip-hop bands that hail from all over the world. After the performance you can dance in room number two, or sit down with a drink in the comfortable bar.

Fonclea
Via Crescenzio 82a - (06) 6896302
Open daily 8pm-2am. Cover charge: 10,000 lire.
Once you've stepped down into what looks like an uncomfortable basement jazz joint, you'll be pleasantly surprised to see that it's really a simple, solid, unpretentious

pub. The atmosphere is lively, the menu offers appetizing little snacks, and the audience looks like a Benetton commercial: all ages, all colors. In a small room off to the side, live bands play rock, soul, R&B, or jazz—the program changes regularly.

Locale
Vicolo del Fico 3 - (06) 6879075
Open 10:30pm-3am. Closed Mon.
A new favorite with the young crowd that gravitates around the Bar della Pace, Jonathan's, and the Bar del Fico (see above). There's always a line outside the Locale, which presents live bands nightly. The music is the kind that keeps kids dancing: country, blues, soul, and funk acts are featured. And there are two bar/lounges for relaxing with a drink between sets.

Palladium
Piazza Bartolomeo Romano 11 - (06) 5110203
Open 9pm-2am when concerts are scheduled. Closed summer. Cover charge: 20-35,000 lire.
The Palladium is the most exciting addition to Rome's club scene in years. It's the brainchild of six music-loving chums, who transformed a splendid old theater from the 1920s into a live-music venue inspired by similar spots in London and New York. The Palladium books name acts—jazzman Lyle Mays, Duran Duran, rai master Cheb Khaled, acid-jazz bands Incognito and Galliano—as well as interesting local talent, like Avion Travel. Saturday nights are devoted to rock and dance music.

Saint Louis Music City
Via del Cardello 13a - (06) 4745076
Open 8:30pm-3am. Closed Sun. Cover charge: 15,000 lire.
The Saint Louis is roomy and modern—a good place to listen in comfort to live music that ranges from jazz and soul to funk, salsa, or Brazilian sounds. On Friday and Saturday nights, there's dancing after the band winds up its set. It's wise to book ahead if you want a table in the bar (the best place to hear the music) or in the restaurant, which serves dinner from 8:30pm.

Plan to travel? Look for *Gault Millau's* other *Best of* guides to Chicago, Florida, France, Germany, Hawaii, Hong Kong, London, Los Angeles, New England, New Orleans, New York, Paris, San Francisco, Thailand, Toronto, and Washington, D.C.

Shops

CONTENTS

We have limited our sampling of Roman shops to the capital's prime commercial district, a vast triangle formed by Piazza del Popolo, Piazza Navona, and Piazza di Spagna. Yet we should mention that many excellent stores may be found around Via Cola di Rienzo and Via Ottaviano, and in Rome's so-called "African" district (Viale Libia and Viale Eritrea).

Rome's shopkeepers rest on Sundays, except for the three weeks preceding Christmas. Many shops also remain closed on Monday mornings, opening for their usual afternoon hours—generally around 3:30pm.

ANTIQUES

Antique fanciers who wish to add to their collections in Rome should head straight for two streets: Via dei Coronari for fine furniture and art objects, and Via del Babuino for rare and costly antiques of the highest order. Twice a year, in May and October, an exhibition of antique furniture is held on Via dei Coronari. The street is festively decorated with glowing torches, and the shops stay open late.

Ad Antiqua Domus
Via Paola 25-27
(06) 6861530, fax (06) 68802561
Via dei Coronari 227 - (06) 6875384
Open 9am-1pm & 4pm-8pm. Closed Mon am.
An excellent collection of antique Italian furniture dating from the earliest times to the nineteenth century is on view at this respected gallery.

ArtImport
Via del Babuino 150 - (06) 6796585
Open 9am-1pm & 3:30pm-7:30pm. Closed Mon am.
A veritable bazaar of fascinating antiques, chosen with discernment and duly certified. Silver is the shop's strong suit, but browsers (whatever their budget) are sure to find some irresistible treasure here.

Atelier d'Horlogerie Lebran
Piazza del Parlamento 9 - (06) 6871358
Open 10am-1pm & 4pm-8pm. Closed Mon am.
Antique clocks and timepieces are repaired, appraised, and sold at this busy workshop. Browsers will find fascinating old-fashioned pocket watches and ornate grandfather clocks with complex mechanisms. Some Romans find it ironic that the shop is situated directly opposite Parliament, where politicians have made an art of losing, wasting, and outright killing that precious commodity, time.

Adolfo di Castro
Via del Babuino 80-81 - (06) 3207684
Open 9am-1pm & 3:30pm-7:30pm. Closed Mon am.
This shop is a lovely place to browse among a huge selection of antique furniture and bibelots.

Alberto di Castro

Piazza di Spagna 5 - (06) 6792269
Open 9am-1pm & 3:30pm-7:30pm. Closed Sat.
Alberto di Castro has been called the king of Italian antiques, and it's easy to see why. All along Via del Babuino, from Piazza di Spagna to Piazza del Popolo, is a veritable dynasty of antique-dealing di Castros (Alberto's relations all).

Curiosità e Magia

Via in Aquiro 70 - (06) 6784228
Open 9am-1pm & 3:30pm-7:30pm. Closed Mon am.
Those intrigued by esoteric cults, magic, and the great unknown will find a wondrous array of instruments and paraphernalia for reading the future, summoning spirits, and deciphering life's little mysteries. Many antique items can be unearthed among the tarot cards and crystal balls.

Di Nepi Antiquitas

Via del Babuino 87-88 - (06) 3207654
Open 9am-1pm & 3:30pm-7:30pm. Closed Mon am.
A prestigious collection of antiques, art, and precious objects is displayed at this high-profile gallery.

Cesare Lampronti

Via del Babuino 67 - (06) 6795800
Open 9am-1pm & 3:30pm-7:30pm. Closed Mon am.
This gallery specializes in Flemish and Dutch paintings and in Italian pictures of the seventeenth and eighteenth centuries. An exhibition of the choicest works is mounted every year, in October.

Tanca

Via dei Coronari 230 - (06) 68806052
Open 10am-1pm & 4pm-7:30pm. Closed Mon am.

Bramante's Tempietto

On the spot where Saint Peter is said to have been crucified stands one of the finest Renaissance works in Rome: Bramante's little temple, in the cloister of the church of San Pietro in Montorio.

This gallery is a worthwhile source for fine nineteenth-century Italian furniture and objets d'art.

BOOKS

Anglo American Book

Via delle Vite 102 - (06) 6795222
Open 9am-1pm & 3:30pm-7:30pm. Closed Mon am.
As one might expect, fiction, history, and all manner of books on Rome written in or translated into English are available here. But those with a scientific bent will be pleased to find that their interests have not been neglected. The firm also offers a wide range of scientific and technical volumes, available down the street at Via delle Vite 27 (second floor).

Antiquaria Scarpignato

Via di Ripetta 156 - (06) 6875923
Open 10am-1pm & 4:30pm-7:30pm. Closed Mon am.
An excellent source of venerable engravings (including a fine selection of views of Rome) and maps, this Antiquaria will thrill the bibliophile with its wealth of rare and early printed books.

L'Asterisco

Via Silla 109-111 - (06) 3211483
Open daily 9am-1pm & 3:30pm-8pm.
L'Asterisco's ground floor is entirely devoted to books for babies, toddlers, and young children just learning to read. Granted, the words are in Italian, but the illustrations are so charming (as they usually are in Italian children's books) that your kids may not notice, and surely won't mind.

The Corner Shop

Via del Moro 48 - (06) 5836942
Open 9:30am-1:30pm & 3:30pm-7:30pm. Closed Mon am.
The volumes sold in this Trastevere bookshop cover a broad range of topics, but they have one point in common: all are in English.

Dell'Automobile

Via Marsala 14 - (06) 491741
Open 9am-1pm & 4pm-7pm. Closed Sat pm.

Appropriately situated across from the Roma Termini train station, this bookstore offers everything a visitor might need in the way of guidebooks, maps, and cultural commentaries. But as the name of the shop suggests, Dell'Automobile specializes in books on cars and racing, two peculiarly Italian passions.

Economy Book & Video Center

Via Torino 136 - (06) 4746877
Open 9am-8pm (Mon 3pm-8pm). Closed Sun.
Books in English exclusively are stocked in this shop, which also sells audio and video cassettes, greeting cards, and gifts. A catalog is available for shopping by mail.

Feltrinelli

Largo Torre Argentina 5a - (06) 68803248
Via del Babuino 41 - (06) 6797058
Via Vittorio Emanuele Orlando 83-86
(06) 484430
Open 9am-8pm. Closed Mon am.
The best-stocked bookstores in the city, with a wide selection of titles in many different areas of interest. Special promotional sales are held year round.

Librars & Antiquaria

Via Zanardelli 3 - (06) 6875931
Open 10am-1pm & 4pm-8pm. Closed Mon am.
Volumes on art, photography, and theater are an invitation to browse at this pretty bookstore just off Piazza Navona. Some of the titles on display are quite rare, a bonanza for the book collector.

Libreria del Viaggiatore

Via del Pellegrino 78 - (06) 68801048
Open daily 10am-8pm (Mon 3pm-8pm).
A bookshop for dedicated travelers. Not just guidebooks, but a full array of travel literature from the earliest times to the present is offered here, in Italian and in original-language versions, many in English.

Lion Bookshop

Via del Babuino 181 - (06) 3225837
Open 9:30am-1:30pm & 3:30pm-7:30pm. Closed Mon am.
In a neighborhood traditionally favored by Rome's English community—Byron, Shelley, and Keats all inhabited this area around Piazza di Spagna—is this elegant cultural center, which has a long-established reputation for offering a wide range

of classic and current English and American literature.

Rizzoli

Largo Chigi 15 - (06) 6796641
Via Tomacelli 156
(06) 68802513, fax (06) 68602514
Open 9am-7:30pm. Closed Mon am.
Rizzoli's size and huge stock are rather daunting, but the visitor should take note that here, in one of Rome's largest bookstores, he will find a gratifyingly wide selection of volumes in his own language, whatever it may be.

DEPARTMENT STORES

Coin

Piazzale Appio 15 - (06) 7080020
Viale Libia 61 - (06) 86214660
Via Mantova 1f-1h - (06) 68416238
Open 9am-1pm & 3:30pm-7:30pm. Closed Mon am.
A large, practical, all-around department store that is notable for its selection of clothing. The Via Mantova branch boasts a particularly novel and attractive setting that is worth a visit.

La Rinascente

Piazza Colonna - (06) 6797691
Piazza Fiume - (06) 8841231
Open 9:30am-7:30pm. Closed Mon am.
Known for its efficient service and its own well-priced line of good-looking clothing, Ellerre, La Rinascente is an upscale department-store chain with an excellent selection of merchandise. What's more, you can pay for your purchases in dollars or with traveler's cheques.

Standa

Corso Francia 124 - (06) 3338719
Corso Trieste 200-226 - (06) 86219587
Via Cola di Rienzo 173 - (06) 3243319
Viale Regina Margherita 117-123
(06) 8417289
Viale Trastevere 60 - (06) 5896322
Open 9am-1pm & 3:30pm-7:30pm. Closed Mon am.
The ubiquitous Standa is stocked with all the usual department-store basics. The em-

phasis is on goods of moderate quality and price.

Upim

Piazza Santa Maria Maggiore - (06) 4465579
Via Alessandria 160 - (06) 8554281
Via Nazionale 211 - (06) 484502
Via del Tritone 172 - (06) 6783336
Open 9am-7:30pm. Closed Mon am.
Like Standa, Upim is a popular chain of middle-of-the-road department stores. It's a fine place to stock up on basics.

FASHION

■ CLOTHING

Alexander

Piazza di Spagna 49-50 - (06) 6791351
Via del Corso 417-418 - (06) 6871506
Open 9:30am-7:30pm. Closed Mon am.
Almost aggressively chic casual clothes for women are Alexander's drawing card.

Giorgio Armani

Via Condotti 77 - (06) 6991460
Via del Babuino 140 (Emporio Armani)
(06) 6788454
Open 9:30am-1pm & 3:30pm-7:30pm. Closed Mon am.
The current emperor of Italian fashion dresses men, women, and children in superb fabrics—for a price! Emporio Armani is the home of the sportier, less expensive lines.

Basile

Via Mario de' Fiori 29 - (06) 6789244
Open 9:30am-1pm & 3:30pm-7:30pm. Closed Mon am.
The fashion firm for which Gianni Versace once worked now features styles by designer Luciano Soprani. Basile's lower-priced Titolo line gives you more fashion for your money.

Laura Biagiotti

Via Borgognona 43-44 - (06) 6791205
Open 9:30am-1pm & 3:30pm-7:30pm. Closed Mon am.
Superbly cut clothing in luxurious fabrics (cashmere, linen) for men and women from one of Italy's top designers. Though

undeniably costly, the clothes are a bit less expensive here than in the U.S.

Cenci

Via Campo Marzio 1-7 - (06) 6990681
Open 9am-1pm & 3:30pm-7:30pm. Closed Mon am.
Classic English styling is the hallmark of this well-known Roman men's and women's clothier. Cenci's window displays are traditionally an attraction for fashion-conscious strollers (and *all* Romans fit that description!).

Discount dell'Alta Moda

Via Gesù e Maria 16 - (06) 3613796
Open 9:30am-1pm & 3:30pm-7:30pm. Closed Mon am.
The end lots of high-fashion clothing on display include loads of worthwhile sportswear and city clothes at irresistible prices—the only hitch is finding the right piece in the right size! And you can accessorize your purchase with the belts, bags, and scarves also sold here.

Fendi

Via Borgognona 36-40 - (06) 6797641
Open 9:30am-7:30pm. Closed Mon am.
Come here to admire the designing sisters' complete line of luxuriously fashionable merchandise: butter-soft leather goods; their famous, fabulously expensive furs; and clothing and accessories that range from the almost-reasonable to the frankly extravagant. Fendi's more youthful Fendissime line is presented at Via Fontanella Borghese 56a.

Salvatore Ferragamo

Via Condotti 66 (menswear) - (06) 6781130
Via Condotti 73-74 - (06) 6791565
Open 10am-7pm. Closed Mon am.
An excellent selection of Ferragamo's world-famous and much-beloved footwear, all of which is exquisitely crafted, comfortable, and eminently tasteful. But these shops offer a full line of luxurious ready-to-wear as well, in addition to an abundance of signature accessories (the scarves and ties make nice gifts).

> **Monday,** *like* **Sunday,** *is a day of rest for many shopkeepers.*

Gianfranco Ferré

Via Borgognona 6 (menswear) - (06) 6797445
Via Borgognona 42 - (06) 6790050
Open 9:30am-7:30pm (N°6); 10am-1:30pm & 3:30pm-7:30pm (N°42). Closed Mon am.
Stunning, high-priced, quintessentially Italian fashion for women and men is sold in these two sleek shops. The designs are intriguing and a bit offbeat.

Mr. Magic Meets His Match

A pinch of Hollywood and Las Vegas at the Forum? Well, not quite. It's true that actors Tyrone Power and Linda Christian were married in the church of Santa Francesca Romana in a 1960s Hollywood-style bash. But the church is famed for something slightly more impressive: the grand magic match of Simon Magus, a sorcerer from Samaria, and Saints Peter and Paul. The sorcerer challenged the apostles to a show of magic, saying he was more powerful than God. A group assembled to watch, and Simon cheerfully took to the sky, levitating far above the stupefied crowd. At this point Peter and Paul got down on their knees and started praying, calling on God to help them unveil Simon's tricks. Their pleas were heard and the flying sorcerer took a precipitous tumble. Peter had been praying so hard that when he stood up, the imprint of his knees was left in the stone. You can still see the marks on the floor of the church. They are *not* the hand prints of Tyrone Power!

Gasbarri

Via Condotti 38-39 - (06) 6782569
Open 10am-2pm & 3:30pm-7:30pm. Closed Mon am.
This elegant emporium specializes in clothing for well-dressed women with classic tastes.

Gattinoni

Piazza di Spagna 91 - (06) 6795361

Open 9:30am-1pm & 3:30pm-7:30pm. Closed Mon am.
Classic lines combined with fresh, novel details distinguish the fashions of this noted Roman designer. The clothes are for women who prefer an elegant but not extravagant look.

Gucci

Via Condotti 8 - (06) 6789340
Open 10am-7pm. Closed Mon am.
What else would you expect to find at Gucci but high-status (high-cost!), beautifully crafted clothing and leather accessories for men and women?

Marchetti Sport

Piazza Firenze 25 - (06) 6893445

Marchetti Time

Via Cassia 927b - (06) 30310388
Open 9:30am-1pm & 3:30pm-7:30pm. Closed Mon am.
Sportswear and casual clothing for men and women have traditionally been Marchetti's strong suit, and the energetic Marchetti brothers have also opened a couple of stores that specialize in chic sporting gear for the mountains and the beach.

Max Mara

Via Frattina 28 - (06) 6793638
Via Condotti 46 - (06) 6787946
Open 10am-2pm & 3:30pm-7:30pm. Closed Mon am.
Classy, smart designs with a touch of wit are Max Mara's specialty. The coats are especially dashing.

Missoni

Via del Babuino 96-97 (Missoni Sport) (06) 6797971
Piazza di Spagna 78 (boutique) - (06) 6792555
Open 10am-7:30pm (Via del Babuino); 9:30am-1pm & 3:30pm-7:30pm (Piazza di Spagna). Closed Mon am.
Missoni's renowned knits in subtle colors and decorative weaves can be found here, for less money than you'd spend in the U.S. (but don't kid yourself: the prices are still high). The stores also carry Missoni's complete line of women's wear, including suits and wonderful patterned stockings.

Find the address *you are looking for, quickly and easily, in the index.*

Eddy Monetti

Via Condotti 63 (menswear) - (06) 6783794
Via Borgognona 24 (women's wear)
(06) 6796996
Open 9am-7:30pm (Via Condotti); 9:30am-7:30pm (Via Borgognona). Closed Mon am.
Monetti's clothing for both men and women is stylish yet classic in cut and design, with a faintly British touch.

Marisa Padovan

Via delle Carrozze 81 - (06) 6793946
Open 9am-1pm & 3:30pm-7:30pm. Closed Mon am.
Frilly and delicate lingerie for women and an alluring collection of swimwear make this address a favorite with discerning *Romane.*

Polidori

Via Belsiana 69 (women's wear) - (06) 6784842
Via Borgognona 4c (menswear)
(06) 69941171
Via Condotti 61 (fabrics) - (06) 6783917
Open 9am-1pm & 3:30pm-7:30pm. Closed Mon am.
If a man can't find what he wants in the Polidori boutique, he can have clothing made to his specifications, in the high-fashion Italian fabrics produced by this internationally known firm.

Prada

Via Nazionale 28-31 - (06) 4882413
Open 9am-1pm & 3:30pm-7:30pm. Closed Mon am.
Prada sells high-profile fashions as well as superb loungewear and underthings for men and women. Sumptuous fabrics are also on display.

Romagnoli

Via Crispi 52 (at Via Sistina) - (06) 4874341
Open 9am-1pm & 3:30pm-7:30pm. Closed Mon am.
For men who want their clothes to convey a quiet sense of elegance, Romagnoli offers beautifully tailored, classic haberdashery.

Mila Schön

Via Condotti 64-65 - (06) 6784805
Open 10am-1:30pm & 2:30pm-7:30pm. Closed Mon am.
Schön's distinctive, expensive, and rather austere styles for men and women

have met with great success in Italy. Cashmere shawls and men's ties are specialties.

Schostal

Via del Corso 158 - (06) 6791240
Open 9am-7:30pm. Closed Mon am.
Rome's most traditional men's shop—founded in 1870—carries everything from undershorts and (superb) socks to cashmere overcoats. The house style suits the "quiet man" who does not wish to call attention to his clothes, but who demands top-quality apparel. Considering the caliber of the clothing, prices are most moderate. And the distinguished staff is devoted to serving customers with courteous efficiency.

Sermanti

Via del Corso 165 - (06) 6790986
Open 9:30am-1:30pm & 3:30pm-7:30pm. Closed Mon am.
The menswear versions of Alexander's (see above) signature fashions: luxurious casual clothing for discriminating dandies.

Angelo Sermoneta

Via Borgognona 5b (women's wear)
(06) 6791220
Via Frattina 34a - (06) 6794555
Open 9:30am-7:30pm. Closed Mon am.
These casual clothes for men are attractive and anything but run-of-the-mill. Angelo Sermoneta is one of the best indicators of new fashion trends sweeping the capital.

Luisa Spagnoli

Via Frattina 116 - (06) 6795517
Via del Corso 133 - (06) 6793474
Open 9:30am-7:30pm. Closed Mon am.
Elegant, tasteful, and finely crafted clothing for women, with an accent on knits and fluid silk. On the whole, prices are manageable.

Tebro

Via dei Prefetti 46-54 - (06) 6873441
Open 9am-1pm & 3:30pm-7:30pm. Closed Mon am.
Beautifully crafted clothing for men and women. Both casual and dressier styles are on hand, along with handsome pajamas, dressing gowns, and underthings.

The prices in this guide reflect what establishments were charging at press time.

Testa

Via Frattina 42-43 - (06) 6790660
Via Frattina 104-106 - (06) 6791296
Via Borgognona 13 - (06) 6796174
Open 9:30am-1pm & 3:30pm-7:30pm. Closed Mon am.
Testa specializes in traditional men's haberdashery with a distinctive "Anglo-Italian" flair. The outerwear is particularly appealing.

Tusseda

Via Frattina 25 - (06) 6793576
Open 9:30am-1pm & 3:30pm-7:30pm. Closed Mon am.
Frilly lingerie for ladies and, in season, a huge selection of swimwear.

Valentino

Via Condotti 22 (corner of Via Mario de' Fiori) (menswear) - (06) 6783656
Via Bocca di Leone 15-18 (women's wear) (06) 6795862
Via del Babuino 61 (Oliver boutique) (06) 6798314
Open 10am-7pm. Closed Mon am.
The first address is home to Valentino Uomo, the acclaimed designer's menswear collection. The second, the flagship store, is a temple to *alta moda* for women. Both are must-visits for anyone even remotely interested in fashion. At both locations you'll find attentive service, ready-to-wear and made-to-order clothing, gorgeous accessories—and prices that would make even a Greek shipping magnate blink.

Versace

Via Bocca di Leone 26 (women's wear & home) (06) 6780521
Via Borgognona 24 (menswear) - (06) 6795292
Via Borgognona 33/34 (Versus menswear & women's wear) - (06) 6783977
Open 10am-7:30pm (9am-1:30pm & 3:30pm-7:30pm Via Borgognona 24). Closed Mon am.
Gianni Versace's go-for-baroque fashions are as expensive as they are extravagant. The prolific designer's lines are divided into four categories—menswear, women's wear, accessories, and home décor—all exhibited in sleek surroundings. The Versus line is more youthful and slightly more affordable.

> *Some establishments change their* **closing times** *without warning. It is always wise to check in advance.*

■ JEWELRY

As you stroll the streets of Italy's capital, you'll be astounded at the number of jewelry shops, both large and small, selling precious and costume pieces. We cannot possibly describe them all for you here; those listed below are the most eminent names. But do browse around the vicinities of these jewelry giants, poking into the smaller stores, where you're more likely to find a bargain. It is still possible, for example, to stumble across an antique Roman semiprecious stone, which may be transformed into a unique ring or pendant.

Ansuini

Via del Babuino 150 - (06) 6795835
Corso Vittorio Emanuele II 151 - (06) 68806909
Open 9:30am-1pm & 3:30pm-7:30pm. Closed Mon am.

Broggi–Van Cleef & Arpels

Via Condotti 78-79 - (06) 69941933
Open 9:30am-1:30pm & 3:30pm-7:30pm. Closed Mon am.

Mario Buccellati

Via Condotti 31 - (06) 6790329
Open 10am-1:30pm & 3pm-7pm. Closed Mon.

Bulgari

Via Condotti 10 - (06) 6793876
Open 10am-7pm. Closed Mon am.

Cartier

Via Condotti 82 - (06) 6782580
Open 10am-7pm. Closed Mon am.

Nessis

Via Sistina 34 - (06) 4881561
Open 9:30am-1pm & 3:30pm-7:30pm. Closed Mon am.

Petochi

Piazza di Spagna 23 - (06) 6793947
Open 9:30am-1pm & 3:30pm-7:30pm. Closed Mon am.

■ LEATHER & LUGGAGE

Casuccio & Scalera

Via Frattina 47-49 - (06) 6794302
Open 9:30am-7:30pm. Closed Mon am.
Prestigious luggage, bags, and shoes for men and women can be found here, along

with top-quality small leather accessories crafted with distinctive Italian flair.

El Charro

Via Condotti 40 - (06) 6789171
Open 10am-2pm & 3:30pm-7:30pm. Closed Mon am.

Supple boots, fine-grained belts, and buttery-soft leather clothing all sport the red-rose logo of Charro, an icon adored by Italian youth.

Gherardini

Via Belsiana 48b - (06) 6795501
Open 10am-1pm & 3:30pm-7:30pm. Closed Mon am.

This collection of refined handbags, luggage, and other leather articles produced by a renowned Florentine manufacturer, is housed in a former church in the heart of Rome's shopping district. Dizzying prices.

Gucci

Via Condotti 8 - (06) 6789340
Open 10am-7pm. Closed Mon am.

Rome's Gucci headquarters (a tourist mecca) is fully stocked with the complete line of loafers and other shoes, fine bags and luggage, and all manner of smart leather accessories, from key chains to desk sets.

Hermès

Via Condotti 67 - (06) 6797687
Open 10am-7pm. Closed Mon am.

Dashing leather goods from the famed French firm; the celebrated silk scarves are reputed to be cheaper here than in Paris.

Ibiz

Via dei Chiavari 39 - (06) 6547297
Open 9:30am-1pm & 3:30pm-7:30pm. Closed Mon am.

This leather workshop turns out supple, handsomely finished bags, wallets, and key rings. The handworked belts are particularly fine.

Nazareno Gabrielli

Via Condotti 36-37 - (06) 6790862
Open daily 10am-2pm & 3pm-7pm.

Nazareno Gabrielli has earned its pre-eminent reputation with a line of exclusive tweed-and-leather bags, beautiful luggage, and a host of desirable leather accessories for women.

Saddlers Union

Via Condotti 26 - (06) 6798050
Open 9:30am-1pm & 3:30pm-7:30pm. Closed Mon am.

Since 1958 Dario Petrini, Gino Munalli, and Angelo Conversi have filled their workshop with handsome leather goods and shoes for men and women. The bags are particularly striking: supple shoulder bags, classy briefcases, and roomy overnight bags. Belts and other accessories are all handcrafted, making this one of the capital's best sources for fine leather accessories.

Tipsy Soldier Wounds Virgin Mary

One of the most moving sights in Rome is the church of Santa Maria della Pace, in the square of the same name. To visit it, you must ask the concierge at number 5 Via dell'Arco della Pace. The church was built in 1480 by Baccio Pontelli. In 1656 Pietro da Cortona added the superb façade and the piazzetta in front. The cloister is an early work by Bramante. Another distinguished artist, Raphael, painted the frescoes of the sibyls of Frigia, Cumae, Tiburtina, and Persica speaking to the angels. (Remember, the sibyls were accepted in the Christian church because they were supposedly the first to foretell the coming of Christ.) Also gracing Santa Maria della Pace is a miraculous painting of the Virgin Mary. The ancient image was attacked hundreds of years ago by a drunken soldier who cut the Virgin's breast; tradition has it that blood flowed from the wound. Pope Sixtus IV ordered the church be built to commemorate the miracle.

Trussardi

Via Condotti 49 - (06) 6792151
Open 10am-1:30pm & 2:30pm-7pm. Closed Mon am.

Currently quite the rage in Italy, Trussardi proposes handsome, fine-quality leather goods and clothing, including such frivolous necessities as leather saddlebags and bicycle bags. Much of the merchandise sports the company's greyhound logo. The canvas and vinyl items are considerably cheaper, but don't have half the cachet of the genuine leather articles.

Vivace
Via Fontanella Borghese 47 - (06) 6876126
Open daily 9:30am-1pm & 3:30pm-7:30pm.
Leather and wool are the materials of choice at Vivace, where women will find an attractive collection of sweaters and leather goods.

■ SHOES & ACCESSORIES

Barrilà
Via Condotti 29 - (06) 6793916
Via del Babuino 33 - (06) 6783830
Open 9:30am-1:30pm & 3:30pm-7:30pm. Closed Mon am.
Custom-made shoes for women and men are Barrilà's specialty, but the Via del Babuino address also offers an interesting selection of quality ready-made shoes.

Borsalino
Via IV Novembre 157b - (06) 6794192
Open 9am-8pm. Closed Mon am.
Urbane or sporty toppers, ranging from opera hats to berets, are all displayed at Borsalino, the capital's most elegant source of headgear.

Bozart
Via Bocca di Leone 4 - (06) 6781026
Open 9:30am-7:30pm. Closed Mon am.
Bozart purveys extravagant, original costume jewelry crafted in top-quality (though not precious) materials. Definitely worth a look.

Burma Bijoux
Via Condotti 27 - (06) 6798285
Open 9:30am-1:30pm & 3:30pm-7:30pm. Closed Mon am.
Covetable costume jewelry is the attraction here. We adore Burma's flawless imitations of drop-dead jewels—in fact, Burma is a fine place to have copies made of your heirloom ornaments.

Camomilla
Piazza di Spagna 85 - (06) 6793551
Open 9:30am-1pm & 3:30pm-7:30pm. Closed Mon am.
Fake leopard-skin sheaths, inky-black capes, flashy accessories, and gaudy jewelry are just a few of the finds you'll discover at Camilla, an utterly eccentric shop for women who just love to be noticed.

Campanile
Via Condotti 58 - (06) 6783041
Open 9:30am-7:30pm. Closed Mon am.
Campanile sells its own make of classy footwear for women and men.

Tanino Crisci
Via Borgognona 4h-i - (06) 6795461
Open 9am-1pm & 3:30pm-7:30pm. Closed Mon am.
Supple leathers and exquisite craftsmanship characterize Crisci's highly desirable handmade boots and shoes for men and women. The styles, especially much of the men's line, are on the classic side.

Dal Cò
Via Vittoria 65 - (06) 6786536
Open 9:30am-1pm & 3:30pm-7:30pm. Closed Mon am.
A superbly elegant shop that sells handmade shoes for women (made to measure on request). After you slip into your divine new pumps, you can choose a coordinating handbag from Dal Cò's mouthwatering collection.

Diego Della Valle
Via Borgognona 45-46 - (06) 6786828
Open 9:30am-1pm & 3:30pm-7:30pm. Closed Mon am.
These sophisticated, expensive shoes are designed for women who are not impressed by faddish footwear.

Furla
Via Tomacelli 136 - (06) 6878230
Open 10am-1pm & 3:30pm-7:30pm. Closed Mon.
Known as a quality manufacturer of women's handbags, Furla also presents a line of costume jewelry, belts, umbrellas, and silk scarves, all bearing the house label.

Grilli
Via del Corso 166 - (06) 6793650
Open 9am-1pm & 3:30pm-7:30pm. Closed Mon am.
  Both sexes will find a selection of elegant shoes and boots at Grilli's.

A Plump Pachyderm and a Ghetto Maker

  There's a fabulous lot of miscellanea in and around Piazza della Minerva. In the center stands Bernini's elephant, with an Egyptian obelisk balanced on its back. The Romans call it the *porcin della Minerva*, because the pachyderm is as plump as a piglet. The monument was commissioned by Pope Alexander VII to symbolize the notion that only a strong mind can withstand the weight of wisdom. The Dominican church of Santa Maria Sopra Minerva has a Renaissance façade but a Gothic heart (1280), and it's bursting with art and religious treasures, including frescoes by Filippino Lippi, a statue of *Christ with the Cross* by Michelangelo, and a crucifix by Giotto. Saint Catherine of Siena is entombed here as is that sublime artist, Fra Angelico. Also buried in the church is Pope Paul IV Carafa, infamous for his creation of the Jewish ghetto (the first was in Rome). When he died in 1559 his statue at the Campidoglio was promptly beheaded.

Jako Bijoux
Via Mario de' Fiori 37b - (06) 6796901
Open 9:30am-1:30pm & 3:30pm-7:30pm. Closed Mon am.
  Costume jewelry by famous designer firms—Valentino, Sharra Pagano, Moschino—is sold here, along with fetching headdresses for brides.

Laudadio
Via Gregoriana 1-2 - (06) 6790583
Open 9am-1pm & 3:30pm-7:30pm. Closed Mon am.
  Master shoe designer Ennio Laudadio has shod the most discerning feet in the capital since 1953. His superb footwear has the singular quality of becoming even more beautiful the longer it is worn.

Pollini
Via Frattina 22-24 - (06) 6798360
Open 9:30am-1pm & 3:30pm-7:30pm (Sat 9:30am-7:30pm). Closed Mon am.
  Meticulously crafted shoes for women in a wide range of fashionable (but not trendy) styles. High quality and good value are guaranteed.

Fratelli Rossetti
Via Borgognona 5a - (06) 6782676
Open 9:30am-1:30pm & 3pm-7:30pm. Closed Mon am.
  This is the Roman source for the Rossetti brothers' famous footwear, as comfortable as it is chic.

Mario Valentino
Via Frattina 84a - (06) 6791242
Open 9:30am-1pm & 3:30pm-7:30pm (Sat 9:30am-7:30pm). Closed Mon am.
  Vivid, light-hearted footwear for flamboyant fashion plates.

FOOD

■ GOURMET SHOPS

Castroni
Via Cola di Rienzo 196 - (06) 6874383
Via Flaminia 28-32 - (06) 3611029
Via Ottaviano 55 - (06) 39723279
Open 8am-1:30pm & 3:30pm-8pm (Via Cola di Rienzo); 7:30am-1:30pm & 4pm-8pm (Via Flaminia); 7am-8pm (Via Ottaviano). Closed Thu pm (exc Via Ottaviano).
  For a large segment of the Roman population, Castroni is synonymous with the kind of old-fashioned grocery store that stocks a little of everything. Ask for licorice for your kids, and a clerk will oblige; request "that strange Eastern bread that puffs up when you throw it in boiling oil," and poppadums will appear as if by magic from some corner of the shop. Such domestic treats as mustard-pickled fruits from Emilia, herbs from southern Italy, and dried fruit from Sicily, all of excellent quality, may be purchased here as well.

Confetteria Moriondo & Gariglio
Via della Pilotta 2 - (06) 6786662
Open 9:30am-1pm & 3:30pm-7:30pm. Closed Mon am.

For the finest chocolate in town, come to this tiny shop near the Trevi Fountain. Every sweet on view here is handmade of superior ingredients. The nut clusters, chocolate-covered cherries, and cioccolatini (filled chocolates) are sublime; but there are slabs of chocolate too, for munching or cooking, and famously good glazed chestnuts. Prices are commensurate with the high quality.

Diotallevi
Via Santa Maria del Pianto 68 - (06) 68802944
Open 8am-1:30pm & 5:30pm-8pm. Closed Thu pm.

Among the many treats obtainable in this interesting shop is an excellent Sardinian bottarga (dried mullet roe), sometimes known as the "poor man's caviar." Located in what was formerly the Ghetto, where Jews were obliged to live until the late nineteenth century, Diotallevi also sells a selection of kosher foods, duly approved by rabbinical authorities.

La Fantasia del Fornaio
Via Venezia 11-13 - (06) 4742339
Open 7am-2pm & 5pm-8pm. Closed Thu pm, Sat, Aug.

This bakery has caught the fancy of many jaded Roman gourmets with its diverse range of top-quality breads and other baked goods.

Fior Fiore
Via della Croce 17-18 - (06) 6791386
Open 8am-1:30pm & 5pm-8pm. Closed Thu pm.

Get your fresh pasta here for a thoroughly authentic fettuccine all'Alfredo (did you know that the dish is genuine only if the pasta is boiled in Roman water?). And you can buy the Parmesan for the creamy sauce as well, along with an appetizing assortment of premium Italian, French, and Swiss cheeses.

Franchi
Via Cola di Rienzo 204 - (06) 6874651
Open 8am-9pm. Closed Sun.

Glorious food: a top name in Rome for gourmet groceries and gustatory treats, Franchi presents a mouthwatering array of perfectly delicious prepared foods to carry out. Cheeses and truffles are house specialties.

Palombi
Via Vittorio Veneto 114 - (06) 4885817
Open 7:30am-1:30pm & 5pm-7:30pm. Closed Thu pm.

Even the sophisticated shoppers and strollers on Via Veneto, Rome's most cosmopolitan thoroughfare, stop to inhale the warm, yeasty aroma that wafts forth from Palombi. The smell of bread fresh from the oven holds universal appeal, and the loaves sold in this traditional bakery are well-nigh irresistible.

Panella
Largo Leopardi 2 (corner of Via Merulana 54)
(06) 4872344
Open 8am-1:30pm & 5pm-8pm. Closed Thu pm.

All sorts of special foods for people on restricted diets can be found at this vast emporium. Sufferers of diabetes, digestive difficulties, hypertension, or obesity will appreciate the range of tasty substitutes for forbidden goodies, and the selection of whole foods will interest anyone who cares about healthful eating.

Ricercatezze Alimentari
Via D. Chelini 17-21 - (06) 8078904
Open 7:30am-1:30pm & 7pm-8pm. Closed Thu pm.

Caviar and premium smoked salmon top the roster of epicurean treats to be had in this large, abundantly stocked grocery store, but the humbler bottarga (dried mullet roe) is on hand as well. Wine buffs can ogle the admirable collection of vintage bottles, and those with sweet tooths are bound to break down at the sight of the pastry selection. But dieters are not neglected, either—they'll find a section of low-calorie foods just for them.

Settespighe
Via Crescenzio 89d - (06) 68805566
Open 10am-1pm & 3:30pm-7:30pm. Closed Mon am.

Organic and biodynamic edibles form Settespighe's healthful stock. No need to be a natural-food fanatic to appreciate the full-flavored provisions on offer here.

Teichner

Piazza San Lorenzo in Lucina 17 - (06) 6871557
Open 8:30am-7:30pm. Closed Sun.
  Good coffee is nectar to Italians. Romans are particularly finicky about the precious brew, and the fussiest of them tend to buy their beans at Teichner, a shop famous for fine roasted coffees since 1922. But that's not all: this is also the place to stock up on hard-to-find (and truly sublime) Peirano's chocolate. Gourmet groceries, such as superior olive oils, truffles, Oriental culinary exotica, and excellent Scottish smoked salmon, round out Teichner's mouthwatering inventory.

■ HERBALISTS

Antica Drogheria Condotti

Via Mario de' Fiori 24a - (06) 6791454
Open 10am-2pm & 3:30pm-7pm. Closed Mon am.
  An old-fashioned herbalist's shop with a fragrant profusion of dried aromatic plants and herbs, the Antica Drogheria also carries exotically scented soaps, curious herb teas, and a group of absolutely natural cosmetics.

La Bottega di Lunga Vita

Via delle Colonnelle 19 - (06) 6787408
Open Tue-Fri 9:30am-7:30pm (Sat 9:30am-1pm & 3:30pm-7:30pm). Closed Mon am.
  The "Long Life Shop" carries major brands of American-made vitamins, cosmetics, and diet foods.

Erboristeria Maurice Mességué

Piazza San Silvestro 8 (Galleria RAS)
(06) 6797294
Open 9:30am-1:30pm & 3:30pm-7:30pm. Closed Mon am.
  Specially selected herbs with guaranteed active properties are the mainstay here, along with an appealing line of natural cosmetics.

Ai Monasteri

Piazza delle Cinque Lune 76 - (06) 68802783
Open 9am-1pm & 4:30pm-7:30pm. Closed Thu.
  Monks from seven different abbeys prepare the herbal specialties sold here. The offerings range from plant-based cosmetics to fragrant herb candies, extra-virgin olive oil, and essential oils for perfumes. The staff willingly mails your purchases anywhere in the world.

■ WINE

Arcioni Centrovini

Piazza Crati 22-25 - (06) 82206616
Open 9am-1:30pm & 4pm-8pm. Closed Thu pm.
  Spirits, various bubblies, premium Chianti Classico, and lively wines from the Alto Adige region share shelf space with Venetian grappas (grape brandies), regional sweets, and elaborate gift boxes at this estimable emporium founded in 1932.

Chiarotti

Piazza Martiri di Belfiore 6-10 - (06) 3217789
Open 8am-1:30pm & 5pm-8pm. Closed Thu pm.
  This well-regarded wine merchant carries an extensive stock of wines, Champagnes, and spirits.

Chirra

Via Torino 133 - (06) 485659
Open 6:30am-2am. Closed Sun.
  In addition to an interesting selection of wines, this shop purveys a wide range of imported gourmet delicacies.

Ciarla All'Eur

Via Canzone del Piave 3 - (06) 5010102
Open 8am-2pm & 5:15pm-9pm. Closed winter: Thu pm.
  A courteous and knowledgeable wine expert will help you choose the bottle you want from the shop's vast selection. Gift packages are available, too.

Del Frate

Via degli Scipioni 128a - (06) 3211612
Open 8:30am-1:30pm & 4:30pm-8pm. Closed Thu pm.
  A prestigious assortment of quality wines and domestic and imported spirits... all the best brands are on hand, and the staff is willing and able to offer reliable advice. Gift packages are a specialty.

Guerrini

Viale Regina Margherita 205-207
(06) 8845389
Open 8am-2pm & 4pm-8:30pm. Closed Thu pm.
  Inside this shop are shelves upon shelves of Italian wines and top-quality imports from France, Spain, and Portugal. The bot-

tles of your choice can be elegantly packaged and sent anywhere you like.

Lucantoni

Largo Vigna Stelluti 33 - (06) 3293743
Largo San Godenzo 9 - (06) 3310622
Open daily 9am-2:30pm & 4:30pm-9:30pm (Largo Vigna Stellitu); 8am-2pm & 4:30pm-9pm (Largo San Godenzo).

Even on Thursday afternoon, when most of their confrères are closed, Lucantoni is open, ready to help you choose from a broad array of Italian and imported vintages. If you're in search of a rare bottle, there's a good chance you'll find it here. Italian Champagne-method sparkling wines, venerable Barolos, and hard-to-find Rhine and Moselle wines are all in stock.

Rocchi

Via Alessandro Scarlatti 7 - (06) 8551022
Via della Balduina 120a - (06) 343694
Open 8:30am-1:30pm & 5:15pm-8pm. Closed Thu pm.

During its nearly 90 years of existence, this firm has established a reputation for offering fine wines and spirits produced in Italy and elsewhere. Rocchi's wines can also be sent to any destination you choose.

Roffi Isabelli

Via della Croce 76a - (06) 6790896
Open 11am-midnight. Closed Sun.

Formerly a popular bar established early in the last century, today Roffi Isabelli is an upscale wine merchant featuring a select stock of French and Italian vintages.

Trimani

Via Goito 20 - (06) 4469661
Via Cernaia 37b (Wine Bar) - (06) 4469630
Shop: open 8:45am-1:30pm & 4pm-8pm. Closed Thu pm. Wine Bar: open 11am-3pm & 5:30pm-midnight. Closed Sun.

Wine merchants in Rome since 1821, Trimani carries a complete range of wines, spirits, Champagnes, Spumantes, regional sweets, and gourmet treats. Upon request, your order can be packed up and sent to practically anywhere in the world. The same firm operates a smart wine bar nearby (see *Quick Bites*).

> **Find the address** you are looking for, quickly and easily, in the index.

GIFTS

Barduagni

Via del Tritone 99-100 - (06) 4884324
Open 9am-1pm & 3:30pm-7:30pm. Closed Mon am.

The Barduagni family, established in Rome since 1912, has a solid tradition of bringing fine objects to light and of helping to educate the taste of many eminent collectors. On view in their vast shop and gallery is the best that Europe has to offer in the way of china and crystal. The experienced, professional staff can be trusted for sound advice and suggestions.

C.U.C.I.N.A.

Via del Babuino 118a - (06) 6791275
Open 9:30am-1pm & 3:30pm-7:30pm. Closed Mon am.

Original designs and unusual materials distinguish the tableware and home accents sold at C.U.C.I.N.A., a shop whose specialty, however, is sleek, efficient kitchen equipment.

Decò

Piazza San Lorenzo in Lucina 2 - (06) 6871395
Open 9:30am-1pm & 3:30pm-7:30pm. Closed Mon am.

The home furnishings and decorative accents from Decò are always in the best of taste; and usually carry a hefty price tag!

Fornari & Fornari

Via Frattina 133 - (06) 6780105
Open 9am-1pm & 3:30pm-7:30pm. Closed Mon am.

Along with Barduagni and Tupini, Fornari offers Rome's premier selection of decorative items, tableware, and collectible bibelots.

Richard Ginori

Via Cola di Rienzo 223 - (06) 3243132
Via del Tritone 177 - (06) 6793836
Open 9:30am-1:30pm & 3:30pm-7:30pm. Closed Mon am.

Ginori is famous throughout the world as a manufacturer of superbly patterned china, fine crystal, and table ornaments.

Limentani

Via Portico d'Ottavia 47-48 - (06) 68806949

Open 9:30am-1pm & 3:30pm-7:30pm. Closed Mon am.

Just behind the synagogue of Rome's ancient Jewish district, Limentani's impressive shop is a treasure trove of table, kitchen, and housewares. Pieces from fashionable manufacturers share shelf space with odd bits that have piled up in the back of the shop over the years. Interesting prices.

Naj-Oleari

Via di San Giacomo 25a - (06) 6780045
Via dei Greci 32 - (06) 6794803
Open 9am-1pm & 3:30pm-7:30pm. Closed Mon am.

Naj-Oleari is Italy's answer to Laura Ashley. The firm is famous for its imaginative fabrics, characterized by brilliant colors and enchanting motifs. These lively cotton prints cover all manner of useful items— eyeglass cases, jewelry bags, address books, and the like—and they may also be purchased by the yard, or in the form of delightful clothing for the entire family.

Ricordi

Via C. Battisti 120 (at Piazza Venezia)
(06) 6798022
Via Giulio Cesare 88 - (06) 3251589
Via del Corso 506 - (06) 3612331
Open 10am-7:30pm. Closed Mon am.

The huge stock of records, CDs, and cassettes can satisfy just about any musical taste, but lovers of the lyric art will be particularly pleased with Ricordi's vast selection of operatic recordings.

Spazio Sette

Via dei Barbieri 7 - (06) 68307139
Open 9:30am-1pm & 3:30pm-7:30pm. Closed Mon am.

A wonderland of high-tech or whimsical designer accents and homewares. Each piece simply oozes that inimitable Italian flair. On hand are fabrics, linens, lamps, glasses, serving pieces, and much more.

Stilvetro

Via delle Carrozze 18 - (06) 69941009
Via Frattina 56 - (06) 6790258
Open 9:30am-1pm & 3:30pm-7:30pm. Closed Mon am.

Both Stilvetro shops feature (appropriately) high-style glass and ceramic tableware. The contemporary home accents make pleasing gifts.

Stock Market

Via dei Banchi Vecchi 51-52 - (06) 6864238
Open 10am-8pm. Closed Mon am.

Stock Market is Rome's answer to London's famous "reject shops," and a bargain hunter's dream. But the china you'll find here is not just end lots and imperfects: there are perfectly good pieces from importers and manufacturers that are not (or not yet) in fashion. Prices are low, low, low.

Tupini

Piazza San Lorenzo in Lucina 8 - (06) 6871458
Open 9:30am-1pm & 3:30pm-7:30pm. Closed Mon am.

Sober classicism characterizes Tupini's elegant decorative objects for the house and the table.

STREET MARKETS

For those who like to browse and poke around in hopes of discovering a bargain, Rome's flea market is a mandatory stop. Every Sunday morning, the streets around **Porta Portese** are transformed into a teeming bazaar where oddities, rarities, and amusing curiosities are set out for sale (the best access is from Piazza Ippolito Nievo). Funky new and vintage clothing can be found at the **Via Sannio** market, near Porta San Giovanni; it's open every morning (except Sunday) as well as Saturday afternoon.

An Evil Stone but a Good Cure for Dog Bites

The so-called pietra scellerata, or evil stone, is in the church of Santi Vito e Modesto. Many a Christian martyr was decapitated on the stone, thus the infelicitous name. In the Middle Ages the Romans would scrape the surface of the stone and use the dust to cure dog bites.

Museums

Galleria dell'Accademia Nazionale di San Luca

Piazza dell'Accademia di San Luca 77
(06) 6798850
Open Mon, Wed, Fri & last Sun of the month: 10am-1pm.

The Academy's collection was started in the eighteenth century with gifts and bequests from the academicians themselves. Today it includes a remarkable group of works by minor painters of the seventeenth and eighteenth centuries as well as Titian's *Portrait of Hippolyte Riminaldi*, a fragment of a fresco by Raphael, *Judith and Holofernes* by Piazzetta, a Van Dyck Madonna, and an allegorical painting by Peter Paul Rubens, *Nymphs Crowning Abundance*.

Galleria Aurora Pallavicini-Casino dell'Aurora

Via XXIV Maggio 43 - (06) 4744019, Casino (06) 4827224
Galleria: open by appt. Casino: open 1st day of the month 10am-noon & 3pm-5pm.

The Casino dell'Aurora is so called for the celebrated fresco of *Aurora* by Guido Reni that decorates the ceiling. The Galleria contains works by Botticelli (*Transfiguration with Saints*) and Filippino Lippi, as well as thirteen panels depicting *Christ and the Apostles* by Rubens, two portraits by Van Dyck, and works by Poussin, the Carraccis, Claude Lorrain, and Luca Giordano.

Galleria & Museo Borghese

Villa Borghese, access from Via Pinciana (06) 8548577
Open 9am-1:30pm (Sun 9am-1pm). Closed Mon, hols.

Quadreria della Galleria Borghese al San Michele

Complesso Monumentale del San Michele a Ripa
Via di San Michele 22 - (06) 5816732

Open 9am-1pm & 4pm-8pm (hols 9am-1pm). Closed Mon.

This jewel among the world's private art collections was begun by Cardinal Scipio Borghese, nephew of Pope Paul V. To house it, he had the Casino Borghese built by architect Giovanni Vasanzio in 1618. The collection encompasses antique sculpture, masterpieces by Bernini (*David and the Sling, Apollo and Daphne*) and Canova (*Pauline Borghese*). Owing to restoration work in the museum's upper wing, the Quadreria (picture gallery) Borghese has been temporarily transferred to the Complesso Monumentale del San Michele a Ripa in Trastevere, opposite the Piazza di Porta Portese. Among the paintings on view are Raphael's *Descent from the Cross*, Titian's enigmatic *Sacred and Profane Love*, Cranach's *Venus and Cupid*, several fine works by Caravaggio, and Correggio's sumptuous *Danaë*.

Galleria Colonna

Via della Pilotta 17 - (06) 6794362
Open Sat 9am-1pm.

This is one of the richest patrician art collections in Rome. It includes works by Italian and foreign artists from the fifteenth to the eighteenth century displayed with a decorative (rather than a didactic) intent, forming a harmonious whole with the palazzo's superb furnishings (note the ebony screen inlaid with ivory). Among the paintings hung here are *Venus with Cupid and a Satyr* by Bronzino, *Portrait of a Gentleman* by Veronese, various seventeenth-century works, and an epic fresco, the *Battle of Lepanto*, by Coli and Gherardi.

Galleria Doria Pamphili

Palazzo Doria Pamphili, Piazza del Collegio Romano 1a - (06) 6797323
Open Tue & Fri-Sun 10am-1pm.

This gallery houses the prestigious collection of primarily sixteenth- and seventeenth-century paintings amassed by members of the patrician Pamphili family, beginning with Olimpia Maidalchini, sister-in-law of Pope Innocent X Pamphili (see the bust of Olimpia by Algardi, the bust of Innocent X by Bernini and the pontiff's portrait by Velásquez, all displayed in the gallery). Among the many masterpieces to be admired in the splendidly furnished rooms are Raphael's *Double Portrait*, *Herodias* by Titian, *Rest on the Flight into Egypt* by Caravaggio, Rubens's *Portrait of a Franciscan*, and a naval battle scene by Pieter Breughel.

Galleria Nazionale d'Arte Antica Palazzo Barberini

Via Quattro Fontane 13 - (06) 4814591
Open 9am-1:30pm (Tue, Thu & Sat 9am-6:30pm; Sun & hols 9am-12:30pm). Closed Mon.
The noble Palazzo Barberini is a sublime example of Baroque architecture that was built for Pope Urban VIII by Borromini and Bernini. The picture gallery on the first floor, decorated with lovely frescoes by Pietro da Cortona, contains a remarkable collection of thirteenth- to eighteenth-century paintings. Raphael's *La Fornarina* is here, as is Holbein's renowned *Portrait of Henry VIII*, along with works by Filippo Lippi, Bronzino, El Greco, Caravaggio (the haunting *Judith and Holofernes*), Canaletto, and Guardi.

Galleria Nazionale d'Arte Antica Palazzo Corsini

Via della Lungara 10 - (06) 68802323
Open 9am-1:30pm (Sun & hols 9am-12:30pm). Closed Mon.
This gallery contains seventeenth- and eighteenth-century works by noted Italian and foreign artists. The collection includes *Saint Sebastian* by Rubens, Caravaggio's *Saint John the Baptist* and *Narcissus at the Pool*, paintings by Murillo, Ribera, Van Dyck, Guido Reni, and a fine still life, *Flowers and Fruit*, by Breughel.

Galleria Nazionale d'Arte Moderna e Contemporanea

Viale delle Belle Arti 131 - (06) 3224209
Open 9am-7pm (Sun & hols 9am-1pm). Closed Mon.
Perhaps the richest and most important collection of modern art in Italy is on view in the Fine Arts building, which was designed by Bazzani. Italian art of the nineteenth century is represented by the *Macchiaioli*, Tuscan painters who favored a pointillist technique and clear, bright colors; by Divisionists, whose works are characterized by highly imaginative subject matter; by the Neapolitan school; and by northern Italian landscape painters. Works from the twentieth century include paintings by Modigliani, Marini, and Carlo Carrà, as well as by such non-Italian artists as Cézanne, Klimt, Utrillo, Kandinsky, Henry Moore, and Jackson Pollock.

Slaughter in Saint Stephen's

Lions and tigers and bears once gave up the ghost where a curious round church called Santo Stefano Rotondo (on the street of the same name) now stands. The church was built in the fifth century, probably over the remains of the ancient *macellum magnum*, the grand market and slaughterhouse of the Emperor Nero's day. Inside the church is a cycle of Counter-Reformation frescoes unusual for their grisly vividness. The ruined but restored works by Pomarancio, Tempesta, and others show the *Martyrdom of the Saints* in 34 gruesome panels. Poor souls are crushed by boulders, their guts bursting every which way and eyes popping out of their sockets; lions claw other martyrs to death; saints are drowned with weights around their necks, or are burned alive, or maimed with an alarming array of instruments.

Galleria Spada

Piazza Capodiferro 3 - (06) 6861158
Open 9am-1:30pm (Sun & hols 9am-12:30pm). Closed Mon.
This small but interesting collection of pictures dating from the late fifteenth to the eighteenth century boasts works from the Italian and Flemish-Dutch schools. Assembled mainly by Cardinal Bernardino Spada (1594–1661), the collection has

come down to us virtually intact and is displayed in its original setting, providing an important record of seventeenth-century patrician taste. Among the works on view are the *Portrait of Cardinal Bernardino Spada* by Guido Reni, a landscape by Jan Breughel, and Gentileschi's *David*.

Istituto Nazionale per la Grafica - Gabinetto Nazionale dei Disegni e delle Stampe

Via della Lungara 230 - (06) 6861375
Open by appt (exc Mon & hols).
Situated near the Villa Farnesina, the National Institute for Graphic Arts boasts the largest collection of prints and drawings in Italy. The group of Piranesi engravings housed here is unparalleled.

Keats-Shelley Memorial House

Piazza di Spagna 26 - (06) 6784235
Open 9am-1pm & 2:30pm-5:30pm (summer 3pm-6pm). Closed Sat-Sun, hols.
A small museum occupies the Casina Rossa (to the right of the steps leading to Trinità dei Monti), where English poet John Keats died in 1821. On display are relics, manuscripts, and memorabilia from Keats, Percy and Mary Shelley, and their circle. The house also contains an impressive library of English Romantic literature.

Museo dell'Alto Medioevo

Viale Lincoln 3 - (06) 5925806
Open daily 9am-2pm (Sun & hols 9am-1pm).
Early medieval artifacts dating from the fourth to the tenth century are preserved here: funerary objects, ceramics, bronzes and jewels, reliefs from Rome and Latium (eighth to tenth century), as well as treasure from Lombard burial sites at Nocera Umbra and Castel Trosino (sixth to seventh century). The items recovered from a Lombard knight's tomb are particularly remarkable.

Museo Archeologico Ostiense

Excavation site at Ostia Antica (24 km SW)
(06) 5650022
Open daily summer 9am-4pm; winter 9am-1pm.
Major archaeological finds uncovered at the site of Rome's ancient port are displayed here in the sixteenth-century Casone del Sale, a dwelling built with excavated materials. Among the many fine works on view, visitors can admire a

second-century sarcophagus depicting a battle of centaurs, a bust of *Aesculapius*, a portrait of the *Emperor Trajan*, and a colossal statue believed to represent Maxentius.

Museo Barracco

Corso Vittorio Emanuele 168 - (06) 68806848
Open 9am-1:30pm (Tue & Thu 9am-1:30pm & 5pm-8pm; Sun & hols 9am-1pm). Closed Mon.
This small but significant collection of ancient sculpture from Rome and the Near East was presented to the city by Baron Giovanni Barracco in 1920. It is displayed in the sixteenth-century Palazzetto Farnesina. Outstanding pieces include the head of a *Greek Youth* from the end of the sixth or the early fifth century B.C., an Egyptian bas-relief depicting a court functionary from the Third Dynasty, and a *Bust of Epicure* (270 B.C.).

Musei Capitolini

Museo Capitolino di Palazzo Nuovo, Piazza del Campidoglio - (06) 67102475
Open 9am-1:30pm (Tue & Sat 9am-1:30pm & 5pm-8pm; Sun & hols 9am-1pm). Closed Mon. A single ticket provides access to the Museo Capitolino & the Museo del Palazzo dei Conservatori.
The Capitoline Museums occupy the Palazzo Nuovo, built to Michelangelo's design by Rainaldi in 1655. It houses an exceptional collection of antique marble statues, busts, and bas-reliefs, including the Amendola sarcophagus (second century B.C.), the well-known mosaic depicting four doves taken from Hadrian's Villa, and several fine Roman copies of ancient Greek and Hellenistic statues, including the famous *Capitoline Venus*.

Museo del Palazzo dei Conservatori & Pinacoteca Capitolina

Palazzo dei Conservatori, Piazza del Campidoglio - (06) 67102071
Open 9am-1:30pm (Tue & Sat 9am-1:30pm & 5pm-8pm; Sun & hols 9am-1pm). Closed Mon. A single ticket provides access to the Museo Capitolino & the Museo del Palazzo dei Conservatori.
A vast, important, and diverse collection of artworks is housed in the Palazzo dei Conservatori. Its façade, which is identical to that of the Palazzo Nuovo, was also

built to Michelangelo's design, in 1568. In the courtyard are the grandiose remains of a statue of the Emperor Constantine, and the portico holds a colossal head of Constantine II. Inside, the sumptuous Sale dei Conservatori are adorned with frescoes, precious tapestries, statues (Bernini's *Urban VIII*), and bronzes. The Museo del Palazzo dei Conservatori preserves superb examples of ancient Greek, Hellenistic, and Roman sculpture, including the famed *Capitoline She-Wolf*, an Etruscan bronze from the fifth century (the young Romulus and Remus were added in the sixteenth century, by Pollaiolo). On display in the Pinacoteca Capitolina are masterpieces of sixteenth-, seventeenth- and eighteenth-century painting by (among others) Palma Vecchio, Tintoretto, Rubens, Velásquez, Van Dyck, and Caravaggio.

Museo della Civiltà Romana

Piazza Agnelli 10 - (06) 5926135
Open 9am-1:30pm (Sun 9am-1pm; Tue & Thu 9am-1:30pm & 3pm-6pm). Closed Mon.

An important collection of plaster casts, models, and relief maps documents Roman history from its origins to the sixth century A.D. and illustrates the spread of Roman culture throughout the known world. A model of Rome at the time of Constantine (1:250 scale) is the largest and most complete mock-up of its kind in the world.

Museo del Folclore

Piazza Sant'Egidio 1b - (06) 5816563
Open 9am-1pm (Tue & Thu 9am-1pm & 5pm-7:30pm; Sun & hols 9am-12:30pm). Closed Mon.

This curious "folklore" museum occupies some rooms in what was once the convent of the Barefoot Carmelites. On display are reconstructions of life as it used to be in the countryside around Rome, illustrated with traditional costumes and pictures of festivals.

Museo Napoleonico

Piazza Ponte Umberto I - (06) 68806286
Open 9am-1:30pm (Tue & Thu 9am-1:30pm & 5pm-7:30pm; Sun & hols 9am-1pm). Closed Mon.

Count Giuseppe Primoli, son of Carlotta Bonaparte, amassed a wide-ranging collection of artworks and memorabilia from the Napoleonic period, which he bequeathed to the city of Rome. Exhibits include books that belonged to the emperor during his exile on Saint Helena, and many portraits, among which is David's *Princesses Zénaïde and Carlotta, Daughters of King Joseph.*

Museo Nazionale delle Arti e Tradizioni Popolari

Piazza Marconi 8 - (06) 5926148
Open daily 9am-2pm (Sun & hols 9am-1pm).

The folklore, folk art, and traditions of every region of Italy are presented in exhibits on agricultural, pastoral, and seafaring life, on music and dance, on religion and popular beliefs. The collection of regional costumes from the nineteenth century is fascinating.

Museo Nazionale di Castel Sant'Angelo

Lungotevere Castello 50 - (06) 68805133
Open 9am-2pm. Closed 2nd & 4th Tue of the month.

The monumental mausoleum that the Emperor Hadrian commissioned for himself and his successors, which has in fact served over the centuries as a fortress, a papal residence, a prison, and an armory, now houses a rich collection of art objects, paintings, furniture, architectural fragments, and weapons. It is one of the most interesting museums in Rome. The Antiquarium holds pieces of the castle's marble decoration from Hadrian's time; the apartments and chapels of the Renaissance popes preserve precious ceramics, statuary, and frescoes; and the prisons are properly shivery. One may visit the cell of Cagliostro, the infamous Italian impostor.

Museo Nazionale Romano

Baths of Diocletian, Piazza dei Cinquecento (06) 4882364
Open 9am-1pm. Closed Mon.

This staggering collection of ancient Greek, Roman, and Hellenistic art occupies parts of the Baths of Diocletian and a former Carthusian monastery (which was built in the baths' ruins in the sixteenth century). The museum's long restructuring is now nearly complete, and the holdings will soon be redistributed among the baths (monumental Roman sculpture) and the nearby Palazzo Massimo (Roman art from the Republic to the late Empire). At present, though many sections of the museum are closed, visitors can count on seeing the Ludovisi Throne, the *Discus Thrower*, and the beautiful Grand Cloister designed by Michelangelo.

Museo Nazionale degli Strumenti Musicali

Piazza Santa Croce in Gerusalemme 9a
(06) 7014796
Open 9am-1:30pm. Closed Sun.

Of the 3,000 items that make up this superb collection of musical instruments, less than a third are on view at any given time. Among the fascinating exhibits are bronze percussion instruments from ancient Egypt, Greece, and Rome, horns and stringed instruments from medieval and Renaissance times, the Barberini harp designed in the early seventeenth century, and a pianoforte built by the instrument's inventor, Bartolomeo Cristofori, in 1722.

Museo Nazionale di Villa Giulia

Piazzale di Villa Giulia 9 - (06) 3201951
Open 9am-7pm. Closed Mon.

The suburban villa built for Pope Julius III in the mid-sixteenth century is now a treasure house of Etruscan art. Outstanding among the remarkable exhibits are an archaic statue, *Man Astride a Sea Monster*, a magnificent life-size terra-cotta statue of Apollo from the sixth century B.C. and, from the same period, the famous *Sarcophagus of a Husband and Wife*. Here, too, is the Castellani collection of ceramics dating from the eighth century B.C. to the late Hellenistic era, as well as exciting archaeological finds from Etruscan and Etrusco-Italic burial sites, and objects in ivory, gold, silver, and bronze from the Barberini and Bernardini tombs (mid-seventh century B.C.).

Museo del Palazzo Venezia

Via del Plebiscito 118 - (06) 6798865
Open 9am-1:30pm (Sun & hols 9am-1pm). Closed Mon.

An enormous and diverse collection of bronzes, enamels, seals, silver, gold, and ivory objects, mosaics, fabrics, painting, and sculpture is assembled in this crenellated palazzo built for Venetian Cardinal Pietro Barbo in the mid-fifteenth century.

A thirteenth-century enamel, *Christ Pantocrater*, is outstanding. The museum's medieval section just reopened after a ten-year hiatus.

Museo Preistorico ed Etnografico

Palazzo delle Scienze dell'EUR,
Viale Lincoln 1 - (06) 5919132
Open daily 9am-7pm (Sun & hols 9am-1pm).

This is one of the largest museums of its type in Europe, freshly emerged from a thorough overhaul. Exhibits include a wide-ranging collection of prehistoric, Neolithic, and Bronze Age artifacts, chiefly from the region of Latium. The ethnographic material includes African art and musical instruments, pre-Columbian ceramics and textiles, feathered objects from Amazonia, and a stunning inlaid wooden mask from Mexico (fifteenth century).

Museo della Basilica di San Pancrazio

Piazza San Pancrazio 5d - (06) 5810458
Open daily 6:15am-noon & 4:30pm-5:30pm.

Sculpture, pagan and Christian inscriptions, a sarcophagus, and some fragments from the ancient fifth-century basilica of San Pancrazio (rebuilt in the seventeenth and restored in the nineteenth century) are preserved here.

Museo Storico dell'Arma dei Carabinieri

Piazza del Risorgimento 46 - (06) 68801020
Open 8:30am-12:30pm. Closed Mon.

Italy's flamboyant military police, the *carabinieri*, are honored in this interesting museum, which displays artworks, weapons, armor, medals, and other relics relating to the corps.

Museo Storico dei Bersaglieri

Porta Pia, Via XX Settembre - (06) 486723
Open Tue, Thu & Sat 9am-1pm.

The *bersaglieri* were the Italian army's famed sharpshooters. Their museum—containing weapons, souvenirs, and historic documents—is located right next to the breach in the Aurelian Wall through which King Victor Emmanuel II's troops entered Rome to capture it (from France) and complete the reunification of Italy on September 20, 1870.

Museo Storico della Fanteria

Piazza Santa Croce in Gerusalemme 9
(06) 7027971
Open Tue, Thu & Sat 9am-1pm.

These statues, medals, banners, arms, and other relics bear witness to the glorious tradition of the Italian army. Exhibits are arranged chronologically, from the earliest times through the Risorgimento, the colonial campaigns, and the World Wars. Next door, at number 7, the Museo Granatieri Sardegna contains memorabilia of the Savoy Guard Regiment, which in 1861 became the Sardinian Brigade of Guards.

Museo Storico della Liberazione di Roma

Via Tasso 145 - (06) 7003866
Open Tue, Thu & Fri 4pm-7pm; Sat & Sun 9:30am-12:30pm. Closed Mon, Wed.

Installed in rooms where political prisoners were detained during the Occupation, this small museum displays photographs, documents, and underground newspapers that recall the battle for Rome's liberation.

Museo & Pinacoteca di San Paolo

Basilica di San Paolo Fuori le Mura, Via Ostiense 186 - (06) 5410341
Open daily 9am-noon & 3pm-6pm.

Displayed in the medieval cloister are many architectural fragments from the adjoining basilica of San Paolo Fuori le Mura ("outside the walls"), which was erected by Constantine on the site of Saint Paul's tomb, ravaged by fire in 1823 and subsequently rebuilt. A museum has been created in the upper rooms of the monastery to hold an extremely interesting collection of Christian epigraphs, tombstones, and medieval frescoes found in and around the original basilica. In addition, a picture gallery in the vast hall just off the cloister (open by appointment) presents religious paintings, prints (some by Piranesi), and antique manuscripts. Also on view are painted panels and frescoes rescued from the ancient basilica.

Orto Botanico

Largo Cristina di Svezia 24 (Villa Corsini)
(06) 6864193
Open 9am-5:30pm (greenhouses 9am-12:30pm). Closed Sun, hols, Aug.

Pope Alexander VII established Rome's Botanical Gardens in 1660 with specimens of plants from all over the world. Situated in the park of the Palazzo Corsini, the garden boasts more than 8,000 different plants, including an exceptional collection of palms and conifers. Greenhouses harbor fascinating examples of orchids, succulents, and ferns.

Piccolo Museo delle Anime del Purgatorio

Chiesa del Sacro Cuore del Suffragio, Lungotevere Prati 12 - (06) 68806517
Open daily 7:30am-11am & 5pm-7:30pm.

The little Museum of the Suffering Souls in Purgatory is undoubtedly the only one of its kind in existence. It presents objects of piety and such testimonies as clothing, Bibles, breviaries, and wooden tables, all of which were allegedly marked by the burning hands of souls in purgatory, who have returned to bear witness to their suffering and to implore the prayers of the living.

Raccolta Teatrale del Burcardo

Via del Sudario 44 - (06) 68806755
Open 9am-1:30pm (Thu 9am-5:30pm, exc in summer). Closed Sun, hols, Aug.

In addition to prints, drawings, photographs, memorabilia, and a huge library, this impressive theatrical museum displays masks, costumes, busts of famous Italian actors, and a charming collection of eighteenth- and nineteenth-century puppets. The German Gothic building in which the collection is housed was erected in 1504.

The Vatican Museums and Galleries

Viale Vaticano - (06) 6983333
Open Jul 1-Sep 30 & 1 wk before & after Easter 9am-5pm; Oct 1-Jun 30 & Sat 9am-2pm. Final admission 1 hour before closing time. Closed Sun & hols (exc last Sun of the month when admission is free).

Visits to the Vatican Museums and Galleries follow four different but fixed itineraries, from which one may choose at the entrance. The museums listed below all share the same opening hours, unless otherwise noted.

Appartamento Borgia

These rooms, decorated with enchanting frescoes by Pinturicchio, were the private apartments of Pope Alexander VI, the

253

famous Borgia pope. The Sala della Vita dei Santi (a room decorated with paintings depicting episodes of the lives of the saints) is exceptionally fine: Saint Catherine of Alexandria (whose features are said to be those of Lucrezia Borgia) is undoubtedly Pinturicchio's masterpiece.

Braccio Nuovo

The Braccio Nuovo ("New Wing") is a Neoclassical gallery that contains Greek and Roman sculptures and a group of second-century mosaics. Here are displayed the famed Prima Porta Augustus, which shows the emperor at the age of 40 wearing superbly crafted armor, and a colossal Roman statue of the Nile, carved in the first century A.D. and rediscovered in 1513.

Cappella di Niccolò V

This small chapel was Pope Nicholas V's private oratory. The inspiring frescoes that adorn it, which were executed by Fra Angelico and his pupil, Benozzo Gozzoli, depict the lives of two martyr saints, Laurence and Stephen.

Cappella Sistina

It is in the Sistine Chapel that the College of Cardinals continues to meet to elect a new pope. The walls and ceiling are adorned with frescoes not only by Michelangelo, who was responsible for the decoration of the back wall (Last Judgment) and ceiling (Creation, Sibyls and Prophets, monumental nudes, and Biblical scenes), but by such eminent artists as Botticelli, Ghirlandaio, Perugino, Pinturicchio, and Signorelli. Yet it is Michelangelo, commissioned by Pope Julius II, who one immediately associates with the Cappella Sistina. His work astounds with its immense power, apocalyptic vision, and virile beauty. These masterpieces have regained their original splendor after thirteen years of painstaking (and highly controversial) restoration work. The first round of cleaning and restoring was completed in 1989; the second—which removed centuries' worth of candle soot and grime from the Last Judgment—ended in early 1994. The frescoes' colors once again display their original intensity: note the sublime ultramarine blue that Michelangelo obtained by mixing powdered lapis lazuli with his pigments.

Collezione d'Arte Religiosa Moderna

Just beyond the Borgia Apartments is the Vatican's collection of modern religious art. No fewer than 55 rooms hold some 800 works by artists from all over the world including Rodin, Rouault, Klee, Kandinsky, Modigliani, Picasso, Chagall, and others. In addition to paintings, the collection contains sculpture, brilliant tapestries, and some striking works in stained glass.

Galleria degli Arazzi

The ten superb tapestries depicting the life of Christ were woven in Brussels by Pieter Van Aelst in 1530 according to cartoons executed by students of Raphael. The gallery also displays glowingly beautiful sixteenth- and seventeenth-century tapestries from the Barberini and Vigevano looms.

Galleria dei Candelabri

This gallery takes its name from the pairs of first- and second-century marble candelabra set in the archways that punctuate its sweeping length. Some of the fine classical statues on view are the Sleeping Satyr in basalt, the Artemis of Ephesus (second century), and a sarcophagus with reliefs depicting the myth of Orestes. At the end of the gallery is the Sala della Biga, which displays a first-century B.C. marble biga (two-horse chariot) and a copy of the Greek Discus Thrower.

Museo Chiaramonti

Sculptor Antonio Canova was commissioned by Pope Pius VII Chiaramonti to create a museum in a long gallery of the Vatican designed by Bramante. Here the visitor will find a remarkable collection of Greco-Roman works, including a fragment of an original Greek relief of Penelope from the fifth century B.C., Roman busts, and a large group of carved sarcophagi.

Museo Gregoriano Egizio

In 1839 Pope Gregory XVI commissioned a disciple of Champollion, the noted Egyptologist, to establish a museum devoted to Egyptian art and civilization, based on the papal collections and recent finds from Hadrian's Villa. It was the first such museum in the world. Among the haunting artworks and artifacts on view are a sandstone head of Pharaoh Men-

tuhotep IV (2054–2008 B.C.) and a colossal statue of *Queen Tewe* (1280 B.C.).

Museo Gregoriano Etrusco
Open Mon & Fri.

This remarkable museum, established in 1836 by order of Pope Gregory XVI, displays sarcophagi, bronzes, urns, terra-cotta busts, and jewelry excavated from Etruscan sites. Of particular interest is the collection of Greek and Etruscan vases, and another collection of sculpture fragments and reliefs from the fifth and sixth centuries B.C. The graceful *Todi Mars*, a rare example of Greek bronze statuary from the fourth century B.C., is also on exhibit.

Museo Gregoriano Profano
Roman sculpture from the first century B.C. to the third century A.D. is displayed here (note the fine replica of Myron's *Athena and Marsyas*), in addition to urns, reliefs, portrait busts, sarcophagi, and funeral altars.

Museo Pio-Clementino
Early in the sixteenth century Pope Julius II amassed the nucleus of this impressive collection of antique sculpture, which succeeding generations have enriched. Perhaps the most famous work on view in the twelve rooms of this imposing museum is the *Belvedere Torso*, sculpted by Apollonius in the first century B.C. Some well-known ancient copies of Greek statues are on display as well, such as the *Cnidos Venus*, after Praxiteles. The dramatic *Laocoön*, a famed Hellenistic group that thrilled Michelangelo and Bernini, is one of the museum's more spectacular treasures.

Museo Profano della Biblioteca Apostolica
This museum in the sumptuous Apostolic Library houses a diverse collection of Etruscan, Roman, and medieval artifacts. Worthy of particular note are a second-century Roman mosaic from Hadrian's Villa, a head and arm from an original Greek statue of Athena (fifth century B.C.), and a bronze head of *Nero* from the first century A.D.

Museo Sacro della Biblioteca Apostolica
This branch of the Apostolic Library's museum was instituted in the mid-eighteenth century by Pope Benedict XIV to bring together the Vatican's early Christian holdings. Today the Museo Sacro offers a broad panorama of applied Christian art—gilded glass, fabrics, enamels, and ivory and bronze artifacts. Among the many interesting items on display are the disk with the oldest known image of Saints Peter and Paul, a Byzantine mosaic of Saint Theodore, and a tenth-century reliquary crucifix.

Pinacoteca Vaticana
The Vatican picture gallery was established under the pontificate of Pius VI (1775–1799) and enriched by canvases recovered from France after the Congress of Vienna. Today, it occupies a building designed in 1932 by Luca Beltrami. This extremely important art collection focuses on paintings of the Italian school from the Byzantine period through the eighteenth century, with special emphasis on the Renaissance and Baroque eras. Visitors to the gallery may admire the *Stefaneschi Triptych* by Giotto and his pupils, Fra Angelico's *Scenes from the Life of Saint Nicholas of Bari*, and Raphael's *Transfiguration* (his last work), his *Madonna di Foligno*, and his *Coronation of Mary*, along with the famous series of tapestries woven from Raphael's cartoons. Here as well are Caravaggio's *Descent from the Cross*, Domenichino's *Communion of Saint Jerome*, and the *Crucifixion of Saint Peter* by Guido Reni.

Le Stanze di Raffaele
The four chambers that make up the Stanze were decorated by Raphael at the behest of Pope Julius II and are generally considered to be the artist's masterpiece. Of the frescoes in the Chamber of the Borgo Fire, only the principal one shows Raphael's hand. But the second, or Chamber of the Signature, is entirely his work—it contains the majestic *School of Athens*, in which the philosophers of antiquity are portrayed with the features of contemporary artists (Leonardo, Michelangelo, Sodoma, Bramante). The Chamber of Heliodorus glorifies Raphael's papal patron: in the *Mass of Bolsena*, a kneeling Julius II is depicted among the worshippers. The astonishing veracity of the portraits and the sublime treatment of light

255

in this fresco make it perhaps the finest thing that Raphael ever painted. The fourth chamber was completed by Giulio Romano after Raphael's death. Beyond the Stanze is Raphael's Loggia, decorated with frescoes of Old and New Testament scenes designed by Raphael and executed by the artists who collaborated with him on the Stanze.

Tesoro di San Pietro

Basilica di San Pietro - (06) 6982
Open Apr-Sep 9am-6pm; Oct-Mar 9am-2pm.
The fabulous Treasury of Saint Peter's in the Vatican has been repeatedly pillaged over the centuries (by the Saracens in 846, during the Sack of Rome in 1527, by Napoleon according to the terms of the Tolentine Treaty in 1797), but its collections are nonetheless of the highest cultural and artistic importance. Some of the most significant items on display are the Crux Vaticana (sixth century), a cross donated by Justinian II, the Emperor of the East; a glittering ciborium (eucharistic bowl) by Donatello; the Tomb of Pope Sixtus IV della Rovere, Antonio Pollaiolo's masterpiece; two candelabra attributed to Benvenuto Cellini; and the sarcophagus of Junius Basso, prefect of Rome in 359.

Notorious Nudes at the Vatican

Oddities abound in this solemn place. One pope would order the naked truth, another would clothe it. Pope Paul III Farnese's funeral monument is adorned with statues of his mother and sister in the guise of Prudence and Justice. The all-too-beautiful Justice, with the features of comely Giulia Farnese, raised eyebrows and it was put under wraps by papal order (Bernini sadly fashioned her metallic mufti). A straitlaced Counter-Reformation crowd also took offense at all the stiff necks staring at the bare bodies in the Sistine Chapel. So, during the pontificate of Pius IV in 1564, Daniele da Volterra was ordered to dress several paintings that were considered "too nude." Obediently, he drew drawers on those whose pants were down, earning himself the nickname il Braghettone, Mr. Baggy Britches. And a thorough job he made of it, too: not even the professionals who recently restored the Sistine Chapel could remove Volterra's handiwork.

Asclepius and the Sacred Serpent

The Isola Tiberina which lies in a bend of the Tiber, is linked to city's left bank by the Ponte Fabricio, the oldest bridge in Rome. The island is home to a major hospital and indeed since antiquity has been associated with health and medicine. Legend says that in 293 B.C. during an outbreak of plague, Rome sent a delegation of wise men to the temple of Asclepius, the Greek god of healing, to find a cure. The Romans returned from their mission with a most unusual remedy—a sacred serpent. Just as the ship touched shore, the snake wriggled overboard and hid beneath the island. The divine message was clear: ever since, the Isola Tiberina has been dedicated to Aesculapius (the god's Roman name) and the medical arts.

Useful Telephone Numbers

Rome Area Code: 06

Airports: Ciampino, 794941; Fiumicino, 65951; Urbe, 8120571
Ambulance: 5510
City Hall: 67101
City Police Department: 67691
CO.TRA.L.: 3610441
Fire Department: 115
Medical Emergency: 4826741

Pharmacy: 1921
Police Emergency: 112; 113
Post Office and Telegraph: 160
Public Transportation Information: 46951
Radio Taxi: 3750; 4994
State Railway Information: 4775
Tourist Information: 4883748
Wake-up Call: 114
Weather Service: 144

A Day at the Races

Toga-clad sports fans in ancient Rome gathered at Domitian's Stadium to see gymnastic events, or at the Colosseum to witness blood-curdling gladiatorial games and wild-animal combats; but when they wanted to watch a Ben Hur–style chariot race, they headed for the Circus Maximus. Drivers of bigas and quadrigas (racing chariots drawn by two or four horses, respectively) were as rich and famous as any Formula One champ today. Young boosters of the "greens" and "blues"—the two top teams—would wear their idols' colors and even comb their hair to resemble their favorite charioteers. Fans didn't hesitate to defend their team with fisticuffs, either: most chariot races concluded with an all-out brawl. For a fine view of the remains of the Circus Maximus, look down from atop the Palatine Hill.

Roman Skyscrapers

Ancient Rome was a real disaster area: when houses weren't catching fire they were caving in! As the city's population ballooned, land speculators tried to cash in on the situation by building taller and taller dwellings. Finally, as collapses became a daily occurrence, Augustus decreed that no house should exceed a height of 69 feet, a limit which Trajan later reduced to 60 feet. However, Rome did have its equivalent of the Empire State building: the Felicula, was situated in the Campo Marzio district between the Pantheon and the Theater of Marcellus. No one knows exactly how high it rose, but in the reign of Septimius Severus (193–211) the Felicula was famed throughout the Empire. Alas, no vestige remains of that marvel, though it is known to have survived at least into the fifth century.

257

VENISE

An Enchanted Labyrinth

In Venice where, as French poet Jean Cocteau once remarked, "pigeons walk and lions fly," it is soon apparent even to visitors with only modest powers of observation that normal rules simply don't apply. In the first place, Venice isn't even really a city, despite the compact geography of its streets and canals. No, Venice is six cities, one per *sestiere*, or district: Castello, San Marco, and Cannaregio on one side of Canal Grande, and San Polo, Dorsoduro, and Santa Croce on the other. To further complicate matters, each *sestiere* is made up of numerous parishes, all clustered around their own public wells and bell towers; some, in fact, are little islets unto themselves.

So the first image that Venice presents to us is of a labyrinth, a mystifying maze of alleys, islands, houses, and canals, constructed and then somehow connected to make a city. All around, in the salt air and underfoot in the city's very shape, is the shimmering presence of the lagoon, fashioned by sandbanks and by the beds of ancient rivers, whose course Canal Grande follows as it flows into the sea. Venice, it has been calculated, consists of more than 100 islets, linked together by nearly 400 bridges. Little wonder, then, that navigating the city is a complicated business.

The sensation of entering a mysterious labyrinth is accentuated by the lack of open space, so typical of Venice yet so atypical of most Italian cities, where public squares—think of Florence, Rome, Naples—suffuse the urban landscape with light and greenery. Venice boasts just one such square (though it is, admittedly, one of the finest on Earth): Piazza San Marco. Many of the city's narrow, twisting streets are nothing more than alleys bounded by high, blank walls. Goethe observed that a man could measure the width of these streets with his arms outstretched; he added, "In the narrowest, standing with arms akimbo, one's elbows touch the walls."

In Venice, visitors naturally have difficulty getting their bearings. The city's central thoroughfare, the Grand Canal, plays much the same role as the *corso* (main boulevard) in other Italian towns. Shaped like a vast, inverted S, it flows over the bed of a river long since expired amid the shoals of the lagoon. Venice's second-most-important artery, the Mercerie, stretches from San Marco to the Rialto Bridge. The Mercerie is, in fact, a series of streets edged with luxury boutiques. Now, with a winding waterway and a main street that is actually several streets, it's only to be expected that one will stray off course occasionally.

But don't worry. Though you may lose your way, you will never get hopelessly lost. Just follow the flow of the crowd, which will invariably carry you back to one of the two poles around which Venetian life has always revolved: the Rialto Bridge or Piazza San Marco—Saint Mark's Square.

Tradition has it that when Saint Mark was sailing back to preach in the West after a sojourn in Egypt, a violent storm cast him up on a deserted shore—the Rialto—where he fell asleep. While he slept, an angel appeared to him and said, "This will be your eternal resting place." Tintoretto, the sixteenth-century Venetian master, left us a marvelous painting of *Saint Mark's Dream*, and another of the recovery of the evangelist's relics. For it is said that after his death, Mark's body remained in Alexandria, where Christians feared that it would be profaned. Two bold Venetian sailors resolved to recapture the relics and bring them to Italy. One stormy night, they wrapped the saint's remains in animal skins and carried them aboard ship. When port authorities questioned them about what they were transporting, they replied, "Pork." They knew that the customs agents, good Muslims for whom the meat was anathema, would not inspect such a cargo too closely. And that is how, in 828, the body of Saint Mark the Evangelist, whose symbol, the winged lion, is synonymous with Venice, was brought to rest as the angel had predicted.

To house these distinguished relics, the Doge commissioned a new private chapel to be built, a modest church that ultimately became one of the most magnificent sanctuaries in Christendom. Saint Mark's Basilica, built to its present design between 1063 and 1071, represents the visible heart of Venice—one might say its Byzantine, Oriental heart. Modeled on Byzantium's Church of the Holy Apostles, the basilica brings East and West together in typically Venetian fashion. To enter Saint Mark's for the first time is to be overtaken by a feeling of mystery. The greatest achievement of Byzantine art, of which the basilica is a masterpiece, is to have made light even more mysterious than shadow. Sunlight filters into San Marco discreetly, almost timidly. What illuminates the dim, candlelit interior is the glow of golden mosaics, which cover the walls with their subdued shimmer. For Easterners who believe that dawn inevitably follows the darkness, darkness is not an enemy. It is this notion, which goes against the very grain of Western art, that San Marco illustrates so powerfully.

Leaving the basilica (which, we repeat, was the Doges' chapel, not the cathedral of Venice), we pass into the courtyard of the Palazzo Ducale, the Doges' Palace, the repository and compendium of Venice's eventful history. When the first Doge fled the islet of Malamocco under the threat of foreign invaders, he established a fortress at this site early in the ninth century. Even then, the upheavals that were a permanent feature of Venetian political life were gathering momentum. In 976 a popular uprising destroyed the original ducal residence, though it was quickly rebuilt. In 1106, it was devastated by fire. Only in the fourteenth century did

the fortress become a palace, where patrician councils convened and elected the Doges, limited sovereigns who embodied the power of the Serenissima Repubblica: the Most Serene Republic, so called for the remarkable stability of its political institutions. The Doges' portraits hang in the Palace's Sala del Maggior Consiglio (the Great Council Hall), a testimony to the continuity of Venetian history (one frame, that of Doge Marin Falier, beheaded for treason in 1355, is empty).

It is fascinating to follow the evolution of Venice's destiny inscribed in the very stones of the Palazzo Ducale. Paradoxically, the structure presents an inverted chronology: the newest parts stand on the ground level, while the most archaic forms are on top. The colonnaded portico (altered in the sixteenth century) is Renaissance; above it rises the delicate openwork of a Venetian-Gothic loggia; crowning the whole is a series of Venetian-Byzantine finials. On the façade of pink, white, and gray marble, the rectilinear pediments of classical windows alternate with small ogival arches, whose angular lines abruptly flow into undulating (we are tempted to say "maritime") curves, an involuntary but appropriate reminder of Venice's long supremacy on the seas. In the Palazzo's splendid courtyard, an attentive observer can begin to comprehend the weight, solidity, and perpetuity of Venice simply by "reading" the architecture of the massive Palace of the Doges.

While the Republic's political and spiritual power was centered on the islet of Castello ("the Castle"), since its earliest days Venice's urban life has had another center: the Rialto. As its name indicates (rivo alto means "the high bank"), this part of Venice was less at the mercy of flood waters than the surrounding islets and was thus one of the first to be inhabited. Here the merchant republic's flourishing trade developed, without which the splendors of San Marco, the Doges' Palace, and the city's patrician palazzi would have been inconceivable. Even now, an observant eye can spot signs of this early commercial activity—like the Rialto Bridge itself, squat and ponderous. Until the nineteenth century it was the sole link between the two halves of Venice, providing the only passage for foot traffic over the Grand Canal.

At first a mere wooden span, the present bridge was built in 1588 by an architect with a predestined name—Antonio da Ponte—whose design, it seems, was favored for its technical features over projects submitted by such brilliant architects as Palladio and Michelangelo. Across the bridge runs a central passageway; behind the twin rows of stores are ramps that afford splendid views of the canal and its teeming life.

On the western bank of the Grand Canal you'll find the Rialto market, still the largest in Venice, where all the riches of the Orient—pepper, cinnamon, Syrian brocades—were once unloaded onto the Republic's docks. Since the fourteenth century, sly, greedy gulls have circled and screeched above the Pescheria (fish market) and the neighboring Erbaria (vegetable market). Standing amid the bright heaps of vegetables and glistening displays of Adriatic fish and other creatures from the lagoon, you can observe a slice of real Venetian life, as merchants and customers bargain and chatter in their curious, lisping dialect. Your whetted appetite will surely lead you into one of the many small, dim osterie (taverns) nearby. Go ahead and treat yourself to a glass of wine from the hills of Treviso (strawberry-scented red Fragolino, or spritzy, aromatic Prosecco) and to some of the marvelous Venetian bar snacks called cicchetti: fried squid, tiny cuttlefish, anchovies, bits of hot tripe or ham, and so on.

At the foot of the Rialto Bridge, on the San Marco side, stands the hulking sixteenth-century Fondaco dei Tedeschi, the German merchants' warehouse, built for the numerous traders from Germany who thronged to Venice to purchase glass, spices, and cotton, and to sell their cargoes of fustian cloth and silver from northern mines. It is now the city's central post office. To return to San Marco, follow the Mercerie, a warren of shopping streets where, as they have done since the Renaissance, stores display elegant merchandise to tempt foreign buyers. Nowhere else does one get a better sense of the mercantile Venice that once proudly named itself "the most opulent of cities."

Less easily accessible than San Marco or the Rialto, the Arsenale, in the eastern section of the city, reveals another essential facet of Venice: its long preeminence on the seas. The Arsenale was until quite recently a military zone; it is now open to the public. When we say "arsenal" today, we mean an arms depot. But that is not at all what the Venetians meant by the term. Venice's Arsenale was the shipyard where the Republic's warships and trading vessels were built. It was a site of immense strategic importance, for while Venice was a world power, her fleet bore the responsibility of protecting the coastlines of her possessions and allies. Founded early in the twelfth century, the Arsenale swiftly developed into a huge industry, a model of technology, employing 3,000 to 4,000 workers in the Middle Ages, and as many as 16,000 in its heyday. Dante, who visited the Arsenale as an ambassador to Venice, was struck by the vision of men laboring with vats of boiling pitch; an echo of that scene found its way into his Inferno.

The Arsenale's monumental entrance, celebrated in innumerable engravings, is the first example of Renaissance architecture in Venice. It offers a striking image of the Serenissima's military might. The portal, a triumphal arch of pure, classic lines, displays a fierce Lion of Saint Mark who seems about to let loose with a terrifying roar. Set around the portal are four more marble lions, war prizes captured in Greece in the late seventeenth century, further reminders of Venice's domination of the eastern Mediterranean. The lion farthest to the left has a curious history: transported from the Greek port of Piraeus, where it served as a fountain, its body bears inscriptions in runic characters carved by Norwegian or Swedish Vikings, mercenary soldiers who had helped quell a popular uprising in Athens. This well-traveled feline, who came from Greece to Venice bearing a message from northern warriors, is one of the city's more endearing landmarks.

This labyrinth for which we have tried to provide a few waymarkers is fascinating not only for its visual splendors and glorious past; Venice is, quite literally, a place of enchantment. The spell it casts is difficult to define, but it has to do with the feeling of unreality, close to a dream state, that the city inspires. The simple fact that one walks all day, rather than riding in cars, cabs, or buses; the absence of traffic noises (save the occasional backfire of a motorboat); the ever-present smell and sound of water—all this contributes to the impression of being in an unfamiliar, other-worldly place.

And in Venice time flows in a peculiar fashion, just as it does in dreams. The city seems to stand outside of time, with its past set out for us to admire, marvel at, and touch as we wish. In Venice no effort of the imagination is needed to picture what life must have been like generations before, for its past is so obviously present and compelling. Unlike Rome, a city that

assails the visitor with the violent chaos of its history, Venice stirs in us sensations that are insistently and magnificently repeated, like recurrent themes in a sonata or symphony. They envelop us in a closed, harmonious world wrought of reflections in water, faded-pink brick, gliding gondolas, endless stone steps leading up numberless bridges, blind alleys, a faint salt smell from the lagoon, the incessant slap of waves against the quays, crumbling palazzi, and the sleek hulls of watercraft... At the heart of the Venetian labyrinth we discover a rare lesson in harmony.

Death in Venice

The Serene Republic had some of the most horrifying prisons known to man, called I Piombi e Pozzi, meaning the Leads and Wells. The Leads were so named because they were rooms right under the leaden roof of the Palazzo Ducale—warm in summer, cool in winter, as you can imagine. The least desirable accommodations were the Wells, also in the Palazzo Ducale. For a shivery bit of sightseeing, they may still be visited today. Once reserved for hardened criminals and political prisoners, these cells are as narrow as water wells, each with one tiny opening on the inner hallway. No light enters. The walls are covered with planks carefully fashioned to resemble the insides of a coffin. Each cell has a name—Mocenigo, Galeotta, Vulcano, Forte, Orba, Liona—and a hideous story to go with it. After less inhumane prisons were built elsewhere, the Council of Ten continued to use the Wells for temporary incarcerations, assuming that the chilling atmosphere of the Pozzi would induce detainees to talk...

Boxing
the Collective Ear

"The gang's all here!" they would shout, and then have at it on the Ponte dei Pugni (Bridge of Blows) at San Barnaba. The *Castellani* and *Nicolotti* were allowed to meet here from September until Christmas and beat the daylights out of one another. The punch-drunk rivals lived on opposite sides of town and dressed differently. The *Castellani* donned red caps and scarves and lived in the Castello district in east Venice; the *Nicolotti* wore black berets and neckerchiefs and hailed from Dorsoduro in the west. The feuding went on for centuries until one wild day in 1705, when the fisticuffs got out of hand. From then on, the custom was outlawed, but the bridge kept its pugilistic name.

Restaurants

It seems appropriate, somehow, that the food one encounters in Venice should turn out to be as startling and unique as the city itself: curious seafood ("creatures from the lagoon"), brown spaghetti, red lettuce, black rice... An authentic Venetian repast mirrors the watery landscape that produced it. The Adriatic sea and Venetian lagoon yield delicate fish, shellfish, and crustaceans that are not found anywhere else: granseole (spider crabs), moleche (soft-shell crabs), gô (whitebait), and capesante (scallops) as well as baby squid, miniature clams, mussels, tiny cuttlefish, spiny lobsters, octopus, mantis shrimp, and prawns. Marinated in a light blend of lemon juice and olive oil, seasoned with more than a little pepper and perhaps some parsley, these seafarers make exquisite antipasti, worlds away from the hearty stuff that neighboring Lombardy serves to start off a meal.

But like the Lombards, Venetians love rice, though they prefer it considerably wetter. Their classic risi e bisi (rice and peas) is nearly a soup, and their risottos are served all'onda, liquid enough to make "waves." Risottos in the Venetian tradition usually incorporate seafood, or the superb vegetables cultivated in nearby Treviso (famous for radicchio, that beautiful, slightly bitter red lettuce) or Chioggia (source of tender, flavorful artichokes). Risotto al nero is a local standard whose unusual inky hue has put off many a first-time taster. The rice is dyed black by cuttlefish ink, which also lends its color to the sauce of stewed cuttlefish (seppie alla veneziana), a popular main dish, often ladled over a bed of golden polenta for maximum visual impact.

Tradition prevails in Venetian kitchens. Ingredients tend to be indigenous (the aforementioned seafood) or else customary, like the raisins and pine nuts that go into sfogi in saor (soused baby sole, an antipasto) or the spices—cinnamon, cloves, saffron, pepper—that hark back to Venice's long history of trade with the East.

Time-honored ways of preparing tripe, cuttlefish, liver, and bigoli (brown wholewheat vermicelli) alla veneziana haven't altered a whit in generations. What's more, it would seem that an enduring fondness for certain dishes is inscribed in Venetians' genetic code: eel (bisati or anguille), for instance, which they grill (all'ara), bake (in tecia), fry, stew, marinate, or sprinkle with lemon juice (alla veneziana); and dried cod, the famous baccalà, which is most often served creamed (mantecato) or alla vicentina (with onions, anchovies, and a whiff of cinnamon).

Restaurant offerings reflect this culinary conservatism as well as diners' preference for regional specialties: sfogi in saor hasn't been bumped off of menus in favor of Norwegian smoked salmon. In Venice, traditional trattorias featuring local dishes are not lacking. The problem is finding those which serve creditable (and fairly priced—food is expensive in this town) versions of a cuisine that, if not capably prepared, palls quicker than most (by your fifth batch of botched, sickly sweet risotto al nero, you'll swear you never want to see the stuff again). So follow this guide, and choose your trattoria with care.

A word about dessert. Tiramisù is certain to be featured as the "house sweet" in five out of seven Venice restaurants. When properly prepared with a light hand, this concoction of creamy mascarpone cheese and rum- or liqueur-soaked cake is heavenly. Unfortunately, it is too often a stodgy cliché. If your preceding meals lead you to suspect that the tiramisù may disappoint, a much better bet, when they're available, are the buttery, typically Venetian biscotti (cookies) called baicoli, lightly perfumed with orangeflower water.

Venetian flavors are best matched with local wines, many of which are familiar from home, but which taste so much better on their native turf: Valpolicella, Bardolino, Pinot Grigio, and Soave.

Antica Besseta
Santa Croce 1395 - (041) 721687
Closed Tue, Wed, Jul. No cards.
Nereo Volpe clings to the culinary traditions of his forebears, preparing simple but satisfying Venetian favorites. Quality ingredients put his dishes a couple of cuts above the ordinary: superbly fresh fish arrives still flipping from the nearby Rialto market, and the vegetables taste just-picked. A recent meal composed of an excellent seafood antipasto, delicious bigoli (whole-wheat spaghetti), a rich frittura mista featuring the tiniest, crispiest little fish imaginable, plus salad, mixed fresh fruit, white wine *della casa*, coffee, and a tot of grappa added up to the very reasonable tab of 60,000 lire. **C** 60,000 lire.

The Oldest Trattoria in Town

Old but not infirm, the Aquila Nera has been serving the neighborhood of San Bartolomeo for at least 445 years. The first document related to the venerable establishment dates to July 12, 1550. It's a death certificate for "the waiter at the Aquila Negra" (sic). But who knows how long the poor man had been dashing from table to table? Like Venice itself, the exact age of this trattoria is shrouded in the mists of time.

Antico Martini
San Marco, Campo San Fantin 1983 (041) 5224121
Dinner only. Closed Tue, Dec 1-Mar 20. All major cards.
In the beginning there was a caffè, one of the oldest in Venice. Situated across from La Fenice, Antico Martini was destined to become a favorite venue for actors and theater goers, and such it has been for nearly two-and-a-half centuries.

The cuisine navigates between "international" offerings and authentic Venetian classics. Needless to say, we far prefer the latter: radicchio braised with beef marrow and Parmesan cheese, tiny sole in a white-wine marinade with raisins and little onions (sfogi in saor), calf's liver alla veneziana (fried with onions), and a variety of fresh fish cooked with skill and respect. For dessert, don't even try to resist the exceptionally airy meringue. Host Emilio Baldi, a connoisseur of French and Italian wines, is responsible for the magnificent cellar. He opened "Italy's first wine bar" next door, see Vino Vino, in *Quick Bites*. **C** 65,000 lire.

Antico Pignolo
San Marco, Calle degli Specchieri 451 (041) 5228123
Closed Tue (exc in summer), Jan. All major cards.
This capacious establishment near Piazza San Marco, (the garden alone can handle 200 diners!) pursues its vocation of serving nicely prepared seafood to lots (and lots) of tourists. The surroundings are rustic, with elegant touches here and there: paintings on the wall, handcrafted tableware. Firm raw scampi or spider crabs (granseole) set the theme for what is to follow: spaghetti sauced with cuttlefish in their ink, curried scampi tossed with tagliolini pasta, risotto garnished with seafood, fish soup, and so on. Fresh fish, whether fried, baked, or broiled, is the backbone of the main-course roster. Give the ice creams a try for dessert. Owner Riccardo Di Pietri is particularly proud of his cellar. **C** 80,000 lire.

Arcimboldo
Castello, Calle dei Furlani 3219 (041) 5286569
Dinner only. Closed Tue, Aug, 10 days before or after Carnival. All major cards.
This quiet corner of Castello near the Arsenale is part of "Venetians' Venice," barely touched by the tourist tide. Arcimboldo, you may recall, was the Renaissance painter who composed vegetables and fruits into fantastical portraits; chef Ivano Borghese makes similarly creative use of his ingredients. Not long ago he served us a salad of sardines and wild rice presented in an ice sculpture, followed by an escalope of sea bass in a pool of ocean-blue sauce, and a dessert dubbed "indigo

sublime" that featured a navy-tinted wild-blueberry sauce. Even if his "blue mood" has passed when you come to dine, you'll be pleased with Borghese's Venetian-style offerings: whole-wheat bigoli spaghetti sauced with anchovies, shellfish soup served under a golden pastry crust, or breast of capon with a mellow sauce of shallots and balsamic vinegar. Turbot given an unnecessary dredging of flour was less thrilling, though, and we do wish that owner Luciana Boccardi would give the wine list an overhaul. **C** 80,000 lire.

Caffè Orientale
San Polo, Rio Marin 2426
(041) 719804
Closed Sun dinner, Mon, Aug 10-23, Nov. All major cards.

Gondoliers often drop by here for a glass of wine, an *ombra* as they say in Venice; we like this spot too, for its inviting ambience and short but attractive seafood menu. A shellfish sauté might pave the way for a splendid dish of tagliatelle cooked with lobster in a covered casserole or ravioli stuffed with sea bass; main-course options run to the savory likes of grilled tuna with polenta, baked monkfish, or an assortment of prime, just-caught specimens presented in a mixed grill. Good desserts; pertinent wine list. **C** 60-70,000 lire (wine incl.).

Canova
Hotel Luna Baglioni,
San Marco, Calle Vallaresso 1243
(041) 5209550
Closed Sun, Mon lunch (in Jul), Aug. All major cards.

A tavern called Alla Luna stood in this spot as far back as the twelfth century. Today, the dining room of the handsomely renovated Luna Baglioni hotel is anything but fusty. Stylish waiters navigate around the tables, serving highly polished renditions of Venetian specialties. Outstanding among the starters are a delicate salad of zucchini and scampi, bean velouté dotted with taglierini (a sophisticated take on the rustic pasta e fagioli), summery zucchini gnocchi sparked with fresh herbs, and a salad of pearly scallops dressed with balsamic vinegar. To follow, you can choose duck breast in peppery peverada sauce, calf's liver alla veneziana on a bed of polenta, or monkfish paired with artichokes and perfumed with fresh chives.

A separate menu is devoted to desserts, and the wine list impresses with its wealth of noble labels. **C** 80,000 lire.

La Caravella
San Marco, Calle Larga XXII Marzo 2397 - (041) 5208901
Closed Wed (exc May-Nov). All major cards.

The nautical décor, which is frankly over the top, immediately arouses suspicion about the food—suspicion that the leather-bound, book-length menu and the eclectic listings (bouillabaisse, paella, "sole à la Carmen," "veal kidneys à la Duc de Guise") do little to disperse. But resist the temptation to flee, order an aperitivo (not the house cocktail, which tastes like cough syrup), and seek out the good regional specialties, like bigoli (whole-wheat pasta) with anchovies, gnocchi with Gorgonzola, excellent stuffed squid, or beef fillet Caravella. Children are given appropriately sized cutlery, the tables are prettily set, the staff is impeccably trained, and the desserts are simply delicious. See? Aren't you glad you stayed? **C** 100-120,000 lire.

Cipriani
Hotel Cipriani,
Giudecca 10 - (041) 5207744
Closed mid Nov-Mar. All major cards.

The Cipriani, surely one of the world's most enchanting hotels, is also home to an exceptional table. Residents are joined for lunch or dinner by a select group of food lovers who know that this is one of the very best restaurants in Venice. What this fortunate group sits down to, on the flower-decked terrace or in the exquisite dining room, bears little resemblance to "hotel food" as it is usually practiced. The kitchen has adopted a pared-down approach, sending out dishes that are visually restrained but which explode with fresh herbal aromas and primal flavors. Rare and exotic foodstuffs are eschewed in favor of local ingredients purchased at their seasonal peak—this is Italian cooking at its streamlined best. Some cases in point are stracci ("little rags") of house-made pasta sauced with a fragrant ragù of veal and celery; a salad of baby spinach leaves combined with morsels of sweetbreads and mild cheese; a splendid mold of mussels and rice that recalls Apulia's famous tiella, a "poor man's" dish made fit for a king; gnocchetti of scampi in a featherlight sauced dotted with spring-green peas; and spiny lobster tail roasted in a shell of spinach pasta and served with Chioggia artichokes: the sweet lobster meat plays beautifully off the vegetable's gentle astringency. The Cipriani's patrons obviously have the means to dine anywhere they choose; their preference for this table proves that refined simplicity may be the rarest form of luxury. **C** 130,000 lire.

Club del Doge

Hotel Gritti Palace,
San Marco, Campo Santa Maria del Giglio 2467 - (041) 794611
Open daily. All major cards.
This stunningly posh setting (the ceiling is painted in the same soft pastels as the terrazzo floor) perfectly suits the tony international clientele that stays at the Gritti Palace. While taking in the view of Canal Grande from the terrace, patrons dine on refined versions of traditional Venetian recipes: raviolini stuffed with fish and garnished with tiny shrimp in a saffron-tinged sauce, golden saffron risotto enriched with chicken livers, Adriatic crabs, anise-scented sea-bream fillet, and breast of guinea hen encased in a crisp crust and garnished with chicken livers. All the fish is impeccably fresh and cooked with care. The cellar spotlights regional wines. Distinguished service. **C** 110,000 lire.

Corte Sconta

Castello, Calle del Pestrin 3886
(041) 5227024
Closed Sun, Mon, Jan, mid Jul-mid Aug. V, AE.
With its affable owner, two small dining rooms, and wee kitchen where traditional dishes are skillfully prepared, Corte Sconta ("Hidden Courtyard") is seductive in its utter simplicity. This Venetian seafood restaurant is quite unlike those "picturesque" eateries around the Rialto and San Marco, all crawling with tourists. Set in a working-class neighborhood not far from the Scuola di San Giorgio degli Schiavoni and its glorious Carpaccios, it attracts artists, filmmakers, and politicians of every stripe. (Reservations are a must, and should be made well in advance.) After sampling from the unbeatable antipasti assortment (ask your waiter to bring you whatever looks good that day), move on to a primo of tuna and artichoke gnocchetti or tagliatelle tossed with anchovies and por-

cini mushrooms, and thence to one of the splendid main courses: John Dory showered with fresh herbs, squid stuffed with vibrant red chicory (radicchio), eel in a sparky vinegar reduction scented with bay, or rockfish with potatoes and "runaway salami" (the sausage adds its zing to the dish, then is removed before serving). Fish and shellfish barely off the boat also come flawlessly fried or grilled. **C** 70,000 lire.

Al Covo

Castello, Campiello della Pescaria 3968
(041) 5223812
Closed Wed, Thu, Jan, 2 wks in Aug. V, AE.
Cesare Benelli is a vivacious host; just watch as he helps his guests put together a meal (Al Covo doesn't have a menu): his enthusiasm is infectious! And don't worry about a language barrier, for Cesare's wife, Diana, is American. On offer is ultrafresh seafood from local waters, prepared with admirable restraint. The offerings change according to the day's catch, so we suggest that you rely on Cesare's excellent judgment. Just don't forget to save room for Diana's scrumptious desserts. **C** 70,000 lire (wine incl).

Brothers of the Good Death

The Scuola di San Fantin in Campo San Fantin was the original headquarters of the Confraternità di San Girolamo and Santa Maria della Giustizia. The brotherhood was in charge of conducting convicts to the gallows, which earned them the name, *Scuola della buona morte*, or, "A good death to you, sir!"

Danieli Terrace

Hotel Danieli,
Castello, Riva degli Schiavoni 4196
(041) 5226480
Open daily. All major cards.
Perched atop the elegant, Neoclassical Hotel Danieli, this terrace restaurant affords an incomparable view of the lagoon and San Giorgio. The restaurant's winter quarters aren't bad either, with their huge

bay windows that take in all of Venice. Surrounded by such beauty and comfort, you would probably expect to feast on first-rate cuisine. Don't get your hopes up *too high*... The strategy we suggest is to stick to the Venetian dishes: braised radicchio with soppressa sausage in a sprightly vinegar-touched sauce, risotto ai porcini, tagliolini tossed with seafood, sea bass with radicchio. Finish with a wonderfully fresh salad and save dessert for another time, another place. The service is polished to a high sheen, but the wine list lacks luster. **C** 120,000 lire and up.

Do Forni
San Marco, Calle degli Specchieri 468
(041) 5232148
Closed Thu (exc in summer), Nov. All major cards.
The cooking at Do Forni has its ups and down (though the check, we've noticed, rarely dips below 100,000 lire). Choose a fresh seafood antipasto (like the delicate granseole served in the crab's shell) and then, if there are two of you, by all means order one of the excellent seasonal risottos, here served "all'onda," as native tastes require—with considerably more liquid than in Piedmont or Lombardy. A fine Adriatic fish baked in parchment or grilled to a turn is preferable, we think, to turkey breast "allo Sherry" or kidneys in mustard sauce. There's a decent wine list, and the service, like the setting, aspires to elegance. **C** 100,000 lire (wine incl).

Do Leoni
Hotel Londra Palace,
Riva degli Schiavoni 4171 - (041) 5200533
Open daily. All major cards.
The kitchen is manned by a versatile crew, equally at ease with French haute cuisine and Italian regional fare. In recent months, Venetian dishes have been holding the spotlight: seasonal risottos, braised cuttlefish, garlicky sautéed shrimp presented on a bed of polenta, and a classic anatra in peverada (duck in a peppery sauce) can be enjoyed, of an evening, to the accompaniment of live guitar music. The setting incites guests to linger over their lush Black Forest cake and admire the view from the veranda (weather permitting) or bask in the elegance of the indoor dining room. The service is first-class but, oddly, the wine list isn't. **C** 100,000 lire and up.

Ai Due Vescovi
San Marco, Calle Fiubera 813
(041) 5236990
Closed Sun. V, AE.
The "Two Bishops" have garnered rave reviews in the press for a clever, ambitious menu (sole stuffed with shrimp and strawberries, steak topped with coffee-flavored butter...) that is often revised. We give high marks to the monkfish with onions, oysters swirled with truffle sauce, and spaghetti with Pernod-laced mussels. But we'll hold back on the bravos until the kitchen performs more consistently and gives desserts their due. **C** 70,000 lire.

Excelsior Lido
Hotel Excelsior,
Lido di Venezia, Lungomare Marconi 41
(041) 5260201
Closed Nov-Mar. All major cards.
An opulent dining room, an equally splendid summer terrace, and the entire litany of the Veneto's culinary repertory are on offer in this palatial hotel's trio of restaurants. Chef Piero Alzetta is at the top of his form when working with such local foodstuffs as the cuttlefish for risotto al nero, the scallops that garnish an airy feuilleté, and the scampi that embellish his excellent fettuccine. Carpaccio (thin slices of raw beef tenderloin) with grana cheese and a hint of celery makes a fine, light main course, as does the elegant turbot with porcini mushrooms. Decent cellar; dazzling service. **C** 90-130,000 lire.

Favorita
Via Francesco Duodo 33
(041) 5261626
Closed Mon, Jan. All major cards.
This enchanting spot may well become one of your favorites. Luca Pradel purchases all of his seafood from fishermen who let down their nets in the waters around Chioggia. They bring him briny shellfish for the enticing antipasto assortment and glossy fresh fish which are grilled, fried, or baked in parchment and garnished with seasonal vegetables. The kitchen also produces velvety Venetian-style risotto and golden, handmade pasta. Fresh fruit desserts and a worthwhile wine list complete this charming picture. **C** 70,000 lire.

Fiaschetteria Toscana

Cannaregio, San Giovanni Crisostomo
5719 - (041) 5285281
Closed Tue, Jul 15-Aug 5. All major cards.
Albino and Mariuccia Busatto extend a
cordial welcome to patrons of their inviting restaurant, which boasts a pretty terrace on the piazzetta out front. There's
nothing Tuscan about the menu, which
looks unwaveringly out to sea, from the
antipasto assortment featuring many rare
varieties of crustaceans, to the glistening
fresh fish prepared with skill and a minimum of fuss. Among the famously tasty
sweets, we're partial to the crêpes folded
over a creamy Grand-Marnier filling. Tip-
top service; exceptional wine list (though
the house Prosecco, served by the carafe,
should not be overlooked). Reservations
are advisable, particularly for dinner.
C 60,000 lire.

 Fiore

San Polo, Calle del Scaleter 2202a
(041) 721308
*Closed Sun, Aug, 2 wks at Christmas. All major
cards.*
An extraordinarily charming restaurant,
and a popular one: don't dream of dining
here without a reservation. The fish and
crustaceans that form the backbone of
Mara Martini's menu are chosen with utmost discernment; she prepares her briny
bounty with a light, deft hand—no needless
complications get in the way of the
seafood's pure, essential flavors. Desserts
are strictly homemade and perfectly
yummy (if it's on offer, do try the flaky,
golden fig tart). Worthwhile wine list. **C** 75-
80,000 lire.

 Ai Gondolieri

Dorsoduro, Fondamenta Ospedalet-
to 366 - (041) 5286396
Closed Tue, 3 wks end Jul-Aug. V, AE.
If a surfeit of seafood has you longing to
sink your teeth into a nice, juicy steak,
book a table at the Gondolieri. Start out
with an earthy soup of onions and porcini
mushrooms or a pretty squash-blossom
flan, then treat yourself to lamb cooked
with aromatic herbs, venison braised in
brawny Barolo wine, rabbit partnered with
ruby-red radicchio, duck confit with
prunes—or a nice, juicy steak! Wine buffs
take note: the cellar holds a cache of
first-rate Italian reds. **C** 45,000 lire.

 Grand Canal

Hotel Monaco & Grand Canal,
San Marco, Calle Vallaresso 1325
(041) 5200211
Closed Tue. All major cards.
The restaurant's terrace is poised at the
water's edge, where Canal Grande flows
into the Bacino di San Marco. The indoor
dining room also has its charms, and both
venues benefit from the services of a supremely polished staff. As in so many
hotels, the menu is something of a hybrid,
with "international" offerings listed alongside dishes typical of the region. We prefer
to choose from the Venetian specialties:
tagliolini tossed with fresh scampi, saffron-
spiced fish soup, sautéed John Dory sprinkled with giant capers, rabbit fricassée,
and calf's liver alla veneta served with
delicious polenta. Of course, if your tastes
lean toward Chateaubriand, roast saddle
of lamb, or shrimp in Cognac, they are
expertly prepared as well. Superior cellar;
elegant desserts, enticingly described on a
separate menu. **C** 95,000 lire (wine incl.).

Harry's Bar

San Marco, Calle Vallaresso 1323
(041) 5286931
Closed Mon. All major cards.
On the face of it, nothing has changed at
Harry's. For more than 50 years this
modest English-style bar near the San
Marco vaporetto stop has offered warmth,
drink, and sustenance to the beautiful
people of the world. English gentlemen—
and their imitators—with silver-headed
canes rub tailored elbows with top
models, literary lions, showbiz folk, and
other exotic or distinguished individuals.
Regulars still gossip at the bar while waiting for their tables, sipping Bellinis (Prosecco and peach juice) in summer, Tizianos
and Tiepolos (same fizz with red or white
grape juice) in autumn. The seafood
ravioli, the risottos, the calf's liver alla
veneziana, the carpaccio, the chocolate
cake, and the intensely flavorful sorbets
still display a commitment to quality and a
respect for Giuseppe Cipriani's old
recipes. And yet, Harry's has indeed
changed somehow. The waiters appear to
think only of dispatching the customers
with all possible haste; tourists in
shirtsleeves and shorts jam the downstairs
room; and the prices, traditionally high
even for Venice, have grown utterly ex-

travagant. On the surface, Harry's Bar is probably pretty much as it was when Hemingway made it famous. Only now, we wonder if Hemingway would even go near the place... **C** 150,000 lire.

Hosteria Franz
Castello, Fondazione Sant'Isepo 754 (041) 5227505
Closed Tue, Jan. All major cards.
The first Franz was an Austrian soldier who opened what was then a modest tavern for fishermen. The Hosteria's current owner, Gian Franco, runs a slightly more upmarket operation, patronized by the city's gourmets. Venetians are understandably finicky about seafood; here they find such rare and unusual specimens as soasso (a type of turbot that haunts a special corner of the lagoon), soft-shell crabs (during their short season), or the prized clams known as caperozzoli. We harbor fond memories of Gian Franco's delicious oyster risotto, delicate scallops partnered with melon, fat marinated shrimp served atop colorful sweet peppers, and a wonderfully moist grilled eel. Incidentally, if you have a hankering for deep-fried seafood, this is the place to indulge it! Top wines from the Veneto cohabit with more exotic bottles in the excellent cellar. **C** 65-80,000 lire.

Locanda Cipriani
Island of Torcello - (041) 730150
Closed Tue, Nov-mid Mar. All major cards.
The island of Torcello lies some ten kilometers across the water from Venice, and is easily reached via the number 12 vaporetto, which departs several times daily from the Fondamente Nuove. Torcello's days of glory are long past, but the ancient cathedral, with its awe-inspiring mosaic of the *Last Judgment* draws art lovers to this sleepy isle. A very few travelers also come to Torcello as residents of the enchanting and exclusive Locanda Cipriani. Still, even if you haven't managed to book one of the inn's half-dozen rooms, you can while away a couple of unforgettable hours at the Locanda's table, savoring uncomplicated dishes—pasta, risotto, seafood from the lagoon—and wines that meet the Cipriani family's customary high standards. **C** 110-120,000 lire.

Maddalena
Island of Mazzorbo, Canale Santa Caterina - (041) 730151
Closed Thu, Dec 20-Jan 10. No cards.
Linked to charming island of Burano by a long wooden bridge, Mazzorbo is home to a handful of fishermen's cottages surrounded by vines and tidy gardens. Seasonal vegetables, game hunted in the sandbanks nearby, and fish from the lagoon sustain the hardy population, and make up the menu served at Maddalena. The food is simple, incomparably fresh, and modestly priced. For dessert, don't miss the crunchy almond cookies called buranelli, accompanied by a glass of strawberry-scented Fragolino wine. **C** 40-45,000 lire (wine incl).

Alla Madonna
San Polo, Calle della Madonna 594 (041) 5223824
Closed Wed, Jan. V, AE.
This busy trattoria is thoroughly Venetian in its allegiance to seafood prepared according to local custom. The Rialto fish market provides the irreproachably fresh shellfish that appear in varied guises as antipasti. First courses run to spaghetti with clams, fish soup, and black risotto colored with cuttlefish ink. The latter is touted as the house specialty, but it occasionally has a sweetish flavor that is not to everyone's taste. For the main course, patrons choose the fish they want from the large variety proposed, and have it cooked to their specifications: poached, grilled, fried, or baked in parchment. Desserts are made in-house, and the unpretentious wines hail mostly from Friuli and the Veneto. **C** 50,000 lire and up.

Ai Mercanti
San Polo, Campo delle Beccarie 1588 (041) 5240282
Closed Sun, 3 wks in Aug. All major cards.
A tireless trio—Diego, Renato, Bruno—runs this fine seafood spot just next door to the Rialto market. In a jolly ambience you can savor spaghetti tossed with eggplant and tiny squid, delicious monkfish sparked with fresh herbs and tomatoes, or sea bream paired with meaty porcini mushrooms (skip the salmon, though: it's not locally caught). For a change of pace from fish, try the veal bocconcini in a lively caper sauce. Laudable wine list; good torta

di ricotta for dessert. **M** 50,000 lire, 80,000 lire.

Al Milion

Cannaregio, San Giovanni Crisostomo 5841 - (041) 5229302
Closed Wed, Aug. No cards.

The restaurant's name pays homage to the Venetian explorer, Marco Polo, who spent his youth in this part of the city (*Il Milione* or *Book of Marvels* is Polo's fabulous account of his travels in the Far East). As you explore the menu, you won't discover anything terribly new. The fare is hard-core Venetian (whipped dried cod, black risotto, whole-wheat spaghetti in anchovy sauce, et al), but the dishes are ably prepared and the fish is always extra-fresh: we sampled a fine John Dory in a tangy caper sauce. The wine list is sure to pique your interest, and the tab won't break the bank. **C** 45,000 lire.

Ostaria a la Campana

San Marco, Calle dei Fabbri 4720 (041) 5285170
Lunch only. Closed Sat. No cards.

Guido Bortoluzzi oversees this un-prepossessing tavern near Saint Mark's Square, a place where you can stop for a glass or two of wine and cicchetti ("little tastes") chosen from an array on the big wooden bar, or sit down to a meal of Venetian soul food: pasta e fagioli, cuttlefish with rice, crispy fried whitebait, and other modest fare. The food is fresh and skillfully cooked (a miracle considering the turnover: the action begins around noon and goes on nonstop until it's nearly dinnertime); and prices are unbeatably low. The rustic local wines are served straight from the cask. **C** 15-25,000 lire.

Poste Vecie

San Polo, Rialto Pescheria 1608 (041) 721822
Closed Tue, Jul 15-Aug 15. V, AE, DC.

A logical stop after a visit to the bustling Rialto fish market, this ancient seafood restaurant is accessible via a little wooden bridge that spans a miniature canal. The premises are divided into several small dining rooms with coffered ceilings and a centuries-old stone fireplace. Fresh shellfish, shrimp, spider crabs, and clams make up the antipasti. Follow them up with a light mixed fry of crispy squid and shrimp flanked by ultrafresh vegetables, or

a letter-perfect risotto al nero colored with cuttlefish ink. Other appetizing options are turbot alla greca (with zesty olives and capers), fried soft-shell crabs, and grilled fish brochettes. The dessert cart is laden with homemade sweets, and the cellar harbors some worthwhile bottles. In summer, the waterside garden is a most romantic spot to dine. **C** 70,000 lire and up.

Quadri

Piazza San Marco 120 - (041) 5289299
Closed Mon, Jan. All major cards.

The setting, rich with gilt and rosy velvet, recalls the opulent Venice of the Doges, whose palace stands just a few steps away. The great writers Marcel Proust and Stendhal frequented Quadri in their day; the latter noted that he paid two francs for a meal here. One now pays considerably more for the pleasure of dining on the upper floor of this famous caffè, on dishes that display a certain studied elegance: fennel soup spiked with Pernod, agnolotti pasta stuffed with lobster, zucchini, and pungent fresh herbs, turbot with almonds and a *pizzico* of ginger, sea bass in a pool of chive velouté... The chef's skill is undeniable, but these dishes summon up a sense of culinary *déjà vu*. And the price of nostalgia at Quadri is high, very high. **C** 100,000 lire and up.

Tiepolo

Hotel Europa e Regina,
San Marco, Calle Larga XXII Marzo 2159 (041) 5213785
Open daily. All major cards.

The Europa e Regina occupies the former Palazzo Tiepolo, home of the patrician family who produced not only one of the great artists of the eighteenth century, but distinguished diplomats, military leaders, and two doges as well. It is fitting, then, that the hotel's restaurant, named in their honor, should piously preserve the traditions of the Venetian table. Every Saturday evening from April through October, Chef Luigi Piccinini orchestrates a *serata veneziana*, a festive dinner composed of ancient Venetian dishes served to the strains of live classical music. The menu modulates with the chef's inspiration, but Adriatic seafood plays the starring role. Exquisite atmosphere; polished service. **C** 100,000 lire.

Vini da Gigio

[13] Cannaregio, Calle de la Stua 3628
(041) 5285140
Closed Mon, 2 wks in Aug & in Jan. All major cards.

Paolo Lazzari's wine list may just be the best in Venice. Yet Vini da Gigio is not a casual wine bar, but a bona fide restaurant serving food that gets better every year. Signora Lazzari has honed her repertoire of family recipes to a fine, keen edge: try her rousing version of penne dressed with rosemary and bacon, or tagliatelle stained black with cuttlefish ink and tossed in a lusty marinara sauce, followed by beautifully moist swordfish rolls or the day's catch baked with a garnish of potatoes and tomatoes. For dessert, we suggest you sample the unusual polenta cake with red-wine sauce. The fine wines are accessibly priced. **C** 50,000 lire.

In Marghera   6 km

Autoespresso

[16] Via Fratelli Bandiera 34 - (041) 930214
Closed Sun, 2 wks at Christmas, 3 wks in Aug. All major cards.

The enchantment of Venice seems very far away, out here amid the smokestacks of Marghera's industrial zone. But if you want to taste some of the best seafood on the Adriatic, you should make the four-mile trip to Autoespresso (no, the name's not very charming, either), a former trattoria that once catered mostly to truckers. Franco and Luciana turned the place into a first-rate restaurant, thanks to their rare discernment in choosing the cream of each day's catch, and to Luciana's talent for enhancing seafood's delicate savors. Improbably flavorful spider crabs, scallops, razor-shell clams, poached baby octopus, grilled miniature squid are the antipasti that lead into (for example) fabulous black tagliatelle embellished with scampi and tomatoes, or a lush shrimp risotto. The main event could be a generous platter of mixed grilled or fried fish, or John Dory with a piquant garnish of black olives and capers, or sea bream baked in parchment. A hazelnut tart tasted a mite too sweet on a recent visit, but a gratin of fresh figs with pistachio ice cream made a splendid finale. The cellar, oddly, is awash in premium red wines; but if, like us, you prefer white with your fish, there are plenty of aromatic examples on hand. **C** 80,000 lire.

In Mestre   9 km

Dall'Amelia

[17] Via Miranese 113 - (041) 913951
Closed Wed. All major cards.

Inauspiciously sited in Mestre's industrial zone, this high-class trattoria attracts a posh clientele of literary and political grandees. Owner Dino Boscarato is a prize-winning chef and former president of the Italian association of sommeliers (his wine list is said to put oenophiles in a trance). Choosing from the huge menu, we recently made a memorable meal of plump tortelli stuffed with vermouth-scented sea bass, crispy deep-fried shrimp and squash blossoms, baked sculpin escorted by potatoes and olives, and a dainty ice-cream sundae strewn with wild berries. Another time, we plan to try the polenta topped with a brochette of small game birds, a regional dish given a "surf-and-turf" twist with the addition of shrimp from the lagoon. The service is occasionally slow, but in the main keeps to the same high standards as the kitchen and the wine cellar. **C** 70-80,000 lire.

Il Valeriano

[14] Via Col di Lana 18 - (041) 926474
Closed Sun, Mon, Aug. All major cards.

The small, elegantly paneled dining room sparkles with pretty lamps and handsome silver table settings. Chef Valeriano handles the usual Venetian specialties with a welcome personal touch. His mixed seafood antipasto is fresh and generous, with baby octopus, crayfish, sea snails and spider crabs. Little gnocchi alla buranea (with scampi and Pernod) makes a pleasant change from pasta or rice, though spaghetti liberally garnished with shellfish is lusty and good. Main courses are Venetian classics, all competently turned out: liver with onions, cuttlefish in their ink, fried fresh anchovies, whipped dried cod. Attractive fruit tarts make a bright-tasting finale after all that fish. Courteous, affable service. The cellar is stocked with wines from Trentino–Alto Adige, Friuli, and the Veneto; make a point of sampling the house brandy flavored with a hint of orange. **C** 60,000 lire.

Quick Bites

CONTENTS

CAFES

Florian
Piazza San Marco 56 - (041) 5285338
Open 7:30am-midnight. Closed Wed.

A Venetian institution founded by Floriano Francesconi in 1720, Florian stands in the arcades of Piazza San Marco. Its eighteenth-century rooms, with their mirrors and lacquer, their marble floors and elegant chairs, are surely among the most poetic settings in the city. Light meals, ice cream, and five o'clock tea may be enjoyed in the caffè or on the enormous outdoor terrace, along with drinks of every kind. The little house orchestra gives charming concerts in the evening. Need we mention that prices are high?

Lavena
Piazza San Marco 133 - (041) 5224070
Open 8am-midnight. Closed Tue in winter.

Wagner, and after him Artur Rubinstein, patronized this grandiose caffè aglitter with marble, mirrors, and crystal chandeliers. The outdoor terrace is a favorite with tourists who want to soak up some sun and drink in the stupendous view of Venice's foremost landmarks. Lavena's coffee and pastries are excellent, though not inexpensive.

Quadri
Piazza San Marco 120 - (041) 5289299
Open daily 8am-midnight.

Giorgio Quadri, a native of Corfu, introduced Turkish coffee to Venice in the eighteenth century. Coffee, along with Italian aperitifs, wines, and cocktails, still draw a faithful clientele to Quadri, Florian's chief rival on Piazza San Marco. There's no reason not to patronize both establishments, spending an evening over drinks in one, then an afternoon sipping cappuccino in the other.

QUICK BITES

Alfredo Alfredo
Castello, Campo Santi Filippo e Giacomo 4294 (041) 5225331
Open 11am-2am. Closed Mon.

A café-restaurant close to Piazza San Marco, serving a broad selection of decent Italian-style dishes. Youthful ambience; low prices.

Antico Dolo
San Polo, Rialto 778 - (041) 5226546
Open 10am-3pm & 6:30pm-10pm. Closed Sun.

A heartwarming Venetian tavern that serves a short menu of sturdy specialties: baccalà with polenta, tripe (the pride of the house), various types of bruschetta (toasted bread drizzled with olive oil and a vegetable topping), and delicious grilled radicchio (red chicory from nearby Treviso).

Agli Assassini
San Marco, Rio Terrà degli Assassini 3695 (041) 5287986
Open 11:30am-3pm & 6:30pm-11:30pm. Closed Sun.

You couldn't do better than this Venetian tavern for a swiftly served meal of un-

273

pretentious Italian "soul food." Daily specials reappear weekly, with soups and white meats featured on Mondays, braises and stews on Tuesdays, pasta and beans, and calf's-foot or beef-muzzle salad on Wednesdays, baccalà (salt cod) and "boiled dinner" on Thursdays, and fresh fish on Fridays. Saturday? Chef's surprise! Meatballs in tomato sauce are a specialty of the house. Good wines.

The Unstoppable Serenissima

Ships have been sailing serenely out of the Arsenale, located on the Gemelle islands (the Twins), since 1104. Venice's mercantile flotillas, fearsome fleets of warships, and the barks of poets and adventurers were built and repaired at the Arsenale, the grand shipyard of the *Serenissima Repubblica* (Most Serene Republic). At one time in the Middle Ages there were 16,000 workers in the shipyard. Dante was so impressed that he dedicated two tercets of the *Inferno* (XXI, v. 7) to the scene. The shipyard was damaged or destroyed by fire several times, most notably in 1569. But the following year, the Arsenale was once again afloat, in record time. Its fleet sailed out to a decisive victory for all of Europe: La Serenissima routed the Turks at Lepanto and set sail for another 200 years of glory.

Bar Latteria–Da Zorzi
San Marco, Calle dei Fuseri 4539
(041) 5252350
Open 7:30am-3pm & 4pm-8pm. Closed Sun.
At tables covered with fresh, colorful Liberty cloths, students and office workers from the neighborhood focus on devouring every crumb of their tasty crostini (toasted bread with all sorts of toppings—the specialty of the house). Cold starters, vegetarian dishes, and good cheeses are available, though at lunchtime only. Zorzi's whipped cream and caramel custard are the best in Venice.

Bar Novo
San Marco 5456 - (041) 5237327
Open 7:30am-2pm & 3:30pm-8pm. Closed Sun.
Frankly terrific sandwiches filled with crab or roast suckling pig are the main attractions, but don't overlook the steaming pot of fresh fish risotto that's always placed invitingly on the counter of this engaging little bar.

Bar Sottosopra
Dorsoduro 3740 - (041) 5285320
Open 11am-midnight. Closed Sun.
The work of local photographers hangs on the walls of this popular spot, where the neighborhood's young crowd likes to congregate. Hot sandwiches with a host of savory fillings are the specialty, but in summer the menu also lists an assortment of refreshing cold dishes. Slowcoach service.

Bar Torino
San Marco 1501 - (041) 5223914
Open 8am-8:30pm. Closed Sun.
Sure it's fast food, but with a genuine Venetian twist: alongside the scores of different sandwich combinations, you'll find several good dishes featuring seasonal vegetables. Note, too, that this corner of Campo San Luca is where Venice's under-30 set gathers nightly.

Burghy
San Marco, Calle Larga San Marco (corner of Mercato dell'Orologio)
Open 10am-1am. Closed Mon.
Fast-food hamburgers, cheeseburgers, and the rest all within sight of Saint Mark's. If you're on a tight budget—or crave a french-fry fix—you could do worse...

Le Chat Qui Rit
San Marco 1131 - (041) 5229086
Open 10am-10:30pm. Closed Sat.
While you can get a simple grilled steak at this old-fashioned self-service cafeteria, Le Chat's real claim to fame is traditional Venetian fare, like stewed cuttlefish spooned over a bed of polenta.

Leon Bianco
San Marco 4153 - (041) 5221189
Open 7:30am-3pm & 4pm-8:30pm. Closed Sun.
Come by early to claim your fair share of Leon Bianco's renowned risotto or cicchetti (Venetian tavern snacks): take our

word for it, they disappear fast. But a charming smile may persuade the owner to part with the portion he often sets aside for late-arriving friends.

Maddalena

Cannaregio 2348 - (041) 5220723
Open 7:30am-9pm. Closed Sun.
When a full-dress meal just seems like too much, this is a fine place to come for a sandwich, a plate of spaghetti, or a warming bowl of noodles and beans. A few hearty Venetian main dishes are on the menu as well.

Osteria alle Botteghe

San Marco 3454 - (041) 5228181
Open 8am-10pm. Closed Sun.
Savory prosciutto and suckling pig straight from the farm fill the famous hot sandwiches prepared here. The cheese crostini are delicious, too. For a light, satisfying lunch or an evening aperitivo, this osteria is a must.

Piccolo Martini

San Marco 1501 - (041) 5285136
Open 7:30am-8pm. Closed Mon.
Once you round the corner of the long bar, you'll discover an atmosphere reminiscent of a turn-of-the-century café. If the staff suggests you try the spaghetti al ragù (meat sauce), by all means do so—it's the best version in town.

Al Ponte

Santa Croce, Ponte del Megio 1666
(041) 719777
Open 8am-1am. Closed Sat eve & Sun (exc in Festival periods).
Forget *nuova cucina*, Al Ponte sticks to old-time Venetian standards like bigoli in salsa (whole-wheat spaghetti in anchovy sauce), tripe alla veneziana, and crispy deep-fried fish. The locals love it, because the food tastes just like what their grannies used to make!

Al Profeta

Dorsoduro 2671 - (041) 5237466
Open 9:30am-3pm & 6pm-midnight. Closed Fri.
By day, it's a sandwich shop popular with university students; by night, Al Profeta turns into a pizzeria patronized by their professors. In high season, the noise can get noisome, but the garden is a delight.

Rosticceria San Bartolomeo

San Marco, Calle della Bissa 5424
(041) 5223569
Open 9am-2pm & 4pm-9pm. Closed Mon.
This is the top spot in town for fast food, Venetian-style. Even if you're pressed for time, you can sample such gutsy regional specialties as baccalà alla vicentina (salt cod simmered in milk with herbs). The deep-fried mozzarella ("in carrozza") and rice balls (arancini) are terrific.

Rosticceria al Teatro Goldoni

San Marco 4747 - (041) 5222446
Open 10am-9pm. Closed Wed.
Pizza is served here all day long, and so is the famed house specialty: deep-fried mozzarella with anchovies or prosciutto. If you're hankering for a quick bowl of mushroom risotto or a pasticcio di pesce (fish pâté), you'll find them on the menu, too.

Alla Zucca

Santa Croce, Ponte del Megio 1762
(041) 5241570
Open 10am-3pm & 6:30pm-midnight. Closed Sun.
Friendly young owners run this likable trattoria, located in a quiet corner of Venice. The menu lists an appetizing assortment of dishes that give vegetables a starring role. Tasty wines on offer, too.

SWEET SNACKS

■ ICE CREAM

Bar Gelateria Al Cucciolo

Dorsoduro, Fondamenta delle Zattere 782
(041) 5289641
Open 9am-7:30pm. Closed Mon.
Along with Da Nico, mentioned below, Al Cucciolo is a favorite with Venetians, who punctuate their strolls along the Zattere with a pause for ice cream. The hazelnut and coffee ice varieties are memorable, but the supremely simple crème Chantilly served with crisp almond cookies should not be overlooked.

Caffè Causin—Da Renato

Dorsoduro 2996 - (041) 5236091
Open 8am-8:30pm. Closed Sat.

A mandatory stop for fanciers of divinely creamy Italian-style frozen custards and ices. Don't miss the nougat-flavored ice cream, a minor masterpiece. Causin is so cherished by the locals that its fame is sung in popular Venetian *canzoni*.

Al Do Porte

San Polo 1131 - (041) 5231184
Open 7am-10:30pm. Closed Sun.
If you're a true ice-cream epicure, make a point of sampling Al Do Porte's delicate, delectable flavors. After a visit to the spectacular Frari church next door, this is an ideal place to pause for refreshment.

Da Nico

Dorsoduro, Fondamenta delle Zattere 922
(041) 5225293
Open 7am-9:30pm (summer 7am-11pm). Closed Thu.
Only ice cream is sold here, but we think it's the best in town. Situated across from the Giudecca on a popular promenade, Da Nico is the exclusive purveyor of a fabulous chocolate treat called the Gianduiotto—invented by Nico himself—which consists of a thick bar of chocolate buried under a drift of whipped cream. More conservative hedonists may content themselves with the Cardinale, a traditional ice cream sundae napped with chocolate.

Paolin

San Marco, Campo Santo Stefano 3464
(041) 5220710
Open 8am-midnight. Closed Thu.
Paolin, on Campo Santo Stefano, is a classic spot for whiling away the hours of a Venetian evening. The barman will serve you any soft or spirited drink you like, but keep in mind that ice cream is the house specialty. One can imagine worse fates than sitting at a little table out on the square, plunging a spoon into a delicious sundae lavished with whipped cream and cherries or a semifreddo rich with frozen cream and chocolate chips.

Al Todaro

Piazza San Marco 3 - (041) 5285165
Open 9am-midnight. Closed Thu.
Al Todaro does double duty as a bar and an ice-cream shop. Enviably situated across from the Doges' Palace, it has long been a favorite place to socialize over a sundae, a semifreddo, or an ice-cream cone. We urge you to try the Bacio ("kiss"), a cone filled with chocolate-glazed mousse and a sprinkling of hazelnuts.

■ PASTRIES

Da Bonifacio

Castello 4237 - (041) 5227507
Open 7:30am-1:30pm & 3:30am-8:30pm. Closed Thu.
Signora Antonia knows everything there is to know about pastry, as her irresistible fruit and ricotta tarts convincingly attest. And if you happen by at cocktail time, by all means order an Americano, made here by its inventor, Signor Armando himself. The delicious cocktail nibbles, baked on the premises, are positively addictive.

Ermenegildo Rosa Salva

San Marco, Ponte Ferai 951 - (041) 5210544

Andrea Rosa Salva

San Marco, Campo San Luca 4589
(041) 5225385
Open 8:30am-8pm (Ponte Ferai); 7:45am-8:45pm (Campo San Luca). Closed Sun.
The Rosa Salvas are the latest offshoots of an old and respected dynasty of Venetian pastry chefs founded long ago by Salvatore Rosa, known as "Salva." His descendants continue the family tradition of baking outstanding pastries and cookies. If you are in Venice in November, look for the fave veneziane and triestine, crunchy little cookies that are traditionally served around All Saints' Day.

Pasticceria Da Colussi

Dorsoduro 2867 - (041) 5231871
Open 7:30am-1pm & 3:30pm-8pm. Closed Tue.
The Colussi brothers prepare a whole calendar full of Italian treats right before your eyes: fritters for Carnival, fave cookies for All Saints' Day, special breads for Christmas and Easter. They also offer seductive ricotta pies baked according to an ancient Venetian recipe and a rainbow of homemade jams (the fig marmalade is sublime).

---

*Some establishments change their **closing times** without warning. It is always wise to check in advance.*

Pasticceria Dal Col
San Marco 1035 - (041) 5205529
Open 8am-1:30pm & 3:30pm-8:30pm.
Closed Sun pm, Mon.
If you happen to be in Venice for the
Christmas or Easter holidays, make sure to
stop by to sample the golden batches of
traditional focaccia (flat bread) and panet-
tone (sweet yeast bread) turned out by
Signor Luciano. Equally memorable are
crispy fruit fritters and lush galani, rich with
pastry cream and zabaglione.

Pasticceria Marchini
San Marco 2769 - (041) 5287507
Open 7:30am-8:30pm. Closed Tue.
Marchini is one of the most renowned
pastry shops in Venice and one of the most
rich in tradition. It's the place to sample
distinctive Venetian *dolci*, particularly
such regional cookies as cornmeal-based
zaleti, orange-scented baicoli, almond-
studded buranelli, and zesty, peppery
peverini.

Pasticceria Martini
Cannaregio 1302 - (041) 717375
Open 6:30am-1pm & 2pm-9pm. Closed Wed.
Though he's a big man, Signor Gianni has
a special fondness for miniature pastries.
He bakes an adorable selection of tiny
sweets, including almond and coconut
cookies and traditional Venetian marzipan
figures.

Pasticceria Targa
San Polo 1050 - (041) 5236048
Open 6am-8pm. Closed Mon.
Sweets for every Venetian holiday, including yummy San Martino tartlets (short
pastry with a quince topping, sold on and
around November 11), sinfully good
chocolates, and light, crisp meringues.

Pasticceria Tonolo
Dorsoduro 3764 - (041) 5237209
Open 8am-9pm. Closed Mon.
If your business in Venice takes you near
the university, make a point of stopping at
this popular pastry shop to taste Signor
Franco's airy brioches and cream-filled krap-
fen (a—distant—relative of our filled doughnut). The almond-based torta greca is one of
the most famous native Venetian pastries.

Da Giancarlo Vio
Dorsoduro 1192 - (041) 5227451
Open 7:30am-9pm. Closed Tue.
Giancarlo Vio, a master baker, is one of
the few remaining practitioners of the art
of Venetian pastry. He possesses a particular knack with marzipan, the almond
paste developed in Venice in 1500 and
known as *pane di San Marco*, or Saint
Mark's bread. Other distinctive specialties
are Doges' bread and Doges' cake, both
based on almond meal and dried fruit. And
here alone will you find a characteristic but
now rare Venetian sweet, the Nicolotta,
made with day-old bread soaked in milk,
and dried fruit.

Pasticceria Zanon—Da Mario
Dorsoduro 1169 - (041) 5222619
*Open 7:30am-1pm & 3pm-7:30pm. Closed
Wed.*
Mario is the city's undisputed master of
pastine al riso (rice cookies). And students
from the neighboring schools of econo-
mics and art stand in line for his deliciously
brittle meringues and his sweet apple pastries, perfect partners for morning coffee.

WINE BARS

Da Aciugheta
Castello, Campo Santi Filippo e Giacomo 4537
(041) 5224292
*Open 9am-3pm & 5:30pm-10pm. Closed Wed
in winter.*
Deservedly popular, this osteria/piz-
zeria/ristorante provides a wide variety of
options for appetites of every size. You
can step up to the counter for a sandwich
or snack (squid salad, fried squash blossoms, anchovy mini-pizzas...) or sit down
at a table for a more substantial meal. The
wines are choice, and many are offered by
the glass.

Bistrot ai Do Draghi
Dorsoduro, Campo Santa Margherita 3665
(041) 5289731
Open 10am-1pm & 5pm-midnight. Closed Sun.
A cozy, friendly wine bar, with red-
lacquered walls, tall mirrors, and a profusion of plants. Do Draghi is known for its
spritzes (wine, bitters, and fizzy mineral
water) and tingly Prosecco, but the plea-

sant, slightly fruity Marzemino from the Trentino–Alto Adige region is also worth getting to know. In autumn, the year's new wine (*vino novello*) is fêted.

Il Caffè

Dorsoduro, Campo Santa Margherita 2963
(041) 5287998
Open 8am-midnight. Closings not available.
Fine wines, sandwiches (tramezzini), and bar snacks feed a non-stop stream of customers at this pleasant address, which boasts an outdoor terrace on one of the city's prettiest, most unspoiled squares.

Canottieri

Cannaregio, Fondamenta del Macello 690
(041) 5215408
Open 6:30pm-2am. Closed Sun in winter.
If, after visiting the Cannaregio district in the neighborhood of San Giobbe, you feel the need for refreshment, Canottieri is a convenient place to stop for a delicious, homemade piadina romagnola (flat bread topped with sautéed greens or prosciutto) and a glass of wine. On Thursday evenings, live bands entertain the youngish crowd of drinkers, and the mood warms up considerably. Tuesday is "cabaret" night.

Cantina "Do Spade"

San Polo, Calle do Spade 860 - (041) 5210574
Open 9am-1pm & 5pm-midnight. Closed Sun.
Tucked away under an arcade behind the fish and fruit market, this historic *bacaro* (wine bar) serves tongue-tingling Prosecco and addictive miniature sand- wiches.

Da Ciccio

Lido di Venezia, Via San Gallo 241
(041) 5265489
Open 10am-4pm & 6pm-11pm (summer until 2am). Closed Tue.
If you're spending the day at the Lido, find some time between a stroll and a swim to pause at this adorable wine bar and inn. Bepi, the friendly master of the house, will seat you outside, if you like, under a wide, cool pergola, where you can enjoy a delicious heap of tiny fried fish and a glass—indeed, a bottle!—of his modest but tasty white wine.

Da Codroma

Dorsoduro, Ponte del Soccorso 2540
(041) 5204161

Open 10am-1:30am. Closed Thu.
The sign outside announces that Da Codroma is a "typical Venetian inn," and indeed a convivial spirit reigns at this osteria set in a working-class district well off the tourist circuit. The tiny bar holds just four tables, where groups of young people chatter, play chess, and sip wine or beer. The list is not long, but you can be sure that Stefano, the serious young owner, will serve you an excellent little wine, be it a sparkling Prosecco, a Marzemino or, in season, a newly fermented Torbolino. Occasional poetry readings, jazz concerts, and art exhibits are hosted here.

Al Mascaron

Castello, Calle Lunga Santa Maria Formosa 5225 - (041) 5225995
Open 11am-3pm & 6:30pm-12:30am. Closed Wed.
Like any self-respecting Venetian wine bar, this one serves a selection of cicchetti (as Venetian bar snacks are called): the mussels (peoci), baby octopus, scallops, sardines, and the rest are first-rate. We would like to draw your attention in particular to an outstanding white wine from the Colline Trevigiane (hills near Treviso) that is poured here with a measure of regional pride. While you sip, admire the imaginative motifs painted on the paneled walls. More substantial fare (and very good it is, too) appears at meal times.

Da Patatina

San Polo, Ponte San Polo 2741a
(041) 5237238
Open 9:30am-2:30pm & 4:30pm-9pm. Closed Sat pm, Sun.
This family-run establishment, one of the most authentic *bacari* (wine bars) in Venice, stands poised on a bridge near the church of the Frari. It offers all the sights and smells of a traditional Venetian tavern along with frisky red and white wines from the Colline Trevigiane: the year's young Torbolino, spritzy Prosecco, and Fragolino redolent of strawberries. From the array of steaming cicchetti (bar snacks) set out to nibble along with your wine, try the crispy rings of fried squid, the french-fried potatoes (patatine), or the tiny, tasty cuttlefish.

Find the address *you are looking for, quickly and easily, in the index.*

Nuova Rivetta
Castello, Campo Santi Filippo e Giacomo 4625
(041) 5237238
Open 11am-10:30pm. Closed Mon.
This perfectly representative Venetian trattoria is located in the heart of the city's historic center, nestled close to the foot of an old bridge. It's an excellent choice for a genuine Venetian lunch or for a snack and a glass of wine. The house produces a creditable mixed fry of fish, best accompanied by a tingly Prosecco—unless, of course, you prefer the more full-bodied red *della casa.*

Alla Vedova
Cannaregio, Ramo Ca' d'Oro 3916
(041) 5285324
Open 11:30am-3pm & 6pm-11pm. Closed Thu.
This is a classic spot for an early evening aperitivo, where young Venetians languidly sip a spritz (white wine, fizzy mineral water, a dash of bitters, a squeeze of lemon), a glass of sparkling Prosecco, red Marzemino, or strawberry-scented Fragolino. An assortment of little nibbles accompany these libations: grilled vegetables, deep-fried tidbits, baby cuttlefish in their ink, tiny meatballs. Alla Vedova ("The Widow's Place") will give you a feel for the social side of this rather closed city. At lunchtime, order some soppressa (salami-like sausage), bussolai (toasted ring-shaped rolls), a carafe of Marzemino, and you'll fit right in.

Vino Vino
San Marco, Ponte delle Veste 2007a
(041) 5237027
Open 10am-midnight. Closed Tue.
An impressive selection of "serious" wines may be found at this wine bar just behind La Fenice. Sit yourself down at a marble table and explore the extensive list of the best vintage wines in Venice: Spumante, Champagne, Prosecco, modest local red and white wines, lordly Brunello di Montalcino, Barolo, Amarone Mazzano (a specialty of the Veneto), and French Château Rayas all lie quietly in the cellar, just waiting for you to pop their corks. An appealing variety of snacks is offered as well, and there is a take-out service.

Vivaldi
San Polo, Calle de la Madoneta 1457
(041) 5238185
Open 10am-3pm & 5pm-10pm. Closed Sun.
Vivaldi's cellar has been assembled with obvious discernment; come sample from their interesting store and accompany your selection with a plate of assorted cicchetti (whipped salt cod, sardines in saor, cuttlefish...).

Al Volto
San Marco, Calle Cavalli 4081 - (041) 5228945
Open 5pm-9pm. Closed Sun.
Al Volto is tiny, typically Venetian, and one of the few genuine wine bars to be found in the center of town. The cellar covers the Italian regions pretty thoroughly: all the DOC (*Denominazione di Origine Controllata*) wines are represented, as are some worthwhile local growths. If you prefer not to drink on an empty stomach, look to the beguiling assortment of cicchetti (Venice's answer to tapas) arrayed on the bar. Delicious hot sandwiches, sausages, little pizzas, and brochettes highlight the menu of savory snacks and nibbles. Wine isn't your tipple? Then look into the remarkable selection of aquavits, whiskies, and 70 different domestic and imported beers.

La Fenice Rises from the Flames

The jewel-box Fenice theater has a long and fiery history, as befits its name (which means "phoenix"). It was built in 1791 over an ancient Roman garden plot and was inaugurated on May 16, 1792, to the warbling poetry of Alessandro Pepoli and music of Giovanni Paisiello in the opera *I Giochi d'Agrigento*. But on December 13, 1836, a raging blaze burned the fabulous bird to the ground. The theater was redesigned by the Meduna brothers and rebuilt in just seven months, rising from the ashes to break into song.

Hotels

Hotel Ala

San Marco, Campo Santa Maria del Giglio - (041) 5208333, fax (041) 5206390
Open year-round. 80 rms 90-212,000 lire, bkfst incl. All major cards.

Owned by the Salmaso family, like the Pensione Accademia (see below), the Ala is a pleasant hotel situated on a beautiful square near Piazza San Marco. You'll love the view from the panoramic terrace, and you'll feel snug and comfortable in the attractive, air conditioned rooms equipped with satellite TV and minibar. Note the antique suit of armor that stands guard by the reception desk!

Agli Alboretti

Dorsoduro, Accademia 884
(041) 5230058, fax (041) 521058
Open year-round. 20 rms 120-180,000 lire, bkfst incl. Restaurant. All major cards.

Ideally situated for visiting the glorious Accademia museum, this charming hotel is housed in an ancient Venetian dwelling adjoined by a small garden. Cheerful rooms, all with either bath or shower. Venetian and creative cooking by Mirella Bettio is featured in the restaurant, where sommelier Anna Linguerri presents an attractive list of Italian wines. Half-board available.

Antica Casa Carettoni

Cannaregio, Lista di Spagna 130
(041) 716231
Closed Aug, Feb. 15 rms 30-54,000 lire. No cards.

If you're looking for basic, no-frills accommodations in the heart of Venice, the Casa Carettoni is a good choice. In operation for more than 135 years, this venerable address has changed little since its early days—many of the spacious, airy rooms are still furnished in authentic nineteenth-century style.

Bauer Grünwald

San Marco, Campo San Moisè 1459
(041) 5207022, fax (041) 5207557
Open year-round. 4 stes 981-1,308,000 lire. 210 rms 273-523,000 lire. Restaurant. Conf. V, AE, DC.

Late in the last century, Herr Bauer and his son-in-law, Herr Grünwald, became so enamored of Venice that they built a hotel here in the Venetian ogival style, incorporating the remains of a fifteenth-century cloister (the unlovely façade on the Campo San Moisè dates from Mussolini's time). It is now one of the best hotels in the city, with an admirable location on Canal Grande, two terraces (one reserved for tour groups), and a private embarcadero for hotel guests. The rooms with views of La Salute and the canal are especially attractive, but all are fully renovated and air conditioned, with well-appointed marble bathrooms and handsome antique desks, chests, and gilded mirrors. Service is swift, courteous, and efficient.

Bel Sito

San Marco, Campo Santa Maria del Giglio 2517
(041) 5223365, fax (041) 5204083
Open year-round. 38 rms 80-215,000 lire, bkfst incl. All major cards.

A convenient location on a romantic square, modern comforts, and a typically Venetian atmosphere are among the Bel Sito's assets. Rooms are tidy and decorated with restraint; doubles come equipped with a full bathroom (showers only in the singles). Air conditioning incurs a supplemental charge per person, per day. In fine weather, breakfast is served outdoors, and there is a little bar where guests may relax after a long day of sightseeing.

Bonvecchiati

San Marco, Calle Goldoni 4488
(041) 5285017, fax (041) 5285230
Open year-round. 86 rms 95-260,000 lire, bkfst incl. Restaurant. All major cards.

Conveniently located close to Piazza San Marco and the Rialto, the Bonvecchiati is a commendable address, with guest rooms that feature authentic Venetian antiques. If you're willing to forego a private bathroom, the savings will be considerable.

Cipriani

Giudecca 10
(041) 5207744, fax (041) 5203930
Open year-round (in winter stes only). 35 stes 1,400-3,300,000 lire. 70 rms 550-990,000 lire. Restaurant. Conf. Pool. Tennis. All major cards.

Heaven on earth is just a boat ride away from Piazza San Marco at the glorious Cipriani hotel compound on the island of Giudecca. Peace, pleasure, and luxury are assured in a setting of princely refinement. The rooms are furnished with both antiques and stunning contemporary pieces; many of the marble bathrooms are equipped with Jacuzzis; and several suites boast private, shaded terraces. The immense heated swimming pool is surrounded by a verdant, blooming garden that all the guests may enjoy. Also at their disposal are tennis courts and an elegant restaurant. The adjacent Palazzo Vendramin is the last word in luxury; guests are pampered with private butler service in addition to all the other amenities provided by the Cipriani. The staff is at once courteous and discreetly friendly—the head concierge will respond to any question or problem in the language of one's choice. Such joys, of course, are reserved for the privileged few for whom price is never a consideration. The Cipriani belongs to the Relais et Châteaux association. For a review of the hotel's superb dining room, see *Restaurants*.

Concordia

San Marco, Calle Larga San Marco 367
(041) 5206866, fax (041) 5206775
Open year-round. 55 rms 170-390,000 lire, bkfst incl. All major cards.

The management boasts that this is the "world's most photographed hotel"—not because the façade is particularly distinctive, but because the Concordia is the only hotel that looks directly onto Piazza San Marco, and therefore right into the cameras of innumerable tourists. Don't expect a stupendous view from inside, however: just a few rooms offer glimpses of one side of the basilica. The hotel is modern, comfortable, and fully air conditioned; there is a cozy bar, a lounge, and a pretty wood-paneled breakfast room that overlooks the piazza. Bright, attractive guest rooms are equipped with hairdryers, satellite TV, and electronic safes. Attentive service. Room rates vary significantly with the seasons.

Danieli

Castello, Riva degli Schiavoni 4196
(041) 5226480, fax (041) 5200208
Open year-round. 9 stes 1,052-1,952,000 lire. 222 rms 361-592,000 lire. Restaurant. Conf. Pool. Tennis. Garage pkg. All major cards.

The palazzo that houses this legendary establishment was built in the fourteenth century. Its vocation as a luxury hotel dates from 1822, when it was taken over by a certain Giuseppe Dal Niel, alias Danieli. Long a favorite with crowned heads, artists, and celebrities, the Danieli is enviably situated next to the Bridge of Sighs and across from the island of San Giorgio. Inside, the lobby and public rooms are majestic with marble columns, Murano glass fixtures, and a monumental staircase. The rooms are handsomely appointed and equipped, but the more recently constructed annex is less charming, though perfectly comfortable. We have found the service to be just a tad chilly. For an account of the panoramic Danieli Terrace, see *Restaurants*.

Conspicuous Consumption

Talk about money to burn! Rich Venetians of old used to toss their gold into the canal to show how rich they were. One such boggling episode occurred at Palazzo Labia, on Campo San Geremia. In 1646 the impossibly wealthy family became members of Venice's patrician class. The clan's founding father, Gian Francesco Labia, happily plunked 300,000 ducats into the Republic's war chest. And then he threw a little supper party for 40 gentlemen. The table settings were of gold. After dinner he tossed them proudly into the canal. Today, visitors may tour the palazzo (by appointment) and admire the ballroom's fabulous frescoes, painted by Giambattista Tiepolo.

Des Bains

Lido di Venezia, Lungomare Marconi 17 - (041) 5265921, fax (041) 5260113 *Closed Nov-Apr. 19 stes 600-900,000 lire. 172 rms 205-400,000 lire. Restaurant. Conf. Tennis. Golf. Garage pkg. All major cards.*
This distinguished hostelry, immortalized by Thomas Mann, is set in an immense, leafy park with a lovely swimming pool and tennis courts, just a few yards from the beach. Though modernized, the guest rooms, lobby, and salons preserve the refined, elegant atmosphere of the hotel's golden age at the turn of the century, when Italian and other European nobility spent their days strolling along what was then the most beautiful beach on the Adriatic coast, and their nights squandering fortunes in the nearby casino. This member of the Ciga hotel chain offers guests all manner of services (shuttle to Venice, babysitting, hair-dresser...) and first-rate sports facilities.

Street Lights and Beardless Knaves

For centuries, shaven cheeks were a sure sign that a fellow was either a priest or a servant; during the Serenissima era, only patricians and citizens were allowed to grow beards. After the sixteenth century, the law was only rarely respected, although it remained on the books until the eighteenth century.
Another law, passed in 1128, forbade the use of false beards. The disguise was all the rage among muggers. Their favorite haunt was known as *il ponte dei delitti*, the Bridge of Crimes, which, appropriately, spanned the Rio degli Assassini. The city hung lanterns (*cesendeli*) there to light the perilous passage. The *rio* (little canal) was eventually filled in and paved, and is now the Street of Assassins.

Domus Cavanis

Dorsoduro, Accademia 896
(041) 5222826
Open Jun-Sep. 19 rms 30-50,000 lire. No cards.

This establishment houses university students the better part of the year, and is open to the public only in summer. The rooms, naturally, are simple and sparsely furnished. Yet the hotel is situated in one of the most elegant neighborhoods in Venice, where many noble families reside and where the cream of the city's academic population tends to gather.

Do Pozzi

San Marco, Calle Larga XXII Marzo 2373 - (041) 5207855, fax (041) 5229413 *Open year-round. 35 rms 100-212,000 lire, bkfst incl. Restaurant. All major cards.*
A perfectly charming place to stay, in a quiet spot only a few hundred feet from the bustle of Piazza San Marco. The pretty little rooms are air conditioned, with TV and minibar in each. Antique weapons and Russian icons accent the public rooms, and there is a lovely patio out front where breakfast is served in fine weather. Guests are accorded a ten-percent discount on meals taken at the Da Raffaele restaurant.

Europa e Regina

San Marco, Calle Larga XXII Marzo 2159 - (041) 5200477, fax (041) 5231533 *Open year-round. 20 stes 750-950,000 lire. 172 rms 250-470,000 lire. Restaurant. Conf. Pkg. V, AE, DC.*
The Ciga hotel group owns five of the most splendid hotels in Venice: the Danieli, Gritti Palace, Des Bains, Excelsior, and Europa e Regina. The latter has been the focus of major investments. The guest rooms have been renovated, with marble bathrooms, handmade copies of period furniture, and rubbed-lacquer walls. The public spaces are superbly decorated with authentic eighteenth-century antiques. Many artists and journalists like to stay at the Europa e Regina when in town for the film festival, the Biennale, and other cultural events, and competition is stiff for the choicest rooms, which look out onto La Salute. In cold weather one dines in the glassed-in Tiepolo restaurant (see *Restaurants*) with a view of the hotel garden and Canal Grande, but in summer the feast moves out onto the enchanting terrace.

> *Remember to call ahead to* **reserve your room***, and please, if you cannot honor your reservation, be courteous and let the hotel know.*

🏰 Excelsior

Lido di Venezia, Lungomare Marconi 41 - (041) 5260201, fax (041) 5267276 *Closed end Oct-beg Apr. 18 stes 890-1,300,000 lire. 179 rms 300-470,000 lire. Restaurant. Conf. Pool. Tennis. Golf. Garage pkg. All major cards.*

Yet another jewel in the crown of the Ciga hotel group, the Excelsior is a favorite with politicians, movie stars, and other celebrities, all of whom value the comfort and rare cachet that this renowned hotel provides. All the rooms were fully renovated in 1991; they are air conditioned and provide dreamy ocean views. Summer days on the private beach and nights on the Excelsior's terrace are the stuff of life-long memories. See the Excelsior Lido, in *Restaurants.*

🏰 La Fenice e des Artistes

San Marco, Campo La Fenice 1936 (041) 5232333, fax (041) 5203721 *Open year-round. 65 rms 120-265,000 lire, bkfst incl. V, EC, MC.*

A charming hotel that recently benefited from a full-scale renovation, La Fenice offers both a central location and quiet surroundings. Guest rooms are equipped with air conditioning and TV; three of them (354, 355, and 406) have access to a lovely terrace.

🏰 Flora

San Marco, Calle Larga XXII Marzo 2283a - (041) 5225324, fax (041) 5228217 *Open year-round. 44 rms 185-245,000 lire. All major cards.*

A peaceful place to stay, close to Piazza San Marco. A pretty garden and a fine wrought-iron staircase dress up the outside; inside, you'll find a damask-hung breakfast room, a small bar, and guest rooms of varying sizes with tasteful, personalized décor. Authentic Venetian atmosphere.

🏰 Gritti Palace

San Marco, Campo Santa Maria del Giglio 2467 - (041) 794611, fax (041) 5200942 *Open year-round. 9 stes 1,356-2,486,000 lire. 78 rms 430-673,000 lire. Restaurant. Conf. Pool. Tennis. Golf. Garage pkg. All major cards.*

From Churchill to Hemingway to the Aga Khan, the Gritti has hosted a stellar list of the world's celebrities. The hotel's reputation is built on a tradition of incomparable comfort and flawless service—and, of course, its stunning location on Canal Grande. The guest rooms are sumptuously decorated with Fortuny fabrics, are all air conditioned, and supplied with room service around the clock. The Ciga group, which owns the Gritti, has acquired valuable furnishings to add to the hotel's collection of museum-quality pieces. The summer terrace, priv-ate beach, and pool are additional attrac- tions. For an account of the noted Club del Doge, see *Restaurants.*

Saint Mark's Salute

Saint Mark the Evangelist was sailing home to Aquileia from his bishopric in Alexandria when a storm forced him into the Venetian lagoon. While asleep that night, he had a chat with an angel who told him that one day his bones would lie in Venice. The prophecy came true in the year 828, when two fervent merchants of Venice, Buono da Malamocco and Rustico da Torcello, swiped the saint's remains from a church in Alexandria. They hid the bones among salted pork bellies in the guts of their freighter, to discourage the Ottoman Turks from too careful a customs check. Years after the Doge, Giustiniano Partecipazio, had the basilica of San Marco built to house the saint's remains, no one could find the spot where the bones had been interred. So on January 25, 1094, the Venetians gathered en masse in the church and prayed to God to help them find Saint Mark's body. Suddenly a pilaster split open and Saint Mark's arm popped out in salute.

🏰 Kette

San Marco, Piscina San Moisè 2053 (041) 5207766, fax (041) 5228964 *Open year-round. 1 ste 250-400,000 lire. 55 rms 100-240,000 lire, bkfst incl. All major cards.*

Here's a hotel with character, situated on a charming canal close to La Fenice and just steps from Piazza San Marco. The spanking-clean rooms are air conditioned and equipped with satellite TV, a safe, hairdryer, and minibar. The public rooms are warm and inviting, and a friendly staff attends cheerfully to your needs.

Londra Palace

Castello, Riva degli Schiavoni 4171
(041) 5200533, fax (041) 5225032
*Open year-round. 3 stes 450-600,000 lire. 65 rms
160-440,000 lire. Restaurant. Conf. Garage pkg.
All major cards.*

Nearly as well situated as its famous neighbor, the Danieli, the Londra Palace has been astutely renovated to best advantage by its owners. Guest rooms are appointed with antique and reproduction Venetian furniture, and the wood-paneled bathrooms boast makeup vanities that look as if they were meant for Hollywood stars. Sun worshippers will appreciate the spectacular solarium on the hotel's sixth floor, as well as the private beach on the Lido. The hotel provides all the usual amenities and then some: hip boots for amateur fishermen, umbrellas and wellies when it rains, and jogging suits in every size. The Do Leoni restaurant is reviewed in *Restaurants*.

Luna Baglioni

San Marco, Calle Vallaresso 1243
(041) 5289840, fax (041) 5287160
*Open year-round. 16 stes 750-1,200,000 lire.
102 rms 185-530,000 lire. Restaurant. Conf.
All major cards.*

An excellent hotel in its category, housed in a palazzo that dates from 1474, the Luna Baglioni has been splendidly renovated in classic Venetian style. Crystal chandeliers shimmer in the salons, shedding brilliant light on the frescoes and elegant furnishings. Guest rooms are decorated in delicate monochromes, different on each floor; the bathrooms are all clad in marble. Executive suites, situated on the fourth and fifth floors, enjoy a ravishing view of Saint Mark's Basin. Fine dining in the Canova restaurant (see *Restaurants*).

Marconi

San Polo, Riva del Vin 729
(041) 5222068, fax (041) 5229700
*Open year-round. 30 rms 60-270,000 lire,
bkfst incl. All major cards.*

The Marconi gazes out over Canal Grande from its picturesque location near the Rialto Bridge. Refurbished in 1991, the rooms and lounges offer Venetian style and modern comforts, including air conditioning, hairdryers, and safes. The hotel's bar spreads out on a terrace by the canal and is a fine place to sip an aperitivo and watch

the world go by (the fascinating Rialto market is just a few yards away).

Metropole

Castello, Riva degli Schiavoni 4149
(041) 5205044, fax (041) 5223679
*Open year-round. 72 rms 165-440,000 lire, bkfst
incl. Restaurant. Conf. Pkg. All major cards.*

The Metropole looks out over the lagoon from the Riva degli Schiavoni, just a moment's walk from Piazza San Marco. The lounges, as well as the pink and white guest rooms, delight the eye with antique furnishings and bibelots (including rare pieces purchased from Christie's and Sotheby's). A full range of amenities includes a private embarcadero. Advantageous room rates are offered from November to mid-March, making a stay at the Metropole a nearly irresistible proposition.

Monaco & Grand Canal

San Marco, Calle Vallaresso 1325
(041) 5200211, fax (041) 5200501
*Open year-round. 5 stes 550-850,000 lire.
65 rms 210-470,000 lire. Restaurant. Conf. All
major cards.*

Admirably situated near San Marco and the historic center of Venice, this romantic and luxurious hotel overlooks the Grand Canal; consequently, many rooms offer stunning views of La Salute, San Giorgio, and the Lido. Although they are not large, the rooms are faultlessly equipped and furnished with refined taste. In summer, guests may lunch or dine on the terrace and exchange banter with the gondoliers. In winter, the bright dining room is cozy and inviting (see the Grand Canal, in *Restaurants*). The comfortable hotel bar boasts an enormous picture window that affords a wide-angle vista of the canal.

Hotel Santo Stefano

San Marco, Campo Santo Stefano
2957 - (041) 5200166, fax (041) 5224460
*Open year-round. 20 rms 100-200,000 lire,
bkfst incl. All major cards.*

Housed in a narrow Gothic-style building on Campo Santo Stefano, this small hotel is done up in soothing pastel shades in a typically Venetian style. Just over half of the accommodations have bathrooms in the rooms; guests in singles have adjacent (private) baths. But there are direct telephones, color TV, and minibars throughout, the location is ideal, and the service is most obliging. Air conditioning incurs an extra charge.

Pensione Accademia

Dorsoduro 1058
(041) 5210188, fax (041) 5239152
Open year-round. 27 rms 100-200,000 lire, bkfst incl. All major cards.

Here is a lovely place to stay: a seventeenth-century villa swaddled in a quiet garden near Canal Grande and the Accademia museum. Formerly the Russian consulate, the villa is now one of the prettiest hotels in its category. The Salmaso family has a long tradition of hotel-keeping, reflected in the personalized service provided here. The public rooms are welcoming, the guest accommodations are very well kept. Breakfast is served in the garden as soon as the days grow warm.

Pensione La Calcina

Dorsoduro, Fondamenta delle Zattere 780 - (041) 5206466, fax (041) 5227045
Open year-round. 37 rms 90-160,000 lire, bkfst incl. All major cards.

This tidy pensione boasts a splendid location overlooking the Giudecca Canal, and a summer terrace that juts out over the water. After breakfasting (if the day is fine) on said terrace, it will take you some fifteen minutes to reach Piazza San Marco and the center of town. Guest rooms are quiet, clean, and decorated with pleasing simplicity. Accommodations with the choicest views cost a bit more than the rest, but the sight of the Redentore from one's bedroom window is surely worth the extra lire.

Pensione Seguso

Dorsoduro, Fondamenta delle Zattere 779 - (041) 5286858, fax (041) 5222340
Open Mar-Nov. 36 rms 165-250,000 lire (half-board for 2). V, AE.

The most romantic—and best known—pensione in Venice (the late novelist Patricia Highsmith set one of her thrillers here). The Seguso stands at the water's edge on the Zattere, Venetians' favorite spot for an afternoon stroll. The best rooms here are spacious with tall ceilings and antique furniture; there is a warm, comfortable lounge as well, and a beamed dining room where residents take their meals. Accommodations should be booked well in advance.

Saturnia & International

San Marco, Calle Larga XXII Marzo 2398 - (041) 5208377, fax (041) 5207131

Open year-round. 95 rms 200-420,000 lire, bkfst incl. Half-board 65,000 lire per person. All major cards.

This patrician palazzo dates from the fourteenth century. The Serandrei family has operated the Saturnia for four generations, keeping a great deal of the building's aristocratic magnificence intact, as evidenced by the sumptuous first-floor salon and the ornate coffered ceilings. Some of the rooms are on the small side, but all are quiet and comfortable, particularly those overlooking the garden or the rooftops of Venice. Along with such amenities as air conditioning and TV, you will find a truly charming and resourceful staff. Room rates vary significantly according to season; attractive all-in packages are offered in winter. For a review of the hotel's restaurant, La Caravella, see *Restaurants.*

The Storm of the Spirits

Making hay in Venice is nothing new. The Ponte della Paglia on the Riva degli Schiavoni owes its name to the *paglia*, or hay boats, that once moored there. It was also the setting for a medieval legend. On February 15, 1340, a poor fisherman saved himself from a terrible storm by mooring his boat under the Ponte della Paglia. A mysterious man appeared and asked the fisherman to take him across to San Giorgio Maggiore. Another man showed up and demanded to go to San Nicolò del Lido. When a third traveler arrived, the fisherman was forced to take to the sea. Far from shore, another boat suddenly appeared, brimming with evil spirits. The three unknown travelers stood up and flung lightening bolts at the demons. The sea calmed. The travelers turned out to be Saint Mark, Saint George, and Saint Nicholas. You can see the legend depicted in a painting by Paris Bordone, hanging in the Accademia.

Nightlife

CONTENTS

I s there life after dark in Venice? No swinging club scene, that's for sure; nor did we discover much live entertainment. But if the night owl in you simply must fly, check out the venues listed below, and look into the wine bars and cafés described in the *Quick Bites* section.

BARS

Le Bistrot de Venise
San Marco, Calle dei Fabbri 4685
(041) 5236651
Open 10am-1am. Closed Thu.
French and Venetian treats—crêpes, bruschetta, pizzas, canapés—keep company with an array of good wines at this charming address, which boasts a lovely outdoor terrace. On Monday nights, comedy sketches or live bands are featured for your entertainment. And for your comfort, the room is air-conditioned in summer. By the way, if you know how to play, don't feel shy about sitting down at the piano!

Linea d'Ombra
Dorsoduro, Punta della Dogana 19
(041) 5285259
Open 7pm-2am. Closed Wed.
This small seafood restaurant and piano bar has a terrace overlooking the lovely Canale della Giudecca and a stupendous view of the island of San Giorgio and the church of the Redeemer. Linea d'Ombra serves full meals, but you can order just a cocktail, if you like, and soak up the atmosphere.

Al Muro
San Marco, Calle Sant'Antonio 4118
(041) 5205205
Open 9am-2am. Closed Sun.
This small bar tucked away on a narrow street near San Marco is a well-known fixture of Venetian nightlife. The Liberty-style décor holds particular appeal for young people, artists, and intellectuals, all of whom settle into these cozy quarters to share drinks and good talk far into the night.

The Doge's Dream

One night in 1234, two angels bearing incense-filled censers swooped down on Doge Giacomo Tiepolo in a delightful, nostril-tickling dream. Soon after, he generously gave the Dominican friars a swamp (it was either that or water) so they could build a church and convent there. The result is the splendid Gothic church of Santi Giovanni e Paolo (Venetians call it "San Zanipolo") and the lovely Campo of the same name. The church is a treasure house of fine art; Doge Tiepolo's tomb therein is decorated with two sculptures—representing the angels of his dream.

Paradiso Perduto
Cannaregio, Fondamenta Misericordia 2540
(041) 5220581
Open 7pm-1am (summer 7am-2am). Closed Wed.

Once upon a time, this classic Venetian wine bar was the semiofficial headquarters of the dissident student movement. Today, artists and young hipsters still gather at "Paradise Lost" to drink wine, listen to poetry readings, admire the paintings and photographs exhibited on the walls, or hear the jazz groups who play here on Tuesday and Saturday nights. Your two hosts will be pleased to help you select from the fine wines assembled in their cellar. To go with, try a plate of delicious homemade bigoli (whole-wheat spaghetti) in anchovy sauce.

CASINO

Il Casinò Municipale di Venezia
Summer: Lungomare Marconi 4, Lido di Venezia - (041) 5297111
Winter: Ca' Vendramin-Calergi, Cannaregio 2040 - (041) 5297111
Open daily from 4pm.
From October until April, you can try your luck in the splendid sixteenth-century rooms of the Palazzo Vendramin-Calergi, overlooking the Grand Canal. And you can pause for a drink or spend your winnings in the Casanova club. In summer, the roulette, craps, blackjack, and chemin-de-fer tables move to the Lido, with its fresh sea breezes. In tune with the times, the

Casino now offers slot machines, video poker, and other video games.

DISCO

Club El Souk
Accademia 1056a - (041) 5200371
Open 8:30pm-3am. Closed Sun (bar only).
A cocktail bar by day, Club El Souk becomes a private disco by night. Find a member to go along with you and you'll be admitted with no problem; you need only ring at the little iron door. Inside, barmen pour exotic drinks, and a DJ mixes the dance music.

NIGHTCLUB

Martini Scala Club
San Marco, Campo San Fantin 1983
(041) 5224121
Open 10pm-3:30am. Closed Tue.
The late-night scene in Venice offers pretty slim pickings, but the Martini Scala Club, situated just around the corner from La Fenice, provides the basics: an animated bar, live music, and a restaurant that operates until the wee hours.

Twelve Brides with a Headache

The venerable church of San Pietro di Castello has been a bishopric since the year 775. Every January 31st, for centuries, the Venetians celebrated a mass wedding there. Twelve of the prettiest and poorest girls in town were given a dowry and a grand marriage celebration as a gift from the Commune. It all went smoothly until, in the year 942, villains arrived on the wedding night. These pirates from Istria holed up out of sight and the next morning swept the newly wed ladies—and their trousseaus—off their feet. The Doge, Candian III, formed a sea posse and gave chase. In a cove near Caorle, they found the pirates, who were in the act of dividing up the plunder and pawing the damsels (the port there has been named Porto delle Donzelle ever since). The Venetians cut the Istrians to pieces, of course, and shipped the wives, no worse for wear, back home.

Shops

CONTENTS

During the tourist season, which runs from April to the end of September, many of the shops listed below remain open without interruption from 9 or 10am until 7:30pm every day of the week, including Sundays.

ANTIQUES

Calle Larga XXII Marzo, the street that links Campo Santo Stefano to Piazza San Marco, is the principal showcase for Venice's antique dealers. The shops listed below all specialize in furniture and art objects made in Venice or the Veneto region.

Antichità e Oggetti d'Arte
San Marco, Frezzeria 1691 - (041) 5235666
Open 10am-12:30pm & 4pm-7pm. Closed Mon.
Beautiful heirloom jewelry and vintage fabrics are presented here, along with a small but significant collection of antique furniture. The textiles in particular are worthy of notice: among the fine velvets are some stamped designs produced according to an ancient Venetian process.

Casellati
San Marco 3130 - (041) 5230966
Open 9:30am-12:30pm & 4pm-7pm. Closed Mon am.
Casellati recently moved from its former (rather grand) quarters to these more modest premises. Nonetheless, the pieces on view are prestigious antiques: marble statues, and smaller figures carved in wood, semiprecious stones, and precious metals. All are Venetian in origin, dating from various periods.

Francesco Mirate
San Marco, Calle della Verona 1904
(041) 5227600
Open 9:30am-12:30pm & 4pm-7pm. Closed Mon.
Antique occasional furniture (nothing too bulky), elegant frames and mirrors, and a discerning selection of pictures and sculptures are offered for sale at this interesting shop.

Pietro Scarpa
San Marco 1464 - (041) 5222697
Open 9:30am-12:30pm & 4pm-7pm. Closed Mon.
Pietro Scarpa is a reputable source for signed paintings and drawings by such immortal Venetian artists as Titian, the Tiepolos, Canaletto, and their most talented disciples.

Zancopé
San Marco 2674 - (041) 5234567
Open 10am-12:30pm & 4pm-7pm. Closed Mon am.
Shimmering antique Venetian glass draws admirers to Zancopé. On view here are perfume bottles, decanters, and goblets dating from 1500 to 1800, the superb results of an art perfected over centuries in such ateliers as Cenedese, one of Venice's most famous glassworks, today considered a highly prestigious "label" for Venetian glass.

BOOKS

Fantoni
San Marco 4121 - (041) 5220700
Open daily 9am-12:30pm & 3:30pm-7:30pm.
Fantoni sells sumptuous books on the fine and applied arts, from jewelry and pottery to ikebana and fashion. Many selections are available in English.

Filippi
Castello 5763 - (041) 5235635
Open daily 9am-12:30pm & 3:30pm-7:30pm.
Filippi is not just a bookstore. It's also a publishing house, one of the most respected establishments of its kind in book-loving Venice. Here visitors may lose themselves in handsomely produced volumes about the city, its history, art, and legends. Filippi also publishes a collection of tales written and illustrated by prominent Venetian artists; they make lovely souvenirs of this enchanted city.

Goldoni
San Marco, Calle dei Fabbri 4742-4743
(041) 5222384
Open daily 9am-12:30pm & 3:30pm-7:30pm.
Goldoni claims to be the best-stocked bookshop in town, and we see no reason to contradict that. It's a fine source of books on the history of Venice, including a selection of volumes in English.

The Original Ghetto

The Ghetto was established in Venice in 1516 in the Cannaregio district. The Jews of Venice were compelled to live there until 1797. A populous place, the Ghetto reached its peak—4,000 residents—in 1633. From sunset to sunrise the gates to the Ghetto were locked and guarded by armed sentinels. Visit the Museo Comunità Ebraica at Cannaregio 2902b (closed Sat) to learn more about the history of the Jewish community in Venice.

Alla Toletta
Dorsoduro, Calle della Toletta 1214
(041) 5232034
Open daily 9am-12:30pm & 3:30pm-7:30pm.
All the books sold here are marked down by 50 percent, which makes the dictionaries (including many English-Italian volumes) and art books unbeatable bargains.

FASHION

■ CLOTHING

Agnona
San Marco, Calle Vallaresso 1307
(041) 5205733
Open 9am-12:30pm & 3:30pm-7:30pm. Closed Mon am.
If your idea of luxury runs to simple lines and opulent fabrics, don't miss Agnona: silk and cashmere in warm, flattering colors make wearable, comfortable, and very classy clothes for women.

L'Ape
San Polo, Calle Botteri 1697 - (041) 5241957
Open 10am-12:30pm & 4pm-7:30pm. Closed Mon.
Patrizia, the owner, is as busy as the proverbial bee for which her shop is named. She hand-prints glowing fabrics that she then transforms into fresh-looking, one-of-a-kind outfits. This little boutique also carries handmade sweaters ornamented with silk appliqués, beads, and sequins as well as sportier cotton-knit pullovers for summer.

Arnold's Shop
San Marco, Calle Mandola 3720b
(041) 5235039
Open 9:30am-12:30pm & 3:15pm-7:30pm. Closed Mon am.
Arnold's is Venice's best-known purveyor of classic English menswear. That translates into Burlington's argyle socks and sweater vests, sheepskin jackets with wool-pile linings, herringbone and tweed jackets, Irish sweaters, and Scottish-tartan flannel shirts. The source for these smart, sporty clothes is located between Campo San Luca and Campo Sant'Angelo.

Laura Biagiotti

San Marco, Calle Larga XXII Marzo 2400
(041) 5203401
Open 9am-12:30pm & 3:30pm-7:30pm. Closed Mon am.
Superbly cut women's clothing in luxurious fabrics (cashmere, linen). The way Biagiotti's knits drape over the body flatters even fuller figures.

Brocca

San Marco 4610 - (041) 5287924
San Polo 974 - (041) 5225451
Open 10am-12:30pm & 4pm-7:30pm. Closed Mon am.
Brocca is renowned for its attractive menswear. The store near the Rialto stocks classic (but not necessarily conservative) apparel, including Marzotto tweed jackets, and offers a custom-tailoring service. The smaller branch near Teatro Goldoni is more closely attuned to current fashion, with younger-looking colors and fabrics, designer sportswear, and such nifty accessories as bright silk boxer shorts.

Roberto Cavalli

San Marco, Calle Vallaresso 1314
(041) 5205733
Open 9am-12:30pm & 3:30pm-7:30pm. Closed Mon am.
Dolce & Gabbana, Italy's highly original and slightly mad designing duo, are showcased here, with an extensive array of fashions for day and evening.

Ceriello

San Marco, Campo Santi Filippo e Giacomo
(041) 5222062
Open 9am-12:30pm & 3pm-7:30pm. Closed Mon am.
The enticing window displays showcase men's sportswear by such top Italian designers as Armani, Valentino, Nino Cerruti, and Brioni.

Corner

San Marco 4855 - (041) 5286924
Open 9am-12:30pm & 3:30pm-7:30pm. Closed Mon am.
Corner carries a full range of casual clothing for men and women from the Marlboro collection, CP Company, Stone Island, Zanone, and other quality Italian makers, as well as men's underwear bearing the label of no less a fashion eminence than Giorgio Armani.

La Coupole

San Marco, Frezzeria 1674 - (041) 5206063
San Marco, Calle Larga XXII Marzo 2366
(041) 5224243
Open 9am-12:30pm & 3pm-7:30pm. Closed Mon am.
The gang's all here: Dolce & Gabbana, Claude Montana, Moschino Couture, Verri, cashmere by Malo, and more. La Coupole clothes men and women in avant-garde style. There are shoes, too, by Maud Frizon and Stéphane Kélian, and lots of handsomely finished leatherwear.

Enrico Coveri

San Marco 1136a - (041) 5221241
Open 9am-12:30pm & 3:30pm-7:30pm. Closed Mon am.
Coveri creates stylish casual clothing for men and youthful, imaginative fashions for women.

Al Duca d'Aosta

San Marco 4922 - (041) 5220733
Open daily 9am-12:30pm & 3:30pm-7:30pm.
Classic elegance is the trademark of Duca d'Aosta, a famous fashion emporium for both women and men in the center of Venice. The selection of menswear is particularly fine, from the silk boxer shorts to the superb sheepskin jackets and luxurious cashmere overcoats. The quality is high, and the prices are thought-provoking. Among the famous labels in stock are Ralph Lauren, Jil Sander, Prada, and Burberry's.

Elite

San Marco 284 - (041) 5230145
Open daily 9am-12:30pm & 3:30pm-7:30pm.
A showcase for such designers as Missoni, Gucci, and Ralph Lauren, along with some more traditional lines.

Elysée Due

San Marco, Frezzeria 1693 - (041) 5223020
Open 9am-12:30pm & 3:30pm-7:30pm. Closed Mon am.
The city's major source for Giorgio Armani's top-of-the-line designs (his more moderate range is sold at Emporio Armani, below).

Elysée 1

San Marco, Calle Goldoni 4485
(041) 5236948
Open 9am-12:30pm & 3:30pm-7:30pm. Closed Mon am.
Lots of up-to-the-minute fashions here for women and men (Blumarine, Eddi, Brooksfield, Ruffo...). Cashmere is a specialty of the house.

Emporio Armani

San Marco, Calle dei Fabbri 989
(041) 5237808
Open daily 9am-12:30pm & 3:30pm-7:30pm.
The Emporio presents Giorgio Armani's less expensive and somewhat sportier clothing for men, women, and children.

Fendi

San Marco, Salizzada San Moisè 1474
(041) 5205733
Open 9am-12:30pm & 3:30pm-7:30pm. Closed Mon am.
Fendi's Venice outpost sells the complete Fendi line of dashing, extravagant furs, ready-to-wear clothing, and fine leather goods. This branch is notable for its small discount area, which often displays some good bargains.

La Fenice

San Marco, Calle Larga XXII Marzo 2255
(041) 5231273
Open 9:30am-12:30pm & 4pm-7:30pm. Closed Mon am.
All the big names are on hand, with their lines for men and women: Moschino, Romeo Gigli, Byblos, Genny, and an impressive French cohort, too (Alaïa, Thierry Mugler, Claude Montana). To finish off your fashionable ensemble, choose a pair of Stéphane Kélian's exquisite braided-leather shoes.

Gianfranco Ferré

San Marco, Calle Larga San Marco 287
(041) 52225147
Open daily 9am-12:30pm & 3:30pm-7:30pm.
Glamorous, high-priced fashion for women and men, by one of Italy's foremost designers. Stunning accessories.

Krizia

San Marco 4948-9 - (041) 5212762
Open 9am-12:30pm & 3:30pm-7:30pm. Closed Mon am.
Krizia's spacious, two-level boutique offers a mouthwatering selection of the designer's coveted Italian-made creations for women; very good prices (considerably less than in the U.S.). Frothy, feminine accessories abound, and the collection of evening wear will tempt you to whip out your credit card.

La Tour

San Marco, Calle Larga San Marco 287
(041)5225147
Open 9am-12:30pm & 3:30pm-7:30pm.
Fashion insiders know that Allegri, Bagutta, and Aida Barni are labels worth seeking out: they are all on hand here, alongside ready-to-wear from Ferré (including togs from his more affordable Studio 0001 line).

Max Mara

San Marco, Calle dei Mori 268-269
(041) 5226688
Open 9am-12:30pm & 4pm-7:30pm. Closed Mon am.
Smart, modern women's wear with occasional whimsical touches. Wonderful coats, knits, and for summer, snappy linen suits.

Missoni

San Marco, Calle Vallaresso 1312
(041) 5205733
Open 9am-12:30pm & 4pm-7:30pm. Closed Mon am.
Despite minimal floor space, this branch of the Missoni empire carries a considerable selection of women's and men's clothing, with the accent on the firm's nubbly, mossy, subtly shaded sweaters.

Ortolani

Piazza San Marco 86-89 - (041) 5225719
Open 9am-12:30pm & 3:30pm-7:30pm. Closed Mon am.
A prime source for fine menswear, Ortolani can be found under the arcades of the Piazza San Marco. The shop's elegant windows and mahogany shelves display classically tailored clothing; the accessories have an unmistakable English flair. Particularly attractive are the collections of shirts, casual slacks, double-breasted suits, and evening clothes.

> **Monday**, *like* **Sunday**, *is a day of rest for many shopkeepers.*

Luisa Spagnoli

San Marco 741-743 - (041) 5206131
Open daily 9am-12:30pm & 4pm-7:30pm.
Elegant, tasteful, and finely crafted women's wear, with an emphasis on knits, at prices that aren't too daunting.

Trussardi

San Marco, Spadaria 695 - (041) 5285757
Open daily 9am-12:30pm & 3:30pm-7:30pm.
Venice's branch of this popular leather-goods maker has surprisingly attractive prices. Along with leather bags, totes, wallets, accessories, and the like, Trussardi sells its own line of high-fashion ready-to-wear for women and men.

Valentino

San Marco, Salizzada San Moisè 1473
(041) 5205733
Open 9am-12:30pm & 3:30pm-7:30pm. Closed Mon am.
A smaller selection that at Valentino's showcases in Milan, Rome, and Florence. But the gorgeously detailed fashions and glamorous accessories are no less fearsomely expensive than at any other Valentino outpost.

Versace

San Marco, Frezzeria 1722 - (041) 5236369
Open daily 9am-7:30pm.
All the best of Gianni Versace's multifarious designs—menswear, women's wear, leather goods, accessories—are sold under this one Venetian roof. Every piece of merchandise is exciting, flamboyant, ultrafashionable—and devastatingly dear!

Versus

San Marco, Calle Larga XXII Marzo 2359
(041) 5232162
Open 9am-12:30pm & 3:30pm-7:30pm. Closed Mon am.
The casual, young-spirited clothes for both sexes that bear Versace's less expensive labels are collected here: Versus by Gianni Versace, Istante, and Jeans Couture.

Volpe

San Marco, Campo San Bartolomeo 5257
(041) 5222524
San Polo, Campo Sant'Aponal 1228
(041) 5238041
Open daily 9am-12:30pm & 3:30pm-7:30pm.

Fashions for women and men by contemporary designers (Byblos, Blumarine, Mani by Armani, Moschino, Le Garage shirts) share space with more conservatively cut (though still quite sleek) apparel. We found the leather jackets exceptionally attractive, and the silk shirts are pure delight. A full range of accessories is sold as well.

■ JEWELRY

Codognato

San Marco 1295 - (041) 5225042
Open 10am-12:30pm & 4pm-7:30pm. Closed Mon am.
Not for the timid, Codognato's sumptuous jewels are designed to attract notice. An enormous lion's head with a ruby in its mouth, a Moor's head in gilded ebony, a diamond-encrusted gold spiral bracelet—such pieces make strong fashion statements (not to mention strong financial statements). Many one-of-a-kind jewels and sublime antique ornaments are also presented.

Missaglia

San Marco 125-127 - (041) 5224464
Open 9:30am-12:30pm & 4pm-7:30pm. Closed Mon am.
A small, select shop on Piazza San Marco, Missaglia is the only place in town where you can purchase the high-status, high-priced jewelry, scarves, perfumes, and leather goods made by Hermès.

Must de Cartier

San Marco, Campo San Zulian - (041) 5207484
Open 9am-12:30pm & 4pm-7:30pm. Closed Mon.
Cartier occupies opulent new digs on Campo San Zulian; the new store is decked out in the company's corporate colors: (royal!) purple and gold. All the latest additions to the "Must" line are on view, along with the other expensive trifles and baubles that have made Cartier a synonym for luxury.

Nardi

Piazza San Marco 69 - (041) 5225733
Open 9:30am-12:30pm & 4pm-7:30pm. Closed Mon am.

The sparkle of Nardi's display cases causes many a stroller to stop in her tracks: who wouldn't be mesmerized by the displays of fabulous jeweled animal pins, splendid Art Deco jeweled pieces, and exclusive ornaments in gold, platinum, and gems? A Venetian jeweler with international renown, Nardi also carries timepieces by Piaget.

Salvadori

San Marco, Mercerie 5022 - (041) 5230609
Open 9am-12:30pm & 3:30pm-7:30pm. Closed Mon am.

Distinctive timepieces by the world's most prestigious watchmakers dominate Salvadori's brilliant showcases. Prominently featured are all the status collections by Rolex.

■ LEATHER & LUGGAGE

Bottega Veneta

San Marco, Calle Vallaresso 1337
(041) 5228489
Open 10am-1pm & 3:30pm-8pm. Closed Mon am.

Bottega Veneta's beautifully supple woven-leather bags are sold in the firm's flagship store at prices significantly lower than anywhere else. In addition to the handbags and leather goods, you'll find sensational shoes and a choice collection of fashion accessories—the shawls are stunning.

Bussola

San Marco 4608 - (041) 5229846
Open 9am-12:30pm & 3:30pm-7:30pm. Closed Mon am.

First-class leather goods—bags, suitcases, belts, wallets—by such major Italian designers as Armani, Versace, and Trussardi are on view in the white-marble cases of this alluring shop, situated in the heart of Venice, just steps from the Rialto Bridge. The complete lines of matching leather luggage for him and her are irresistible (or would be, if they weren't so terrifyingly expensive).

Furla

San Marco, Mercerie 4954 - (041) 5230611
San Polo, Rialto Arcades 53-54 - (041) 5235862
Open 9am-12:30pm & 3pm-7:30pm. Closed Mon am.

Furla has conquered a loyal clientele with a complete line of leather bags, luggage, and accessories and a dazzling collection of unusual costume jewelry. Bags in every size, shape, and color are a specialty: whether you need a classic clutch in a conservative tint or a zany leopard-print carry-all, Furla is sure to have one in stock. And you'll find coordinated change purses, wallets, and belts to go with it.

Grano Pelletterie

San Marco, Mercerie 4928 - (041) 5222272
Open 9:30am-12:30pm & 3:30pm-7:30pm. Closed Mon am.

If you want a piece of Samsonite luggage to complete your collection, this small but incredibly well-stocked store can provide it. There's a large assortment of matching luggage sets by other manufacturers as well, along with some lovely leather traveling bags. Grano also specializes in luxurious crocodile bags and accessories.

Gucci

San Marco, Mercerie 259 - (041) 5229119
Open 9:30am-12:30pm & 3:30pm-7:30pm. Closed Mon am.

Italy's top name in leather has rejuvenated its image without losing an ounce of class. What woman wouldn't want one of Gucci's colorful, beautifully crafted bucket bags flung over her shoulder? From key cases to luggage, the leather accessories display impeccable workmanship; for the quality, the prices are not so very unreasonable.

Marforio

San Marco, Campo San Salvador 5033
(041) 5225734
Open 8:30am-12:30pm & 3:30pm-7:30pm. Closed Mon am.

Luggage and handbags are the specialty of this well-regarded leather-goods store located in the center of Venice. Not only will you find useful and attractive small leather items, such as key holders and shaving kits, you will also discover the entire lines of Samsonite, Fila, and Invicta luggage, backpacks, and other sporting accessories, as well as folders and briefcases for the executive set.

Vogini

San Marco, Calle Seconda dell'Ascension
1257a - (041) 5222573
Open 9am-12:30pm & 3pm-7:30pm. Closed Mon am.

Just off Piazza San Marco, Vogini's windows dazzle passersby with their witty and imaginative displays: tortoise-shell evening bags, gilded minaudières shaped like seashells, suede and patent-leather handbags aglitter with sequins or rhinestones. Of course, there are plenty of quietly tasteful bags, too, including some desirable braided-leather items. Vogini also stocks an impressive array of luggage, some of it classic and some of it decidedly funky (check out the Moschino bags). Don't overlook the buttery-soft suede jackets, available in a gorgeous palette of colors.

Louis Vuitton

San Marco 1461, Campo San Moisè
(041) 5224500
Open 9am-12:30pm & 4pm-7:30pm. Closed Mon am.

Those universally known initials are printed on trunks, suitcases, handbags, folders, briefcases. And the L.V. theme continues on the accessories (wallets, umbrellas, and much more). If wearing other people's initials is not for you, take a look at Vuitton's Épi lines, in handsomely worked green and brilliant yellow leathers.

■ SHOES & ACCESSORIES

Atelier Segalin

San Marco, Calle dei Fuseri 4365
(041) 5222115
Open 9am-12:30pm & 3:30pm-7:30pm. Closed Mon am.

Since 1932, discriminating Venetians have called upon the Atelier Segalin to cobble custom footwear to their size and style specifications. Expensive, and the work takes considerable time.

La Bauta

San Marco, Mercerie 729 - (041) 5223838
Open 9am-12:30pm & 3:30pm-7:30pm. Closed Mon am.

Fetching, original footwear and leather gear presented in elegant surroundings. La Bauta is the city's source for leather designs by Prada.

La Corte delle Fate

Castello 5690, San Lio - (041) 5286611
Open 9am-12:30pm & 3:30pm-7:30pm. Closed Mon am.

La Corte delle Fate's shoes are superbly designed (by Romeo Gigli and Giorgio Armani, among others) and highly original. For evening, you'll find a stunning selection of models in satin or metallic tints. You're sure to covet a pair of the exclusive, glove-soft walking shoes, the most elegant of their type we've seen in many a moon.

Bruno Magli

San Marco 1302 - (041) 5227210
San Marco 1583-1585b - (041) 5223472
Open 9am-12:30pm & 4pm-7:30pm. Closed Mon am.

Bruno Magli's name is a familiar one to fanciers of high-quality footwear, who admire his casual and formal designs for women and men. A glance at the shop's extensive displays proves that Magli has an equal talent for creating classic styles and outlandish ones (we love his bare, high-heeled evening sandals for women).

Mori & Bozzi

Cannaregio, Strada Nuova 3822
(041) 5203455
Open 9am-12:30pm & 3pm-7:30pm. Closed Mon am.

This designing couple has a wild sense of style that translates into eccentric, extravagant, elegant footwear. Elbow your way past the admiring crowd in front of the store, and see for yourself: mocassins adorned with feathers, spotted leathers, patent-leather pumps in outrageous hues. Sensible shoes they're not, but they're marvelously chic.

La Pantofola

San Marco, Calle della Mandola 3718
(041) 5222150
Open 9am-12:30pm & 3pm-7:30pm. Closed Mon am.

You can't leave Venice without a pair of traditional handcrafted Friulian *pantofole* (slippers), with velvet uppers and "bicycle-tire" soles. They are the specialty of this store, which also purveys footwear for sensitive or hard-to-fit feet.

Pollini

San Marco 186 - (041) 5237480
Open 9am-12:30pm & 3pm-7:30pm. Closed Mon am.
Shoes to please a wide range of tastes. The skins are of excellent quality, and the styles show sure-footed fashion sense, never falling over into faddishness.

Fratelli Rossetti

San Marco 1477 - (041) 5220819
San Marco 4800, Campo San Salvador
(041) 5230571
Open 9am-12:30pm & 3:30pm-7:30pm. Closed Mon am.
This famous Venetian firm favors futuristic window displays, the better to set off its classic footwear. The men's line is the last word in restrained elegance, while the women's collections, fashioned in beautiful colored leathers, combine timeless grace with contemporary chic.

Mario Valentino

San Marco 1255, Bocca di Piazza
(041) 5231333
Open 9:30am-12:30pm & 3:30pm-7:30pm. Closed Mon.
Zany, colorful footwear for men and women, along with stylish leather gear.

FOOD

■ GOURMET SHOPS

Aliani

Ruga Rialto 654-5 - (041) 5224913
Open 9am-12:30pm & 3:30pm-7:30pm. Closed Mon pm.
After a tour of the Rialto market, visit Aliani to purchase cheeses, premium olive oils, salami, and wine. The stracchino and ricotta cheeses are remarkable, and there is also a selection of prepared foods for take-out, including terrific, creamy baccalà mantecato (whipped dried cod).

Dietaverde

Dorsoduro 1358, Fondamenta Romite
(041) 5231007
Open 9am-1pm & 3:30pm-7:30pm. Closed Wed pm.
Mother Nature herself would surely shop at Dietaverde, choosing from among the whole foods and macrobiotic specialties that line the shelves. Fresh tofu is a staple here, as are phosphate-free detergents that are guaranteed to be gentle on both your clothes and the environment.

Drogheria Caberlotto

Cannaregio, San Felice 3689 - (041) 5228258
Open 9am-1pm & 3:30pm-7:30pm. Closed Wed pm.
One of the oldest grocery stores in Venice, Caberlotto sells its own brand of several typically Venetian items, such as baicoli (twice-baked cookies). The displays of foodstuffs in great glass jars and wooden crates have an old-fashioned charm, but the shop is up on all the latest culinary trends—you'll even find fixings for a Mexican feast!

Macrobiotica El Quetzal

Dorsoduro, Campo Santa Margherita 2932
(041) 5237444
Open 9am-12:30pm & 4pm-7:30pm. Closed Mon am.
Get your whole-wheat bread here, fresh every Monday and Thursday. You'll also find a full line of whole foods and organic and biodynamic provender at this well-stocked macrobiotic shop.

Luciano Mascari

San Polo 381 - (041) 5229762
Open 8am-1pm & 5pm-7:30pm. Closed Wed pm.
This is one of the few grocery shops in town with a complete range of spices and dried fruit. For subtle palates that appreciate nuances of flavor, there are several varieties of cocoa and many different coffees.

Giacomo Rizzo

Cannaregio 1538 - (041) 5217494
Salizzada San Giovanni Crisostomo
(041) 5222824
Open 9am-1pm & 4pm-8pm. Closed Wed pm.
The best fresh pasta in Venice is on sale in Rizzo's two shops; the dusky tagliatelle dyed with cuttlefish ink or cocoa are memorable indeed. The other specialty of these fascinating stores is a vast array of exotic essentials for Chinese, Thai, Greek, and Turkish cookery.

295

Salumeria San Marco

San Marco, Frezzeria 1580 - (041) 5222527
Open 8am-1pm & 4:30pm-8pm. Closed Wed pm.
A very classy address. You want truffles? Salmon? Caviar? They're here, and of the finest quality to boot. You'll also find a trove of such gourmet supplies as cider, raspberry and balsamic vinegars, black bread from Merano, and a collection of pungent Spanish condiments and sauces.

■ HERBALISTS

Erbalido

Lido di Venezia, Via Negroponte 4c
(041) 5260375
Open 9am-12:30pm & 3:30pm-7:30pm. Closed Sat pm, Sun.
This is the only herbalist's shop on the Lido, and it's certainly one of the most fashionable in Venice. From plant-based tanning oils to herbal teas for whatever ails you, there are scores of examples of the herbalist's art to be discovered here, including fresh and appealing scents for the home.

Erboristerie Riunite

Dorsoduro 1321 - (041) 5210688
Open 9:30am-12:30pm & 4pm-8pm. Closed Sun-Mon.
Hidden away in a little *calletta* near the university, on the edge of a canal, this herbalist offers a range of natural foods in addition to the usual plants and essential oils. The whole-wheat spaghetti is excellent, and the all-natural sweets are more appealing than such things usually tend to be. Refreshing vegetable drinks and fruit cocktails are served at the juice bar.

Il Melograno

Dorsoduro 2999 - (041) 5285117
Open 9:30am-12:30pm & 3:30pm-7:30pm. Closed Sun-Mon.
This astonishing collection of herbs for medicinal, cosmetic, and culinary uses includes even the most arcane varieties. For those who are unfamiliar with the art of concocting herbal mixes and other preparations, Melograno carries a line of ready-made teas and potions.

■ WINE

Cantina Aziende Agricola

Cannaregio, Rio Terrà Farsetti 1847a
(041) 718699
Open 9am-2pm & 4:30pm-9pm. Closed Sun.
Sample the fresh and delicious wines of the Veneto, sold straight from the cask. Choice bottles from all over Italy are on offer, too.

GIFTS

Burelli

Dorsoduro, Campo San Barnaba 2729
(041) 5224309
Open 9am-12:30pm & 4pm-7:30pm. Closed Mon am.
Artists prize Burelli's top-quality powdered pigments, which are sold here along with all manner of supplies for the fine arts, from paints and lacquers to hardware and specialized tools. If Venice brings out the artist in you (and how could it not?), nip round to Burelli for the necessary kit.

Gianni Cavalier

San Marco, Campo Santo Stefano 2863a
(041) 5238621
Open 9am-12:30pm & 4pm-7:30pm. Closed Mon am.
The art of gilding survives among a handful of Venetian craftsmen, including Gianni Cavalier. In his shop set on a lovely square, you may admire the soft, golden glow of angels, Carnival masks, lamps, and mirrors, all gilded by hand.

Cenedese

Piazza San Marco 40-41 - (041) 5225487
Fondamenta Venier 48a, Murano
(041) 739877
Open 9am-1pm & 3pm-7pm. Closed Sun pm.
The fragile, finely wrought wine glasses, decorative accents, jewelry, and sculpture produced at the Cenedese glassworks are renowned throughout the world. Glorious colors, and a wide range of pieces in both contemporary and classic styles.

The prices in this guide reflect what establishments were charging at press time.

Color Casa

San Polo 1990 - (041) 5236071
Open 9am-12:30pm & 4pm-7:30pm. Closed Mon am.
A profusion of vivid and attractive homewares: the warm colors and rich textures are typically Italian. You'll find household linens, upholstery and curtain fabrics, and beautiful wallpapers, too.

Ex Libris

San Marco 3633 - (041) 5231459
Open 9am-12:30pm & 4pm-7:30pm. Closed Mon am.
Give your library special cachet with personalized bookplates from Ex Libris; or write impressive letters with a Venetian-glass pen dipped in perfumed, all-natural ink, on marbleized stationery sealed with scented wax! All of these exquisite supplies are available here, along with handsome leather desk accessories.

Frette

San Marco, Calle Larga XXII Marzo 2070a
(041) 5224914
Open 9am-12:30pm & 4pm-7:30pm. Closed Mon am.
Lavished with lace, embroidered borders, scalloped edgings, and delicate openwork, Frette's linens look almost too pristine to use! But they're as long-wearing (given proper care, of course) as they are lovely. The firm's wool blankets are famous for their snuggly warmth and incomparable feel. Frette also provides custom-made linens for the ultimate in personalized luxury. If a full set of sheets and pillowcases is beyond your budget, take a look at the irresistibly frothy lingerie and sleepwear.

Graffiti

San Polo, Campo ai Frari 3045
(041) 5228843
Open 9am-12:30pm & 4pm-7:30pm. Closed Mon am.
This little shop brims over with colorful art posters and unusual postcards. There is an interesting collection of reproductions of works by Matisse, De Chirico, Picasso, and other greats.

L'Isola

San Marco, Campo San Moisè 1468
(041) 5231973
Open 9:30am-7:30pm. Closed Mon am.
Glass designer Carlo Moretti's distinctive, stylized vases, plates, and tumbler sets, many adorned with his signature spiral motif, rate star billing in this glittering emporium.

Jesurum

San Marco, Ponte della Canonica 4310
(041) 5206177
Piazza San Marco 60-61 - (041) 5229864
Open 9:30am-12:30pm & 3:30pm-7pm. Closed Mon am.
Lace from Jesurum has for decades trimmed the trousseaus of the world's elegant brides (and the bibs and booties of their babies). The Ponte della Canonica store, housed in a former church, is worth a visit if only to view Jesurum's Lace Museum, where the firm's most precious pieces are collected. If you bring plenty of money, you can purchase a lovely set of lace-edged napkins, or sheets frothed with lace and embroidery, or a sumptuous tablecloth encrusted with appliqués. A more modest sum will buy a delicate lace-edged handkerchief.

Laboratorio Artigiano Maschere

Castello, Barbaria delle Tole 6657
(041) 5223110
Open 9am-12:30pm & 4pm-7:30pm. Closed Mon.
Fantastic masks are still handcrafted in leather or papier-mâché at this historic atelier. Masks portraying the characters of the Commedia dell'Arte are on hand, along with strange and wonderful sun and moon masks, and still others representing Medusa or the Valkyries.

Legatoria Piazzesi

San Marco 2511 - (041) 5221202
Open 9am-12:30pm & 4pm-7:30pm. Closed Mon am.
At this, one of the oldest bookbinder's shops in Venice, splendid handcrafted marbleized papers, in dozens of delicate nuances and designs, are still created according to time-tested methods. These papers are used (alone or in combination with leather) to cover highly desirable notebooks, date books, address books, pencils, and picture frames.

Find the address *you are looking for, quickly and easily, in the index.*

Mondo Nuovo

Dorsoduro, Campo Santa Margherita 3063
(041) 5287344
Open 10am-12:30pm & 4pm-7:30pm. Closed Mon am.

Gianni Lovato is one of Venice's grand masters of masks. His minuscule shop is alive with expressive faces fashioned of papier-mâché, all of them his original creations. Particularly impressive are the series of Egyptian pharaohs, animals, and mythological figures.

Paolo Olbi

San Marco, Calle della Mandola 3653
(041) 5285025
Open 9:30am-12:30pm & 3:30pm-7pm. Closed Mon am.

A gold mine of gift ideas for book lovers and writers: uncommon small leather goods are displayed alongside precious marbleized papers, bound notebooks, curious pens, and other desktop paraphernalia.

Paropamiso

San Marco, Frezzeria 1701 - (041) 5227120
Open 10am-12:30pm & 4pm-7:30pm. Closed Mon am.

Ethnic ornaments from the far reaches of the Orient mingle here with shimmering Venetian glass beads, both antique and modern, in a dizzying range of tints. The mix produces an uncommonly beautiful array of jewelry.

Pauly

San Marco, Ponte Consorzi - (041) 5209899
Open 9:30am-12:30pm & 3:30pm-7pm. Closed Mon am.

Glassmaker in Venice since 1866, Pauly is renowned for its superb vases, goblets, lamps, and bottles crafted with infinite skill. Pauly's artisans work in the traditional, rather ornate style that is typically Venetian; prices are not low, but the quality is irreproachable. A small flacon, candle holder, or bibelot from this firm makes a splendid gift or memento.

Il Prato

San Marco, Frezzeria 1770 - (041) 5203375
Open daily 9am-12:30pm & 3:30pm-7:30pm.

A smart clientele of artists, politicians, and entertainers loves to browse in Giulio Secco's shop, admiring the rare and elegant art objects on display, fingering the delicate laces, satins, and silks of the antique clothing collection, and choosing a gift from among the curious masks, Art Deco ornaments, mother-of-pearl fountain pens, velvet hats, ivory fans, and silver-headed walking sticks that compose Secco's varied and precious inventory.

Il Quadrifoglio

Castello, San Lio 5576 - (041) 5222822
Open 9am-12:30pm & 3:30pm-7:30pm. Closed Mon am.

The china, crystal, silver, lamps, and bibelots showcased here are the work of top designers (Pozzi, Munari...). Don't miss the Wright tea sets and the lovely vases by Portoghesi.

Seguso Archimede

San Marco 1236-1237 - (041) 739065
San Marco 143 - (041) 793048
Open daily 9am-8pm.

For Venetians, Seguso Archimede is synonymous with art glass. Master craftsmen fashion the exquisite objets d'art, tumblers, wine glasses, mirrors, and jewelry that sparkle and glimmer in the window displays. The firm's particular pride is its collection of beautifully wrought figurative and abstract sculptures.

Signor Blum

Dorsoduro, Calle Lunga San Barnaba 2864
(041) 5226367
San Marco, Campo San Zulian 602a
(041) 5210436
Open 9:30am-12:30pm & 4pm-7:30pm. Closed Mon am.

For an original souvenir of your stay in Venice, consider a handcrafted wooden puzzle depicting one of the city's famous monuments. At Signor Blum's wonderful woodworking atelier, you can watch young craftsmen carve colorful wooden toys, dolls, and animals, which children will enjoy taking apart and putting back together.

Venetia Studium

San Marco, Calle Larga XXII Marzo 2425
(workshop) & 2403 (shop)
(041)5229281
Open summer: 9am-7:30pm; winter: 9am-12:30pm & 3:30pm-7:30pm. Closed Mon am.

The ornate and highly decorative silk shades you may have seen photographed in upscale shelter magazines can be purchased here. The range of patterns and delicate tints will make you gasp in amaze; we particularly admired the elongated models finished with a tassel and a glass bead.

Venini

San Marco 314, Piazzetta Leoncini
(041) 5224045

Open summer: 9am-7:30pm; winter: 9am-12:30pm & 3:30pm-7:30pm. Closed Mon am.

Certainly one of the most prestigious names in Venetian art glass, Venini is noted for the sublime simplicity of its opaque, monochromatic vases and for the shimmering transparency of its fragile bowls and bottles. In addition to an enchanting assortment of precious bibelots in a distinctive spiral design, Venini presents a striking collection of lamps and lighting fixtures.

Saint Mark's Vision
and the Brotherhood of the Grape

The seal of Venice bears the motto, *Pax Tibi Marce Evangelista Meus* ("Peace unto you, Mark, my evangelist"). The story goes that Saint Mark took shelter in Venice during a storm and was visited by an angel who gave him the word (in Latin, we wonder?). A small church—not the famous cathedral of San Marco—was erected on the site. Somehow it disappeared and was replaced by a vineyard. Marco Ziani, son of Doge Pietro Ziani, bequeathed the vineyard to the Franciscan brothers in 1253. Soon after, they built another tiny church, still standing today, named San Francesco della Vigna: Saint Francis of the Vineyard. Inside are a *Sacra Conversazione* by Veronese and Giovanni Bellini's *Madonna and Saints.*

Tit for Tat
and Tattler

Until a few years ago, the Riva del Carbon at San Luca was lined with the shops of the *carbonai*, or coal merchants. They formed a guild, or *corpo*, way back in 1476 and held their special prayer sessions in the church of San Salvatore. Under the Serenissima, they avoided military service by supplying the Arsenale and Zecca (mint) with coal free of delivery charge. In early 1551, Pietro Aretino, the immensely successful and frequently lewd satirist, gossip hound, and womanizer, moved into a house on the Riva del Carbon. It is said that the wife of a coalman lit Aretino's fire and took the sting out of his pen. He lived there until his death in 1556.

299

Museums

Visitors may purchase a *single ticket* that admits them to the **Palazzo Ducale** and all of **Venice's Civic Museums** (the Correr, Casa Goldoni, Ca' Pesaro, Ca' Rezzonico, and more). Currently priced at 16,000 lire, the ticket offers significant savings and is on sale at the Palazzo Ducale and other *musei civici*.

La Biblioteca Nazionale Marciana

Piazzetta San Marco 13 - (041) 5208788
Open summer 9am-1pm; winter 10am-6pm. Closed Sun, hols.
On the walls and ceiling of the Marciana's public rooms are paintings by Titian, Veronese, and Tintoretto. In addition viewing the temporary exhibits, visitors may admire some of the library's vast holdings of illuminated manuscripts and incunabula, ornate Byzantine and Italian bindings, and the magnificent *Grimani Breviary*, a late-fifteenth-century codex with illuminations by Flemish masters.

Casa Goldoni

San Polo, Calle dei Nomboli 2794
(041) 5236353
Open 8:30am-1:30pm. Closed Sun, hols.
The fifteenth-century Palazzo Centani near Campo San Tomà, where playwright Carlo Goldoni was born in 1707, is now an international institute for theatrical research. It houses a collection of Goldoni memorabilia, manuscripts, and first editions of his acerbic comedies.

Civico Museo Correr

Piazza San Marco 52 - (041) 5225625
Open 10am-4pm (Apr-Sep 10am-5pm). Closed Tue.
The museum's holdings include both historic and artistic collections. The former evoke the glorious past of the Venetian Republic—its government, commerce, ceremonies, military battles, and the daily lives of its citizens. The upper floor is given over to the Correr's renowned art gallery, the Quadreria, with important works by such Venetian masters as Vivarini, Giovanni Bellini (*The Transfiguration, The Dead Christ*) and Carpaccio (*Two Venetian Women*), as well as fine German and Flemish paintings. The Museo del Risorgimento, an annex to the Museo Correr, documents the history of Venice from the fall of the Venetian Republic in 1797 to the end of World War II.

Collezione Peggy Guggenheim

Dorsoduro, San Gregorio 701 - (041) 5206288
Open 11am-6pm. Closed Tue.
The eighteenth-century Palazzo Venier dei Leoni holds Peggy Guggenheim's magnificent collection of modern art. Works from all the important avant-garde movements are represented, from Dadaism to Abstract Expressionism, by such artists as Picasso, Duchamp, Braque, Ernst, Kandinsky, Giacometti, Francis Bacon, Mark Rothko, and Jackson Pollock. The great patroness of the arts herself, who died in 1979, is buried in the garden.

Gallerie dell'Accademia

Dorsoduro, Campo della Carità - (041) 5222247
Open daily 9am-2pm.
The Accademia contains the world's finest and most complete collection of Venetian painting from the fourteenth to the eighteenth century. Among the treasures it contains are sublime Madonnas by Giovanni Bellini, Giorgione's enigmatic *Tempesta*, Veronese's *Coronation of the Virgin* and *Feast in the House of Levi*, the mysterious *Miracles of Saint Mark* by Tintoretto, Carpaccio's *Saint Ursula Cycle*, *The Brazen Serpent* by Giambattista Tiepolo, and Piazzetta's saucy *Fortune-teller*.

> *Some establishments change their* **closing times** *without warning. It is always wise to check in advance.*

Galleria Giorgio Franchetti-Ca' d'Oro

Cannaregio, Palazzetto Giusti, Calle della Ca' d'Oro - (041) 5238790
Open daily 9am-2pm.

The collection bequeathed to the nation in 1915 by Baron Giorgio Franchetti contains outstanding works of fifteenth- to eighteenth-century art, among which are frescoes by Giorgione and Titian removed from the Fondaco dei Tedeschi, and paintings by Carpaccio, Mantegna, Luca Signorelli, and Francesco Guardi. On view as well are interesting exhibits of Venetian ceramics and Italian medals.

Galleria Internazionale d'Arte Moderna-Ca' Pesaro

Santa Croce, San Stae 2078 - (041) 721127
Open 10am-4pm (Apr-Sep 10am-5pm). Closed Mon.

Housed in the Palazzo Pesaro, a masterpiece of Venetian Baroque architecture, this collection encompasses paintings, drawings, and sculptures by Italian and international artists from 1800 to the present. Particularly worthy of note is Gustav Klimt's haunting *Salome.* Certain sections of the museum are currently closed for restoration.

Museo Archeologico

Piazza San Marco 52 - (041) 5225978
Open daily 9am-7pm.

The Archaeological Museum was founded in the sixteenth century with a legacy of Roman bronzes and marbles bequeathed to the Republic by Cardinal Domenico Grimani. It was later enriched by a collection of Greek sculptures donated by the cardinal's nephew, Giovanni Grimani, Patriarch of Aquileia. Among the items most worthy of note are statues of Greek goddesses from the fourth and fifth centuries B.C., the Hellenistic Grimani altar, and the Zulian cameo, which is carved in agate.

Museo di Arte Ebraica

Cannaregio, Campo del Ghetto Nuovo 2902b - (041) 715359
Open 10am-7pm. Closed Sat, Jewish hols.

Situated in the Ghetto Nuovo where the Jews of Venice were compelled to live from 1516 until the fall of the Republic in 1797, this museum houses a collection of religious objects and relics relating to the city's Jewish community. Guided tours of the nearby synagogues leave the museum on the half-hour, from 10:30am to 5:30pm.

Museo d'Arte Orientale Marco Polo

Santa Croce, San Stae 2078 - (041) 5241173
Open 9am-2pm. Closed Mon.

Located on the third floor of the Ca' Pesaro, just over the Modern Art Gallery (see above), the Oriental Museum houses Italy's most important collection of Far Eastern antiquities. Outstanding exhibits include Japanese weapons and suits of armor from the seventeenth to the nineteenth century and exquisite Chinese lacquer work, porcelain, and jade.

A Fly in the Ointment of the Fair

Back when a lily-white complexion was all the rage, the ladies of Venice bought their beauty marks in Campiello Mosca in the San Pantalon neighborhood. In Italian, *mosca* means fly, as in insect. That's what the locals rather irreverently called the gentleladies' beauty marks, which were made of black taffeta and glued onto pearly cheeks to highlight their whiteness.

Museo dell'Arte Vetraria di Murano

Fondamenta Giustinian 8 - (041) 739586
Open 10am-4pm (Apr-Sep 10am-5pm). Closed Wed.

Prepare to be dazzled by exhibits that illustrate the glassmaker's art from the Roman Empire through the nineteenth century. The crowning glory of this unique collection is the deep-blue Barovier wedding cup, an extremely rare example of fifteenth-century Venetian glass.

Museo Civico di Storia Naturale

Santa Croce, Fondaco dei Turchi 1730 (041) 5240885
Open 9am-1pm. Closed Mon.

Collections of fossils and interesting rocks are mounted for your inspection, along with exhibits on wild beasts, birds, bugs, and butterflies.

Museo Diocesano d'Arte Sacra Sant'Apollonia

Castello, Ponte della Canonica 4312
(041) 5229166
Open 10:30am-12:30pm. Closed Sun.

A permanent exhibit of liturgical objects, silver, books, and vestments from Venetian churches may be seen here, along with a number of artworks, including Titian's *Saint James the Apostle.*

Museo Dipinti Sacri Bizantini

Castello, Ponte dei Greci 3412 - (041) 5226581
Open 9am-1pm & 2pm-5pm. Closed Sun, hols.

Founded in 1959, the Institute for Byzantine Studies displays icons dating from the fourteenth to the sixteenth century, sacred vessels, and a collection of rare manuscripts.

Museo Fortuny

San Marco, San Beneto 3780 - (041) 5200995
Open 9am-2pm. Closed Mon.

Artist Mariano Fortuny's home is filled with his legacy of curious bibelots and paintings, but the museum is best known for its displays of the precious fabrics and costumes Fortuny designed and collected. During special exhibitions, the museum remains open until 7pm.

Museo Marciano

Basilica di San Marco, Piazza San Marco
(041) 5225205
Open 9am-1pm. Closed Sun.

On display are mosaic fragments from the twelfth and fourteenth centuries, fifteenth-century Flemish tapestries, Persian carpets, sacred vessels and vestments. The four Greek horses from the façade of the basilica of San Marco are conserved here, and there is a fine polyptych by Paolo Veneziano.

Museo del Risorgimento

See *Museo Correr.*

Museo del Settecento Veneziano-Ca' Rezzonico

Dorsoduro, San Barnaba - (041) 5224543
Open 10am-5pm. Closed Fri.

The splendid Baroque Ca' Rezzonico, begun in 1649 and completed in the following century, forms a magnificent setting for this collection of furnishings, tapestries, costumes, puppets, precious objets d'art, and paintings by Giambattista Tiepolo, Piazzetta, and Guardi. Visitors also discover an important collection of Pietro Longhi's charming canvases, as well as frescoes by Giandomenico Tiepolo. The ensemble of these works creates an extraordinarily evocative picture of eighteenth-century Venetian life.

Museo Storico Navale

Castello, Arsenale 2148 - (041) 5200276
Open 9am-1pm. Closed Sun, hols.

The glorious maritime history of Venice is recorded in this, one of Italy's most important naval museums. On display is a model of the *Bucintoro*, the galley on which the Doge would each year reenact the nuptials of Venice and the sea by casting a wedding ring into the lagoon (the actual ship was destroyed when the Republic fell in 1797). Other ship models are exhibited, along with an interesting collection of compasses, weapons, uniforms, and sundry works of art.

Museo di Torcello

Island of Torcello, Palazzi dell'Archivio & del Consiglio - (041) 730761
Open 10am-12:30pm & 2pm-5:30pm. Closed Mon, hols.

The museum's archaeological section, housed in the Palazzo dell'Archivio, displays Greek and Italic ceramics, Greek and Roman marbles, small Paleo-Venetian bronzes, and finds from the lagoon. In the Palazzo del Consiglio are medieval marbles from Torcello, church paintings and statuary, as well as relics and documents relating to the island's civil and ecclesiastical history.

Palazzo Ducale

Piazza San Marco - (041) 5224951
Open daily 9am-4pm (Apr-Oct 9am-7pm).

The Venetian-Gothic Doges' Palace was built essentially in the thirteenth and fourteenth centuries, but after two disastrous fires the interior was almost entirely redecorated in the late sixteenth century. Visitors may admire frescoes, panels, ducal portraits, and historical and mythological subjects by Veronese, Titian, Bassano, and Tiepolo. Don't miss the colossal *Paradiso*, painted by Jacopo Tintoretto and his son Domenico, when the elder was over 70 years old.

Palazzo Mocenigo

Santa Croce, San Stae 1992 - (041) 721798
Open 8:30am-1:30pm. Closed Sun, hols.
A fascinating collection of textiles, costumes, and accessories draws fashion and history buffs alike to the Palazzo Mocenigo. Several rooms are gloriously furnished and be-frescoed, providing a splendid example of eighteenth-century Venetian interior decoration.

Pinacoteca Querini Stampalia

Castello, Palazzo Querini Stampalia
(041) 5225235
Open 10am-3pm (summer 10am-4pm). Closed Mon.
This sixteenth-century palazzo contains a riveting gallery of mostly Venetian paintings arranged in an authentic eighteenth-century setting. Several works by Palma Vecchio (notably *Portrait of Francesco Querini and his Wife*) and two series of paintings by Pietro Longhi (including *Duck Shoot on the Lagoon*) are outstanding.
N.B.: As of this writing, the Pinacoteca is closed indefinitely for restoration.

Scuola Grande dei Carmini

Dorsoduro, Campo dei Carmini
(041) 5289420
Open 9am-noon & 3pm-6pm. Closed Sun, hols.
Housed in a seventeenth-century edifice, the Scuola dei Carmini was a charitable society established under the patronage of Our Lady of Carmel. The rich interior decoration includes the most complete series of paintings by Giambattista Tiepolo to survive in Venice; executed between 1739 and 1744, they are perhaps his finest works. The luminous central fresco, *Our Lady of Carmel Presenting the Scapular to Blessed Simon Stock*, is particularly striking for its graceful composition.

Scuola Grande di San Rocco

San Polo, Campo San Rocco 3054
(041) 5234864
Open daily 9am-5:30pm.
This is the largest and the richest of the Venetian *scuole* (schools), and the only one to have kept its original decoration intact. It houses a remarkable series of 56 paintings by Jacopo Tintoretto, who won the right to decorate the school over such rivals as Paolo Veronese. The works display rare inventiveness and a great virtuosity in the rendering of light.

Scuola di San Giorgio degli Schiavoni

Castello, Ponte dei Greci 3259a
(041) 5228828
Open 9:30am-12:30pm & 3:30pm-6pm. Closed Sun pm, Mon.
The extraordinary series of nine paintings by Vittore Carpaccio displayed on the ground floor of the school illustrates the lives of Saints George, Tryphone, and Jerome, patrons of the Dalmatians ("Schiavoni"). A fantastic, poetic atmosphere pervades these pictures, particularly *Saint George Slaying the Dragon* and *Saint Jerome's Funeral*.

Tesoro della Basilica di San Marco

Piazza San Marco - (041) 5225205
Open daily 9:25am-4pm (summer 9:25am-5pm, Sun 2pm-5pm).
The Treasury of San Marco contains precious Byzantine relics, many of which were brought to Venice after the fall of Constantinople in 1204: altarpieces, icons, reliquaries, and sacred vessels. The altarpiece for the basilica's main altar is a masterpiece of silversmithing that dates from the thirteenth century.

The Columns of Death

The gallows of Republican Venice were set up between the two twelfth-century columns that stand in the Piazzetta San Marco. One column is topped by the winged Lion of Saint Mark, the other by Saint Theodore, first patron saint of Venice. These were brought over from Constantinople along with a third column, which fell into the sea and was never retrieved.

Useful Telephone Numbers

Venice Area Code: 041

Airport Information: Marco Polo, 661262
Ambulance: 5230000
City Hall: 788111
Fire Department: 115
Foreigners' Assistance: 5203222
Lost and Found: 2708225
Medical Emergency: 781456

Pharmacy: 5230573
Police Emergency: 112; 113
Post Office and Telegraph: 5220606
Public Transportation Information: 5287866
State Railway Information: 715555
Tourist Information: 5298711; 5226356
Wake-up Call: 114
Water Taxis: 5222303
Weather Service: 191

The Mori Brothers, Anonymous

The Campo dei Mori, near the church of the Madonna dell'Orto, takes its name from the statues in the wall of Palazzo Mastelli. Tradition has it that they represent the Mastelli brothers: Rioba, Sandi, and Alfani. They were called "Mori" (Moors) not because they were black, but because their family came from Morea (the medieval name of the Peloponnesus). The corner statue is known as Sior Antonio Rioba. Back in the days when free speech could cost a life, the statue was used by anonymous satirists as a pen-name personality. They wrote their biting, witty verse and signed "Sior Antonio Rioba." His neck of stone was harder to slit than theirs.

Plague-free but Impoverished

Talk about the rising cost of health care... The church of Santa Maria della Salute (*salute* means "health") was built to fulfill a pledge made during the devastating pestilence of 1630, which knocked Venice's population down from 142,804 to 98,244 sorrowful souls. The survivors had budgeted 50,000 ducats for the construction job, but by the time the church was completed 54 years later, they had wound up spending 500,000. Yet this masterpiece of Baroque architecture, designed by Baldassare Longhena, has won a place among the best-loved landmarks of Venice.

Keeping Abreast of the Competition

There once was a bridge near San Cassiano called the Ponte delle Tette, so named because the prostitutes there hung their goods out of the windows to attract the passersby. The government encouraged this baring of breasts as a means of combating sodomy, which was rampant during the days of the Doges. Pederasty became so widespread that the Council of Ten appointed two noblemen per neighborhood to keep an eye on the habits of the menfolk. For many years at Carnival, the Bridge of Bosoms was re-created for a bit of bawdy good fun.

MENU SAVVY

A GUIDE TO ITALIAN FOOD TERMS

A

Abbacchio: milk-fed lamb
Acciughe: anchovies
Aceto: vinegar
Affumicato: smoked
Aglio: garlic
Agnello: lamb
Agnolotti: crescent-shaped, meat-filled pasta
Agrodolce: sweet-and-sour
Albicocca: apricot
Alici: anchovies
Amaretti: crunchy almond macaroons
Anatra (also Anitra): duck
Anguilla: eel
Animelle: sweetbreads
Aragosta: spiny lobster
Arrosto: roasted meat
Arzilla: skate
Astice: lobster

B

Baccalà: dried (salt) cod
Bagna cauda: hot, savory dipping sauce for raw vegetables
Beccaccia : woodcock
Bigoli: whole-wheat spaghetti
Biete: Swiss chard
Biscotti: cookies
Bistecca (alla fiorentina): charcoal-grilled T-bone steak (seasoned with pepper and olive oil)
Bollito misto: mixed boiled meats
Bombole: fritters
Brace (alla): charcoal grilled
Braciole: thin steaks, usually rolled around a savory filling
Brasato: braised; beef braised in wine
Bresaola: air-dried spiced beef
Brodetto: fish soup
Brodo: broth
Bruschetta: toasted garlic bread topped with tomatoes or other vegetables
Bucatini: hollow spaghetti
Budino: pudding

Burro (fuso): (melted) butter
Busecca alla milanese: tripe with herbs and vegetables
Bussechina: dried chestnuts simmered in milk

C

Cacciagione: game
Cacciucco alla livornese: seafood stew
Calamari (calamaretti): (baby) squid
Calzone: stuffed pizza turnover
Cannellini: white beans
Cappellacci alla ferrarese: pasta stuffed with pumpkin
Cappelletti: meat- or cheese-stuffed pasta ("little hats")
Capperi: capers
Cappesante (or capesante): scallops
Cappone: capon
Capretto: kid
Carciofi (alla giudia): (flattened and deep-fried baby) artichokes
Cartoccio (in): baked in parchment paper
Casalinga: homestyle
Cassata: ice-cream bombe
Cassata alla siciliana: sponge cake layered with sweetened ricotta and candied fruit, iced with chocolate buttercream
Castagna: chestnut
Castagnaccio: Tuscan chestnut cake
Caviale: caviar
Cavolfiore: cauliflower
Cavolo (nero): (red) cabbage
Ceci: chickpeas
Cernia: grouper
Cervelle: brains
Chiodini: small, nail-shaped mushrooms
Cicchetti: Venetian bar snacks; tapas
Cime di rape: turnip tops
Cinghiale: boar
Cipolla: onion
Coda (di bue); (di rospo): Tail (oxtail); (monkfish)
Conchiglie: pasta shells
Coniglio: rabbit
Contorni: side dishes

Coppa: cured pork fillet encased in sausage skin
Costata: rib steak
Costoletta (alla milanese): (breaded veal) chop
Cotechino: large, spicy sausage
Cotoletta: cutlet
Cozze: mussels
Crescione: watercress
Crespelle: crêpes
Crocchette: croquettes
Crostacei: crustaceans
Crostata: tart

Gnocchi: dumplings made of cheese (di ricotta), of potatoes (di patate), cheese and spinach (verdi) or semolina (alla romana)
Gramigna: short, curly, tubular pasta
Grana: hard cheese for grating
Granchio: crab
Granita: sweetened, flavored ice
Granseola: Venetian spider crab
Granturco: corn
Grigliata mista: mixed grill
Grissini: breadsticks
Guazzetto: light stew

D

Dolci: desserts

F

Fagiano: pheasant
Fagioli: beans
Fagiolini: string beans
Faraona: guinea hen
Farro: a type of wheat; used as soup base in Tuscany
Fedelini: very thin spaghetti
Fegatini di pollo: chicken livers
Fegato (alla veneziana): (calf's) liver (sautéed with onions)
Ferro (al): grilled
Fetta: a slice
Fichi: figs
Finocchio: fennel
Focaccia: crusty flat bread
Formaggio: cheese
Forno (al): oven baked or roasted
Fragole: strawberries
Fragoline: wild strawberries
Frittata: Italian omelet
Fritto misto: mixed fry of meats or fish
Frittura: fried foods
Frutta (di stagione): (seasonal) fruit
Frutti di mare: seafood (esp. shellfish)
Funghi (trifolati): mushrooms (sautéed with garlic and parsley)
Fusilli: spiral-shaped spaghetti

G

Gamberi: shrimp
Gamberi di fiume: crayfish
Gamberoni: prawns
Gelato: ice cream

I

Indivia: Belgian endive
Insaccati: sausages
Insalata: salad
Involtini: stuffed meat or fish rolls

L

Lamponi: raspberries
Lattuga: lettuce
Lavarello: salmon trout
Lenticchie: lentils
Lepre: hare
Lesso: boiled
Lombatina: loin
Luganega: fresh pork sausage
Lumache: snails

M

Maccheroni: macaroni pasta
Maiale: pork
Mandorle: almonds
Manzo: beef
Mela: apple
Melanzana: eggplant
Miele: honey
Minestra: soup; pasta course
Minestrone: vegetable soup
Molluschi: mollusks
Mondeghili: breaded meatballs, a Lombard dish
Moscardini: baby octopus
Mortadella: large, mild Bolognese pork sausage
Mostarda: fruit preserved in syrup, flavored with mustard (used as a relish with boiled meat)
Mozzarella di bufala: fresh cheese made from water-buffalo milk

N

Nasello: whiting
Nervetti: chewy bits of calf's foot or shin (a northern Italian antipasto)
Nocciola: hazelnut
Noce: walnut

O

Oca: goose
Orate: sea bream
Orecchiette: ear-shaped pasta
Ortaggi: vegetables
Ortolana (all'): with garden vegetables
Osso buco: braised veal shanks
Ostriche: oysters

Pignoli: pine nuts
Piselli: peas
Pizzoccheri: buckwheat-flour noodles with potatoes and Swisschard
Polenta: cornmeal porridge
Pollame: poultry
Pollo (ruspante): (farm-bred) chicken
Polpette, polpettone: meatballs, meatloaf
Polpo: octopus
Pomodoro: tomato
Pompelmo: grapefruit
Porchetta: roast suckling pig
Porcini: boletus mushrooms
Prezzemolo: parsley
Prosciutto: air-dried ham
Prugna: prune
Puntarelle: wild chicory greens

P

Padella (in): pan-roasted or sautéed
Pajata: stewed calf's innards served with rigatoni pasta, a Roman dish
Palomba: wood pigeon
Palombo: firm-fleshed fish of the shark family
Pane: bread
Panettone: brioche-like sweet bread
Panforte: Siennese fruit cake
Panna: heavy cream
Pancetta: rolled, herbed pork belly
Pansotti: pasta stuffed with cheese and greens, usually served with a walnut sauce
Panzanella: bread and tomato salad, a Tuscan dish
Pappardelle: wide noodles
Pasta asciutta: pasta served plain or with a sauce
Pasticceria: pastry; pastry shop
Pasticcio: pie or mold of pasta, sauce, and meat or fish
Patate: potatoes
Pecorino: hard sheep's-milk cheese
Penne: quill-shaped pasta
Peperoncini: tiny hot peppers
Peperoni (ripieni, farciti, imbottiti): (stuffed) green, red, or yellow sweet peppers
Pernice: partridge
Pesca: peach
Pesce: fish
Pesce persico: perch
Pesce spada: swordfish
Petto (di pollo): chicken breast
Piccione, piccioncino: (squab) pigeon

Q

Quaglia: quail

R

Radicchio: red chicory
Ragù: meat sauce
Rane: frogs (usually frogs' legs)
Ricotta: fresh sheep's-milk cheese
Riso: rice
Risotto: braised rice
Rognoncini: kidneys
Rognoni: kidneys
Rombo: turbot
Rosmarino: rosemary
Rospo (pescatrice): monkfish (anglerfish)
Rucola: rocket (arugula)

S

Salsa (verde): sauce (of parsley, capers, anchovies and lemon juice or vinegar)
Salsicce: fresh sausage
Saltimbocca: veal scallop with prosciutto and sage
Salvia: sage
San Pietro: John Dory
Sarde: sardines
Scalogno: shallot
Scarola: escarole
Scorfano: scorpionfish (sculpin)
Sedano: celery
Selvaggina: wild game
Semifreddo: frozen dessert, usually ice cream with or without cake

Seppia (seppiolina): (baby) cuttlefish; its black ink is used in risotto and sauces for pasta

Sfogi in saor: marinated baby sole, a Venetian dish

Sfoglia: pastry or egg pasta dough

Sformato: mold, mousse, or flan, usually of rice or vegetables

Sgombro: mackerel

Sogliola: sole

Soppressata: dried pork sausage studded with lard

Speck: spicy cured pork, served as an antipasto

Spezzatino: stew

Spiedino: brochette

Spigola: sea bass

Spumone: light, foamy ice cream

Stinco di vitello: veal shank

Storione: sturgeon

Stracotto: beef braised in red wine

Strangolaprete: "priest chokers": small pasta nuggets

Stufato: stew

Sugo: sauce

T

Tacchino (petto di): turkey (breast)

Taccole: snowpeas

Tartufi: truffles

Tegame (in): cooked in a covered casserole

Testaroli: wild mushrooms

Timo: thyme

Tiramisù: creamy dessert of rum-spiked cake and triple-crème cheese

Tonnarelli: square spaghetti

Tonno: tuna

Torrone: nougat

Torta: cake

Tortelli: pasta dumplings stuffed with greens and ricotta

Tortellini: ring-shaped dumplings stuffed with meat or cheese and served in broth or in a cream sauce

Totani: squid

Trenette: thin noodles served with potatoes and pesto sauce

Triglia: red mullet

Trota: trout

U

Uccelletti, uccellini: small roasted or grilled birds

Umido (in): simmered in a sauce

Uovo, uova (sodo): (hard-boiled) egg, eggs

Uva: grapes

Uva passa: raisins

V

Vellutata: cream soup or velouté sauce

Verdura: greens, vegetables

Verza: Savoy cabbage

Vitello: veal

Vongole (verace): (carpetshell) clams

Z

Zabaglione (or Zabaione): warm whipped egg yolks flavored with Marsala

Zafferano: saffron

Zampa di vitello: calf's foot

Zampone: spicy stuffed pig's trotter

Zucca: pumpkin

Zucchero: sugar

Zucchine: zucchini

Zuccotto: dome-shaped mold of liqueur-soaked sponge cake, whipped cream, chocolate and nuts

Zuppa: soup

Zuppa inglese: cake steeped in rum-flavored custard sauce

BE SMART. BOOK US.

"Gault Millau is the toque of the town." — *San Francisco Examiner*

THE "BEST OF" SERIES

In 18 comprehensive guidebooks to destinations
around the world, we'll take you to the best in restaurants,
hotels, nightlife, shopping, sights, arts, events and more.

NEW!

GAYOT'S

THE BEST OF

FRANCE

MORE THAN 7,000 FRANK
AND WITTY REVIEWS OF
RESTAURANTS AND HOTELS.

THE ONLY GUIDES
THAT DISTINGUISH THE TRULY
SUPERLATIVE FROM THE MERELY OVERRATED.

Gault Millau

- Chicago
- Florida
- Germany
- Hawaii
- Italy
- London
- Los Angeles
- LA Restaurants
- New England
- New Orleans
- New York
- Paris
- San Francisco
- Thailand
- Toronto
- Washington D.C.
- Wineries of
  North America

*(See order form at
the back of the
book for prices)*

Winner "BEST GUIDEBOOK"
Lowell Thomas/Society of American Travel Writers

ORDER TOLL FREE 1(800) LE BEST 1

INDEX

Arte Antica, 170
Arte della Cera (L'), 183
Attanasio, 158
Aurora, 152

B

Bacco, 182
Balbi (Salvatore), 185
Bar dell'Ovo, 168
Barone Pio, 173
Bars, 166
Benetton, 174
Bersagliera (La), 145
Bilancioni, 158
Blanche, 166
Blasi, 174
Body (The), 167
Body of Naples, 167
Books, 172
Bottega della Carta, 183
Bottega
  dell'Erborista (La), 180
Bowinkel, 184
Brandi, 156
Brinkmann (Theo), 176
Britannique, 160
Burn the Belfry!, 190

C

Cachaca (La), 168
Cacharel, 174
Caffè
  - Megaride, 168
  - Nobile, 168
Caflisch, 158
Cage (La), 185
Cambusa (La), 154
Cantina di Triunfo (La), 145
Cantinella (La), 145
Canzone del Mare (La), 152
Capannina (La), 153
Caravella (La), 151
Carmagnola, 185
Carraturo, 158
Caruso, 155, 184
Caruso Belvedere, 165
Casanova Grill, 146
Castel dell'Ovo, 169
Catacombs (The), 177
Cavin, 182
Chez Black, 154
Chez Moi, 166
Cimmino, 158
'53 (Al), 146
Ciro a Mergellina, 146
Ciro a Santa Brigida, 147
City Hall, 191
City Hall Café, 166
City Police, 191
Clinica dell'Accendino, 184

Clothing, 173
Codrington & Co., 179
Coin, 173
Coloniali, 179
Colonnese, 172
Corcione, 182
Crêperie (La), 156

D

Da
  - Gemma, 151
  - Giovanni, 148
  - Luigi, 182
Dal Vecchio, 180
Damiani, 166
Damiano, 153
D'Amodio, 170
D'Andrea, 185
D'Angelo (Mario), 170
Daniele, 158
D'Aria, 177
De Simone (Livio), 174
Delicato (Il), 147
Department Stores, 173
Deperro, 172
Discos, 166
Dizzy Club, 166
Don Alfonso, 155
Don Salvatore, 147
Donna Marianna, 143
Down with Rome, Long Live
  Toledo!, 175
Drugs, 179

E

Eddy Monetti, 175
Emporio Armani, 174
Enoteca
  - Belledonne, 182
  - del Buon Bere, 182
Erba Voglio (L'), 180
Ettore, 147, 156
Eugenio Marinella, 178
Europa Palace, 162
Excelsior, 160
  - restaurant, 146
  - Vittoria, 165

F

Fabbrini, 171
Faraglioni (I), 153
Fashion, 173
  - Accessories, 177
  - Clothing, 173
  - Jewelry, 176
  - Shoes, 177
Fendi, 174
Fenestella (A), 168
Ferragamo (Salvatore), 177

Ferré (Gianfranco), 174
Ferrigno, 184
Ferry Service, 191
Fiaba, 176
Fiorentino, 172
Fire Department, 191
Florida, 171
Fontana, 158
Fontana
  dell'Immacolatella, 146
Food, 179
  - Gourmet Shops, 179
  - Herbalists, 180
  - Wine, 181
Footloose Fountain, 146
Fratelli Montagna, 182
Fratelli Piccini, 178
Friggitoria del Vomero, 156

G

Gabbiano (Il), 169
Gabriella Spatarella, 176
Gabrielli (Nazareno), 178
Galiano, 177
Galleria dell'Accademia di
  Belle Arti, 186
Gallerie Nazionali di
  Capodimonte, 187
Gallo Nero, 147, 169
Gambrinus, 166
Garibaldi Slept Here, 191
Gay Odin, 180
Gennaro, 153
Gennaro Brandi, 170
Gianfranco Ferré, 174
Giannotti, 178
Giardini Eden, 154
Gifts, 183
Giorgio, 174
Gorizia, 148
Gourmet Shops, 179
Grand Hotel
  - Excelsior, 161
  - Oriente, 160
  - Punta Molino, 163
  - Quisisana, 162
Grande Albergo Vesuvio, 160
Grimaldi, 172
Grotte Risto-Club (Le), 169
Gucci, 174
Guida, 172
Guinness Club, 169

H

Happy Rock, 156
Hard Rock, 156
Head (The), 143
Head of Naples, 143
Herbalists, 180

319

B

Babington's English
   Tearoom, 214
Bacaro (Il), 201
Bar
 - del Fico, 229
 - della Pace, 229
 - del Tennis, 212
Barduagni, 246
Barocco, 221
Barrilà, 242
Bars, 229
Basile, 237
Basilica Emilia, 222
Basilica San Pancrazio, 252
Bella Napoli, 218
Bernasconi all'Argentina, 218
Bevitoria (La), 229
Biagiotti (Laura), 237
Biblioteca Apostolica, 255
Big Bang & Tatum, 231
Big Mama, 233
Birreria
 - L'Orso Elettrico, 214
 - Tiroler Keller, 214
 - Viennese, 214
Bocca della Verità, 204
Boccione, 218
Boning Up on Franciscan
   History, 216
Bonne Nouvelle, 201
Books, 235
Borgia (Apparmento), 253
Borromeo, 221
Borsalino, 242
Bottega di Lunga
   Vita (La), 245
Bottega del Vino
   da Bleve, 214
Bozart, 242
Braccio Nuovo, 254
Bramante, 229
Bramante's Tempietto, 235
Broggi–Van Cleef
   & Arpels, 240
Brotherhood of the Last
   Wish, 228
Buccellati (Mario), 240
Bulgari, 240
Burghy, 214
Burma Bijoux, 242

C

Cabarets, 231
Cafes, 212
Caffè
 - Greco, 211, 212
 - Latino, 233
 - Vigna Clara, 215
Caffettiera (La), 212
Calisè, 214

Camiscioni, 201
Camomilla, 242
Campanile, 242
Campo de' Fiori, 221
Cannavota, 202
Cappella di Niccolò V, 254
Cappella Sistina, 254
Cardinale (Il), 202
Carriage, 221
Cartier, 240
Casino dell'Aurora, 248
Castro (Adolfo di), 234
Castro (Alberto di), 235
Castroni, 243
Casuccio & Scalera, 240
Cavalletti, 218
Celio, 221
Cenci, 237
Cesare Lampronti, 235
Charro (El), 241
Checchino dal 1887, 202
Chez Albert, 203
Chiarotti, 245
Chirra, 245
Ciampini, 215
Ciarla (Alberto), 200
Ciarla All'Eur, 245
Cigno (Il), 218
Circus Maximus, 257
City Hall, 257
City Police, 257
Clothing, 237
Coin, 236
Collezione d'Arte Religiosa
   Moderna, 254
Colosseum, 198, 257
Columbus, 222
Confetteria Moriondo
   & Gariglio, 244
Convivio, 203
Coriolano, 203
Corner Shop (The), 235
Cornucopia (La), 203
CO.TRA.L., 257
Cottini, 218
Crêperie (La), 215
Crisci (Tanino), 242
Crowne Plaza Minerva, 222
C.U.C.I.N.A., 246
Cul de Sac 1, 215
Cupola (La), 204
Curiosità e Magia, 235

D

Da Lucia, 206
Dal Cò, 242
Day at the Races (A), 257
Decò, 246
Department Stores, 236
Di Nepi Antiquitas, 235
Diana, 222
Diego Della Valle, 242

Dino e Toni, 204
Diotallevi, 244
Discos, 231
Discount dell'Alta Moda, 237
Divina, 231
Domitian's Stadium, 257
Doney, 212
Douce Vie (La), 217
Drappo (Il), 204

E

Economy Book & Video
   Center, 236
Eddy Monetti, 239
Eden, 222
 - restaurant, 210
Elettra, 204
Erboristeria Maurice
   Mességué, 245
Étoiles (Les), 205
Euclide, 215
Europeo, 219
Evil Stone but a Good Cure
   for Dog Bites (An), 247
Excelsior, 222
 - restaurant, 204

F

Fantasia del Fornaio (La), 244
Fashion, 237
 - Accessories, 242
 - Clothing, 237
 - Jewelry, 240
 - Leather, 240
 - Luggage, 240
 - Shoes, 242
Felice, 205
Felicula, 257
Feltrinelli, 236
Fendi, 237
Ferragamo (Salvatore), 237
Ferré (Gianfranco), 238
Filettaro a Santa Barbara
   (Dar), 215
Fior Fiore, 244
Fire Department, 257
Follia, 231
Fonclea, 233
Fontanella (La), 205
Food, 243
 - Gourmet Shops, 243
 - Herbalists, 245
 - Wine, 245
Fornari & Fornari, 246
Forum, 223
Franchi, 244
Frate (Del), 245
Fratelli Rossetti, 243
Furla, 242

Deep in the Southern Rockies lie two hundred and fifty spectacular square miles known as Forbes Trinchera. Its tallest peak reaches 14,345 feet into the Colorado sky, and its mountains sweep down into valleys as green and fertile as a Kentucky meadow.

This historic tract of land was bought by publisher Malcolm S. Forbes in 1969 as a natural escape to a place far from Wall Street and corporate stress. And now, for the first time, it is being offered to Incentive Planners looking for something unique.

The buildings of Forbes Trinchera have been remodeled to provide superb accommodation, but it is still, essentially, a ranch.

Whilst there, guests can ride the land on horseback, or on trail-bike. They can fly-fish on its miles of streams, or hike its thousands of trails. They will have special rights at a nearby golf club, or they can shoot skeet until every clay looks as big as a house. And, as you can imagine, the cross-country skiing and snowmobile rides are nothing short of breathtaking. When there's work to be done, the main conference room can seat up to sixty.

However they choose to use it, Forbes Trinchera will provide a lookout point from which to view the world. Two hundred and fifty square miles. Fifty staff. Mountains. Valleys. Lakes. Streams.

Call 1-800-FORBES-5, and allow us to tell you more.

FORBES TRINCHERA RANCH
A Forbes Executive Retreat

GAYOT PUBLICATIONS ARE AVAILABLE AT
ALL FINE BOOKSTORES WORLDWIDE.

INTERNATIONAL DISTRIBUTION IS COORDINATED
BY THE FOLLOWING OFFICES:

MAINLAND U.S. & CANADA
Publishers Group West
4065 Hollis St.
Emeryville, CA 94608
(800) 788-3123

HAWAII
Island Heritage
99-880 Iwaena
Aiea, HI 96701
(800) 468-2800

AUSTRALIA
Little Hills Press Pty. Ltd.
Regent House, 37-43 Alexander St.
Crows Nest (Sydney) NSW 2065
Australia
(02) 437-6995

TAIWAN
Central Book Publishing
2nd Floor, 141, Section 1
Chungking South Rd.
Taipei, Taiwan R.O.C.
(02) 331-5726

HONG KONG & CHINA
Pacific Century Distribution
14 Lower Kai Yuen Ln.
Ground Floor
North Point, Hong Kong
(852) 881-5505

SINGAPORE
Periplus Editions
2A Paterson Hill
Singapore 0923
(65) 73-48-42

UK & EUROPE
World Leisure Marketing
Downing Rd.
West Meadows Industrial Estate
Derby, Derbyshire
DE21 6HA England
(01) 332-343-332

FRANCE
Gault Millau
61 Avenue Hoche
75611 Paris Cedex 08
France
(1) 40-54-33-05

TO ORDER THE GUIDES FOR GIFTS, CUSTOM EDITIONS AND
CORPORATE SALES IN THE U.S. CALL OUR TOLL-FREE LINE.

ORDER TOLL-FREE
1 (800) LE BEST 1

RECEIVE A **FREE**

SUBSCRIPTION

TO **"TASTES"**

(A $40 VALUE)

BY FILLING OUT THIS QUESTIONNAIRE YOU'LL RECEIVE
A COMPLIMENTARY ONE YEAR SUBSCRIPTION TO
"TASTES," OUR INTERNATIONAL NEWSLETTER.

NAME _____

ADDRESS _____

CITY_____STATE _____

ZIP_____COUNTRY _____

PHONE ( )   -

The AGP/Gault Millau series of guidebooks reflects your demand for insightful, incisive reporting on the best that the world's most exciting destinations have to offer. To help us make our books even better, please take a moment to fill out this anonymous (if you wish) questionnaire, and return it to:

Gault Millau Inc., P.O. Box 361144, Los Angeles, CA 90036;
Fax: (213) 936-2883.

1. How did you hear about the AGP guides? Please specify: bookstore, newspaper, magazine, radio, friends or other.

2. Please list in order of preference the cities or countries which you would like to see AGP cover.

3. Do you refer to the AGP guides for your own city, or only when traveling?
A. (Travels) ....   B. (Own city) ....   C. (Both) ....

Please turn over

4. Please list, starting with the most preferred, the three features you like best about the Gault Millau guides.

A. .... B. ....

C. ....

5. What are the features, if any, you dislike about the Gault Millau guides?

6. Please list any features you would like to see added to the Gault Millau guides.

7. If you use other guides besides Gault Millau, please list below.

8. Please list the features you like best about your favorite guidebook series, if it is not Gault Millau.

A. .... B. ....

C. ....

9. How many trips do you make per year, for either business or pleasure?

Business: International: ....   Domestic: ....

Pleasure: International: ....   Domestic: ....

10. Please check the category that reflects your annual household income.

$20,000-$39,000 .... $40,000-$59,000 ....
$60,000-$79,000 .... $80,000-$99,000 ....
$100,000-$120,000 ....   Other (please specify) ....

11. If you have any comments on the Gault Millau guides in general, please list them in the space below.

12. If you would like to recommend specific establishments, please don't hesitate to list them:

Name	City	Phone

We thank you for your interest in the Gault Millau guides, and we welcome your remarks and recommendations about restaurants, hotels, nightlife, shops, services and so on.

TASTES

THE WORLD DINING & TRAVEL CONNECTION

Want to keep current on the best bistros in Paris? Discover that little hideaway in Singapore? Or stay away from that dreadful and dreadfully expensive restaurant in New York? André Gayot's *Tastes* newsletter gives you bi-monthly news on the best restaurants, hotels, nightlife, shopping, airline and cruiseline information around the world.

☐ **YES,** please enter/renew my subscription to TASTES newsletter for six bi-monthly issues at the rate of $40 per year.
(Outside U.S. and Canada, $50.)

SPECIAL OFFER!
Receive a free book of your choice when you subscribe/renew or order a gift subscription to TASTES. Select the title you want from the following page and submit your $40 check or pay using your **VISA** card.

Name _____

Address _____

City _____ State _____

ZIP _____ Country _____

Phone (   )   -

☐ Enclosed is my check or money order made out to Gault Millau, Inc.

☐ $_____

☐ Charge to: _____ **VISA** _____AMEX _____MASTERCARD   Exp. _____

Card#_____ Signature _____

308/95

FOR FASTER SERVICE CALL 1 (800) LE BEST 1

"Gault Millau is provocative and frank."
—*Los Angeles Times*

"You will enjoy their prose."
—*US News & World Report*

"Gault Millau is the toque of the town."
—*San Francisco Examiner*

Please send me the "Best of" books checked below:

❏ Chicago $18.00	❏ London $20.00	❏ Paris $20.00
❏ Florida $17.00	❏ Los Angeles $18.00	❏ San Francisco . . .$18.00
❏ France $20.00	❏ LA Restaurants . .$10.00	❏ Thailand $18.00
❏ Germany $20.00	❏ New England . . .$15.95	❏ Toronto $17.00
❏ Hawaii $18.00	❏ New Orleans . . .$17.00	❏ Washington, D.C. $16.95
❏ Italy $20.00	❏ New York $18.00	❏ Wineries of North America $18.00

Mail to:

Gault Millau, Inc., P.O. Box 361144, Los Angeles, CA 90036

Or, order toll-free: **1 (800) LE BEST 1** • **FAX: (213) 936-2883**

In the U.S., include $4 (shipping charge) for the first book, and $3 for each additional book. Outside the U.S., $7 and $5.

❏ Enclosed is my check or money order made out to Gault Millau, Inc.
for $ _____.

❏ Please charge my credit card: ❏ **VISA** ❏ MC ❏ AMEX

Card # _____ Exp. ___/___

Signature_____ Telephone _____

Name _____

Address _____

City _____ State_____ ZIP_____

Country _____

308/95